FOURTH EDITION

Secondary School Reading Instruction

THE CONTENT AREAS

Betty D. Roe
Tennessee Technological University

Barbara D. Stoodt
University of North Carolina at Greensboro

Paul C. Burns
Late of University of Tennessee at Knoxville

HOUGHTON MIFFLIN COMPANY   *BOSTON*

Dallas   Geneva, Illinois   Palo Alto   Princeton, New Jersey

To Mike
and
To Linda and Susan

Cover illustration by Margery Mintz.

Figure in Example 7.3 from *An Introduction to Teaching the Language Arts* by Elinor P. Ross and Betty D. Roe. Copyright © 1990 by Holt, Rinehart and Winston, Inc. Reprinted by permission of the publisher.

Example 4.14, "U.S. Air and Water Pollution Map," Example 4.16, "Immigration to the United States, 1830–1970, Bar Graph," and Example 4.18, "Cotton Production in the United States, 1790–1840," from *The Free and the Brave*, 1980, by Henry F. Graff. Courtesy of the Riverside Publishing Company. Copyright © 1980 by Houghton Mifflin Company. Used with permission.

Printed in the U.S.A.

Library of Congress Catalog Card Number: 90–83049

ISBN: 0–395–43233–2

ABCDEFGHIJ-D-99876543210

Secondary School Reading Instruction

THE CONTENT AREAS

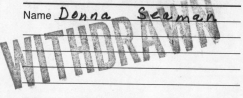

CONTENTS

3

READING COMPREHENSION   60

4

READING-STUDY SKILLS   107

5

"AT RISK" READERS   172

6

ADJUSTING READING ASSIGNMENTS TO FIT ALL STUDENTS

7

READING AND WRITING IN THE CONTENT AREAS

8

READING IN THE CONTENT AREAS: PART I   294

9

READING IN THE CONTENT AREAS: PART 2   358

10

ASSESSMENT PROCEDURES   409

II

SECONDARY SCHOOL READING PROGRAMS 465

PREFACE

Audience and Purpose

Secondary School Reading Instruction: The Content Areas, fourth edition, has been written primarily for preservice teachers preparing for secondary school certification in teacher-training programs and for experienced high school teachers who want to help their students read content assignments with more understanding. Neither group is likely to have background knowledge in reading. This book has thus been written at an introductory level, with the needs and concerns of these teachers in mind. The text also contains much information that is useful for reading specialists who work cooperatively with content teachers in helping secondary students with reading difficulties and for secondary school administrators who must know about the reading needs of secondary school students if they are to set school policies appropriately.

The aim of this book is to prepare secondary school teachers to teach content of their subject areas more efficiently. Much secondary content area material is written at a high difficulty level and students are required to read extensively. Teachers who know how to teach the reading strategies appropriate to their content area enhance their students' success in the classroom. This book provides a strategy-based approach to content reading.

Revisions in This Edition

The fourth edition of *Secondary School Reading Instruction: The Content Areas* has been thoroughly updated and revised to cover current research in the field of reading instruction. In particular, new research studies on reading comprehension; vocabulary development; approaches to teaching reading; the connections between reading, writing, and thinking; and the instructional needs of an increasingly diverse classroom population have offered insights for reading instruction within the secondary school setting. A revised chapter organization places coverage of the reading process up front, and students are guided through the reading process toward understanding and application of theory and strategies.

Two new chapters have been written for the fourth edition. The first, Chapter 5, addresses the changing makeup of today's secondary school classrooms, and the second, Chapter 7, covers the integration of writing and reading in the content areas. More specifically, Chapter 5, "'At Risk' Readers," takes a strategy-based approach to meeting the needs of diverse students who are experiencing reading difficulties in the classroom. This chapter presents strategies and activities to help exceptional students and students from diverse social, cultural, and economic backgrounds get the most from their reading of content area materials. Chapter 7, "Reading and Writing in the Content Areas," makes strong connections between reading, writing, and thinking skills, showing how writing activities can increase students' comprehension of content area materials. Students are encouraged to write journals and logs to enhance their understanding of subject area material and are guided through the process approach to writing.

In addition to the new chapters, Chapter 2, "Developing a Meaningful Vocabulary," and Chapter 3, "Reading Comprehension," have been extensively updated to emphasize the interactive approach to reading and to link reading and schema theory more, as well as to encourage the development and activation of readers' background knowledge. These chapters feature concrete applications of theory by using content area materials to demonstrate vocabulary development and comprehension skills and strategies.

Every chapter has been reworked to reflect the latest developments in reading instruction. Chapter 1, "Reading in the Secondary School," has a new section on the literacy demands facing secondary school students. Chapter 4, "Reading-Study Skills," and Chapter 6, "Adjusting Reading Assignments to Fit All Students," have been revised to offer more activities, more strategies, and more suggestions on increasing reading comprehension across the content areas. The two content area chapters, Chapter 8 and Chapter 9, have been updated to reflect changes in the way content area subjects are taught. Both chapters contain new facsimile textbook pages. Chapter 10, "Assessment Procedures," has also been updated to cover new information on formal and informal assessment, including process and holistic assessment in secondary schools. Chapter 11, "Secondary School Reading Programs," stresses involvement of all school personnel in creating schoolwide reading programs. All chapters feature new examples from secondary level textbooks in fourteen content areas to show application of reading theories and strategies to actual content area classroom materials.

Features of the Text

This text presents a balance of theory and applications related to secondary school reading. Throughout, reading is viewed as an interactive process in which the reader both brings information to the text and takes information from the text. *Secondary School Reading Instruction: The Content Areas*, fourth edition, provides unique emphasis on the content areas with practical strategies and illustrations of content materials from all high school subject areas. In all chapters, extensive use is made of actual secondary school material to explicitly bring theory into practice. A major strength of this book is the guidance it provides teachers in helping students improve their reading performance through mastery of reading and study skills. To help the reader gain a more complete understanding of content, each text chapter contains the following features:

Overview. A brief description of the most important concepts and themes of each chapter. Readers can use the overview to provide a mental set for reading the chapter.

Purpose-Setting Questions. Purpose-setting questions focus readers' attention on the important aspects of chapter content.

Key Vocabulary. Terms from the chapter are highlighted, calling attention to their importance. Placed at the beginning of the chapter, key terms alert readers to important ideas and concepts.

Summary. The summary pulls together the main ideas of the chapter. Readers can use the summary to review their own knowledge and reinforce chapter content.

Self-Test. Multiple-choice questions on important concepts require student recall of chapter material. Self-tests can be used as self-monitoring aids both as post-reading activities and as study aids for exams. Answers to self-tests are provided in the text appendix.

Thought Questions. Higher-level essay questions that teachers can use as homework assignments or as the basis of class discussion are provided for each chapter.

Enrichment Activities. Application activities that go beyond chapter content provide students with opportunities to practice what they have learned in each chapter. These range from ideas for research papers to creating lesson plans and using strategies.

In addition, the *Instructor's Resource Manual with Test Items* offers chapter-by-chapter sets of examination items, including essay, true-false, multiple-choice, and completion questions. Each chapter also offers ideas for extra teaching materials and suggested teaching strategies. The *Instructor's Resource Manual* also includes a study skills learning activity packet, a listing of extra reading materials, and bibliographic information.

Acknowledgments

We are indebted to many people for their assistance in the preparation of our manuscript. Although we would like to acknowledge the many teachers and students whose inspiration was instrumental in the development of this book, it is impossible to name them all. Grateful recognition is also given to the following reviewers whose constructive advice and criticism helped greatly in the writing and revision of the manuscript: Donald Cushenbery, University of Nebraska, Omaha; Betsy Hobbs, West Virginia University; Sylvia Hutchinson, University of Georgia, Athens; Gary Negin, University of California, San Bernardino; Desmond Rice, Lamar University; Sherrie Shugarman, University of Dayton; Linda Smetana, Holy Names College; Timothy Standal, University of Washington. In addition, appreciation is expressed for those who have granted permission to use sample materials or citations from their respective works.

Betty D. Roe, Tennessee Technological University

Barbara D. Stoodt, University of North Carolina at Greensboro

Secondary School Reading Instruction

THE CONTENT AREAS

READING IN THE SECONDARY SCHOOL

OVERVIEW

This chapter opens with a discussion of the nature of reading, followed by a look at the literacy demands on secondary school students. An overview of the secondary school reading program is presented, including a discussion of the relationship of reading instruction to the secondary school curriculum. Faulty assumptions about teaching reading are examined, and then reading achievement levels of students and minimum competency requirements for students are addressed.

PURPOSE-SETTING QUESTIONS

As you read this chapter, try to answer these questions:

1. What occurs during the reading process?
2. What literacy demands do secondary school students face?
3. What are the major phases of a secondary school reading program?
4. What are some faulty assumptions about teaching reading in secondary schools?
5. What are some concerns about reading achievement levels of secondary school students?
6. What is the purpose of minimum competency testing?

KEY VOCABULARY

As you read this chapter, check your understanding of these terms:

word identification
   skills
study skills
content area reading
comprehensive reading
   program
developmental reading

corrective/remedial
   reading
capacity level
recreational reading
minimum competency
   tests

A Content Area Teacher's Challenge

"My students aren't doing their reading assignments for my class. I don't know whether they *can't* or just *won't* read the material. Either way, my lessons haven't been going smoothly," a new secondary school teacher complained to a colleague.

"First, you need to find out if they *can* read the material," the colleague replied. "Do you know how to construct a *cloze test* or a *group reading inventory*?"

"No. Are they hard to do?" the new teacher responded.

"Cloze tests are easier to construct. However, you may feel that you get more specific information from the inventory," the colleague answered.

"Will you show me how to make these assessments?" asked the new teacher. "And will you help me interpret the results?"

"I'll lend you a book that describes them," the colleague said. "I got it for a college methods course. I'm sorry that I don't have more time to help, but you might ask the special reading teacher or the reading consultant for some assistance too."

"I didn't think of that," the new teacher admitted. "Thanks for your advice."

After studying the book's description of the two assessment measures, the teacher chose to prepare and administer a cloze test to the students. The results surprised her. Only a small number of the students appeared to be capable of reading the text independently. The majority could read it with teacher assistance, but some could not read it with understanding, even with teacher assistance.

"Thank goodness for the independent level group," she thought, "but what can I do to help the others?"

She returned to her colleague with her new question. He replied, "Check out that book some more. It suggests strategies that help prepare students for reading, guide them through reading, and direct them in analysis after reading. It describes study methods and ideas for study guides and other instructional activities for those students who can learn from the text with help. It suggests alternative materials and strategies for the other less capable readers, but I still think you should talk to the reading specialists about this as well."

The teacher examined more sections of the recommended book and gained ideas from it. Then she talked to the reading staff in her school. She now had a better idea of what she needed to do, and she had more specific questions to ask them.

"Where can I locate lower-level reading material for the students who can't read this text?" she asked.

"Enlist the help of the media specialist," she was told. "Also make some transcripts of class discussions that can be duplicated and used as reading material for these students."

"Oh, yes. I remember that idea," she said. "The book called it use of language experience materials. What would you suggest that I do to prepare the ones who can read the text with help for successful reading?"

"For *all* your students, try developing the new vocabulary through semantic webs or semantic feature analysis. Provide purposes for their reading that involve higher-level thinking. Perhaps use anticipation guides," she was told.

"The book explains all those activities," she said with relief. "I guess I had better get busy."

"If you need help when you get into the process, call me," the reading consultant said. "I'll be glad to lend a hand with specifics."

"It's sure good to have some direction for this," the teacher sighed. "Who would have thought I'd be so concerned about *reading*? I'm a *science* teacher."

Although this scenario is not based on the experience of a particular teacher, the plight of this teacher is a common one. Teachers who have not had courses in secondary reading methods often find themselves in this situation. How good it would be if they could all find colleagues with the right books and advice to offer! This text is designed to help teachers know what to do about their students' reading problems and whom to ask for assistance when it is needed.

What Is Reading?

Reading is described in many ways by different people. Some describe it as a thinking process. Others say it is the reconstruction and interpretation of meanings behind printed symbols. Still others say it is the process of understanding written language. All these explanations of reading are accurate. Despite continuing disagreement about the precise nature of the reading process, there are some points of general agreement among reading authorities. One such point is that comprehension of written material is the purpose of reading instruction. In fact, we consider *reading comprehension* and *reading* to be synonymous, because when understanding breaks down, reading actually has not occurred.

4

Many reading authorities agree that during reading the eyes sweep across a line of print in jerks (*saccadic movements*) and stops (*fixations*), sending messages to the brain during the stops. When the brain associates meaning with these sensory-perceptual messages, reading occurs. The word identification skills of sight word recognition, use of context clues, structural analysis, phonic analysis, and use of the dictionary's respellings for pronunciation facilitate understanding by helping readers associate printed words with the words in their oral and listening vocabularies. Readers who lack word identification abilities are not able to make these associations; thus, they require assistance with reading.

During the reading process, there is an interplay between the reader's preexisting knowledge and the written content. Competent reading is an active process in which the reader calls on experience, language, and schemata (theoretical constructs of knowledge related to experiences) to anticipate and understand the author's written language. Thus, readers both bring meaning to print and take meaning from print.

The nature of the reading process alters as students mature. In the early stages of reading, word identification requires a reader's concentration. Eventually, however, readers are able to use their reading ability (ability to interpret written language) for pleasure, appreciation, knowledge acquisition, and functional purposes. Thus, reading competence has many faces. Competent readers locate materials and ideas that enable them to fulfill particular purposes, which may be to follow directions, to complete job applications, or to appreciate Shakespearean plays. In addition, competent readers adjust reading style as they move from narrative to expository content. Finally, they read with various types of understanding — literal, interpretive, critical, and creative.

The terms *literal, interpretive (inferential), critical,* and *creative* refer to the types of thinking that are commonly associated with reading comprehension. *Literal understanding* refers to the reader's recognizing or remembering ideas and information that are explicitly stated in printed material. *Inferential comprehension* occurs when the reader synthesizes ideas and information from printed material with knowledge, experience, and imagination to form hypotheses. This type of comprehension requires that the reader use ideas and information that are not stated on the printed page. It requires the reader to "read between the lines," to use deductive reasoning, and to make assumptions based on the facts given. *Critical comprehension (evaluation)* requires that the reader make judgments about the content of a reading selection by comparing it with external criteria. The reader may have developed these criteria through experience, through reference to resource materials, or through access to information provided by authorities on the subject. *Creative understanding (reading beyond the lines)* has to do with the reader's emotional responses to printed material (appreciation) and his or her ability to produce new ideas based on the reading experience. Creative understanding is built on literal, inferential, and critical understanding. A reader's intellectual understanding provides a foundation for his or her emotional reaction. For example, a reader may respond to an author's style or may identify with a certain character, story incident, or the author's use of symbolism.

Good readers exercise comprehension monitoring (metacognitive) strategies as they read. They constantly ask if the material they are reading makes sense, and if not, what they should do to remedy their lack of understanding.

Literacy Demands on Secondary School Students

Literacy is said by some to be the ability to respond to the daily reading tasks that are required (Taber, 1987). Secondary school students face the need to read content textbooks and outside assignments in school, but they have even more extensive literacy needs in their everyday activities. They need to read road signs, signs posted in or on buildings, recipes, menus, manuals for operating equipment, instructions for assembling items purchased unassembled, job applications, television schedules, transportation schedules, road maps, labels on food or medicine, newspapers, weather maps, public notices, advertisements, bank statements, bills, and many other functional materials, even if they ignore purely recreational reading. Failure to read some of these materials with adequate understanding can result in their commission of traffic violations, becoming lost, having unpleasant reactions to food or medicine, being ejected from unauthorized areas, missing desirable programs, failing to make connections with needed transportation, losing money, losing employment opportunities, and other undesirable outcomes. Our culture places a high value on literacy, and every member is inundated with reading demands in order to carry out everyday tasks.

In everyday situations, all people, secondary students included, must determine the information that they need and must seek this information. In a model secondary classroom, much instruction would center on issues and problems that are relevant to the students in everyday life, providing instruction in finding and understanding information, comparing and evaluating sources of the information, and going beyond the printed material by interpreting, generalizing, synthesizing, and applying the information. In fact, however, this type of activity does not seem to be typical in secondary classrooms, either in reading classes or in content classes (Feathers and Smith, 1987).

Perhaps secondary school teachers should think about how students need the material from their classes in everyday life, and then in many cases they could formulate a curriculum devised to help the students apply this information to real-life situations. In order to accomplish this, reading sources that are more varied than just the textbook would need to be incorporated

6

into the lessons, and teachers would need to offer the students guidance in approaching the reading of both the textbook and the supplementary materials, integrating the information gained from these print sources with other information from lectures, demonstrations, class discussions, and audiovisual presentations.

The job market also affects students' literacy needs. Research shows that there is a decrease in low-literacy jobs, and even jobs considered to be low in literacy demands may require the ability to read such materials as manuals for operating equipment. According to Mikulecky (1989, p. 124), "Workplace literacy calls for regular use of higher-level application and metacognitive reading skills (i.e., setting purposes, self-questioning, summarizing, and monitoring), while school reading is primarily fact gathering." Workers have to put together information from a variety of sources to solve problems and perform job requirements. High school students may not have opportunities to practice such uses of printed material. In fact, Mikulecky (1982) found that high school juniors read less than all types of workers except blue-collar ones, and this included reading for homework completion. Added to these findings are those of a study by the College Board showing that newspapers, magazines, and job-related reading materials averaged at tenth- and eleventh-grade levels in difficulty (Mikulecky, 1989).

Whimbey (1987) says that reading at grade level is not good enough in today's schools. He points out that a score of twelfth grade on the *Nelson Denny Reading Test* (a commonly used reading survey test) corresponds to a verbal score of only 370 on the *Scholastic Aptitude Test* (SAT). Most major universities expect students to score 900 (combined score) on the SAT. If the verbal score is considered to be about half of the combined score, a verbal score of 450 (grade equivalent of 14.4 on the *Nelson Denny Reading Test*) would be required of entering college students.

Providing a variety of reading experiences using varied materials can help students develop the backgrounds to read material needed in the real world. These students need some assignments in which their reading involves problem solving. Reading short textbook assignments in order to answer factual check-up questions is not enough (Mikulecky, 1989).

The Secondary School Reading Program

In recent years the need to provide well-conceived secondary school reading programs has grown as the population in secondary schools has increased and the importance of comprehensive curricula has been recognized. Comprehensive programs for reading instruction at the secondary level are described in detail in Chapter 11. This section serves as a brief orientation to the program.

The population being served in secondary schools today is diverse in a variety of ways: culturally, linguistically, mentally, physically, and economically. Teachers must try to reach *all* the students, not just the advantaged and gifted ones, who are the easiest to teach. See Chapter 5 for more on the diversity of students.

How Does Reading Instruction Fit into the Secondary School Curriculum?

This section is designed to explain the general relationship of reading/study skills to content reading and to show the content area teacher's position in the overall picture. It also shows the general organization and approach of this text. The concepts discussed here are analyzed in greater detail in later chapters.

Word Identification Skills

Word identification skills include sight word recognition, contextual analysis, structural analysis, phonic analysis, and use of the dictionary's respellings to determine pronunciation. The goal of word identification instruction is to develop students' independence in identifying words.

Sight words are words students have memorized and are able to identify immediately. Secondary students usually have a good store of sight words that help them read content materials with understanding. Each time a content teacher introduces a new technical or specialized term that is important to understanding the content area, the teacher hopes to turn the new word into a sight word for the students; the study of the subject would be inefficient if many of the important words had to be analyzed carefully before recognition occurred. The content teacher can help impress new words on the students' memories, and thus turn them into sight words, by writing them on the chalkboard, pronouncing them, and discussing them with the students. Knowledge of sight words also enables students to use contextual analysis.

Contextual analysis is use of the context (surrounding words and sentences) in which an unknown word occurs in order to identify the word. Contextual analysis skills are powerful tools for secondary students to use in reading content area materials, and content area teachers will benefit greatly from helping students become aware of the context and its usefulness in word identification. Contextual analysis not only plays a role in word identification but also is an important tool for determining word meaning.

Structural analysis involves the use of word parts such as affixes, root words, syllables, and smaller words that are joined to form compound words to help in the identification of unfamiliar words. Structural analysis is extremely helpful in analysis of content area words because in many cases certain prefixes, suffixes, and root words appear repeatedly in the related technical terms of a discipline. Learning to recognize these word parts can be very helpful in decoding the vocabulary of the discipline.

Phonic analysis involves breaking words into basic sound elements and blending these sounds together to produce spoken words. Phonic analysis is not generally stressed by the content area teacher but lies in the province of the special reading teacher.

Use of the dictionary's respellings to determine pronunciation is an important skill for students to master. Lessons in use of the dictionary's pronunciation key to help in decoding the respellings are needed by many students. Practice in using the respellings to determine pronunciation is also essential for complete learning of the skill.

Comprehension

Reading comprehension is an interactive process of meaning construction. The reader's background knowledge structures (schemata), the information in the text, and the context in which the reading takes place all interact to produce comprehension. Schemata related to the reading material must be activated if students are to comprehend material as fully as possible.

Word identification skills help students pronounce words, but word meanings must be understood before reading comprehension can occur. Many of the words that content readers encounter represent labels for key concepts in the content areas. A reader learns word meanings through experience, word association, discussion, concept development, contextual analysis, structural analysis, and use of a dictionary and a thesaurus. Content teachers can help students comprehend content materials by teaching them the meanings of key vocabulary terms. Structural analysis plays an important part in the determination of word meaning in content area classes. Morphemes, the smallest meaningful units of a language, include prefixes, suffixes, and root words. Each content area has common word parts such as these that are frequently found in instructional materials for the class. Analogy exercises, semantic feature analysis, word sorts, and word webs (or semantic webs or arrays) are all good vocabulary development activities.

To read with comprehension, readers must also be able to perceive the internal organization of reading materials, understand the various writing patterns used to structure content materials, and understand the material at the appropriate cognitive levels.

A reader's perception of the internal organization of a selection is based on the ability to identify main ideas and supporting details as well as on familiarity with various organizational writing patterns. Expository writing patterns may include cause-effect, comparison-contrast, sequence of events, or one or more of a variety of other organizations. For narrative materials, knowledge of story grammar (or story structure) is important. Readers understand content better when they are able to follow the particular writing pattern and organization used. Content area teachers need to be familiar with the types of writing patterns encountered frequently in their particular disciplines, so that they can help students to better understand these patterns.

When reading, students must comprehend material literally, interpretively, critically, and creatively, as each type of comprehension is appropriate. Modeling, discussion, a problem-solving approach to reading, visualization strategies, and judicious use of questioning techniques serve as five vehicles for developing these types of understanding. Because most content area teachers use commercial materials, such as textbooks, to teach their subject areas, they need to be familiar with the types of questions used in these materials. Some textbooks focus too heavily on literal questions and therefore do not provide the means for encouraging higher-level thinking about the content and certainly fail to offer enough challenge for better students. Other textbooks may be too heavily laden with higher-order questions, without first laying the groundwork with literal understanding, thereby overtaxing the abilities of less able students.

Content reading requires flexible use of reading rate. The concept of rate can be examined best as it relates to comprehension. Rate is governed by purpose for reading, type of comprehension desired, familiarity with content, and type of content. Content area teachers need to help students learn to vary their reading rates to fit particular instructional materials and different purposes for reading.

Study Skills

In the secondary school, students are expected to become more independent in applying their reading skills in work-study situations. Study skills involve application of reading skills to learning written content area material. There are three basic types of study skills: those that involve locating information through reading; those that are concerned with understanding and remembering content; and those that are concerned with the organization of information once it has been located and read. Content area teachers need to help students learn to use these study skills efficiently, so that they can study the content assignments more effectively. Teaching study skills in the situations in which they are expected to be used is more effective than teaching them in isolation. Examples of study skills can be found in Chapter 4, and application of these skills to particular content areas is discussed in Chapters 8 and 9.

Phases of the Reading Program

The total, or comprehensive, reading program should consist of at least four interrelated phases.

1. *The content area phase.* This phase of the program is for all students enrolled in a content area course. Here the student is helped to comprehend

the specific subject matter. Reading skills required for effective reading of the content area material are considered. Within each content area — English, mathematics, social studies, science, and so forth — reading materials with which students can experience reading success must be utilized. Such materials may include multilevel texts, materials from library sources with lower levels of reading difficulty, films, and tapes.

2. *The developmental phase.* This phase of the program is for average and above-average readers who elect to enroll in it. A special reading teacher, who directs the program, helps students to further develop comprehension skills, vocabulary knowledge, rate of reading, and study skills.

3. *The corrective and remedial phase.* This portion of the program is for students who are reading at levels that are below their *capacity,* or *potential reading levels.* Corrective readers generally read from six to eighteen months below potential. They are generally served by the regular classroom teacher through in-class adjustments to assignments and materials. Remedial readers may have gaps of two or more years between instructional and potential levels. These students usually need to work on basic word recognition and comprehension strategies and skills. As these strategies and skills improve, the students learn how to apply general study skills. This part of the program is directed primarily by the special reading teacher, generally in a separate class.

4. *The recreational phase.* Since the ultimate goal of all reading instruction is to develop good reading habits that will last a lifetime, this phase is an important, although frequently neglected, aspect of the comprehensive reading program. All personnel involved with reading responsibilities should take an active part in encouraging recreational reading.

Although English teachers and reading specialists have particularly strong reasons for motivating students to read for pleasure, all content area teachers should share the responsibility of motivating students to read recreationally. There are three major reasons for this:

1. The content area teacher may have a special rapport with several students who do not like to read and with whom no other secondary teacher has established this special relationship.

2. A certain content area may be the only one that holds a student's interest at a particular time. For example, a physical education teacher might be able to motivate a particular boy or girl to read extracurricular books on sports.

3. Particular subject matter becomes more "real" as a reader experiences events through imaginative literature. For example, the topic of the American Revolution, which might take up only one chapter in a social studies text-

book, will be more meaningful to a student who reads Esther Forbes' *Johnny Tremain* and becomes involved in Johnny's experiences of that period's political intrigue and his preparation for war. *Across Five Aprils* by Irene Hunt gives students broadened perspectives on the Civil War, and students who read *Talking in Whispers* by James Watson, a novel set in Chile, will have a better idea of what can happen to civil rights in a military dictatorship. Good nonfiction selections can also add interest to the study of history. Teachers may want to recommend *The Eagle and the Dragon* (about the United States' relationship with China) by Don Lawson and *Eyes on the Prize: America's Civil Rights Years, 1954–1965* by Juan Williams. Science teachers can enrich their programs by supplementing course material with readings in nonfiction — for example, *The Quest for Artificial Intelligence*, by Dorothy Hinshaw Patent. Teachers of agriculture can use literature to sustain student interest; for example, Henry Billings' *All Down the Valley* is an interesting story of the Tennessee Valley Authority. Teachers of composition may find Lois Duncan's *Chapters: My Growth as a Writer* useful, and music teachers may want to suggest *Nothing but the Best: The Struggle for Perfection at the Juilliard School* by Judith Kogan. Extra effort by each content area teacher to find interesting supplementary reading material may lead to enduring reading habits and tastes in the students.

Gee and Forester (1988) surveyed subscribers to the *Journal of Reading* and concluded that most secondary schools either did not have an organized reading program or offered reading instruction only in a class called "Reading." Some of these programs resulted from mandates from state agencies or local administrations; others came about through efforts by teachers. The researchers found that teachers' awareness of the reading needs of the students in their classes appeared to support the development of successful content reading programs.

Some Faulty Assumptions About Teaching Reading

There are several faulty assumptions about the teaching of reading that should be considered.

1. *Teaching reading is a concern only in the elementary school.* In many school systems, formal reading instruction ends at the sixth grade. The idea that a child who has completed the sixth grade should have mastered the complex process of reading fails to take into account the fact that learning to read is a continuing process. People learn to read over a long period of time, attempting more advanced reading materials as they master easier ones. Even after encountering all the reading skills through classroom instruction, readers continue to refine their use of them.

2. *Teaching reading in the content areas is separate and distinct from teaching subject matter.* Teaching reading and study skills is an integral part of teaching

any subject matter. A teacher is obligated to teach students how to use the printed materials that are assigned. When a teacher employs printed materials to teach a content area, that teacher is using reading as a teaching and learning aid — and should use it for maximum effectiveness. Teaching reading in subject matter areas is a complementary learning process, inseparable from the particular subject matter. Teachers' efforts to teach reading in various content areas are an important element in the success of any junior or senior high school reading program.

3. *Reading needs in the secondary school can be met through remedial work alone.* Some schools fail to make an essential distinction between *developmental reading,* which is designed to meet the needs of all students, and *corrective* or *remedial reading,* which provides specific assistance to readers who are having difficulties. Not only should developmental (as well as remedial) classes be made available, but within each class the content teacher can promote developmental reading by helping students learn the concepts and vocabulary of that content area, and they can enhance their students' reading comprehension by assisting them in interpreting and evaluating the text material. Corrective reading assistance can also be given within each class, as needed.

Additionally, teachers can help students develop better reading study skills and other specialized skills associated with the particular content areas. For example, reading and understanding written directions are skills that are needed in every secondary classroom. Other universally needed skills include reading to discover main ideas, details, and inferences. Even more important than absorbing the vast amount of printed material that they encounter every day is the secondary school students' development of critical reading ability. Before they leave secondary school, students should know how to sort out fact from opinion, truth from half-truth, information from emotion.

4. *A reading specialist or an English teacher should be responsible for the teaching of reading.* Reading specialists have distinct responsibilities in secondary reading programs, but the results of their efforts are negligible without the help of classroom teachers. Reading as a tool for learning is no more important in English class than it is in most other classes, and English teachers do not necessarily have any better preparation for teaching reading skills than do other teachers. Responsibility for teaching reading cannot be delegated solely to English teachers. All content teachers (English, science, health, social studies, mathematics, computer science, home economics, business education, industrial arts, agriculture, physical education, music, art, and others) have a responsibility to teach the language and organization of their particular content areas, and to do so they must help students read that content.

5. *The teaching of reading and the teaching of literature are one and the same.* Reading skills are important to the study of literature, as they are to the study of every content area. It should be understood, however, that teaching litera-

ture, even in junior high school, should not consist merely of having students read stories and then giving vocabulary drills and exercises to find details and main ideas. It is dangerous to assume that a student will improve content reading skills by practicing with only literature selections, for reading in other content areas involves primarily expository, rather than narrative, selections and the need to integrate information gained from graphic aids such as pictures, maps, graphs, charts, and diagrams with the written text.

Reading Achievement Levels and Minimum Reading Competency

In recent years, concern has been voiced repeatedly about the reading achievement levels of secondary students. A movement has developed to attempt to ensure that students attain a minimum level of reading competency. These issues are considered here.

Reading Achievement Levels

The wide range in reading abilities among junior and senior high school students presents secondary school teachers with one of their most vexing problems. For example, in a group classified as seventh graders, there may be boys and girls whose reading skills equal those of many tenth or eleventh graders. Some twelfth graders may have a fifth- or sixth-grade reading ability, whereas others may read at the level of college seniors. Teaching reading in the secondary schools includes both strengthening the performances of students who are reading well for their grade placements *and* giving more basic assistance to students who are reading at levels significantly below their grade placements.

The reading abilities of students in classes above the sixth grade commonly have a range of at least eight school years. Complicating this problem is the large number of remedial readers among secondary school students. Nearly 20 percent of all junior and senior high school students may be in need of small group or individual remedial work to correct specific reading disabilities (Wolfthal, 1981). Teachers in secondary schools should know that a student's grade placement may mean nothing in terms of his or her reading ability.

The National Assessment of Educational Progress (NAEP) is a study to determine competence in a number of learning areas, including reading. NAEP assessments in reading, involving nationally representative samples of students in the fourth, eighth, and twelfth grades, take place every two years. Currently, overall assessment results are analyzed by placement on a single proficiency scale, showing the kinds of tasks the subjects can perform at different achievement levels. National, regional, and subgroup (e.g., gender, ethnic group) results are reported. In 1990, there will be provisions for voluntary state-by-state comparisons in mathematics for the eighth grade level; by 1992, these comparisons will be available for the fourth grade level in both reading and mathematics (Salinger, 1989–1990).

The subpopulations that formed the basis for the first reports were composed of students of ages nine, thirteen, and seventeen and adults between the ages of twenty-six and thirty-five. The findings included the following information:

1. Relatively few young Americans could read and interpret graphs, maps, or tables.
2. Less than one-half of the nation's seventeen-year-olds and young adults could accurately read all parts of a ballot (Ahmann, 1975).

The Commission on Reading of the National Academy of Education has estimated that in the year 2000 an individual will need a higher level of literacy than was necessary to get by in 1950 (Anderson and others, 1985). If this is true, students will need to be able to perform better on literacy assessments as time passes.

There have been some bright spots related to the reading achievement of secondary school students. Roger Farr's historical analysis of reading achievement over several decades suggests that in 1976 secondary students were reading at about the same level as or better than students had been reading in 1944–1945 (Farr and others, 1978). Reading scores from the National Assessment of Educational Progress have improved somewhat over the years of the study. There was evidence that the reading skills of nine-, thirteen-, and seventeen-year-old students improved from 1971 to 1984. As a matter of fact, between 1980 and 1984 the reading skills of seventeen-year-old students improved for the first time since the assessments began.

The 1984 results indicated that almost all thirteen- and seventeen-year-old students had rudimentary reading skills (those necessary to perform simple, discrete reading tasks) and that almost 99 percent of the seventeen-year-olds and about 94 percent of the thirteen-year-olds had basic reading skills (those necessary to comprehend specific or sequentially related information). Unfortunately, however, only about 39 percent of the seventeen-year-olds and about 10 percent of the thirteen-year-olds had skills described as adept (those necessary for finding, comprehending, summarizing, and explaining fairly complicated information), and only about 5 percent of the seventeen-year-olds and 1 percent of the thirteen-year-olds had skills described as advanced (those necessary for synthesizing and learning from specialized reading materials) (*Reading Today*, 1986).

The results of the 1986 NAEP at grades three, seven, and eleven reveal several issues that educators need to consider. First, students still show a need for instruction in higher-level reading skills. Students at all grade levels tested had trouble elaborating on or defending their interpretations and evaluations of material that they read. Second, the assessment revealed that good readers do more independent reading and school reading than poor readers and that teachers use a wider range of instructional approaches with good readers than with poor readers. Teachers place more emphasis on comprehension and critical reading with good readers and more emphasis on decoding skills with poor readers. Another finding was that "at grade 11 . . . average proficiency levels for minority and disadvantaged urban students are only slightly above the seventh-grade level for students nationally" (Applebee and others, 1987, p. 6).

There have been concerns among reading educators and researchers that "the NAEP assessment is too limited in scope, is not innovative, and doesn't incorporate the latest information on the reading process and how to measure it well" (Thelen, 1990, p. 2). The participants at the Delegates' Assembly of the International Reading Association in 1988 passed a resolution that says, in part, "Reading assessment must reflect advances in the understanding of the reading process. As teachers of literacy we are concerned that instructional decisions are too often made from assessments which define reading as a sequence of discrete skills that students must master to become readers. Such assessments foster inappropriate instruction." Farstrup (1989–1990) feels that the objectives for the 1990 NAEP reading assessment represent a more current view of reading as an interactive, constructive process than did those for previous assessments, but he points out that the assessment instrument only marginally reflects these new objectives, largely because of restraints imposed by NAEP authorities to retain reading trend data.

Another major concern voiced by many is that there should not be state-by-state comparisons of reading competency because of the different approaches to education in the different states. Farr, however, disagrees that there is a problem with such comparisons. He feels that the comparisons can be used to promote positive change in state practices, but he wisely cautions against making decisions based on a single measure (Farstrup, 1989–1990).

Harste raises two points about the NAEP. He feels that the planned state-by-state comparisons are a waste of money because educators already know how the states rank, and he asserts that "[s]tandardized tests that reduce literacy to a single scale are, put bluntly, invalid, and invalid, generic tests of literacy have zero instructional usefulness" (Farstrup, 1989–1990, p. 12). He feels that the money for state-by-state testing would be better spent in seeking alternative testing procedures that reflect current knowledge of the reading process. Valencia and Guthrie also feel that the NAEP currently is invalid for use with state-by-state comparisons. They believe that the NAEP must reconceptualize reading assessment, considering it as more than a single test score. Noneducational determinants of test scores, such as poverty; educational determinants, such as instructional strategies; and literacy factors, such as metacognitive process measures, should be included in an assessment system, with the test scores as only a part. The test itself should make use of a variety of materials, responses to texts at a variety of levels of comprehension, consideration of processes of reading (e.g., use of prior knowledge, comprehension monitoring), and reading and writing interests and dispositions. Valencia and Guthrie also believe that the focus on collection of trend data leads to use of old test items, which may not reflect the literacy needs of today's population. In addition, the reports should be structured to provide teachers with more implications for improving instruction (Farstrup, 1989–1990).

John Bormuth (1979) pointed out additional trends in literacy in this country. Since 1947 the percentage of young people enrolled in colleges has risen, as has the percentage of workers employed in white-collar jobs. Thus, the populations being tested now often contain greater percentages of students in the lower range of academic achievement. Any apparent decline in scores (such as the SAT score decline during the 1970s) must be viewed with this fact in mind. Any stabilization of scores (such as that of the SAT scores in 1980 and 1981) or increase in scores (such as that indicated by the NAEP trend) may be viewed as even more encouraging than they would have been without this shift in population.

However, whether students as a group are reading better now than they did in the past is not the main issue for the secondary school classroom teacher. It is clear that there is, indeed, a very wide *range* of achievement levels in many classrooms and that many secondary students are not reading as proficiently as they should be in order to understand and learn from content materials.

In spite of acknowledged inadequacies of assessment tests, a fair-minded interpretation of the data surely should give teachers reason to be concerned. About 20 percent of the students in a typical middle-class suburban high school are likely to read below their grade levels; in a typical inner-city high school, at least 50 percent of the students may read below grade level.

Minimum Competency Programs

A development stemming from students' failure to achieve minimum reading competencies is the requirement by some state boards of education that students must acquire certain measurable abilities before they can be awarded a high school diploma. Local school systems or state departments of education have to consider many questions: What competencies should be assessed? How should they be measured? Where should the "passing" cut-off point be placed? What should be done for those who "fail" the test?

A number of states now have published minimum requirements for graduation. Oescher and Kirby (1989) reported that seventeen states require students to "pass" a minimum competency test in order to graduate from high school. Such tests are basically of two types: one is a "survival skills" reading test, asking the student to read a schedule, a medicine bottle label, or the like; the other is the "basic skills" test in which reading skills such as identifying meanings of prefixes or making inferences are tested. Both types of tests assess specific skills and are scored on the basis of specific cut-off points, but there is frequent disagreement as to what cut-off point should be set as "passing."

Competency tests have been developed at the state level in some states and at the local level in others. Instructional objectives commonly included on these tests are identifying main ideas and details, finding sequence and cause-and-effect patterns, making inferences, following written directions, using an index and table of contents, using a dictionary, extracting information from graphic aids, and interpreting and completing common forms. Some secondary schools use a commercially available standardized survey reading test (such as the *Gates-MacGinitie Reading Test: Survey*); other schools use commercially available standardized reading tests that measure survival reading skills or basic skills.

The cut-off point for "passing" depends on the arbitrary judgment of the local school system or the state department of education. Berk (1987) and many other educators believe that an arbitrary passing score can result in unfair and incorrect educational decisions. Additionally, there is a lack of uniformity in "preventive" or "follow-up" plans with students who are poor achievers or who do not obtain the required score.

In some situations, nonpassing students are assigned to a remedial reading class in high school. Credit for the English requirement may be given when a student successfully completes the class. The student may be assigned to a reading class throughout high school, depending on the degree of improvement. Remediation programs are very expensive, and they may not receive funding, even though they are state-mandated. Complicating this problem is the fact that a higher proportion of minority students than nonminority students fail the tests. These failing students may come from relatively poorer districts that can least afford the remedial programs, leading to situations in which the areas that need the remediation programs most may be least likely to implement them (Oescher and Kirby, 1989). If fairness to all students is the objective of the state programs, it is probably not obtained in these circumstances.

Singer and others (1988) studied the results of two types of placement on high school students who failed their district's reading competency test (one that had a reading grade equivalent of grade 8.8) but were reading at grade 5.5 or higher as assessed by a standardized reading test. They found that these students were "more likely as a group to benefit from placement in a regular English class than in a remedial reading class that does not provide diagnostically based instruction" (p. 519). The researchers believed that the students benefited more from the regular English class because they were beyond the stage of reading acquisition and into a stage of reading to learn

18

from text, in which they needed more stress on metacognitive strategies, higher-level reasoning skills, abstract vocabulary, and knowledge of things beyond their immediate experiences.

One concern about minimum competency testing is that teachers may just teach to have students pass the test, which would provide only *minimum* competency for everyone, rather than helping students reach their full potentials (Oescher and Kirby, 1989). Urzillo (1987) feels that members of school boards, school administrators, and teachers have a duty to ensure that the curriculum is more than preparation for test taking.

Another concern is that failure on minimum competency tests may have adverse psychological effects on students. Richman and others (1987) found that, when high-academic-risk students failed a minimum competency test, self-esteem was adversely affected and neuroticism and apprehension increased. When such students passed the test, measures of dominance/ assertiveness increased, but there were no changes in self-esteem, neuroticism, or apprehension. The evidence from this study appears to support those who believe that the test may be detrimental to some students. Catterall (1989) found that, although educators did not tend to see the tests as threatening to students, students tended to feel that in some cases the tests could result in their dropping out of school. There was also a strong association between failure on the competency test and reduced belief by the students that they would finish school.

Some educators have felt that minimum competency tests are unfair to some subgroups of our population. Airasian (1987, p. 407) sees two sides of this concern: "state-mandated standardized testing may be consistent with the desire for social justice when the criteria for attaining social justice are equal treatment, constancy of standards, and uniformity of judgments. However, state-mandated testing may be inconsistent with the desire for social justice when the criteria for attaining social justice are conditional on pluralistic standards and sensitivity to the differential attributes of individuals. Obviously, different perspectives on social justice will provoke quite different reactions to state-mandated testing programs." Some teachers feel that standardized curricula, brought about because of minimum competency testing requirements, impair their ability to match learning objectives to particular student needs. They worry about covering all the skills with all the students, even though some students have not mastered the skills already presented. Such concerns often result in inappropriate instructional pacing, which, according to research, accounts for poor reading performance on the part of students of low socioeconomic levels (Rosenholtz, 1987).

Ellman (1988) feels that the tests used are not valid for testing verbal skills. He points out such problems with all standardized tests that focus on speed, remarking that some students work more slowly than others and are adversely affected by the timing of the tests. He also believes that the test producers overlook individual differences in students' development of skills and knowledge, assuming that they all should have mastered the same material or skills by the same date. He states that the tests discourage holistic teaching approaches because isolated factors are easier to test, and that generally they do not attempt to test for creativity and higher-order thinking skills.

Some educators are concerned that diplomas should not be denied on the basis of a test. A legal decision was made about this in *Debra P. v. Turlington*, a case in which diploma denials were declared defensible if the tests cover material presented in the curriculum (Catterall, 1989). Some programs address the testing problem by trying to reflect the entire curriculum in the tested objectives (Oescher and Kirby, 1989). States have sometimes had high failure rates initially with their tests and have subsequently lowered the cutoff scores to offset this situation (Catterall, 1989). This attack on the problem does not seem as beneficial as changing the objective to reflect the curriculum.

Although many schools use minimum competency tests, the International Reading Association (IRA) has issued a caution in its position on minimum competencies in reading that was adopted by its Board of Directors in 1979. This position has been retained because it is still considered to be an appropriate concern. It is reproduced below.

> No single measure or method of assessment of minimum competencies should ever be the sole criterion for graduation or promotion of a student. Multiple indices assessed through a variety of means, including teacher observation, student work samples, past academic performance, and student self-reports, should be employed to assess competence.
>
> Furthermore, every effort should be made through every possible means to remediate weaknesses diagnosed through tests. Retention in grade or non-promotion of a student should be considered only when all other available methods have failed.
>
> For these reasons, the Board of Directors of the International Reading Association is firmly opposed to the efforts of any school, state, provincial or national agency which attempts to determine a student's graduation or promotion on the basis of any single assessment (*The Reading Teacher*, 1979).

The Minimum Competency Programs and Reading Committee of the IRA conducted a survey in 1983 and 1984 that was designed to investigate the extent and nature of minimum competency testing and programs in reading in the United States. The survey failed to show the degree of interest in such testing that Chall found in 1979 (Gambrell, 1985; Chall, 1979). Gambrell (1985, p. 737) notes that "the present trend appears to be toward testing across several grade levels and providing remediation across several grade levels for students who fail rather than using minimum competency testing results as a criterion for retention or graduation."

Today, minimum competency testing is still controversial, and there are serious questions about its benefits. Although W. J. Popham and others (1985) conceded that it was too early to tell whether most competency testing programs were beneficial, they described four programs (instituted in Detroit,

Maryland, Texas, and South Carolina) that had had positive influences on student learning.

SUMMARY

Knowledge and understanding of the reading process enable teachers to develop effective reading instruction. Reading is a complex process with many facets.

Of the four phases of the reading program, the content area phase is the primary focus of this text. The content area teacher has responsibility for this phase and for the corrective part of the corrective and remedial phase. The developmental phase and the remedial part of the corrective and remedial phase are generally the responsibility of the special reading teacher. Responsibility for the recreational phase should be assumed by all personnel who are involved with students' reading development.

There are a number of misconceptions about the teaching of reading at the secondary school level. These faulty assumptions include the notions that (a) teaching reading is a concern only in the elementary school; (b) teaching reading in the content areas is separate and distinct from teaching subject matter; (c) reading needs can be met through remedial work alone; (d) a reading specialist or English teacher should be totally responsible for the teaching of reading; and (e) the teaching of reading and the teaching of literature are one and the same.

Factors that influence secondary reading programs include the wide range in reading ability among junior and senior high school students and dissatisfaction with school reading achievement levels and the resulting trend toward minimum competency testing.

SELF-TEST

1. What is a good definition of reading? (a) Reconstructing, interpreting, and evaluating what the author of written content means by using knowledge gained from life experience (b) Pronouncing a series of words correctly (c) Looking at all the words on a page in rapid succession (d) None of the above
2. Which of the following statements is correct? (a) Readers bring meaning to print. (b) Readers take meaning from print. (c) Both of the above (d) Neither of the above

3. What type of reading program reflects the fact that learning to read is a continuing process? (a) Developmental (b) Corrective/remedial (c) Content area (d) Recreational

4. Which of the following is a true statement? (a) Reading instruction is the concern of only the elementary school. (b) Teaching reading is an integral part of teaching any subject. (c) Only a remedial reading program is needed in secondary schools. (d) Reading and literature instruction should be considered synonymous.

5. Who should bear responsibility for encouragement of recreational reading? (a) English teacher (b) Special reading teacher (c) Content area teacher (d) All these teachers

6. Who should bear responsibility for the teaching of reading in the secondary school? (a) English teacher only (b) Special reading teacher only (c) All secondary teachers, including content area teachers (d) Nobody, because students learn to read in elementary school

7. What range of reading ability commonly appears in classes above the sixth grade? (a) Two years (b) Four years (c) Six years (d) Eight years

8. What is a true statement about the cutoff points for passing minimum competency tests? (a) They depend on someone's arbitrary judgment. (b) They are determined with precision. (c) Both of the above (d) Neither of the above

THOUGHT QUESTIONS

1. Which "faulty assumptions" seem most evident in your school situation?
2. Do you believe that it is possible to increase learning in the content areas by providing appropriate help to students in their study of printed materials? Give as many examples as possible.
3. In your content area, how might recreational reading be promoted most effectively?
4. In your opinion, what factors account for many secondary school graduates' inability to read well enough to cope with basic reading requirements? Give reasons for your answer.
5. In your opinion, what factors account for the wide range of reading ability of secondary school students? Defend your answer.

ENRICHMENT ACTIVITIES

*1. What do you think are the most important things about reading that a content area teacher should know? Interview a content area teacher about this question. Compare the findings with your own views.

---

*Activities with asterisks are designed for in-service teachers, student teachers, and practicum students.

22

2. Keep a log of your reading activities for a week. What do your findings suggest about reading to meet the daily needs of young adults?

*3. Interview three students, one of each of the following types: (a) accelerated reader, (b) average reader, and (c) remedial reader. Try to learn each student's perspective as to the effect of his or her reading ability in terms of school achievement, self-image, and life goals. Share your findings with the class.

4. Visit a secondary classroom. Try to identify the range of reading abilities. Compare your impressions with those of the teacher.

BIBLIOGRAPHY

Ahmann, J. Stanley. "A Report on National Assessment in Seven Learning Areas." *Today's Education,* 64 (January–February 1975), 63–64.

Airasian, Peter W. "State Mandated Testing and Educational Reform: Context and Consequences." *American Journal of Education,* 95 (May 1987), 393–412.

Anders, Patricia. "Tests of Functional Literacy." *Journal of Reading,* 24 (April 1981), 612–619.

Anderson, Richard C., et al. *Becoming a Nation of Readers: The Report of the Commission on Reading.* Washington, D.C.: The National Institute of Education, The National Academy of Education, 1985.

Applebee, Arthur N., Judith A. Langer, and Ina V. S. Mullis. *The Nation's Report Card: Learning to Be Literate in America.* Princeton, N.J.: Educational Testing Service, 1987.

Applebee, Arthur N., Judith A. Langer, and Ina V. S. Mullis. *The Nation's Report Card: Who Reads Best?* Princeton, N.J.: Educational Testing Service, 1988.

Berk, Ronald A. "Setting Passing Scores on Competency Tests." *NASSP Bulletin,* 71 (February 1987), 69–76.

Bormuth, John R. "Trends, Level, and Value of Literacy in the U.S." *Slate Newsletter,* 4 (August 1979), 2.

Catterall, James S. "Standards and School Dropouts: A National Study of Tests Required for High School Graduation." *American Journal of Education,* 97 (November 1989), 1–34.

Chall, Jeanne S. "Minimum Competency in Reading: An Informal Survey of the States." *Phi Delta Kappan,* 60 (January 1979), 351–352.

Ellman, Neil. "The Impact of Competency Testing on Curriculum and Instruction." *NASSP Bulletin,* 72 (February 1988), 49–52.

Farr, Roger, et al. *Then and Now: Reading Achievement in Indiana (1944–45 and 1976).* Bloomington, Ind.: Indiana University, 1978.

Farstrup, Alan E. "Point/Counterpoint: State-by-State Comparisons on National Assessments." *Reading Today,* 7 (December 1989/January 1990), 1, 11–15.

Feathers, Karen M., and Frederick R. Smith. "Meeting the Reading Demands of the Real World: Literacy Based Content Instruction." *Journal of Reading,* 30 (March 1987), 506–511.

Forbes, Roy H. "Test Score Advances Among Southeastern Students: A Possible Bonus of Government Intervention." *Phi Delta Kappan,* 62 (January 1981), 332–334, 350.

Gambrell, Linda B. "Minimum Competency Testing Programs in Reading: A Survey of the United States." *Journal of Reading,* 28 (May 1985), 735–738.

Gambrell, Linda B., and Craig J. Cleland. "Minimum Competency Testing: Guidelines for Functional Reading Programs." *Journal of Reading,* 25 (January 1982), 342–344.

Gee, Thomas C., and Nora Forester. "Moving Reading Instruction Beyond the Reading Classroom." *Journal of Reading,* 31 (March 1988), 505–511.

Literacy Among Youth 12–17 Years. Washington, D.C.: U.S. Government Printing Office, 1973.

Mikulecky, Larry. "Job Literacy: The Relationship Between School Preparation and Workplace Actuality." *Reading Research Quarterly,* 17, No. 3 (1982), 400–419.

———. "Real-World Literacy Demands: How They've Changed and What Teachers Can Do." In Diane Lapp, James Flood, and Nancy Farnan, *Content Area Reading and Learning: Instructional Strategies.* Englewood Cliffs, N.J.: Prentice-Hall, 1989.

Monteith, Mary K. "How Well Does the Average American Read? Some Facts, Figures and Opinions." *Journal of Reading,* 23 (February 1980), 460–463.

Oescher, Jeffrey, and Peggy C. Kirby. "The Effects of Graduation Test Policies on Student Subgroups." *Administrator's Notebook: The University of Chicago,* 33, No. 5 (1989), 1–4.

O'Rourke, William J. "Research on the Attitude of Secondary Teachers Toward Teaching Reading in Content Classrooms." *Journal of Reading,* 23 (January 1980), 337–339.

Patberg, Judythe P., et al. "The Impact of Content Area Reading Instruction on Secondary Teachers." *Journal of Reading,* 27 (March 1984), 500–507.

Popham, W. James, and Stuart Rankin. "Minimum Competency Tests Spur Instructional Improvement." *Phi Delta Kappan,* 62 (May 1981), 637–639.

The Reading Report Card: Progress Toward Excellence in Our Schools. National Assessment of Educational Progress. Princeton, N.J.: Educational Testing Service, 1985.

The Reading Teacher, 33 (October 1979), 54–55.

Reading Today, 3 (December 1985/January 1986), 1, 18–19.

Reed, Arthea J. S. *Comics to Classics: A Parent's Guide to Books for Teens and Preteens.* Newark, Del.: International Reading Association, 1988.

Richman, Charles L., Kathryn P. Brown, and Maxine Clark. "Personality Changes as a Function of Minimum Competency Test Success or Failure." *Contemporary Educational Psychology,* 12 (1987), 7–16.

Rosenholtz, Susan J. "Education Reform Strategies: Will They Increase Teacher Commitment?" *American Journal of Education,* 95 (August 1987), 534–562.

Salinger, Terry. "Background on NAEP." *Reading Today,* 7 (December 1989/January 1990), 11.

Singer, Harry, Irving H. Balow, and Robert T. Ferrett. "English Classes as Preparation for Minimal Competency Tests in Reading." *Journal of Reading,* 31 (March 1988), 512–519.

Swift, John S., Jr. "Accountability, Testing, and Minimum Proficiency May Undermine Educational Change." *Clearing House,* 60 (March 1987), 329–330.

Taber, Sylvia Read. "Current Definitions of Literacy." *Journal of Reading,* 30 (February 1987), 458–461.

"Testing Students May Raise Legal Issues for Reformers." *Phi Delta Kappan,* 68 (February 1987), 481–483.

Thelen, Judith N. "Commentary: What's 'Dreadfully Inadequate' in Reading?" *Reading Today,* 7 (April/May 1990), 2.

Urzillo, Robert L. "Competency Testing: Blessing or Bane?" *Contemporary Education,* 59 (Fall 1987), 13–14.

Whimbey, Arthur. "A 15th-Grade Reading Level for High School Seniors?" *Phi Delta Kappan,* 69 (November 1987), 207.

Wolfthall, Maurice. "Reading Scores Revisited." *Phi Delta Kappan,* 62 (May 1981), 662–666.

2

DEVELOPING A MEANINGFUL VOCABULARY

OVERVIEW

Helping students acquire word meanings and concepts that will enable them to learn independently is an important focus of content reading instruction. Teachers of history, science, mathematics, home economics, physical education, music, art, and other subjects must help students acquire the terms essential for these subjects. Many of the words used in content materials are labels for concepts, and conceptual development is a major goal of content area instruction. Content materials frequently contain a high proportion of unknown words, so teachers may find it impossible to teach students every unknown word. Teachers must identify and teach words that are the most useful to students.

This chapter focuses on the relationships among word meanings, conceptual development, and comprehension. Research shows that readers with a rich store of word meanings comprehend written text better than students whose vocabularies are limited in range and depth.

PURPOSE-SETTING QUESTIONS

1. How are concepts related to word meanings?
2. How should a teacher choose words to teach?
3. Identify three strategies that you can use to develop word meanings in your class effectively.

KEY VOCABULARY

As you read this chapter, check your understanding of these terms:

analogy	key words
attributes	context
association	denotation
categorization	hierarchy
concept	structured overview

Introduction to Vocabulary

Vocabulary knowledge is fundamental to reading — a reader cannot under-stand text without knowing what most of the words mean (McKeown and Curtis, 1987; Nagy, 1988). The size and depth of vocabulary and ability to use it are strongly related to a student's reading comprehension, intelligence, thinking abilities, and academic achievement (Freebody and Anderson, 1983; Styles and Cavanagh, 1980).

Students who do not recognize important words in a reading assignment will find it difficult, if not impossible, to acquire new concepts and ideas from the written content. A significant number of the words in content reading materials are technical words necessary to comprehension. Dale (1975) stated that to know a content subject one must "learn its key concepts; that is, its language." Vocabulary is central to formation of concepts, acculturation, and all other learning.

Students need more than superficial word knowledge for adequate com-prehension. They need depth of word meaning and the ability to relate words to concepts and experiences. Words and concepts are so closely intertwined that researchers like Klausmeier and Sipple (1980) define concept knowledge in relation to word knowledge and identify a concept as a socially accepted meaning of one or more words. Naming is associating words with concepts constructed from our experiences. In the process of conceptualizing and label-ing, we mentally categorize or group our experiences, making associations among ideas. There are often many levels of categorization. For instance, we may group animals as pet animals, wild animals, exotic animals, and zoo animals, although all of these fit into a broad category named "animals." We create more and more categories for group experiences and knowledge as our experiences accumulate.

Reading as an Interactive Process

In this book, reading is described as an interactive process because we recog-nize the importance of readers' experiences in constructing their understand-ing of the text. *Schemata* (related clusters of concepts based on knowledge and experiences) are related to word knowledge and to the comprehension pro-cess. Readers combine their background knowledge with information in the text to comprehend printed material. Word meanings are a large part of the

26

background knowledge that readers use to infer meaning. Some aspects of this process are illustrated in the following passage:

> When Barbara arrived in Florida, a representative of the convention hospitality committee greeted her and gave her registration materials.

In this example, the first phrase cues the reader to use his or her existing knowledge of Florida. This may include information gleaned from reading, watching television, or having conversations with people who have visited Florida. Such clusters of background knowledge allow the reader to anticipate ideas and interrelationships among ideas. The information regarding conventions creates another set of expectations based on readers' knowledge about such meetings.

What Does It Mean to Know a Word?

Knowing a word involves being able to process it in several ways. The processes include pronouncing the word, associating it with a range of experiences, associating it with individual concepts, explaining one's understanding of it, using the word to express ideas, and recognizing synonyms, metaphors, and analogies that employ the word (Graves and Prenn, 1986). Learning a word thoroughly requires a number of exposures in a variety of contexts.

As indicated above, knowing a word means having a concept or concepts to associate with it. Most words are labels for generalized ideas, or concepts, about classes of objects. Concepts are the products of experience; they are the abstracted and cognitively structured mental experiences acquired by individuals in the course of their lives. The process of conceptualizing involves grouping specific objects, experiences, or information with common features into categories. The learner compares and contrasts items with which he or she is familiar and assigns specific examples to appropriate categories. For example, John Kennedy, Lyndon Johnson, Dwight Eisenhower, and Harry Truman can be classified under the category of "U.S. presidents." Concepts are a mental filing system that enable a person to sort out and organize relationships among specific items and instances.

Many concepts and the words that label them embrace a group of referents. The word *measurement* can include the referents *meter, ounce, gram,* and *inch,* and each of these words represents a concept. A word also can refer to a series of related experiences. The word *butterfly* can represent many different referents: *monarch, painted lady, kallima,* or even the opera *Madame Butterfly.* In this instance, the context helps readers know whether the author is talking about the insect or the opera. Readers refine word meanings and concepts gradually as they acquire experiences and encounter words in different contexts.

A solid knowledge of vocabulary helps us communicate through oral and written language. People with large vocabularies are well informed and use a wide variety of words with precision. The number of word meanings a reader knows is an excellent indication of his or her ability to understand content. Nagy and Herman (1984) estimate that high-achieving students know 4,500 to 5,400 words more than low-achieving students. Knowing word meanings enables students to read and listen with understanding and to select the words they need to express their own thoughts in writing and talking.

Students display widely varying levels of word knowledge. Beck and others (1979) identified three levels of knowing words: unknown, acquainted, and established. Obviously, the unknown level is the one at which the student has no understanding of a word. At the acquainted level the student recognizes a word, but only with deliberate attention. At the established level, the word meaning is easily, repeatedly, and automatically recognized. This last level is reached when the reader has a deep, fluent understanding of a word, meaning that he or she knows the word in the fullest sense (Pearson, 1985).

Each of us has four vocabularies: speaking, listening, reading, and writing. Speaking and writing vocabularies are substantially smaller than reading and listening ones. People recognize many words they read and hear, but they do not speak and write those words because they are often uncertain about their pronunciations or precise meanings. For example, *cacophony* represents an experience that teachers encounter daily, yet few people use this word in conversation because they are not quite sure how to say it. They also may not use *cacophony* in writing because of uncertainty regarding its precise meaning and appropriate context.

Many teachers and parents assume that students who have in-depth word knowledge know more definitions of words. But definitions alone provide only superficial word knowledge. Looking up words in a dictionary or memorizing definitions does not reliably improve reading comprehension (Nagy, 1988). Many teachers who have tried this method with their students can attest to its failure. A strictly definitional approach to teaching word meanings fails for a variety of reasons. First, many definitions are not very clear or precise, as illustrated in the following examples:

> *sedimentary*: Of, containing, resembling, or derived from sediment.
> *hogweed*: Any of various coarse, weedy plants.

These definitions are accurate, but they would not help a person who did not already know the word meanings. Most of the words in a definition should be familiar to students if they are to understand the definition. In addition, using a form of the defined word in its definition further obscures the meaning, and this occurs in both examples above.

Second, definitions are not always appropriate to the context of the material that students are reading, and the students may have difficulty choosing the correct definition for that context from several that are given in a dictionary or glossary. Third, definitions often do not give enough information to help students understand words for concepts with which they are unfamiliar. Fourth, definitions do not help learners use a new word. Research shows that youngsters have difficulty writing meaningful sentences utilizing new words when given only definitions of those words (Miller and Gildea, 1987). Definitions do not convey concepts.

Sheffelbine (1984) recommends that teachers take some definitions of words that represent truly unfamiliar concepts — such as those listed below — and try to do what students are frequently asked to do: "Write a sentence for each word in which it is used correctly."

persiflage: light, bantering style in writing or speaking
febrifacient: a substance that causes a fever
heterotrophic: obtaining nourishment from organic substances

The point of this discussion is not to suggest that definitions should never be used in teaching word meanings but to emphasize that they are only one aspect of understanding words. Therefore, they should be used in combination with synonyms, context, and conceptual instruction.

At the outset of this section, we posed a question: "What does it mean to know a word?" The answer to this question is that students who know a word can give examples of it, think of synonyms and antonyms, explain its meaning in their own words, and use it with confidence to express their own ideas and to comprehend written language. They have in-depth word knowledge, which permits them to use the word fluently in reading and writing. The purpose of vocabulary instruction is to develop students' word knowledge fluency.

Choosing Words to Teach

Research shows that students benefit from direct vocabulary instruction (Anderson and Freebody, 1981; Graves and Prenn, 1986; Stahl, 1986). Direct vocabulary instruction improves understanding of the specific words taught. Teachers must plan to teach key words before students read a selection in order to ensure understanding (Beck, Perfetti, and McKeown, 1982; Kameeniu, Carnine, and Freschi, 1982). Students also need to learn words that they are likely to encounter in subsequent reading in the subject area (high utility words). Since developing in-depth word knowledge is time-consuming and teachers have limited instructional time, they must carefully choose the words to teach (Beck, Perfetti, and McKeown, 1982).

Three categories of words are needed by students. The first is *general vocabulary*, consisting of common words that have generally accepted meanings. These words appear in both content reading materials and general reading materials. Words such as *neutral* and *mobilize* are in this group. The second category, *special vocabulary*, consists of words having both general and specialized meanings. The word *matter* is in this group. In general use, *matter* has the meaning reflected in the sentence "What is the matter?" The word *matter* also has a technical meaning in science content. The last category is *technical vocabulary*, consisting of words representing specific concepts that are applicable to specific content subjects. *Photosynthesis* is an example of a technical word used in scientific content.

The vocabulary in all these categories appears not only in textbooks but also in the reading materials that students encounter in daily life. Newspapers, magazines, advertising materials, and general fiction or nonfiction books include terms that students need to know. The widespread use of these words means that teachers can use real-life reading materials to enhance vocabulary development.

Students are likely to encounter many unknown, or partially known words as they read all kinds of content. Teachers generally find it impossible to teach all the unknown words that students will encounter. If an assignment has twenty-five or thirty unfamiliar words and a teacher devotes one minute to each word, twenty-five to thirty minutes have been spent in vocabulary development, which cuts into other instructional time. Since time and energy constraints make it impossible to devote this amount of time to vocabulary instruction on a regular basis, teachers need to focus on words that are essential to comprehension of the major points in the selection.

Key words are those that are essential to understanding the ideas and concepts developed in a text. These words are combined to form main ideas and important supporting details. In content area reading, key words are often technical terms whose referents are central to understanding the concepts of the content area. Teachers should examine textbook reading assignments carefully to determine whether the author has assumed that students know certain concepts which they actually do not know. After carefully determining which concepts are necessary for student comprehension, the teacher can develop those concepts and their related labels in class. Teachers should also call students' attention to how authors use words and language in content textbooks. Example 2.1 shows some questions that will help students think about concepts.

E X A M P L E **2.1**

Business Concepts

How does the author help you understand the nature of the business cycle?

If prosperity is the high point in the business cycle, what do you think the low point in the business cycle is called?

A *cycle* is a repeating period or time. The term we use to describe how the economy moves from good times to bad times and back again is **business cycle**. Sometimes this series of changes is like a roller coaster. For a while, everything seems to be going very well. Jobs are plentiful, and anyone who wants to work can find a job. People feel good about the economy and are willing to spend their money. Because people are buying, business is good. And when business is good, we say we are enjoying prosperity. **Prosperity** is the high point of a business cycle. Sometimes it's called a *boom*. Employment is way up, the demand for goods and services is high, and businesses are turning out goods and services as fast as they can.

Source: Betty J. Brown and John Clow, *General Business: Our Business and Economic World* (Boston: Houghton Mifflin Company, 1982), p. 144. Reprinted by permission of Houghton Mifflin Company.

Assessment

Assessment plays an important role in identifying vocabulary to teach. The content teacher may construct a vocabulary inventory to assess student knowledge of the key terms in a chapter. A vocabulary inventory is an informal teacher-made test — it may consist of matching words with synonyms or may simply provide students with a list of words to assist in identifying known and unknown vocabulary. Words that are known can be eliminated from further study so teachers and students can concentrate on unknown words. Known words can be used as context or synonyms for teaching unknown words.

Teachers should use assessment activities primarily when they are unsure of students' vocabulary and concept knowledge. If a teacher observes that students know the meanings of most of the words in a selection, instruction can proceed without formal assessment. On the other hand, if observation indicates that students do not know the meanings of many of the words, vocabulary instruction should generally be based on assessment.

A teacher may also use assessment strategies at the end of a chapter or unit of study to determine whether students have learned the important concepts in the chapter. If assessment indicates that students do not understand key concepts, these concepts need to be retaught. The strategies suggested later in this chapter may be used as either teaching or reteaching activities.

Dale and O'Rourke (1971) suggest four methods of testing vocabulary:

1. Identification — the student responds orally or in writing by identifying a word according to its definition or use.
2. Multiple choice — the student selects the correct meaning of the tested word from three or four definitions.
3. Matching — the tested words are presented in one column and the matching definitions are presented out of order in another column.
4. Checking — the student checks the words he or she knows or doesn't know.

Identification

In testing with the first method, identification, the students are allowed to respond orally or in writing to a list of words the teacher has supplied. Such a list should begin with easy words and move on to more difficult ones. Students may self-check their responses in this testing situation, thereby obtaining immediate feedback. This technique is particularly useful for alerting students to their own vocabulary strengths and weaknesses. The following example of an identification vocabulary test uses words drawn from a science book.

_____ observe
_____ describe
_____ hypothesis
_____ molecules
_____ atoms
_____ substance
_____ element
_____ interact

Multiple-Choice Testing

The second method of testing vocabulary, multiple choice, presents words in context. After students complete the exercise, the teacher should discuss their responses with them. Following is an example of a multiple-choice exercise:

Susan broke a window. "You're a big help," her mother said.

Susan's mother was being _____. (appreciative, sarcastic, ironic)

Matching Exercises

The third method of evaluating vocabulary development is to use matching exercises. The following set of words comes from a social studies textbook.

1. Census	a. A town near a large city
2. Human geography	b. The study of where people live and carry on their activities
3. Urban	c. A count of people
4. Population distribution	d. Areas where people live close together in villages, towns, and cities
	e. Where people live on the surface of the earth

Self-Checking

The fourth method of vocabulary evaluation is self-checking by the student; it is useful for alerting both students and teachers to vocabulary strengths and weaknesses. Dale and O'Rourke (1971) suggest the following self-checking code:

+ means "I know it well, I use it."
√ means "I know it somewhat."
− means "I've seen it or heard it."
0 means "I've never heard of it."

The following list of words for self-checking was taken from a mathematics book.

_____ commutative
_____ metric
_____ symmetrical
_____ pentagon
_____ hexagon

Teacher Judgment

With experience, content teachers become aware of the words that give students problems year after year. They should examine content reading materials to identify potentially difficult words prior to giving reading assignments. They should also decide which vocabulary development technique is most likely to be helpful for each identified word. Example 2.2 shows a page from a content textbook with troublesome words underlined by the teacher.

E X A M P L E **2.2**

Identifying Difficult Words in Content

Introduction

As mentioned in Chapter 1, we will use the computer language BASIC in this book. It is one of the most commonly used programming languages today. Different computers have different versions of BASIC; whenever possible, we will use a general form that will work on most computers. Where there are significant differences, we will give the necessary changes for the *Apple, IBM,* and *TRS-80* microcomputers. For other machines, differences can be explored in the Lab Activities that appear throughout the book.

In the first two sections of this chapter, you will learn how to use the computer as a calculator. Certain words in the BASIC language can be used to give the computer instructions, or *commands,* that it will perform as soon as you press the < RETURN > or < ENTER > key after typing the command. When a computer is used in this fashion, it is said to be in *immediate mode.* Later in the chapter, you will see how to store instructions in the computer's memory as a *program,* a technique that makes the computer a much more useful and powerful tool than a simple calculator. In the final section of this chapter, a short introduction to *graphics* is presented for the *Apple, IBM,* and *TRS-80* microcomputers.

2-1 The PRINT Command

One of the most useful words in the BASIC language is PRINT. The PRINT command allows the computer to communicate with you. It can be used to display on the screen any combination of letters, numbers, and symbols (such a combination is called a *string*), or to evaluate numerical expressions and show the results on the screen. When strings are used with the PRINT command, they must be enclosed in quotation marks, as in the following example:

Example 1

```
a. PRINT "HELLO THERE"        ←——— command
   HELLO THERE                ←——— output

b. PRINT "NOW WE CAN COMMUNICATE"    ←——— command
   NOW WE CAN COMMUNICATE            ←——— output
```

The result, or *output*, of a PRINT command appears on the screen beneath the command on the next line. PRINT causes the computer to display on the screen exactly what is typed inside the quotation marks, including spaces, as you can see in Example 2 on the next page. (The small shaded rectangles in that example are used to represent spaces in this book.)

Source: David L. Myers, Valarie Elswick, Patrick Hopfensperger, and Joseph Pavlovich: *Computer Programming in BASIC* (Boston: Houghton Mifflin Company, 1986), p. 17. Reprinted by permission of Houghton Mifflin Company.

Text: *Computer Programming in BASIC*				
Word	Page	Context	Structural Analysis	Glossary, Dictionary
commands	17	X		
immediate mode	17	X		X
graphics	17			X
output	17		X	
versions	17	X		
numerical	17		X	

As is shown in the example, words that can be recognized and understood through meaning clues are taught via context, words that can be analyzed through the chunks forming them are taught through structural analysis, and words that cannot be solved with the aforementioned clues must be located in reference materials such as a glossary, dictionary, or thesaurus. These techniques are described later in this chapter.

Effective Vocabulary Instruction

Effective vocabulary instruction includes concept development, expanding students' experiences and associations, using contextual information, and defining words (Nagy, 1988). Combining these elements results in a concept-oriented approach to vocabulary instruction. Students develop fluency when they work intensively with words, generating meanings and concepts. Working through activities such as those shown in later sections of this chapter will develop greater depth of word understanding than copying or memorizing definitions from reference books.

Contextual learning activities are effective in helping students acquire word meanings because they give students a deeper understanding of words. In-depth word knowledge also develops when students have opportunities to create networks of word meanings such as those established in associational activities.

Students learn conceptually when they develop an understanding of relationships among ideas rather than deal with lists of independent facts. For example, developing a concept of *river* would include linking it to other related concepts such as *waterway, transportation, tributaries*, and *recreation*. Of course, the word *river* can also be used metaphorically or figuratively to describe something that flows like a river, as in "a river of lava flowed down the mountain" (Blachowicz, 1986).

Existing concepts can be used as a basis for acquiring new concepts. For example, a student who knows what a horse is can relate the new concept of *unicorn* to *horse* in order to understand the new concept. The attributes of the related concepts can be compared using *semantic feature analysis*. Semantic feature analysis works best with words that are related, such as those related to a single concept or within a specific content area. Some of the words in the feature analysis should be familiar to the students, so they have a basis for comparison with the new words. For example, in the following semantic feature analysis (Example 2.3), students could begin with the more familiar sports of football and baseball and then add a less familiar sport, such as *soccer*, later. The teacher may develop the grid of vocabulary words and features, or attributes, related to them and let the students complete the grid by putting ×s in appropriate cells — the ones in which the rows for specific terms intersect with columns that are features related to the terms — or the students and teacher may develop the grid together as the terms are discussed.

EXAMPLE **2.3**

Physical Education Attributes

	bases	yards	rules	ball	field	official
football		×	×	×	×	×
baseball	×		×	×	×	×

The following example, Example 2.4, is the beginning of a grid. Students will need to add the attributes to be compared and then make the comparisons.

EXAMPLE 2.4

Mathematics Attributes

rational numbers	
irrational numbers	

Example 2.5 is an example of a type of semantic feature analysis for a geology chapter. This type was described by Anders and Bos (1986) for use in

EXAMPLE 2.5

Geology Terms and Ideas

Text: _Geology_

Topic: _Earth Materials_   Chapter 6

Important Ideas

Important vocabulary	interfaces between earth materials	abundant elements	rare metal deposits	predominant minerals	atom & molecule	element & compound	
interface							
minerals							
isotopes							
silicates							
carbonates							
sulfates							
halides							
oxides							

Source: William Matthews III, Chalmer Roy, Robert Stevenson, Miles Harris, Dale Hesser, and William Dexter, *Investigating the Earth,* 4th ed. (Boston: Houghton Mifflin Company, 1984), pp. 145–159. Reprinted by permission of Houghton Mifflin Company.

helping students in content classes learn relationships among important vocabulary and important ideas in textbooks. Teachers can create similar grids for significant vocabulary in many reading selections they assign. Students can use the charts to become aware of important concepts related to specific vocabulary as they study content chapters.

For a more complete understanding of all the facets of a new concept, teachers should include both positive and negative examples during instruction. In developing a concept of democratic government, students should identify governments that are not democratic as well as ones that are democratic and be prepared to explain why a particular government is a negative or positive example of the concept. Example 2.6 shows an activity that can be used as the basis for discussion of positive and negative examples of a concept.

E X A M P L E **2.6**

Mathematics Examples

Directions: Place a + on the line before each positive example and a − on the line before each negative example. Be prepared to explain your answers.

The concept is triangle.

_____ scalene
_____ adjacent
_____ isosceles
_____ equilateral
_____ left
_____ vertical
_____ acute
_____ right
_____ obtuse

In the following sections we examine vocabulary instruction and the role of experience, association, context, structural analysis, reference materials, and computer instruction in learning words.

Experience

Reading comprehension depends on having a large store of information about the world. Experience is vital to word knowledge, contextual analysis, and concept development. Words are learned more effectively when they are attached to real experience; therefore, real and vicarious experiences should be used to support vocabulary development. A student who encounters the term *intersect* in a mathematics text will understand it better because of his or her familiarity with street intersections. However, students cannot have direct experience with every concept they encounter in reading. Thus, teachers must help students build both direct and indirect experience through field trips, exhibits, dramatizations, films, television, resource persons, and pictures. They need to help students relate their own experiences to the passages they read.

Actual experience is more concrete than vicarious experience. The further an experience is removed from actual activity, the more abstract it becomes. Edgar Dale summarizes the degrees of abstractness of experiences in his "Cone of Experience," which is shown in Figure 2.1. Note that in his hierarchy verbal symbols (spoken words) and visual symbols (printed words) are the most abstract sources of experience.

Association

Association strategies are based on the notion that students should relate concepts and the words that represent them. Unknown words are learned by connecting them with known words that have similar meanings.

Association activities can help students learn vocabulary they will encounter on a field trip, when viewing a film, or when listening to a speaker. Teachers can write appropriate words on the chalkboard, pronounce them, and discuss their meanings, thus giving students opportunities to associate the visual forms of the words with the pronunciations and the meanings. This practice will help students retain these words. For example, students who are visiting a local courthouse may encounter such terms as *attorney, litigation, defendant,* and *prosecutor.*

Research shows that students need many encounters with new words in order to learn them (Stahl, 1986; McKeown and Curtis, 1987). *Discussion* is one means of increasing students' experiences with new words. Discussion helps students associate word pronunciation and meaning. Vocabulary discussions may be conducted in large or small group sessions. Students may brainstorm word associations for key words the teacher has identified and write down the words and phrases thus generated. They may identify synonyms and antonyms and create networks for target words. Many of the vocabulary activities in this chapter can be used orally with large or small groups.

In addition to discussion, association activities include matching exercises, in-depth word study, crossword puzzles, analogies, sorts, and graphic organizers, which can be used for prereading activities or for review and reinforcement after students have read a textbook chapter. Example 2.7 is an association activity based on a science text chapter on rockets; Example 2.8 is based on a science chapter entitled "States of Matter;" and Example 2.9 is based on a chapter on disease in a biology textbook.

FIGURE **2.1**

Dale's Cone of Experience

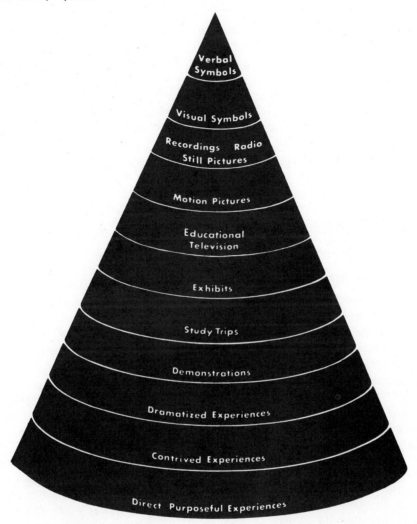

Source: "Cone of Experience" from *Audiovisual Methods in Teaching,* Third Edition, by Edgar Dale. Copyright © 1969 by Holt, Rinehart and Winston, Inc., reprinted by permission of the publisher.

E X A M P L E **2.7**

Science Association Activity

Directions: Draw a line to connect the words in Column A with the words that have almost the same meaning in Column B.

A	B
combustion	pushes forward
thrust	burn
propellant	supplying oxygen
oxidizer	pushing force
propels	burning chemicals or expanding gases

E X A M P L E **2.8**

Science Association Activity

Directions: Write S on the line beside a set of words if they have the same meaning. Write D on the line if the words have different meanings.

_____ hardness — rigidity
_____ brittle — will shatter
_____ tensile strength — can be pulled apart easily
_____ matter — gas
_____ malleability — lumpiness
_____ ductility — can be drawn into wires

E X A M P L E **2.9**

Science Association Activity

Directions: Write each word from the list below on the line beside its meaning.

_____ the science of disease
_____ departure from a state of health
_____ noninfectious disease
_____ biologically inherited disease
_____ signs of illness
_____ germ disease
_____ resistance to disease

pathology	hereditary disease
disease	symptoms
immunity	infectious disease
deficiency disease

In-depth word study is another way to increase knowledge of word meanings through association. This means that students study all the aspects of a word along with words that are related to it. The content teacher may identify specific words for such study or ask students to identify words they feel they need to study in greater depth. Students may use their textbooks, a dictionary, and a thesaurus to obtain the necessary information. This activity is illustrated in Example 2.10, which is an in-depth word study of the word *economy*, selected from a social studies text.

E X A M P L E **2.10**

In-Depth Word Study

Economy: "The management of the resources of a country, community, or business: the American economy."

RELATED WORDS AND MEANINGS

economy: (a second meaning) The careful or thrifty use or management of resources; freedom from waste, thrift.

economics: The science of the production, distribution, and consumption of wealth.

ecology: The branch of biology that deals with the relationship of living things to their environment and to each other.

WORD FORMS

economic, economical, economically, economics, economize, economization, economizer

Opposing Concepts	Related Concepts
liberal	frugal
generous	thrifty
wasteful	save
careless	accumulate
bounteous	amass
beneficent	chary
munificent	miserly
improvident	parsimonious
lavish	penurious
extravagant	curtail
impoverished	retrench

42　　Crossword puzzles are another approach to developing word associations. Content teachers may construct crossword puzzles for students to complete, or students may demonstrate their word knowledge by making up their own puzzles. Example 2.11 is a crossword puzzle that was devised to accompany a chapter in a mathematics textbook.

EXAMPLE **2.11**

Mathematics Crossword Puzzle

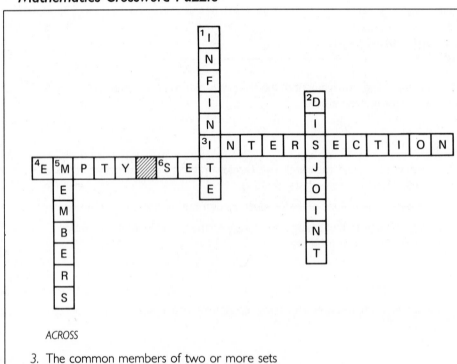

ACROSS

3. The common members of two or more sets
4. A set that has no members is an _____ set.
6. A collection of objects or things

DOWN

1. A set whose members cannot be counted is an _____ set.
2. Sets that have no members that are the same are _____ sets.
5. Things or objects that belong to a set

Concepts are taught through associational activities that encourage students to establish connections among the words and ideas. These activities encourage students to label and to think of likenesses and differences among words and to perceive how they are related. Among the activities that help develop concepts are categorizing exercises such as making analogies, performing sorts, and constructing graphic organizers, such as hierarchical and linear arrays.

Analogies show a relationship or similarity between two words or ideas. Analogy activities are conceptual and associational, comparing two similar relationships. On one side of the analogy, the two objects or concepts are related in a particular way; on the other side, the objects are related in the same way. For example, in the analogy *triangle : three :: square : four*, the relationship is "geometric figure is to number of sides." An analogy has equal or balanced sides similar to those in a mathematical equation. Analogies help students build associations among words.

Content teachers may construct analogy exercises for students. After learning how to form analogies, students can construct their own. This is a very important form of vocabulary study for college-bound students because analogies are frequently used to evaluate the word knowledge of students who are taking college entrance examinations. Unfortunately, many secondary school students are unfamiliar with the format of analogies; therefore teachers should explain that the colon (:) represents the words *is to*, and the double colon (::) represents the word *as*. Teachers can provide examples of analogies for the entire class to work through in preparation for analogy practice activities. When working through an analogy example, students should identify the relationship, complete the analogy, and explain their reasoning.

The relationships usually expressed by analogies are

a. opposites
b. origin
c. synonyms
d. plural
e. part-to-whole
f. function
g. homonyms
h. number
i. classification
j. process
k. degree
l. characteristic

Example 2.12 shows an analogy worksheet that was prepared for a chapter in a science textbook.

EXAMPLE **2.12**

Science Analogy Worksheet

Directions: Select the answer that completes each analogy. Identify the relationship expressed in the analogy and be prepared to explain your answer.

1. water : dehydration :: vitamins : (mumps, deficiency, diseases, jaundice, appendicitis)
2. taste buds : tongue :: villi : (mouth, stomach, small intestine, colon)
3. pepsin : protein :: ptyalin : (oils, fats, starch, sucrose)

4. liver : small intestine :: salivary glands : (mouth, stomach, small intestine, colon)
5. mouth : large intestine :: duodenum : (esophagus, jejunum, ileum, cecum)
6. protein : organic compound :: magnesium : (peptide, vitamin, mineral, salt)
7. pancreas : pancreatic fluid :: stomach : (water, saliva, gastric juices, intestinal fluid)
8. saliva : ptyalin :: pancreatic fluid : (trypsin, amylase, lipase, peptones)

Sorts are categorization activities, also based on common characteristics, which are useful in a conceptual approach to word meanings. The most common types of sorts are open-ended and closed-ended. In closed-ended sorts, the common properties of category members are stated at the outset and the identified category gives students a basis for including or excluding a class of concepts. In open-ended sorts, no category is stated in advance and no examples are given. Students seek to identify the relationships among the concepts, grouping them together and defining the connection that has served as a basis for inclusion or exclusion in that category.

Examples 2.13 and 2.14 present closed-ended sort categorization activities: the feature that all words in a group must share is stated in advance. Examples 2.15 and 2.16 present open-ended sorts, in which there are no stated sorting criteria.

E X A M P L E **2.13**

Closed-Ended Sort for Social Studies Content

Directions: Draw a line through the name in each group that does not belong. The common characteristic of each group is identified by the word in parentheses.

1. Bob La Follette, Jane Addams, Upton Sinclair, Theodore Roosevelt, Jacob Riis (progressives)
2. Edward Bok, Joseph Pulitzer, Carl Schurz, Samuel Gompers, Ole Rölvaag, Benjamin West (immigrants to the United States)

E X A M P L E **2.14**

Closed-Ended Sort for Home Economics

Directions: Sort the list of words into the following categories: protein, carbohydrates, calcium.

fish	nuts	bread	apples
spaghetti	cheese	kale	broccoli
eggs	sugar	peaches	milk
potatoes	cereal		

EXAMPLE **2.15**

Open-Ended Sort for Biology

Directions: Draw a line through the word in each group that does not belong and identify the common characteristic (category) of the remaining items.

1. intestinal juice, gastric juice, maltose, pancreatic juice
2. amylase, gastric proteinase, lipase, polypeptides, peptidases, disaccharidases
3. fats, amino acids, maltose, glycerol, simple sugars

EXAMPLE **2.16**

Open-Ended Sort for Secretarial Office Procedures

Directions: Classify the following list of words into groups and identify the common characteristic of each group.

sales invoice	multicopy
purchase order	purchase invoice
bills	horizontal spaces
sales order	binding space
credit memorandum	credit approval
purchase requisition	vertical line
business firm heading	

Graphic organizers illustrate hierarchical and/or linear relationships among the key concepts in a content textbook, chapter, or unit. Graphic organizers called *structured overviews* are based on Ausubel's (1978) theory that an orderly arrangement of concepts helps students learn them. A graphic organizer gives students a structure for incorporating new concepts, thus helping them anticipate the words and concepts in a content selection.

Hierarchical graphic organizers are used when the relationships portrayed fit into a subordinate-superordinate array. The social studies content in Example 2.17 and the biology content in Example 2.18 fit into hierarchical arrays.

Barron (1969) recommended the following steps for developing structured overviews.

1. Identify the words (concepts) that are important for students to understand.
2. Arrange the words (concepts) into a structure that illustrates the interrelationships among them.

3. Add to the structure words (concepts) that the students understand in order to show the relationship between the specific learning task at hand and the discipline.
4. Analyze the overview. Are the major relationships shown clearly? Can the overview be simplified and still communicate the important relationships?

The relationships in a structured overview are usually arranged in the following manner:

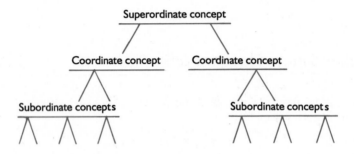

EXAMPLE **2.17**

Graphic Organizer for Social Studies

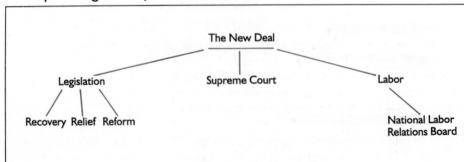

EXAMPLE **2.18**

Graphic Organizer for Biology

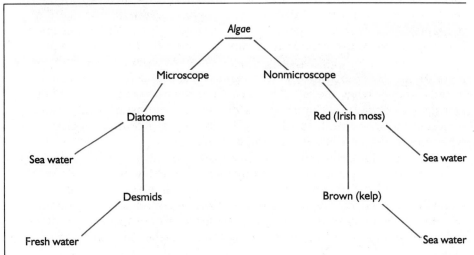

Linear arrays are created on a horizontal line, showing gradations of meanings for related terms. This is illustrated in Example 2.19.

EXAMPLE **2.19**

Linear Array

Euphoric	Joyful	Delighted	Happy	Glad

Contextual Instruction

Mature readers use contextual knowledge to understand and remember word meanings. Context consists of the words surrounding the target word. One of the ways we acquire vocabulary is by encountering a particular word in a variety of contexts. Each experience with a word helps us refine our understanding. Readers use context to narrow a word's field of reference and to specify its meaning. Context alone usually does not provide adequate knowledge about unknown words; in fact, context is most useful when the reader already knows what the word means. Consider the sentence, "Although Donald was skinny, his brother was obese." A contrasting relationship is indicated by the context, but the exact nature of the contrast is clear only when the reader knows the meaning of *obese*.

Context is important in vocabulary development. Presenting words in isolation does not lead to understanding them. Context helps students understand word use and provides a model for subsequent use of the words. To use written context effectively, students need to be fluent readers who automatically recognize most of the words in a sentence. Fluent readers can devote more of their attention to understanding the text rather than to figuring out individual words.

Although contextual strategies can be introduced in various ways, discussion is one of the most meaningful ways to clarify students' understanding of words and to encourage them to use newly acquired words. Students should deliberately try to employ new words in speaking, reading, writing, and listening. As they use new words, both in and outside class, students can make inferences about word meanings and tie them to their own concepts and experiences.

Research shows that instructing students in how to derive word meaning from context improves their ability to acquire vocabulary (Jenkins, Matlock, and Slocum, 1989). This research also shows the importance of practice in deriving meaning from context. Students need considerable practice in deriving word meaning from context in order to learn to use context clues effectively. Teachers should encourage students to identify the various types of contextual aids in their reading materials. Having students use examples of context clues in their own compositions will increase their understanding of them. After using context clues in their own writing, students may exchange papers with others in the class for additional practice with finding context clues. The following examples show semantic and syntactic clues.

Semantic clue: The harshness in his voice and the scowl on his face told that father was in a *captious* mood.

Syntactic clue: His *truculent* criticism of the article revealed his deepest feelings.

In the first example, the meaning of *captious* is suggested by the meanings of other words in the sentence, such as *harshness in his voice* and *scowl on his face*. In the second example, the reader who finds the word *truculent* unfamiliar can tell by its position in the sentence that the word is not a noun or a verb. Its position indicates that it describes a type of criticism; therefore, it is an adjective.

The following list shows types of context clues that can be helpful to students.

1. Definition	A *micrometer* is an instrument used for measuring minute distances.
2. Restatement	A cockroach has two *antennae,* or feelers, at its head.
3. Example	"The ship plows the sea" is an example of a *metaphor*.
4. Comparison/contrast	A *machete,* like a sword, can be very dangerous. In bright light, the pupils of the eyes contract; in the dark, they *dilate*.
5. Description	The *ginkgo* is a tree of eastern China that has fan-shaped leaves and provides much shade.
6. Synonyms/antonyms	The *mercury* in the thermometer was dropping — the *quicksilver* was contracting. The *acid,* not the *base,* reddened the litmus paper.
7. Familiar experience or language	*Artificial respiration* was applied to the nearly drowned man.
8. Association	He ate as *ravenously* as a bear.
9. Reflection of mood	All alone, Jim heard the creaking sound of the opening door and saw a shadowy figure standing suddenly before him. Jim was literally *stupefied*.
10. Summary	Even though he was sixty-five years old, he continued to love sports. He played a skillful game of tennis and seldom missed his daily swim. He was very *athletic*.

Context clues can be developed with special types of words such as homonyms (That is the only *course* he could take. The dress was made from *coarse* material.), synonyms (*drill — bore*), antonyms (*talkative — taciturn*), and homographs. Homographs are words that look alike but have different meanings and pronunciations (Did you *record* the science experiment? Jim broke

Tom's *record* for the most interceptions in one game.). Multiple meanings of words can cause confusion for readers. The word *base* may appear in mathematics class with a very specific meaning, but the student may already know the word with a different meaning as used in "the *base* of the lamp" or "Jim is stationed at the air *base*."

As illustrated in this section, context clues are not only useful, but essential, in understanding words and the specific meanings used in a particular instance. However, use of context clues is contingent on students' knowledge and abilities. Students must use reasoning abilities when encountering an unknown word. They must consider what has been said earlier in the passage that might help reveal the word's meaning. In addition, they must consider whether any other words might fit into that slot in the sentence.

Students must have a sizable store of word meanings if they are to use context clues. They must know most of the surrounding words in the sentence in order to use them to determine the meaning of the unknown word. They also need background information about the topic. A reader who knows a great deal about cars, for example, will be better able to read and understand words like *generator, transmission, chassis, accelerator, gasket, lubrication,* and *ignition system* and even more technical terms like *bore, stroke, displacement, valve, compression, drive shafts, axle, distributor, plug thread,* and *exhaust system.*

Students need to be encouraged to keep reading backward and forward to where clues may be, to generate hypotheses and test alternative possibilities, to demand sense, and to recognize a wide variety of language clues. To refine word meaning, readers must frequently use context clues in combination with the dictionary.

An activity like sentence completion can be used in discussion groups. For example, if students were studying the words *bizarre, beguiling, astounding,* and *illustrious,* they might choose the appropriate word to complete this sentence: "She was a(n) _____ young woman." Then they should be prepared to explain their choice, and this strategy could be elaborated by providing more extensive context or description to influence students' inferences. For example, the context could explain that the young woman in question had gained notoriety by going over Niagara Falls in a barrel. A sound vocabulary program includes many activities that require students to use, not just to state, the meanings of words they are learning.

Figurative Language

Figurative language is an aspect of the context, a form of rhetoric used to persuade or otherwise communicate with others. It is usually vivid and imaginative, as in the second of the following two sentences.

The man was bigger than the boy.
The man was a giant next to the terrified boy.

The figurative language in the second sentence expresses the idea effectively and interestingly. The first sentence is literal, whereas the second relies on picturesque, imaginative language to heighten the comparison. We all use figurative speech as we talk; therefore, students will be familiar with many figurative expressions. However, they should carefully consider how authors use figures of speech to convey meaning.

The most common types of figurative language are personification, simile, metaphor, and hyperbole. Euphemism and allusion are also forms of figurative language, but they occur less frequently. The following are examples of each type of figurative language:

1. *Personification*. Human or personal qualities are given to inanimate things or ideas. A ship is called "she," and we speak of "Mother" Earth. Personification is used in the following sentence: "The moon smiled down on the lovers."
2. *Simile*. A direct comparison is made between things. The words *like, as . . . as,* and *so . . . as* are frequently used in making the comparisons in similes. Similes are useful because they help us illustrate our thoughts and ideas. An example of a sentence containing a simile is, "The thunder reverberated like an entire corps of bass drums."
3. *Metaphor*. This figure of speech helps writers and speakers create clearer pictures through direct comparisons. These comparisons do not use clue words such as *like* or *as*. An example of a sentence containing a metaphor is, "Her blistering remark burned in Jim's mind."
4. *Hyperbole*. This is an exaggeration used for effect. The speaker or writer deliberately stretches the truth, as in "I haven't seen you for a million years."
5. *Euphemism*. Euphemism is used to express disagreeable or unpleasant facts indirectly. Death is often described as "passing away," "going to one's reward," or "the final rest."
6. *Allusions*. Allusions may refer to Greek and Roman mythology, historical characters, or literature. Allusions are based on the assumption that the reader knows the characters, that the allusions will cause the reader to make associations, and that the allusions will clarify a point. For instance, a person may be declared "a silent Sphinx" or said to have a "Cheshire cat grin" or to be "carrying coals to Newcastle."

Instruction to help students understand figurative language should focus on the ways authors convey meaning through their word choices. Teachers should be aware of the particular difficulty that figurative language presents to students who are learning English as a second language. References such as these will help teachers in this area: Maxine Bortner and John Gares, *A Dictionary of American Idioms*, rev. ed. (Woodbury, N.Y.: Barron's Educational Services, Inc., 1975); and Richard Boning, *Interpreting Idioms* (Baldwin, N.Y.: Barnell Loft, Ltd., 1979).

52

Structural Analysis

Structural analysis, which is also called morphological analysis, contributes to students' vocabulary growth (White, Power, and White, 1989). Nagy and others (1989) found that students' morphological knowledge enabled them to identify words more rapidly and accurately.

Morphological analysis is based on word roots and affixes. A root carries the base meaning of the word, whereas affixes are primarily prefixes and suffixes. *Graph* is a root that means "write," as in *autograph*. Prefixes are word parts added to the front of roots, and *suffixes* are word parts added to the end of roots. Many of the roots used in content area writing originated in Greek or Latin. Affixes have two major functions. *Inflectional* affixes relate to grammatical functions, such as creating plurals and altering verb tense. *Derivational* affixes change word meanings, and they may also change the grammatical class to which a word belongs.

Inflectional affixes	Derivational affixes
en — soften	un — unannounced
ed — wanted	dis — dissect
s — hands	ness — arbitrariness
	able — serviceable

Morphological analysis is especially valuable when used in combination with context clues, which help students determine the correct meaning of an affix. Many affixes have multiple meanings, so all affixes that occur frequently should be taught. For example, the suffix *ways* in the word *sideways* can mean "course," "direction," or "manner." When a multiple-meaning affix occurs, students can use context clues to determine which meaning is appropriate.

Teachers may have students practice using morphological (structural) analysis through having them build new words by adding various prefixes and suffixes to the given root word or combining form. For instance, the word *construct* can be changed in a variety of ways, some of which are illustrated below.

construct

construction	reconstruct
constructing	reconstruction
constructed	reconstructing

The teacher can pose questions that will stimulate students to examine the structural aspects of words. Sample questions that might be used to develop vocabulary in a science class follow:

1. If *thermos* means hot, what is a *thermostat*? a *thermometer*?
2. If *hydro* means water, what do these words mean: *dehydrate*? *hydrophobia*?
3. How is *hydroplane* related to *hydrant*?

4. If *tele* means far, what is the meaning of these words: *telescope? television?*
5. If *zoo* means animal, what is the meaning of *zoology?* Who is a *zoologist?*
6. If *tome* is the act of cutting, what is an *appendectomy?*
7. If *micro* means small, what is a *microscope?*
8. Why would you call *dynamite* and *dynamo* first cousins?

Students can create a web of words structured upon a root. Webs may be developed by groups of students or by students working alone. Example 2.20 illustrates a web for the root *migr*.

EXAMPLE **2.20**

Web for Root Word

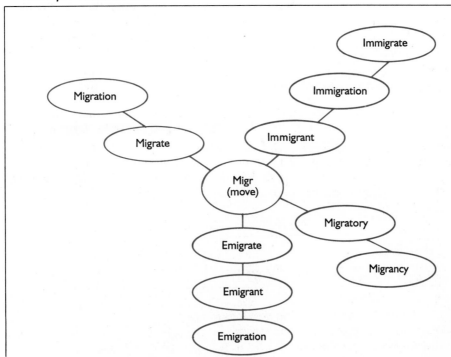

The Dictionary and the Thesaurus

Dale's "Cone of Experience" illustrates the abstract nature of printed materials as a source of understanding. Nevertheless, a dictionary and a thesaurus can be valuable sources of information. Students need to learn to use these references in conjunction with experience, context, and structural analysis in developing their understanding of word meanings. The following guidelines are useful for using the dictionary in content classrooms:

1. Help students select the appropriate dictionary definition by using the context in which the word appears. The multiple meanings included in dictionaries can create problems for students because they find it difficult to choose the appropriate meaning from those listed in the dictionary. With practice, most students can learn how to use content context to identify the appropriate meaning.

2. Identify only a few key concepts for dictionary study. It is perfectly legitimate for teachers to tell students the meanings of unknown words. Secondary students generally are more willing to use the dictionary when they need it if the teacher has not forced them to use it on a constant basis.

A thesaurus also is helpful for developing an understanding of words. Some students find it easier to understand and remember the synonyms provided in a thesaurus than to remember dictionary definitions. The dictionary format of recent editions of the thesaurus makes it easier for students to use as a reference.

Expanding Definitions of Words

Learners need to integrate instructed words with other knowledge (Nagy, 1988). As stated elsewhere in this book, comprehension is based largely on prior experience and knowledge. Words are understood and retained best when they are related to existing knowledge. Definitions that students generate help them relate new words to prior experiences. Defining activities like the one shown in Example 2.21 are useful in developing students' understanding.

EXAMPLE **2.21**

Defining Words in Different Ways

1. Use the word in a sentence that shows its meaning.
   Magnanimous people make good friends.
2. Give a synonym for the word.
   magnanimous — generous
3. Give an antonym for the word.
   magnanimous — selfish
4. State a classification for the word.
   Magnanimity can be classified as a quality of mind and soul.
5. Provide an example of the word. Either draw an illustration or locate a picture to illustrate it.
6. Make a comparison of the word with another word.
   Magnanimity is like generosity, but it implies more noble unselfishness.

Computer Instruction

Computers use programs that can help students to develop extensive word understanding. Computer programs are motivational learning tools for students, and students can use them independently. The most common types of computer software for vocabulary instruction are cloze passage programs; structural analysis programs; homonym, synonym, and antonym programs; computer dictionaries; and computer thesauruses. The specific software selected depends both on the type of computer available and on the instructional objectives. Software and computers are constantly being changed and upgraded; therefore, it is difficult to recommend specific materials. We do recommend that teachers read the sections in this book on vocabulary development to establish criteria for the software they wish to use and evaluate available materials based on their own requirements. Many computer companies and/or salespeople will provide demonstration disks of software to potential customers for examination before purchase. It is wise to take advantage of this opportunity.

SUMMARY

Students who have large stores of word meanings comprehend content materials better than students who have limited vocabularies. Research shows that direct teaching of vocabulary increases students' word knowledge and that students need practice to develop their fluency in applying vocabulary skills. Definitions derived from dictionaries and glossaries have limited value, unless they are combined with other approaches to understanding words. Conceptual approaches to developing word meanings are the most effective.

Since many of the words used in content materials are labels for concepts, concept development is an important goal of content area instruction, as well. Knowing a word means understanding the concept it represents. Vocabulary in content materials falls into three general categories: general, special, and technical. Because content materials frequently contain a high proportion of unknown words, it is impossible for teachers to teach students every word they do not know. Therefore it is important for teachers to focus on key vocabulary.

Assessment strategies are useful in identifying both known and unknown words and should be used by teachers who are planning vocabulary instruction. The following strategies are valuable in developing students' word knowledge and in providing them with practice in developing word

56

meanings: experiential, associational, contextual, structural analysis, use of reference materials, expanding word definitions, and use of computer instruction.

SELF-TEST

1. Why is experience an important factor in vocabulary instruction? (a) Experience helps the reader identify main ideas. (b) Experience helps students understand the concepts that support vocabulary development. (c) Experience provides a purpose for reading. (d) All readers have experience that is directly related to the subjects in their textbooks.
2. Why is it impossible for content teachers to teach all the unknown words in a content chapter? (a) There may be a large number of new words in a selection. (b) Teachers are not interested in doing this. (c) The students usually know all the terms. (d) All of these reasons.
3. How is the relationship between concept development and vocabulary development best described? (a) No relationship (b) A labeling relationship (c) A spiral relationship (d) None of these
4. Which of the following processes operates in concept development? (a) Comparisons (b) Petrology (c) Concretion (d) Signaling
5. Which of these activities enhances concept development? (a) Categorizing (b) Finding connections (c) Finding common properties (d) All of these
6. A check (√) in the code suggested by Edgar Dale means what? (a) I know the word well and use it. (b) I know it somewhat. (c) I've seen it or heard of it. (d) I've never heard of it.
7. What is general vocabulary, as it is defined in this chapter? (a) Common words with generally accepted meanings (b) Words with both general and specialized meanings (c) Technical vocabulary (d) All of these
8. When should word meanings be taught in content instruction? (a) As readiness for reading a chapter (b) As a follow-up to reading a chapter (c) In the middle of a content chapter (d) Both *a* and *b*
9. Which of the following is *not* a recommended approach to teaching word meanings? (a) Concept development (b) Association (c) Phonics (d) Structural analysis
10. Which of the following describes an open-ended sort categorization? (a) Examples are provided. (b) Categories are provided. (c) Neither examples nor categories are given. (d) Essential characteristics are given.
11. Why does a word in isolation lack a clear-cut meaning? (a) Words in English derive meaning from interaction with other words. (b) Words are hard to define. (c) A dictionary is necessary to determine the meaning of a word. (d) None of these.
12. Which answer best describes figurative language? (a) Literal language (b) Picturesque, imaginative language (c) Language based on artists' illustrations (d) Language rarely found in English

13. Which of the following is a weakness of definitional approaches to word meanings? (a) Students do not know the meanings of some of the words in the definitions. (b) Definitions do not show students how to use the word. (c) Words have multiple meanings. (d) All of these are weaknesses of definitional approaches.
14. Which of the following is a synonym for structural analysis? (a) Phonics (b) Contextual analysis (c) Morphological analysis (d) All of these

THOUGHT QUESTIONS

1. Why is experience of paramount importance in vocabulary instruction?
2. What does it mean to know a word?
3. What are the weaknesses of a definitional approach to developing vocabulary?
4. What are concepts? Explain them in your own words.
5. What are the strengths and weaknesses of context clues in deriving word meanings?
6. Why do you think practice is so important in developing students' ability to derive meaning from context?

ENRICHMENT ACTIVITIES

1. Prepare a categorization activity, as illustrated in Examples 2.13 through 2.16, for a chapter from a content area textbook of your choice.
2. Prepare an assessment using words from a chapter in a content area book; use one or more of the four methods of testing vocabulary that are described in this chapter.
3. Prepare a crossword puzzle for a set of important terms associated with a unit of work in your content area.
4. Select a chapter in a content area book and identify the vocabulary you would teach to a class. Plan ways to teach the chosen terms. Following is a list of content areas and the key concepts that might be found in a chapter in each area.

   Auto mechanics: thermostat, radiator, carburetor, ammeter, armature, commutator, generator, oscilloscope, polarize, camshaft, valve-tappet

   Music: choreographer, prologue, prompter, score, overture, prelude, libretto, aria

   Health: bacteria, virus, protozoa, metazoa, fungi, carbuncle, psoriasis, shingles, scabies, eczema

   Foreign language: masculine, feminine, gender, predicate, cognates, singular

   Art: introspective, murals, appreciation, technique, expression, properties, exhibitions, contemporary, interpret

Driver education: awareness, controlled emotions, maturity, irresponsibility, behavioral patterns, compensate, fatigue, carbon monoxide, medication, alcohol, depressants, visual, auditory

Psychology: learning curve, plateau, hierarchies, massed practice, feedback, frame, negative transfer, retention, overlearning

Government: delinquent, incorrigibility, omnibus, exigency, indeterminate, adjudicated, arbitrariness, interrogation, formulation, juvenile

5. Develop a worksheet for in-depth study of a word.
6. Make a graphic organizer for a selection in a content area textbook.
7. Prepare an analogy exercise sheet (similar to the one in Example 2.12) for a chapter or unit in a content area text.

BIBLIOGRAPHY

Afflerbach, P., R. Allington, and S. Walmsley. "A Basic Vocabulary of U.S. Federal Program Applications and Forms." *Journal of Reading*, 23 (January 1980), 332–336.

Anders, P., and C. Bos. "Semantic Feature Analysis: An Interactive Strategy for Vocabulary Development and Text Comprehension." *Journal of Reading*, 29 (April 1986), 610–616.

Anderson, R., and P. Freebody. "Vocabulary Knowledge." In J. Guthrie (ed.), *Comprehension and Teaching*. Newark, Del.: International Reading Association, 1981.

Anderson, R., and P. Freebody. "Reading Comprehension and the Assessment and Acquisition of Word Knowledge." In B. Hutson (ed.), *Advances in Reading/Language Research*. Greenwich, Conn.: JAI Press, 1983, pp. 231–256.

Ausubel, D. *Educational Psychology: A Cognitive View*, 2nd Ed. New York: Holt, Rinehart and Winston, 1978, pp. 523–525.

Barron, R. "The Use of Vocabulary as an Advance Organizer." In H. Herber and P. Sanders (eds.), *Research in Reading in the Content Area: First Year Report*. Syracuse: Syracuse University Press, 1969, pp. 29–39.

Bean, T., H. Singer, and S. Cowan. "Analogical Study Guide: Improving Comprehension in Science." *Journal of Reading*, 29 (November 1985), 246–250.

Beck, I., M. McKeown, E. McCaslin, and A. Burkes. *Instructional Dimensions That May Affect Reading Comprehension: Examples from Two Commercial Reading Programs*. Pittsburgh: University of Pittsburgh, Learning Research and Development Center, 1979.

Beck, I., C. Perfetti, and M. McKeown. "Effects of Long-Term Vocabulary Instruction on Lexical Access and Reading Comprehension." *Journal of Educational Psychology*, 74 (1982), 506–521.

Blachowicz, C. "Making Connections: Alternatives to the Vocabulary Notebook." *Journal of Reading*, 29 (April 1986), 643–649.

Carr, E., and K. Wixson. "Guidelines for Evaluating Vocabulary Instruction." *Journal of Reading*, 29 (April 1986), 588–595.

Carroll, J. "Words, Meanings, and Concepts." *Harvard Educational Review*, 34 (Spring 1964), 180–181, 193–194.

Dale, E. *The Word Game: Improving Communications*, Fastback 60. Bloomington, Ind.: Phi Delta Kappa Educational Foundation, 1975.

Dale, E., and J. O'Rourke. *Techniques of Teaching Vocabulary*. Palo Alto, Calif.: Field Educational Publications, 1971.

Duin, A., and M. Graves. "Teaching Vocabulary as a Writing Prompt." *Journal of Reading,* 32 (December 1988), 204–212.

Freebody, P., and R. Anderson. "Effects of Vocabulary Difficulty, Text Cohesion and Schema Availability on Reading Comprehension." *Reading Research Quarterly,* 18 (1983), 277–294.

Gillet, J., and C. Temple. "Developing Word Knowledge: A Cognitive View," *Reading World,* 21 (December 1978), 132–140.

Gipe, J., and R. Arnold. "Teaching Vocabulary Through Familiar Associations and Contexts." *Journal of Reading Behavior,* 11 (Fall 1979), 281–285.

Graves, M., and M. Prenn. "Costs and Benefits of Various Methods of Teaching Vocabulary." *Journal of Reading,* 29 (May 1986), 596–602.

Hayes, D., and R. Tierney. "Developing Readers' Knowledge Through Analogy." *Reading Research Quarterly,* 17, No. 2 (1982), 229–255.

Jenkins, J., B. Matlock, and T. Slocum. "Two Approaches to Vocabulary Instruction: The Teaching of Individual Word Meanings and Practice in Deriving Word Meaning from Context." *Reading Research Quarterly,* 24, No. 2 (1989), 215–234.

Kameenui, E., D. Carnine, and R. Freschi. "Effects of Text Construction and Instructional Procedures for Teaching Word Meanings on Comprehension and Recall." *Reading Research Quarterly,* 17, No. 4 (1981), 367–388.

Klausmeier, H., and T. Sipple. *Learning and Teaching Concepts.* New York: Academic Press, 1980.

McKeown, M., and M. Curtis (eds.). *The Nature of Vocabulary Acquisition.* Hillsdale, N.J.: Erlbaum, 1987.

Miller, G., and P. Gildea. "How Children Learn Words." *Scientific American,* 257 (1987), 94–99.

Moore, D. "Vocabulary." In D. Alvermann, D. Moore, and M. Conley (eds.), *Research Within Reach: Secondary School Reading.* Newark, Del.: International Reading Association, 1987, pp. 64–79.

Moore, D., and J. Readence. "A Quantitative and Qualitative Review of Graphic Organizer Research." *Journal of Educational Research,* 78 (1984), 11–17.

Nagy, W. *Teaching Vocabulary to Improve Reading Comprehension.* Newark, Del.: International Reading Association, 1988.

Nagy, W., R. Anderson, M. Schommer, J. Scott, and A. Stallman. "Morphological Families and Word Recognition." *Reading Research Quarterly,* 24, No. 3 (1989), 262–282.

Nagy, W., and P. Herman. "Breadth and Depth of Vocabulary Knowledge: Implications for Acquisition and Instruction." In M. McKeown and M. Curtis (eds.), *The Nature of Vocabulary Acquisition.* Hillsdale, N.J.: Erlbaum, 1987.

Pearson, P. "Changing the Face of Reading Comprehension Instruction." *The Reading Teacher,* 38 (May 1985), 724–738.

Schatz, E., and R. Baldwin. "Context Clues Are Unreliable Predictors of Word Meanings." *Reading Research Quarterly,* 21 (1986), 429–453.

Sheffelbine, J. *Teachers' Decisions about the Utility of Dictionary Tasks and the Role of Prior Knowledge.* Paper presented at the Annual Meeting of the National Reading Conference, St. Petersburg, Fla., 1984.

Stahl, S. "Three Principles of Effective Vocabulary Instruction." *Journal of Reading,* 29 (May 1986), 662–668.

Styles, K., and G. Cavanagh. "Language Across the Curriculum: The Art of Questioning and Responding." *The English Journal,* 69, No. 2 (September 1980), 24–27.

White, T., M. Power, and S. White. "Morphological Analysis: Implications for Teaching and Understanding Vocabulary Growth." *Reading Research Quarterly,* 24, No. 3 (1989), 283–335.

3

READING

COMPREHENSION

A long-range purpose of education is to prepare students to understand and use the printed matter they encounter in life. The morning paper, the news magazines, tax forms, instructions for assembling a bicycle, professional materials, and voting information — all these and other printed materials provide knowledge to those who can comprehend them.

This chapter develops your understanding of the cognitive process called comprehension. "Comprehension is the dynamic interactive process of constructing meaning by combining the reader's existing knowledge with the text information within the context of the reading situation" (Cook, 1986). Three major factors interact in reading comprehension: the reader, the text, and the context. Each of these is examined in this chapter.

Current reading instruction focuses on developing active, responsible readers (Brown, 1980). Teachers focus on guiding students in developing strategic learning that fosters higher-levels of literacy and the ability to monitor their own cognitive processes (metacognitive ability). "To foster higher-level literacy skills is to place a new and special emphasis on thoughtful, critical elaboration of ideas and understandings drawn from the materials students read and from what they already know" (National Assessment of Educational Progress, 1985).

A model reader is an active, strategic, constructive thinker who links new information to prior knowledge. Our explanation of the comprehension process stresses the active role of readers in creating meaning. We recommend comprehension strategies that are based on research; some are implemented before reading, some during reading, and others after reading.

PURPOSE-SETTING QUESTIONS

As you read this chapter, try to answer these questions:

1. What is reading comprehension?
2. How is reading comprehension related to content reading?
3. What is the student's role in reading comprehension?
4. Which reading strategies are available to be used during reading to enhance comprehension?
5. How is metacognition related to the reading comprehension process?

KEY VOCABULARY

As you read this chapter, check your understanding of these terms:

comprehension   main idea
inference   critical (evaluative)
schemata   metacognition
visualization   literal
creative

What Is Reading Comprehension?

The ultimate goal of secondary reading instruction is reading maturity. Reading comprehension is a major aspect of reading maturity and of fluent reading. Although many aspects of reading are controversial, reading comprehension is unquestionably important; it is universally agreed that students cannot learn unless they comprehend reading material, and they cannot remember what they read unless they understand it.

Reading comprehension is a covert process because it cannot be observed directly. What we see during the process are its products, such as answers to questions based on textual material. Students can discuss reading content, answer questions, and verbalize how they have arrived at answers, but their actual mental processes of comprehension are not observable. A good way to explore the reading comprehension process is self-examination of one's own reading experiences. The passage that follows should help you think about your own reading comprehension. It illustrates the reading experience of a mature reader.

As the reader sat down with a cup of coffee and the newspaper, her eyes fell on the front-page headline that read: BRRR BOWL . . . ZIP WIN WARMS FANS. The reader knew from this headline that she was reading sports news because her schemata (background knowledge) provided the information that the word *Zip* referred to the University of Akron football team, "The Zips." The team was so named because zeppelins are made of rubber, and Akron is the "rubber capital of the world." Knowing that she was reading sports news provided her with a mental set (expectation) to read quickly and superficially because she was not deeply interested in sports. However, the subject was an important local game, so she decided to read about it.

Recognizing that she was reading sports news activated a mental set for this reader for the way sports news is organized. The headline stating that "Zip win warms fans" indicated that the University of Akron team had won the game. The language "brrr bowl" and "warms fans" also indicated that the game was played in very cold weather. This was about all the information that the reader wanted regarding the game. Then, however, she remembered over-hearing a conversation about a championship competition, and so she established another purpose for reading the article: to find out the title for which the Zips were competing. She skimmed the first two paragraphs and learned that the team had played a national semifinal game for the NCAA Division II teams. At this point, she decided to find out how close the game was, so she scanned the third paragraph for numerals indicative of a game score and found that the final score was 29 to 26 in an overtime game. Thus the reader satisfied her purposes for reading and decided that she had missed an exciting game.

Although this account is of a single reading experience, with only one type of content and a reader who read for rather specific purposes, examining it gives considerable insight into the comprehension process. Notice that the reader did not read the first word in the headline first. Instead, her eyes moved to a more meaningful word, *Zip*, a noun that enabled her to predict the type of content in the article. The fact that this was sports news created a mental set for the writing style. Identifying this one word enabled her to predict the topic, and reading a few more words enabled her to use prior knowledge to predict the content of a large portion of the article, which covered one-third of the newspaper's front page. Detailed reading confirmed the reader's predictions based on her sampling of text information and her schemata. The reader used her knowledge of the organization of sports information to achieve her reading purposes. She inferred that the quickest way to determine the score of the game was to scan the article for numbers. She also evaluated the information — and regretted missing the game.

The reader used schemata (background information), semantic and syntactic knowledge, and thinking skills to comprehend the information. She used strategies for understanding that included establishing purposes for reading; relating schemata to written text; thinking at literal, inferential, critical, and creative levels; and reading for main ideas and details. She integrated prior knowledge regarding the Zips, football, and the weather with new knowledge acquired from reading. This brief analysis reveals some of the complexities of reading comprehension and shows how this reader used knowledge and skills to interact with the article and thus create meaning.

By now you realize that reading comprehension is a complex process that does not yield to simple definitions and explanations. Therefore, we have compiled the following list of generalizations to represent our theory of reading comprehension. Research supports each of these assertions, and they are the basis for understanding this chapter.

Comprehension is a process of creating meaning.

Comprehension is making sense out of text.

Comprehension is an active, constructive process.

Comprehension is an interactive process. The reader, the text, and the context interact in this process.

Comprehension is a thinking process that takes place before, during, and after reading.

Competent readers strive to understand and to regulate their own learning.

Comprehension strategies enable students to understand text, learn from text, and correct misunderstandings.

"Reading is a process in which information from the text and the knowledge possessed by the reader act together to produce meaning. Good readers skillfully integrate information in the text with what they already know" (Anderson et al., 1985). The resulting meaning will be processed and will further elaborate the reader's existing knowledge (Ruddell, 1986). Competent readers fluently integrate prior knowledge with text information; they have advanced beyond letter-by-letter and word-by-word reading so they can use their schemata to derive meaning from the text (Pearson and Spiro, 1980). Readers who are stuck at the word-by-word level laboriously work their way through texts, so intent on getting the words right that they overlook meaning. They read so slowly that they cannot attend to meaning (Lesgold, Resnick, and Hammond, 1985). They are unable to acquire information from the text to combine with their schemata and subsequently to construct meaning.

Figure 3.1 illustrates the interactive reading process in which readers are central. Readers use word knowledge, language, schemata, and reading strategies to process text. Their manner of processing is influenced by cognitive and metacognitive abilities and by their affective states. Cognitive abilities enable readers to hold ideas in their minds and to relate them to their schemata; cognition also enables them to address reading purposes and to solve problems. Metacognitive abilities enable them to monitor and evaluate

FIGURE **3.1**

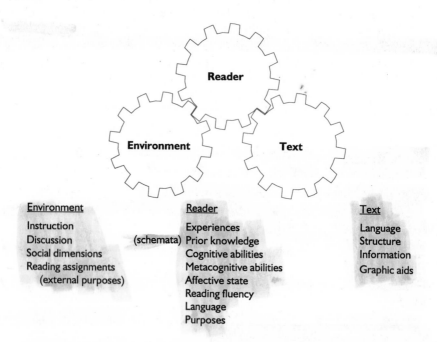

Environment	Reader	Text
Instruction	Experiences	Language
Discussion	(schemata) Prior knowledge	Structure
Social dimensions	Cognitive abilities	Information
Reading assignments	Metacognitive abilities	Graphic aids
(external purposes)	Affective state	
	Reading fluency	
	Language	
	Purposes	

their understanding of what they read. The affective states of the readers (emotions) determine purposes and create expectations and attitudes toward the content.

The text itself may facilitate or deter understanding. Authors who have a strong sense of their audience structure texts well and employ language that is "user friendly." The inclusion of reader aids such as glossaries, tables of contents, structured overviews, and anticipation guides contributes to comprehension.

Schemata

One of the most universal conclusions emerging from recent research is the importance of readers' *prior knowledge* in facilitating comprehension. Readers combine structures of prior knowledge (schemata) with text information to create meaning. When we hear or read something we've never heard or read before, it doesn't imprint on our brains directly the way print remains on paper. Instead, we respond to it by searching through our minds for information and understanding that we already have to see how our existing knowledge connects with the new information (Vygotsky, 1962). Prior knowledge is the foundation for comprehending new ideas.

Schemata are cognitive structures that are variously described as frameworks, scripts, and knowledge structures. They are related to ideas, thoughts, or concepts. These abstractions of reality are acquired from experience (Anderson and Pearson, 1984). We use schemata to cluster memory representations of experience and knowledge about a given topic (Pearson and Johnson, 1977). For instance, anyone who flies frequently has schemata of airplanes, of the procedures involved in flying, and of airports — the ticketing counter, the security check procedure, checking baggage, the boarding gate, and the baggage claim area. When well-traveled individuals enter a new airport, they use schemata to identify the specific locations of the ticket counter, baggage claim area, and boarding gate, which are located at various places in different airports. Each traveler's schemata provide a framework for integrating new information.

Efficient readers use their schemata to predict the words and ideas they will read and to form hypotheses about text content; then they read to see if their hypotheses are confirmed. They use schemata to create expectations about text organization and meaning. Anticipating the author's ideas increases comprehension (Adams and Collins, 1986). Students who have many experiences outside the classroom are able to anticipate the author's ideas and words better than students with more limited experiences.

Content Schemata

Content schemata help a reader make sense of written content by providing a context or frame of reference. For instance, a home economics student who has baby-sitting experiences with younger brothers and sisters will have greater understanding of a child development text than a student who has not been exposed to young children. Content schemata help us anticipate an author's ideas and provide a cognitive framework for relating what we know to what we read and for organizing, understanding, and remembering content.

Because they involve knowledge of the world, content schemata are extremely important for the comprehension of content materials. Students who have not had experiences related to certain topics lack the schemata necessary to understand written material about these topics. One has only to reflect on how different a sports-loving student's comprehension of the sports section of the newspaper is from his or her understanding of a chapter of social studies to see what an important role schemata play in comprehension. When reading the sports section, sports fans can use schemata that they have developed from years of experience. The same students may not have had experiences that would develop their schemata for understanding international events because they have not traveled in or read about other countries. Consequently, to aid comprehension, teachers must help students develop schemata for content topics. Activities such as discussion, viewing television shows and films, examining models, and participating in simulations develop schemata for content reading.

In addition to providing background experiences that expand and refine students' schemata, such as those referred to in the previous paragraph, teachers can also implement techniques for activating students' schemata to increase comprehension. Preteaching vocabulary is another important instructional technique in preparing students to read with understanding. As you learned in Chapter 2, word knowledge is related to background experience and to conceptual development.

Textual Schemata

Readers create schemata about a broad range of experiences; however, the schemata of written discourse are of particular interest in developing reading comprehension. We develop schemata for different types of discourse as a result of exposure to them. Textual schemata consist of a reader's knowledge of the structural characteristics of written content. "Textual schemata provide the general outline for material which we read. For example, we expect a newspaper article to have a special form, and that form is quite different from a research article" (Bowman, 1981). In a well-written research article, we know where to find the review of related literature, the methods used, and the results of the study. When we read fictional stories, we expect to encounter plot, characters, and setting.

Readers use their knowledge of a particular genre or type of writing to anticipate, follow, and organize the materials they read. Research shows that text organization is an important component of reading comprehension in both fiction and nonfiction (Fitzgerald and Spiegel, 1983; Buss, Ratliff, and Irion, 1985; Berkovitz, 1986). Content reading instruction should guide students to perceive text organization and the relationships it reflects.

Activating Schemata

Readers do not automatically activate their schemata; therefore, teachers must plan to help them connect their background knowledge to the text. Activating schemata involves recalling existing knowledge that is related to a specific subject and/or story or text structure and connecting it to the content being read. When students activate appropriate schemata, they can anticipate the author's ideas and information and make inferences regarding content (filling in missing ideas and information) when the author does not concretely explain ideas.

Many of the strategies and activities in this chapter are designed to be used for activating students' existing schemata. For instance, posing purpose questions helps students to relate the text to their existing knowledge and activates their schemata.

Strategies that encourage prediction also develop students' expectations for reading content and create a mind set for following the author's ideas and information. Therefore prediction activities are related to activating schemata. Advance organizers and purpose questions serve to encourage prediction.

Advance organizers, based on Ausubel's (1978) concept and research, are short reading passages that precede a longer selection and deal with the same topic as the selection. They give students a conceptual framework for the content and help them to predict the author's ideas.

A teacher usually writes advance organizers for students to use, although some more recent textbooks include advance organizers for each chapter. You have probably noticed that each chapter in this text begins with an overview — an advance organizer designed to aid your comprehension. It is well worth a teacher's effort to construct advance organizers for textbook chapters. These passages are especially valuable when the teacher explains their relationship to the chapters.

Purpose questions build readers' anticipation of the author's ideas. They focus on the important ideas in a selection and should be broad enough to guide the reader through an entire selection. Questions that are too specific cause students to read only for details.

Good sources for purpose questions are the review questions that many textbooks provide at the end of each chapter. Reading these questions before starting the chapter gives students a sense of the important ideas it covers. Other sources of purpose questions are a textbook's chapter titles and subheadings. These headings point out the important ideas in each chapter, and students can turn these ideas into questions, thus devising purpose questions that they can answer as they read. Finally, students may read the first paragraph of a selection and then formulate questions based on the information it provides.

The following are some examples of questions designed to give students reading purposes:

1. What is this section about?
2. What is the main idea of the selection?
3. What is the author's point of view? This includes identification of the author's bias, sources, and so forth.
4. Do you agree with the author?
5. How do ideas in this selection relate to what you already know about this topic?

Students must learn to read and understand a variety of text forms and types. Some texts are "considerate" and some are "inconsiderate." A considerate text has a number of specific characteristics. Factors such as text organization and structure determine how considerate text is. When readers understand text organization and structure, their comprehension is enhanced. For example, texts that present clearly identified main ideas and supporting details are easier to understand than those that do not have these features. The clarity and coherence of the writing further contribute to text comprehensibility, as do the accuracy and consistency of the information in the text.

The comprehensibility or readability of a text is also determined by the vocabulary and concepts it develops, as discussed in Chapter 6. The factors involved in selecting appropriate textbooks and matching texts' difficulty levels with students' reading levels are discussed in Chapters 6 and 11. Students can comprehend better when they are reading materials that enable them to complete assignments. However, they must learn to use structural and organizational factors to increase their comprehension.

Metacognition

Metacognition refers to the knowledge and control students have over their own thinking and learning activities (Baker and Brown, 1984; Brown and Palincsar, 1982). Metacognition involves two separate components: (1) an awareness of the skills, strategies, and resources needed to perform a task effectively, and (2) the ability to use self-regulatory mechanisms to ensure the successful completion of the task, such as checking the outcome of attempts to solve a problem, planning the next move, or evaluating the effectiveness of attempted actions (Baker and Brown, 1984).

Metacognition (metacomprehension) is functioning when students realize whether they understand or do not understand what they are reading (self-monitoring) and know how to correct lapses in understanding. When students are conscious of their own thinking and comprehension, they can try different strategies if comprehension breaks down. Students who have well-developed metacognitive skills are more likely to be independent readers.

Research shows that skilled comprehenders are aware of different purposes for reading and of ways of adjusting their own knowledge to the demands of the task; they monitor their comprehension and implement corrective strategies when it fails (Baker and Brown, 1984). Unskilled readers do not seem to be aware that they have failed to understand material they read (Paris and Myers, 1981). Apparently, they read assignments but do not reflect on their understanding of the text. Competent readers are active comprehenders with better developed metacognitive skills (Cook and Mayer, 1983). The metacognitive process is illustrated in the following example.

Molly Rose, a secondary school student, read a selection in her mathematics text that introduced sampling. Her purpose was to understand sampling as a basis for statistical analysis. She asked herself questions to ascertain whether she had achieved her purpose. After answering her questions, she realized that she understood the overall process of sampling but could not define the terms *variance, population,* and *population parameter.* Thus, she was aware of what she understood and did not understand and was able to reread specific portions of the text to locate and further study the needed information. Such self-regulation requires awareness of one's cognitive processes.

Competent students, aware of the cognitive demands of their reading assignments, identify important parts of the text and focus on them. The example in the preceding paragraph demonstrates this process; the reader recognized the importance of focusing on the key terms related to the process she was learning.

Students need instructional strategies to develop an awareness of their own cognitive processes, as well as ways of remedying comprehension failures. Teachers can demonstrate metacognition to students through modeling. This strategy is presented later in this chapter. Teachers often find it helpful to use content from their own subject areas to demonstrate metacognition, since they have larger backgrounds of experience with that content.

Mary Heller (1986) suggests using a worksheet like that given in Example 3.1, which is based on social science content. The students fill in the topic, purpose, and section A before reading a selection. They complete sections B and C and the answer to the purpose question after reading the selection.

E X A M P L E **3.1**

Social Science Worksheet

Topic: Imperialism

Purpose Question: How does imperialism relate to me?

A What I already knew	B What I now know	C What I don't know
Imperialism is extending power. Britain is an imperialist country.	Power can be extended through economic, military, and political means. U.S. used "dollar diplomacy" in Latin America.	Other countries that U.S. practices imperialism on. Does imperialism cause war? Is imperialism good or bad?

Answer to purpose question: The U.S. practices imperialism and sends U.S. tax money to Latin America.

Self-questioning also facilitates metacognitive development (Tierney and Cunningham, 1984). A number of researchers have demonstrated the value of self-questioning and have established that students can learn to control their own thought processes by using it (Palincsar, 1982; Singer and Donlan, 1982;

Andre and Anderson, 1978). Self-questioning can be initiated by asking questions such as "What is the main idea in this paragraph (selection)?" and "Is there anything I don't understand in this paragraph?" Teachers can teach students about the different types of questions (literal, inferential, critical, and creative) and teach them to generate different types of questions. Students may work in pairs formulating questions related to their readings. (See the section in this chapter on Types of Thinking and Reading for more information about question types.)

A worksheet like that in Example 3.2 is also useful in guiding students to generate questions after instruction on question types.

E X A M P L E **3.2**

Worksheet for Generating Questions

Directions: Read the assigned selection, then write a question at each level indicated and answer the remaining questions.

1. Literal question:
2. Inferential question:
3. Evaluative question:
4. Creative question:
5. Give an example of the concept presented:
6. What is the main idea of the selection?
7. List the things that you do not understand:

Understanding the Components of Text Structure

Authors use specific patterns of organization to structure the ideas presented in the text. Reading researchers have identified five structures that appear most frequently in content materials — time order (chronological), list structure, comparison-contrast, cause-effect, and problem solution (Horowitz, 1986). However, these patterns are often used in combination and they also occur together with other patterns, such as narrative, description, example, process, definition, and classification (Hoskins, 1986).

Recognizing text structure is important to both reading comprehension and writing (Armbruster, Anderson, and Ostertag, 1989). It is helpful to think about a text structure as analogous to an outline — as the bare bones of the selection. Sensitivity to selection structure increases comprehension and memory and serves as a model for students to structure their own writing (Meyer, Brandt, and Bluth, 1980; Taylor, 1985).

One of the reasons students find content area textbooks difficult to read is their lack of knowledge about how texts are structured (McGee and Richgels, 1985; Piccolo, 1987). Students need to learn the basic differences between narration and exposition. They need to read all kinds of texts — considerate, well-written, and well-organized ones, and some that are inconsiderate, poorly written, and/or disorganized.

Considerate Texts

Effective readers are active readers who use a variety of strategies and processes to construct text meaning. They understand the components and patterns of text structure, such as paragraphs, main ideas, and story grammar. The initial sections of this chapter addressed the current emphasis on the reader's active role in comprehension. However, in order to read actively and responsibly, students also must understand the nature of considerate and inconsiderate text, so that they can compensate for text limitations.

Five characteristics account for the ease or difficulty a student is likely to encounter when reading a text:

1. Organization and structure
2. Whether the text addresses one concept at a time or tries to explain several at once
3. The clarity and coherence of the explanations
4. Whether the text is appropriate for the students' reading levels and the purpose
5. Whether the information is accurate and consistent (Armbruster and Anderson, 1981)

Organizational Patterns

Research reveals that students who recognize the various patterns of written discourse understand and recall text content better. In addition, researchers report that students who use the author's top-level organizational structure (the basic structure of the text) as an aid to comprehension tend to perform better on recall, summarization, and other comprehension tasks than do readers who do not use this structure (Shannon, 1986).

Hoskins' (1983) research shows that 80 percent of the college freshmen examined were not aware of organizational patterns in textbooks. This is a disappointing figure when one considers the importance of structural (content) schemata in comprehension (Brooks and Dansereau, 1983). Researchers have also found that educating students to recognize organizational patterns increases their understanding of main ideas (Readence, Bean, and Baldwin, 1981). In the following sections, organizational patterns of both selections and paragraphs are explored further. Examples of the most common organizational patterns follow.

72

1. *Sequential or chronological order:* Paragraphs in sequential or chronological order present information in the order of its occurrence to clarify the ideas presented. Readers can use time or sequential order patterns to organize and remember this information. Some words that may signal the use of this organization are *after, before, begin, beyond, during, first, finally, next, now, second, then, third, until,* and *when.* Chronological order is illustrated in the following example.

> *The Federalist Party disappears.* During Jefferson's administrations the Republican Party grew stronger. The Republicans elected the next two Presidents — James Madison, who served from 1809 to 1817, and James Monroe, who was President from 1817 to 1825. During these years, on the other hand, the Federalist Party became weaker and weaker. Finally, in Monroe's first term, it disappeared, and Monroe was re-elected without opposition. Because there was only one political party, the years of Monroe's presidency are called the *Era of Good Feeling* (Wilder et al., 1982).

2. *Comparison and contrast:* Authors use comparison and contrast to clarify certain points. Questions like the following may help readers to understand this structure: What is the author's main idea? What similarities and/or differences does he or she use to illustrate the point? Student-constructed tables that list similarities and differences also enhance understanding. Some words that may signal the use of this pattern are *although, but, yet, nevertheless, meanwhile, however, on the other hand, otherwise, compared to, despite,* and *similarly.* The next paragraph illustrates the comparison and contrast pattern.

> Some individual health policies are filled with loopholes. The average individual health policy pays out only about 50 per cent of the premiums in benefits — compared to 90 per cent for group insurance plans. Sales commissions, other costs, and profits eat up the remainder of the premiums of individual plans.
>
> Mail-order health plans are usually the worst buy. This insurance is advertised in newspapers, on television, and by direct mail. Consumer's Union says that some of these policies return only a third of their premiums in benefits (Morton and Renzy, 1978).

3. *Cause and effect:* Authors use this pattern to explain relationships among facts and ideas. Readers need to identify both the causes and the related effects, which may be either stated or implied. The following words may signal the use of cause and effect: forms of the verb *cause* or *because, since, so that, thus, therefore, if, consequently,* and *as a result.*

An example of a cause-and-effect paragraph follows.

> When your body produces an antibody in response to an invading pathogen, the antibody protects you against a disease. It works for your benefit. Antibodies can also be produced in response to other materials such as pollen, the yellow powder produced by the male reproductive organs of some plants. If you have an **allergy,** your body is extra sensitive to certain substances. It

works against you. Antibodies react with the pollen, dust, or other substance. A chemical called **histamine** (HIS tuh meen) is produced. Histamine causes the symptoms of allergy, including sneezing, coughing, and itching. Antihistamines, the major medicines for relieving symptoms of allergies, block some of the effects of histamine (Rosenberg et al., 1978).

4. *Definition or explanation:* This pattern explains a concept or defines terms. The reader should be alert for paragraphs of definition and note them for future reference because they are essential to understanding in many of the content areas. An example of a definition or explanation pattern follows.

Gravitational force pulls together masses of gas and dust into clouds in many places in space. **Gravitational force** is the attraction that pulls things toward one another. You experience gravitation every day. Because of it, your pencil falls to the floor when you let it go. Gravitation brings a pole-vaulter back to Earth and makes it hard for you to learn to ride a bike. The particles in the dust cloud attract each other because of gravitation. As time passes, all the matter in the cloud is crowded into a smaller space. When the particles begin to squeeze each other, the temperature in the dense part of the cloud rises higher and higher. The cloud begins to glow with a reddish color, like a burner on an electric stove or the wires in a toaster (Jackson and Evans, 1980).

5. *Enumeration or simple listing pattern:* Paragraphs in this pattern list items of information (such as facts or ideas), either in order of importance or simply in logical order. Readers often must determine the relative importance of the items listed. Clues to this pattern are the words *one, two, first, second, third, to begin, next, finally, most important, when, also, too,* and *then.* An example follows.

Chemical energy is a stored form of energy. Fuels such as coal, oil, and natural gas have chemical energy. When they are burned, the energy is released as heat light. Batteries also have chemical energy. Cars, portable radios, and other battery-operated devices convert chemical energy to electric energy. Food, too, has stored energy. Your body changes the chemical energy in food to heat and mechanical energy (Hill and May, 1981).

Paragraphs

Intriguing stories and understandable text consist of simple, clear paragraphs. Stories should not be complicated by tangled paragraphs, and information should not be buried in badly composed paragraphs. Paragraphs are important components of content structure. Successful readers adjust their thinking to the organization of the selection and follow the author's line of thought.

Well-developed paragraphs are easier to understand. Each of them focuses on a single major topic, and a logical sequence of sentences is used in the structure. The sentences have coherence; they are related to the para-

74

graph topic and to each other. In contrast, a poorly organized paragraph does not establish a focus, and the sentences frequently are not related to each other and are not presented in a logical order.

The following are examples of both a well-developed paragraph and a poorly developed paragraph.

PARAGRAPH A

Flowers bloom throughout the world. They grow on high mountains at the edges of the snow. Other flowers grow in the shallow parts of oceans. Even hot, dry deserts have bright blossoms. The only places where flowers do not grow are on the ice-covered areas of the Arctic and Antarctic and the open seas.

PARAGRAPH B

Flowers are the reproductive parts of flowering plants. Flowers bloom throughout the world. They grow on high mountains and in the oceans. Many flowers have a smell that attracts birds and insects. Flowers bloom in the hot, dry desert during the rainy season. The only places flowers do not grow are the Arctic, the Antarctic, and the open seas.

If you identified Paragraph A as the well-developed paragraph, which is easier to understand, you are correct. Notice that this paragraph sticks to the subject — the fact that flowers grow throughout the world. The ideas are presented in a logical order, and the sentences have coherence. No loosely related ideas are introduced to divert the reader's attention. On the other hand, Paragraph B does not have a clear focus because botany and geography are mixed. The sentences are not cohesive.

Main Ideas and Details

The writing in most content area materials is structured around or built on details and main ideas. Both paragraphs and entire selections include these structural elements. The main idea of a paragraph is the big idea that the author develops and supports with details throughout the paragraph. Most of the content in informative writing is organized around main ideas and details; therefore, developing the ability to identify the main ideas of paragraphs and entire selections has a high priority in most reading programs.

Details are the smaller pieces of information or ideas that are used to support the "big idea." Main idea is not a single concept; it is an umbrella term that encompasses nine specific types of important ideas (Cunningham and Moore, 1986). These nine types of main ideas are

1. Gist
2. Interpretation
3. Key word

4. Selective summary/selective diagram
5. Theme
6. Title
7. Topic issue
8. Topic sentence/thesis sentence
9. Other (unclassified responses)

The common thread that relates these various types of main ideas is the fact that each addresses important information that is explained in the text. Knowing the types of main ideas permits teachers to guide students in identifying and stating them.

Main ideas are interrelated with organizational patterns because they can be expressed in patterns such as cause and effect, contrast, sequential order, enumeration, and explanation. For example, a paragraph in a cause-and-effect pattern has a main idea and supporting details that are expressed through this pattern. The main idea of such a paragraph could be "causes and effects of erosion." The details would be the specific causes and effects. Similarly, in a paragraph written with a comparison and contrast pattern, the details might be the contrasting points and the main idea the overall comparison (Palincsar and Brown, 1984). Helping students to identify this organizational pattern will help them to state the main idea and comprehend the selection better.

Research shows that instructions requiring students to generate the main idea of a selection or paragraph lead them to recall and understand content better than those requiring them to identify the main idea from multiple-choice items (Taylor and Berkowitz, 1980). Therefore, whenever possible, students should be asked to write the main idea in their own words. Palincsar and Brown (1984) found that students who learned to summarize main ideas improved their ability to answer questions and to identify important information. To help you communicate this strategy to your students, you may wish to refer to the summarization strategies suggested in Chapter 4.

Main ideas and supporting details should be taught through informational content, with students being asked to identify stated and unstated (implied) main ideas. After students learn to identify and restate main ideas, they should learn to use text structures (organizational patterns) to assist their understanding of the content.

Locating key words in sentences is a means of identifying important details. Teachers can direct students to compose telegrams conveying crucial information, which helps them learn to focus on key words, usually nouns and verbs. For the message "Mother has had a heart attack and is very ill. Please hurry home," students would probably select the following key terms: "Mother ill. Hurry home." Telegram construction activities should be used with sentences selected from content textbooks.

Activities for locating key words in sentences can be expanded to finding the key words in a paragraph. After identifying the key words, students can use them to find the larger idea they point to. Readers should sum up the relationships among the key words. Then they can select the sentence that best states the main idea. If no one sentence sums up the main idea (some main ideas are implied), students can compose such a sentence. The following is a paragraph with the key words underlined.

> A dog is a useful animal. It guards our homes from burglars and alerts us when guests are coming. The dog will warn members of the household if fire breaks out in the home. Some dogs serve as seeing-eye dogs for blind people. Perhaps most important of all, dogs are loyal, loving companions who provide many hours of pleasure for their owners and families.

The main idea of this paragraph is the first sentence, "A dog is a useful animal." The key words of each sentence clearly point to this idea.

The telegram strategy is useful for teaching students to identify important details, which is an important skill for readers of content materials. Important details develop and support the main idea. Sometimes authors include details that are interesting but that do not give additional information about the main idea.

Categorization activities help students separate important from unimportant details. For instance, students can write down the details they have identified in a paragraph and categorize them as either important or unimportant to communication of the main idea. Having students state reasons that they classified details into either of these categories permits the teacher to clear up any misconceptions about the points being stressed by the author.

Important Details	Unimportant Details

Main Idea and Detail Activities

Activities such as the following ones give students help with and practice in identifying and stating main ideas and supporting details.

1. Model the procedure of finding main ideas for students before asking them to locate main ideas themselves. See the examples of modeling that are included in this chapter.

2. Have students ask themselves these questions: What is this sentence or paragraph about? What do most of the key words seem to point to? What words occur most frequently? What do these frequently occurring words relate to? What idea is related to most of the supporting details? What sentence would best summarize the frequently occurring ideas? Is the main idea stated or implied? Where is the main idea located in the paragraph (at the beginning, in the middle, or at the end)?

3. Teach students to look for words and phrases that often indicate the main idea, for instance, *first, last, the most important factor, the significant fact.*

4. Prepare blank diagrams on which students can place main ideas and supporting details. Following are two examples: the first example is a generic diagram; the second is a diagram developed for the following paragraph.

A mutation is a change in a gene, which is the part of the cell that determines the inherited characteristics of the offspring. The changed gene is then passed on to succeeding generations. Some mutations produce only a slight change in the offspring, whereas others produce more drastic changes.

Main Idea
Detail #1
Detail #2
Detail #3
Detail #4

A mutation is a change in a gene
inherited characteristic
passed to offspring
slight change
drastic change

5. Have students create their own diagrams for main ideas and supporting details.

6. Encourage students to write, in their own words, concise statements of main ideas.

Selection Organization

Selections are longer units of discourse composed of series of paragraphs. In content reading, we are concerned largely with expository discourse, which is explanatory in nature. The organizational patterns presented earlier in this chapter (sequential, comparison and contrast, cause and effect, definition or explanation, and enumeration) are found in many selections, and they are frequently combined in structuring discourse. When these patterns are identified in longer selections, they can be interpreted in the same ways as in paragraphs. However, these common patterns become parts of a macrostructure in longer discourse.

Well-written expository content — such as a content textbook chapter — begins with an introductory section, which previews the subject. This introduction can be compared to an inverted triangle, because it starts with a

FIGURE **3.2**

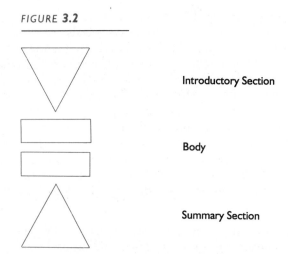

Introductory Section

Body

Summary Section

broad, general idea of the topic and narrows the topic to a more specific point. This section may be developed in a variety of ways, including comparison and cause and effect.

The second part of a selection is the *body,* which develops the ideas that have been stated in the introduction. Each of the paragraphs that make up the body usually has a main idea and details that relate to the topic presented in the introductory section. These paragraphs may be developed through any organizational pattern the author chooses.

The chapter or selection usually concludes with a summary paragraph that pulls together the ideas presented in the body. A triangle can be used to illustrate this section, which begins with a specific idea and broadens and becomes more general as it develops. The pattern of the summary is the reverse of that of the introductory section. A diagram of a selection based on this pattern is shown in Figure 3.2.

Content teachers can use a textbook chapter to show students the introductory section, the body, and the summary section. Students should be encouraged to read the book's preface, because it usually identifies the author's overall organization. Then they can compare the author's organization as stated in the preface with the actual development of material in the text. Students should also learn to use the detailed table of contents, which often contains the chapter headings and subheadings, to help with their understanding of a selection's organization. The table of contents can be used as a study outline, to which important details can be added.

Story Grammars

In the preceding sections we examined the common structures found in expository and descriptive text. Now we will examine the structural elements of short stories. Structure is in some ways a container, the means through which the content is communicated. A story is a particular form of narrative that has plots, characters, and themes. It usually contains a problem or a conflict or both, revolves around characters' goals, and has action and resolution. The various story elements are related in time and causation. Many stories have entertainment and/or esthetic value, and they may evoke the reader's emotional responses.

Story structure is sometimes referred to as story schema (singular of schemata) or story grammar. In this instance, *grammar* means structure. A story grammar is an internal (mental) representation of the parts of a typical story and the relationships among those parts (Mandler and Johnson, 1977). Students identify the important elements in stories and relate these elements to one another through mapping them.

Various researchers have evolved story grammars that differ from one another in minor ways. Our discussion is based on the six major story elements posited by Mandler and Johnson (1977). These elements are *setting, beginning, reaction, attempt, outcome,* and *ending.* The *setting* introduces the main character and the time and place. A precipitating or initiating event occurs in the *beginning,* and the main character's response to the precipitating event is identified as the *reaction. Attempt* is the next component of story structure, and it is concerned with the main character's efforts to attain his or her goal. The success or failure of the attempt is identified in the *outcome.* The *ending,* the last component of story structure, is the long-range consequence of the action, the final response of a character, or an emphatic statement. A story may be composed of one story grammar or it may include a series of story grammars. In an episodic story, each episode has a story grammar.

Example 3.3 is a story grammar for the novel for adolescents, *The Goats,* by Brock Cole.

EXAMPLE **3.3**

Story Grammar

The Goats by Brock Cole

Setting	A small island and the area near two summer camps — one a boys' camp and the other a girls' camp. Bryce, a camper in the boys' camp, and Julie, a camper in the girls' camp.
Beginning	As a joke, Bryce and Julie are stripped of their clothes and possessions and marooned on a small island for the night by their respective campmates.
Reaction	They join forces because they are alone and scared.

Attempt	Together they escape the island but decide that they're not going back to the camp. They find the world is dangerous and they run because no place is safe, and things are never going to be the same.
Outcome	Gradually, they discover how strong they are and how much they can depend on one another.
Ending	Julie discovers that her mother cares about her. She and Bryce make plans for the future because they can depend on one another.

Readers use their knowledge of story structure to guide their expectations, understanding, recall, and production of text. They produce text when retelling stories, reviewing books, and writing their own stories. When reading, listening, and writing, students use a structural outline of the major story components in their minds to make predictions and hypotheses about information they will encounter in stories. These expectations focus students' attention on story events, help them understand the unfolding of time and sequence, and cue recall of story information. When writing their own essays or analyses, students use knowledge of text structures as an aid in shaping discourse.

Teaching Comprehension

Current research on effective teaching defines the role of teachers as "mediators," or helpers who support the learner and influence the nature of the student's interaction with the text (Brown and Palincsar, 1982). In this view of instruction, teachers provide in-depth explanations, guidance, modeling, demonstrating, support or "scaffolding," assistance during reading, guided practice, coaching, encouragement when students are confused, and conscious connections to previous and future learning (International Reading Association, 1988).

Initially, students comprehend reading materials with assistance, but eventually they are able to do so by themselves (Gavelek, 1986). Many students do not develop effective learning strategies unless they receive explicit instruction in their use. Furthermore, students learn reading strategies and skills best when the instruction is incorporated into regular subject matter classes (Weinstein, 1987). To acquire and integrate most cognitive processing skills, students need guided practice and feedback (Anderson et al., 1985). By providing these experiences, content area teachers can play an important role in helping students develop effective learning and study strategies. Then the teacher gradually turns over the responsibility for learning to the students, thereby enabling them to become independent learners.

Instructional approaches that emphasize students' awareness of their own reading strategies, alternative strategies, and how to choose appropriate strategies and that deal with techniques for self-monitoring have been found to result in sizable gains in reading comprehension (Palincsar and Brown, 1986). Students can learn reading strategies that will improve their learning skills.

Instructional activities for reading comprehension should focus on meaning and encourage students to view the reading process as one of acquiring meaning. They should employ "real" reading materials, which are read for authentic purposes. For example, students in business education should read actual memos and accounts from operating businesses as well as the business sections of newspapers and magazines. They should read these materials to solve problems encountered in a business operation. Such activities actively engage students in reading and problem solving in their fields of study.

The first instructional approach we discuss is the use of questions to direct students' thinking. Reading comprehension involves thinking about reading content, and questions stimulate thinking; therefore, they are essential to understanding. Effective questions introduced in a stimulating environment encourage cognitive development.

Thinking and Questioning

Thinking is more likely to flourish in an environment in which ideas are valued. Teachers create such an environment when they accept students' answers that differ from their own and when they encourage different points of view. In such an environment, students' answers and ideas are accepted, clarified, and expanded, often by the teacher's asking, "Why do you think that?" Ample time should be provided for students to think about their responses; when a student must answer questions quickly, the quality of his or her answers may be lowered.

Over 2,000 years ago, Socrates demonstrated the power of questioning to stimulate thinking. Educators today know that the way a teacher structures a question influences the nature of the thinking required to respond (McTighe and Lyman, 1988). We also know that follow-up discussion strategies, such as asking for elaboration, influence the degree and quality of classroom discussion. Despite this knowledge, Goodlad (1984) reports that most classroom questions require only factual responses, and that generally students are not involved in thought-provoking discussions.

Questioning can effectively guide and extend comprehension. In addition, asking and answering questions often reveal our thoughts and feelings, to ourselves as well as to others (Christenbury and Kelly, 1983). Strategies such as providing relevant questions before students read the selection help them focus on major ideas and concepts. Asking questions that require interpretation and critical thinking gives students practice in higher types of cognitive processing. However, asking too many literal questions requiring single correct answers limits thinking, because students can memorize the text to answer them. Higher-order questions encourage students to go beyond the text and to apply knowledge in different situations.

Teachers should ask questions that have more than one correct answer. Questions that focus on right and wrong answers do not stimulate thinking. The really stimulating questions are those that have several appropriate responses; such questions give students good opportunities to experience success in expressing their ideas as related to their reading. Teachers should also ask questions that require multiple-word answers, because they foster cognitive growth. When students offer one-word answers, they should be encouraged to expand their answers. As they formulate answers and express them in sentences, they are thinking more than when they respond with a simple "yes" or "no." In order to encourage students to expand their answers, a teacher may say, "Can you tell me any more about . . . ?" or "Why do you think that?" or "Can you give me examples of this?"

"Wait time" is very important to the quality of students' answers. Teachers should wait 3 to 5 seconds after asking a question, allowing students time to process the question and formulate a response (Conley, 1987).

Questions can be posed before, during, and after reading. Questions asked before reading activate schemata and focus attention on important ideas and concepts. Before reading, students can generate questions about a topic or concept; after reading, teachers can ask questions such as "Did you find the answers to your questions?" "What are they?" "Which questions are still unanswered?" "What did you learn that we didn't ask questions about?" "What did the writer do to make readers feel or think a certain way?" "How did the writer use language to convey a particular idea?" "What evidence to support a particular idea did the writer give?" (Hammond, 1983). Students who read a passage and answer questions about it generally learn more than students who only read the passage (Klauer, 1984; Tierney and Cunningham, 1984).

Teaching students who are unsuccessful readers to raise questions as they read helps them acquire the ability to comprehend complex verbal material (Andre and Anderson, 1978). It appears that students who ask themselves questions engage in self-monitoring of their understanding, which leads them to independent comprehension (Hammond, 1983).

All questioning should be carefully planned, so that teachers ask questions related to important ideas and concepts in a reading selection. Poorly chosen questions and questions that emphasize insignificant details are detrimental to the growth of thinking abilities. For example, the question "What color was Mary's dress?" would probably be an unimportant one that would not enhance comprehension. Teachers who are preparing questions for a discussion should first review the following points:

1. What are the important ideas in this selection?
2. What ideas and concepts do I want the students to remember from this selection?
3. What questions will lead students to understand these ideas and concepts?
4. What thinking abilities have the students in this group already developed?
5. What thinking abilities do the students in this group need to develop?

Types of Thinking and Reading

Four aspects of thinking and problem solving are addressed in the following paragraphs: literal, inferential, critical, and creative. These types of thinking are interrelated and interactive. Some reading situations involve all four types of thinking, whereas others focus on only one or more.

Literal Thinking/Reading

Literal reasoning is concerned with facts and ideas that are directly stated in the reading content. Readers often quote the text to answer literal questions. A reader reproduces the author's ideas to achieve literal understanding and should address the question, "What did the author say?" Literal comprehension includes identification and recall of stated main ideas and details. Literal understanding is basic to comprehension.

The main forms of literal thinking are recognizing and recalling stated main ideas; recognizing and recalling stated details; recognizing and recalling stated sequences; following stated directions; and recognizing stated causes and effects. The following are some examples of literal-level questions that are asked about a story entitled "A New England Nun," which is a high school literature selection (Freeman, 1976). This story concerns a young woman who was engaged to a man for fourteen years; yet, after waiting all those years for her fiancé, she decided to break the engagement just before the wedding. Literal questions for this selection include:

1. What activities gave Louisa pleasure?
2. How would you describe Joe in a short paragraph?
3. Who was the "New England Nun"?
4. What events led to the broken engagement?

Teachers should model the process of answering questions before asking students to answer them. For example, for the first question based on "A New England Nun," the teacher might say, "The activities that gave Louisa pleasure are directly stated in this story. The text states that she enjoyed cleaning, baking, sewing, and gardening."

Inferential Thinking/Reading

Inferential thinking and reading are concerned with deeper meanings and are difficult to define because they involve several types of reasoning. In order to make inferences, readers must relate facts, generalizations, definitions, and values. Inferential questions emphasize finding relationships among elements of the written text. Essentially, making inferences involves using one's schemata to fill in information that the author assumes the reader knows. An author cannot tell everything he or she knows about a subject because of space and time limitations. For example, in the sentence "Nancy pulled on her mittens and her parka before opening the door," the reader draws upon personal experience with winter clothing to infer that Nancy is going outdoors into cold weather.

Students need to learn how to make inferences. They also need to realize that inferences are necessary to comprehension (International Reading Association, 1988). In making inferences about reading content, readers should examine the author's words, reading between the lines to arrive at meanings that are not explicitly stated in the text. They must combine information from their own experiences with information from the text. The main types of inference are: *location* inferences, in which the reader infers the place; *agent* inferences, which require the reader to infer the person acting; *time* inferences, which are concerned with the time of day; *action* inferences, which have to do with the action occurring in the text; *instrument* inferences, which are concerned with tools or devices involved in the text; *object* inferences, which require readers to infer objects the author has implied; *cause and effect* inferences, which have to do with implied causes and/or effects; *category* inferences, which require the reader to infer a category to which objects mentioned in the text belong; *problem-solution* inferences, which have to do with problems and solutions implied by the author; and *feeling-attitude* inferences, which are concerned with the feelings and attitudes implied by the author (Johnson and Johnson, 1986). Students should have opportunities to identify these various types of inference in written content.

Inferential questions often have more than one "correct" answer. When evaluating student answers, the teacher should be concerned with the logical thinking processes used to arrive at a synthesis of ideas. The student should be asked to support and explain his or her answers. This is a very important comprehension strategy that is easy to use.

Inferential questions based on "A New England Nun" follow:

1. Why do you think this story is called "A New England Nun" when it is about a woman who is engaged?
2. What caused the broken engagement?
3. What was the result of the broken engagement for Joe, for Lily, and for Louisa?
4. Why did the author tell the reader about Caesar in such detail?

The teacher can model the process of inferential thinking by thinking aloud as he or she reasons to arrive at an answer for one of the above questions. For instance, for question 4, the teacher might say, "The author described Caesar as a vigorous, active animal who delighted in running free and exploring. The author also described the way that Louisa restrained Caesar by chaining him up. The vivid descriptions lead to comparing Joe with the dog. They are both vigorous and healthy and enjoy freedom and exploration, but Louisa tries to restrain Joe the same way that she restrains Caesar."

To understand implied relationships, such as comparison, contrast, cause and effect, and sequence, students should use their experiential backgrounds to interpret written content. Content activities such as the following can help students develop their ability to make inferences:

Comparing and contrasting two historical figures
Comparing and contrasting two cities
Citing examples of concepts and ideas students are reading about
Identifying generalizations in their content textbooks

Critical Thinking/Reading

Critical readers question what they read; they suspend judgment, evaluate, and decide. Critical thinking is "reasonable reflective thinking focused on deciding what to believe or do" (Ennis, 1989). To make such judgments, the reader compares text with external criteria derived from experience, research, teachers, and experts in the field; therefore, background knowledge is essential to critical reading. Critical reading also depends on a person's ability to engage in literal and interpretive thinking. Critical readers must be able to recognize the author's purpose and point of view and to distinguish fact from opinion. Readers should test the author's assertions against their own observations, information, and logic. In order to read critically, readers must begin with an understanding of what the author is saying, because grasping the author's ideas is fundamental to critical thinking. The major facets of critical reading are summarized in Figure 3.3.

Critical readers logically and objectively evaluate content, suspending their judgment while gathering the necessary information. Suspending judgment requires that the reader avoid jumping to conclusions. The critical reader must have background experience that provides a basis for making judgments. The critical reading task should be approached with an open-minded, problem-solving attitude. Critical readers should constantly ask questions about the text they are reading.

Critical reading questions based on "A New England Nun" follow:

1. Does this story provide an accurate picture of life in the late 1800s? What story material supports your answer?
2. What was the real reason Louisa broke the engagement?

FIGURE **3.3**

Critical Reading

Reader	Author
Reader suspends judgment.	Author should be objective.
Reader's attitude is open-minded toward problem-solving.	Author should be qualified.
Reader is knowledgeable.	Author researches topic and presents current information.
Reader discerns author's purpose.	Author should be logical.
Reader evaluates author's qualifications.	Author should support conclusions and generalizations.
Reader evaluates validity of material.	Author should avoid overuse of emotional language.
Reader evaluates use of propaganda.	
Reader evaluates author's logic.	
Reader evaluates author's use of language.	

3. Which incident in this story most accurately reveals Louisa's character? Why did you select this incident?
4. Do you think Louisa acted suitably when she broke the engagement? Why or why not?

When modeling critical thinking, the teacher might say, "To answer question 1, we must examine our knowledge about life in the late 1800s in Massachusetts. What do you know about this period?"

After some discussion, the students could brainstorm ideas, which the teacher would write on the chalkboard. Ideas that might arise from the discussion are that the majority of people at that time lived a rural existence, farming and preserving their own foods, churning butter, and making their clothing.

The teacher might then say, "This information is congruent with the picture that the author creates. In addition, the author shows that many people were leaving established lives in settled towns to move to the frontier, where they encountered hardships. This fact of life in the 1800s is an important aspect of the story. The life-style, foods, clothing, conversation, and issues portrayed in this story coincide with those described in your social studies text."

Critical reading such as that described in the preceding paragraphs involves three major types of abilities: semantics, logic, and evaluating authenticity (Wolf et al., 1967). Semantics abilities include understanding the denotative and connotative uses of words, the use of vague and precise words, and the use of words in a persuasive manner. Logic skills include understanding the reliability of the author's argument; understanding the reliability of the author's statements; recognizing the use of propaganda; distinguishing fact from opinion; and recognizing the various forms of persuasive writing. Authenticity skills include determining if adequate information is included, comparing this information with other relevant information, examining the author's qualifications, and using authoritative research sources.

In subject-matter instruction, students are encouraged to think and read about the subject critically, and general principles and applications of critical thinking are made explicit (Ennis, 1989). Critical thinking in content area materials is discussed in Chapters 8 and 9.

Teaching suggestions for general critical reading are given in the following section.

SEMANTIC LEARNING ACTIVITIES

1. Students should become sensitive to an author's efforts to influence readers with "loaded" words that play on their emotions. For example, many readers have negative reactions to the words *un-American, communist,* and *radical* while reacting favorably to words such as *freedom, peace,* and *human rights.* Ask students to find examples of the use of loaded words in newspapers, magazines, and textbooks.

2. Critical readers need to be alert for words used in vague, general ways (for example, the expressions "Everyone is doing it" and "They say"). Students should locate examples of vague uses of words in their reading material.

LOGIC LEARNING ACTIVITIES

1. Have students create syllogisms that state an author's premises and conclusions. The following example is based on a chapter from a social studies textbook:

PREMISES

People with undesirable characteristics were rejected. Some "new" immigrants had undesirable characteristics.

CONCLUSION

Those "new" immigrants were rejected.

2. Have students verify the facts found in local newspaper stories through research.

3. Although authors may not state whether they are giving facts or opinions, sometimes there are indicators of opinion, such as the following qualifying words: *think, probably, maybe, appear, seem, believe, could,* and *should.* Have students examine sentences with the purpose of locating "opinion words." The following sentences might be used:
   a. I believe this is the best cake I have ever eaten.
   b. This symptom could mean that you are getting the flu.
   c. Jane will probably come home for vacation.

4. Making a graphic representation (chart) of the facts and opinions presented by an author will help the reader examine ideas critically. Example 3.4 is a chart based on information taken from a social studies textbook.

E X A M P L E **3.4**

Graphic Representation

Facts	Opinions
"Old" immigrants from British Isles, Germany, Scandinavia	"Old" immigrants acceptable
"New" immigrants from Slavic countries, Italy, Greece	"New" immigrants unacceptable, ignorant, greedy, diseased, criminals, insane, wild-eyed, bad-smelling

5. Recognizing propaganda is one of the abilities required for critical reading. Discussions of propaganda techniques and methods for analyzing propaganda could be held in class. Make sure that students realize that these propaganda techniques are usually used in combination.
   a. Bad names — Disagreeable words are used to arouse distaste for a person or a thing.
   b. Glad names — Pleasant words are used to create good feelings about a person or a thing.
   c. Plain folks — This kind of propaganda avoids artificiality and sophistication. Political candidates use this technique when they shake hands, kiss babies, and play with dogs.
   d. Transfer — This type of propaganda attempts to transfer to a person or thing the reader's respect for the flag, the cross, or some other valued symbol.
   e. Testimonial — This technique is like transfer except that a famous person gives a testimonial for a product or a person. Positive feelings for the famous person are supposed to be transferred to the product.
   f. Bandwagon — This is an attempt to convince readers that they should accept an idea or purchase an item because "Everyone is doing it."

    g. Card stacking — This technique utilizes accurate information but omits some data so that only one side of a story is told.

6. After learning to identify propaganda techniques, the reader should analyze the propaganda using the following questions:

    a. What technique is used?

    b. Who composed the propaganda?

    c. Why was the propaganda written?

    d. To what reader interests, emotions, and prejudices does the propaganda appeal?

    e. Will I allow myself to be influenced by this propaganda?

AUTHENTICITY LEARNING ACTIVITIES

1. Writers should support their conclusions in the text. Occasionally a reader must seek additional data before evaluating the validity of an author's writing. Assign students an article to read, having them check other sources of information on the topic to evaluate the validity of the information given in the article.

2. Ask students to evaluate the author's qualifications for writing on the topic at hand. Questions like these help this evaluation:

    a. Would a lawyer be qualified to write a book on writing contracts?

    b. Would a football player be qualified to write a book on foreign policy?

    c. Would a chef be a qualified author for a book on menu planning?

    d. Would a physician be qualified to write a book on music theory?

Creative Thinking/Reading

Creative reading employs the creative process, which involves original or novel thought. Creative thinkers find new ways of viewing ideas, incidents, or characters that stimulate novel thinking or production of new materials. They strive for originality and ideas that are fundamental, far-reaching, and powerful (Perkins, 1984). Creative thinkers are able to view their experiences in different ways. Critical thinking and creative thinking are closely interrelated because creative thinkers generate possibilities, then critically sift through and rework them. Critical and creative readers both go beyond the literal understanding of printed materials.

    Some psychologists contend that thinking ability is closely related to the level of one's specialized knowledge (Glaser, 1984). It appears that people who are knowledgeable about a subject are more able to think creatively about it. Brandt (1986) recommends that schools concentrate on teaching science, reading, and mathematics in ways that help students learn to think through these content areas better. This approach to cognitive development means students engage in genuine problem solving, genuine inventive tasks, and genuine critical appraisal.

    Creative thinkers/readers may come up with several ways of solving a math problem or of performing an experiment in science class. They may turn a situation from a literature selection into a puppet show, a skit, or a painting. They may make a unique table in woodshop or develop a design in home economics that surpasses those suggested in the book. To do these things, creative thinkers translate existing knowledge into new forms. Creativity is stifled if all school activities must be carried out according to the precise specifications of the teacher and if deviations from prescribed forms are always discouraged.

Creative thinking is based on knowledge regarding the subject and opportunities to solve problems and to respond to authentic situations. Creative thinking/reading activities related to "A New England Nun" follow.

CREATIVE THINKING/READING ACTIVITIES

1. Write a new ending in which Louisa does not break the engagement.
2. Paint, draw, sketch, or model Louisa's home as you envision it.
3. Rewrite this story, setting it in modern times. One student created a story in which Louisa "jilted" Joe because he did not want her to be a professional woman. Lilly was portrayed as a woman who preferred homemaking to a profession.
4. Reread the introduction to the story. Analyze how history would have changed if more early pioneers had been timid.
5. Write about how you would feel if you were each of these characters: Louisa, Joe, Lilly.
6. Dramatize the scene you think might have occurred when Louisa told Joe that she would not marry him.

Strategies to Increase Comprehension

Throughout this text, strategies and activities are introduced to improve students' comprehension. Some of these suggestions should be implemented before reading, some during reading, and some following reading. Some strategies are used throughout the reading process. Figure 3.4 summarizes these instructional strategies and relates them to the reading process.

Questions and discussions are essential for increasing comprehension. They are tools that a teacher can use to encourage cognitive development.

Discussion

Discussion is important both as a communication skill and as a means for developing higher-order thinking (Alvermann et al., 1987). Discussion offers a teaching and learning alternative to the lecture method. In discussions, participants interact as they present multiple points of view and listen to counterarguments (Alvermann et al., 1987). Meanings shared in discussion

FIGURE **3.4**

Reading Comprehension Instruction

Before reading	Develop word meanings
	Build background (schemata)
	Activate prior knowledge
	Establish reading purposes (e.g., through questioning and anticipation guides)
During reading	Use metacognitive strategies
	Self-question
	Visualize
	Relate new knowledge to existing knowledge
After reading	Summarize
	Evaluate
	Discuss
	Apply

groups are more than a collection of individual ideas; they are part of new sets of meanings developed as members talk and listen to one another (Pinnell, 1984).

In a well-planned discussion, students interact with one another as well as with the teacher, and they are encouraged to make comments and ask questions that are longer than two- or three-word phrases. Such discussions offer students opportunities to enrich and refine knowledge gained from the text and to hear information discussed from others' points of view. Example 3.5 illustrates a model for classroom discussion.

E X A M P L E **3.5**

Classroom Discussion Model

Chapter Synopsis

"The Shady Side of the Marketplace" discusses fraudulent business practices. Fraud is defined as "getting money through some kind of deception." The authors present four examples of fraud, including "bait-and-switch advertising," "referral selling," "the free gimmick," and "the fear sell." The authors imply that the desire of the public to get something for nothing is a major reason that people are defrauded.

The teacher identified the following important ideas that served as focal points in the discussion.

1. What is fraud?
2. What are the four basic types of fraud?
3. Is "getting something for nothing" the major cause of fraud?

The teacher asked the students to explain the chapter title ("The Shady Side of the Marketplace") as an introduction to the chapter. This gave them opportunities to use background experiences and to anticipate the ideas in the chapter.

Student. "Shady" means dishonest to me, so I think this chapter is about dishonesty in stores because "the marketplace" probably refers to stores.

Teacher. Good response. This title is a good example of figurative language. Can you think of dishonest or fraudulent business practices reported in the news during the last week?

Student. I heard dishonest contractors were stopping at people's houses and offering to fix their roofs. But they got their pay in advance and never came back.

Student. I heard that people were going around selling magazines, but the people who bought them never received any.

Teacher. Certainly, these are examples of dishonest business. Fraud is getting money through deception. Can anyone tell us the meaning of "deception"?

Students. Telling a lie. Tricking another person.

Teacher. Both of these explanations are good. Now, read Chapter 7 to find out why some people are easily cheated [inferential question]. And identify the most common kinds of fraud the author describes [literal thinking].
(Silent reading takes place).

Teacher. Now, tell me why some people are easily cheated [inferential].

Several students in unison. Because they want something for nothing.

Teacher. Why does wanting something for nothing make people easy to fool?

Student. Because they are willing to believe in schemes that will give them something for almost nothing.

Teacher. Can you think of examples of this that happened in Greensboro?
Several students respond with examples from their own experiences.

Teacher. Can you think of other reasons that people are easily defrauded?

Student. Some people are afraid they won't have enough money to pay for things they need.

Teacher. What kinds of fraud are described in the textbook?

Student. Bait-and-switch, referral selling, the free gimmick, the fear sell.

Teacher. How can you as a customer prevent a seller from swindling you?

Students. We don't know.

Teacher. Look back in your textbook at the four examples. What could you do in the situation described on page 102 to avoid being cheated? For instance, the woman could have gone to some large stores and compared prices as well as the performance of the sweeper and other sweepers.

Student. She could have read the contract before she signed it.

Student. She could have checked with discount stores and catalogs to see what they charged for the same vacuum cleaner.

Teacher. Look at Example 2 on page 103. How could you avoid this swindle?

Student. The buyers should have shopped around for the carpet because they probably paid too much for it. The store used "bait-and-switch," which probably means the store can't be trusted. The customers would also have to pay finance charges, which means they would end up paying more than the carpet was worth.

Teacher. We have discussed fraudulent practices used by sellers. How do customers swindle business people?

Student. By shoplifting, stealing towels and blankets at motels, and not telling anyone when they aren't charged enough.

Question/Answer Relationships

Use of question/answer relationships (QAR) (Raphael, 1986) is another questioning strategy to increase comprehension. This procedure focuses on the processes for generating answers to questions and on the relationships between questions and answers. Students are encouraged to think of sources for answers to questions. The following ideas are included to guide teachers in using the procedure.

1. The first question-answering strategy is called RIGHT THERE. The student finds the words used to create the question and looks for these words in a sentence to answer the question. In this instance, the answer is within a single sentence.

2. The second question-answering strategy is called THINK AND SEARCH. This strategy involves a question that has an answer in the story, but the answer uses information from more than one sentence or paragraph.

3. The third question-answering strategy, ON MY OWN, involves a question that can be answered from the reader's own knowledge.

4. The fourth question-answering strategy, WRITER AND ME, is for inferential questions. The answer may be found in the reader's background knowledge but would not make sense unless the reader had read the text.

5. When teaching QARs, give students immediate feedback, start with short texts and work up to longer ones, and start with group activities and move to independent ones.

6. Students should learn all four strategies and how to tell the differences among them. Research shows that understanding the question–answer relationships increases student achievement.

Think Alouds

Think alouds are strategies that can be used to demonstrate the comprehension process or specific aspects of it. The think aloud process makes thinking public and gives students a model for the kinds of thinking that a reader may do while reading text (Davey, 1983). Initially, teachers demonstrate think alouds to the class. After observing them, students can work in pairs, doing think alouds for one another.

When planning a think aloud, teachers should select passages that contain information requiring clarification, such as contradictions, ambiguities, or word meanings that need clarification. As the teacher reads the passage aloud, students follow along silently, listening to ways of thinking through each trouble spot as it is encountered. The teacher may also choose specific instances from a text to demonstrate ways of coping when comprehension breaks down.

Although think alouds generate many types of thinking, teachers should plan to focus on specific thinking abilities. For example, the teacher may choose to demonstrate the use of background knowledge to understand text and to make predictions about the reading. Describing the images the text creates helps students understand the role of visualization in thinking. Another form of thinking commonly used in think alouds is analogies, in which the reader compares prior knowledge to new information in the text. The teacher may question confusing points aloud to help students understand that many texts contain confusing material. The teacher may also demonstrate strategies, such as rereading, that the student can use when he or she does not understand the text. The following think aloud is based on the first part of a story by Roald Dahl.

E X A M P L E **3.6**

"Think Aloud" for Inferencing

Directions: While the teacher reads the story or text aloud, the students follow along, reading the selection silently, listening to the teacher verbalize his or her thoughts as the reading progresses.

Story Summary for "The Landlady" (Dahl, 1978)

Billy Weaver was searching for cheap lodging in London. The Bell and Dragon was recommended, but while on his way to this hotel, he noticed a "Bed and Breakfast" sign in the window of a warm, inviting-looking house. The house was so attractive and well cared for that he thought this lodging would be too expensive for him. He was about to turn away and go on to the hotel when. . . . "Each word was like a large black eye staring at him through the glass, holding him, compelling him, forcing him to stay where he was and not to walk away from that house, and the next thing he knew, he was actually moving across from the window to the front door of the house, climbing the steps that led up to it, and reaching for the bell."

Modeling Dialogue

Teacher. From the title, I predict that this story will be a character sketch about an unusual landlady. The story seems quite ordinary until we encounter the description of each word staring at him "like a large black eye." These visual images are unusual and mysterious. The author seems to be preparing us for unusual events to happen. Suspense is mounting. My experiences with television stories and previous reading make me anticipate a mystery.

Teacher. The next hint of something unusual comes when the author says, "But this dame was like a jack-in-the-box. He pressed the bell — and out she popped! It made him jump." Apparently, the landlady knew Billy was at the door before he rang the bell. He jumped because he was tense.

Teacher. The next hint of the unusual occurs in the following paragraph. Billy says, "I saw the notice in the window," and the landlady responds, "Yes, I know." Billy says, "I was wondering about a room," and the landlady replies, "It's all ready for you, my dear." She had a round pink face and very gentle blue eyes. Did you notice that she talked as if she knew he was coming? This story is getting more and more mysterious because there are so many unexplained events.

Teacher. Then they discuss the price, which was so low — less than half of what Billy had been willing to pay. The landlady said, "If that is too much, then perhaps I can reduce it just a tiny bit." This sounds as if she is really determined to get Billy to stay with her, no matter how low she has to make the price. A very suspicious incident . . . why is she so willing to lower the price?

Teacher. Billy thinks that she is "slightly off her rocker," "slightly dotty." He still thinks that she is harmless, but is she?

Teacher. When Billy signs the guest book, he notices and recognizes the names of earlier guests, although he can't place how he knows them. The landlady assures him that he couldn't possibly know the preceding boarders. But his memory will not let go, and he finally remembers that these boarders disappeared under strange circumstances. Then Billy grows more tense. The landlady tries to divert his attention to the tea and to discuss other things, which makes me more apprehensive. I anticipate that he is in danger.

Problem Solving

A problem-solving approach to reading encourages students to read actively. In this approach the teacher introduces various methods of problem solving and poses problem situations that lead students to an understanding of significant points relating to content area reading.

When initiating problem solving, the teacher encourages students to identify the problem and state it in their own words. The next stage is brainstorming possibilities for solving the problem; after brainstorming, students should critically examine the possibilities generated and eliminate those that will not work. Students can compare this problem with others that they know about. Discussing the problem with another person can help them clarify their thinking about it. In addition, students may gather relevant information and find out how other people have solved similar problems. A problem may be broken into parts and/or restated to expand students' understanding. Finally, writing out a problem often helps them solve it.

After identifying the problem and restating it, students often find that additional reading will help them solve it. They may gather relevant information from textbooks, fiction and nonfiction books, television, newspapers, and magazines. After introducing the problem, the teacher should give students opportunities to participate in a discussion period, during which they may ask questions that will clarify the problem-solving reading activities. The teacher may help by developing guiding questions for students' reading. The following are examples of problems that could be used in problem-solving reading activities.

PROBLEM-SOLVING ACTIVITIES

SOCIAL STUDIES

1a. When studying a Civil War unit, give students a quotation from a Southern sympathizer and one from a Northern sympathizer. Then ask them to read to determine which point of view they believe is correct, and why.

1b. Ask students why people from the South refer to the "War between the States," whereas people from the North call it the "Civil War."

SCIENCE

2a. During the reading of material for a unit on environmental disease, present the following problem: The water purification, sewage disposal, trash, and garbage collection procedures in Greensboro, North Carolina, were completely disrupted for a two-week period as the result of a tornado and fires. What diseases could have become rampant? Why?

2b. Ask students what emergency measures could be taken to control the diseases identified in question 2a.

INDUSTRIAL ARTS

3. While studying a unit on lumber types and uses, give students the following problem: After showing them pictures of various buildings and pieces of furniture, ask them to identify the best type of wood for each purpose and to explain their choices.

HOME ECONOMICS

4. When studying a unit on nutritional needs for individuals with various diseases, pose the following problem to students: Plan menus for individuals who have diabetes, an allergy to milk, and an allergy to wheat.

Controversial issues provide material for the problem-solving approach to content area reading (Lunstrum, 1981). In such an approach, teachers may select issues related to assigned reading or may use an approach wherein students research current issues. Issues may be selected from newspapers, news magazines, and television programs. Teachers should use the same steps in developing these problems as they use in other problem-solving activities. The following are examples of controversial issues.

1. The president's economic changes at the beginning of a new term of office (economics class)
2. The moral and/or scientific issues in genetic engineering (science class)
3. The role of computers in education and other facets of life. Will computers conflict with humanism? (social studies class)

The Reciprocal Questioning Procedure

The reciprocal questioning (ReQuest) procedure, which was developed by Manzo (1969), improves reading comprehension and helps students develop questioning skills. This strategy is used most effectively in the classroom when the teacher models the process with a student and then pairs students to do it. The basic steps in ReQuest follow.

1. Both student and teacher silently read the first sentence of the selection. Then the student asks the teacher (or paired student) as many questions as possible about the sentence — with the book closed. The student attempts to ask the kind of questions that the teacher would normally pose to the class.
2. The teacher (or paired student) answers all the student's questions, asking the student to restate any question that was poorly stated. The teacher or partner restates any answers that the student does not fully understand.
3. After all the questions have been answered, the second sentence is read — and the teacher or second student now asks thought-provoking questions to ensure comprehension of the content. The teacher should act as a questioning model for the student and go on to pose questions that require evaluation of prior student responses.

ReQuest is continued until the student can confidently answer the questions, *What do you think is going to happen in the rest of this selection?* and *What have you read that causes you to make this prediction?* Then the student reads to the end of the selection to determine if the prediction was correct.

Reciprocal Teaching

Reciprocal teaching (Palincsar and Brown, 1986) is similar to ReQuest. In this approach, the teacher models the process, and then gradually turns it over to the students while providing feedback and encouragement. This activity may be done with pairs or triads (three students, or one adult and two students). Reciprocal teaching involves four strategies. First, the teacher or leader summarizes the paragraph or assignment in one sentence. Then this person asks a higher-level question or two, which a student answers. Any difficult parts are clarified at this time. Then a student predicts what the next paragraph or section will discuss.

Writing Strategies

Research shows that writing improves reading comprehension (Kronoblauch and Brannon, 1983; Emig, 1977). Writing is a way of understanding, because it is a mode of language processing along with listening, speaking, and reading. Writing helps students understand and remember ideas and information. When you ask students to write, you are forcing them to shape and form their responses to the text — to bring these thoughts to conscious awareness (Blatt and Rosen, 1984). Students who put the concepts they are reading and studying into their own language are able to understand and evaluate their own learning more fully. Writing serves as a catalyst for further study and reflection on a topic; therefore, teachers of all subject areas should incorporate writing into their instructional programs. The reading and writing chapter in this text (Chapter 7) includes activities that will stimulate understanding.

Visualization Strategies

Visualization is the process of forming mental images of the content that one is reading. Through visualization, one's schemata are used to understand and remember content. Written language is translated into visual images that depict various elements of reading material: story settings, characters, story action, geographic areas, famous historical figures, scientific experiments, steps in mathematical problems, and problem-solving situations.

Teachers can help students create visual images by discussing the language an author has used. Activities that encourage the visualization of scenes, situations, or people help students learn to use their schemata to comprehend reading content. Students can practice visualization by forming mental images of places, people, things, and situations they have experienced, such as a play in a football game, a building or meeting place in the community, the school principal, or their homes. Visualization activities should be followed by discussion of the students' feelings and reactions to the images they have created.

The following are some visualization activities that can be used to increase content reading comprehension.

ACTIVITIES

1. *Social Studies:* Develop a "You-Are-There" activity. The students could be asked to visualize Abraham Lincoln as he delivered the Gettysburg Address. They could discuss the sounds, smells, and emotions engendered by the occasion. Students could visualize a battle in a war they are studying, discussing the placement of various battle lines and giving descriptions of weapons and uniforms.
2. *Science:* As a preparation for performing an experiment, students could be asked to visualize the steps of the experiment as well as its possible outcome.
3. When working with problem-solving activities in any subject, students can be asked to visualize alternative solutions that will help them work through the various ways of solving a problem.

SUMMARY

Reading comprehension, the primary goal of reading instruction, is especially important in teaching students to read content materials. In order to understand written language, readers use schemata, vocabulary, and metacognition. They also use their understanding of language and of the ways that authors organize and structure content. Reasoning plays a significant role in reading comprehension, with particular stress on the higher levels of thinking.

Reading comprehension strategies provide students with independence in reading and learning. The strategies emphasized in this chapter focus on activating schemata, metacognition, prediction, visualizing content, writing, different types of reading and thinking, questioning, and reciprocal teaching. Schemata activation strategies are concerned with activating the schemata that will be most useful to readers as they predict information, ideas, and language in written content. Teaching strategies encourage students to develop and use schemata. Metacognitive strategies are those that students use when they search for understanding; when comprehension falters, students "de-bug" the process by rereading and rethinking selected portions of the text. Self-questioning strategies are especially important to metacognition. Questions are a major tool in developing thinking abilities in comprehension, which is a cognitive process. Teachers need to address the cognitive levels of literal, inferential, critical, and creative thinking in guiding comprehension and discussion. Teachers can use discussion, ReQuest, and reciprocal teaching as strategies for developing students' thinking and question-answering abilities. Students' writing contributes to comprehension because students who write are more able to understand the ways that authors express ideas in written language. Visualization of content enhances understanding of content area text. The basic ideas and strategies introduced in this chapter will help you implement the content reading instruction presented in Chapters 8 and 9.

SELF-TEST

1. What do we deal with when we examine reading comprehension? (a) An unimportant process (b) The product of the process (c) An observable process (d) A controversial process
2. What are schemata? (a) Organized stores of information and experience (b) Word recognition schemes (c) Printed letters (d) Purposes
3. How do schemata help readers? (a) They enable students to anticipate an author's ideas. (b) They present formal definitions of key terms. (c) They provide a teaching model. (d) They are a word recognition strategy.
4. According to this chapter, what is reading? (a) Identifying words (b) Processing information from print (c) A delegated process (d) A structured overview

5. What is the purpose of activating schemata? (a) To improve readers' eye movements (b) To create entirely new cognitive structures (c) To help students relate their experiences to written content (d) To increase the number of pages read in an assignment

6. Which of the following answers describes prediction as it relates to reading comprehension? (a) Print (b) Anticipating ideas, information, and language (c) Being able to spell the words that occur in a text (d) Random information

7. Which answer best describes metacognition? (a) Knowing when you have comprehended (b) Knowing when you have not comprehended (c) Both a and b (d) Neither a nor b

8. What conditions are necessary for metacognition to occur? (a) Establishing a purpose and awareness of cognitive processes (b) Decoding and encoding (c) Textual schemata, story grammar, and think time (d) Propaganda, think time, application, and experience

9. What is a story grammar? (a) The correct English to use in telling a story (b) Story structure (c) Expository (d) All of these

10. Why is writing a way of comprehending? (a) Because it is a mechanical process (b) Because it requires editing (c) Because it is a mode of language processing (d) Because it is not creative

11. What is one purpose of problem-solving activities? (a) To teach word recognition skills (b) To develop thinking abilities (c) To teach schemata (d) To teach psycholinguistics

12. How can a preview guide help readers? (a) It helps them relate personal experiences to the reading content. (b) It makes the pictures easier to understand. (c) It makes reading some parts of the material unnecessary. (d) It tells the reader what pages to read.

13. What is the purpose of the structured overview in developing readiness for a reading assignment? (a) It helps the reader understand syntax. (b) It helps the reader fit personal experience into a conceptual framework that will help in understanding the text. (c) It structures the entire book for the student. (d) It helps the student recognize similarities and differences.

14. What type of understanding is sought at the inferential level? (a) The meaning stated in the content (b) Evaluation of ideas read (c) Meanings that are not stated in the text (d) Application of ideas to new situations

15. What type of thinking is recognizing stated main ideas? (a) Literal (b) Inferential (c) Critical (d) Creative

16. What information do readers use to make inferences? (a) Information stated in the selection (b) Background experience (c) Evaluative (d) Both a and b

17. What type of thinking is making generalizations? (a) Literal (b) Inferential (c) Evaluative (d) Creative

18. What is one of the aspects of textual schemata? (a) Semantics (b) Concepts (c) Paragraph structure (d) Phonics

19. Why do purposes for reading improve comprehension? (a) They are interesting. (b) They speed up reading. (c) They cause students to share ideas. (d) They focus readers' thinking.
20. What types of thinking are presented in this chapter? (a) Survey, review, and rereading (b) Tropic, directed, submerged (c) Literal, inferential, critical, and creative (d) Literal, inferential, and interest
21. "What did the author say?" is a good question for what type of thinking? (a) Literal type (b) Inferential type (c) Critical type (d) Creative type
22. What type of thinking is needed for understanding propaganda? (a) Literal (b) Inferential (c) Critical (d) Creative
23. Why should teachers allow students time to think? (a) Being given more time makes students think. (b) Being given more time enables students to answer questions better. (c) It is the polite thing to do. (d) It provides students with a break in the work routine.
24. Which of these is a basic element of structure in content reading materials? (a) Main ideas (b) SQ3R (c) Vocabulary (d) Strategies
25. What strategy helps students learn to ask and answer questions? (a) ReQuest (b) Reciprocal Teaching (c) Neither of these (d) Both of these

THOUGHT QUESTIONS

1. How is prediction related to reading comprehension?
2. What are textual schemata? How do they function in reading comprehension?
3. Why is it important to be an active reader?
4. What is the relationship between reading comprehension and content reading?
5. What are main ideas, and how are they related to content reading instruction?
6. Compare and contrast critical reading and creative reading.
7. What strategies and activities can a teacher use before having students start a reading assignment to aid their comprehension?
8. How is discussion related to reading comprehension?

ENRICHMENT ACTIVITIES

1. Read an article in the local newspaper and write down all the thinking processes that you use to understand what you are reading.
2. Read a chapter in a book of your choice and write a question for each type of thinking related to the chapter. Share your questions with your classmates.
3. Read a current best seller and write a brief paragraph that paraphrases the theme of the book. Have a classmate who has read the same book analyze your comprehension.

4. Visit a secondary school classroom for the purpose of watching questioning procedures. What type of questions is used most often? How much time are the students allowed for formulating answers?
5. Find examples of paragraphs in content area textbooks that follow organizational patterns illustrated in this chapter. Bring these examples to class to share and discuss.
6. Use the "key word" idea to analyze several paragraphs in a content textbook.
7. Select a chapter in a content textbook and make a plan to help other students comprehend the chapter, using the strategies suggested in this chapter.
8. Adapt one of the metacognitive activities presented in this chapter to a reading selection in your content area.
9. Examine the activities suggested in this chapter and plan ways to adapt them to your content area.

BIBLIOGRAPHY

Adams, M., and A. Collins. "A Schema-Theoretic View of Reading," in H. Singer and R. Ruddell (eds.), *Theoretical Models and Processes of Reading.* Newark, Del.: International Reading Association, 1986, pp. 404–425.

Alverman, D., D. Dillon, and D. O'Brien. *Using Discussion to Promote Reading Comprehension.* Newark, Del.: International Reading Association, 1987.

Anderson, R., E. Hiebert, J. Scott, and I. Wilkinson (eds.). *Becoming a Nation of Readers: The Report of the Commission on Reading.* Washington, D.C.: National Institute of Education, 1985.

Anderson, R., and P. D. Pearson. "A Schema-Theoretic View of Basic Processes in Reading Comprehension." In P. D. Pearson (ed.), *Handbook of Reading Research.* New York: Longman, 1984, pp. 255–291.

Andre, M., and T. Anderson. *The Development and Evaluation of a Self-Questioning Study Technique,* Technical Report No. 87. Cambridge, Mass.: Bolt, Beranek and Newman, 1978.

Armbruster, B., and T. H. Anderson. *Content Area Textbooks.* Reading Education Report No. 23. Urbana, Ill.: University of Illinois Center for the Study of Reading, 1981.

Armbruster, B., T. Anderson, and J. Ostertag. "Teaching Text Structure to Improve Reading and Writing." *The Reading Teacher,* 43 (November 1989), 130–136.

Ausubel, David. *Educational Psychology: A Cognitive View* (2nd ed.). New York: Holt, Rinehart and Winston, 1978.

Baker, L., and A. Brown. "Metacognitive Skills and Reading." In P. D. Pearson (ed.), *Handbook of Reading Research.* New York: Longman, 1984, pp. 353–394.

Berkowitz, S. "Effects of Instruction in Text Organization on Sixth Grade Students' Memory for Expository Reading." *Reading Research Quarterly* 21, No. 2 (1986), 161–178.

Blatt, G., and L. Rosen. "The Writing Response to Literature," *Journal of Reading,* 28 (October 1984), 8–12.

Bowman, M. "A Comparison of Content Schemata and Textual Schemata or the Process of Parachuting." *Reading World,* 21 (October 1981), 14–22.

104   Brandt, R. "On Creativity and Thinking Skills: A Conversation with David Perkins." *Educational Leadership* (May 1986), 12–18.

Brooks, L., and D. Dansereau. "Effects of Structural Schema Training and Text Organization on Expository Prose Processing." *Journal of Educational Psychology,* 75, No. 6 (1983), 811–820.

Brown, A. "Metacognitive Development and Reading." In R. Spiro, B. Bruce, and W. Brewer (eds.), *Theoretical Issues in Reading Comprehension.* Hillsdale, N.J.: Erlbaum, 1980.

Brown, A., and A. Palincsar. "Inducing Strategic Learning from Texts by Means of Informed, Self-Control Training." *Topics in Learning and Learning Disabilities,* 2 (1982), 1–17.

Buss, R., R. Ratliff, and J. Irion. "Effects of Instruction on the Use of Story Starters in Composition of Narrative Discourse." In J. Niles and R. Lalik (eds.), *Issues in Literacy: A Research Perspective.* Rochester, N.Y.: National Reading Conference, 1985, pp. 55–58.

Christenbury, L., and P. Kelly. *Questioning a Path to Critical Thinking.* Urbana, Ill.: National Council of Teachers of English, 1983.

Conley, M. "Teacher Decisionmaking." In D. Alvermann and D. Moore (eds.), *Research within Reach: Secondary School Reading.* Newark, Del.: International Reading Association, 1987.

Cook, D. (ed.). *A Guide for Curriculum Planning: Reading.* Madison, Wis.: Wisconsin Department of Public Instruction, 1986.

Cook, L., and R. Mayer. "Reading Strategies Training for Meaningful Learning from Prose." In M. Pressley and J. Levin (eds.), *Cognitive Strategy Research: Educational Applications.* New York: Springer-Verlag, 1983, 87–131.

Cunningham, J., and D. Moore. "The Confused World of Main Idea." In J. Bauman (ed.), *Teaching Main Idea Comprehension.* Newark, Del.: International Reading Association, 1986, pp. 1–17.

Davey, B. "Think Aloud — Modeling the Cognitive Processes of Reading Comprehension." *Journal of Reading,* 27 (October 1983), 44–47.

Emig, J. "Writing as a Mode of Learning." *College Composition and Communication* (May 1977), 123–124.

Ennis, R. "Critical Thinking and Subject Specificity: Clarification and Needed Research." *Educational Researcher,* 18 (April 1989), 4–10.

Fitzgerald, J., and D. Spiegel. "Enhancing Children's Reading Comprehension Through Instruction in Narrative Structure." *Journal of Reading Behavior,* 15 (1983), 1–17.

Freeman, M. "A New England Nun." In M. Spring (ed.), *Where We Live.* New York: Scholastic Book Services, 1976, pp. 689–695.

Gavelek, J. "The Social Contexts of Literacy and Schooling: A Developmental Perspective." In T. Raphael (ed.), *The Contexts of School Based Literacy.* New York: Random House, 1986, pp. 3–26.

Glaser, R. "Education and Thinking: The Role of Knowledge." *American Psychologist* 39 (February 1984), 93–104.

Goodlad, J. *A Place Called School.* New York: McGraw Hill, 1984.

Hammond, D. "How Your Students Can Predict Their Way to Reading Comprehension." *Learning,* 12 (1983), 62–64.

Heller, M. "How Do You Know What You Know? Metacognitive Modeling in the Content Areas," *Journal of Reading,* 29 (February 1986), 415–422.

Hill, F., and J. May. *Spaceship Earth: Physical Science,* rev. ed. Boston: Houghton Mifflin Company, 1981, p. 102.

Horowitz, R. "Text Patterns: Part I," *Journal of Reading,* 29 (March 1986), 448–454.

Hoskins, S. "Text Superstructures." *Journal of Reading,* 28 (February 1986), 538–543.

Hoskins, S. "The Use of Top-Level Structure of Exposition by Entering College Freshmen." Ph.D. dissertation, Texas Women's University, Denton, Texas, 1983.

International Reading Association. *New Directions in Reading Instruction.* Newark, Del.: International Reading Association, 1988.

Jackson, J., and E. Evans. *Spaceship Earth: Earth Science,* rev. ed. Boston: Houghton Mifflin Company, 1980, p. 19.

Johnson, D., and B. Johnson. "Highlighting Vocabulary in Inferential Comprehension Instruction." *Journal of Reading,* 29 (April 1986), 622–625.

Klauer, K. "Intentional and Incidental Learning with Instructional Texts: A Metaanalysis for 1970–1980." *American Educational Research Journal,* 21 (1984), 323–340.

Kronoblauch, C., and L. Brannon. "Writing as Learning Through the Curriculum," *College English,* 45 (September 1983), 465–474.

Lesgold, A., L. Resnick, and K. Hammond. "Learning to Read: A Longitudinal Study of Word Skill Development in Two Curricula." In T. Waller and G. MacKinnon (eds.), *Reading Research: Advances in Theory and Practice.* (Vol. 4, pp. 107–138). New York: Academic Press, 1985.

Lunstrum, J. "Building Motivation Through the Use of Controversy." *Journal of Reading,* 24 (May 1981), 687–691.

Mandler, J., and N. Johnson. "Remembrance of Things Passed: Story Structure and Recall." *Cognitive Psychology,* 9 (1977), 111–151.

McGee, L., and D. Richgels. "Teaching Expository Text Structure to Elementary Students." *The Reading Teacher,* 38 (May 1985), 739–748.

McTighe, J., and F. Lyman. "Cueing Thinking in the Classroom: The Promise of Theory Embedded Tools." *Educational Leadership,* 45, 7 (1988), 15–18.

Manzo, A. "The ReQuest Procedure." *Journal of Reading,* 13 (November 1969), 123–126.

Meyer, B., D. Brandt, and G. Bluth. "Use of Top-Level Structure in Text: Key for Reading Comprehension of Ninth-Grade Students." *Reading Research Quarterly,* 16 (1980), 72–103.

Morton, J., and R. Renzy. *Consumer Action.* Boston: Houghton Mifflin Company, 1978, p. 308.

National Assessment of Educational Progress. *The Reading Report Card* (Report No. 15-R-01). Princeton, N.J.: Educational Testing Service, 1985.

Palincsar, A., and A. Brown. "Interactive Teaching to Promote Independent Learning from Text." *The Reading Teacher,* 39 (May 1986), 771–777.

Palincsar, A., and A. Brown. *Reciprocal Teaching of Comprehension Monitoring Activities,* Technical Report No. 269. Champaign, Ill.: University of Illinois, Center for the Study of Reading, 1984.

Paris, S., and M. Myers. "Comprehension Monitoring, Memory and Study Strategies of Good and Poor Readers." *Journal of Reading Behavior,* 13 (Spring 1981), 5–22.

Pearson, P., and D. D. Johnson. *Teaching Reading Comprehension.* New York: Holt, Rinehart and Winston, 1977.

Perkins, D. "Creativity by Design." *Educational Leadership,* 42 (September 1984), 19–26.

Pearson, P. D., and R. Spiro. "The New Buzzword in Reading Is Schema." *Instructor* 89 (1982), 46–48.

Piccolo, J. "Expository Text Structure: Teaching and Learning Strategies." *The Reading Teacher,* 40 (June 1987), 838–847.

Pinnell, G. "Communication in Small Group Settings." *Theory into Practice,* 23 (1984), 246–254.

Raphael, T. "Teaching Question Answer Relationships, Revisited." *The Reading Teacher,* 39 (1986), 516–555.

Readence, J., T. Bean, and S. Baldwin. *Content Area Reading: An Integrated Approach.* Dubuque, Iowa: Kendall/Hunt, 1981.

Richek, M. "5 Variations That Facilitate Independence in Reading Narratives." *Journal of Reading,* 30 (April 1987), 632–636.

Ruddell, R. "Vocabulary Learning: A Process Model and Criteria for Evaluating Instructional Strategies." *Journal of Reading,* 29 (April 1986), 581–587.

Rosenberg, E., H. Gurney, and V. Harlin. *Investigating Your Health,* rev. ed. Boston: Houghton Mifflin Company, 1978, p. 313.

Shannon, D. "Use of Top-Level Structure in Expository Text: An Open Letter to a High School Teacher." *Journal of Reading,* 28 (February 1986), 426–431.

Singer, H., and D. Donlan. "Active Comprehension: Problem-Solving Schema with Question Generation for Comprehension of Complex Short Stories," *Reading Research Quarterly,* 27 (1982), 901–908.

Taylor, B. "Text Structure and Children's Comprehension and Memory for Expository Material." *Journal of Educational Psychology,* 74 (1985), 323–340.

Taylor, B., and S. Berkowitz. "Facilitating Children's Comprehension of Content Material." In M. Kamil and A. Moe (eds.), *Perspectives on Reading Research and Instruction.* Twenty-ninth Yearbook of the National Reading Conference. Washington, D.C.: National Reading Conference, 1980, pp. 64–68.

Tierney, R., and J. Cunningham. "Research on Teaching Reading Comprehension." In P. D. Pearson, et al. (eds.), *Handbook of Reading Research.* New York: Longman, 1984, pp. 609–656.

Vygotsky, L. *Thought and Language.* Cambridge, Mass.: The M.I.T. Press, 1962.

Weinstein, D. "Fostering Learning Autonomy Through the Use of Learning Strategies." *Journal of Reading,* 30 (1987), 590–595.

Wilder, H., R. Ludlum, and H. Brown. *This Is America's Story.* Boston: Houghton Mifflin Company, 1982, p. 238.

Wolfe, W., C. Huck, and M. King. *The Critical Reading Ability of Elementary School Children.* Columbus, Ohio: Ohio State University Research Foundation, 1967, Project No. 5-1040, supported by the U.S. Office of Education.

READING-STUDY

SKILLS

OVERVIEW

In this chapter consideration is given to the development of additional skills that enhance both comprehension and retention of information contained in printed material. These skills are important in helping a student manage reading assignments in content area classes.

Study methods such as SQ3R, EVOKER, SQRQCQ, and REAP are described, and their usefulness in different subject areas is discussed. Teaching procedures such as GRASP and PSRT are also discussed. Attention is given to the organizational skills of outlining, summarizing, and note taking and to location skills related to use of the library, books, and computer databases.

Ways to help students learn to read to follow directions are suggested. Consideration is given to helping students learn from the graphic aids (maps, graphs, tables, diagrams, and pictures) in their content area reading materials, as well as to helping them learn to adjust their reading rates to fit their purposes and the materials to be read. The two final topics of discussion are retention and test taking.

PURPOSE-SETTING QUESTIONS

As you read this chapter, try to answer these questions:

1. What are some study methods designed for use with content area reading selections, and how do they help?
2. What are some teaching procedures for helping students learn study skills and helping them to read with more comprehension, and why are they effective?
3. What organizational skills are helpful to students who are reading material that is to be used later in some manner?

4. What location skills do secondary school students need in order to use the library? To use books? To use computer databases?
5. How can a teacher help students learn to follow written directions accurately?
6. What are the types of graphic aids found in textbooks, and what must students know about each one to read it effectively?
7. What are some factors to consider in instruction related to reading rate?
8. What are some suggestions that can help students retain what they read?
9. How can teachers help students read test questions with understanding?

KEY VOCABULARY

As you read this chapter, check your understanding of these terms:

SQ3R	graphic aids	databases
EVOKER	map scale	pacers
PSRT	map projections	controlled reading
SQRQCQ	map legend	projectors
REAP	line graphs	tachistoscopes
GRASP	bar graphs	skimming
PORPE	circle or pie graphs	scanning
metacognitive skills	picture graphs (picto-	
paraphrase	graphs)	

Importance of a Study Method

According to Simons (1989, p. 419) "[s]tudies show that up to 50% of the students in secondary classrooms cannot read and learn from their content area textbooks." These students can often read narrative material effectively, but they have difficulty with expository text. Students also often do not study effectively because they *do not know how.* They have never been given instruction in how to focus on the important material, identify the organization of material, make use of graphic aids, vary reading rates and study procedures to fit the material, or tie in new learning to things they already know. They often approach all content reading material with the same attention and speed used for narrative materials that they read for pleasure.

Students often also fail to make use of metacognitive skills — that is, they do not monitor their comprehension of the material that they read as they are reading it. Metacognition involves knowing what is known already, knowing when understanding of new material has been accomplished, knowing how the understanding was reached, and knowing why something is or is not known (Guthrie, 1983). Students frequently look at or pronounce the words in a selection and feel that they have read it, without checking to see if they have located important ideas and understood the content and how it fits in with information that they already know. They fail to ask the questions, "Do I understand this point?" and "Does this make sense?" Even if they ask these questions, when the answers are negative, they may not think through the reading strategies that they have for understanding text and try to remedy the situation by applying appropriate ones, such as rereading, checking word meanings in a glossary or dictionary, looking for relationships among ideas, and identifying the organizational pattern of the text in order to clear up problems with meaning (Babbs and Moe, 1983). All these activities are part of effective studying. Students with a high maturity level can learn aspects of comprehension monitoring if teachers guide them toward use of these skills (Meir, 1984). This means that teachers must show students the importance of deciding what they already know about a topic, relating new information to their prior knowledge, and realizing whether the new information makes sense in light of previous knowledge. They must also make students aware of the strategies that they have at hand to help them figure out meanings that are not immediately apparent. Teacher modeling of the thinking process of self-questioning about meaning and deciding on strategies to use when meaning is unclear is a good approach for increasing metacognitive activities among students.

Having purposes for their reading activities can increase the likelihood that students will apply metacognitive skills. If they have purposes for reading, they can check to see if those purposes were met. If they have no purposes, they may not know what to look for or what questions to ask about the material.

Study methods have been developed that help students to approach content material in ways that make comprehension and retention of the material read more likely. These methods help students to establish purposes for reading the material and to monitor their reading to determine if understanding of the concepts was attained. They often cause the student to look at the material more than once for different purposes, thereby making retention of the ideas more likely.

Students need to be told the advantages of using a study method so that they will be more likely to use one when they read independently. Students also need to be told how to apply each method and how to decide when to apply it. For example, neither SQ3R nor any of the other study methods described in this chapter is appropriate for use with recreational reading in fiction. Having this knowledge constitutes a metacognitive skill that is very valuable. (See Chapter 3, Reading Comprehension, for more about metacognitive skills that allow students to monitor their comprehension and make adjustments when difficulties in comprehension arise.)

Students who do not know what study method to use when reading content area assignments may resort to pronouncing all the words in the selections as they read without actually thinking about the content. They may then rely on rote memorization to get them past the tests given on the material. If students rely on rote memorization for learning content, they may never find meaning in the content they are studying (Clarke et al., 1989), because such memorization does not require understanding.

Teaching Procedures

There are some teaching procedures that teachers find particularly helpful in enhancing students' study skills. GRASP, the PSRT strategy, and some recitation techniques can be useful approaches.

GRASP — the Guided Reading and Summarizing Procedure — is based on the Guided Reading Procedure (Manzo, 1975), with a focus on the process of summary writing. The goals of this procedure are development of a skill students can apply independently in writing reports, sharpening of their abilities to recall material they read, encouragement of self-correction, and improvement in their organizational skills. The steps in the procedure are as follows: "prepare students for the lesson, have them read for remembering details, help them group remembered details, and show them how to convert grouped details into a prose summary" (Hayes, 1989, p. 96). In the preparation phase, the teacher explains the purpose of the procedure. The selection that is given to the students to read should be 500 to 1,500 words long. The students make a list of all remembered facts. Rereading takes place in order to complete the information needed and make corrections in the original listing. Then major topics in the text are determined, and the information is categorized by topic. Finally, a summary is formed by including only important information, compressing and combining information, and adding any information needed for a coherent account (Hayes, 1989).

Simons (1989) suggests use of the PSRT strategy. The steps in this strategy are *Prepare, Structure, Read,* and *Think.* The *Prepare* step includes finding out what the students already know about the concepts in the material and, if necessary, supplementing this background information. Brainstorming about the key concepts should take place during this step. The *Structure* step involves helping students grasp the text's organization through use of a blank graphic overview that is partially completed with them on the board. During the *Read* step, the students read the text independently for a purpose and individually complete the overview presented in the previous step. During the *Think* step, a discussion of the text is held, the overview on the board is completed as a class activity, and the students summarize the text and answer higher-order, teacher-developed questions about it. This procedure is effective because of its high levels of teacher-student interactions. It also takes into account the importance of background knowledge and text organization to reading comprehension.

Classroom recitation techniques can be used to encourage good study practices. Recitation involves saying aloud the information to be remembered. It may serve as a motivational factor for studying material because students feel the need to prepare when they may be required to make presentations in class. It also can strengthen the memory for the material, as a student must think about the information, say it, and hear the result. Some forms of recitation include paraphrasing previous contributions to the content discussion, telling something that was learned from the day's lesson, discussing answers to questions constructed by students, brainstorming about possible test questions, and responding simultaneously with the rest of the class, through signals, to true/false or multiple-choice questions. The total-class response activities allow students to respond without feeling the pressure of being singled out. They simply hold up a "true" or "false" symbol at the same time that others do. The teacher can probe for thinking behind responses when some confusion exists among the students (Rakes and Smith, 1987).

Teacher modeling of the steps in study skills procedures before students are asked to perform the steps can be a very useful technique. The teacher can move through a procedure, verbalizing the steps being used and letting the students see how each step is accomplished.

In teaching the use of study methods, it is important that teachers provide students with opportunities to practice the methods before asking them to use the methods independently. The teacher should guide students through use of each study method during a class period, using an actual reading assignment. At the teacher's direction, the students should be expected to perform each step in the chosen method. For example, with the use of SQ3R, all students should be asked to survey the material together, reading the chapter title, the introduction to the chapter, the boldface and/or italicized headings, and the chapter summary. At this time they should also be asked to inspect graphic aids within the chapter. Each of the other steps, in turn, should be carried out by all students simultaneously. This technique can be applied to any of the study methods described in this chapter.

Specific Study Methods

Many methods of approaching study reading have been developed. The one that is probably best known and most widely used, especially for social studies and science selections, is the SQ3R method, developed by Robinson (1961). Other study methods have been designed for poetry, prose, and drama (EVOKER) (Pauk, 1963) and for mathematics (SQRQCQ) (Fay, 1965). Each of these methods will be considered in turn, as will a general study method, REAP (Eanet and Manzo, 1976).

SQ3R

When the five steps of the SQ3R method are applied to a content area reading selection, a variety of reading activities must be employed. The five steps of SQ3R "are metacognitive in nature: Prior to reading students preview the text and establish purposes for reading; while reading, they monitor their comprehension; and after reading, they summarize and review the content"

(Jacobowitz, 1988, p. 127). The details related to the different steps are discussed below.

1. *Survey.* During the survey step, the readers read the chapter title, the introductory paragraph(s), the boldface and/or italicized headings, and the summary paragraph(s). At this time the readers should also inspect any graphic aids, such as maps, graphs, tables, diagrams, and pictures. This survey provides readers with an overview of the material contained in the reading assignment and a framework into which they can organize the facts contained in the selection as reading progresses. Having this knowledge about what they are going to be reading and this grasp of the macrostructure (gist) of the text makes better comprehension of the material likely. This step also gives the readers enough information to generate individual purposes for reading the text (Jacobowitz, 1988).

2. *Question.* During this step, readers formulate questions that they expect to find answered in the selection. The author may have provided purpose questions at the beginning of the chapter or follow-up questions at the end. If so, the students may utilize these questions as purpose questions for the reading. If not, the readers can turn the section headings into questions and read to answer self-constructed questions.

3. *Read.* This is the step in which the students read to answer the purpose questions formulated in the previous step. Notes may be taken during this careful reading. Active involvement in the reading is important if the students are to obtain maximum benefit from it.

4. *Recite.* In this step, the students try to answer the purpose questions formulated during the second step without referring to the book or any notes that they have made. This step helps to "set" the information in memory, so that it can be recalled at a later time. This rehearsal process aids the transfer of information from short-term to long-term memory (Jacobowitz, 1988).

5. *Review.* At this point each student reviews the material by rereading portions of the book or notes taken during the careful reading, to verify the answers given during the previous step. This activity helps the students retain the material better; immediate reinforcement of ideas helps them overcome the tendency to forget material shortly after reading it.

The SQ3R method, like other study techniques, seems to be learned best when taught in situations where it is expected to be used. Brazee (1979) compared the effect of *skill-centered* reading instruction (focusing on a skill apart from the situation in which it will be applied) with that of *content-centered* reading instruction (focusing on application of a skill for content learning) in social studies classes. One group of students was instructed in the SQ3R study method and rate flexibility before, and separate from, their social studies lesson; the teacher was "teaching general reading skills, assuming that such general skills would 'automatically' transfer to the content area." With this group, "at no time did the instructors indicate that the reading skills might be effectively used in the context of each social studies lesson." The other group received instruction in the same two skills, but the skills were taught within the framework of the social studies material. The material itself determined the skills to be taught, a situation that did not exist in the control group's instruction. The second group actually received less instructional time on the reading skills, but that group showed greater improvement in both rate flexibility and the ability to use the survey part of SQ3R without specific instructions to do so. The difference in improvement between the two groups was greatest on the flexibility measure. Therefore, it seems that the reading skills involved in this study are more efficiently learned and utilized when taught in the context of content materials and during, rather than before, the content class.

EVOKER

This procedure should be applied when students are reading prose, poetry, and drama, rather than expository text. It is a method for "close reading." The steps are as follows:

1. *Explore.* Read the entire selection silently to gain a feeling for the overall message.
2. *Vocabulary.* Note key words. Look up those words with which you are not familiar. Also look up unfamiliar places, events, and people mentioned in the selection.
3. *Oral reading.* Read the selection aloud with good expression.
4. *Key ideas.* Locate key ideas to help you understand the author's organization. Be sure to determine the main idea or theme of the selection.
5. *Evaluate.* Evaluate the key words and sentences with respect to their contributions to developing the key ideas and the main idea.
6. *Recapitulation.* Reread the selection.

SQRQCQ

Since mathematics materials present special problems for readers, this study method was developed for use with statement or word problems in mathematics. The steps are discussed briefly below.

1. *Survey.* The student reads the problem rapidly to obtain an idea of its general nature.
2. *Question.* In this step, the student determines the specific nature of the problem, that is, "What is being asked in this problem?"
3. *Read.* The student reads the problem carefully, paying attention to specific details and relationships.
4. *Question.* At this point, the student must make a decision about the mathematical operations to be carried out, and, in some cases, the order in which these operations are to be performed. The student asks what operations must be performed and in what order.

5. *Compute*. The student does the computations decided on in the previous step.
6. *Question*. The student checks the entire process and decides whether or not the answer seems to be correct. He or she asks if the answer is reasonable and if the computations have been performed accurately.

Notice that, like SQ3R, this method encourages use of metacognitive skills. Students preview the problem in the survey step, set purposes in the first two question steps, and monitor their success with the problem in the final question step.

REAP

This study technique encourages students to demand meaning from the reading because it requires an overt response. Not only reading skills, but also thinking and writing skills, are sharpened by using this approach. The four steps of the technique are described below.

1. *Read*. The student reads to find out what the writer is saying.
2. *Encode*. The student translates the writer's message into his or her own language.
3. *Annotate*. During this step, the student writes the message. Any one of several forms of annotation may be used. Heuristic annotations consist of quotations from the selections; they suggest the essence of the selections and stimulate responses. Summary annotations are brief restatements of the author's main ideas and the relationships among them. A thesis annotation states the author's main premise or theme. A question annotation is a formulation of the question or questions that the annotator feels the author is answering in the selection. A critical annotation includes a statement of the author's thesis, a statement of the reader's reaction to this thesis, and a defense of the reader's stated reaction. An intention annotation states the author's purpose as it is understood by the reader. In a motivation annotation, the annotator speculates about the probable motives of the writer (Eanet and Manzo, 1976). Probe annotations give emphasis to verification, consequence, and alternatives. Personal view annotations answer the question, "How do personal experiences, views, and feelings stack up against the thesis or main idea?" Inventive annotations take a creative approach, drawing from other contexts or synthesizing ideas (Manzo, 1985).
4. *Ponder*. The student thinks about the author's message. Discussion with others may be a part of this step.

Organizational Skills

When participating in study activities such as writing reports, secondary school students need to organize the ideas they encounter in their reading.

Three helpful organizational skills are outlining, summarizing, and note tak-ing. All require recognition and recording in an organized form of important ideas from the materials read. The act of organizing information helps stu-dents comprehend and retain it better.

Outlining

Teachers should help their students to understand that outlining is recording information from reading material in a way that makes clear the relationships between the main ideas and the supporting details. Before it is possible for students to learn to construct an outline properly, they must know how to identify main ideas and supporting details in reading selections. Information on how to assist students in locating main ideas and recognizing related details is found in Chapter 3.

Readiness for formal outlining tasks may be developed by having stu-dents work with arrays, which are free-form outlines. When constructing arrays, students are required to arrange key words and phrases in ways that show the relationships set forth by the author. They can use words, lines, and arrows to do this. It is important to use a simple, familiar story for this activity, so that the students can focus on the logical arrangement of the terms rather than worrying about the details of the story. Example 4.1 shows a story array for the familiar story "Johnny Appleseed."

E X A M P L E **4.1**

Story Array

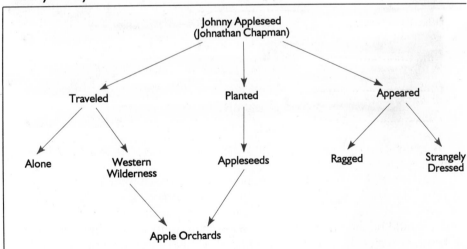

Teachers can guide students to learn how to make arrays by first supply-ing the words and phrases and then letting the students work in groups to complete the arrays. First the students read the selection; then they arrange the words and phrases appropriately, using lines and arrows to indicate relationships. The teacher questions students about the positioning and direction of arrows, asking for reasons for the choices made. In addition, the teacher is available to answer students' questions. Eventually, the students are expected to choose key words and concepts themselves and arrange them without the teacher's help.

Two types of outlines that students may find useful are the sentence outline and the topic outline. In a sentence outline, each point is stated in the form of a complete sentence; in a topic outline, the points are written in the form of key words and phrases. The sentence outline is generally easier to master because the topic outline involves an extra task — condensing main ideas, already expressed in sentence form, into key words and phrases.

The first step in making an outline is extracting the main ideas from the material and listing them beside Roman numerals in the order in which they occur. The next step is locating the details that support each of the main ideas and listing them beside capital letters below the main idea that they support. These details are indented to indicate subordination to the main idea. Details that are subordinate to these details are indented still more and preceded by Arabic numerals. The next level of subordination is indicated by lower case letters. Although other levels of subordination are possible, secondary school students will rarely need such fine divisions.

The following are some ideas about outlining that a teacher may wish to stress:

1. The degree of importance of ideas in an outline is shown by the numbers and letters used, as well as by the indentation of entries. Points that have equal importance are designated by the same number or letter style and the same degree of indentation.
2. A topic should not be subdivided unless two points of equal value can be noted under it. (For example, the student should not use a I without a II or an A without a B.)
3. An outline should not incorporate unimportant or unrelated details.

A generic outline form may be helpful in demonstrating proper form. Example 4.2 shows such a form.

Teachers can help students see how a textbook chapter would be outlined by showing them how the headings within the chapter indicate different levels of subordination. For example, in some textbooks the title for the outline would be the title of the chapter. Roman numeral headings would be centered, or major, headings in the chapter, capital letter headings would be side headings, and Arabic numeral headings would be italic or paragraph headings.

EXAMPLE **4.2**

Outline Form

TITLE

I. Main idea
  A. Detail supporting I
  B. Detail supporting I
    1. Detail supporting B
    2. Detail supporting B
      a. Detail supporting 2
      b. Detail supporting 2
  C. Detail supporting I
II. Main idea
  A. Detail supporting II
  B. Detail supporting II
  C. Detail supporting II
    1. Detail supporting C
    2. Detail supporting C

Another approach to helping students learn to outline their reading as-signments is for the teacher to supply the students with partially completed outlines of the material and then have them complete the outlines. The teacher can vary the difficulty of the activity by gradually leaving out more and more details until the students do the entire outline alone. In Example 4.3, a progression of assignments in outlining is suggested.

EXAMPLE **4.3**

Progression of Outlining Assignments

First Assignment

TITLE (GIVEN BY TEACHER)

I. (Given by teacher)
  A. (Given by teacher)
    1. (To be filled in by student)
    2. (To be filled in by student)
  B. (Given by teacher)
    1. (To be filled in by student)
    2. (Given by teacher)
      a. (To be filled in by student)
      b. (To be filled in by student)

II. (Given by teacher)
    A. (Given by teacher)
    B. (To be filled in by student)

Second Assignment

TITLE (GIVEN BY TEACHER)

I. (Given by teacher)
    A. (To be filled in by student)
    B. (To be filled in by student)
        1. (To be filled in by student)
        2. (To be filled in by student)
II. (Given by teacher)
    A. (To be filled in by student)
    B. (To be filled in by student)

Third Assignment

TITLE

I.
    A.
    B.
    C.
        1.
        2.
II.
    A.
        1.
            a.
            b.
        2.
    B.

Outlining practice should probably be offered in every subject area because of the differences in organization of material among the disciplines. A standard form of outlining, used throughout the school, will decrease confusion among the students.

Summarizing

Summaries of reading assignments can be extremely valuable to secondary school students when they are studying for tests. The summaries have to be good ones in order to be helpful, however. To write a good summary, a student must restate what the author has said in a more concise form. The main ideas and essential supporting details of a selection should be preserved in a summary, but illustrative material and statements that merely elaborate on the main ideas should not be included. The ability to locate main ideas is therefore a prerequisite for learning how to write good summaries. (Development of this skill is discussed in Chapter 3.)

The topic sentence of a paragraph is a good summary of the paragraph, if it is well written. Practice in finding topic sentences of paragraphs, therefore, is also practice in the skill of summarizing paragraphs.

Summaries of longer selections may be constructed by locating the main ideas of the component paragraphs and combining these ideas into a summary statement. Certain types of paragraphs can generally be disregarded when summaries of lengthy selections are being written. Introductory and illustrative paragraphs do not add new ideas and therefore are not helpful in constructing a concise overview of the material. Students who write summaries of their reading assignments may wish to compare their summaries with concluding or summary paragraphs written by the author, to make sure that they have not omitted essential details.

When writing summaries, students should try not only to limit the number of sentences they use but also to limit the number of words they use within sentences. Words that are not needed to convey the meaning of the sentences can be omitted. For example:

> *Original sentence.* A match, carelessly discarded by an unsuspecting tourist, can cause the destruction by fire of many acres of trees that will take years of work to replace.

> *Changed sentence.* Carelessly discarded matches can result in extensive destruction of forested areas by fire.

Teachers should show students that in order to make good summaries, they must delete trivial and redundant material. They should use superordinate terms to replace lists of similar items or actions (for example, "animals" for "pigs, dogs, and cats"). A superordinate action can be used to replace steps in an action (for example, "made spaghetti sauce" for "took tomato sauce, sliced mushrooms, fried ground beef, chopped onion, oregano, and salt, . . . and placed on the stove to cook on low heat"). As mentioned above, each paragraph can be represented by an implied main idea sentence or a directly stated topic sentence. Paragraphs can then be examined to see which ones are most needed. Only necessary ones should be kept, and some that are kept can be combined (Brown and Day, 1983; Brown, Day, and Jones, 1983; Hare and Borchardt, 1984; Recht, 1984).

One method of teaching summarization has been discussed earlier in this chapter under the heading "Teaching Procedures." It is the Guided Reading and Summarizing Procedure described by Hayes (1989).

Practice in summarizing is most effective if the material being summarized is taken from textbooks the students are currently using or from other material that they are expected to read in connection with classwork. The teacher may give students a section of the textbook to read, along with three or four summaries of the material. The students can be asked to choose the best summary from those presented and asked to tell why the other summaries are not as good. This is good preparation for independent student writing of summaries.

Précis writing is a form of summarizing. This form of summarizing is discussed in detail in Chapter 7.

Note Taking

Taking notes on material read for classes can be a helpful memory aid. Well-constructed notes can make rereading of the material at a later time unnecessary and thus can save students time and effort. In order to take good notes, students must think about the material they are reading; as a result, they will be more likely to remember the material when they need to use it. It is also true that the simple act of writing ideas helps fix them in students' memories. Smith and Tompkins (1988, p. 46) point out that "[t]he farther students move along the continuum from verbatim notes to elaborated notes, the greater the benefit they receive." This increased benefit comes from increased active mental involvement with the text.

Notes on Reading Assignments

Students should be encouraged to use the form of note taking that helps them the most. Some students may utilize outline form when taking notes on an assignment in a textbook. Others may write a summary of the textbook materials. Still others may wish to use what Smith and Tompkins (1988, p. 48) call structured notes. "Structured notes are graphic organizers in which the top level structure used by the author or the structure inferred by the reader is explicit in the graphic." In other words, the notes show description, time/order, cause-effect, problem-solution, comparison-contrast, and definition-examples patterns visually through the form in which the notes are taken. For example, the description pattern could have notes taken in a sunburst shape, with the concept being described in the center of the circle and the descriptive details on the rays, and the time/order pattern could have a stairstep numbered listing of events in order. Teachers should teach each pattern and the structure for notes taken in that pattern.

Before notes are taken for a research paper, the questions that should be answered in the paper must be determined. The questions can be listed under categories important to the topic, and students can go to appropriate reference sources to find out about the categories. For example, "What types of printers exist?" and "What are some advantages of a dot matrix printer?" could be categorized under the topic "Printers." All notes taken on the topic "Printers" could be labeled with this term, to facilitate organization of notes. Other categories might be "Monitors," "CPUs," and "Keyboards," for example.

Notes for a research paper can be especially effective when made on index cards that can later be sorted into topics to be covered in the paper. If note cards are used, each one should include the source of information so that the paper is well documented. Sample note cards are shown in Example 4.4. Some guidelines for note taking that may be helpful to students follow:

1. Key words and phrases should be used in notes.
2. Enough of the context must be included to make the notes understandable after a period of time has elapsed.
3. The bibliographical reference should be included with each note card or page.
4. Direct quotations should be copied exactly and should be used sparingly.
5. Notes should differentiate clearly between direct quotations and re-worded material.
6. Notes should be as brief as possible.
7. Use of abbreviations can make note taking less time-consuming. Examples: ∴ for therefore; w/ for with; = for equals.

E X A M P L E **4.4**

Note Cards

First reference from source:

Fishel, Wesley R. "Indochina." *The World Book Encyclopedia,* 1978, X, 168.

Indochina includes the following countries: Cambódia, Laos, Vietnam.

Source previously used:

Fishel, page 168

A variety of racial and language groups are found in Indochina, resulting in a lack of uni-formity and unity among the people.

Incomplete sentences:

Fishel, page 169

Khmer tribesmen — ancestors of present-day Cambodians — empire famous for art, architecture and government.

Teachers may be able to help their students learn to take good notes by "thinking through" a textbook assignment with them orally in class, emphasizing the points that should be included in a good set of notes. This provides them with a model of the process of note taking. Students then can be encouraged to take notes on another assignment and compare them with a set of notes the teacher has constructed on the same material.

Taking Classroom Notes

Another way to help students develop note-taking skills is the *Guided Lecture Procedure* (GLP), devised by Kelly and Holmes (1979). The steps in the GLP are as follows:

1. Before the lecture begins, the teacher writes the lecture objectives (maximum of four) in brief form on the chalkboard, accompanied by new terms to be presented in the lecture.
2. Students copy this material from the board before the lecture begins. This gives them a purpose for listening.
3. The lecturer speaks for approximately thirty minutes while the students listen *without* taking notes.
4. The lecturer stops and gives the students approximately five minutes to write down all that they recall from the lecture. Students are encouraged to categorize and relate ideas.
5. Students are divided into small groups to discuss the lecture and organize their notes. The lecturer serves as an assistant during this phase, helping students find the answers they seek.
6. After the class, students reflect on the material and the class activities. This step helps promote long-term memory.
7. Finally, students write from memory a narrative covering the main points of the lecture and the conclusions drawn.

This procedure, which is excellent as a note-taking strategy, is also a study approach and, to a large degree, a teaching procedure. Teachers will find it helpful to use in many content classes.

Location Skills

In order to take part in many study activities (primarily content area reading and writing assignments), students need to be able to locate specific reading materials. The teacher can help students by showing them location aids that exist in libraries and books.

Libraries

Teachers may not wish to teach students location skills connected with the library because they feel that the librarian should perform this task. The librarian, however, may feel that he or she is not supposed to function as an instructor. Because of these conflicting viewpoints, students may receive no instruction in using the library, even though they are encouraged to use it for both reference work and recreational reading. This problem can be solved if teachers and librarians work cooperatively to help students develop the skills needed for effective library use.

The librarian can help by showing students the location of books, periodicals, card catalogs, computer terminals, and reference materials (dictionaries, encyclopedias, atlases, *Readers' Guide to Periodical Literature,* and others) in the library; by explaining the procedures for checking books out and returning them; and by clarifying the rules relating to behavior in the library. The librarian can also demonstrate use of the card catalog and the *Readers' Guide* and explain the arrangement of books in the library. (The Dewey Decimal System is the arrangement most commonly used in school libraries in the United States for classifying nonfiction books, although some libraries classify books by Library of Congress numbers.) Posters can be constructed and displayed in the library to remind students of checkout procedures, library rules, and arrangement of books. A poster might, for example, list the major divisions of the Dewey Decimal System. These divisions are indicated below:

000–099: Generalities
100–199: Philosophy and Psychology
200–299: Religion
300–399: The Social Sciences
400–499: Language
500–599: Pure Sciences
600–699: Technology (Applied Sciences)
700–799: The Arts
800–899: Literature
900–999: General History and Geography (Dewey, 1971)

Other posters that might profitably be displayed in the library include samples of the different types of cards that are found in the card catalog. Sample cards are shown in Example 4.5.

The librarian can be extremely helpful to teachers. He or she may

1. help teachers locate both printed and other materials related to current units of study;
2. help teachers plan a unit on use of reference materials in the library;
3. help teachers discover reading interests of individuals and specific groups of students;

E X A M P L E **4.5**

Card Catalog Cards

Subject Card:

> Animal Stories
>
> A   Adams, Richard
>   *Watership Down*
> Rex Collings, Ltd. (c) 1972

Author Card:

> A   Adams, Richard
>
>   *Watership Down*
> Rex Collings, Ltd. (c) 1972

Title Card:

> *Watership Down*
> A   Adams, Richard
>   *Watership Down*
> Rex Collings, Ltd. (c) 1972

Cross-Reference Card:

> Zeus
> see
> Greek Mythology

4. alert teachers to professional reading materials in their content areas;
5. give presentations to students on the availability and location of materials for particular content areas; and
6. put materials on particular content topics on reserve for a class.

If students seek material in popular magazines, the teacher might review or initially teach the use of the *Readers' Guide to Periodical Literature*, which indexes articles from approximately 160 popular magazines. Each article is indexed under both the subject and the author's name. Sometimes an article is also included under the title.

Social studies teachers may wish to teach students to use *The New York Times Index*, which is a subject index of articles from the *New York Times*. Since dates of publication of the articles are included, students can use this index as an aid to locating articles on the same subjects in local papers.

Features Within Books

Teaching students how to locate material within informational books and special reference books (encyclopedias, dictionaries, almanacs, atlases) found in the library is also a concern of the content area teacher. Most informational books include special features that students can use to locate needed material. Content area teachers will find that explaining the functions of prefaces, tables of contents, indexes, appendixes, glossaries, footnotes, and bibliographies is well worth the effort in increasing students' efficiency as they use books.

Secondary level teachers tend not to teach textbook use to their students, possibly because they think it has been covered previously. Since elementary teachers do not appear to give such instruction frequent attention, secondary school content teachers need to strongly consider adding this component to their classes (Davey, 1988).

Preface. When a content area teacher presents a new textbook to secondary school students, he or she should ask the students to read the preface and/or introduction to obtain an idea about why the book was written and the manner in which the material is presented.

Table of Contents. The table of contents of a textbook should also be examined on the day the textbook is distributed. Students can be reminded that the table of contents tells what topics the book includes and the pages on which those topics begin. A brief drill with the textbook can help to emphasize the functions of the table of contents. Questions such as these can be asked:

1. What topics are covered in this book?
2. What is the first topic that is discussed?

3. On what page does the discussion about _____ begin? (This question can be repeated several times with different topics inserted in the blank.)

Indexes. Students need to understand that an index is an alphabetical list of the important items and/or proper names mentioned in a book, with the pages where each item or name appears. Students generally need practice in using index headings and subheadings to locate information in their books.

A preliminary lesson on what an index is and how to use it to locate information can be presented. Afterward, the teacher can use the students' own textbooks to teach index use. The lesson idea shown in Example 4.6 can be modified for use with an actual index in a content area textbook. (The sample index is not from an actual textbook.)

E X A M P L E **4.6**

Sample Index and Questions

Sample Index

Absolute value, 145, 174–175
Addition
    of decimals, 101
    of fractions, 80–83
    of natural numbers, 15–16, 46–48
    of rational numbers, 146–148
    of real numbers, 170
Angles, 203
    measurement of, 206–207
    right, 204
Axiom, 241
Base
    meaning of, 5
    change of, 6–7

Index Questions

1. On what page would you look to find out how to add decimals? Under what main topic and subheading did you have to look to discover this page number?
2. On what pages will you find base mentioned?
3. What pages contain information about absolute value?
4. On what pages would you look to find out about measurement of angles? What

main heading did you look under to discover this? What subheading did you look under?

5. Where would you look to find information about adding real numbers? Would you expect to find any information about real numbers on page 146? Why or why not?

6. Is there information about addition of natural numbers on pages 46–48? Is information on this topic found on any other pages?

   (The following questions could be incorporated into the lesson if an actual index were being used.)

7. Find the meaning for <u>base</u> and read it aloud. Did you look in the index to find the page number? If not, could you have found it more quickly by looking in the index?

Appendixes. Students can be shown that the appendixes in textbooks and other books contain helpful information, such as bibliographies, maps, and tables.

Glossaries. Glossaries are often found in content area textbooks. Students can be taught that glossaries are similar to dictionaries but include only words presented in the books in which they are found. Glossaries of technical terms can greatly help students in understanding a book's content. The skills needed for proper use of a glossary are the same as those needed for using a dictionary. (See Chapter 2 for further discussion of dictionary use.)

Footnotes and Bibliographies. Footnotes tell the source of information included in the text. If further clarification of the material is needed, a student may use the footnote as a guide to the original source. Bibliographies may refer students to other sources of information about the subjects discussed in a book. The bibliography at the end of a chapter in a textbook is generally a list of references that the author(s) consulted when preparing the chapter and also references that contain additional information about the subject. Bibliographies are extremely valuable aids for students doing assigned research activities.

Special Reference Books

Secondary school students are often called on to find information in reference books such as encyclopedias, dictionaries, almanacs, and atlases. Unfortunately, many students reach junior high or high school without knowing how to use such books effectively.

Important aspects related to effective use of reference books include

1. Knowledge of alphabetical order of entries (Most secondary school students have mastered the principles of alphabetical order, but a few need help.)

2. Knowledge that information in encyclopedias, dictionaries, and some atlases is arranged in alphabetical order

3. Ability to use guide words (that is, knowing the location of guide words on a page and understanding that they represent the first and last entry words on a dictionary or encyclopedia page)
4. Ability to use cross-references (related primarily to use of encyclopedias)
5. Ability to use pronunciation keys (related primarily to use of dictionaries)
6. Ability to choose from several possible word meanings the one that most closely fits the context in which the word was found (related to use of dictionaries)
7. Ability to interpret the legend of a map (related to use of atlases)
8. Ability to interpret the scale of a map (related to use of atlases)
9. Ability to locate directions on maps (related to use of atlases)
10. Ability to determine which volume of a set will contain the information being sought (related primarily to use of encyclopedias)
11. Ability to determine key words under which related information can be found

Because encyclopedias, almanacs, and atlases are often written on extremely high readability levels, teachers should use caution in assigning students work in these reference books. Students are not likely to profit from trying to do research in books written on a level they find frustrating. When students are asked to look up material in books that are too difficult for them to read with understanding, they tend to copy the material word for word instead of trying to extract the important ideas.

Encyclopedias

A surprising number of junior high school students and a few high school students do not realize that, when you look up the name of a person in the encyclopedia, it will be alphabetized by the last name, not the first. A student who had to write a report on James Otis came to one of the authors of this text and announced that James Otis was not in the encyclopedia. Puzzled, the author asked the student to show her how he had proceeded in looking for the name. He went to the "J" volume of the encyclopedia and began to look for "James." He seemed surprised when he was told that proper names are listed alphabetically according to last name and then the first name. Example 4.7 can be used as a diagnostic measure to determine whether students know how to look up people's names; when used in this way, it should be followed by appropriate explanations for those students who are unable to answer all the items correctly. This activity (or a similar one) may also be used as a reinforcement exercise following such explanations. If the activity was used initially as a diagnostic instrument, it should be modified when used for reinforcement.

EXAMPLE **4.7**

Activity for Using the Encyclopedia

Directions: Pretend you have an encyclopedia whose volumes are arranged so that there is one volume for each letter of the alphabet. Look at the following names and decide which volume of the encyclopedia you would have to use to find each name. Write the letter of the volume in the space provided beside the name. When you finish, use the answer key to check your work. If you don't understand why you made your mistakes, ask the teacher for an explanation.

_____ Richard Nixon
_____ Marie Curie
_____ Clara Barton
_____ Martin Van Buren
_____ Martin Luther King
_____ Robert Louis Stevenson
_____ John Paul Jones

Answer key: N, C, B, V, K, S, J

Example 4.8 gives students practice in locating various types of information in the encyclopedia. To complete this activity (or one modeled on it), the students decide which key words to look under in order to find certain information. For example, for "Education in Sweden" they would need to look first under Sweden and then find the section on education. When completed, this activity should be discussed in class to show students why they made the errors they made and how to approach the task correctly.

EXAMPLE **4.8**

Activity for Using the Encyclopedia

Directions: Look up each of the following topics in the encyclopedia. On the line beside each topic; write the letter of the volume in which you found the topic and the page number on which the topic is discussed.

1. Tennis   _____
2. Solar system   _____
3. U.S. Constitution   _____
4. Lobster   _____
5. Oleander   _____
6. Sampan   _____
7. Education in Sweden   _____
8. Computer use in library systems   _____

Because encyclopedias vary in content and arrangement, students should be taught to use several different sets. They should be asked to compare the entries in these sets on a specified list of topics. They may also be asked to compare different sets of encyclopedias on an overall basis, noting features such as type of index used, number of volumes, ease of reading, and date of publication.

Dictionaries

Students frequently are not extremely familiar with dictionary content and use. A few, but not a large number, have some trouble with alphabetical order. A much larger number have trouble with guide words and use of the pronunciation key, and many do not realize the variety of information that is found in a dictionary entry. Spending some time to familiarize students with dictionary use can pay good dividends in their future learning.

Example 4.9 shows a page from a dictionary that is recommended for use with grades 9 through 12 and provides some instructional commentary that could be helpful to use with students who show a need for better understanding of the dictionary.

Dialogues similar to that in Example 4.9 can be held for other words until all of the features of the dictionary have been highlighted. For example, the teacher could read a sentence containing the word *knot* and have students decide which definition fits the context, and why. Principal parts of verbs and degrees of adjectives should also receive attention.

Since dictionary skills are presented to students repeatedly during their school careers, even though they may not be thoroughly learned, these skills may seem boring to students. The introduction of games, audiovisual presentations, and other motivational activities may enhance interest in the instruction. For example, paper-and-pencil scavenger hunts in the library might be fun for students. They might be asked to find a book by Herman Melville (write down its name, call number, and location), the dictionary definition of *catamaran,* and the volume and page number of the *World Book Encyclopedia* that contains a discussion of catamarans. Each student or small group of students could have a different list.

Using Computer Databases

The location skills that students need in today's schools include one type that has not received much attention in the past. Students need to know how to retrieve information stored in computer databases, either ones that the students have compiled themselves or others that are available in the school.

A database is an organized collection of information. Conceptually, a database is like a filing cabinet (or several cabinets), with separate file folders for each article in the database. The information may be categorized by subject or by another categorization scheme and is indexed for easy access. Typi-

EXAMPLE 4.9

Dictionary Page and Instructional Commentary

knelt (nĕlt) v. var. p.t. & p.p. of KNEEL.

Knes·set (knĕs′ĕt) n. [Heb. *Kéneseth*, assembly < *kanas*, he gathered.] The Israeli parliament.

knew (nōō, nyōō) v. p.t. of KNOW.

Knick·er·bock·er (nĭk′ər-bŏk′ər) n. [After Diedrich *Knickerbocker*, fictitious author of *History of New York*, by Washington Irving.] **1. a.** A descendant of the Dutch settlers of New York. **b.** A New Yorker. **2. knickerbockers.** Full breeches gathered and banded just below the knee.

knick·ers (nĭk′ərz) pl.n. [Short for KNICKERBOCKERS.] **1.** Long bloomers once worn as underwear by women and girls. **2.** KNICKERBOCKERS 2.

knick·knack (nĭk′năk′) n. [Redup. of KNACK.] A trinket.

knife (nīf) n., pl. **knives** (nīvz) [ME *knif* < OE *cníf*.] **1.** A cutting instrument having a sharp blade with a handle. **2.** A cutting edge : BLADE. —v. **knifed, knif·ing, knifes.** —vt. **1.** To use a knife on, esp. to cut, stab, or wound. **2.** *Informal.* To hurt, defeat, or betray by underhand means. —vi. To cut or slash a way with or as if with a knife. —**knif′er** n.

knife-edge (nīf′ĕj′) n. **1.** The cutting edge of a blade. **2.** A sharp knifelike edge <felt the *knife-edge* of criticism> **3.** A metal wedge used as a low-friction fulcrum for a balancing beam or lever.

knight (nīt) n. [ME < OE *cniht*.] **1.** A medieval tenant giving military service as a mounted man-at-arms to a feudal landholder. **2.** A usu. high-born medieval gentleman-soldier raised by a sovereign to privileged military status after training as a page and squire. **3.** The holder of a nonhereditary dignity conferred by a sovereign in recognition of personal merit or services to the country. **4.** A member of an order or brotherhood designating its members knights. **5. a.** A zealous defender or champion of a principle or cause. **b.** A lady's devoted champion. **6.** A chess piece moved either two squares horizontally and one vertically or two vertically and one horizontally. —vt. **knight·ed, knight·ing, knights.** To raise (a person) to knighthood. —**knight′li·ness** n. —**knight′ly** adj.

knight er·rant (ĕr′ənt) n., pl. **knights errant. 1.** A knight of medieval romance who wandered in search of adventure. **2.** One given to adventurous or quixotic conduct. —**knight′-er′rant·ry** (nīt′ĕr′ən-trē) n.

knight·hood (nīt′hŏŏd) n. **1.** The rank, profession, or dignity of a knight. **2.** Behavior of or qualities worthy of a knight : CHIVALRY. **3.** Knights as a group.

Knight of Co·lum·bus (kə-lŭm′bəs) n. A member of a philanthropic fraternal society of Roman Catholic men.

Knight of Pythias n. A member of a secret philanthropic fraternal order.

Knights of the Round Table pl.n. The knights of the court of King Arthur in Arthurian legend.

Knight Templar n., pl. **Knights Templars.** A member of a 12th–14th cent. order of knights founded to protect pilgrims in the Holy Land during the Second Crusade.

knish (kə-nĭsh′) n. [Yiddish < R.] Dough stuffed with potato, meat, or cheese and baked or fried.

knit (nĭt) v. **knit** or **knit·ted, knit·ting, knits.** [ME *knitten* < OE *cnyttan*, to tie in a knot.] —vt. **1.** To make by intertwining yarn or thread in a series of connected loops. **2.** To unite securely and closely. **3.** To draw (the brows) together in wrinkles : FURROW. —vi. **1.** To make a fabric or garment by knitting. **2.** To come or grow together securely. **3.** To come together in wrinkles or furrows. —**knit′** n. —**knit′ter** n.

knit·ting needle (nĭt′ĭng) n. A long, thin, pointed rod used for knitting.

knit·wear (nĭt′wâr′) n. Knitted garments in general.

knives (nīvz) n. pl. of KNIFE.

knob (nŏb) n. [ME *knobbe*, prob. < MLG.] **1. a.** A rounded protuberance. **b.** A rounded dial. **2.** A prominent rounded hill or mountain. —**knobbed** adj. —**knob′by** adj.

knob·ker·rie (nŏb′kĕr′ē) n. [Afr. *knopkierie* : *knop*, knob (< MDu. *cnoppe*) + *kieri*, club < Hottentot *kirri*.] A short club with one knobbed end, used by South African tribesmen as a weapon.

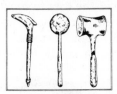

knobkerrie
Three types of knobkerries

knock (nŏk) v. **knocked, knock·ing, knocks.** [ME *knokken* < OE *cnocian*.] —vt. **1.** To strike with a hard blow. **2.** To cause to collide. **3.** To produce by hitting <*knocked* a hole in the fence> **4.** To instill as if with blows <*knocked* some sense into their

heads> **5.** *Slang.* To criticize adversely : DISPARAGE. —vi. **1.** To strike a blow or series of blows. **2.** To collide. **3. a.** To make a clanking or pounding noise. **b.** To undergo engine knock. —**knock around** (or **about**). *Informal.* **1.** To be rough or brutal with : MALTREAT. **2.** To wander from place to place. **3.** To discuss or consider. —**knock back.** *Informal.* To gulp (an alcoholic drink). —**knock down. 1.** To disassemble into parts. **2.** To declare sold at an auction, as by striking a blow with a gavel. **3.** *Informal.* To reduce, as in price. **4.** *Slang.* To receive as wages : EARN. —**knock off. 1.** *Informal.* **a.** To take a break or rest from : STOP. **b.** To cease work. **2.** *Informal.* To make, accomplish, or consume hastily or easily. **3.** *Informal.* To eliminate : deduct <*knocked* 15% off the bill> **4.** *Slang.* To kill. **5.** *Slang.* To hold up or rob. **6.** *Informal.* To copy the design or production of. —**knock out. 1.** To render unconscious. **2.** To defeat by knocking down to the canvas for a count of ten in boxing. **3.** *Informal.* To render useless or inoperative <power *knocked out* by a storm> **4.** *Informal.* To exert or exhaust (oneself or another). —**knock together.** To make or assemble quickly or carelessly. —**knock up. 1.** *Chiefly Brit.* To gain the attention of or wake up by knocking at the door. **2.** To wear out : EXHAUST. —n. **1.** An instance of knocking : BLOW. **2.** The sound of such a tap on a hard surface : RAP. **3.** A clanking, pounding noise made by an engine, esp. one in poor operating condition. **4.** *Slang.* A cutting, often petty criticism. —**knock cold.** To knock out. —**knock dead.** *Slang.* To affect strongly, usu. positively <a virtuoso piano performance that *knocked us dead*> —**knock for a loop.** *Slang.* To surprise greatly : ASTONISH. —**knock out of the box.** *Baseball.* To force the removal of (an opposing pitcher) by heavy hitting.

knock·a·bout (nŏk′ə-bout′) n. A small sloop with a mainsail, a jib, and a keel but no bowsprit. —adj. **1.** Boisterous and rowdy. **2.** Appropriate for rough wear or use <*knockabout* clothes>

knock·down (nŏk′doun′) adj. **1.** Forceful enough to knock down or overwhelm : POWERFUL <a *knockdown* punch> **2.** Designed to be assembled and disassembled easily and quickly <*knockdown* office furniture> —n. **1.** An act of knocking down. **2.** An overwhelming blow. **3.** A device or mechanism designed to be assembled and disassembled quickly and easily.

knock·down-drag·out (nŏk′doun-drăg′out′) adj. Marked by roughness, violence, and acrimony.

knock·er (nŏk′ər) n. One that knocks, as a fixture for knocking on a door.

knock-knee (nŏk′nē′) n. An abnormal condition in which one knee is turned toward the other or in which each is turned toward the other. —**knock′-kneed** adj.

knock·off (nŏk′ôf′, -ŏf′) n. *Informal.* A usu. inexpensive copy, as of a garment <a *knockoff* of a designer original>

knock·out (nŏk′out′) n. **1.** The act of knocking out or the state of being knocked out. **2.** The knocking out of an opponent in boxing. **3.** *Slang.* One that is very impressive or attractive.

knockout drops pl.n. *Slang.* A solution, as of chloral hydrate, put into a drink to render the drinker unconscious.

knock·wurst (nŏk′wûrst′, -wŏōrst′) n. var. of KNACKWURST.

knoll¹ (nōl) n. [ME *knolle* < OE *cnoll*.] A small rounded hill or mound : HILLOCK.

knoll² (nōl) n. [ME *knollen*, prob. alteration of *knellen*, to knell < OE *cnyllan*.] *Archaic.* —vt. & vi. **knolled, knoll·ing, knolls.** To ring or sound mournfully. —**knoll** n.

knop (nŏp) n. [ME *knoppe* < OE *cnop*.] A decorative knob.

knot¹ (nŏt) n. [ME < OE *cnotta*.] **1. a.** A compact intersection of interlaced material, as cord, ribbon, or rope. **b.** A fastening made by tying together lengths of material, as rope, in a prescribed way. **2.** A decorative bow of ribbon, fabric, or braid. **3.** A unifying bond, esp. a marriage bond. **4.** A tight group or cluster <*knots* of spectators> **5.** A difficult problem. **6. a.** A hard node, esp. on a tree, at a point from which a stem or branch grows. **b.** The circular, often darker cross section of such a node as it appears cross-grained on a piece of cut lumber. **7.** A protuberant growth in living tissue. **8.** *Naut.* **a.** A division on a log line used to measure the speed of a ship. **b.** A unit of speed, one nautical mile per hour, approx. 1.15 statute miles per hour. **usage:** *Knot* is a unit of nautical speed with the built-in meaning of "per hour." Therefore, a ship would properly be said to travel at ten *knots* (not at ten *knots per hour*). **c.** A distance of one nautical mile. —v. **knot·ted, knot·ting, knots.** —vt. **1.** To tie in or fasten with a knot. **2.** To entangle. **3.** To cause to form knots. —vi. **1.** To become entangled. **2.** To form a knot. —**knot′ted** adj.

knot² (nŏt) n. [Orig. unknown.] A shore bird, *Calidris canutus* or *C. tenvirostris*, related to the sandpiper.

knot·grass (nŏt′grăs′) n. **1.** A low-growing weedy plant, *Polygonum aviculare*, having tiny greenish flowers. **2.** A grass having jointed stems.

knot·hole (nŏt′hōl′) n. A hole in lumber where a knot used to be.

knot·ty (nŏt′ē) adj. **-ti·er, -ti·est. 1.** Tied or snarled in knots. **2.** Covered with knots or knobs : GNARLED. **3.** Difficult to compre-

â pat   ā pay   âr care   ä father   ĕ pet   ē be   hw which   ĭ pit
ī tie   îr pier   ŏ pot   ō toe   ô paw, for   oi noise   ōō took

Instructional Commentary

Notice the two words at the top of the page. These words are called guide words. The first word is *knelt*. Find it in the body of the dictionary page. Where is it? (Students indicate that it is the first word on the page.) The second word is *knotty*. Find it in the body of the dictionary page. Where is it? (Students indicate that it is the last word on the page.)

Look at the bottom two lines of the righthand column on this page and the lefthand column on the next page. (Only the first part of this is shown in the figure.) That is the pronunciation key. It has the special letter markings found in the phonetic respellings beside the entry words and a common word that has the sound each marking represents. The letter or letters that represent the sound are in bold print in the common word.

Find the word *knobkerrie* on this page. Look at its phonetic respelling in the parentheses following it. Notice that the first *k* does not appear in the respelling because it is not heard when the word is pronounced. Checking the pronunciation key, note that the *o* is pronounced like the *o* in *pot*. Looking again at the respelling, notice that the first syllable has the darkest, biggest accent mark, meaning that it gets the heaviest emphasis. Checking the pronunciation key once more, decide what sound the vowel in the second syllable has. (Students should decide that it sounds like the *e* in *pet*.) How strongly is the second syllable accented? (Students should say that it is accented less strongly than the first syllable, but more strongly than the third syllable.) How did you know? (Students should indicate that the size of the accent mark told them.) What does the final vowel in the word sound like? (Students should indicate that it sounds like the *e* in *be*.) Where did you look to find out? (Students should respond that they looked in the pronunciation key.)

Notice the *n.* just after the phonetic respelling. It tells you the part of speech of the word. What part of speech is *knobkerrie*? (If students cannot answer this question, point out the page in the dictionary that has the key to abbreviations and labels used.)

Look at the material in brackets following the *n.* It tells the etymology, or history, of the word. What does *Afr.* stand for? What does *MDu.* stand for? (If the students cannot answer immediately, refer again to the page of abbreviations.) Notice that the word is derived from words meaning "knob" and "club." Now read the definition. If, after reading the definition, you still could not decide what a knobkerrie was, you could study the illustration provided in the dictionary. Do all knobkerries look exactly alike? (After examining the illustration, students should be able to respond that they do not.)

cally, the computer system supporting a database allows the user to construct complicated search requirements, for example, "Find all articles on distortion in optics used for telescopes published after 1980 in Sweden." Databases can be user created (student created) or preexisting, large or small, general or specific.

Ben Johnson, English actor and author, observed that there are two kinds of knowledge: what we know and what we know how to find. Increasingly, finding information is becoming a computer-oriented task involving databases. More and more occupations rely on the use of such databases, making the need for information retrieval skills and an understanding of database maintenance more and more relevant for today's students (Oley, 1989). The variety of databases available covers agriculture, business, computers, finance, forestry, health and medicine, national and world news, and social sciences, among other topics. Access to these sources has traditionally been through trained intermediaries, often qualified librarians, but increasingly the end user has direct access to the materials via computer. Cost-effective use of these sources requires knowledge of how to construct search questions for the database system in use, of the organizational scheme of the subject matter, and of search techniques in general (Oley, 1989). The user must be able to phrase complex questions that limit the retrieval process to pertinent information without omitting any desired information.

A database can be very broad or very specific in scope, and it can be organized in a wide variety of ways. A limited database might contain the names, symbols, and basic properties of chemical compounds used in the manufacture of paper, or the names, dates of inauguration, and birthplaces of the presidents of the United States. An example of a large database is the Encyclopedia of Associations, covering over 16,500 labor unions, professional societies, trade associations, fraternal associations, and professional associations. It is updated annually. Another large database is Who's Who in America. The contents are the same as those in the printed volume, but its structure as a database allows searching by such things as birthplace (for example, what famous people are from Claysville, Idaho), or profession, or college of matriculation.

Schools now have access to both local and remote databases. A local database resides on the computer system of the user, whereas a remote database resides on a computer system other than the user's. Typically, remote databases reside on large mainframe systems and are accessed through telephone lines. Although access to large, remote databases requires some special equipment (such as a modem and a communication port on the computer), these are sometimes available to educators.

A local database in a classroom might range from a small quantity of information collected as part of a class project to a complete encyclopedia. Both *The New Grolier Electronic Encyclopedia* and *Compton's Multimedia Encyclopedia* are available in computer-readable form, by use of technology similar to the compact disks (CDs) used for music. An entire multivolume encyclopedia can be contained on a single disk. In addition to text, the Compton's encyclopedia includes pictures, maps, animated diagrams, and a limited number of voice recordings of excerpts from historic speeches. The cost of the additional equipment to read these special disks makes it unavailable in most individual classrooms, but the cost is not prohibitive for a school's media center or library. The cost of the encyclopedias in computer format is comparable to the cost of printed copies, but the additional computer equipment may cost twice as much as the encyclopedia.

Since access to databases, especially remote ones, is limited, techniques should be used to maximize the effectiveness of their use. A mock demonstration using slides or overhead transparencies can demonstrate the procedure for signing on to the database and the structure of search questions. Examples can be given of good and bad techniques, with emphasis on likely problem areas.

Creating small databases in the classroom can give students valuable experience in categorizing and organizing material. For this type of work on the computer, the teacher needs access to a database utility program of some kind. Examples of such programs are AppleWorks (for Apple computers) and dBase (for IBM computers). After the information for the database has been collected and entered into the computer, the database system can be used for critical analyses, such as comparing similarities and differences (for example, "What do rapidly growing population centers have in common? How are these areas different from declining areas?"); analyzing relationships; examining trends; and testing and refining hypotheses (Lapp, Flood, and Farnan, 1989).

One application of databases that is important for students, especially when they reach college, is the computerized card catalog in many libraries. Students access the catalog by using a computer keyboard to request information that is transferred to the student on the computer's screen. Such databases replace the traditional card catalogs, providing the traditional indexing plus complex search capabilities. Many libraries also provide access to the ERIC (Educational Resources Information Center) index of educational material.

Reading to Follow Directions

Another skill that secondary school students need in order to study effectively is the ability to read to follow directions. Students are constantly expected to follow written directions both in the classroom and in everyday experiences. Teachers write assignments on the chalkboard and distribute duplicated materials that have directions written on them. Textbooks and workbooks in different content areas contain printed directions that students are expected to follow. This is particularly true of science, mathematics, and vocational education books, but it applies to all subject areas. There are also many aspects of everyday activities that require us to follow directions: reading traffic signs, recipes, assembly and installment instructions, forms to be completed, voting instructions, and registration procedures, to name a few. A traffic sign gives a single direction that is vital for a person to follow in order to avoid bodily injury, misdirection, fines, or other penalties. The other activities mentioned above involve multiple steps to be followed. Failure to complete the steps properly may result in various penalties: inedible food, non-working appliances, receipt of incorrect merchandise, and so forth.

Many people fail at a task either because they do not know how to follow written directions or because they ignore the directions and try to perform the task without understanding the sequential steps that compose it. Almost everyone is familiar with the saying, "When all else fails, read the directions." This tendency to take printed directions lightly may have been fostered in the classroom. Teachers hand out printed directions and proceed to explain them orally. Teachers also often tell students each step to perform as they progress through the task, rather than asking them to read the directions and point out which parts they need to have clarified. These actions promote a general disregard for reading directions. Maybe it should not be surprising that even "good readers follow directions well only 80% of the time and poor readers are fortunate to achieve a 50% success rate" (Henk and Helfeldt, 1987, p. 603).

Following directions requires two basic comprehension skills — the ability to locate details and the ability to detect sequence. Because each step in a set of directions must be followed exactly and in the appropriate sequence, reading to follow directions is a slow and deliberate task. Rereading is often necessary. The following procedure may prove helpful.

1. Read the directions from beginning to end to get an overview of the task to be performed.
2. Study any accompanying pictorial aids that may help in understanding one or more of the steps or in picturing the desired end result.
3. Read the directions carefully, visualizing each step to be performed. Read with an open mind, disregarding any preconceived ideas about the procedure involved.
4. Take note of such key words as *first, second, next, last,* and *finally.* Let these words help you picture the order of the activities to be performed.
5. Read each step again, just before you actually perform it.
6. Carry out the steps in the proper order.

Students will learn to follow directions more easily if the presentation of activities is scaled in difficulty from easy to hard. Teachers can start with one-step directions and then progress to two-step, three-step, and longer sets of directions as the students' proficiency increases.

Some activities for developing skills in following directions are suggested below.

ACTIVITIES

1. Give students a paragraph containing key direction words (*first, next, then, last, finally,* and so forth) and ask them to underline the words that help to show the order of events.

2. Prepare duplicated directions for Japanese paper-folding activities. Provide the students with paper, and ask them to follow the directions.
3. Make it a practice to refer students to written directions instead of telling them orally how to do everything. Ask students to read the directions silently and then tell you in their own words what they should do.
4. Teach the meanings of words commonly encountered in written directions, such as *affix, alphabetical, array, estimate, example, horizontal, phrase,* and *vertical.* Some other words that might need special attention are listed in an article by Newcastle (1974).
5. Have students follow directions to make something from a kit.
6. Use activities similar to those in Examples 4.10 and 4.11 to make a point about the importance of following directions.

EXAMPLE **4.10**

Activity on Following Directions

Questionnaire

Read this entire questionnaire before you begin to fill in the answers. Work as quickly as you can. You have five minutes to finish this activity.

Name _____

Address _____

_____

Phone Number _____

Age _____

What is your father's name? _____

What is your mother's name? _____

What is your mother's occupation? _____

Do you have any brothers? _____ If so, how many? _____

Do you have any sisters? _____ If so, how many? _____

Do you plan to go to college? _____ If so, where? _____

What career are you most interested in? _____

How many years of preparation past high school will be necessary if you pursue this career? _____

Who is the person that you admire most? _____

What is this person's occupation? _____

After you have completed reading this questionnaire, turn the paper over and write your name on the back. Then give the paper to your teacher. You should have written nothing on this side of the page.

EXAMPLE **4.11**

Activity on Following Directions

Carefully follow the directions given in the sentences below:

1. Circle the numeral that stands for the largest number: 11, 52, 4, 16, 21, 32, 35, 15.
2. Underline the first and last numerals in this list: 2, 7, 1, 4, 3, 8.
3. Draw a line through the third word in this sentence.
4. Circle each word in this sentence that begins with the letters *th*.
5. Add 44 and 76. Take the result and subtract 10. Divide that result by 10. Place your answer on this line. _____
6. Circle every noun in this sentence.

Any exercises for improving their ability to understand details and detect sequence will also help students in their efforts to improve their skills in following directions. Activities in which students must integrate information from graphic aids, such as charts or diagrams, with printed information in the text will also be helpful.

Graphic Aids

Textbooks contain numerous graphic aids that are often disregarded by students because they have had no training in the use of such aids. Maps, graphs, tables, charts and diagrams, and pictures can all help students understand the textbook material better if they receive assistance in learning to extract the information from these graphic aids.

Fry (1981) developed a taxonomy of graphic aids that he feels should receive instructional time. Example 4.12 illustrates this taxonomy.

Maps

Maps may be found in social studies, science, mathematics, and literature textbooks, although they are most common in social studies (particularly geography) textbooks. Since maps are generally included in textbooks to help clarify the narrative material, students need to be able to read them to understand fully the material being presented.

Some students may have received background in map-reading techniques in elementary school, but many have not had any structured preparation for reading maps. Therefore, secondary school students may vary greatly

EXAMPLE **4.12**

An Illustrated Version of a Taxonomy of Graphs

1. Lineal

  a. Simple   story

  b. Multiple   history

  c. Complex

    Hierarchy   organization

    Flow   computer

    Process   chemicals

    Sociogram   friendship

2. Quantitative

  a. Frequency Polygon   growth

  b. Bar graph   production

  c. Scattergram   test scores

  d. Status Graph   scheduling

  e. Pie Graph   percentage

  f. Dials   clock

3. Spatial

a. Two Dimensions
(single plane)   map

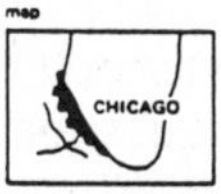

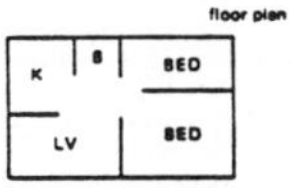

floor plan

b. Three Dimensions
(multiplane)   relief map

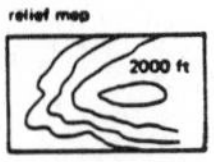

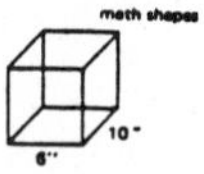

math shapes

4. Pictorial

a. Realistic

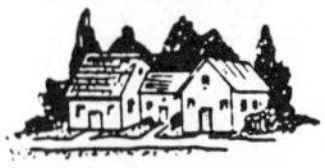

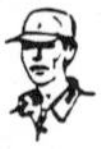

b. Semipictorial

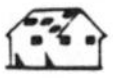

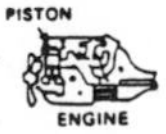

PISTON

ENGINE

c. Abstract

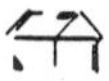

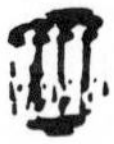

5. Hypothetical

a. Conceptual

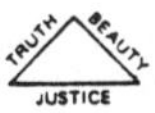

TRUTH BEAUTY

JUSTICE

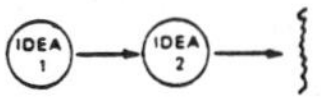

IDEA 1 → IDEA 2 →

b. Verbal

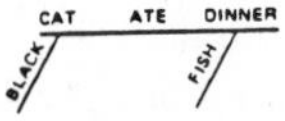

CAT   ATE   DINNER

BLACK   FISH

6. Near Graphs

a. High Verbal Outline   Main Idea
a. Detail
b. Another detail

b. High Numerical

Table	
25	4.2
37	6.1
71	7.3

c. Symbols $ ✚ 🚭

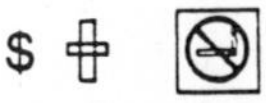

d. Decorative Design

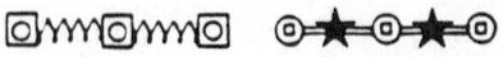

Source: Reprinted by permission of Edward Fry.

in their abilities to handle assignments containing maps. A survey of map-reading skills should be administered early in the school year by teachers who expect map reading to be a frequently needed activity throughout the year. A sample map and some useful questions for surveying map-reading skills are shown in Example 4.13.

EXAMPLE **4.13**

U.S. Air and Water Pollution Map and Questions

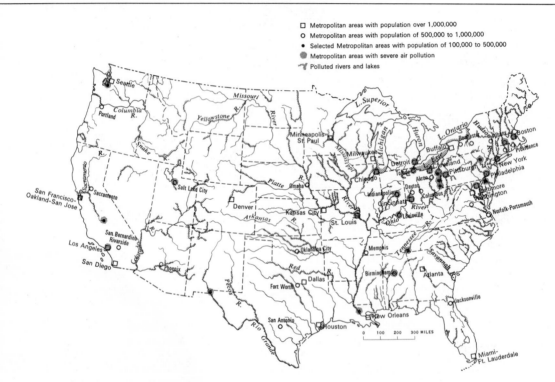

Source: *The Free and the Brave*, 1980, by Henry F. Graff. Courtesy of the Riverside Publishing Company. Reprinted by permission.

Questions

1. What kind of information does this map supply?
2. What symbol indicates a metropolitan area with a population from 500,000 to 1,000,000?
3. What is the distance from Birmingham to Atlanta?
4. What lakes are shown on the northern boundary of this map?
5. What are possible reasons for the areas of severe air pollution shown on the map? The polluted rivers and lakes?

After administering a survey of map-reading skills and evaluating the results, the teacher should systematically teach any of the following skills that the students have not yet mastered:

1. Locating and comprehending the map title
2. Determining directions
3. Interpreting a map's legend
4. Applying a map's scale
5. Understanding the concepts of latitude and longitude
6. Understanding common map terms
7. Making inferences concerning the material represented on a map
8. Understanding projections.

Reprinted with special permission of King Features Syndicate, Inc.

The first step in map reading should be examining the title of the map to determine what area is being represented and what type of information is being given about the area. Map titles are not always located at the tops of the maps, as students often expect them to be. Therefore, students may overlook the title of a map unless they have been alerted to the fact that they may need to scan the map to locate it.

Next, students should locate the directional indicator on the map and orient themselves to the map's layout. They should be aware that north is not always at the top of the map, although many maps are constructed in this manner.

Interpretation of the legend or key of the map is the next step in reading it. The map legend contains an explanation of each of the symbols used on it. If a student does not understand these symbols, the map will be incomprehensible to him or her.

To determine distances on a map, the student must apply the map's scale. Because it would be highly impractical, if not impossible, to draw a map the actual size of the area represented (for instance, the United States), maps show areas greatly reduced in size. The relationship of a given distance on a map to the same distance on the earth is shown by the map's scale.

An understanding of latitude and longitude will be helpful in reading some maps. Understanding the system of parallels and meridians enables a reader to locate places on a map by using coordinates of degrees of latitude and longitude. Parallels of latitude are lines on a globe that are parallel to the equator. Meridians of longitude are lines that encircle the globe in a north-south direction, meeting at the poles.

Students need to understand many common map terms to comprehend maps fully. Among these are *latitude* and *longitude*, of course, as well as *Tropic of Cancer, Tropic of Capricorn, North Pole, South Pole, equator, hemisphere, peninsula, continent, isthmus, gulf, bay*, and many others.

Teachers should encourage students to perform more than simple location activities with maps. They should ask students to make inferences concerning the material represented on maps. For example, for a map showing the physical features of an area (such as mountains, rivers, lakes, deserts, and swamps), the students might be asked to decide what types of transportation would be most appropriate in that area. This kind of activity is extremely important at the secondary school level.

Students may need help in understanding different types of projections. Flat maps and globes can be compared to illustrate distortion. Inexpensive globes can be taken apart and flattened out to show one common type of projection.

It may be helpful to students to relate a map of an area they are studying to a map of a larger area that contains the smaller one. For example, a map of Tennessee can be related to a map of the United States. In this way, the position of Tennessee within the United States becomes apparent.

Further suggestions for working with map-reading skills are given below.

ACTIVITIES

1. Before presenting a chapter in a textbook that requires much map reading, ask students to construct a map of an area of interest to the class (for example, in a health or physical education class, a map of recreation facilities in the town). Help students draw the map to scale. (You may want to call on a mathematics teacher to help with this aspect.) Make sure students include a title, a directional indicator, and a legend. This exercise will give students the opportunity for direct experience with the important tasks in map reading and help prepare them to read the maps in their content textbooks with more understanding.
2. When students encounter a map in a content area textbook, help them use the legend by asking questions such as the following:

Where is there a railroad on this map?
Where do you find a symbol for a college?

Are there any national monuments in this area? If so, where are they located?

3. Help students with map terminology by asking them to point out on a wall map features such as a *gulf* and a *peninsula* when these features are pertinent to the content presentation.

Graphs

Graphs often appear in social studies, science, and mathematics books, and sometimes in books for other content areas. Graphs are used to make comparisons among quantitative data.

Types of Graphs

There are four basic types of graphs:

Picture Graphs (or Pictographs). Picture graphs — graphs that compare quantities by using pictures — are often thought to be the easiest to read. Visualization of data is aided by use of this type of graph. The reader must remember, however, that only approximate amounts can be indicated by pictographs, making it necessary to estimate amounts when interpreting these graphs.

Circle or Pie Graphs. Proportional parts of a whole can be shown most easily through use of circle or pie graphs. These graphs show the percentage of the whole represented by each individual part.

Bar Graphs. Bar graphs are useful for comparing the sizes of several items or the size of a particular item at different times. These graphs may be either horizontal or vertical.

Line Graphs. Line graphs can depict changes in amounts over a period of time. They have vertical and horizontal axes. Each point that is plotted on a line graph has a value on both axes.

Representative samples of each of these types of graphs and accompanying sample questions are shown in Examples 4.14, 4.15, 4.16, 4.17, and 4.18.

Graph Reading Skills

Students can be taught to discover from the title of a graph what comparison is being made or what information is being supplied. They can learn to interpret the legend of a picture graph and to derive needed information from a graph accurately.

EXAMPLE **4.14**

Sample Picture Graph and Questions

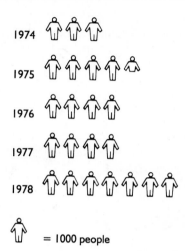

1974

1975

1976

1977

1978

= 1000 people

Questions

1. What does each symbol on this graph represent?
2. What time period does this graph cover?
3. During what year did Kingsley have the largest population?
4. Approximately how many people lived in Kingsley in 1976?

EXAMPLE **4.15**

Sample Circle Graph and Questions

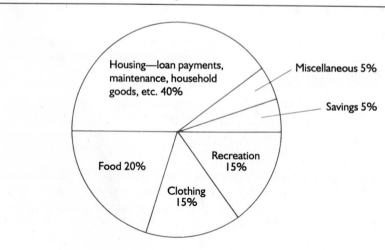

Housing—loan payments, maintenance, household goods, etc. 40%

Miscellaneous 5%

Savings 5%

Recreation 15%

Food 20%

Clothing 15%

Questions

1. What kind of information does this graph contain?
2. What budget item consumes the most money?
3. What percentage of the budget is allocated for food?
4. What does the "Miscellaneous" category contain?

EXAMPLE **4.16**

Sample Bar Graph (Vertical) and Questions

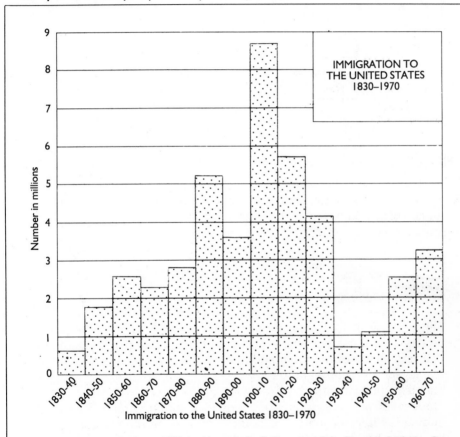

IMMIGRATION TO
THE UNITED STATES
1830–1970

Number in millions

Immigration to the United States 1830–1970

Source: *The Free and the Brave*, 1980, by Henry F. Graff. Courtesy of the Riverside Publishing Company. Reprinted by permission.

Questions

1. What is the topic of the bar graph?
2. How many people immigrated during the years 1910–20?
3. During what ten-year span did the largest number of people immigrate?
4. During what ten-year span did the smallest number of people immigrate?

E X A M P L E **4.17**

Sample Bar Graph (Horizontal) and Questions

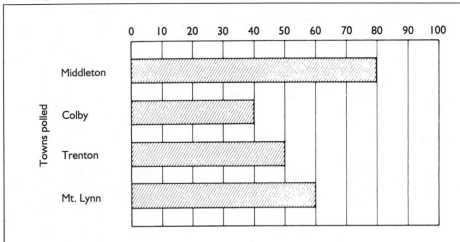

Questions

1. What percentage of the voters from Middleton were for John Drew?
2. In which of the four towns was John Drew least popular?
3. In which of the four towns did John Drew have the most support?
4. In which town were 40 percent of the voters for John Drew?

Teachers can help students discover the following information about the graphs in their textbooks:

1. The purpose of the graph (Usually indicated by the title, the purpose becomes more evident when the accompanying narrative is studied.)
2. The scale of measure on bar and line graphs
3. The legend of picture graphs
4. The items being compared
5. The location of specific pieces of information within a graph (for example, finding the intersection of the point of interest on the vertical axis with the point of interest on the horizontal axis)
6. The trends indicated by a graph (For example, does an amount increase or decrease over a period of time?)
7. The application of graphic information to actual life situations (A graph showing the temperatures for each month in Sydney, Australia, could be used for planning what clothes to take on a trip to Sydney at a particular time of the year.)

Fry (1981, pp. 388–389) points out that "graphical literacy — the ability to both comprehend and draw graphs — is an important communication tool that needs more emphasis in the school curriculum." He urges teachers to include graphing in their assignments, perhaps taking a section of the content textbook or an outside reading and asking students to make as many graphs as they can to illustrate ideas in the material. One of the best ways to help students learn to read graphs is to have them construct their own. The following is a list of types of graphs students can construct to help them develop a graph schema that will enhance their understanding of the graphs found in content area textbooks.

1. A picture graph showing the number of tickets each homeroom purchased for the senior prom
2. A circle graph showing the percentage of each day that the student spends in various activities (sleeping, eating, studying, and so forth)
3. A bar graph showing the number of outside readings that the student completed for English class during each grading period
4. A line graph showing the student's weekly quiz scores for a six-week period

EXAMPLE **4.18**

Sample Line Graph and Questions

Describe the increase in cotton production that took place after the cotton gin came into use

COTTON PRODUCTION IN THE UNITED STATES 1790–1840

Source: *The Free and the Brave*, 1980, by Henry F. Graff. Courtesy of The Riverside Publishing Company. Reprinted by permission.

Questions

1. What time period is depicted on this graph?
2. What does the vertical axis represent?
3. What does the horizontal axis represent?
4. What was the trend in cotton production over the years represented?
5. Did the invention of the cotton gin in 1793 have an effect on cotton production? Describe the effect.

(*Note:* If a teacher has students in the class who have directionality lags, the terms *vertical* and *horizontal* should be explained for them, since these terms are particularly difficult for these students.)

The teacher can construct graphs such as the ones in Examples 4.14 through 4.18 and ask students to answer questions about them. Questions can also be asked about particular graphs in the students' textbooks.

Tables

Tables, which are found in reading materials for all subject areas, contain information arranged in vertical columns and horizontal rows. One problem that students have with reading tables is extracting the needed facts from a large mass of information presented. The large amount of information provided in a small space can confuse students unless the teacher provides a procedure to guide them when reading tables.

Like the titles of maps and graphs, the titles of tables contain information about their content. Also, because tables are arranged in columns and rows, the headings for the columns and rows also provide information. Specific information is obtained by locating the intersection of an appropriate column with an appropriate row. Example 4.19 shows a sample table. The questions that follow the table are presented as models for the types of questions that teachers might ask about the actual tables in students' content textbooks.

E X A M P L E **4.19**

Sample Table and Questions

Average Temperatures in Darby and Deal for June–December 1990 (in degrees)

		Months						
		June	July	August	September	October	November	December
Towns	Darby	70°	72°	75°	74°	65°	65°	60°
	Deal	68°	69°	71°	70°	65°	64°	58°

Questions

1. What type of information is located in this table?
2. What are the column and row headings? What are the subheadings?
3. What time period is covered by the table?
4. Which of the two towns had the lowest average temperatures over the time period represented?
5. What was the average temperature for Darby in October 1990?
6. In what month did Darby and Deal have the same average temperature?
7. What is the unit of measurement used in this table?

Example 4.20 is a table from a computer textbook. It offers a comparison of different generations of computers. It differs from the table in Example 4.19 in that there are no row headings, just column headings. Similar types of information are located in similar rows, however, making comparisons easier. Questions that might be asked concerning this table follow it.

EXAMPLE **4.20**

Table from Computer Textbook and Table Questions

Computer Generations

First	Second	Third	Fourth
1946–1960	1960–1964	1964–1970s	1970s–1980s
Vacuum tubes	Transistors	Integrated circuits	Large-scale integrated circuits
Hundreds of computers in use	Thousands of computers in use	Tens of thousands of computers in use	Millions of computers in use
1000 circuits per cubic foot	100,000 circuits per cubic foot	10 million circuits per cubic foot	Billions of circuits per cubic foot
ENIAC, EDSAC, UNIVAC		Minicomputers developed	Microcomputers developed
	10 times faster than first generation	100 times faster than second generation	10 times faster than third generation
	Magnetic-tape storage	Disk storage	Floppy disks

Source: Barbara L. Kurshan, Alan C. November, and Jane D. Stone, *Computer Literacy Through Applications* (Boston: Houghton Mifflin Company, 1986), p. 81. Reprinted by permission of Houghton Mifflin Company.

Questions

1. What type of information is located in this table?
2. What are the column headings?
3. What would be a good heading for each row, if the rows had headings?
4. In what time period were second generation computers manufactured?
5. How many fourth generation computers are in use?
6. To what generation of computers did UNIVAC belong?
7. How fast are fourth generation computers in relation to second generation computers?
8. What kind of storage did second generation computers use?

Charts and Diagrams

Charts and diagrams appear in textbooks for many different content areas. They are designed to help students picture the events, processes, structures, relationships, or sequences described by the text. At times they may be used as summaries of text material. Example 4.21 is a chart from a history book that summarizes text material.

Students must be made aware of the abstract nature of diagrams and of the fact that they often distort or oversimplify information. Interpretation of the symbols found in diagrams and understanding of the perspective used in diagrams are not automatic; teachers must provide practice in such activities.

Numerous types of charts and diagrams are used in the various content areas. Examples include tree diagrams (English), flow charts (mathematics), and process charts (science). Careful instruction in reading such charts and diagrams must be provided for interpretation of content material. Another example of a diagram is a floor plan. (See Chapter 9 for such a diagram.) Example 4.22 shows a diagram from a science textbook.

The teacher can point out that distortions are frequently found in textbook drawings. Students can be helped to see that the diagrams in Example 4.22 are views of the human body's bone structure, which is not visible because it is covered by flesh and skin. The teacher can also identify the front and rear views and discuss the differences between them. Diagrams such as this might also appear in health textbooks.

Pictures and Cartoons

Content area textbooks contain pictures that are designed to illustrate the material described and to interest students. The illustrations may be photographs offering a realistic representation of concepts, people, and places, or they may be line drawings that are somewhat more abstract in nature.

Students frequently see pictures merely as space fillers, reducing the amount of reading they will have to do on a page. Therefore, they may pay

History Chart

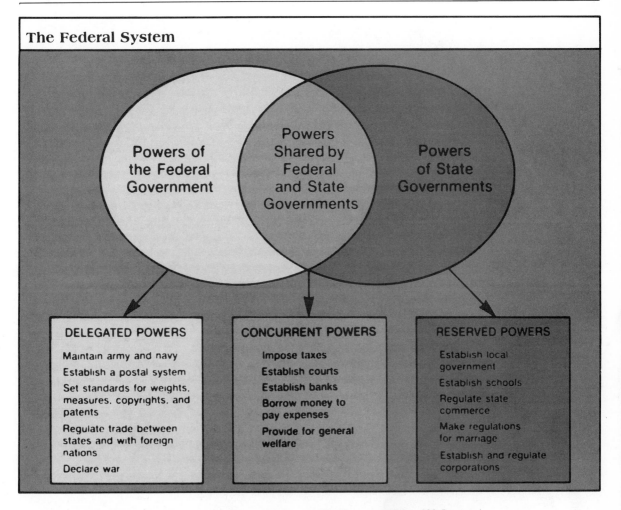

The Federal System

Powers of the Federal Government

Powers Shared by Federal and State Governments

Powers of State Governments

DELEGATED POWERS

Maintain army and navy

Establish a postal system

Set standards for weights, measures, copyrights, and patents

Regulate trade between states and with foreign nations

Declare war

CONCURRENT POWERS

Impose taxes

Establish courts

Establish banks

Borrow money to pay expenses

Provide for general welfare

RESERVED POWERS

Establish local government

Establish schools

Regulate state commerce

Make regulations for marriage

Establish and regulate corporations

Source: Jacobs, William Jay et al. *America's Story*. (Boston: Houghton Mifflin Company, 1990), p. 238. Reprinted by permission of Houghton Mifflin Company.

little attention to pictures, although the pictures are often excellent sources of information.

Since pictures are representations of experiences, they may be utilized as vicarious means of adding to a student's store of knowledge. Teachers should help students extract information from textbook illustrations by encouraging them to study the pictures before and after reading the text, looking for the

EXAMPLE **4.22**

Science Diagram

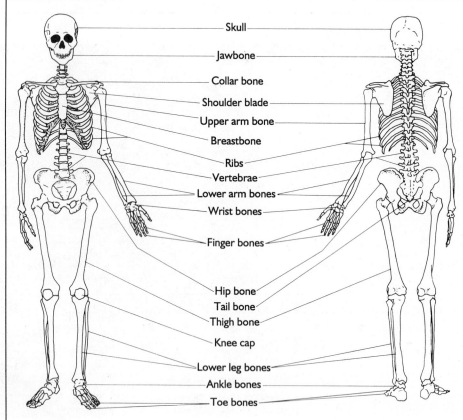

Skull

Jawbone

Collar bone

Shoulder blade

Upper arm bone

Breastbone

Ribs

Vertebrae

Lower arm bones

Wrist bones

Finger bones

Hip bone

Tail bone

Thigh bone

Knee cap

Lower leg bones

Ankle bones

Toe bones

There are 206 bones in the
human skeleton. They make up about 18%
of the body mass.

Source: James E. McLaren et al.: *Spaceship Earth: Life Science*, p. 113. Copyright © 1981 by Houghton Mifflin Company. Reprinted by permission of Houghton Mifflin Company.

purpose of each picture and its specific details. Studying pictures may help students understand and retain the information illustrated.

Example 4.23 depicts the surface of the moon on the nearside and the farside. Because students will not have had a chance to see the moon directly, the vicarious experience and visual imagery gained from this picture are valuable.

E X A M P L E **4.23**

Science Textbook Illustration

FIGURE **19.1**

a, *The nearside of the moon is the side you see from the earth.* **b,** *The farside. How does it differ from the nearside?*

Source: Matthews, William H., III, et al. *Investigating the Earth* (Boston: Houghton Mifflin Company, 1987), p. 431. Reprinted by permission of Houghton Mifflin Company.

Cartoons are special types of pictures that contain special symbols. They often distort the things they represent in order to make a point. Students should be encouraged to read cartoons critically.

Example 4.24 can be used as an exercise in examining how a cartoon delivers a message. Teachers can help the students connect the environmental issue involved with the situation depicted in the cartoon. In the cartoon, recent oil spills in the ocean are referred to indirectly by equating the smell of oil, rather than fresh salt air, with the ocean.

Adjusting Rate to Fit Purpose and Materials

Study time will be used most efficiently if students are taught to vary their reading rates to fit their purposes and the materials they are reading. Making these adjustments, which is important for good comprehension, is called *flexibility of rate*. Good readers adjust rates, thinking, and approaches auto-

154

EXAMPLE **4.24**

Science Textook Cartoon

Source: Joseph H. Jackson and Edward D. Evans: *Spaceship Earth: Earth Science*, p. 511. Copyright © 1980 by Houghton Mifflin Company. Reprinted by permission of Houghton Mifflin Company.

matically and are not aware that they make several changes when reading a single page.

Flexible readers are able to distinguish between important and unimportant ideas and to read important ideas carefully. They do not give each word, phrase, or paragraph equal attention but select the parts that are significant for understanding the selection. Familiar material is read more quickly than new material, because familiarity with a topic allows the reader to anticipate ideas, vocabulary, and phrasing. A selection that has a light vocabulary burden, more concrete concepts, and an easily managed style of writing can be read more rapidly than material with a heavy vocabulary load, many abstract concepts, and a difficult writing style. Light fiction that is read strictly for enjoyment can and should be absorbed much faster than the directions for a science experiment; newspapers and magazines can be read more rapidly than textbooks; theoretical scientific content and statistics must be read more slowly than much social studies content.

Students often think that everything should be read at the same rate. Thus, some of them read light novels as slowly and deliberately as they read mathematics problems. These students will probably never enjoy reading for recreation because they work so hard at reading and it takes so long. Other students move rapidly through everything they read. In doing so, they usually fail to grasp essential details in content area assignments, although they "finish" reading all of the assigned material. Rate of reading should never be considered apart from comprehension. Therefore, the optimum rate for reading any material is the fastest rate at which an acceptable level of comprehension is obtained. Teachers who wish to concentrate on improving their students' reading rates should include comprehension checks with all rate exercises.

Work on increasing reading rate should not be emphasized until basic word recognition and comprehension skills are thoroughly under control. Improvement in these skills often results in increased rate without any special attention to it. For best results, flexibility of rate should be developed with the content materials students are expected to read.

Factors Affecting Rate

Many factors influence the rate at which a person can read a particular selection, including the following:

1. Factors related to the material
   a. Size and style of type
   b. Format of the pages
   c. Use of illustrations
   d. Organization
   e. Writing style of the author
   f. Abstractness or complexity of ideas
2. Factors related to the reader
   a. Background of experiences
   b. Reading ability
   c. Attitudes and interests
   d. Reason for reading

Obviously, these factors differ with each selection. Therefore, different rates are appropriate for different materials.

Poor reading habits may greatly decrease reading rate. Poor habits include excessive vocalizing (forming each word as it is read); sounding out all words, both familiar and unfamiliar; excessive regressing (going back and rereading previously read material); and pointing at each word with the index finger. Concentrated attention to the elimination of these problems can yield good results. Often secondary school students simply need to be made aware of the habits that are slowing them down and to be given some suggestions for practice in overcoming them. Use in a reading laboratory of the equipment described in the next section has proved helpful in correcting some of these problems.

Techniques for Increasing Rate and Flexibility

Many methods have been devised to help students increase or adjust their rates of reading. These approaches include use of special machines, timed exercises, skimming and scanning exercises, and flexibility exercises.

Machines

Using special equipment to increase reading rate generally is not a responsibility of the content area teacher. However, the content area teacher may have students who, despite encouragement and teacher direction, read very slowly, in a word-by-word fashion, with many regressions. These students lack confidence in their ability to read and may claim that they cannot read more rapidly. The content teacher may refer these students to a reading laboratory or clinic for help by a reading teacher who uses rate machines to develop students' speed. Because they cannot regress as they read and are forced to move ahead through the material when rate machines are used, students realize that they can indeed read more rapidly.

The machines most commonly used for increasing rate are controlled reading filmstrip projectors, tachistoscopes, and pacers. These machines help students learn to read faster in a variety of ways.

Controlled reading filmstrip projectors use sets of specially developed filmstrips. They show students one line of text at a time, or successive parts of lines from left to right, at rates that may be adjusted to fit the needs of individual students. Associated workbooks may instruct students to preview the material before the machine is used, offer programmed vocabulary study, and provide comprehension checks.

Tachistoscopes show sections of printed material of various lengths for given periods of time. The time intervals can be adjusted to meet the needs of individual students. Some tachistoscopes can be attached to filmstrip and motion projectors. These devices are designed to encourage students to take in more print in a single fixation and to shorten fixation time.

Pacers have arms, beams of light, or shades that move down the page of printed material from top to bottom at regulated speeds. The student tries to read below the moving bar or within the beam of light.

The computer is now influencing reading rate instruction in the schools. Recently, computer software has been developed to promote speed reading. Some of this software is not very effective, but *Speed Reading: The Computer Course* (Bureau of Business Practices, Waterford, CT) is one program that has received a very favorable review (Damm and Chan, 1986). The program is available for machines compatible with the IBM PC and for the Apple. It includes techniques for broadening peripheral vision, looking for phrases, and focusing on key words in each lesson. Some comprehension skills are also given attention. Students keep records related to their rate and comprehension and, thus, are able to compete with themselves in order to improve. Students can control the speed of materials presented. Teachers should preview all software designed for rate improvement before using it with students, to ensure use of programs that meet the needs of their students.

Timed Readings

To help students increase their rates of reading in material that does not require intensive study-reading, teachers may use timed readings. As Brazee's study (1979) indicates, such skills may be learned best in situations in which they are actually used. Teachers may use timed readings with content materials to help students maintain rate gains achieved by using machines, or timed readings may be the only technique used. In choosing appropriate selections, the content teacher should avoid material that includes many small details (for example, a science experiment or a mathematics statement problem). Materials that present general background and recreational reading in the content area are more useful for this activity (for example, the story of a scientific discovery or the biography of a mathematician).

Two types of timed readings are common: (1) reading for a fixed period of time and then counting the number of words read and computing the words read per minute, and (2) reading a fixed number of words, computing the time elapsed while reading, and deriving a rate score in words per minute.

Timed readings should always be accompanied by comprehension checks. An extremely high rate score is of no use if the student fails to comprehend the material. Teachers should encourage rate increases only if comprehension does not suffer. Some students need help in basic reading skills before they can participate profitably in these rate-building activities.

Graphs can be kept of the results of timed rate exercises over a period of weeks or months. Seeing visible progress can motivate students to continue to work on improving their rates. Comprehension charts should also be kept, so rate increases can be viewed in the proper perspective.

Timed readings are more satisfactory than machine-oriented exercises as rate-building tools. The main reason for this is that machines are not always available to push students to read more rapidly; eventually, students must learn to operate without depending on machines to push them.

Skimming and Scanning Techniques

Skimming and scanning are special types of rapid reading. Skimming refers to reading to obtain a general idea or overview of the material, and scanning means reading to find a specific bit of information. Skimming is faster than rapid reading of most of the words in the material because, when readers skim material, they read selectively. Scanning is faster than skimming because only one piece of information is being sought. When scanning, readers run their eyes rapidly down the page, concentrating on the particular information being sought.

Example 4.25 shows how you might go about skimming an article. Skimming techniques are used in the survey step of the SQ3R method discussed earlier in this chapter. Teachers can help develop skimming skills as they work to teach this study method.

Other skimming activities include the following:

1. Give the students a short period of time to skim an assigned chapter and write down the main ideas covered.
2. Ask students to skim newspaper articles and match them to headlines written on the board. Have a competition to see who can finish first with no errors.
3. Give students the title of a research topic and have them skim an article to decide whether it is pertinent to the topic. Memory and Moore (1981) developed a procedure for doing this that involves group activity: students skim a series of articles and then their reactions.

Scanning activities are easy to design. Some examples follow:

1. Have students scan a telephone directory page to find a specific person's number.
2. Have students scan a history chapter to find the date of a particular event.
3. Have students scan a textbook to find information on a particular person.

Students need to scan for key words related to the specific facts they seek. An exercise in generating key words that are related to a specific topic may be beneficial.

FLEXIBILITY EXERCISES

Since not all materials should be read at the same rate, students need assistance in determining appropriate rates for different materials. The table in Example 4.26 shows three reading rates of a good reader, each of which is appropriate for a particular type of reading material.

One type of flexibility exercise is to ask a series of questions such as the ones below and then discuss students' reasons for their answers:

1. What rate would be best for reading a statement problem in your mathematics textbook?
2. Which could you read most quickly and still achieve your purpose — a television schedule, a newspaper article, or a science textbook?
3. Is skimming an appropriate way to read a science experiment?
4. What reading technique would you use to look up a word in the dictionary?

Skimming

Shown below is a view of how you might skim an article. Notice that you read all of the first and second paragraphs to get an overview. By the third or fourth paragraph you must begin to leave out material; read only key sentences and phrases to get the main ideas and a few of the details. Note also that, since final paragraphs often summarize, it may be worthwhile to read them more fully.

Skimming must be done "against the clock." That is, you must try to go as fast as you possibly can while leaving out large chunks of material. Be careful to avoid getting interested in the story since this might slow you down and cause you to read unnecessary detail. Skimming is work. It is done when you do not have much time and when you wish to cover material at the fastest possible rate.

Usually the first paragraph will be read at average speed all the way through. It often contains an introduction or overview of what will be talked about.　Sometimes, however, the second paragraph contains the introduction or overview. In the first paragraph the author might just be "warming up" or saying something clever to attract attention.　Reading a third paragraph completely might be unnecessary but ... ... the main idea is usually contained in the opening sentence ... ... topic sentence ... ... Besides the first sentence the reader should get some but not all the detail from the rest of the paragraph ... ... names ... ... dates ... ... This tells you nothing	... ... hence sometimes the main idea is in the middle or at the end of the paragraph.　Some paragraphs merely repeat ideas ... ... Occasionally the main idea can't be found in the opening sentence. The whole paragraph must then be read.　Then leave out a lot of the next paragraph ... ... to make up time ... ... Remember to keep up a very fast rate ... ... 800 w.p.m. ... ... Don't be afraid to leave out half or more of each paragraph ... ... Don't get interested and start to read everything ... ... skimming is work	... ... Lowered comprehension is expected ... ... 50% ... ... not too low ... ... Skimming practice makes it easier ... ... gain confidence ... ... Perhaps you won't get anything at all from a few paragraphs ... ... don't worry ... ... Skimming has many uses ... ... reports ... ... newspapers ... ... text ... ... The ending paragraphs might be read more fully as often they contain a summary.　Remember that the importance of skimming is to get only the author's main ideas at a very fast speed.

Source: Reprinted by permission of Edward Fry.

EXAMPLE **4.26**

Rate Chart

Kind of Reading	Rate	Comprehension
Slow: *Study reading* speed is used when material is difficult or when high comprehension is desired.	200 to 300 w.p.m.	80–90%
Average: An *average reading* speed is used for everyday reading of magazines, newspapers and easier textbooks.	250 to 500 w.p.m.	70%
Fast: *Skimming* is used when the highest rate is desired. Comprehension is intentionally lower.	800 + w.p.m.	50%

Source: Reprinted by permission of Edward Fry.

Retention

Secondary school students are expected to retain much of the material they are assigned to read in their content area classes. Retention is demonstrated in different ways. When students recognize words or sound-symbol associations learned previously, they exhibit retention of that information. If students fail to recognize previously learned information, retention is faulty for some reason. If students who have learned a rule for decoding printed words are asked to state the rule and are able to do so, they can be said to have recalled it. Failure to recall the rule indicates lack of retention.

Use of study methods to enhance retention has already been discussed extensively in this chapter. Teachers can help students apply these techniques and others that will facilitate retention of material. Some suggestions that the teacher may offer include:

1. Always read study material with a purpose. If the teacher does not supply you with a purpose, set purposes of your own. Having a purpose for reading will help you extract meaning from a passage, and you will retain material that is meaningful to you longer.
2. Try to grasp the author's organization of the material. This will help you to categorize concepts to be learned under main headings, which are easier to retain than small details and which facilitate recall of the related details. In order to accomplish this task, outline the material.
3. Try to picture the ideas the author is attempting to describe. Visualization of the information being presented will help you remember it longer.

4. As you read, take notes on important points in the material. Writing information down can help you to fix it in your memory.

5. After you have read the material, summarize it in your own words. If you can do this, you will have recalled the main points, and rewording the material will demonstrate your understanding. Shugarman and Hurst (1986) describe paraphrase writing, or writing the material in one's own words, as a means of increasing comprehension and recall. They suggest that students be allowed to consult with one another and to refer to resource material in order to produce good paraphrases. They give ten suggestions for ways teachers can incorporate paraphrase writing into their content area lessons, thereby helping students improve reading and writing abilities while learning content.

6. When you have read the material, discuss the assignment with a classmate or a group of classmates. Talking about the material facilitates remembering it.

7. Apply the concepts that you read about, if possible. Physical or mental interaction with the material will help you retain it.

8. Read assignments critically. If you question the material as you read, you will be more likely to remember it.

9. If you wish to retain the material over a long period of time, use spaced practice (a number of short practice sessions extended over a period of time) rather than massed practice (one long practice session). Massed practice facilitates immediate recall, but for long-term retention, distributed practice produces the best results.

10. If you plan to recite the material to yourself or to another student in order to increase your retention, do so as soon as possible after reading the material. Always check your accuracy and correct any errors immediately, so that you will not retain inaccurate material.

11. Overlearning facilitates long-term retention. To overlearn something, you must continue to practice it for a period of time after you have initially mastered it.

12. Mnemonic devices can help you retain certain types of information. (For example, remember that there is "a rat" in the middle of "separate.")

13. A variety of types of writing can improve retention. Langer (1986) reported the effects of different types of writing tasks on learning from reading in the content areas. Writing answers to study questions fostered recall of isolated bits of information. Essay writing produced more long-term and reasoned learning of a smaller amount of material. Note taking fell somewhere in the middle, causing students to deal with larger chunks of meaning than did study questions, but not involving reorganization of material, as did essay writing.

Concentrating on material as it is read is important to retention. Memory and Yoder (1988) suggest the use of a written guide to help students become aware of techniques for improving concentration on content area assignments. Their guide is very detailed and broad in scope. Teachers would probably want to use only excerpts from it or less extensive guides that they develop themselves. Some of the suggestions in such a guide could be similar to those given above. Others might include the following recommendations:

1. Relate the material you are reading to things you already know. Making such connections can aid in the acquisition of new concepts and in the retention of material read (Jones, 1988).
2. Monitor your reading to determine if you understand the material. If not, reread it or take other steps to ensure understanding.
3. Survey the material for information that could be interesting to you.
4. Take five- or ten-minute study breaks after forty-five or fifty minutes of study.
5. Avoid studying in a distracting setting.
6. Study more difficult and less interesting material when you are most alert (Memory and Yoder, 1988).
7. Anticipate what is coming next as you read a passage, and read to see if your prediction was accurate (Moore et al., 1989).

Teachers can also facilitate student retention of material by offering students ample opportunities for review of information and practice of skills learned and by offering positive reinforcement for correct responses given during the practice and review periods. Class discussion of material to be learned tends to aid retention. Emphasis on classifying the ideas found in the reading material under appropriate categories can also help.

Test Taking

Secondary school students sometimes fail to do well on tests, not because they do not know the material, but because they have difficulty reading and comprehending the test. Teachers can help by giving students suggestions for ways of effectively reading different types of tests.

Essay tests often contain the terms *compare, contrast, trace the development, describe, discuss,* and others. Teachers can explain what is expected in an answer to a question containing each of these terms and any other terms they may plan to use. This will help prevent students from losing points on the test because they "described" instead of "contrasted." Teachers can point out that, if students are asked to compare two things or ideas, both similarities and differences should be mentioned. If students are asked to contrast two things or ideas, differences are the important factors. If students are asked to describe something, they are expected to paint a word picture of it. Sample answers to a variety of different test questions utilizing the special vocabulary may be useful in helping students understand what the teacher expects. An example follows.

> *Question:* Contrast extemporaneous speeches and prepared speeches.
> *Answer:* Extemporaneous speeches are given with little advance thought. Prepared speeches are usually preceded by much thought and research. Prepared speeches often contain quotations and paraphrases of the thoughts of many other people about the subject. Extemporaneous speeches can contain such material only if the speaker has previously become very well informed in the particular area involved. Assuming that the speaker has little background in the area, an extemporaneous speech would be likely to have less depth than a prepared speech, since it would involve only the speaker's immediate impressions. Prepared speeches tend to be better organized than extemporaneous speeches because the speaker has more time to collect thoughts and arrange them in the best possible sequence.

PORPE is a technique developed by Simpson (1986) to help students study for essay examinations. The steps in PORPE are as follows.

1. *Predict.* Construct potential essay questions, based on reading of the material. Use words such as *explain, criticize, compare,* and *contrast.* Focus on important ideas.
2. *Organize.* Organize the information necessary to answer the questions.
3. *Rehearsal.* Memorize material through recitation and self-testing. Space practice over several days for long-term memory.
4. *Practice.* Write out in detail the answers to the questions that you formulated.
5. *Evaluate.* Judge the accuracy and completeness of your answers.

Simpson suggests teaching this procedure through teacher modeling and a series of group and individual activities.

The student must read objective tests carefully. Generally, every word in an item must be considered. Teachers should emphasize the importance of considering the effect of words such as *always, ever,* and *not,* as well as others of this general nature. Students need to realize that all the parts of a true-false question must be true if the answer is to be *true.* They also need to understand that all possible responses for a multiple-choice question need to be read before an answer is chosen.

Teachers can also help students improve their performance on tests by offering the following useful hints:

1. When studying for essay tests:
   a. Remember that your answers should include main ideas accompanied by supporting details.
   b. Expect questions that cover the topics most emphasized in the course, since only a few questions can be asked within the limited time.

    c. Expect questions that are broad in scope.

    d. Consider the important topics covered, and try to guess some of the questions that the teacher may ask. Prepare good answers for these questions and try to learn them thoroughly. You will probably be able to use the points you learn in your answers on the actual test, even if the questions you formulated are not exactly the same as the ones asked by the teacher.

2. When studying for objective tests:

    a. Become familiar with important details.

    b. Consider the types of questions that have been asked on previous tests, and study for those types. If dates have been asked for in the past, learn the dates in the material.

    c. If listing questions are a possibility, especially sequential listings, try preparing mnemonic devices to help you in recalling the lists.

3. Learning important definitions can be helpful for any kind of test and can be useful in answering many essay questions.

4. Apply the suggestions listed in the earlier section on "Retention."

When teachers construct tests, they need to take care to avoid making the test harder to read than the original material. If this situation exists, students may know the material required, but the readability level of the test may be so high that they are unable to comprehend the questions. Students may then make low test scores because of the teacher's inappropriate test preparation rather than because of their lack of knowledge of the concepts involved.

McPhail (1981) developed strategies for teaching test wiseness that have been used with inner-city high school students and others. He felt that this instruction could improve the validity of test results and help provide minorities with equal education, employment, and promotion opportunities.

SUMMARY

Reading-study skills are skills that enhance comprehension and retention of information contained in printed material. They are helpful to students in managing their reading in content area classes.

Study methods such as SQ3R and REAP are applicable to a number of different subject areas, including social studies and science. EVOKER is a study method especially developed for use with prose, poetry, and drama; SQRQCQ is effective for use with statement or word problems in mathematics. Instructional procedures such as GRASP, the PSRT strategy, and some recitation techniques can be used to enhance the development of study skills.

Three helpful organizational skills needed by students who are participating in report writing are outlining, note taking, and summarizing. Also essential for good report writing are the skills of locating information in books, in the library, and in computer databases.

The ability to follow written directions is vitally important to secondary school students. Teachers should plan activities to help students develop this important skill.

Content area textbooks are filled with graphic aids such as maps, graphs, tables, diagrams, and pictures. Teachers should give students guidance in interpreting these aids, so that the students will derive maximum benefit from their textbooks.

Other areas to which teachers should give attention are adjustment of reading rate to fit the purpose for which the reading is being done and the material to be read, retention of material read, and test-taking skills.

SELF-TEST

1. What does SQ3R stand for? (a) Survey, Question, Read, Recite, Review (b) Seek, Question, Read, Review, Report (c) Sequential Questioning, Read, React, Report (d) None of the above
2. For what content area is SQRQCQ designed? (a) English (b) History (c) Science (d) None of the above
3. Which statement is true of outlining? (a) A main topic may have a single subdivision. (b) Indention helps to show the degree of importance of ideas in an outline. (c) Roman numeral headings are subordinate to capital letter headings. (d) None of the above
4. Which of the following are contained in the card catalog? (a) Subject cards (b) Author cards (c) Title cards (d) All of the above
5. Which of the following statements is not true? (a) Glossaries are found in many content area texts. (b) Skills needed to use glossaries are the same as those needed to use dictionaries. (c) Glossaries include mainly general vocabulary words. (d) None of the above
6. What should students know about dictionary guide words? (a) They represent the first and last entry words on a page. (b) They represent the first two entry words on a page. (c) They are found in the preface of the book. (d) None of the above
7. Which skill(s) are involved in reading to follow directions? (a) The ability to locate details (b) The ability to detect sequence (c) Both of the above (d) Neither of the above
8. Which statement describes the legend of a map? (a) It is the history of the area represented in the map. (b) It contains an explanation of each of the

symbols used on the map. (c) It is located in the top left-hand corner of the map. (d) None of the above

9. What is a problem in reading diagrams? (a) They are generally filled with too much unimportant information. (b) They often oversimplify information. (c) Both of the above (d) Neither of the above

10. What is meant by flexibility of rate? (a) Reading all material as rapidly as possible (b) Varying reading rate to fit purposes and materials (c) Rapid reading without regard for comprehension (d) None of the above

11. Which factor(s) affect rate? (a) Size and style of type (b) Author's writing style (c) Reader's background of experiences (d) All of the above

12. What kind of rate machine has an arm that moves down a page of printed material from top to bottom at regulated speeds? (a) Tachistoscope (b) Controlled reading filmstrip projector (c) Pacer (d) None of the above

13. Which of the following represents the fastest reading rate? (a) Skimming (b) Study reading (c) Scanning (d) None of the above

14. Which of the following methods can improve retention? (a) Discussing the assignment with a classmate (b) Applying the concepts presented in the assignment (c) Reading the assignments critically (d) All of the above

THOUGHT QUESTIONS

1. Which of the study methods listed in this chapter is best for use in your content area? Why?

2. How can outlining help students to understand the material in the textbook for your content class?

3. What are helpful guidelines for note taking that you can share with students?

4. How can the librarian and the content area teacher cooperate to teach library skills that students need for research activities?

5. What parts of a book do students need to be able to use effectively if they are going to locate needed information efficiently?

6. What is a useful procedure for teaching students to read directions with understanding?

7. What graphic aids occur most commonly in your content area? What can you do to help students interpret them effectively?

8. What is the best setting in which to offer students instruction concerning flexibility of rate? Why is this so?

9. What are some techniques for helping students increase reading rate with acceptable comprehension?

10. How can you help your students retain as much of the material that they read in their content textbooks as possible?

11. Should you give attention to helping your students develop test-taking skills? Why, or why not?

12. What computer skills may be needed by students making use of today's libraries and media centers?

ENRICHMENT ACTIVITIES

*1. Teach one of the study methods described in this chapter to a class of secondary school students. Work through it with them step by step.

2. Make a bulletin board display that would be helpful to use when teaching either outlining or note taking. Display it either in your college classroom or in a secondary school classroom.

3. Make a set of sample card catalog cards for ten or more books. Plan a lesson on use of the card catalog. Teach this lesson to a group of your classmates. *Teach the lesson in a secondary school classroom, if possible.

4. Plan a lesson on use of the index of a secondary level textbook of your choice. Teach the lesson to a group of your classmates. *Teach the lesson in a secondary school classroom, if possible.

5. Collect materials that include directions that secondary level students often need to read. Discuss with your classmates how you could help the students learn to read the materials more effectively.

6. Take a content area textbook at the secondary level and plan procedures to familiarize students with the parts of the book and with the reading aids the book offers.

7. Visit a secondary school library and listen to the librarian explain the reference materials and library procedures to the students. Evaluate the presentation, and decide how you might make changes if you were responsible for it.

8. Collect a variety of types of maps. Decide which features of each map will need most explanation for students.

9. Collect a variety of types of graphs. Make them into a display that could be used in a unit on reading graphs.

10. Develop a procedure to help secondary school students learn to be flexible in their rates of reading. Use materials of widely varying types.

*11. Examine several of your old tests. Decide what reading difficulties they may present for your students. Isolate special words for which meanings may have to be taught.

12. Read Howard I. Berrent's article "OH RATS — A Note-Taking Technique," *Journal of Reading*, 27 (March 1984), 548–550. Try out Berrent's procedure on a chapter that you have been assigned to study. React to the effectiveness of the procedure for your study. Indicate if you believe it would be as effective with secondary students, and explain your reasons.

*These activities are designed for in-service teachers, student teachers, or practicum students.

13. Read the following article: Victoria Chou Hare and Richard G. Lomax, "Readers' Awareness of Subheadings in Expository Text," in Jerome A. Niles and Rosary V. Lalik (eds.), *Issues in Literacy: A Research Perspective* (Rochester, N.Y.: National Reading Conference, 1985), pp. 199–204. Report on the study to the class, giving your assessment of the implications of this study for secondary school teachers.

14. Read the following article: Lawrence B. Friedman and Margaret B. Tinzmann, "Graphics in Middle-Grade U.S. History Textbooks," in Jerome A. Niles and Rosary V. Lalik (eds.), *Issues in Literacy: A Research Perspective* (Rochester, N.Y.: National Reading Conference, 1985), pp. 151–167. Analyze the graphic aids in one of your content texts in the way that Friedman and Tinzmann did in their study. Compare your results with theirs.

BIBLIOGRAPHY

Askov, Eunice N., and Karlyn Kamm. *Study Skills in the Content Areas.* Boston: Allyn and Bacon, 1982.

Babbs, Patricia J., and Alden J. Moe. "Metacognition: A Key for Independent Learning from Text." *The Reading Teacher,* 36 (January 1983), 422–426.

Bailey, Nancy S. "S-RUN: Beyond SQ3R." *Journal of Reading,* 32 (November 1988), 170–171.

Beers, Penny G. "Accelerated Reading for High School Students." *Journal of Reading,* 29 (January 1986), 311–315.

Brazee, Ed. "Teaching Reading in Social Studies: Skill-Centered Versus Content-Centered." *Colorado Journal of Educational Research,* 18 (August 1979), 23–25.

Brown, A. L., and J. D. Day. "Macrorules for Summarizing Texts: The Development of Expertise." *Journal of Verbal Learning and Verbal Behavior,* 22, No. 1 (1983), 1–14.

Brown, A. L., J. D. Day, and R. Jones. "The Development of Plans for Summarizing Texts." *Child Development,* 54 (1983), 968–979.

Carr, Eileen, and Donna Ogle. "K-W-L Plus: A Strategy for Comprehension and Summarization." *Journal of Reading,* 30 (April 1987), 626–631.

Clarke, John H., James Raths, and Gary L. Gilbert. "Inductive Towers: Letting Students See How They Think." *Journal of Reading,* 33 (November 1989), 86–95.

Cousin, Patricia Tefft. "Toward Better Use of Improved Textbooks." *Reading Research and Instruction,* 29 (Fall 1989), 61–64.

Crain, Sue Ann Kendall. "Metacognition and the Teaching of Reading." *Journal of Reading,* 31 (April 1988), 682–685.

Damm, Bonnie E., and Lawrence D. Chan. "Computer Software." *Journal of Reading,* 29 (January 1986), 373–374.

Dansereau, Donald F. "Transfer from Cooperative to Individual Studying." *Journal of Reading,* 30 (April 1987), 614–619.

Davey, Beth. "How Do Classroom Teachers Use Their Textbooks?" *Journal of Reading,* 31 (January 1988), 340–345.

———. "Team for Success: Guided Practice in Study Skills Through Cooperative Research Reports." *Journal of Reading,* 30 (May 1987), 701–705.

Davis, Susan J. "Applying Content Study Skills in Co-listed Reading Classrooms." *Journal of Reading,* 33 (January 1990), 277–281.

Dewey, Melvil. *Dewey Decimal Classification and Relative Index.* Lake Placid Club, N.Y.: Forest Press, 1971.

Eanet, Marilyn G., and Anthony V. Manzo. "REAP — A Strategy for Improving Reading/Writing/Study Skills." *Journal of Reading*, 19 (May 1976), 647–652.

Fay, Leo. "Reading Study Skills: Math and Science." In J. Allen Figurel (ed.), *Reading and Inquiry*, Newark, Del.: International Reading Association, 1965, pp. 93–94.

Finley, Claudia D., and Martha N. Seaton. "Using Text Patterns and Question Prediction to Study for Tests." *Journal of Reading*, 31 (November 1987), 124–132.

Friedman, Lawrence B., and Margaret B. Tinzmann. "Graphics in Middle Grade U.S. History Textbooks." In Jerome A. Niles and Rosary V. Lalik (eds.), *Issues in Literacy: A Research Perspective*. Rochester, N.Y.: National Reading Conference, 1985, pp. 151–167.

Fry, Edward. "Graphical Literacy." *Journal of Reading*, 24 (February 1981), 383–390.

Guthrie, John T. "Children's Reasons for Success and Failure." *The Reading Teacher* 36 (January 1983), 478–480.

Guthrie, John T. "Research: Context and Memory." *Journal of Reading*, 22 (December 1978), 266–268.

Hancock, Joelie. "Learning with Databases." *Journal of Reading*, 32 (April 1989), 582–589.

Hansell, T. Stevenson. "Stepping Up to Outlining." *Journal of Reading*, 22 (December 1978), 248–252.

Hare, V. C., and K. M. Borchardt. "Direct Instruction of Summarization Skills." *Reading Research Quarterly*, 20, No. 1 (1984), 62–78.

Hare, Victoria Chou, and Richard G. Lomax. "Readers' Awareness of Subheadings in Expository Text." In Jerome A. Niles and Rosary V. Lalik (eds.), *Issues in Literacy: A Research Perspective*. Rochester, N.Y.: National Reading Conference, 1985, pp. 199–204.

Hayes, David A. "Helping Students GRASP the Knack of Writing Summaries." *Journal of Reading*, 33 (November 1989), 96–101.

Henk, William A., and John P. Helfeldt. "How to Develop Independence in Following Directions." *Journal of Reading*, 30 (April 1987), 602–607.

How to Use the Readers' Guide to Periodical Literature. Rev. ed. New York: H. W. Wilson, 1970.

Jacobowitz, Tina. "Using Theory to Modify Practice: An Illustration with SQ3R." *Journal of Reading*, 32 (November 1988), 126–131.

Jeremiah, Milford A. "Summaries Improve Comprehension." *Journal of Reading*, 32 (November 1988), 172–173.

Jones, Janet Craven. "Reading and Study Skills: Problems in the Content Areas." *Journal of Reading*, 31 (May 1988), 756–759.

Kelly, Brenda Wright, and Janis Holmes. "The Guided Lecture Procedure." *Journal of Reading*, 22 (April 1979), 602–604.

Kirsch, Irwin S., and Peter B. Mosenthal. "Understanding Documents: Nested Lists." *Journal of Reading*, 33 (January 1990), 294–297.

Kirsch, Irwin S., and Peter B. Mosenthal. "Understanding Documents: Understanding Forms, Part I." *Journal of Reading*, 33 (April 1990), 542–545.

Kratzner, Roland R., and Nancy Mannies. "Building Responsibility and Reading Skills in the Social Studies Classroom." *Journal of Reading*, 22 (March 1979), 501–505.

Lapp, Diane, James Flood, and Nancy Farnan. *Content Area Reading and Learning: Instructional Strategies*. Englewood Cliffs, N.J.: Prentice Hall, 1989.

Langer, Judith A. "Learning Through Writing: Study Skills in the Content Areas." *Journal of Reading*, 29 (February 1986), 400–406.

Lindquist-Sandmann, Alexa. "A Metacognitive Strategy and High School Students: Working Together." *Journal of Reading*, 30 (January 1987), 326–332.

Manzo, A. V. "Guided Reading Procedure." *Journal of Reading*, 18 (December 1975), 287–291.

McAndrew, Donald A. "Underlining and Notetaking: Some Suggestions from Research." *Journal of Reading*, 27 (November 1983), 103–108.

McPhail, Irving P. "Why Teach Test Wiseness?" *Journal of Reading*, 25 (October 1981), 32–38.

Meir, Margaret. "Comprehension Monitoring in the Elementary Classroom." *The Reading Teacher*, 37 (April 1984), 770–774.

Memory, David M., and Carol Y. Yoder. "Improving Concentration in Content Classrooms." *Journal of Reading*, 31 (February 1988), 426–435.

Memory, David M., and David W. Moore. "Selecting Sources in Library Research: An Activity in Skimming and Critical Reading." *Journal of Reading*, 24 (March 1981), 469–474.

Moore, David W., John E. Readence, and Robert J. Rickelman. *Prereading Activities for Content Area Reading and Learning*. 2nd ed. Newark, Del.: International Reading Association, 1989.

Mosenthal, Peter B., and Irwin S. Kirsch. "Understanding Documents: Intersecting Lists." *Journal of Reading*, 33 (December 1989), 210–215.

Mosenthal, Peter B., and Irwin S. Kirsch. "Understanding Documents: Lists: the Building Blocks of Documents." *Journal of Reading*, 33 (October 1989), 58–60.

Mosenthal, Peter B., and Irwin S. Kirsch. "Understanding Documents: Understanding Graphs and Charts, Part I." *Journal of Reading*, 33 (February 1990), 371–373.

Mosenthal, Peter B., and Irwin S. Kirsch. "Understanding Documents: Understanding Graphs and Charts, Part II." *Journal of Reading*, 33 (March 1990), 454–457.

Newcastle, Helen. "Children's Problems with Written Directions." *The Reading Teacher*, 28 (December 1974), 292–294.

Oley, Elizabeth. "Information Retrieval in the Classroom." *Journal of Reading*, 32 (April 1989), 590–597.

Pauk, Walter. "On Scholarship: Advice to High School Students." *The Reading Teacher*, 17 (November 1963), 73–78.

Pincus, Arlene R. H., Elaine B. Geller, and Eileen M. Stover. "A Technique for Using the Story Schema as a Transition to Understanding and Summarizing Event Based Magazine Articles." *Journal of Reading*, 30 (November 1986), 152–158.

Rakes, Sondra K., and Lana J. Smith. "Strengthening Comprehension and Recall Through the Principle of Recitation." *Journal of Reading*, 31 (December 1987), 260–263.

Reading/Language in Secondary Schools Subcommittee of IRA. "Secondary Perspectives: Summarizing." *Journal of Reading*, 33 (January 1990), 300–302.

Recht, Donna. "Teaching Summarizing Skills." *The Reading Teacher*, 37 (March 1984), 675–677.

Reinking, David. "Integrating Graphic Aids Into Content Area Instruction: The Graphic Information Lesson." *Journal of Reading*, 30 (November 1986), 146–151.

Rickelman, Robert J., and William A. Henk. "Telecommunications in the Reading Classroom." *Journal of Reading*, 43 (February 1990), 418–419.

Robinson, Francis P. *Effective Study*. Rev. ed. New York: Harper & Row, 1961, Chapter 2.

Schmidt, Cynthia Maher, Arlene Barry, Andrea Giese Maxworthy, Winnie R. Huebsch. "But I Read the Chapter Twice." *Journal of Reading*, 32 (February 1989), 428–433.

Shepherd, David L. *Comprehensive High School Reading Methods*. 3rd ed. Columbus, Ohio: Charles E. Merrill, 1982.

Shugarman, Sherrie L., and Joe B. Hurst. "Purposeful Paraphrasing: Promoting a Nontrivial Pursuit for Meaning." *Journal of Reading*, 29 (February 1986), 396–399.

Simons, Sandra McCandless. "PSRT — A Reading Comprehension Strategy." *Journal of Reading*, 32 (February 1989), 419–427.

Simpson, Michele L. "PORPE: A Writing Strategy for Studying and Learning in the Content Areas." *Journal of Reading,* 29 (February 1986), 407–414.

Smith, Patricia L., and Gail E. Tompkins. "Structured Notetaking: A New Strategy for Content Area Readers." *Journal of Reading,* 32 (October 1988), 46–53.

Taylor, Barbara. "Toward an Understanding of Factors Contributing to Children's Difficulty Summarizing Textbook Material." In Jerome A. Niles and Rosary V. Lalik (eds.), *Issues in Literacy: A Research Perspective.* Rochester, N.Y.: National Reading Conference, 1985, pp. 125–131.

Taylor, Karl K. "Teaching Summarization Skills." *Journal of Reading,* 27 (February 1984), 389–393.

5

"AT RISK"

READERS

Once the United States was a melting pot, and new-comers aspired to become assimilated into the population. Now there is an emphasis on retaining our country's diversity and cherishing the differences manifested in a diverse population. However, a common type of individual difference that is a source of diversity in secondary school populations and that has created some problems in our educational system is variation in reading ability. For various reasons, some students experience greater difficulty achieving reading fluency than others. These students are "at risk" of reading failure; they are also "at risk" of failing to learn in accordance with their potential. Reading difficulties are a significant problem for students because reading ability, more than any other ability, empowers students to learn and develop in directions that enable them to achieve their potential.

Student diversity arises from many sources, including factors such as environment, emotions, and physical development (Pallas, Natriello, and McDill, 1989). Diversity in content classrooms is increasing as a result of educational practices such as "mainstreaming." In mainstreaming, exceptional students who formerly were taught in separate classes now spend a large part of the school day in regular classrooms. Thus, teachers in content area classes now teach a broader range of pupils.

Teachers play a central role in educating all students; therefore, they need to recognize and respect their students' different experiences, values, and attitudes. Included in such recognition is an awareness of their own expectations as teachers and the expectations in their social contexts of school and community. One of a teacher's concerns is understanding students' culture, experience, and language.

Teachers need strategies to facilitate disabled or exceptional students' reading strategies and to motivate them to seek higher levels of literacy. Successful reading and learning experiences are highly motivating for students. This chapter will assist you in learning ways to use the knowledge and strategies in this book to help a diverse student population to achieve success.

PURPOSE-SETTING QUESTIONS

As you read this chapter, try to answer these questions:

1. What are the major factors contributing to the wide range of individual differences in the student population?
2. Why is it important that teachers understand student diversity?
3. What are some useful intervention strategies that can be used to assist "at risk" students?

KEY VOCABULARY

As you read this chapter, check your understanding of these terms:

"at risk"	exceptionalities
diversity	individual differences
dialect	Individualized Educational Plan
ESL (English as a Second Language)	mainstreaming

Diversity in the Student Population

The demographics of the student population in the United States are changing rapidly. Today's educators instruct a more diverse (varied) student population than did any preceding generation. Political and economic ferment throughout the world have caused increased numbers of immigrants to move into cultures that are new to them. Vietnamese students and Hispanic students have different, but equally diverse, cultural experiences, as do native American students and some African-American students. They all have cultural experiences that are substantially different from the middle class, mainstream culture of secondary schools. These students may have difficulty acquiring an education due largely to cultural considerations.

Individual differences are respected and encouraged in sound educational programs. Encouraging each individual to realize his or her potential is the major thrust of our educational system. In order to achieve this, teachers must understand and address the diversity among students. Of specific concern in this text is the fact that students demonstrate wide variability in their command of the reading process. Years ago, students who did not read well dropped out of school before entering high school or in the early stages of their high school education. Today schools work to retain such students until graduation.

Secondary school teachers encounter students who exhibit a wide range of reading abilities and who often do not have background knowledge that is related to the subjects they have to study. These students face genuine problems in reading content textbooks. Teachers must be able to help this wide variety of students achieve reading fluency, which distinguishes competent readers from incompetent ones (Anderson et al., 1985). Some students can read a textbook at 400 words per minute with good comprehension. Others plod through the same book at 100 words per minute with much less understanding (Perfetti, 1985). Students who lack fluency need direct teaching and helpful strategies if they are to read successfully.

Less competent readers are usually aware that they are unable to keep up with their classmates, but they do not know what to do about it. As a result of reading difficulties, they tend to rate high in school-related anxiety and low in self-esteem (Thomson and Hartley, 1980; Athey, 1982). Anxiety has a debilitating effect on school performance because anxious students tend to divide their attention between the task at hand and their preoccupation with how well they are doing (Wigfield and Asher, 1984; Willig et al., 1983). Teachers must help these students break the cycle of anxiety, which inhibits their ability to improve reading achievement and perpetuates negative self-concepts (Eldredge, 1981).

Students who are unable to read competently have low achievement levels in the majority of school subjects because they cannot read well enough to comprehend and to work with the concepts presented in their textbooks. Often their problems are not limited to academic areas; their personal adjustment may be inadequate, thus contributing to low self-concepts and poor social adjustment (Bristow, 1985; Quandt and Selznick, 1984).

Reading disability often results in stress and anxiety when students are required to read textbooks and ancillary materials they do not understand (Gentile and McMillan, 1987). When teachers help students acquire the strategies and reading fluency required to deal successfully with their content textbooks, they are helping them reduce the stress and anxiety they normally experience in reading situations. Teachers' attitudes toward students' learning are a major factor in developing fluent readers (Wigfield and Asher, 1984).

Through no fault of their own, many students such as those discussed in this chapter are "at risk" *for learning*. Slavin (1989) identified the "risk factors" associated with school dropouts, including low achievement, retention in grade, behavior problems, poor attendance, low socioeconomic status, and attendance at schools with large numbers of poor students. Pellicano (1987) describes at risk students as being uncommitted to deferred gratification and to competitive school situations. Vobejda (1987) defines at risk students as those whose poverty, family instability, or social backgrounds make them likely candidates for school failure — often falling victim to crime, drugs, teenage pregnancy, or early entry into the ranks of the unskilled unemployable. At risk students often have an impoverished quality of life over which they have no control. When this is compounded by handicapping conditions such as deficits in perceptual, motor, language, and attentional skills that are prerequisites for school success, students are in double jeopardy (Clark-Johnson, 1988).

The school must become a mediating force for those who are powerless to develop their own potential (Pellicano, 1987). Unsuccessful students tend to view teachers as uncaring and the school as unfair and ineffective (Wehlage and Rutter, 1986). Nevertheless, teachers and schools must become the primary agents for addressing the individual differences of students who are at risk for learning.

Factors Contributing to Student Diversity

The sources of variability in learning of at risk students are multiple, and research shows that individual differences in the student population will continue to increase in the future. Hodgkinson (1985) identified the following factors that will increase the variety of students in current and future school populations:

1. More students entering school from poverty-stricken family situations.
2. More students entering school from single-parent households.
3. More students from minority backgrounds.
4. A larger number of premature babies, primarily born to teenage mothers, who are more likely to have learning disabilities.
5. An increase in the number of African-American students.
6. An increase in the number of Asian-American students.

Reading is a complex cognitive process; therefore, it is not surprising that it is subject to a variety of influences. Each factor that affects students' reading abilities contributes to the diversity of reading achievement found in secondary school classrooms. Rarely is a single factor responsible for individual differences in reading ability. In this section, we discuss some of the major factors that shape students' reading ability, including environmental and societal factors, cultural factors, language differences, socioeconomic factors, the family, peer group influences, and educational factors.

The following student descriptions illustrate the kinds of variability in students' reading skills that secondary teachers may encounter in the classroom.

Reading Case 1

John is a tenth-grade student who is passing with the minimum grade in all subjects that require reading ability. John's listening comprehension is high average for his grade placement, and the teacher's observations indicate that John has average ability. However, scores on reading achievement tests show that he is reading at the middle eighth-grade level. John's written assignments are poorly organized and written. His speaking and writing vocabularies are limited, and his scores on the vocabulary sections of reading achievement tests are low.

John appears to require assistance in vocabulary, organization of content, and study skills. These areas of learning can be handled best by the various content teachers because they know the particular needs of their content subjects. Moreover, John can probably be helped by classroom teachers because he has shown that he is quite capable of learning and because his reading difficulties seem to relate in part to a lack of experiences promoting concept and vocabulary development. Reading-study skills and organizational skills can be learned from systematic instruction. This is the kind of assistance a content teacher can provide. Strategies such as those discussed in Chapters 2, 3, 4, 6, 7, 8, and 9 should help John.

Reading Case 2

Mary is a tenth-grade student. She is unable to pass any of the courses that require reading skills or to read any of her textbooks with understanding. Listening comprehension tests indicate that she has below average listening comprehension for her grade, and reading achievement test scores show that she is reading at a third-grade level. The teacher's observations indicate that she has below average ability.

Mary must have assistance from a remedial reading teacher because she is unable to progress in school. A classroom teacher could not provide adequate help in this case. Because Mary reads far below her grade placement, a classroom teacher would not have the time (or perhaps the expertise) to provide the extensive diagnosis and individualized instruction she sorely needs.

Mary's reading difficulties probably arise from multiple sources. She may lack the experiences that would help her construct the meaning of the language she reads, or may come from a cultural background that differs in values, attitudes, and educational expectations from those exhibited in the school. Since she reads at such a low level, she probably lacks basic word knowledge skills that would permit her to read fluently. The factors that identify her and others as at risk students are explored in subsequent sections of this chapter.

Student Exceptionalities

Exceptional students are those who differ from average students in (1) mental abilities, (2) sensory abilities, (3) communication abilities, (4) social behavior, or (5) physical characteristics. "These differences must be to such an extent that the child requires a modification of school practices, or special educational services, to develop to maximum capacity" (Kirk and Gallagher, 1989, p. 5).

According to the United States Department of Education, approximately 4.4 million students received special education services during the 1986–87 school year. Students who have handicapping conditions (also called exceptional students) often receive a portion of their education in public school classrooms since *Public Law 94-142* was passed. This law protects the rights of each child identified as having a handicapping condition and assures the "free, appropriate public education of all handicapped children." Exceptional students include those with the following individual variations:

Intellectual differences, including students who are intellectually superior and students who are slow to learn;

Communication differences, including children with learning disabilities or speech and language impairments;

Sensory differences, including children with auditory or visual impairments;

Behavioral differences, including children who are emotionally disturbed or socially maladjusted;

Multiple and severe handicapping conditions, including children with combinations of impairments (e.g., cerebral palsy and mental retardation, deafness and blindness);

Physical differences, including children with nonsensory handicaps that impede mobility and physical vitality (Kirk and Gallagher, 1989).

Public Law 94-142 stipulates that each handicapped youngster be placed in *the least restrictive environment*. Ordinarily the least restrictive environment that is the most appropriate educational setting for an exceptional student's needs is as much like the regular classroom setting as possible. Therefore, students who have special needs are often *mainstreamed* in regular classrooms, meaning that whenever it is appropriate, as many handicapped students as possible enter the mainstream of education by attending classes with nonhandicapped pupils. Thus, an evaluation is performed for each pupil included under PL 94-142 to determine the extent to which instruction in a regular class is appropriate.

Each student who is identified as handicapped must have an individualized education plan (IEP). The plan includes a description of the student's problem, the program's long-term goals as well as its short-term objectives, the special education services needed for the student and the criteria for assessing the effectiveness of the services. Classroom teachers serve on the committees that develop IEPs for students who are mainstreamed in their classes.

Environmental and Cultural Factors

Students live and grow in different environments that have a strong impact on their desire and ability to learn. The total environment within which students operate includes the home, the school, the social group, and the culture. Understanding these environments helps us understand students and their learning processes (Richek, List, and Lerner, 1989). The five major indicators of poor performance and educational disadvantage in school are all based in the environment: minority racial/ethnic group identity, living in a low-income household, living in a single-parent family, having a poorly educated mother, and having a non–English language background (Hodgkinson, 1985).

Socioeconomic Factors

Students who come from low socioeconomic status backgrounds are at risk for learning to read (Slavin, 1989; Hornbeck, 1988). The relationship between social class and reading achievement is well documented. Socioeconomic status is the single best predictor of students' reading achievement. Low socioeconomic status students experience more failure and lower achievement than students from middle-class homes (Fotheringham and Creal, 1980).

The number of children living in conditions of poverty has been projected to increase from 14.7 million in 1984 to 20.1 million in 2020. Therefore, public education will have to serve a much larger disadvantaged population in the future. New strategies to deal with this problem should be developed. Many educators recommend that schools become more aware of and involved in the family and community contexts of their students, both to understand the problems these contexts present and to learn to draw on the strengths of families and communities to enrich the education of students (Pallas, Natriello, and McDill, 1989).

The Family

The home environment of students exerts a powerful influence on their cognitive growth, intelligence, and language development. Students are profoundly affected by what happens to their parents. In today's society, many students must cope with family moves, divorce and separation of parents, death of close relatives, and leave-taking of older siblings (Richeck, List, and Lerner, 1989). Parents and teachers can often work together to help the student cope with these changes.

Students who come from homes in which parents provide good nutrition, opportunities for adequate rest, and a stable environment have advantages in school. Students from homes where reading materials are available and reading skills are valued by parents also have an advantage in school (Bettelheim and Zelan, 1983). Parents who provide a broad experiential background for their children prepare them to read with understanding.

Peer Group Influences

Students' learning is also influenced by their peer group. Secondary students are especially sensitive to peer group influences. The peer group influence grows more powerful with a sudden downturn in achievement during fourth or fifth grade (Harris and Sipay, 1985). This achievement slump has been attributed to a variety of factors, of which peer group influence is only one; nevertheless, it is a significant variable in achievement. If a gang or social group to which a student belongs is antagonistic toward school, his or her school work will reflect this attitude. A correlation has been shown between delinquency and learning difficulties (Dunwant, 1983). In many cases, students' antisocial behavior and school failure appear to be related to adverse environmental influences (Schonhaut and Satz, 1983).

Cultural Factors

The United States has a rich, multifaceted culture that is a composite of many ethnic and cultural traditions. Culture is defined as the "context in which children develop" (Gage and Berliner, 1988). In students' cultural context we find home, school, and community, from which they learn attitudes, values, customs, and language. These values and customs form an identifiable heritage that may differ substantially from the middle-class values that so strongly influence the activities of the public schools. When this occurs, adaptation problems arise for these students and their teachers (Erikson and Mohatt, 1982; Phillips, 1983; Good, 1987; Kirk and Gallagher, 1989).

Cultural differences produce a variety of results in an educational environment. For instance, a disproportionate number of children from minority cultures receive special education services (Children's Defense Fund, 1987; National Black Child Development Institute, 1986; Salend, Michael, and Taylor, 1984; Messick, 1984). More than three times as many African-American children are labeled mentally retarded as white children (Children's Defense Fund, 1987; National Black Child Development Institute, 1986), and the proportion of African-American youngsters classified as emotionally disturbed is higher than their proportion in the general population. Researchers have found the same kind of discrepancy among Hispanic students, who are represented in larger numbers in the population of children with learning disabilities than they are in the general population (Messick, 1984).

Cultural diversity leads to diverse sets of schemata on the part of students. Competent readers relate their backgrounds to the text and construct meaning as they interact with the text. Thus cultural background is a critical factor in reading comprehension. Nelson (1987) illustrates this point with a vignette involving students from the Middle East who had been living in Minnesota for 4 to 20 years but who had retained many of the characteristics of their native culture. These students read Willa Cather's story, "The Sculptor's Funeral." Its salient point was the mother's exaggerated demonstration of grief, which most Americans perceive as insincere; however, the Middle Eastern students believed that the outward display of grief demonstrated a deep sorrow. Therefore, these students misinterpreted the story. This example illustrates how cultural schemata can interfere with comprehension.

Students whose cultural background differs from that of the dominant culture may also lack the experiences necessary to build new schemata that could assist them in understanding written language. For example, students may lack knowledge regarding famous Americans that is assumed in textbooks. Knowledge of the meanings of figurative expressions is another area in which students may lack background. Students from cultures other than middle-class America may lack many of the concepts that authors assume are a part of students' background knowledge. These students must continuously interact with information outside of their own cultural schemata (LeSourd, 1988).

Students who come to school with a different cultural background often are unable to seek outside assistance in learning. The needs of these students must be met within the public school setting. Teachers can begin by demonstrating their respect for the culture and the language of their students. They need to recognize that students' parents may require assistance with the educational system and the schooling process. Teachers should make a special effort to include parents in the planning process and to keep them informed of their child's progress (Fitzpatrick, 1987).

Nelson (1987) found, not surprisingly, that students with a cultural background different from that of a large part of middle-class America showed improved comprehension when reading about their own culture. Furthermore, these students preferred to read stories and articles about their culture.

Maintaining their cultural backgrounds can help students develop self-respect and healthy self-concepts. Culture determines how people interpret and mentally organize the world (Robinson, 1985). Culture shapes people's views of the world, their behavior, and their interpretation of experiences, all of which are important to educational efforts. Culture also shapes students' attitudes about reading and writing and the value they attribute to these abilities (Field and Aebersold, 1990).

Fillmore (1981) identified six cognitive abilities that influence acquisition of a second language and whose usage appears to vary from culture to culture. Fillmore did not imply differences in students' abilities or cognitive development; she indicated how these abilities are valued and encouraged in different cultures. If a student's culture has encouraged these cognitive abilities, the student will probably acquire proficiency in reading and writing English more easily than will students from cultures not valuing these abilities.

1. *Sustained and systematic attention,* which is concerned with the student's willingness to persevere with a task and with his or her attitude toward the activity.
2. *Verbal memory,* which is memory of language and is related to the amount of memorization that is expected of a student.
3. *Analyticity,* which is the activity of recognizing patterns and generating new material using these patterns.
4. *Playfulness,* which is the willingness to experiment, to manipulate materials.
5. *Mental flexibility,* which is demonstrated through generating guesses, considering alternatives, and hypothesizing.
6. *Field independence,* which is a proclivity toward being able to see relationships without reference to background.

Language Factors

Culture and language are intimately interrelated. Both also have a strong impact on reading and writing. Many secondary students from different cultural backgrounds use language forms that differ from the standard language used in textbooks and in teaching. Teachers need to realize that these students use *alternative* language forms and not *inferior* language forms. In this section, we discuss students who are learning English as a second language (ESL) and dialect-different students, whose dialects differ from the majority of the student body.

Hispanics are the fastest growing population segment in the United States (Valdiviesco, 1986). It is projected that Spanish-speaking individuals will constitute the largest minority group in the United States by the turn of the century (Valero-Figueira, 1988).

ESL Students

The extent of cultural and linguistic differences among students means that teachers must become familiar with the backgrounds and cultures of their ESL students. This knowledge will enable the teachers to make the instructional adjustments necessary to teach these students to read and write. Field and Aebersold (1990) recommend that teachers instructing students learning

English as a second language or students who are bilingual should investigate their students' concepts of reading and its role in society as well as their expectations about reading. Johns (1986) recommends that teachers instructing such students should make a conscious effort to clarify and refine students' concepts of reading as they teach. He recommends that these efforts include attention to the teachers' assumptions about the students and to the terminology used that students might not understand. Furthermore, he recommends that teachers audiotape or videotape their lessons for later evaluation of any assumptions or terminology that students might fail to comprehend.

Teachers would be well advised to follow Johns' recommendations, but they should also try to learn about the home environments of their students and their native cultures. They need to know the extent to which English is used in the home, the number of relatives living in the home, and their level of fluency in English. In addition, identifying the common method of instruction in that culture's schools is very helpful (Field and Aebersold, 1990).

Reading comprehension of ESL students is enhanced when teachers use a variety of means to promote and check reading comprehension. For instance, they may choose to use oral and visual prompts such as pictures, signs, ads, and video clips. Interviewing students about their ideas also will help them to develop oral language, which will serve as a basis for increasing their command of English. These strategies also contribute to integrating the students in the classroom.

Students who are learning English as a second language should continue to maintain their native languages (Kupinsky, 1983). When students have opportunities to develop and maintain their first languages, their self-concepts are enhanced. In our multicultural society, speaking more than one language is a valuable asset and enables students to participate more fully in their family and cultural backgrounds. In order to achieve this parallel language development, students should be exposed to reading materials written in both English and their first languages, when possible. Classroom teachers should understand that students need to learn oral English before they can successfully read it.

ESL students frequently have different experiences from those of students from the dominant culture; therefore teachers should include clarification of cultural terms or concepts in their instruction. These cultural references may encompass information from the fields of art, music, and drama. Many ESL students lack a command of oral English to form a basis for reading and writing English. Because of their inability to communicate effectively in the school environment, they have low self-esteem, which further interferes with their reading success. Their inability to converse in English inhibits both their educational and social development.

ESL instruction is accomplished in a number of ways. In some classrooms, students acquire English through interaction in the regular classroom.

Immersion programs are based on moving the student into the second language as a basis for learning academic subjects (Genesee, 1985). Other ESL programs are "pull-out" programs in which students spend a portion of the school day with a teacher who systematically teaches them the second language. Whatever the program, there is agreement that second language learning should create a desire in the students to learn the language in order to engage in meaningful and interesting communication (Genesee, 1985). This approach is effective for ESL students as well as for dialect-different students.

When students are learning English as a second language, teachers should consider these factors:

1. Cognitive organization is related to the culture and affects metacognition and schemata;
2. Second-language reading is subject to interference from first-language knowledge;
3. Students need a grammatical and lexical base for second-language learning;
4. Direct instruction and extensive reading are important in developing the linguistic base for second-language learning;
5. Reading in a second language can be taught through a reading curriculum that approximates the reading program for a native language reader (Grabe, 1987).

Dialect Different Students

Dialect different students use a language pattern of a subgroup of language speakers. Students who grow up in a specific cultural group speak a dialect of English used in their environment, such as Appalachian or Black English Vernacular (BEV). However, all African-Americans do not use BEV, nor do all residents of the Appalachian region speak the same dialect. Within each dialect there are many variations. It is inaccurate to suggest that there is one BEV or one Appalachian dialect because there are many dialects in each group. Alexander (1985) identifies three facts about BEV that will help teachers understand and work with it in the classroom: (1) African-Americans who use a form of dialect do not use all of the BEV features at all times; (2) their use of these features varies from sentence to sentence; and (3) the type of Black English used is determined by sex, age, socioeconomic status, geographic areas in which one spent formative years, and the speaker's purpose, setting, topic, and audience. Black English dialect is a legitimate linguistic system with its own complex set of rules.

Do dialect-different students have more learning problems than other students? Most research indicates that BEV speakers are not seriously hampered in reading standard English (Holloway, 1985). Students who speak a different dialect have many opportunities to hear and understand standard

English through television and movies. They are also exposed to books written in standard English in elementary school and to the general print media (e.g., newspapers and magazines). By the time these students reach secondary school age, they can comprehend written and spoken standard English.

Teachers of dialect-different students should respect the students' language and culture in the same way they need to respect the language and culture of students who are learning English as a second language. If teachers have negative feelings about their students' language and feel that speakers of some dialects are less intelligent than standard English speakers, they will find it difficult to work with dialect speakers in an objective manner. Therefore, teachers must confront their own reactions and work to eliminate any negative attitudes that may exist.

Educational Factors

Students enter school expecting to learn to read and write, but some experience serious difficulty with these tasks. If they fail over and over again, they give up, and they feel helpless (Coley and Hoffman, 1990). The inability to read prevents many adolescents from acquiring knowledge that is fundamental to human beings in our culture (Athey, 1982). On the other hand, students who succeed in learning to read will develop feelings of autonomy, mastery of their environment, accurate perception of reality, and positive attitudes toward learning. These students can access the accumulated wisdom of their culture through reading.

Some schools use standardized test scores as a basis for assigning instructional materials to students in an attempt to address individual needs. Unfortunately, these test scores may not be a viable basis for grouping or assigning reading materials because they usually indicate a frustration level of reading (the level at which the student cannot succeed). Furthermore, many achievement tests are based on narrative content, whereas secondary students must read content textbooks (expository in nature) to complete their assigned work.

Any school policy or instructional practice that interferes with instructional adjustments to meet individual student needs hinders students' progress in acquiring the skills needed to read content area materials. School policy in some school systems supports promotion by age rather than achievement (this is sometimes called social promotion). When this policy is combined with rigid curriculum policies, it contributes greatly to the reading difficulties of secondary school students. Students are passed from grade to grade without achieving adequate reading skills, but the curriculum is not adjusted to the lower reading levels of the students. Furthermore, many teachers believe that a student whose grade placement is eighth grade should read eighth-grade materials. Therefore, they make impossible demands on at risk students.

The reading curricula in many schools are deficient in providing for the development of study skills and content reading skills. The reading materials used to develop reading skills in elementary schools may be largely composed of story or narrative materials instead of the nonfiction materials necessary for developing the study skills and content reading abilities that students need to learn from content materials, although newer basal reading materials present much expository content as well.

To add to the problem, the reading curricula of many schools end at the sixth-grade level, even though many students have not attained reading maturity by sixth grade. Some students referred to reading clinics could make more progress in public schools if secondary school reading programs were more universally provided. The lack of such programs forces many secondary students to seek help outside the public school system.

Most reading curricula and materials are designed for average, rather than at risk, students. The materials do not address the needs of students whose readiness lags behind that of average students. In most schools, students in the primary grades are introduced to the basic reading strategies necessary for them to transfer from a focus on oral language to processing written language. By fourth grade, students are expected to read fluently enough to learn from written texts. These expectations are predicated on the abilities of students who make average progress in acquiring the reading process.

Some students acquire basic reading abilities, but lack the higher levels of comprehension necessary for learning content through reading. Content instruction must be modified for students who have not yet developed the requisite reading, language arts, and thinking abilities. At risk students also need relevant content materials that relate to their conceptual and reading levels. Before they can understand text, however, students must have the underlying conceptual readiness that makes comprehension possible. Each reading assignment demands a certain level of prior knowledge to facilitate understanding. When this knowledge is missing, teachers must develop it. When it is present, teachers must activate it.

Strategies like those presented throughout this text will help students acquire the needed strategies. Students who cannot read their textbooks and related materials need remedial reading instruction which is beyond the scope of classroom teachers, but the strategies suggested in the next section are ones that teachers find particularly helpful to at risk readers.

Instructional Strategies

Effective reading instruction for all types of students is based on an understanding of reading as a thinking process. A whole language or integrated language arts approach that emphasizes reading, writing, listening, and speaking offers at risk students the greatest opportunities for success. In such an approach students should have as many opportunities as possible to read interesting, comprehensible content. Reading instruction should incorporate daily opportunities to read highly motivational material that will encourage students to read frequently, thus developing their reading fluency.

Reading strategies should involve inferential thinking, problem solving, and critical thinking. Some teachers exhibit a tendency to stress literal level thinking with less able students; however these students can think at higher cognitive levels when they have appropriate background knowledge. Therefore, adapted reading instruction should provide for building and activating schemata in a diverse classroom population.

Building Background Knowledge

Reading is a constructive process for all readers. They construct meaning from written text. No text is completely self-explanatory (Anderson et al., 1985). In interpreting a text, readers draw on their stores of background knowledge about the text topic. For example, in reading the sentence, "Susan searched her bookcase for the book," a student's background knowledge might suggest that books are usually stored in a bookcase, and that the word "the" (a definite article) suggests that a specific book is the object of this search. A reader might also reflect that this could be Susan's personal copy rather than a library book, since it is kept in her bookcase; further, the bookcase suggests that Susan has a number of books because she has a place for storing books. However, the sentence does not indicate whether the book is a textbook or a recreational reading book, nor does it tell what Susan plans to do with the book.

Word recognition processes involve access to mental representations or concepts of words. Knowing or recognizing words enables readers to associate printed words with familiar concepts in their memories (Perfetti, 1985). The reader discussed above first recognizes a word and associates it with his or her schemata (cluster of concepts stored in memory). The reader connects the words and these schemata to construct meaningful ideas about the text. In this process, he or she also uses inferencing ability. At risk students have difficulty making these associations because they have different schemata. The situation of having a bookcase and books in the home may be inconceivable to them. Their homes may be devoid of reading material. They also may not use language with enough precision to consider the role of the definite article. The speech models by which they are surrounded may be careless and imprecise in usage.

Teachers help students activate appropriate schemata and build the appropriate experiences that will help them comprehend content reading materials. They may use photographs, videotapes, models, and guest lecturers to develop schemata. At risk students will probably benefit more from the more concrete experiences than from vicarious ones. Advance organizers and preview guides, which are discussed in Chapters 3, 6, 8, and 9, help activate and develop schemata. Previewing of text, as described in Chapter 4, can also be helpful. Previewing text involves examining the title, photographs, headings, and introduction. In addition, teachers who are instructing students whose native language is not English can help them by providing previews of the text in the students' native language. Teachers who do not speak the students' native language may have another person make audiotapes to use in previewing content. Additional strategies in this area are included later in this chapter.

Teachers also help students integrate new experiences with their previous ones through discussion questions that encourage them to reflect on their experiences and to compare and contrast experiences. Teachers increase reading comprehension when they activate prior knowledge before and during students' actual reading. Student self-questioning is useful in activating prior knowledge about the topic or story. Suggestions to aid in this process are discussed in Chapters 3, 4, 6, 8, and 9.

Discussion plays an extremely important role in teaching at risk students because they often acquire more information and understanding from talking and listening than through reading. Through discussion teachers can introduce the main ideas of a class and review the important ideas from a preceding lesson to create a context for learning new material. At the end of a lesson, summarizing and recapping important ideas by the teacher or the students facilitates understanding and remembering.

As stated earlier, listening plays a large role in teaching at risk students. Students need to learn to listen with pen or pencil in hand when they listen to longer selections. Taking notes makes students more attentive and accurate in recalling material. Listening study guides and the directed listening-thinking activity (DLTA) are approaches that help secondary students, particularly at risk students. Example 5.1 shows a Listening Study Guide, and Example 5.2 identifies the steps in a directed listening-thinking activity that is based on the Directed Reading-Thinking Activity discussed in Chapter 6.

EXAMPLE **5.1**

Listening Study Guide

1. Date, class (e.g., social studies, English, home economics)
2. What is the topic? (e.g., Egypt, gerunds, nutrition)
3. How was the content organized? (Any of the patterns discussed in Chapters 3, 8, and 9 may be used, such as cause and effect, examples, or comparison/contrast.)
4. Did the instructor or discussants stick to the point?
5. Do you agree with the ideas or information given?
6. Why do you agree or disagree?
7. Write the main points in no more than three sentences.

EXAMPLE **5.2**

Directed Listening-Thinking Activity (DLTA)

1. Select a story that has a strong plot. The story should include conflicts or problems to be overcome.
2. Read through the story and identify places for the students to stop reading. These stopping places should occur just prior to an important event in the story so that the listeners can predict what will happen next. Avoid stopping too frequently because this will fragment the story. The number of stops depends on the story length, but two to four stops work best.
3. Introduce the story by telling the students the title and the author and by showing them the cover or the early illustrations in the book. If any students have already heard or read the story, ask them to keep the outcome a secret until the other students have heard it.
4. Read the story, stopping at each point selected. When you stop, ask the students to tell what has happened up to this point (briefly), to predict what will happen next, and to explain why they think so.

Adaptive Instruction

Adaptive instructional practices are important to secondary teachers because they must deal with a tremendous diversity of students *and* large numbers of students. They commonly instruct from 100 to 200 students each day. Normal teaching loads consist of five or six daily classes and two to four daily preparations (Moore and Murphy, 1987). Reading is a basic process that all students must acquire, and students' individual abilities are an important factor in content reading instruction. At risk students need more individual instruction, if they are to experience success.

Intervention strategies are tactics that help students whose reading achievement lags behind the average because of one or more of the factors discussed earlier in this chapter. Throughout this book, we describe instructional strategies that teachers can use and reading strategies that students can use to increase their understanding of written text. A curriculum including learning strategies and instructional modifications such as those described here constitutes an intervention program that will help many students whose reading achievement does not permit them to understand content textbooks.

Generally speaking, students who are of below average intelligence, those who are underachievers because of socioeconomic factors, and learning disabled students can benefit from many of the same instructional modifications. Teachers should avoid frustrating these students by planning lessons that they can accomplish and by giving them materials they can read with some assistance. Avoiding frustration and building students' self-esteem will improve their overall learning (Biehler and Snowman, 1990). Instructional strategies should involve presenting learning tasks that contain a small number of elements, some of which are familiar to the students. Teachers can give a series of very brief lessons because these students find it difficult to sustain concentration and effort. They can also arrange learning in a series of small steps and give students immediate positive feedback as they achieve each step. Frequent review helps build overlearning into lessons, which aids retention, and students enjoy the review because it involves learned material with which they feel more secure.

One method of providing students with the kind of instruction described above is by means of the computer. Computers have an obvious appeal for adolescents and give them a sense of control in the learning situation that helps build self-confidence. Properly written computer programs are non-judgmental about mistakes and exhibit unlimited patience while permitting students to work at their own paces. Additionally, when a student doesn't know a word, he or she does not have to reveal this to the teacher or to other students. The student receives immediate feedback and reinforcement from computers. Computer instruction can also be more game-like than more traditional instruction, making drill and practice more interesting. It can also encourage risk-taking by the students. Many computer programs have branching capabilities that ensure individualized instruction according to the students' needs (Pommer, Mark, and Hayden, 1983; Schiffman, Tobin, and Buchanan, 1982). Branching programs offer different sets of information depending on the students' answers; therefore, each student completing the program may encounter different information.

Motivation and Intervention Strategies

Students with individual differences and needs such as those described in this chapter need to be motivated to read. Reading is an ability that must be exercised. The more students read, the better they read, and the better they read the more they want to read; thus increased reading enhances fluency and the desire to read. However, students must be motivated to read in order to activate this reading fluency cycle. The following strategies are particularly helpful in secondary classrooms:

1. Have newspapers and magazines available in the classroom for students to read. They are more likely to read these materials when they are displayed on counters or tables rather than on shelves.

2. Set aside time each day to do booktalks about books that students might enjoy. You may also choose to read poems, newspaper or magazine articles, or excerpts from books. When giving booktalks, teachers briefly discuss the main character, plot, and theme of a story but do not reveal its

resolution. In giving booktalks about informational books, highlight the important, new, and unusual ideas and relate these to students' existing knowledge. You may select a group of books that relate to a single theme or topic or a wide range of books that appeal to a variety of interests.

3. Make the book review section of the local newspaper available to students.

4. Create bulletin boards and book displays to encourage reading.

5. Invite local authors to discuss their writing.

6. Provide incentives for students to read. These incentives may take the form of adding points to a grade for the course or gift certificates for records, food, or clothing for a certain number of titles read. In some schools, parent organizations or local businesses will donate money or certificates for incentives. At risk students may be more motivated by the more concrete rewards, at least in the early stages.

7. Have regular reading conferences with students. These individualized discussions are highly motivating for many students. Some categories of at risk students get little individualized attention from adults and may respond especially well to the conferences.

8. Develop a "Sustained Silent Reading (SSR)" program. You may begin with one or two days a week and gradually extend the number of days. Start with 5 minutes and gradually extend the time to 15 minutes. Students may read anything they choose. Keep a selection of reading materials in the classroom in case students forget their own. In many schools, the SSR program involves everyone in the school reading at the same time.

9. Provide audiotapes of stories and poems that the students can listen to while following the text. These tapes can be highly motivational for many students.

10. Read aloud regularly to secondary students from prose and poetry selections. As a result of their poor reading abilities, at risk students have not had opportunities to read and enjoy fine literature; therefore, they do not really know what books have to offer them.

Teachers also can use strategies such as those identified in the following paragraphs that have proved helpful for adolescents who lack the academic skills required by secondary schools (Lerner, 1985). These strategies and other similar ones are discussed throughout this book. Useful strategies focus on helping these students learn how to read, how to study, and how to learn rather than tutoring them in content. For instance, an assistance program should focus on ways to organize the material in preparation for a biology test rather than on the specific questions on the test.

Advance organizers establish a mind-set for readers, encouraging them to relate new material to previously learned material before reading. Advance organizers may have a variety of focal or starting points, such as general concepts to be explored in the content, linkages of new material to previously learned ideas, or an introductory paragraph that explains the material to be read.

The Prereading Plan (PReP) (Langer, 1982, 1984) is a way of activating students' prior knowledge that involves associations, reflections about associations, and reformulation of knowledge.

1. Initial association: The teacher identifies a word, phrase, or picture relating to the key concept. Then the students discuss the word, phrase, or picture, and how it is related to the key concept, for example, how the 28th parallel is related to the Korean war.
2. Reflection: students explain their associations.
3. Reformulation: students explain new knowledge they have acquired about the Korean war.

Search strategies are concerned with helping students scan text before they answer questions. The goal is to reduce impulsive, thoughtless answers and to encourage thoughtful responses. They learn to stop, listen, look, and think — to consider alternative answers and problem solutions before responding.

Verbal rehearsal (think-aloud) helps students learn to state comprehension problems to themselves as a means of clarifying their understanding. There are three stages for developing this strategy: (1) the instructor models verbalization of the problem, (2) the students practice verbalizing aloud, (3) the students verbalize independently and silently.

Metacognition (self-monitoring) is an active reading strategy that helps students learn to monitor their own understanding of text. When students become aware of comprehension and exert control over it, their understanding improves. Students need direct instruction in using this strategy so they develop the ability to monitor their own understanding and become conscious of errors or answers that do not make sense.

Self-questioning is a metacognitive strategy that encourages active reading. In this approach, students develop their own comprehension questions. They ask themselves general questions such as, "What did the author say to me?" "Why am I reading this passage?" "What is the main idea?" and "How can I state the main idea?"

Audiotapes can be prepared to accompany textbooks. Students who are not fluent readers can use the tapes with tape recorders and ear phones to help them understand the text. Both teachers and students who are fluent readers can prepare these tapes.

Example 5.3 summarizes teaching strategies for at risk students that are introduced throughout this text and gives chapter numbers indicating where further descriptions of these strategies can be found.

EXAMPLE **5.3**

Reading Strategies for At Risk Students

Strategy	Before Reading	During Reading	After Reading	Discussed in Chapter(s)
Advance organizer	X			3
Audiovisual (photos, video- and audiotapes)	X			2, 3, 4
Preview guides	X			3, 6, 8, 9
Discussion	X	X	X	3, 4, 6
Sustained Silent Reading (SSR)		X		3, 11
Think-aloud	X	X		3, 8, 9
Study guides	X	X	X	3, 6, 8, 9
Self-question	X	X	X	3
Mapping	X		X	3, 6, 8, 9
Word sorts	X		X	2
Structured overview	X		X	2, 6
In-depth word study	X		X	2
Semantic feature analysis	X		X	2
SQ3R	X	X	X	4
Summaries			X	4, 7
Outlining			X	4, 8

SUMMARY

The number of at risk students in public schools is increasing. The population of students in secondary school classrooms reflects greater diversity than ever before. Some factors contributing to diversity in the student population are living in poverty, growing up in a single parent home, and learning English as a second language. The numbers of students from these situations who attend our schools are increasing. In addition, more handicapped students are attending school in regular classrooms, or being mainstreamed because of changes in the way we educate exceptional students.

Reading is a complex process, and its complexity contributes to the wide range of individual differences that students exhibit in secondary classrooms. Much of the student diversity in reading abilities found in secondary classrooms arises from students' varying background experiences and concept development, because these factors are so important in reading comprehension. Some students learn to read, but not well enough to learn from their content textbooks. A common problem encountered by these readers is a lack of knowledge to anticipate and understand the ideas expressed in written language.

Teaching strategies must help students develop their abilities to read and study content textbooks. The specific instructional techniques directed at meeting individual needs, including the needs of so-called exceptional and at risk students, are developed throughout this text.

SELF-TEST

1. Which is an attribute of secondary school disabled readers? (a) Enjoyment of reading (b) Low achievement in the majority of school subjects (c) Average achievement (d) Above average achievement
2. Which of the following statements is true of the reading process? (a) It is a process of constructing meaning. (b) Meaning gained from reading may differ from individual to individual. (c) Readers use their individual experiences and knowledge to understand print. (d) All of these
3. What characteristics are exhibited by competent readers? (a) They are often listless and inattentive. (b) They give up quickly. (c) They read rapidly with good understanding. (d) They read slowly, decoding words as they go.
4. What is the "numbers" problem encountered by secondary teachers? (a) They usually have 100 to 200 students each day. (b) They teach 5 or 6 classes a day. (c) Both *a* and *b* (d) Neither *a* nor *b*
5. Why do the authors of this text state that "no text is completely self-explanatory?" (a) Because readers must draw on their store of knowledge about the topic in order to interpret text. (b) Because readers must draw on their previous experiences to interpret text. (c) Both *a* and *b* (d) Neither *a* nor *b*
6. What characteristics make computer instruction good for adaptive in-

struction? (a) It forces students to respond quickly. (b) It is patient and nonjudgmental. (c) Both *a* and *b* (d) Neither *a* nor *b*

7. How is the number of students living in poverty projected to change in the future? (a) It will decline. (b) It will rise. (c) It will stay the same. (d) No child will live in poverty by the year 2000.

8. Which type of students are reading curricula and materials designed for? (a) Above average students (b) Below average students (c) Average students (d) Gifted students

9. What is culture? (a) Values (b) Customs (c) Context in which one develops (d) All of these

10. What factor is highly predictive of reading difficulty? (a) Skin color (b) Low socioeconomic status (c) Dialect spoken (d) None of these

THOUGHT QUESTIONS

1. How is culture related to reading and writing?
2. Discuss the pros and cons of mainstreaming in content classes.
3. What steps can a teacher take to help students from another culture learn to read and write English?
4. Describe a disabled reader you might encounter in a secondary school classroom.
5. Describe a competent reader you might encounter in a secondary school classroom.
6. How do you think education will change in the future if an increasing proportion of students live in conditions of poverty?

ENRICHMENT ACTIVITIES

1. Interview disabled readers at the secondary level; ask them what their reading problems are and why they think they have reading problems.
2. Interview the parents of a disabled reader regarding the development of his or her reading problems and their possible causes.
3. Discuss the reading problems of students with teachers of various content areas. How are the reading problems of their students alike and how are they different?
4. Observe in an ESL classroom if possible. What problems do you anticipate these students will encounter in the content area that you intend to teach?

BIBLIOGRAPHY

Alexander, C. F. "Black English Dialect and the Classroom Teacher." In C. Brooks (ed.), *Tapping Potential: English and the Language Arts for the Black Learner.* Urbana, Ill.: National Council of Teachers of English, 1985, pp. 20–29.

Anderson, R., E. Hiebert, J. Scott, and I. Wilkinson. *Becoming a Nation of Readers.* Washington, D.C.: The National Institute of Education, 1985.

Athey, I. "The Affective Domain Reconceptualized." *Advances in Reading/Language Research* (1982), 203–217.

Bettleheim, B., and K. Zelan. *On Learning to Read.* New York: Vintage Books, 1983.

Biehler, R. F., and J. Snowman. *Psychology Applied to Teaching.* Boston: Houghton Mifflin, 1990.

Bristow, P. "Are Poor Readers Passive Readers? Some Evidence, Possible Explanations and Potential Solutions." *The Reading Teacher,* 39 (December 1985), 318–325.

Callaway, B., B. Jerrolds, and W. Gwaltney. "The Relationship Between Reading and Language Achievement and Certain Sociological and Adjustment Factors." *Reading Improvement,* II (Spring 1985), 19–26.

Children's Defense Fund. *A Children's Defense Budget: An Analysis of the FY'87 Federal Budget and Children.* Washington, D.C.: Children's Defense Fund, 1987.

Clark-Johnson, G. "Black Children." *Teaching Exceptional Children,* 54 (Summer 1988), 46–47.

Coley, J., and D. Hoffman. "Overcoming Learned Helplessness in At-Risk Readers." *Journal of Reading,* 33 (April 1990), 497–502.

Cusick, P. *The Egalitarian Ideal and the American High School: Studies of Three Schools.* New York: Longman, 1983.

Dunwant, N. *The Relationship Between Learning Disabilities and Juvenile Delinquency.* Williamsburg, Va.: National Center for State Courts, 1983.

Educational Testing Service. *The Reading Report Card: Progress Toward Excellence in Our Schools, Trends in Reading Over Four National Assessments, 1971–1984.* Report No. 15-R-01. Princeton, N.J.: Educational Testing Service, 1985.

Eldredge, A. "An Investigation to Determine the Relationships Among Self-Concept, Locus of Control, and Reading Achievement." *Reading World,* 21 (1981), 59–64.

Erickson, F., and G. Mohatt. "Cultural Organization of Participant Structures in Two Classrooms of Indian Students." In G. Spindler (ed.), *Doing the Ethnography of Schooling: Educational Anthropology in Action.* New York: Holt, Rinehart and Winston, 1982.

Field, M., and J. Aebersold. "Cultural Attitudes Toward Reading: Implications for Teachers of ESL/Bilingual Readers." *Journal of Reading,* 33 (March 1990), 406–414.

Fillmore, L. "Cultural Perspectives on Second Language Learning." *TESL Reporter,* 14 (1981), 23–31.

Fitzpatrick, J. *Puerto Rican Americans.* Englewood Cliffs, N.J.: Prentice Hall, 1987.

Fotheringham, J., and D. Creal. "Family Socioeconomic and Educational-Emotional Characteristics as Predictors of School Achievement." *Journal of Educational Research,* 73 (July–August 1980), 311–314.

Gage, N., and D. Berliner. *Educational Psychology.* 4th ed. Boston: Houghton Mifflin, 1988.

Genesee, F. "Second Language Learning Through Immersion: A Review of U.S. Programs." *Review of Educational Research,* 55 (Winter 1985), 541–561.

Gentile, L., and M. McMillan. *Stress and Reading Difficulties: Research, Assessment, Intervention.* Newark, Del.: International Reading Association, 1987.

Good, T. "Teacher Expectations." In D. Berliner and B. Rosenshine (eds.), *Talks to Teachers.* New York: Random House, 1987, pp. 469–520.

Grabe, W. "The Transition from Theory to Practice in Teaching Reading." In F. Dublin, D. Eskey, and W. Grabe (eds.), *Teaching Second Language Reading for Academic Purposes.* Reading, Mass.: Addison-Wesley Publishing Co., 1987, pp. 25–48.

Harris, A., and E. Sipay. *How to Increase Reading Ability.* New York: Longman, 1985.

Hodgkinson, L. *All One System: Demographics of Education — Kindergarten Through Graduate School.* Washington, D.C.: Institute of Educational Leadership, 1985.

Holloway, K. "Learning to Talk — Learning to Read." In C. Brooks (ed.), *Tapping Potential: English and the Language Arts for the Black Learner.* Urbana, Ill.: National Council of Teachers of English, 1985, pp. 12–19.

Hornbeck, D. *"All Our Children." An Introduction. School Success for Students at Risk: Analysis and Recommendations of the Council of Chief State School Officers.* Orlando, Fla.: Harcourt Brace Jovanovich, 1988, pp. 3–9.

Johns, J. "Students' Perceptions of Reading: Thirty Years of Inquiry." In D. Yalden Jr. and S. Templeton (eds.), *Metalinguistic Awareness and Beginning Literacy.* Portsmouth, N.H.: Heinemann, 1986, pp. 31–40.

Kirk, S., and J. Gallagher. *Educating Exceptional Children.* Boston: Houghton Mifflin, 1989.

Kupinsky, B. "Bilingual Reading Instruction in Kindergarten." *The Reading Teacher,* 37 (November 1983), 132–137.

Langer, J. "Facilitating Text Processing: The Elaboration of Prior Knowledge." In J. Langer and M. T. Smith-Burke (eds.), *Reader Meets Author/Bridging the Gap: A Psycholinguistic and Sociolinguistic Perspective.* Newark, Del.: International Reading Association, 1982, pp. 149–162.

———. "Examining Background Knowledge and Text Comprehension." *Reading Research Quarterly,* 19 (1984), 468–481.

Lerner, J. *Learning Disabilities: Theories, Diagnosis, and Teaching Strategies.* 5th ed. Boston: Houghton Mifflin, 1989.

LeSourd, S. "Using an Advance Organizer to Set the Schema for a Multicultural Lesson." *Journal of Reading,* 32 (October 1988), 12–18.

Levin, H. *The Educational Disadvantaged Are Still Among Us.* Stanford, Cal.: Stanford University Press, 1986.

Mathewson, G. C. "Toward a Comprehensive Model of Affect in the Reading Process." In H. Singer and R. Ruddell (eds.), *Theoretical Models and Processes of Reading.* Newark, Del.: International Reading Association, 1985.

Messick, S. "Assessment in Context: Appraising Student Performance in Relation to Instructional Quality." *Educational Researcher,* 13 (March 1984), 3–8.

Moore, D., and A. Murphy. "Reading Programs." In D. Alvermann, D. Moore, and M. Conley (eds.), *Research Within Reach: Secondary School Reading.* Newark, Del.: International Reading Association, 1987, pp. 2–13.

National Black Child Development Institute, Inc. *1986 NBCDI Annual Report.* Washington, D.C.: National Black Child Development Institute, 1986.

Nelson, G. "Culture's Role in Reading Comprehension: A Schema Theoretical Approach." *Journal of Reading,* 30 (February 1987), 424–429.

Neville, D., P. Pfost, and V. Dobbs. "The Relationship Between Test Anxiety and Silent Reading Gains." *American Educational Research Journal,* 4 (1987), 45–50.

Pallas, A., G. Natriello, and E. McDill. "The Changing Nature of the Disadvantaged Population. Current Dimensions and Future Trends." *Educational Researcher,* 18 (June–July 1989), 16–22.

Pellicano, R. "At-Risk: A View of 'Social Advantage'." *Educational Leadership,* 44 (1987), 47–50.

Perfetti, C. *Reading Ability.* New York: Oxford University Press, 1985.

Phillips, S. *The Invisible Culture: Communication in Classroom and Community on the Warm Springs Indian Reservation.* White Plains, N.Y.: Longman, 1983.

Pommer, L., D. Mark, and D. Hayden. "Using Computer Software to Instruct Learning Disabled Students." *Learning Disabilities,* 2 (1983), 99–110.

Quant, I., and R. Selznick. *Self-Concept and Reading.* Newark, Del.: International Reading Association, 1984.

Rayner, K., and A. Pollatset. *The Psychology of Reading.* Englewood Cliffs, N.J.: Prentice Hall, 1989.

Richek, M., L. List, and J. Lerner. *Reading Problems: Assessment and Teaching Strategies.* Englewood Cliffs, N.J.: Prentice Hall, 1989.

Robinson, G. *Crosscultural Understanding: Processes and Approaches to Foreign Language, English as a Second Language and Bilingual Educators.* New York: Pergamon, 1985.

Salend, S., R. Michael, and M. Taylor. "Competencies Necessary for Instructing Migrant Handicapped Students." *Exceptional Children*, 51 (1984), 50–55.

Schiffman, G., D. Tobin, and B. Buchanan. "Microcomputer Instruction for the Learning Disabled." *Journal of Learning Disabilities*, 15 (1982), 557–559.

Schonhaut, S., and P. Satz. "Prognosis of the Learning Disabled Child: A Review of the Followup Studies." In M. Rutter (ed.), *Behavioral Syndromes of Brain Dysfunction in Childhood.* New York: Guilford Press, 1983, pp. 89–95.

Slavin, R. "Students at Risk of School Failure: The Problem and Its Dimensions." In R. Slavin, N. Karweit, and N. Madden (eds.), *Effective Programs for Students at Risk.* Needham Heights, Mass.: Allyn and Bacon, 1989, pp. 1–20.

Thomson, M., and G. Hartley. "Self-Concept in Dyslexic Children." *Academic Therapy*, 16 (September 1980), 19–36.

Valdivieso, R. *Must They Wait Another Generation? Hispanics and Secondary School Reform.* New York: ERIC Clearinghouse on Urban Education, 1986.

Valero-Figueira, E. "Hispanic Children." *Teaching Exceptional Children*, 54 (Summer 1988), 47–49.

Vobejda, B. "Children at Risk," *Washington Post*, 11 (October 1987), 22–23.

Wehlage, G., and R. Rutter. "Dropping Out: How Much Do Schools Contribute to the Problem?" *Teachers College Record*, 87 (1986), 374–392.

Weiner, B. "Some Thoughts About Feelings." In S. B. Paris, G. M. Olson, and H. W. Stevenson (eds.), *Learning and Motivation in the Classroom.* Hillsdale, N.J.: Erlbaum, 1983.

Wells, G. (ed.). *Learning Through Interaction.* New York: Cambridge University Press, 1981.

Wigfield, A., and S. Asher. "Social and Motivational Influences on Reading." In P. D. Pearson (ed.), *Handbook of Reading Research.* New York: Longman, 1984, pp. 423–452.

Willig, A. C. et al. "Sociocultural and Educational Correlates of Success-Failure Attributions and Evaluation Anxiety in the School Setting for Black, Hispanic, and Anglo Children." *American Educational Research Journal*, 26 (Fall 1983), 385–410.

6

ADJUSTING READING ASSIGNMENTS TO FIT ALL STUDENTS

OVERVIEW

Not all students are alike in their ability to handle printed instructional material, and the instructional material itself may not be at the difficulty level that teachers assume it to be. For these reasons, teachers have a tremendously important task to perform in adjusting their reading assignments to fit all students. Teachers know that not all students read at the same level, but they do not always know whether a given student can read at the level on which the textbook is written; in fact, they may not know what this level actually is. In order to match students with reading materials that are appropriate for them, teachers need to understand the factors that influence readability and how to use readability formulas and other measures for determining the difficulty of materials.

The variety of reading achievement levels present among students within a classroom makes it important for teachers to have knowledge of how and when to group students for motivational purposes and for differentiated assignments. Also, if assignments truly are to fit all students, teachers need to have knowledge of the means of differentiating assignments by using study guides, directed reading approaches, directed reading-thinking activities, alternate textbooks, rewritten materials, language experience materials, and computer applications. Teaching units can be used as a vehicle for this differentiation, and selection aids can help the teacher locate materials on different topics and levels.

PURPOSE-SETTING QUESTIONS

As you read this chapter, try to answer these questions:

1. How is an understanding of the readability levels of textbook materials important to a teacher?

2. What are some types of study groups that a teacher might wish to form within a classroom, and for what purpose would each be formed?
3. What is the purpose of a study guide?
4. Under what circumstances would a teacher wish to locate alternate textbooks or printed materials for use in his or her classroom?
5. How can a teacher use language experience materials at the secondary level?
6. How can the computer be used to adjust assignments?
7. What four basic types of activities are part of a teaching unit?
8. What selection aids are available to help secondary school teachers locate appropriate books for the readers in their classes?

KEY VOCABULARY

As you read this chapter, check your understanding of these terms:

directed reading approach
high interest, low vocabulary
   materials
language experience materials
multilevel materials
readability
cooperative learning
readability formula

simulation programs
structured overview
student tutorial groups
study guides
teaching units
trade books
word processing programs

Readability of Printed Materials

When educators refer to the readability of printed materials that students are asked to read, they mean the reading difficulty of these materials. Selections that are very difficult to read are said to have high readability levels; those that are easy to read are said to have low readability levels.

Teachers and students in college classes who check the readability of textbooks with readability formulas sometimes find that the textbooks are written at higher levels of difficulty than the grade levels for which they are designed. Teachers are then faced with the question of how to present the material to their students in a way that will help them to learn the content.

Even if textbooks are labeled properly for the intended grade placement (that is, a text that is labeled grade nine is written on a ninth-grade difficulty level), many students in that grade will be unable to benefit from them. Many students in the ninth grade are unable to read with understanding material written on that level. Many ninth-grade students read anywhere from one to five grade levels *below* their placement, and a few are even farther behind than that. This situation obviously presents a difficult problem for the teacher who is working with this wide range of abilities. Furthermore, the teacher will have some students who are reading one to five (and possibly more) grades *above* their ninth-grade placement. A textbook may be adequate for teaching subject-matter concepts to these better students, but it may seem so elementary to them that more challenging supplementary materials will have to be provided to avoid boring them. In view of the fact that secondary school teachers frequently use textbooks for independent homework assignments and often expect that the students will read the complete textbooks, matching the textbooks assigned to students with the students' reading levels is particularly important (Davey, 1988).

A fact that textbook users often overlook is that different sections of the same textbook may have different readability levels, some topics may require more difficult language for their presentation, or different sections may be written by different authors with writing styles that vary in complexity or clarity. English teachers, in particular, should be aware of the wide differences in readability levels of selections in literature anthologies, because different authors have written the materials.

Many factors influence the level of difficulty of printed materials. Some of these are vocabulary, sentence length, sentence complexity, abstract concepts, organization of ideas, inclusion of reading aids (such as underlining, boxing of information, and graphic aids), size and style of type, format, reader interest, and reader background. Concept load seems to be particularly important. If many new or technical concepts are introduced on each page or in each paragraph of text or if many of the concepts presented are abstract rather than concrete, the readability will be more difficult. Of the factors identified that influence the level of difficulty, two are directly related to the uniqueness of the reader: interest and background. A piece of literature may be of great interest to one student and yet have little appeal for another. A reader's areas of interest may be related to his or her background of experience. This background enables readers to understand easily material for which they have experienced vocabulary and concepts either directly or vicariously. (See Chapter 5 for a discussion of background experience as one area in which students exhibit individual differences.)

Although all the other factors mentioned obviously affect difficulty, vocabulary and sentence length have been found by researchers to be the most important ones to use in predicting readability.

Readability Formulas

Various formulas have been developed to measure the readability of printed materials. Most contain measures of vocabulary and sentence difficulty. Some

TABLE **6.1**

Readability Formulas

Formula	Characteristics Measured	
	Vocabulary difficulty	*Sentence difficulty*
Dale-Chall Readability Formula[a]	Percentage of "hard words"	Average sentence length
Flesch "Reading Ease" Formula[b]	Average number of syllables per 100 words	Average sentence length
SMOG Grading Formula[c]	Polysyllabic word count for 30 sentences	
Fry Readability Graph Formula[d]	Average number of syllables per 100 words	Average number of sentences per 100 words

[a]Edgar Dale and Jeanne S. Chall, "A Formula for Predicting Readability," *Educational Research Bulletin* 27 (January 21, 1948), 11–20, 28; also Edgar Dale and Jeanne S. Chall, "A Formula for Predicting Readability: Instructions," *Educational Research Bulletin* 27 (February 18, 1948), 37–54.

[b]Rudolf Flesch, *The Art of Readable Writing* (New York: Harper & Row, 1949).

[c]Harry G. McLaughlin, "SMOG Grading — A New Readability Formula," *Journal of Reading* 12 (May 1969), 639–646.

[d]Edward Fry, "A Readability Formula that Saves Time," *Journal of Reading* 11 (April 1968), 513–516, 575–578; also Edward Fry, *Fry Readability Scale (Extended)* (Providence, R.I.: Jamestown Publishers, 1978).

of the most frequently used formulas are listed in Table 6.1. Teachers should be aware that these formulas have been developed for use with connected prose; their use with other types of text, such as mathematics calculations, is inappropriate and will result in inaccurate scores.

The Dale-Chall Readability Formula is a well-validated formula, but it is relatively difficult and time-consuming to use. Therefore, few secondary classroom teachers are likely to use it on a regular basis, especially if they must do the calculations by hand. However, they can learn to use it with practice and may want to do so in special situations that require a highly valid formula. A number of samples of approximately 100 words each are used for computing readability with this formula. A word from a sample that is on the 3,000-word Dale list (words known by 80 percent of fourth graders) or a word that is an acceptable variation of a word on the list is considered easy; if the sample word is not on the list, it is considered hard. The sample scores are averaged, and a correction table is provided with which to determine the grade score for a selection. Powers, Sumner, and Kearl (1958) revised the formula in order to modernize it.

The Flesch "Reading Ease" Formula is also somewhat complex. When using the Flesch Formula, one must count the number of sentences in the sample, treating each independent unit of thought as a sentence, and must compute the average sentence length. After having determined the "Words per Sentence" and "Syllables per 100 Words" figures, one can use a chart prepared by Flesch to determine the "Reading Ease" score (Flesch, 1951). The Flesch "Reading Ease" Formula was recalculated at the same time that the Dale-Chall Formula was revised (Powers, Sumner, and Kearl, 1958). This formula is also time-consuming for teachers to use; therefore it may not be chosen by secondary classroom teachers for use on a routine basis if teachers must do the calculations by hand.

The SMOG Grading Formula requires the user to count each word of three or more syllables in each of three ten-sentence samples. The approximate square root of the number of such polysyllabic words is calculated (by taking the square root of the nearest perfect square); to this figure the number three is added to give the SMOG Grade. This formula takes less time to calculate than the Dale-Chall and Flesch formulas, and it may be chosen for use by some secondary teachers. It produces a score that reflects an independent reading level, meaning that a student reading at the indicated level could read the tested material with complete understanding.

The Fry Readability Graph is another relatively quick readability measure (Fry, 1972). To use the graph, one needs to select three 100-word samples and to determine the average number of sentences and the average number of syllables per 100 words. (The number of sentences in a 100-word sample is determined to the nearest tenth of a sentence.) With these figures, it is possible to use the graph to determine the approximate grade level of the selection. Fry's Graph and the instructions for using it are reprinted in Figure 6.1. The Fry Graph reflects an instructional reading level, the level at which a student should be able to read with teacher assistance. The authors of this text have found that, in many cases, secondary classroom teachers are more comfortable with this formula than with the other three discussed here. For that reason, it is presented in more detail. There is no implication that it is superior to the other three, and teachers should use their own judgment in choosing a suitable formula to use.

The formulas already discussed are designed for use with long passages. Fry (1990) has developed a formula for use with passages from 40 to 300 words long. The passage should contain at least three sentences. The user selects at least three key words needed to understand the passage, looks up the grade level of each key word in *The Living Word Vocabulary* (Dale and O'Rourke, 1976), and averages the three hardest key words to find the Word Difficulty. Then he or she counts the number of words in each sentence and gives each sentence a grade according to a sentence length chart. An average of the grade levels of all sentences produces the score for Sentence Difficulty. The average of the Word Difficulty and Sentence Difficulty gives the readability estimate. This formula is designed for grades 4 through 12.

Some educators prefer to use the more lengthy and complicated for-

FIGURE **6.1**

203

Fry Readability Graph

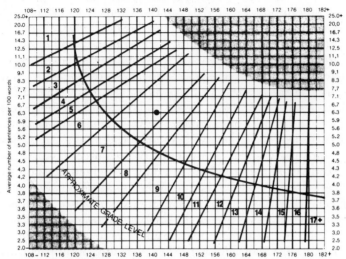

Expanded Directions for Working Readability Graph

1. Randomly select three (3) sample passages and count out exactly 100 words each, beginning with the beginning of a sentence. Do count proper nouns, initializations, and numerals.
2. Count the number of sentences in the hundred words, estimating length of the fraction of the last sentence to the nearest one-tenth.
3. Count the total number of syllables in the 100-word passage. If you don't have a hand counter available, an easy way is to simply put a mark above every syllable over one in each word, then when you get to the end of the passage, count the number of marks and add 100. Small calculators can also be used as counters by pushing numeral 1, then push the + sign for each word or syllable when counting.
4. Enter graph with *average* sentence length and *average* number of syllables; plot dot where the two lines intersect. Area where dot is plotted will give you the approximate grade level.
5. If a great deal of variability is found in syllable count or sentence count, putting more samples into the average is desirable.
6. A word is defined as a group of symbols with a space on either side; thus, *Joe, IRA, 1945,* and *&* are each one word.
7. A syllable is defined as a phonetic syllable. Generally, there are as many syllables as vowel sounds. For example, *stopped* is one syllable and *wanted* is two syllables. When counting syllables for numerals and initializations, count one syllable for each symbol. For example, *1945* is four syllables, *IRA* is three syllables, and *&* is one syllable.

Note: This "extended graph" does not outmode or render the earlier (1968) version inoperative or inaccurate; it is an extension. (REPRODUCTION PERMITTED — NO COPYRIGHT) mulas, which, they feel, are more accurate. Considering the number of factors that formulas fail to take into account, however, no formula can provide more than an approximation of level of difficulty. For this reason, the quick formulas should not be scorned. Determination of the relative difficulty levels of textbooks and other printed materials can be extremely valuable to a teacher. It has been demonstrated that estimating reading difficulty by using a formula produces much more consistent results than estimating without one.

If you are daunted by the prospect of counting syllables, words, sentences, and unfamiliar words, and your school has a computer or a microcomputer, you can use one of these valuable aids to save you time and effort in making calculations (Judd, 1981; Gross and Sadowski, 1985; Kretschmer, 1984). Although a school's mainframe computer may not be available to teachers for such projects, in many cases microcomputers are. A number of programs can analyze the readability levels of texts according to a variety of readability formulas. Some programs run only a single formula on a passage that is typed into the program, as is true of the *Fry Readability Program* (Jamestown Publishers) (Balajthy, 1986). Others run a number of formulas on the passage simultaneously, as is true of the *Readability Analysis Program* (Random House). This latter program performs the analyses for six different formulas: the Flesch, Fog, Dale-Chall, SMOG, Wheeler-Smith, and Spache formulas. The *Reading Level Analysis* (Bertamax, Inc.) runs the Wheeler-Smith and Spache formulas on materials for grades 1 to 3 and the Flesch, Fog, Dale-Chall, and SMOG formulas for grades 4 and above (Rude, 1986). These programs perform the calculations that teachers would ordinarily have to do manually. Teachers just have to type in the passages to be analyzed and read an on-screen menu that allows them to choose such things as which formulas to run.

Degrees of Reading Power

The Degrees of Reading Power (DRP) test is a criterion-referenced test published by the College Entrance Examination Board to measure students' reading ability at different levels of difficulty. DRP units can also be used to measure readability of printed materials. By measuring both the student's reading ability and the readability of printed materials in the same units, the idea is to produce a match between student and material that is more accurate than matching by other means available.

The College Entrance Examination Board's *Readability Report* (1983) lists DRP scores for many materials that are used in schools. In addition, for a fee the Board will calculate DRP readability scores for any material sent to them.

DRP units are based on cloze research done by John Bormuth. Bormuth (1985) admits that the DRP system overestimates the difficulty of easy material for younger readers and underestimates the difficulty of hard materials for older readers. He attributes these tendencies, which are common to readability estimates, to the fact that the DRP formula and other existing formulas do not take into account the background knowledge of the students and the levels of background knowledge that authors assume in their readers.

Cautions and Controversies

All teachers should be familiar with at least one readability formula so that they can check the printed materials used in their classes. Then perhaps students will not be asked so frequently to read textbooks or supplementary materials that are too difficult for them. However, because of the limitations of the available formulas, teachers should always combine results obtained from the formulas with judgment based on personal experience with the materials and knowledge of the abstractness of the concepts presented, the organization and writing style of the author, the interests of the students in the class, the backgrounds of experience of the students, and other related factors such as size and style of type and format of the material. Because sampling procedures suggested by several formulas result in limited samples, teachers should be very cautious in accepting calculated grade levels as absolutes. They also should remember that textbooks vary in difficulty from section to section and should interpret samples with that in mind.

Readability formulas do not have any measure for abstractness or unfamiliarity of concepts covered. Familiar words, such as "run" and "bank," do not always have their familiar meanings in school materials. A social studies text might discuss a "run on the banks," which would present a less familiar situation than reading about "fast movement by water along the shore of a stream," that may be the meaning of these words that comes to mind immediately.

Authors may organize materials clearly or they may have very poor organization, and the clarity of their writing styles may vary immensely, with some choosing to construct sentences in less common ways and others choosing familiar sentence structures. Readability formulas contain no measures for organization or style.

The cohesive structure of a text (the interrelationships of ideas) also affects readability (Binkley, 1988). Cohesive ties may fit under five classifications — reference, substitution, ellipsis, conjunction, and lexical. Standard formulas do not measure cohesion, which is a complex procedure.

Factors within individual students help determine the readability of particular material for those students. Material that is interesting to students is easier for them to read, because they are more motivated to read it. Other people with similar reading skills may find the material uninteresting and, thus, much more difficult to read. Likewise, readers who have had much experience related to the topic will find the material easier to read than those who have had little experience related to it. No formula has the power to foresee the interests and backgrounds of particular readers. (See Chapter 10 for expanded coverage of assessing background knowledge and how differences in this knowledge affect learning.)

Formulas also do not contain measures for mechanical features such as size and style of type and format of the printed material. Type that is too small or too large may adversely affect readability, and some styles of type make reading the material more difficult than do other styles. Additionally, closely packed type, unrelieved by sufficient white space or illustrative material, can make reading more difficult.

Other Methods of Readability Assessment

Formulas may be used to determine which materials should be reasonable to use with a given group of readers. However, there are other means of deciding if material is actually appropriate for specific students. Some of these are discussed below.

Combining Internal and External Factors

Newer approaches to assessing text difficulty are receiving much attention currently. Zakaluk and Samuels (1988) suggest the use of a system that combines consideration of internal factors (level of word recognition skills and knowledge of text topic) and external factors (text readability level and adjunct comprehension aids). They refer to these as "inside the head" and "outside the head" factors. Word recognition skill is rated as either nonaccurate, accurate but not automatic, or accurate and automatic. Knowledge of the text topic is determined by a word association task related to the main idea of the topic of the selection. Readability level is determined by a formula such as Fry's Readability Graph Formula. The adjunct comprehension aids considered are statements of objectives and study questions. Internal and external factors are given values and a special table (called a nomograph) is used to derive a predicted level (high, average, or low) of reading comprehension for a particular student on that passage. Obviously, doing this for each student in the class would be extremely time-consuming, but the results could be valuable in planning more individualized instruction.

Checklists

A checklist approach to assessing readability has been presented by Irwin and Davis (1980). Their excellent checklist is based on accepted psychological research and includes many considerations not covered by readability formulas. Items included in the checklist cover understandability and learnability. Example 6.1 presents the checklist developed by Irwin and Davis.

Phrase Analysis

Another system for assessing comprehensibility has been developed by Clark (1981). It is called the PHAN (phrase analysis) system and considers factors such as reference cohesion, connectives, and vocabulary. The number of phrases between pronouns and their referents and the number of phrases between connected information, the number of inferences the reader must make, and the number of potentially difficult phrase concepts are counted. Using the three totals obtained, passages having the same number of phrases can be compared as to comprehensibility. Higher totals reflect more difficult material. Since the PHAN system does not yield grade-level scores, Clark suggests its use in conjunction with other readability assessments, including formulas.

EXAMPLE **6.1**

Readability Checklist

This checklist is designed to help you evaluate the readability of your classroom texts. It can best be used if you rate your text while you are thinking of a specific class. Be sure to compare the textbook to a fictional ideal rather than to another text. Your goal is to find out what aspects of the text are or are not less than ideal. Finally, consider supplementary workbooks as part of the textbook and rate them together. Have fun!

Rate the questions below using the following rating system:

5 — Excellent
4 — Good
3 — Adequate
2 — Poor
1 — Unacceptable
NA — Not applicable

Further comments may be written in the space provided.

Textbook title: _____

Publisher: _____

Copyright date: _____

UNDERSTANDABILITY

A. _____ Are the assumptions about students' vocabulary knowledge appropriate?

B. _____ Are the assumptions about students' prior knowledge of this content area appropriate?

C. _____ Are the assumptions about students' general experiential backgrounds appropriate?

D. _____ Does the teacher's manual provide the teacher with ways to develop and review the students' conceptual and experiential backgrounds?

E. _____ Are new concepts explicitly linked to the students' prior knowledge or to their experiential backgrounds?

F. _____ Does the text introduce abstract concepts by accompanying them with many concrete examples?

G. _____ Does the text introduce new concepts one at a time with a sufficient number of examples for each one?

H. _____ Are definitions understandable and at a lower level of abstraction than the concept being defined?

I. _____ Is the level of sentence complexity appropriate for the students?

J. _____ Are the main ideas of paragraphs, chapters, and subsections clearly stated?

K. _____ Does the text avoid irrelevant details?

L. _____ Does the text explicitly state important complex relationships (e.g., causality, conditionality, etc.) rather than always expecting the reader to infer them from the context?

M. _____ Does the teacher's manual provide lists of accessible resources containing alternative readings for the very poor or very advanced readers?

N. _____ Is the readability level appropriate (according to a readability formula)?

LEARNABILITY

Organization

A. _____ Is an introduction provided for in each chapter?

B. _____ Is there a clear and simple organizational pattern relating the chapters to each other?

C. _____ Does each chapter have a clear, explicit, and simple organizational structure?

D. _____ Does the text include resources such as an index, glossary, and table of contents?

E. _____ Do questions and activities draw attention to the organizational pattern of the material (e.g., chronological, cause and effect, spatial, topical, etc.)?

F. _____ Do consumable materials interrelate well with the textbook?

Reinforcement

A. _____ Does the text provide opportunities for students to practice using new concepts?

B. _____ Are there summaries at appropriate intervals in the text?

C. _____ Does the text provide adequate iconic aids such as maps, graphs, illustrations, etc., to reinforce concepts?

D. _____ Are there adequate suggestions for usable supplementary activities?

E. _____ Do these activities provide for a broad range of ability levels?

F. _____ Are there literal recall questions provided for the students' self review?

G. _____ Do some of the questions encourage the students to draw inferences?

H. _____ Are there discussion questions which encourage creative thinking?

I. _____ Are questions clearly worded?

Motivation

A. _____ Does the teacher's manual provide introductory activities that will capture students' interest?

B. _____ Are chapter titles and subheadings concrete, meaningful, or interesting?

C. _____ Is the writing style of the text appealing to the students?

D. _____ Are the activities motivating? Will they make the student want to pursue the topic further?

E. _____ Does the book clearly show how the knowledge being learned might be used by the learner in the future?

F. _____ Are the cover, format, print size, and pictures appealing to the students?

G. _____ Does the text provide positive and motivating models for both sexes as well as for other racial, ethnic, and socioeconomic groups?

READABILITY ANALYSIS

Weaknesses

   1) On which items was the book rated the lowest?
   2) Did these items tend to fall in certain categories?
   3) Summarize the weaknesses of this text.
   4) What can you do in class to compensate for the weaknesses of this text?

Assets

   1) On which items was the book rated the highest?
   2) Did these items fall in certain categories?
   3) Summarize the assets of this text.
   4) What can you do in class to take advantage of the assets of this text?

Source: Judith Westphal Irwin and Carol A. Davis, "Assessing Readability: The Checklist Approach." *Journal of Reading* 24 (November 1980), pp. 129–130. Reprinted with permission of Judith W. Irwin and the International Reading Association.

A Questioning Procedure

Clewell and Clifton (1983) decided upon the characteristics of a comprehensible text and then composed a list of questions that teachers should ask about a textbook in an attempt to determine its comprehensibility. The questions are arranged under the headings of textual aids, content, coherence, types of discourse, and language and style. Teachers can use the questions to make decisions related to text adoptions and instructional procedures to use with already adopted texts.

User Involvement Techniques

Some techniques involve trying out representative portions of the material on prospective users. These techniques take into account reader interest, reader background, author's writing style and organization, abstractness of concepts, and, except for the cloze test, they also may include consideration of format and type size and style. Three of these techniques are cloze tests, group reading inventory selections, and informal reading inventory selections. (See Chapter 10 for a more detailed discussion of these three techniques.)

Cloze tests involve systematic deletion of every fifth word in a 250-word passage and substitution of blanks of uniform length for these words (Taylor, 1956; Bormuth, 1968). Students are asked to fill in the blanks. Only exact words are scored as acceptable. Scores of 44 to 57 percent correct indicate instructional level material for the students; lower scores indicate material that is too difficult; higher scores indicate material suitable for independent use by the students. Chance (1985) found the cloze procedure to be a quick and reliable way to determine the readability of specific material for individual students. He also verified that subject matter teachers find it easy to construct cloze tests and use them for determining readability.

Group Reading Inventories (Shepherd, 1982) and Informal Reading Inventories (Betts, 1946; Johnson and Kress, 1987; Valmont, 1972) consist of representative passages chosen from the textbook in question, 1,000 to 2,000 words long for group reading inventories and approximately 200 words long for informal reading inventories. The passages are accompanied by carefully prepared sets of comprehension questions. See the discussions in Chapter 10 for question types, examples, and explanations. Comprehension scores of 75 percent to 90 percent on either type of inventory are considered indicative of instructional level material; higher scores indicate independent level material; and scores below 50 percent indicate material that is too difficult. Scores between 50 percent and 75 percent could be either at the instructional or the frustration level. Teachers should use other indicators, such as signs of student restlessness when reading, frowning, and other signs of discomfort, to help determine whether the material is actually too hard. The informal reading inventory also includes a word recognition indicator of difficulty level: 95 to 99 percent accuracy signals the instructional level; 99 to 100 percent signals the independent level; and under 90 percent signals the frustration level. Both word recognition and comprehension criteria must be met for a passage to be considered independent or instructional level on an informal reading inventory; however, if either frustration level criterion is met, the passage is considered to be too difficult.

Grouping for Motivation and Differentiated Assignments

Grouping is important when students are asked to complete reading assignments because, as has been shown earlier in this text, all students cannot perform reading tasks at the same levels. In content area classrooms grouping is not necessary for all assignments, however, since all students are able to function together when doing many nonreading tasks or performing reading tasks that are easy enough for all participants. As illustrated by the cases presented later in this section, members of different achievement groups (as determined by standardized reading test scores and a readability formula or by one of the informal assessment measures) should be given differentiated reading assignments. One group may read the textbook independently, perhaps in conjunction with a teacher-created study guide or with a list of purposes constructed by the students themselves. Another group may use the textbook as the teacher guides them through a directed reading lesson. Still another group may use only the pictures and graphic aids in the actual text while reading material of a lower level of difficulty on the topic; this less difficult material may have been located by the teacher or it may be textual material that the teacher has rewritten to a lower difficulty level. Tapes, films, filmstrips, and other audiovisual aids may also be used to present material to these students (and to the entire class). After a whole-class discussion of the material covered, the teacher may develop a summary in language experience style and use it for reading material with this group in subsequent study sessions. All these approaches are discussed in more detail later in this chapter.

Teachers who know the results of reading tests that have been administered to their students (see Chapter 10 for a discussion of testing) and know the readability levels of the textbooks to be used can determine if the textbooks are appropriate, too easy, or too difficult for each student in the class. An illustration of grouping procedures based on such information is given in the following case.

CASE: NINTH-GRADE SCIENCE CLASS

Mrs. Jones is a ninth-grade science teacher. After using the Fry Readability Formula, she discovers that the science textbook assigned to her class has a readability level of ninth grade. Examination of norm-referenced reading test results for the students in her class reveals this information:

Reading Grade Level (Instructional)	Number of Students
11	3
10	5
9	10
8	9
7	4
6	2
5	1
	34

Using the science textbook itself, she administers a cloze test to the class to help her confirm that those students reading at a ninth grade instructional level or above can in fact handle this textbook.

In order to have optimum utilization of the textbook, Mrs. Jones divides her class into instructional groups. Group *A* includes the eight students with instructional reading levels of grades 10 and 11. These students can read the textbook independently, without the teacher's constant supervision. They can set their own purposes for reading most of the time, or at least work cooperatively with the teacher on purpose setting.

Group *B* includes the ten students reading at a ninth-grade level, who can profit from the textbook with the aid of the teacher. Mrs. Jones needs to prepare them carefully for the reading, setting purposes for them or helping them set their own purposes. As they proceed with the reading, she needs to be available to help them with any difficulties they might encounter.

Group *C* includes the sixteen students reading at levels ranging from grade 5 to grade 8. These students would be frustrated by the reading demands of the textbook and need to have alternate material. Mrs. Jones provides rewritten text material, alternate textbooks, and supplementary library books for them. Obviously, the span of reading levels within Group *C* is too great for all of the students to use identical materials all of the time. Rewritten text material at the fifth-grade level is utilized by the entire group. Mrs. Jones chooses alternate texts, as well as supplementary library books, to fit each student's reading level. The information learned by each individual from the various sources are synthesized through group discussion and individual presentations of summary statements. Mrs. Jones elicits these statements through the use of the language experience approach (discussed later in this chapter).

Group *C* is able to utilize the textbook to a limited degree. For instance, all members of the group can study the graphic aids offered in the textual material. In addition, at times the nine students reading on the eighth-grade level can use a limited portion of the written text with extensive help from the teacher.

Whole-class discussion follows the study of a topic by the three individual groups. The less able readers are able to contribute to the discussion, having studied the subject from material that they can understand. They learn additional information from the whole class discussion because the better readers have gained more insights into the overall subject through their superior ability to do critical reading. As the better readers discuss the concepts presented in the material, these concepts are clarified for others in the class.

This illustration of grouping procedure is an example of *achievement grouping,* or grouping students on the basis of their general ability to read material at certain levels with understanding. There are other types of grouping within a class that may facilitate differentiation of assignments or provide motivation for completing assignments. These include *needs groups, student tutorial groups, partnerships, interest groups, research groups, cooperative learning groups,* and *friendship groups.* Each type is discussed below.

1. Needs groups. Some students in a class may have trouble with basic reading skills, which may impede their understanding of the content of the subject area textbook. For example, some students may have difficulty identifying main ideas. This will make study of any subject area difficult. Some students may not be able to read to follow directions. Work in science, mathematics, art, and vocational subjects will suffer greatly. Some students may be unable to read maps adequately. Social studies and even science classes often require students to be able to handle map-reading tasks in order to completely understand the material. Some students may not be able to recognize common prefixes and suffixes. This skill is very important in many science and mathematics classes. The examples could go on and on.

A teacher may form needs groups, each consisting of students who lack or are weak in a particular skill. The needs group members may not all be from the same achievement group (or at the same reading level) because many of the best students have gaps in their reading skill development corresponding to those of poorer students. The teacher can use materials specially designed to aid students in applying needed skills to the content area involved. A needs group can be assembled when the rest of the class is involved in other purposeful activity, such as doing research, working on a study guide, or doing supplementary reading from library books.

Needs groups are formed when students exhibit specific needs; they are disbanded when those needs have been met. Some students will require only one or two meetings to achieve the desired goal; others will need more time. No student should be retained in a needs group after he or she has mastered the needed skill.

2. *Student tutorial groups.* While the teacher is busy working with one group of students (either an achievement or a needs group), another group of students can be assisted by a classmate who has achieved mastery in a particular area. Student tutors must be given explicit instructions as to their responsibilities. They must know exactly what they should and should not do to help classmates. (For example, if a tutor merely tells other students answers, which might be considered helpful by the classmates, he or she would not bring about the results desired by the teacher.) Student tutors can be particularly helpful in supervising the completion of study guide assignments, which are discussed later in this chapter.

Student tutorial groups generally prove beneficial to both the tutor and the "clients." The student tutor often achieves a more complete understanding of the material in attempting to explain it to classmates or in attempting to clarify students' incomplete concepts or correct their misconceptions. Being placed in the position of student tutor is also an ego-satisfying experience. While the tutor benefits from his or her experience, classmates generally improve their skills. Some of them may be able to express their difficulties more easily to a fellow student than to a teacher, and the student tutor may be able to explain ideas in the students' own language more adeptly than the teacher.

When student tutorial groups are used, the teacher must be careful to choose students who can work together. Some students tend to be more disruptive when in the presence of certain other classmates. Such combinations should be avoided, since they cannot possibly result in the desired outcomes. It should be clearly understood by all the group members that any disruptive behavior will result in immediate disbanding of the group.

Roles in student tutorial groups should not be static; that is, one or two students should not always be tutors while the others are always in the role of clients. As many different students as possible should be allowed to function in the role of tutor. There should, of course, be the limitation that no student can act as a tutor in a situation where he or she is not competent.

3. *Partnerships*. When two (or possibly more) students have nearly attained mastery of a skill or when they have marginal competence to complete an assigned task, the teacher may decide to set up a partnership grouping. In such a grouping, the students are presented with a task (for example, a study guide) to be completed and are allowed to pool their resources in order to complete it successfully. Each individual is likely to accomplish more in such a partnership than by working alone at a task, and success is strong positive reinforcement for the activity or skill involved. Being successful also tends to motivate the students to continue to try in successive reading tasks.

Teachers must be as careful in choosing students for partnerships as they are in choosing students for tutorial groups. Disruptive partnerships should be dissolved immediately. Setting a very specific task and a time limit for the partners to complete it may help a partnership remain task-oriented. Partners may work together while the teacher is involved with other groups.

4. *Interest groups*. When units are being taught in the content areas, many possibilities for additional student reading are available, often more than the teacher wishes to utilize. In such cases the teacher may allow class members to choose areas of interest for supplementary reading. The students who choose the same area may be formed into an interest group, asked to read individually in the area of interest, and brought together to discuss the material read with the other group members. The group may be charged with the responsibility of communicating its findings to the whole class through a formal report, a panel discussion, a dramatization, or some other means. Individual group members may be on different achievement levels in reading; they can read materials designed for their own individual levels and then can contribute their findings to the group as a whole.

Interest groups are motivational because the students are allowed to pick their own subjects for reading. They also help to avoid the stigma that is sometimes attached to members of low achievement groups because they provide an opportunity for these students to be mixed with students from other groups to work and study.

5. *Research groups*. Research groups are similar to interest groups in that a group of students read independently about a particular topic, discuss it together, and share their findings with the class as a whole. These groups are different from interest groups in that the topics and group members are assigned by the teacher. The teacher may deliberately mix students with varying strengths and weaknesses in order to capitalize on each group mem-

ber's strengths and to enable students with specific weaknesses to learn from those with corresponding strengths. The groups may need to be closely monitored to ensure that these results are achieved. Research groups do not have the built-in motivation for reading content that interest groups do. They do, however, provide an intermingling of students from varying achievement levels.

6. *Cooperative learning groups.* Cooperative learning groups are formed so that students can serve as learning resources for each other. They are small groups of students of mixed abilities formed to learn academic material together (Slavin, 1989).

Researchers have found that significant gains in achievement, self-esteem, and social development occur when instructional techniques involve cooperation and collaboration. In addition to achieving gains in these areas, students display greater motivation to learn, more positive attitudes toward instruction, a decrease in dependence on the teacher, and greater acceptance of student differences, among other positive effects (Wood, 1987).

A variety of techniques are used with cooperative groups. One is the Student Teams-Achievement Divisions (STAD), in which the teacher presents a lesson and, subsequently, students work to master the lesson's content in four-member teams. They may discuss the ideas presented, drill each other on facts, or work cooperatively in solving problems. Although students are tested individually on the material, teams may receive certificates for average team scores (Slavin, 1986).

Johnson and Johnson (1986) have small groups of students work together on worksheet activities. They attempt to come to a consensus on responses. Their grades may be partially affected by the average score attained by the individual members of their groups.

Aronson and others (1978) developed a technique called jigsaw teaching in which each member of a mixed-ability learning group becomes an expert on a particular aspect of the material to be learned. One person from each group has each aspect. Students read about their own aspects and pool information with students in the other groups who are studying the same aspects. Then each group member teaches his or her original group about the aspect of the material on which he or she has become an expert. A form of jigsaw teaching developed by Slavin (1986) is Jigsaw II. It is useful for studying material that is in written narrative form.

In Jigsaw II, heterogeneous groups of students are assigned chapters or stories to be read. A term should "represent a cross section of the class in past performance, race or ethnicity, and sex" (Slavin, 1989, p. 334). The teacher provides Expert Sheets, which specify the different topics on which the team members are to concentrate. Expert groups of students focusing on the same topic meet for discussion of their topics, as in the regular jigsaw arrangement, and they teach what they have learned to their classmates. Testing also oc-

216

curs. In both approaches, interdependence of the students is important — they depend on their teammates to provide information to help them perform well on quizzes (Slavin, 1989).

7. *Friendship groups.* At times, class members can be allowed to work on certain assignments with friends of their choice. This type of grouping is motivational and may be highly beneficial for some students. Other students may be unable to conduct themselves properly under such conditions. Friendship groups should be used with discretion.

Montague and Tanner (1987, p. 716) point out that "research indicates that small group instruction, cooperative learning, and active participation of students and teachers are important elements of effective instruction, particularly for low achieving students." They recommend having students work in small, cooperative groups of individuals who have found that the same reading strategy (for example, SQ3R [see Chapter 4] or DRTA) is the most efficient for them. The group members may use the strategy together to complete the assignment, or they may use it independently but assist each other in its use, as needed.

All teacher-assigned groups should be flexible. In achievement groups, for example, some students may experience sudden spurts in attaining reading skills and should be transferred to higher groups. Other students, because of extensive absences, emotional difficulties, or other reasons, may fall behind the group in which they have been placed. These students should be moved to lower groups, at least temporarily. In needs groups, students are included and dismissed as their needs are detected and met. Student tutorial groups, partnerships, and research groups last only until the assigned task is completed.

As the teacher works with the achievement groups, he or she may discover the need to form needs groups, student tutorial groups, or partnership groups for students who lack the mastery of a specific skill. If all students in the class lack such mastery, whole-class instruction on the skill may be in order.

Especially when a unit approach to teaching is being used in the class, the teacher may find it effective to form some interest groups or research groups or may decide to utilize friendship groups for motivational purposes. Research groups may be formed to capitalize on the special abilities of various class members, and assignments should take varying reading levels into consideration.

Ned Ratekin and others (1985) found from observations in classrooms that the grade 8 and grade 11 English and mathematics teachers in their study did not use small-group instruction, whereas social studies teachers spent 4 percent and science teachers 12 percent of the class time in small group instruction. Instructional strategies involving student interaction, shared predictions, and verification activities can best be carried out in small-group situations. The teachers in the observational study relied heavily on lecture-discussion and on monitoring students working individually.

Strategies for Guiding Content Area Reading

Three effective ways to guide reading assignments are through use of study guides, directed reading approaches, and directed reading-thinking activities. These techniques may be used separately or, in the case of study guides and directed reading approaches, concurrently in some situations. Study guides and directed reading approaches are teacher-directed activities, whereas directed reading-thinking activities are student-centered.

Study Guides

One of the most valuable strategies for increasing students' comprehension of content materials is use of the study guide. Armstrong and others (1988) found study guides to be helpful for narrative materials as well. A study guide is a "set of suggestions designed to lead the student through a reading assignment by directing attention to the key ideas in a passage and suggesting the application of skills needed to read a passage successfully" (Harris and Hodges, 1981, p. 313). It simulates events in the comprehension process to some extent in an attempt to help students comprehend the material better (Armstrong et al., 1988). A study guide creates a point of contact between the student and the written material, showing readers *how to comprehend* content.

The composition of a study guide is determined by the instructor's reasons for having students read the content material and by the students' needs. A study guide may cover a chapter, a larger unit, or merely part of a long chapter. If students are given a study guide to read before they read an assignment, they can respond to the questions and activities in the study guide as they read the content selection. These guides may take a variety of forms. Throughout this text there are examples of a number of different study guides that can be varied to fit particular selections.

A single study guide may set purposes for reading, provide aids for interpretation of the material, or do both. Study guides are particularly valuable when the teacher employs grouping in the content class. They can be designed in such a way that the different groups have differentiated assignments based on the same textbook material, or separate guides can be prepared for different groups and based on assignment of reading materials on different levels of difficulty. Each small group of students can sit together, work through their study guide individually, and then discuss their answers with each other. During the discussion, the group members try to reconcile any differences they discover in their answers. A whole-class discussion may follow the small-group sessions. All class members will have something to contribute from their learning during the guided reading or during their ensuing group discussion.

Handling material this way causes the students to think about the material they are reading; critical thinking is necessary when small groups try to reach a consensus about certain answers. Thinking is also necessary later, when the different groups perceive how all of their findings fit together. Retention of material is aided by the act of critically thinking about it.

Example 6.2 shows a science selection followed by a study guide. The content of this selection is also typical of health and home economics textbooks. The study guide sets purposes for reading (content guidance) and provides aids for interpretation of the material (process guidance).

E X A M P L E **6.2**

Science Selection and Study Guide

Food Additives: A Danger, a Safeguard, or Both?

Every day suppliers deliver tons of food items to grocery stores all over the country. Most of this food has traveled hundreds of miles from farms and processing plants. Food can take days, weeks, or even months to reach your table. Did you ever wonder what kept food from spoiling on its journey?

Since many foods travel long distances before reaching the market, certain chemicals are added to prevent spoilage during shipment and storage. Other chemicals, or food additives, improve texture, prevent caking, or provide extra vitamins and minerals. Some additives make foods look more appealing by adding colored vegetable dyes.

Even though government agencies test foods and additives to be sure they are safe, some research indicates that certain food additives can cause cancer in laboratory animals.

Nitrites and nitrates are common additives in meat, fish, and poultry. At first, these chemicals were added because their interaction with bacteria made the food look fresher longer. Later, scientists found that nitrites act as preservatives. They slow down the growth of bacteria that cause botulism, a food poisoning that is often fatal.

A committee supported by the National Academy of Sciences reported in December, 1981, that the cancer risk to humans from nitrites is small but genuine. The committee recommended that the amounts of nitrites added to foods be lowered, but that enough be added to protect against botulism. One way to safely add nitrites to food is to also add vitamins C and E. Other methods to prevent botulism without adding nitrites are being tested. These methods include using ionizing radiation, which kills bacteria, adding nonpoisonous chemicals such as potassium sorbate, and adding bacteria that lower the meat's pH, inhibiting the growth of botulism bacteria.

Additives can be both helpful and harmful. If you want to eliminate additives from your diet, you might have to give up many foods. For instance, you might have to limit your diet to foods which can be grown in your part of the country. You might also have to prepare many foods "from scratch." On the other hand perhaps the inconvenience and forgoing of certain foods would be safer for us all in the long run. More information is needed before definite conclusions can be drawn.

Analysis

1. What standards or criteria would you set for the use of food additives?
2. Look at labels and find out what additives are in some of your favorite foods.

Source: From SCOTT, FORESMAN BIOLOGY by Irwin L. Slesnick, et al. Copyright © 1985 by Scott, Foresman and Company. Reprinted by permission of HarperCollins, Publishers.

Study Guide

Overview Questions: What are the positive and negative aspects of food additives? How do you feel about eating foods containing additives?

1. Read the first paragraph to find out how long it may take food items to arrive at their final destinations. What does the author mean by the phrase "to reach your table"?
2. Read the second paragraph to find out what food additives are. (Two context clues are there to help you.)
3. What are five different uses of food additives?
4. Read the third paragraph to find out the effect that food additives may have on laboratory animals.
5. Read the fourth paragraph. It tells two advantages of using nitrites and nitrates as additives. What are they?
6. What is a preservative? (Think about the root word of preservative and use the meaning of this word to help you decide.)
7. What is botulism? (Use the context to help you answer.) Why would you want to avoid botulism?
8. Read the fifth paragraph. Is the cancer risk to humans from nitrites real? What word tells you so?
9. How can nitrites safely be added to food?
10. What are some methods being tested to prevent botulism without adding nitrites?
11. Read the last paragraph. If you wanted to avoid additives, what two things might you have to do and why? What does it mean to prepare food "from scratch"? (The words do not mean what they usually do.)

The study guide in Example 6.2 could be used for all students who can read the textbook, with or without teacher assistance; however, if a teacher wanted to reduce the length of the guide, some questions could be assigned to both groups and other questions could be divided between the groups. For example, all students might complete items 1, 2, 4, 5, 8, and 11, which would provide some guidance through the entire selection. The other questions could be divided between the two groups as the teacher thought appropriate, although the items designed to aid in interpretation of the material might be best used with the instructional group. The teacher may work closely with the instructional-level group members as they discuss their assigned questions and may monitor the independent-level group less intensively. The group that cannot handle the text material should be given another reading assignment in order to learn the content. This group should have its own study guide, geared to its assignment. The whole-class discussion that follows the small-group sessions with the guides will help all the students clarify their concepts and see relationships among the ideas.

The instructional intent of the teacher can be seen by looking carefully at the study guide in Example 6.2. First, overview questions are presented. These questions are designed to focus on the understandings that students are expected to have gained when the entire selection has been read. They give purpose to the reading of an entire selection, often require critical and/or creative reading abilities, and lead to more complete comprehension. The remainder of the guide provides a series of questions and guidance statements that are arranged sequentially in the order in which they are needed in the reading. The students are expected to read the first numbered item, read the selection to find the answer to that question or use the skill suggested, and then repeat the process with the next question or guidance statement.

Three-Level Guides

A three-level study guide is one in which the student is guided toward comprehension at the literal level (understanding ideas that are directly stated), the interpretive level (reading between the lines), and the applied level (reading to use information to solve problems) (Herber, 1978). (See Chapter 3, Reading Comprehension, for a discussion of comprehension levels or types and for an explanation of the fact that cognitive skills at different levels are often employed simultaneously.) A three-level guide can be especially useful with literature selections. The guide in Example 6.3 is designed for use with the short story "The Man Without a Country," by Edward Everett Hale.

Riley (1980) emphasizes the value of these three-level guides in stimulat-

EXAMPLE **6.3**

Three-Level Study Guide

Directions: Check the statement or statements under each level that answer the question.

LITERAL — WHAT DID THE AUTHOR SAY ABOUT PHILIP NOLAN?

_____ 1. Philip Nolan said, "I wish I may never hear of the United States again!"
_____ 2. Philip Nolan never actually met Aaron Burr.

_____ 3. The court decided that Nolan should never hear the name of the United States again.

_____ 4. Nolan was placed on board a ship and never allowed to return to the United States.

_____ 5. Nolan was often permitted to go on shore.

_____ 6. Nolan did not intentionally make it difficult for the people who were supposed to keep him from knowing about his country.

INTERPRETIVE — WHAT DID THE AUTHOR MEAN BY HIS STORY?

_____ 1. Nolan never seriously regretted having denied his country.

_____ 2. Nolan spoke against his country without realizing how much it had meant to him.

_____ 3. Nolan never really missed hearing about his country.

APPLIED — HOW CAN THE MEANING BE APPLIED TO OUR LIVES?

_____ 1. People should consider the consequences of their actions before they act.

_____ 2. People can live comfortably away from home.

_____ 3. Punishment is not always physical; it may be mental.

ing the comprehension process. He offers an extensive example of how such guides can be utilized in a content classroom. In his example, a three-level guide was presented with a poem to several small groups. The students in each group examined the statements and then looked in the poem for evidence to support each statement. They discussed these statements in their groups as the teacher listened to the group interaction. The teacher then questioned the groups about their responses to each of the statements that might have caused difficulty or controversy, asking for the supporting evidence from the poem. If insufficient evidence was offered, the teacher asked for further explanation. If there were widely differing views presented in the small-group discussion, the teacher asked about any disagreements. Riley (1980, p. 720) points out that the teacher tried "to *recognize* students' responses, to *infer processes* underlying those responses, and to *value* students' initial responses as ones to build upon" and to encourage "the students to *generalize* their attempts at understanding the material to similar situations." Teachers can and should do all these things when using any study guide, not just three-level guides.

Bean and Ericson (1989) suggested using text previews and three-level guides to promote content area critical reading. Text previews are a type of advance organizer containing three sections: "(1) an interest building section which includes an analogy to students' experience; (2) a brief synopsis of the selection; and (3) an explanation of any difficult vocabulary along with questions that guide the reader" (p. 338). (More on advance organizers can be found in Chapter 3, Reading Comprehension.)

Preview Guides

A preview guide is designed to help students relate what they are about to read to their own experiential backgrounds. Although in its simplest form the preview guide may be a request to, for example, "list everything you already know about word processing," it is likely to be more structured. In one form of the guide, the student is given a list of statements before reading and is asked to place a check mark next to the statements that are substantiated by the reading after it has been completed. Students may also be asked to revise statements that were proved wrong by the reading and to put question marks beside items that were not addressed by the reading. All three types of items should be brought out in class discussion.

In more structured forms of the guide, the teacher may begin the lesson by presenting statements or questions about the material to be read. Before the students have read the material, they can be asked to indicate whether they believe the statements are true or false, or they can be asked to answer the questions. After completing the reading, they should check the accuracy of the answers they gave. Example 6.4 shows a preview guide of the more structured form.

Duffelmeyer and others (1987) refer to the more structured preview guides as "anticipation guides" and suggest that teachers include in them

EXAMPLE **6.4**

Preview Guide

Directions: Before you read the chapter, answer the following question to the best of your ability by placing check marks beside your chosen responses. After you finish reading the chapter, check the accuracy of your responses.

What functions are possible with word processing software that are not possible with a standard typewriter?

1. Straight typing of sentences
2. Deleting a word in a paragraph after the paragraph is typed
3. Typing the material with one set of margins and then changing the margins without retyping
4. Underlining
5. Moving material from one paragraph to another without retyping
6. Setting up typed material in tabular form
7. Inserting material in the middle of a paragraph without retyping the paragraph
8. Copying a paragraph to another section of a document without retyping
9. Inserting material at the end of a selection without retyping the paragraph
10. Using footnotes with superscripts

statements that are compatible with the text, but not intuitively appealing, and statements that are incompatible with the text, but intuitively appealing. They also suggest taking a basic anticipation guide in which the students respond to the statements before reading with "agree" or "disagree" and adding to it a portion to be completed after the reading in which they indicate for which items their predictions were supported by the reading and for which items their predictions were not confirmed. When one of their predictions was not confirmed, the students would write in their own words the information from the text that was counter to the prediction.

Pattern Guides

A pattern guide focuses on the organizational pattern of the text. If a text is organized according to a cause-and-effect pattern, for example, the guide would highlight causes and effects. Some possible focuses for pattern guides other than cause and effect are sequence, comparison/contrast, and categorization (Olson and Longnion, 1982). A pattern guide activates a reader's schema for the particular organizational pattern involved. (Chapters 3, 8, and 9 provide information about organizational patterns frequently found in various subject areas, and Chapter 3 contains information on schema activation.) Below is a comparison/contrast guide for a selection from a biology text (Example 6.5).

E X A M P L E **6.5**

Comparison/Contrast Guide

Directions: Read the selection about flowers and animal pollinators and then fill in the chart below to help you compare and contrast flowers pollinated by bees and moths with flowers pollinated by birds.

Flowers Pollinated by Birds	Flowers Pollinated by Bees	Flowers Pollinated by Moths
Usually red or yellow		
Petals fused into a		
long tube that holds		
nectar		

Flowers and Animal Pollinators: Made for Each Other

With rapidly beating wings the hummingbird hovers over the flower. Its long bill plunges deep inside the flower to gather the sweet nectar. As the bird flies away, its head is covered with a dusting of pollen from the flower's stamens. When the hummingbird visits the next flower, the pollen on its head will be brushed off to pollinate the flower.

Because flowering plants cannot move about as animals do to accomplish fertilization, they rely on other means of transferring pollen. Many flowers are pollinated by birds or insects. Scientists are taking an interest in studying the amazing adaptations of flowers that allow certain animals to pollinate them.

Birds have a poor sense of smell, but have excellent vision. So bird-pollinated flowers rely on color to attract their pollinators. Birds' eyes are most sensitive to the red end of the spectrum, so bird-pollinated flowers are usually red or yellow. Bird-pollinated flowers include hibiscus, red columbine, and fuchsia. Bird-flower petals are usually fused into a long tube that holds large quantities of nectar. When a bird inserts its long bill to reach the nectar, pollen is brushed off the stamens onto its head or breast.

Bee-pollinated flowers are usually brightly colored blue or yellow since bees' vision is most sensitive to this end of the spectrum. Bee-pollinated flowers also give off a sweet scent since bees are attracted to sweet or minty odors. Bee-pollinated flowers are usually open only during the day when bees are flying. Many bee-pollinated flowers have at least one protruding petal that serves as a landing platform for the bees. The nectar is usually hidden deep in the flower, but many flowers have *nectar guides* that point the way to the nectar. In violets and irises the nectar guide is a series of lines; in Turk's-cap lilies it is a cluster of spots in the center of the flower. Petunias and morning glories have a star-shaped pattern that surrounds the nectar opening.

But some nectar guides are not visible to humans. Bees can see them because their eyes are sensitive to ultraviolet light. To the human eye the marsh marigold flower appears solid yellow. But to the bee, only the center of the flower appears yellow. The outer part of the flower reflects a mixture of yellow and ultraviolet light called *bee purple*.

Moth-pollinated flowers are generally white or pale yellow, and are easily visible at dusk or night when moths are most active. Many moth flowers are open only during late afternoon or evening. Moth flowers have a strong, sweet scent and include orchids, evening primroses, and night-blooming cactuses. Since moths hover while feeding, moth-pollinated flowers do not have landing platforms.

The relationship between flowers and their animal pollinators is beneficial to both organisms. The animals secure food and the flowers get pollinated. Many scientists think that flowers and their animal pollinators coevolved to suit each other's needs.

Source: From SCOTT, FORESMAN BIOLOGY by Irwin L. Slesnick, et al. Copyright © 1985 by Scott, Foresman and Company. Reprinted by permission of HarperCollins, Publishers.

Analogical Guides

Bean and others (1985) suggested the use of analogical study guides for science instruction. An example of such a guide on cell structure and function

Cell Structure-Function Analogical Study Guide

Structure	Main Functions	Analogy (comparing the cell to a factory)
cell wall	support; protection	factory walls
cell membrane	boundary, gatekeeper	security guards
cytoplasm	site of most metabolism	the work area
centrioles	cell reproduction	?
chloroplasts	photosynthesis	snack bar
endoplasmic reticulum	intracellular transport	conveyor belts
golgi bodies	storage, secretion	packaging, storage, and shipping
lysosomes	intracellular digestion	clean-up crew
microfilaments	movement	?
microtubules	support; movement	?
mitochondria	cellular respiration	energy generation plant
nucleus	control; heredity	boss's office, copy machine
ribosomes	protein synthesis	assembly line
vacuoles	storage	warehouses

Source: Thomas W. Bean, Harry Singer, and Stan Cowan, "Analogical Study Guides: Improving Comprehension in Science," *Journal of Reading,* 29 (December 1985), 249. Reprinted with permission of Thomas W. Bean and the International Reading Association.

relationships is shown in Example 6.6. In this example, Bean and others compared the parts of a cell and their functions to the parts of a factory. They offered three steps for construction of these guides: "(1) Analyze the reading assignment for appropriate concepts. (2) Create appropriate analogies in a complete or skeletal guide. (3) Instruct students in the use of analogies as reading and retrieval cues" (Bean et al., 1985, p. 250).

Reasoning Guides

A type of guide that may be used to help develop post-reading reasoning skills is called a reasoning guide by Herber (1978, p. 124), who says that it "can be thought of as an applied-level guide standing alone." This guide may look exactly like the applied-level portion of a three-level guide, but it is used after students have read the selection. It may also have a format that differs somewhat from the statements in the applied level of the guide in Example 6.3. For example, rather than having a list of statements, it could contain a list of words, as in Example 6.7.

E X A M P L E **6.7**

Reasoning Guide

Directions: Each of the words below may have something to do with the story "The Man Without a Country." If you think a particular word applies in any way to the story or to a person or event in the story, place a check on the line before the word. Be ready to tell your reason for checking each word.

_____ treason	_____ thoughtlessness
_____ disowned	_____ court-martial
_____ considerate	_____ confined
_____ punishment	_____ prisoner
_____ courage	_____ kindness
_____ isolation	_____ suffering
_____ loyalty	_____ shrine
_____ harsh	_____ compassion
_____ repentant	_____ reconciled

Directed Reading Lessons

A directed reading lesson is a method for guiding students through the reading of a textbook selection. It is used most often with basal reader selections but can be adapted for use with content area selections. Directed reading approaches vary from source to source in the number of steps involved, but the following components are present in all the plans:

1. Motivation and building of background
2. Skill development activities
3. Guided reading of the story
   a. Silent reading
   b. Discussion and oral reading (when appropriate)
4. Follow-up activities

The first step — *motivation and building of background* — consists of the following elements: a discussion of background concepts needed to understand the selection and of the relationship of content to the background experiences of the students; some discussion of difficult vocabulary; and a preview of the selection to see what type of information will be presented. The teacher may wish to help build background by using films, filmstrips, slides, still pictures, models, or other visual aids. These aids ordinarily generate some motivation to study the passage. Discussion of the way the content relates to their own lives can also be motivational for the students. Research has shown that developing students' backgrounds of experiences in a topic before they read about it can improve their comprehension of material on that topic (Stevens, 1982).

The structured overview, explained in Chapter 2, is a technique developed by Barron (1969) that can be used in a directed reading lesson for developing readiness to read. It involves using a graphic arrangement of terms that apply to the important concepts in the passage.

To introduce a reading assignment, the teacher can show the students a structured overview and explain why the terms are arranged in the order chosen. He or she can encourage students to participate in the discussion and to contribute any background information they might have. Then, as the assignment is carried out, the teacher and students continue to relate new information to the overview, which provides a framework for understanding the content. Example 6.8 shows a sample structured overview in the area of atomic structure. Other examples of structured overviews may be found in *Improving Reading in Science,* 2nd ed., by Judith Thelan (Newark, Del.: International Reading Association, 1984).

E X A M P L E **6.8**

Structured Overview

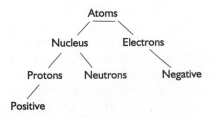

Students are more likely to benefit from structured overviews if they actively participate in the construction. For example, they can be given vocabulary terms on slips of paper and can be encouraged to place them in a logical arrangement that shows relationships. The teacher can then see what initial information the students have and can correct any erroneous impressions. The activity could be repeated after the assignment has been studied in order to assess the students' comprehension of the interrelated concepts presented.

Structured overviews, such as the one illustrated in Example 6.8; chapter overviews; and even chapter summaries all may be used by teachers as advance organizers for students who are about to read material in a textbook. Advance organizers are materials given to the students to read before starting a chapter assignment. Approaching a selection in this way helps the students to grasp the author's organization and to read the body of the text purposefully. (More on advance organizers may be found in Chapter 3, Reading Comprehension.) If a structured overview does not seem to be the best approach for guiding the reading, and if no chapter overview is provided to

228

point out main ideas and important concepts, the teacher may direct the students to read the end-of-chapter summary before they read the chapter. If there is no chapter summary, the teacher may wish to provide a list of main points and important concepts, in simplified terms, as an advance organizer.

Previewing the selection — reading the title, the introduction, the bold-face headings, and the summary — gives students a framework into which they can fit the ideas they gain through reading. A brief examination of the graphic aids — pictures, maps, graphs, and diagrams — may also be helpful.

The second step — *skill development activities* — includes direct teaching of vocabulary, word recognition skills, comprehension skills, and study skills. The skills taught should be those the students will need to use when reading the selection; for example, if the students need to read a map in the story, a map-reading lesson would be in order.

Difficult vocabulary words that are not clearly explained by the context may need to be presented before the students are asked to read the assign-ment. Vocabulary words that have appropriate context clues should *not* be presented; students should use their reading skills to determine the meanings of these words. Students also should be alerted to and encouraged to use the glossaries included in many content area textbooks.

The third step — *guided reading of the selection* — includes both setting purposes for reading and actually reading. Purposes for reading may be de-veloped in different ways. They may be in the form of questions constructed by the teacher. (In this case, a study guide might be used to guide the read-ing.) They may be questions that have been formulated by the students them-selves, perhaps based on the boldface headings picked out during the pre-view of the selection. Or, they may be predictions about what the selection offers, based on clues from the title and illustrations. If the purpose is in the form of a prediction, students read to confirm or deny their hypotheses.

Once the purposes have been set, students read to fulfill them. The initial reading should be silent. Silent reading always precedes oral reading unless a reading teacher is testing for word recognition skills. The content teacher usually should not ask students to read orally unless they have had a chance to read the selection silently first. There are several reasons for this:

1. Reading silently gives the reader an opportunity to decode unfamiliar words without being subject to embarrassment in front of his or her peers.
2. Reading silently allows the reader to become familiar with the phrasing patterns before he or she reads them aloud.
3. Most reading at the secondary level should be done silently because silent reading is more prevalent than oral reading in everyday situations.

After the silent reading, students may discuss the answers to the purpose questions or to additional discussion questions, perhaps reading certain pas-sages orally to verify some of them. Any oral rereading that is done should be purposeful. Purposeful oral rereading would include reading to prove a point, reading to appreciate the beauty of the language (especially in poetry), and reading to interpret characterization (in a play in which different people are reading various parts). Many directed reading lessons at the secondary level do not include an oral reading component.

The fourth step — *follow-up activities* — includes enrichment activities related to the lesson and designed to further develop the topic. Examples might be reading additional books on the same topic or by the same author, illustrating an event or concept from the story, constructing a model, writing a story related to the content, conducting an experiment, or otherwise applying concepts presented in the reading assignment.

Movement through such a sequence of steps may sound time-consuming, but in reality teaching a lesson in this format probably involves no more time than a teacher would typically spend on a section of a content text. Furthermore, after the students have been led through these steps, they will be more likely to understand the material. They will also be more likely to retain it, because they have had adequate preparation for the lesson and have read the material with a purpose in mind.

Example 6.9 shows a directed reading lesson, which is based on an eighth-grade English textbook.

E X A M P L E **6.9**

English Selection and Directed Reading Lesson

The Life of a Word

Our language constantly changes to meet our needs. We adopt words from other languages and maintain their meanings. We adapt words from languages by altering their meanings slightly. Sometimes we completely change the meaning of a word when we take it for our own. Words have origins and histories, many of which are fascinating. The study of words is called **etymology**.

Consider the word *canary*, which originally comes from the Latin word for *dog*, *canis*. What do dogs and canaries have in common? The Romans named a group of Islands off northwest Africa, Canaria Insula, or Dog Island, because of all the dogs that they found there. Songbirds also inhabited the islands. Later, when the birds were exported to Europe, they were called canaries, after their home, the Canary Islands.

Another word that got its name from a place is *mayonnaise*. According to a legend, the town of Mahón on the island of Minorca in the Mediterranean once had a shortage of milk products. Consequently, the usual cream sauces could not be made. One chef began experimenting with eggs and oil. The result was a sauce that took the name of the city, Sauce Mahónnaise. Eventually, the word changed to *mayonnaise*.

Word change is unpredictable. For instance, the word *silly* in Old English was *seely*, meaning "blessed." The Normans were considered *seely*, because they had idle time for hunting and playing. Over time, *seely* came to mean "idle." In contrast, the word *knight* was originally the Anglo-Saxon word for youth, *cniht*. Later, it came to mean "servant," then "servant of a noble." Finally, the meaning was elevated to mean a person who served a noble with great chivalry and daring.

Many dictionaries give whole or partial etymologies. Some dictionaries list the early meanings of a word before its current meanings. Check your dictionary for its etymologies. You may also want to look at the *Oxford English Dictionary* which provides extensive etymologies.

PRACTICE

A. Create your own etymology for each of these words: *mathematics, study, gymnasium, vacation*. What are their real etymologies?
B. What is the etymology for the name of your state, the month of your birth, and the days of the week?

Source: Shirley Haley-James and others: *Houghton Mifflin English* (Boston: Houghton Mifflin Company, 1986), p. 417. Reprinted by permission of Houghton Mifflin Company.

Directed Reading Lesson

MOTIVATION AND BUILDING BACKGROUND

1. Ask the students if they know what a *villain* is. After discussing its current meaning, tell them that it originally meant "a person from a villa" and that its meaning has changed for the worse.
2. Ask the students if they know what *nice* means. After discussing its current meaning, tell them that it once meant "ignorant" and that its meaning has changed for the better.
3. Ask the students if they know any words that have come from place names or names of people. Let them name as many as possible. Be ready to provide some examples for them, such as *pasteurization*.

SKILL DEVELOPMENT ACTIVITIES

4. Remind students that words presented in bold-face print are important words for which to know meanings.
5. Review types of context clues that are often found in textbooks. Give special attention to definition clues, since there is a definition clue for the word *etymology* in the assignment.
6. Review the meaning of *-logy* (the study of). Have students name and define words ending in *-logy* (*biology, geology,* and so forth).
7. Review the meaning of the word part *un-* (not). Have students name and define words with this part (*unhappy, unwanted*).
8. Review the meaning of the word part *-able* (able to be). Have students name and define words with this part (*workable, marketable*).

9. Silent reading — Have students read the selection silently for the following purposes:
   a. Determine the meaning of the word *etymology.*
   b. Find two words whose names have come from the names of places.
   c. Determine the meaning of *unpredictable.*
   d. Find a word that had a negative meaning change over the years.
   e. Find a word that had a positive meaning change over the years.
10. Discussion and oral reading — Choose some students to read aloud and discuss the parts related to the silent reading purposes, especially if the students find the purpose questions difficult to answer.

FOLLOW-UP ACTIVITIES

11. Have the students do the two practice activities at the bottom of the selection and discuss their results in class.
12. Have the students list five words that they find that have interesting etymologies. Have a class discussion of the words.

In their observational study, Ned Ratekin and others (1985) observed that eighth- and eleventh-grade teachers spent little time on readiness activities for textbook reading. In fact, the teachers spent only 20 percent of their time providing any kind of guidance for learning from textbooks. Science teachers used guidance materials slightly more frequently than mathematics, social studies, and English or language arts teachers. The small amount of time that all these teachers spent on readiness activities may be related to the fact that the teachers, and not the textbooks, appeared to be the primary sources of information for the students. The students were not expected to learn concepts from the texts but from explanations by the teachers.

Directed Reading-Thinking Activity

Stauffer (1969) developed the Directed Reading-Thinking Activity (DRTA) to encourage students to think while they read. Stauffer feels that motivation of effort and concentration occurs when students are involved intellectually with the reading material, forming hypotheses, processing information, and evaluating tentative solutions — that is, when they are active participants in the reading process.

Students develop their own purposes for reading when the teacher asks them to predict what the material will be about from the title clues, then from the title clues plus graphic aids available in the section to be read. Predictions may be listed on the board and modified as the students request. They may be withdrawn (erased), and students may change to support predictions made by other students (Richek, 1987). The teacher asks the students why they have made the predictions that they have made, and discussion of the reasons ensues.

The teacher divides the reading material into portions that provide good prediction points. Students are asked to read to a specified point, stop, assess their previous predictions, either confirm or reject the predictions, and make new predictions if they have rejected the old ones. A discussion of the confirmation or rejection of predictions is held, and the students support their decisions by referring to information gathered from the text. This process is continued until the entire selection has been read. (Richek [1987] suggests choosing no more than five or six prediction points for a selection.) The early predictions are likely to be diverse, because the clues from the reading are sparse at that point. The predictions become more convergent as more clues emerge, pointing more obviously to the selection's message.

Richek (1987) feels that the DRTA, with its prediction/confirmation process, provides the students with a general method for approaching narratives. She has found that students become aware of mood and tone clues, foreshadowing, and figurative language in the text as they search for the clues that will help them make decisions about hypotheses during the DRTA process.

Josel (1986) has suggested a Silent DRTA for remedial students, in which they read to marked stopping points, write predictions at these points, and check to see if they missed clues. Students who are embarrassed to respond orally are thereby freed from this problem, and all students can work at their individual paces.

Alternate Classroom Materials

If a content teacher finds that some of the students in a class are unable to benefit from the textbook designated for the class because of the book's readability level, he or she can make several possible adjustments. As mentioned earlier, these include the use of alternate textbooks, supplementary readings, rewritten materials, language-experience materials, computer applications, and audiovisual aids.

Alternate Textbooks or Supplementary Readings

One obvious solution to the problem of an assigned textbook's high readability level would be locating alternate textbooks or supplementary reading materials with lower readability levels. Sometimes this is a practical solution, although in some cases it may be difficult to secure an adequate supply of alternate materials. Many times, however, teachers overlook the possibilities of such materials even when they are readily available.

An ideal situation would be to have several textbooks that cover identical content but that are written at varying levels of difficulty, but availability of such material is unlikely. Even so, teachers should not discard the idea of using textbooks at different levels. Many textbooks on the same subject (for example, biology, chemistry, plane geometry, algebra, American history, civics, or health) are produced by various publishers. One publisher may include in a health text designed for eighth graders many of the same topics that another publisher includes in the health text designed for seniors in high school. A teacher assigned to use the health textbook from the second publisher might acquire some health textbooks from the first publisher to use with the students who cannot read the textbook designated for the course. For the common topics in the two textbooks, part of the class could be assigned reading in one text and part in another. The reading, which of course would be done for specified purposes, could then be followed by class discussion, with both groups taking an active part.

Another possibility that should not escape the teacher's attention is use of material that comes from different publishers but is designed for the same grade. As we have already mentioned, a textbook for a particular grade may not really be written on that grade level. By checking the readability of various publishers' products, a teacher may find a textbook that is considerably easier to read than the one being used, although it has been written for the same grade level and subject.

In some content fields attempts are being made to provide high-interest, low-vocabulary materials for use as regular basal materials. High-interest, low-vocabulary materials contain concepts appropriate for mature readers but have simplified vocabulary and sometimes simplified sentence structure. These materials can be obtained for use by the students in the class whose reading levels are lower than the level for which the class textbook is written. Study guides may be supplied by the teacher for both regular textbooks and for high-interest, low-vocabulary books, and class discussion of a topic can tie together the information students learn from both sources.

High-interest, low-vocabulary text materials for secondary school students are available from many publishers. Some examples are presented in Appendix A of this chapter.

If alternate textbook materials are unavailable, a teacher can still find supplementary material for those who cannot manage the textbook reading. Trade books (books other than textbooks) on various levels of readability are available on almost any topic covered in the school curriculum. Some publishers have made available information on the readability levels of many of the trade books they produce. If such information is not readily available, the teacher can apply readability measures to the books of interest, following the procedures discussed earlier in this chapter.

Trade books are not the only available useful supplementary materials. Pamphlets produced by government agencies; newspaper articles, editorials, and other features; copies of political platforms of candidates; popular maga-

234

zines; and a variety of other materials can be used. The teacher should probably check the readability levels of the portions of this supplementary material earmarked for the less able readers. He or she should keep in mind that material that carries a high enough interest factor for the students may be readable even if it is on a slightly higher reading level than these students can ordinarily manage.

The supplementary materials suggested above should not be limited to use with less able readers. On the contrary, better readers will benefit greatly from having exposure to various points of view, different methods of presentation, and additional information, even though they may use the textbook as the basis for their studies.

Teachers need to be aware that all reading difficulties in content areas will not necessarily disappear magically simply because the student has a book "on the correct level." Regardless of the readability level of the book, students need guidance in approaching content area reading tasks.

Some teachers hesitate to use varied materials because they are bothered by the question of how they are going to test the students on this varied material. Teachers must take several things into consideration when composing tests for students who have to read different materials. For example:

1. The teacher should start by listing the concepts that he or she wishes to transmit to all the students.
2. The teacher then can choose diverse materials that cover these concepts at different levels.
3. The teacher should give special attention in class discussion to any concepts that are not clearly covered at some levels of the materials assigned. Language experience materials could be developed from such discussions to cover these key concepts. Language experience materials in this case would be the class discussion as recorded by the teacher and distributed to the students to study.
4. The teacher should compose tests of items covering those important concepts that have been treated either in all the assigned printed material or in class discussion.

Rewritten Materials

If teachers find that there is not enough supplementary reading material available in their content areas, they should not assume that less able readers have to struggle with the assigned textbook. Secondary school teachers *can* successfully rewrite crucial textbook passages to lower difficulty levels. Experimentation with this activity has been done over a lengthy time span in a secondary reading methods course. Participants in the course are generally in-service classroom teachers, and the results are often excellent: using selections from history, English, literature, and science textbooks, teachers frequently are able to lower the reading difficulty by two to four grade levels without sacrificing meaning. A key to the success of the activity is that the teachers are warned *not* to write "to the formula" but to attempt to express the ideas presented in the original material in a more understandable form and then recheck the new material with the readability formula. Most of the teachers have said that the experience is eye-opening and enjoyable, and several continued rewriting activities after the class ended, although not all felt they had time to do so. Rewritten material can allow many students to learn more from content reading assignments.

In an earlier portion of this chapter, it is mentioned that vocabulary and sentence difficulty are the two most significant indicators of readability. Rewriting a selection to a lower readability level primarily involves simplifying its vocabulary and sentence structure. Easier synonyms can be substituted for more difficult words when appropriate, and teachers can simplify sentences by shortening them or by changing compound and complex sentences into simple sentences. Simplifying sentence structure *must not* be done at the expense of leaving out connectives that help students to see relationships, however. If a sentence originally had a cause-and-effect relationship signaled by *because,* for example, deletion of the explicitly stated *because* would result in more difficult material, rather than simpler text. Therefore, rewriting without thinking about the meanings being conveyed is worse than not rewriting. Teachers must not write to fit the formulas' requirements, but to clarify and simplify. Then they can check the result with the formula. An example of how this can be accomplished follows.

Original sentence: The ancient Phoenicians were the undisputed masters of the sea; they were also adept at business matters, keeping scrupulous records of all transactions that took place during their extensive excursions.

Rewritten material: The Phoenicians who lived in the year 1000 B.C. were the best sailors of their time. People from other nations did not doubt that the Phoenicians were masters of the sea. They were also good at the business deals that took place during their long trips over the seas. They kept careful records of those deals.

Although the rewritten material contains more words, the vocabulary and sentence structure of the original have been simplified. Easier synonyms or explanations have been substituted for words that might have presented problems to less advanced readers: *ancient, undisputed, adept, scrupulous, transactions, extensive, excursions.* A thirty-one word sentence was simplified by being broken down into four sentences, ranging from seven to eighteen words in length. No essential connectives were deleted. Ideas presented in the original were enhanced rather than made more obscure.

Although rewriting does not inevitably result in better comprehension, there is evidence that it is effective in some situations. Duffelmeyer (1979) rewrote selections from the comprehension section of the *Nelson-Denny Reading Test,* substituting concrete nouns for abstract nouns and full verbs for verb-nominalizations. Poor readers understood the revised passages better than the original ones, but average or better readers did not.

Language Experience Materials

Language experience materials are materials written in the students' own words. In the elementary school, language experience stories are often developed by a group of students who have had a special common experience. In the secondary school, experience materials may be written by a group of students who have read about a common topic and wish to summarize their findings. The teacher can record all significant contributions on the chalkboard as they are offered. At the conclusion of the discussion, the teacher and students together can organize the contributions in a logical order (for example chronological or cause-effect). The teacher can then have duplicates of the group-composed material made and can distribute them to the students on the following day.

The members of the groups that are able to handle the textbook with ease may file the experience material to use for review for subsequent tests. A group that is unable to handle the textbook presentation may use the material more extensively. For example, the teacher may meet with this group and guide the members through the reading of the material by using purpose questions. The students are likely to succeed in reading this material because they have seen the content written on the board and because it is in the words of fellow students. Having heard a discussion of the content, the students will find it easier to apply context clues as they read. Any technical vocabulary or multiple-meaning words can be located and discussed thoroughly. These words may be written in a special notebook with accompanying pronunciations and definitions and a reference to the experience material in which they occurred. A booklet made up of experience material can serve as a reference source for these words when they are encountered again. The booklet is also used by this group in studying for tests on the material.

Experience materials may also be developed by individuals and groups who wish to record the results of scientific experiments or the periodic observation of some natural phenomena. These materials may be shared with the rest of the class in oral or written form. Such activities are extremely valuable for students who are not able to gain much information from a textbook that is too difficult for them.

Sharp (1989), Laminack (1987), and Ferguson and Fairburn (1985) found the language experience approach to be effective for use with content instruction in social studies, science, and math story problems. Sharp feels that this approach motivates remedial students, builds their self-esteem, provides them with concepts that allow participation in content classes, builds reading vocabulary (including technical vocabulary), and activates and organizes the students' prior knowledge in the content areas, among other values.

Some Uses of the Computer in Adjusting Assignments

A number of computer utility programs are available that teachers can use when constructing drill-and-practice materials, crossword puzzles, word search puzzles, and multiple-choice tests. These materials also can serve as special assignments for students who need a particular type of practice or a different level of practice or testing material from that currently available.

Word processing programs can be used to prepare simpler materials for students to read, study guides, or tests. The preparation of such materials is made easier with a good word processing program (e.g., WordStar [WordStar International, Inc.], Apple Writer [Apple Computer, Inc.], Bank Street Writer [Scholastic, Inc.], or Magic Slate [Sunburst Communications, Inc.]) because correction of errors, editing, and formatting changes may be made quickly, easily, and neatly without redoing an entire document. Word processing software can also be helpful when recording language experience materials, such as those mentioned in the previous section. If a large monitor is available for use in the classroom, the material can be directly entered on the computer, rather than on the chalkboard, and can easily be modified according to suggestions given during class discussion. This will result in a well-organized, neat handout that can be printed and duplicated for the students' use.

Students may use the computer to write their own accounts about subjects under study and may edit them with teacher assistance, using the easier word processing programs. Teaching proofreading and editing skills can be made easier when students realize that changes can be made without recopying entire documents. Even organization of paragraphs can be changed easily with block moves! Therefore report-writing efforts can be greatly improved, and students can take more pride in their well-developed products.

The teacher can use simulation programs, which simulate real events, to add high-interest reading material to the curriculum. Students can use these programs in independent study activities. The *Oregon Trail* program (Minnesota Educational Computer Consortium) may be used to enrich the reading in a history class; *Ecological Simulations 1 & 2* (Creative Computing) and *Three Mile Island* (Muse Software) can be used in a science class; *Sounds Abound* (Houghton Mifflin) in an accounting class; and *In Search of the Most Amazing Thing* (Spinnaker) in a class in which study skills are being taught. Any one of a wide variety of interactive fiction story programs can be used as recreational reading in an English class. Blanchard and Mason (1985) feel that *In Search of the Most Amazing Thing* may start a trend in study skills/adventure programs.

Because writing and reading skills go hand-in-hand, the many writing skills programs that are available may also enhance reading skills. Students who are involved in producing written products seem to do better at analyzing the written products of others.

Because they need to collect and organize information effectively, students also can benefit from learning to use computerized database management systems. They provide rapid access to filed information, the ability to easily add and update files, and the ability to compare and contrast information in files in a number of ways (Mathison and Lungren, 1989).

Other Audiovisual Materials

A classroom teacher may find that one of the best ways to help less proficient readers gain access to important content information is through the use of supplementary audiovisual materials. Such materials may include computers, audiotapes, videotapes and films, and filmstrips.

Audiotapes

If the teacher feels that certain textbook material is essential in its original form (for example, a poem or a beautifully worded essay), he or she may wish to tape the passage and set up a listening station for students who cannot read the selection themselves. The teacher or a particularly good reader from the class may be the reader on the tapes. (If a class member records the tapes, the teacher should preview the tapes before releasing them for general use.) If students who are unable to read the text for themselves follow along in the book as they listen to the tapes, they may pick up some sight vocabulary as they absorb the content. Some publishers offer commercial tapes to accompany their material. (See the Educational Activities, Inc., listing in Appendix A: High-Interest, Low-Vocabulary Material at the end of this chapter for some examples.) Pendulum Press offers *Read Along* tapes to accompany Shakespearean plays, other classics, and a history series. Bowmar/Noble Publishers has tapes to accompany some texts, such as the *Our Nation's Heritage* programs and the *Reading Incentive Series.*

Tyo (1980) studied the use of tape-recorded social studies textual material for poor readers in junior high school. One group of subjects listened to tapes of assignments while reading along. The other group read without tapes. The comprehension of the group using the tapes was significantly greater than that of the group that did not use tapes, as measured by a cloze test on the content.

Sometimes the tapes of textbook selections may be used by students who can handle reading the textbook assignments but who learn best through the auditory mode, rather than the visual mode. Students can also use these tapes as an alternate way to study for tests on material previously read.

Videotapes and Films

Videotapes of various topics of study can be used to illustrate text materials for the less proficient readers or for students with limited experiential backgrounds. For example, if students are expected to read about the process of pasteurization in their textbooks, a videotape or film depicting the process can be shown before they read the material, thereby supplying background information and visual images for students to associate with the words. Videotapes or films may also help bring a literary selection to life. For example, a videotape of a storyteller telling "The Monkey's Paw" or a film of Shakespeare's *A Midsummer Night's Dream* could be shown to either the less advanced readers or the entire class before these works are studied. By giving poor readers advance knowledge of the plot and characters and a chance to adjust to the type of language used, teachers will be preparing them for interaction with the rest of the class in class discussion. In the case of the Shakespearean play, the entire class may benefit from the opportunity to hear the unfamiliar language patterns spoken aloud. (This becomes a readiness activity.)

Filmstrips and Illustrations

Some concepts covered in class may also be covered in filmstrips, which, like videotapes and films, can help less able readers and those with limited experiential backgrounds by supplying background information about text material and presenting visual images to accompany new terms.

Some publishers offer filmstrips of literary selections that can be used to give less able readers background and motivation for reading the selections. Pendulum Press has filmstrips in its *Illustrated Classics Series*, its *Shakespeare Series*, and its *Basic Illustrated History of America Series*, among others. These series include books illustrated in a style that resembles that of a comic book (dialogue attached to characters) but that has typeset lettering and uncluttered pages. Students respond well to these books. Bowmar/Noble Publishers also has filmstrips to accompany some materials, notably the *Reading Incentive Program*.

Developing Teaching Units

A teaching unit is a series of interrelated lessons or class activities organized around a theme, a literary form, or a skill. Because unit activities are varied in terms of the amount of reading skill and the levels of thinking required to complete them, they offer excellent opportunities to adjust reading assignments to fit all students. Different students may complete different activities, such as reading, listening to, and/or viewing different resource materials, and share the results of these varied activities with their classmates.

Use of teaching units takes a great deal of teacher planning. The teacher must develop objectives for a unit that are in keeping with the overall goals of the class, must decide upon skills to be developed, and must plan activities designed to help meet these objectives and to help develop these skills.

FIGURE **6.2**

Unit Development Web

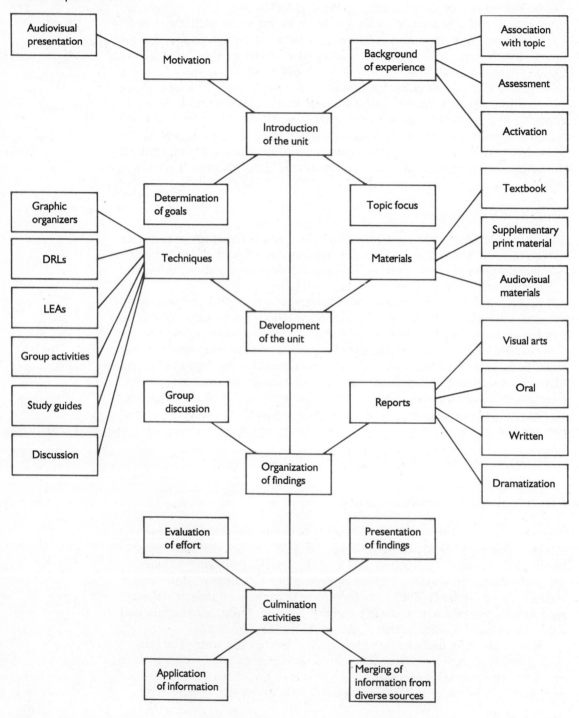

The web shown in Figure 6.2 depicts the parts of a unit graphically. A unit generally involves four basic types of activities:

1. Introduction of the unit
2. Development of the unit
3. Organization of findings
4. Culmination activities

Each of these activities is explained below.

Introduction of the Unit

The students are introduced to the unit's theme or central idea, the literary form to be explored, or the skills to be developed. Through class discussion and/or pretests, the teacher determines the extent to which the students' backgrounds of experience in the area can contribute to the unit activities. The teacher discusses with the students what they already know about the topic under consideration and helps them to evolve questions that they need to answer and to identify areas in which they need clarification. During this discussion, the teacher helps the students relate the area of study to their own personal experiences or needs. Semantic webs of concepts or terms related to the unit theme may be effective in activating the students' background knowledge and in facilitating the discussion (Cooter and Griffith, 1989). The teacher may supply motivation for participating in the unit activities by showing a film or filmstrip or by playing records or tapes related to the subject.

Development of the Unit

The teacher begins teaching the unit by presenting core instructional material to the whole class. This material will probably consist of the textbook material and supplementary material that the teacher has carefully chosen for those students who cannot benefit from reading the text because of its difficulty level. The teacher may develop directed reading lessons (DRLs) for both the textbook material and the supplementary material.

During the first step of some of the directed reading lessons, the teacher may use structured overviews to develop readiness for reading. Next, using techniques presented in Chapters 2, 3, and 4, he or she may teach needed vocabulary, comprehension, and study strategies and skills that are vital to the understanding of the particular passages involved. As a part of the directed reading lesson, the teacher may guide the actual student reading of the material by means of a study guide. All the students can combine what they have learned through class discussion and language experience activities. The follow-up activities will be included among the independent assignments for different research groups formed by the teacher after the reading of the core material has taken place.

After the core instructional presentation, the teacher assigns areas of concern to the students or allows them to choose areas in which they have a particular interest. Self-selection may have the advantage of providing internal motivation for the unit study. Students form several small groups that attempt to answer specific questions, clarify specific areas of concern, or analyze particular literary works. The teacher may meet with each group to discuss the possible reference sources that are available: textbooks, library books (fiction and nonfiction), encyclopedias, other reference books, magazines, newspapers, original documents, films, filmstrips, and a variety of other audiovisual aids. Whenever possible, books that reflect a multicultural environment should be chosen, and there should be access to large-type books, Braille materials, or audiotapes that cover the class material if there are visually impaired students in the class. Multicultural resources provide the students with a realistic picture of the world at large, even if the cultural diversity within the particular school is narrow, and they allow students whose cultural backgrounds vary from the mainstream culture to feel more comfortable and see how their culture fits into the overall picture. Materials for students with physical handicaps allow these children to participate in unit activities without undue stress and difficulty.

The teacher must be alert to the variety of reading abilities within the group and must help the group members expend their efforts in fruitful ways, making available books and reference aids on a number of different levels. Some resources should be easy to read for the lowest level readers in the class; others should challenge the best reader. A review of study skills such as using the card catalog, using encyclopedias, outlining, taking notes, skimming, and scanning may be helpful for some members of each research group. (See Chapter 4 for a discussion of these skills.) Needs groups encompassing members from all of the research groups may be formed for these purposes. (See the discussion of grouping in this chapter.)

Each member of each research group is responsible for collecting data. Differentiated assignments within the groups may be developed by the teacher or by group leaders, who are guided by the teacher.

Organization of Findings

The research groups meet after ample time has been allowed for individual members to collect data. Each group then reviews the information collected from the various sources, discusses and attempts to resolve differences of opinion, and forms the findings into a coherent report. The discussion allows the students to share the information they have discovered and find out what others have learned. The report may be oral or written and may be accompanied by audiovisual aids such as charts, tables, maps, graphs, pictures, filmstrips, or tapes. It may be in one of a number of forms, including an oral report, a panel discussion, a skit, a more complete dramatization, or a mural.

TABLE **6.2**

Unit Development

Introduction	Development	Organization of Findings	Culmination
1. Build background and motivation 2. Connect unit to students' experiences	1. Core lessons presented through a directed reading approach, use of structured overviews, teaching of needed skills, study guides, language experience approach 2. Research groups 3. Needs groups	1. Discussion 2. Oral or written reports	1. Merging of information from diverse sources 2. Evaluation of effort 3. Application of information

Culmination Activities

At the end of the unit study, the different research groups present their findings in a variety of ways. The class critically examines the information that is presented, merges it with the core of information learned from the textbook and supplementary materials, and determines if the purposes of the unit have been met. If the class feels that not all of the original purposes have been met, the members may regroup to finish the task.

The teacher should help the students relate the findings to events in their own lives. An activity that immediately applies the findings to real situations would be beneficial because it would emphasize the relevance of the unit.

Table 6.2 presents the steps in unit development.

Sample Unit Ideas

A unit in health might be arranged around a theme such as "The Four Basic Food Groups." A discussion of the theme could make apparent the background knowledge that the group has concerning the theme. A film or filmstrip on the topic could clarify the composition of each of the four basic food groups. Four research groups could be set up, one for each food group. Additional groups might be formed to study fad diets.

Each group studying a basic food group could investigate the importance of the foods in its group, setting out to answer these questions: What are the benefits from eating these foods? What are the problems that could result from not eating them? Groups on fad diets could weigh the benefits and dangers of these diets. A variety of sources should be available, including current paperbacks, newspaper articles, and magazine articles concerned with nutrition and dieting. Textbooks and reference books, such as encyclopedias, should also be utilized.

The group reports could take a variety of forms: one possibility would be to have a student describe what happened when he or she went on a fad diet. In the whole-class discussion following the group reports, relationships among the reports should be emphasized. For example, the fad diets that sometimes have bad results often leave out some of the basic food groups.

A unit in literature might be developed around a type of literature, such as "Tall Tales of the United States." The opening discussion could include an attempt to define "tall tales" and could provide opportunities for the students to name tall tales with which they are familiar. The teacher might use a film, filmstrip, or tape during the introductory stage to clarify the nature of tall tales. Different groups could be formed to read tall tales about different superhuman individuals, for example, Old Stormalong, Paul Bunyan, Mike Fink, and Pecos Bill. Other groups could concentrate on tall tales of other types, such as Washington Irving's "Rip Van Winkle" and "The Legend of Sleepy Hollow" or Mark Twain's "The Celebrated Jumping Frog of Calaveras County." As a culminating activity, each student could write a tall tale of the general type that he or she has read. The tales could be shared in oral or written form with the rest of the class.

SUMMARY

In order to adjust reading assignments to fit all students, teachers need to know the difficulty levels of classroom reading materials so they can match the materials to the students' reading levels. The difficulty levels can be determined by using readability formulas or other readability measures in conjunction with teacher judgment.

Assignments can be adjusted more readily if a teacher utilizes a number of grouping procedures in the classroom. Study guides, directed reading approaches, directed reading-thinking activities, alternate textbooks, supplementary reading, rewritten materials, language experience materials, computer applications, and other audiovisual aids can all be used to differentiate assignments. Teaching units are a natural vehicle for differentiated assignments.

1. Which statement is incorrect? (a) Textbooks placed at grade 9 often are written at a tenth-grade readability level or above. (b) Content textbooks tend to be written by reading specialists. (c) Literature anthologies often vary widely in readability from selection to selection. (d) Many students in any given grade are unable to read at that grade level.

2. What are the two factors that researchers have found to be the most useful in predicting readability? (a) Vocabulary and sentence length (b) Vocabulary and reader background (c) Sentence length and abstract concepts (d) Idea organization and format

3. What is true of student tutorial groups? (a) The tutor is allowed to plan his or her own lessons. (b) The tutor does not benefit from the activity, although the "clients" do. (c) One or two especially good students should always act as tutors. (d) None of the above

4. What should teachers who use groups within their classes remember? (a) Needs groups should continue for a minimum time period of a semester. (b) All groups should be flexible. (c) Both *a* and *b* (d) Neither *a* nor *b*

5. Which statement is true of study guides? (a) They are not helpful for less able readers. (b) They are useful when the teacher is employing grouping with the content class. (c) They can be designed to help students focus on particular information by offering purpose questions. (d) Both *b* and *c*.

6. Which kind of guide is designed to help students relate what they are about to read to their own experiential backgrounds? (a) Content (b) Pattern (c) Preview (d) Reasoning

7. Which statement is true of structured overviews? (a) They involve a graphic arrangement of terms that apply to the important concepts in the passages. (b) They contain a list of purpose questions. (c) They cannot be used with mathematics materials. (d) All of the above

8. Which one of the following is *not* a step in a directed reading lesson? (a) Motivation and building background (b) Oral reading, paragraph by paragraph, without specific purposes (c) Skill development activities (d) Guided reading of the story

9. If secondary school students cannot read the textbooks assigned for their classes, what can the teacher do? (a) The teacher can rewrite the material to a lower difficulty level. (b) The teacher can find an alternate textbook or other alternate printed material. (c) The teacher can tape portions of the textbook for student use. (d) All of the above are possibilities.

10. Which statement is true of language experience materials? (a) They consist of the students' own words. (b) They are inappropriate for use above ninth grade. (c) They must be developed in small groups. (d) All of the above

11. For what purposes can word processing programs be used? (a) To prepare simpler materials for students to read (b) To prepare study guides

(c) To allow students to write their own accounts about subjects under study (d) All of the above

12. Which statement is true if teaching units are utilized? (a) Separate lessons are unrelated. (b) Research groups can be profitably employed. (c) All students engage in identical activities. (d) None of the above

THOUGHT QUESTIONS

1. Why is it helpful for a content area teacher to know how to use a readability formula? Are there some readability formulas that would be more appropriate for you to use in your particular situation? Why, or why not?
2. Do readability formulas provide absolute grade level values? Why, or why not?
3. What are some measures other than readability formulas that could be used to test readability? Why would you use, or not use, one of these methods instead of a formula?
4. What are some types of groups that you might choose to use in your classroom? What advantages would there be to using these groups?
5. What can study guides do to enhance the learning of students in your content area classes?
6. How can structured overviews be used in a content area class? What are the advantages of using them?
7. What are the steps in a directed reading lesson? How does each step enhance the learning of the content of the textbook?
8. What procedures might you follow in locating alternate textbooks to use with readers for whom the assigned textbook is not appropriate? Are there sources other than textbooks that you also might utilize? If so, what are they?
9. If you decide to rewrite materials to a lower readability level, what factors should you take into account in your rewriting?
10. How can tapes and films be used to further content learning when not all students can manage the textbook?
11. How are language experience materials helpful to both poor and good readers in content classrooms?
12. What are some ways that the computer can be used to adjust assignments?
13. How does unit teaching lend itself to differentiation of assignments?
14. How is the DRTA different from a directed reading lesson?

ENRICHMENT ACTIVITIES

1. Apply the Fry Readability Graph Formula to a 100-word sample from the science textbook selection in Example 6.5. Start counting your 100-word sample with the first paragraph, which begins: "With rapidly beat-

ing. . . .'' After you have completed the formula application, check your answer against the answers obtained by your classmates.

2. Construct a study guide that could be used with the English selection found in Example 6.9. Discuss your guide with your classmates.

*3. Construct a study guide for a secondary level textbook that you are currently using. Try it with your students and report to the class concerning the results.

4. Write out a plan for a directed reading lesson for the science selection in Example 6.2. Discuss your results with your classmates.

*5. Write out a plan for a directed reading lesson for a section of a textbook that you are currently using. Try it with your students and report to the class concerning the results.

6. Choose a topic and locate printed materials, both textbook and nontextbook, on a variety of difficulty levels that could be used by students when studying this topic.

7. Learn to use a readability formula other than Fry's formula. Test a passage of a secondary level textbook of your choice using this formula, and then test the passage using the Fry formula. Discuss the results of your activity with your classmates.

*8. Try using a language experience activity with students in one of your secondary classes. Report the results to your college class.

*9. Plan a unit from your chosen subject area. Try it with students in your class. Decide how you could improve the unit if you were to teach it again.

10. Arrange the vocabulary terms at the beginning of the chapter in the form of a structured overview. You may need to add some terms. Explain your arrangement to the class.

11. Choose a chapter from a content area textbook or a short story from a literature textbook. Choose prediction points for the selection that would allow you to use it for a DRTA. Discuss the stopping points that you have chosen with your college classmates.

12. Select four articles on the topic of readability formulas from the Bibliography at the end of this chapter or from other sources. Compare and contrast the viewpoints reprinted in these articles in a two- or three-page paper. Conclude with your own viewpoint.

BIBLIOGRAPHY

Armstrong, Diane P., Judythe Patberg, and Peter Dewitz. "Reading Guides — Helping Students Understand." *Journal of Reading*, 31 (March 1988), 532–541.
Aronson, E., et al. *The Jigsaw Connection.* Beverly Hills, Calif.: Sage, 1978.

*These activities are designed for in-service teachers, student teachers, or practicum students.

248

Balajthy, Ernest. *Microcomputers in Reading & Language Arts.* Englewood Cliffs, N.J.: Prentice Hall, 1986.

Barron, Richard F. "The Use of Vocabulary as an Advance Organizer." In Harold Herber and Peter Sanders (eds.), *Research in Reading in the Content Areas: First Year Report.* Syracuse, N.Y.: Syracuse University Press, 1969, pp. 29–39.

Bean, Thomas W., and Bonnie O. Ericson. "Text Previews and Three Level Study Guides for Content Area Critical Reading." *Journal of Reading,* 32 (January 1989), 337–341.

Bean, Thomas W., Harry Singer, and Stan Cowan. "Acquisition of a Topic Schema in High School Biology Through an Analogical Study Guide." In Jerome A. Niles and Rosary V. Lalik (eds.), *Issues in Literacy: A Research Perspective.* Rochester, N.Y.: National Reading Conference, 1985.

————. "Analogical Study Guides: Improving Comprehension in Science." *Journal of Reading,* 29 (December 1985), 246–250.

Betts, Emmett A. *Foundations of Reading Instruction.* New York: American Book Company, 1946.

Binkley, Marilyn R. "New Ways of Assessing Text Difficulty." In Beverley L. Zakaluk and S. Jay Samuels (eds.), *Readability: Its Past, Present, & Future.* Newark, Del.: International Reading Association, 1988, pp. 98–120.

Blanchard, Jay S., and George E. Mason. "Using Computers in Content Area Reading Instruction." *Journal of Reading,* 29 (November 1985), 112–117.

Bormuth, John. "A Response to 'Is the Degrees of Reading Power Test Valid or Invalid?' " *Journal of Reading,* 29 (October 1985), 42–47.

————. "Cloze Test Readability: Criterion Reference Scores." *Journal of Educational Measurement,* 5 (Fall 1968), 189–196.

Carver, Ronald P. "Is the Degrees of Reading Power Test Valid or Invalid?" *Journal of Reading,* 29 (October 1985), 34–41.

————. "Measuring Readability Using DRP Units." *Journal of Reading Behavior,* 17, No. 4 (1985), 304.

Chance, Larry. "Use Cloze Encounters of the Readability Kind for Secondary School Students." *Journal of Reading,* 28 (May 1985), 690–693.

Clark, Charles H. "Assessing Comprehensibility: The PHAN System." *The Reading Teacher,* 34 (March 1981), 670–675.

Clewell, Suzanne F., and Anne M. Clifton. "Examining Your Textbook for Comprehensibility." *Journal of Reading,* 27 (December 1983), 219–224.

Cooter, Robert B., Jr., and Robert Griffith. "Thematic Units for Middle School: An Honorable Seduction." *Journal of Reading,* 32 (May 1989), 676–681.

Dale, Edgar, and Joseph O'Rourke. *The Living Word Vocabulary.* Elgin, Ill.: Dome, 1976.

Davey, Beth. "How Do Classroom Teachers Use Textbooks?" *Journal of Reading,* 31 (January 1988), 340–345.

————. "Using Textbook Activity Guides to Help Students Learn from Textbooks." *Journal of Reading,* 29 (March 1986), 489–494.

Donlan, Dan. "Using the DRA to Teach Literary Comprehension at Three Response Levels." *Journal of Reading,* 28 (February 1985), 408–415.

Dreyer, Lois Goodman. "Readability and Responsibility." *Journal of Reading,* 27 (January 1984), 334–338.

Duffelmeyer, Frederick A. "The Effect of Rewriting Prose Material on Reading Comprehension." *Reading World,* 19 (October 1979), 1–11.

Duffelmeyer, Frederick A., Dale D. Baum, and Donna J. Merkley. "Maximizing Reader-Text Confrontation with an Extended Anticipation Guide." *Journal of Reading,* 31 (November 1987), 146–150.

Estes, Thomas H., and Joseph L. Vaughan, Jr. *Reading and Learning in the Content Classroom.* Boston: Allyn and Bacon, 1978.

Ferguson, Anne M., and Jo Fairburn. "Language Experience for Problem Solving in Math." *The Reading Teacher*, 38 (February 1985), 504–507.

Fitzgerald, Gisela G. "How Many Samples Give a Good Readability Estimate? The Fry Graph." *Journal of Reading*, 24 (February 1981), 404–410.

Flesch, Rudolph. *The Art of Readable Writing*. New York: Harper & Row, 1951.

Fry, Edward. "A Readability Formula for Short Passages." *Journal of Reading*, 33 (May 1990), 594–597.

––––––. "Fry's Readability Graph: Clarifications, Validity and Extension to Level 17." *Journal of Reading*, 21 (December 1977), 242–252.

––––––. *Reading Instruction for Classroom and Clinic*. New York: McGraw-Hill, 1972.

Gold, Patricia Cohen. "The Directed Listening-Language Experience Approach." *Journal of Reading*, 25 (November 1981), 138–141.

Gross, Philip P., and Karen Sadowski. "FOGINDEX — A Readability Formula Program for Microcomputers." *Journal of Reading*, 28 (April 1985), 614–618.

Haggard, Martha Rapp. "An Interactive Strategies Approach to Content Reading." *Journal of Reading*, 29 (December 1985), 204–210.

Harris, Theodore L., and Richard E. Hodges, eds. *A Dictionary of Reading and Related Terms*. Newark, Del.: International Reading Association, 1981.

Herber, Harold L. *Teaching Reading in Content Areas*. 2nd ed. Englewood Cliffs, N.J.: Prentice Hall, 1978.

Irwin, Judith Westphal, and Carol A. Davis. "Assessing Readability: The Checklist Approach." *Journal of Reading*, 24 (November 1980), 124–130.

Johnson, D. W., and R. T. Johnson. *Learning Together and Alone*. 2nd ed. Englewood Cliffs, N.J.: Prentice Hall, 1986.

Johnson, M. S., R. A. Kress, and J. J. Pikulski. *Informal Reading Inventories*. 2nd ed. Newark, Del.: International Reading Association, 1987.

Josel, Carol A. "A Silent DRTA for Remedial Eighth Graders." *Journal of Reading*, 29 (February 1986), 434–439.

Judd, Dorothy H. "Avoid Readability Formula Drudgery: Use Your School's Microcomputer." *The Reading Teacher*, 35 (October 1981), 7–8.

Klare, George R. "Understanding the Readability of Content Area Texts." In Diane Lapp, James Flood, and Nancy Farnan (eds.), *Content Area Reading and Learning: Instructional Strategies*. Englewood Cliffs, N.J.: Prentice Hall, 1989, pp. 34–42.

Kretschmer, Joseph C. "Updating the Fry Readability Formula." *The Reading Teacher*, 29 (March 1976), 555–558.

––––––. "Computerizing and Comparing the Rix Readability Index." *Journal of Reading*, 27 (March 1984), 490–499.

Laminack, L. "Mr. T Leads the Class: The Language Experience Approach and Science." *Science and Children*, 24 (1987), 41–42.

Mathison, Carla, and Linda Lungren. "Using Computers Effectively in Content Area Classes." In Diane Lapp, James Flood, and Nancy Farnan (eds.), *Content Area Reading and Learning: Instructional Strategies*. Englewood Cliffs, N.J.: Prentice Hall, 1989, pp. 304–318.

Montague, Marjorie, and Michael L. Tanner. "Reading Strategy Groups for Content Instruction." *Journal of Reading*, 30 (May 1987), 716–723.

Olson, Mary W., and Bonnie Longnion. "Pattern Guides: A Workable Alternative for Content Teachers." *Journal of Reading*, 25 (May 1982), 736–741.

Powers, R. D., W. A. Sumner, and B. E. Kearl. "A Recalculation of Four Adult Readability Formulas." *The Journal of Educational Psychology*, 49 (April 1958), 99–105.

Ratekin, Ned, et al. "Why Teachers Resist Content Reading Instruction." *Journal of Reading*, 28 (February 1985), 432–437.

Readability Report: 1983–84 Academic Year. New York: College Entrance Examination Board, 1983.

250   Richek, Margaret Ann. "DRTA: 5 Variations that Facilitate Independence in Reading Narratives." *Journal of Reading*, 30 (April 1987), 632–636.

Riley, James D. "Statement-Based Reading Guides and Quality of Teacher Response." *Journal of Reading*, 23 (May 1980), 715–720.

Roe, Betty D. "Teacher Prepared Material for Slow Readers." *Journal of Reading*, 15 (January 1972), 277–279.

Rude, Robert T. *Teaching Reading Using Microcomputers.* Englewood Cliffs, N.J.: Prentice Hall, 1986.

Sharp, Sidney J. "Using Content Subject Matter with LEA in Middle School." *Journal of Reading*, 33 (November 1989), 108–112.

Shepherd, David. *Comprehensive High School Reading Methods.* Columbus, Ohio: Charles E. Merrill, 1982.

Slavin, Robert. "A Cooperative Learning Approach to Content Areas: Jigsaw Teaching." In Diane Lapp, James Flood, and Nancy Farnan (eds.), *Content Area Reading and Learning: Instructional Strategies.* Englewood Cliffs, N.J.: Prentice Hall, 1989, pp. 330–345.

———. *Using Student Team Learning.* 3rd ed. Baltimore, Maryland: Center for Research on Elementary and Middle Schools, Johns Hopkins University, 1986.

Spiegel, Dixie Lee, and Jill D. Wright. "Biology Teachers' Use of Readability Concepts When Selecting Texts for Students." *Journal of Reading*, 27 (October 1983), 28–34.

Stauffer, Russell G. *Teaching Reading as a Thinking Process.* New York: Harper & Row, 1969.

Stevens, Kathleen C. "Can We Improve Reading by Teaching Background Information?" *Journal of Reading*, 25 (January 1982), 326–329.

Taylor, Wilson L. "Recent Developments in the Use of Cloze Procedure." *Journalism Quarterly*, 33 (Winter 1956), 42–48, 99.

Tyo, John. "An Alternative for Poor Readers in Social Science." *Social Education*, 44 (April 1980), 309–310.

Valmont, William J. "Creating Questions for Informal Reading Inventories." *The Reading Teacher*, 25 (March 1972), 509–512.

Whimbey, Arthur. "A 15th-Grade Reading Level for High School Seniors." *Phi Delta Kappan*, 69 (November 1987), 207.

Wood, Karen D. "Fostering Cooperative Learning in Middle and Secondary Level Classrooms." *Journal of Reading*, 31 (October 1987), 10–18.

Zakaluk, Beverley L., and S. Jay Samuels, eds. *Readability: Its Past, Present, & Future.* Newark, Del.: International Reading Association, 1988.

Zakaluk, Beverley L., and S. Jay Samuels, "Toward a New Approach to Predicting Text Comprehensibility." In Beverley L. Zakaluk and S. Jay Samuels (eds.), *Readability: Its Past, Present, & Future.* Newark, Del.: International Reading Association, 1988, pp. 121–144.

CHAPTER APPENDIX A: HIGH-INTEREST, LOW-VOCABULARY MATERIAL

BOWMAR/NOBLE PUBLISHERS, INC.

1. *United States Government,* by J. R. Reich and Michael S. Reich. A comprehensive government text for below-average readers in grades 7–12.

CHARLES E. MERRILL

1. *Reading for the Real World.* Reading level, grades 4–7.5; grade level, grades 7–10.

EDUCATIONAL ACTIVITIES, INC.   **251**

1. *Mythology Alive,* by Ronald A. Feldman and Lynn B. Goldman. Reading level, grades 3–4; grade level, grades 7–12. Books, cassettes, dittos.
2. *Biographies from American History,* by Michael Harrison, Alice Keener, and Deborah O'Brien-Smith. Reading level, grades 2–3; interest level, all ages. Idiom controlled. Books, cassettes.

FOLLETT PUBLISHING COMPANY

1. *Skills for Understanding Maps and Globes,* by Kenneth Job and Lois Weiser. Reading level, grades 4–5; grade level, grades 7–12.
2. *American History,* 5th ed., by Jack Abramowitz. Reading level, grades 5–7; grade level, grades 8–12.
3. *Civics,* 5th ed., by Grant T. Ball and Lee J. Rosch. Reading level, grades 6–7; grade level, grades 8–12.
4. *World History,* 3rd ed., by Jack Abramowitz. Reading level, grades 6–8; grade level, grades 9–10.
5. *The Adventures of Primero Dinero,* by Steve Jackstadt and Yukio Hamada. Reading level, grades 5–7; grade level, grades 7–12.
6. *Superheroes of Macroeconomics,* by Steve Jackstadt. Reading level, grades 6–8; grade level, grades 7–12.
7. *Foundations of Freedom,* by Jack Abramowitz. Reading level, grades 6–8; grade level, grades 7–12.
8. *The American Nation: Adventure in Freedom,* by Jack Abramowitz. Reading level, grades 4–7; grade level, grades 7–8.
9. *Follett Coping Skills Series.* Reading level, grade 3.5; grade level, grade 9–Adult. Sixteen titles.

FRANK E. RICHARDS PUBLISHERS

1. *Your Government and You,* by John H. Hock.
2. *Meeting Basic Competencies in Reading,* by Eileen L. Corcoran.
3. *The World Around Us,* by Helen Prevo.
4. *Useful Science,* by Jerry J. Danley.

GLOBE BOOK COMPANY

1. *Exploring United States History,* by John R. O'Connor et al. Reading level, grades 7–8; grade level, senior high.
2. *Minorities U.S.A.,* revised edition, by Milton Finkelstein et al. Reading level, grades 5–6; grade level, intermediate through senior high.
3. *Exploring World History,* by Sol Holt and John R. O'Connor. Reading level, grades 5–6; grade level, senior high.
4. *Inquiry: Western Civilization,* by Sidney Schwartz and John R. O'Connor (five softcover texts). Reading level, grade 7; grade level, junior and senior high.
5. *Exploring a Changing World,* revised edition, by Melvin Schwartz and John R. O'Connor. Reading level, grade 7; grade level, junior high.
6. *Exploring the Urban World,* by John R. O'Connor et al. Reading level, grades 5–6; grade level, junior and senior high.
7. *Unlocking Social Studies Skills,* by John R. O'Connor and Robert M. Goldberg. Reading level, grades 5–6; grade level, junior and senior high.

252

8. *Science Workshop*, by Seymour Rosen (twelve books). Reading level, grades 4–5; grade level, junior and senior high.

9. *Pathways in Science*, revised edition, by Joseph M. Oxenhorn (twelve books). Reading level, grades 5–6; grade level, junior high.

10. *Pathways to Health*, by J. Keogh Rash. Reading level, grades 4–5; grade level, junior high.

11. *Exploring Metrics*, by Frank D. Mark. Reading level, grades 3–4; grade level, middle school and above.

12. *The World of Vocabulary*, revised edition, by Sidney J. Rauch et al. (seven books). Reading level, grades 2–7; grade level, junior and senior high.

13. *An Edgar Allan Poe Reader*, adapted by Ollie DePew. Reading level, grades 6–7.

14. *Tales Worth Retelling*, adapted by Herzl Fife. Reading level, grades 5–6.

15. *Language Workshop: A Guide to Better English*, revised edition, by Robert R. Potter. Reading level, grades 4–5; grade level, senior high.

16. *Spell It Out: Reading/Spelling Workshop*, by Philip Trocki (four books). Reading level, grades 3–7; grade level, junior and senior high.

HOUGHTON MIFFLIN COMPANY

1. *New Directions in Reading*, by Jo M. Stanchfield and Thomas G. Gunning (ten books). For less successful readers in grades 4–12.

JANUS PUBLICATIONS

1. *Job Application Language*, by Jim Richey.
2. *Reading and Following Directions*, by Winifred Ho Roderman.
3. *Supermarket Language*, by Jim Richey.
4. *Using the Want Ads*, by Wing Jew and Carol Tandy.

McGRAW-HILL

1. *Challenges to Science: General Science for Tomorrow's World*, by William L. Smallwood. Reading level, grade 6–6.5; grade level, junior and senior high.

SCHOLASTIC MAGAZINES AND BOOK SERVICE

1. *Action*, edited by Mel Cebulash. Reading level, grades 2–3; grade level, grades 7–9.
2. *Scope*, edited by Katherine Robinson. Reading level, grades 4–6; grade level, grades 8–12.
3. *Search*, edited by Eric Oatman. Reading level, grades 4–6; grade level, grades 8–12.

STECK-VAUGHN COMPANY

1. *Wonders of Science*, by Joan S. Gottlieb. Reading level, grades 2–3; grade level, grades 7–12.
2. *Living in America Series*, by Thomas A. Rakes, Annie De Caprio, and J. Ralph Randolph (four titles). Reading level, grades 3–6; grade level, mature learner.
3. *America's Story*, by Vivian Bernstein. Reading level, grades 2–3; grade level, older students in elementary and secondary grades.

4. *Health and You,* by Vivian Bernstein. Reading level, grades 2–3. Health program for students with learning disabilities who are reading below grade level.
5. *World History and You,* by Vivian Bernstein. Reading level, grade 4; grade level, grades 5–10.
6. *Panorama Reading Series.* Reading level, grades 2–4; grade level, junior and senior high.
7. *Reading for Winners,* by Norman Schacter and John K. Whelan. Reading level, grades 4–6; grade level, junior and senior high.
8. *Superstars in Action Series,* by Randall C. Hill. Reading level, grades 4–6; grade level, grades 5–12.
9. *Spotlight Series,* by Randall Hill. Reading level, grades 2–4; grade level, grades 4–8.
10. *Great Disasters, Great Rescues, Great Escapes, Great Mysteries,* by Henry Billings and Melissa Stone. Reading level, grades 2–4; grade level, intermediate and secondary school.

SULLIVAN ASSOCIATES

1. *Programmed Math for Adults.* Reading level, grades 2–5; interest level, 12 years and older.

CHAPTER APPENDIX B: SELECTION AIDS

A number of selection aids can help secondary school teachers locate appropriate books for the variety of readers in their classes. Following is a list of some of the especially useful aids:

Abrahamson, Richard, and Betty Carter (eds.). *A Booklist for Senior High Students.* Urbana, Ill.: National Council of Teachers of English, 1988.
Books for the Teenager, 1985 Annual. New York: New York Public Library, 1985.
Blackburn, Meredith, III: *Index to Poetry for Children and Young People, 1982–1987.* New York: H. W. Wilson Company, 1988. (This title is also available for earlier years.)
Carlsen, G. Robert. *Books and the Teenage Reader: A Guide for Teachers, Librarians, and Parents.* 2nd revised edition. New York: Harper & Row, 1980.
Carter, Betty, and Richard F. Abrahamson. "The Best of the Hi/Lo Books for Young Adults: A Critical Evaluation." *Journal of Reading,* 30 (December 1986), 204–211.
Dole, Janice A., and Virginia R. Johnson. "Beyond the Textbook: Science Literature for Young People." *Journal of Reading,* 24 (April 1981), 579–582.
Donelson, Kenneth. "200 Adolescent Novels Worth Reading 1972–1977." *Illinois English Bulletin,* 65 (Fall 1977).
Eble, Mary, and Jeanne Renton. "Books Unlimited: A School-Wide Reading Program." *Journal of Reading,* 22 (November 1978), 123–130.
Fader, Daniel N. *The New Hooked on Books.* Revised edition: New York: Berkley Medallion Books, 1981.
Gallo, Donald R., ed. *Books for You: A Booklist for Senior High Students.* Urbana, Ill.: National Council of Teachers of English, 1985.
Halpern, Honey. "Contemporary Realistic Young Adult Fiction: An Annotated Bibliography." *Journal of Reading,* 21 (January 1978), 351–356.
Junior High School Library Catalog. 5th ed. New York: H. W. Wilson Company, 1985.
Matthews, Dorothy, ed. *High Interest — Easy Reading: For Junior and Senior High School Students.* 5th ed. Urbana, Ill.: National Council of Teachers of English, 1988.
Metzner, S. *World History in Juvenile Books: A Geographical and Chronological Guide.* New York: H. W. Wilson Company, 1973.

254

Reed, Arthea J. S. *Comics to Classics: A Parent's Guide to Books for Teens and Preteens.* Newark, Del.: International Reading Association, 1988.

Ryder, Randall J., Bonnie B. Graves, and Michael F. Graves. *Easy Reading: Book Series and Periodicals for Less Able Readers.* 2nd ed. Newark, Del.: International Reading Association, 1989.

School Library Journal. New York: R. R. Bowker. Published monthly September through May.

Senior High School Library Catalog. 13th ed. New York: H. W. Wilson Company, 1987.

Spache, George. *Good Reading for Poor Readers.* Revised edition. Champaign, Ill.: Garrard Press, 1978.

Stensland, A. E. *Literature by and About the American Indian: An Annotated Bibliography for Junior and Senior High School Students.* 2nd ed. Urbana, Ill.: National Council of Teachers of English, 1979.

Stroud, Janet G. "The Handicapped in Adolescent Fiction." *Journal of Reading,* 24 (March 1981), 519–522.

Tway, Eileen, ed. *Reading Ladders for Human Relations.* 6th ed. Washington, D.C.: American Council on Education, 1981.

Vugrenes, David E. "North American Indian Myths and Legends for Classroom Use." *Journal of Reading,* 24 (March 1981), 494–496.

Walker, Elinor. *Doors to More Mature Reading.* 2nd ed. Chicago: American Library Association, 1981.

Wilton, Shirley M. "Juvenile Science Fiction Involves Reluctant Readers." *Journal of Reading,* 24 (April 1981), 608–611.

7

READING

AND

WRITING

IN THE

CONTENT AREAS

OVERVIEW

The language arts are highly interrelated, and reading and writing are complementary skills. For these reasons, this chapter considers the relationships among reading, writing, and thinking in content area classes; the process approach to writing instruction; and types of writing-to-learn strategies that content teachers may employ. The aim of this chapter is to help content area teachers learn to use writing to advantage in their classes. James Upton has rightly pointed out that "the emphasis must be on the quality of the content, not on language arts skills" (Sensenbaugh, 1989, p. 463).

The explanation of the process approach to writing covers prewriting, drafting, revision, and publication procedures. The types of writing-to-learn strategies in content areas that are discussed are the language experience approach, content journals or learning logs, dialogue journals, RAFT assignments, research reports, and laboratory reports. The process approach to writing can be used with many types of content area writing, especially research reports and RAFT assignments, as well as creative writing endeavors.

Results of teachers' attempts to initiate writing across the curriculum have not been uniformly successful. Some teachers have trouble becoming collaborators in learning with students because they hold on to the traditional role of examiner. They also have trouble looking at writing as process rather than product (Sensenbaugh, 1989). Part of the reason for this may be that they tend to teach the same way they were taught, and emphasis on the writing product was common in classrooms in the past. Focus on the product alone, however, may leave students unfamiliar with the steps that must be taken to produce written materials that communicate well. The process approach involves the student with concern for the message and the audience for the writing from the beginning, whereas focus on the product often gives inordinate attention to the mechanics of writing without emphasizing the development of the message.

PURPOSE-SETTING QUESTIONS

As you read this chapter, try to answer these questions:

1. What is the relationship between reading and writing activities in content area classes?
2. What are some types of writing that are useful in the content areas?
3. What are the steps in the process approach to writing instruction?

KEY VOCABULARY

As you read this chapter, check your understanding of these terms:

dialogue journals   paraphrasing
focused freewriting   process approach
language experience approach   RAFT

The Relationships among Reading, Writing, and Thinking

Values of Writing in the Content Areas

Study in the content areas is designed to promote the learning of facts, principles, and procedures related to the disciplines involved. Such learning involves both literal and higher-level thinking skills and retention of material studied.

Writing is a tool for thinking. Glatthorn points out that "conscious, deliberative thought makes extensive use of symbols as a representation of reflection." Writing also is helpful in the development of thinking skills. Its "linear and structured form imposes its own sense of order on our attempts to think about relationships. And, as 'frozen speech,' it makes metalinguistic reflection more easily accomplished" (Glatthorn, 1989, p. 284). Writing can help readers explore what they know. Through writing, students come to terms with their own thoughts, solve problems, and discover new ideas. As Britton and others (1975, p. 28) explain, "*An essential part of the writing process is explaining the matter to oneself.* . . . There are plenty of things we are sure we know but cannot articulate: 'tacit knowledge,' Polanyi calls it. There are many more where we may still be working towards a satisfactory understanding, and others where we surprise ourselves by only realizing after we've said or written something that we've succeeded in bringing to light an idea we thought was only half-formed." Elbow (1978) expresses a similar sentiment. He not only feels that writing enhances thinking, but he also feels that it leads to an ongoing process of self-knowledge. For reasons such as these, Jenkinson (1988b, p. 716) calls writing "a powerful catalyst for learning."

Maimon (1988) encourages the frequent use of writing activities of various types, pointing out that such activities will also help students become more fluent writers. Fluency is an aspect of writing that is achieved only with practice. It also seems likely that the advantages of writing as a tool for thinking are more available to fluent writers than to writers who have not achieved fluency.

The Relationship Between Reading and Writing in Content Area Classes

There is no question that secondary school students need both reading and writing skills. They are asked to read textbooks, supplementary books, and articles as a means of obtaining content information. The writing they are asked to do, however, is often used to prove what they have learned, rather than as a learning device.

Teachers of content area classes have generally perceived reading as a means of learning content. Few, however, have viewed writing as a means of learning. Consequently, there is a noticeable lack of writing activities in most content area classes. Applebee studied writing activities in content classrooms and found that little class time (less than 5 percent) involved writing at least a paragraph. Most of the writing done was mechanical, not involving idea generation, or informational, including only notetaking or extremely brief written responses. Personal and imaginative uses of writing were extremely rare (Applebee, 1984). These findings are unfortunate, since both reading and writing are valuable learning techniques for students in these classes.

Reading and writing have the obvious link of being written language skills. They both involve prediction and anticipation of outcomes. They are both concerned with communication: readers consider the author's purposes and believability, and writers the needs of their audiences (Shanahan, 1988). Because both make use of written words that represent thoughts and oral language, vocabulary development is a key ingredient in successful reading and writing activities.

Another link between reading and writing is that the construction of meaning in reading has a relationship to the organization of written material (Shanahan, 1984). Raphael and others (1986) have found that teaching students about expository text structure has a positive effect on both report writing and content area reading. (See Chapter 3, Reading Comprehension, for more on teaching expository text structure.) As Konopak and others (1987) point out, the characteristics of generating, organizing, drafting, and revising ideas are common to both reading and writing. Learning to write using a particular organizational pattern has the potential to help students understand material that others write in that pattern, but students need to "have been actively involved in significant, purposeful writing before, during, or after reading" (Oberlin and Shugarman, 1988, p. 720).

The fact that reading is a thinking process has been stated several times earlier in this text. Elaboration on this idea can be found in Chapter 3, Reading Comprehension. This relationship to thinking is another link between reading and writing.

Techniques of Combining Reading and Writing Effectively

Despite the connections between reading and writing, use of random writing activities in a content course may not help students in reading. Ferris and Snyder (1986) found that use of a process approach to writing instruction increased writing skills, but not reading skills, for students in eleventh grade English classes. Therefore, use of random writing assignments in an effort to improve reading performance is not advisable. Assignments must focus on the relationships between the two disciplines. For example, Shanahan (1988) suggests that after students read a selection from a text, teachers can discuss its organization in relation to the organization of some of the students' own compositions. Another suggestion is that teachers have students write explanations of a difficult text to help them understand it better and make them more aware of their levels of understanding. Shanahan (1988, p. 637) also cautions that, because "reading and writing do not overlap sufficiently to permit complete reading and writing development through an instructional emphasis on one or the other," separate attention should be given to each area.

Konopak and others (1987) did find, however, that, compared to a nonwriting treatment or no treatment, a writing treatment resulted in greater student ability to produce higher level ideas gained from their reading and to synthesize information from various class activities. The writing treatment included making jot lists to activate prior knowledge, brainstorming and classification of ideas, preliminary writing based on the classifications, reading, and further writing.

Writing before starting the reading assignment can help students retrieve background knowledge that is needed to comprehend ideas in the written material. Activation of such knowledge can be beneficial to reading achievement. Oberlin and Shugarman (1988) suggest writing responses to prereading questions; previewing unfamiliar texts; using a short dictated excerpt from the passage to be read as the basis for prereading discussion; and making a conscious effort to tie students' existing knowledge to the content of the passage.

McGinley and Denner (1987) suggest the use of a prereading writing activity called story impressions before reading of narrative events. With this activity, the teacher constructs a series of clue words and phrases to provide the reader with the information necessary to form an overall impression related to the story to be read. The clues are systematic, designed to approximate closely the text's top level structure. Students are asked to take the clues and construct a story of their own that would fit the information provided, thereby predicting what the story will be about. After the writing exercise, students read the story and compare their predictions with the events of the actual story. McGinley and Denner found that this procedure significantly facilitated comprehension of the stories involved, whether or not the stories that the students constructed were close to the originals. This procedure appeared to benefit remedial students more than high ability students. An example of a set of story impressions used by McGinley and Denner and a remedial eighth grader's story prediction are shown in Example 7.1.

Cunningham and Cunningham (1987) suggest reading-writing lessons based on an organizational device as a means of helping students understand and retain knowledge in content area subjects. These instructional sessions may be built around feature matrixes, webs, outlines, or timelines. The teacher first guides the students to begin filling in a class skeleton organizer (one without the information included) that is placed on the chalkboard or a transparency, using their background knowledge of the material to be studied. Then the students read the text selection on which the organizer is based with the purpose of confirming, changing, or adding to the information in it, noting this on their personal copies of the organizer. Following this activity, the students and teacher complete the class organizer together. Disagreements are resolved by returning to the text for supporting evidence. Gaps in the information provided by the text may be used as motivational devices to send the students to reference materials. On another day, the teacher leads the group through the writing of a paragraph based on a portion of the organizer (i.e., an item on a feature matrix, a strand of a web, a main division of an outline), followed by individual or small group writing on other parts of the organizer. Eventually students can write entire compositions from their organizers.

Example 7.2 shows an organizer both in its early stages of development during the prereading period and in completed form. This organizer was developed for information included in a chapter in *Physics: Fundamentals and Frontiers*, by Robert Stollberg and Faith Fitch Hill (Boston: Houghton Mifflin, 1980).

Peresich and others (1990) had good results with the use of cognitive mapping of reading selections to increase writing proficiency. They used this technique to help students elaborate and work with text. Teachers first mapped the ideas in a unit that was about to be taught and then assigned the reading material to the students. After the students had finished the reading,

E X A M P L E **7.1**

Story Impressions

Story Impressions (Prereading) Activity Based on Poe's "The Tell-Tale Heart"

Story Impressions Given to a Class	A Remedial 8th Grader's Story Guess Written from the Story Impressions

house
↓
old man
↓
young man
↓
hatred
↓
ugly eye
↓
death
↓
tub, blood, knife
↓
buried
↓
floor
↓
police
↓
heartbeat
↓
guilt
↓
crazy
↓
confession
	There was a young man and his father, an old man. They lived in a house on a hill out in the bouniey's. The old man hated his son because he had an ugly eye.
	    The young man was asleep in his bedroom when he was awakend by screaming. He went to the bedroom and saw his father laying in the tub. There was blood everywhere and a knife through him.
	    The young man found a tape recording hidden behind the door on the floor. He turned it on there was screaming on the tape. The young man started to call the police, but then he stopped and remembered what his mother had told him. She had told him that he had a split personality. So he called the police and confessed to being crazy and killing his father. His heartbeat was heavy as he called.

Source: William J. McGinley and Peter R. Denner, "Story Impressions: A Prereading/Writing Activity," *Journal of Reading* 31 (December 1987), 250. Reprinted with permission of William J. McGinley and the International Reading Association.

the teachers presented a large blank map to the class and called on students to help fill it in. Later in the process, the teachers often assigned material to be read for homework and then to be mapped by individual students or groups of students, who presented their products on the chalkboard and discussed them. Sometimes students were asked to fill out blank maps designed by the teacher, using supplied lists of headings and subheadings. Finally, students

EXAMPLE **7.2**   261

Incomplete and Completed Organizer

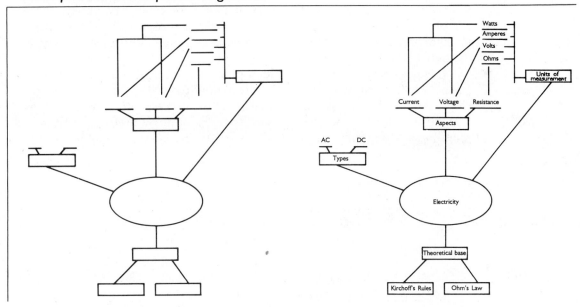

were given blank maps showing the organization of the material and were asked to read the material, fill in the maps, and write essays explaining the ideas shown on the maps.

The Process Approach to Writing in the Content Areas

If writing across the curriculum is to be implemented by teachers, they need to know how to guide students through the writing process, regardless of whether they are writing fiction or nonfiction, stories or reports. Writing has at times been treated in content classes as a two-step process: (1) the writing assignment is given, and (2) the students write a paper and turn it in to the teacher. This is an inadequate and inaccurate picture of what writing in content classes should be. Students are not helped to develop their writing products, but they are graded on their effectiveness.

When a process approach to writing is used, the development of the written material is guided through various stages of development, with students receiving feedback from teacher and peers at each stage. Students are encouraged to think about their topics, the organization for their writing, and their audiences, for the teacher is not the only audience anticipated. The papers may be shared with peers, with younger students, with parents, or with the community at large in letters to the editor of the local paper. Therefore, students tend to produce papers that are more coherent and have more complete explanations when a process approach is used than they produce when they assume that the teacher, who knows all about the topic anyway, is the only audience for the paper.

It is possible to divide the writing process into steps in several different ways, but all the systems of division have multiple stages. Example 7.3 provides an overview of a system of division of the process into four basic steps that are overlapping and recursive: prewriting, writing a draft, revision, and publishing and sharing. Each of these steps is discussed in detail below.

E X A M P L E **7.3**

Overview of Writing Stages

PREWRITING

Select and delimit topic.

Decide on audience for piece.

Choose general approach for writing.

Activate prior knowledge.

Discuss ideas with others.

Organize ideas.

WRITING A DRAFT

Get ideas on paper.

Leave space for revisions.

Share with others.

Conference with teacher.

Conference with peers.

Consult references.

Make changes without regard for neatness.

REVISION

Read draft carefully.

Consider criteria for writing.

Make use of peer editing.

Make changes based on consideration of peer and teacher comments and writing criteria.

Make use of technological aids (such as spelling checkers).

Rewrite neatly for audience, incorporating revisions, if sharing is to be in written form.

PUBLISHING AND SHARING (in one or more of these ways)

Share orally.

Include in personal book.

Include in group book.

Include in class or school magazine or newspaper.

Display in classroom.

Source: From *An Introduction to Teaching the Language Arts* by Elinor P. Ross, Betty D. Roe, copyright © 1990 by Holt, Rinehart and Winston, Inc., reprinted by permission of the publisher.

Students need instruction in the various aspects of the writing process if they are to achieve at the highest possible levels (Manion, 1988; Gahn, 1989; Cunningham and Cunningham, 1987). In her instruction, Manion uses literature as a model of quality writing for the students. One day a week there is a three- to twenty-minute mini-lesson dealing with a topic in areas ranging from class procedures to sentence-combining activities that help students learn to relate, coordinate, and subordinate ideas in their writing. Other possibilities for lessons include choosing topics, techniques for revision, paraphrase writing, feature matrix development, and webbing. Components of effective writing lessons are teacher modeling, guided practice, and feedback. Writing and conferences take place in Manion's class after the mini-lessons and during another complete class period each week. This process allows students to apply what they have learned from the mini-lessons in authentic writing experiences.

Prewriting

Prewriting is a step that is often neglected in content classes. This stage is used for selection and delimitation of the topic, determination of the audience for the writing, decision about the general approach for the writing, activation of the students' prior knowledge of the subject, discussion of ideas with classmates, and organization of ideas. The topic for the writing is sometimes selected by the teacher in a content class, but all the other activities should take place during a prewriting step. In composition classes, and sometimes in other areas, even topic selection needs to be included in the prewriting activities.

Secondary students often do not adequately limit the scope of topics they choose. Therefore, they face researching a seemingly insurmountable amount of material on a broad topic. When they discover the scope of the task ahead of them, their response is often to inquire, "How long does the paper have to be? How many sources do we need to consult?" when they should ask themselves, "What is needed to cover this topic adequately?" A social studies student may decide to write about a topic as broad as "The Civil War" when he or she should be considering something much more specific, such as a single battle, a particular general, or a single theme related to the war. Modeling of topic delimitation by the teacher can be effective in helping students to perform this task effectively.

Students need practice in writing for audiences other than the teacher. Often the audience is their classmates. When a process writing approach is used in a class, peers listen to and/or read each other's drafts during the development of the drafts, and they also often have access to each other's revised writings in the form of classroom "books" composed of the collected writings of several students or of a single student, bulletin board displays, or oral sharing sessions. During peer conferences, students can learn to ask each other questions that request clarification or expansion of the information given. The peers, therefore, let each other know when the needs of the audience are not being taken into consideration.

Teachers may also want to plan lessons that focus on other audiences. Letters to the editor of the local newspaper on timely subjects such as water pollution, unfairness of restrictions on youth gatherings, a local health hazard, or the drug problem in the schools provide students with the larger community as an audience. Students may also be asked to write simplified explanations of concepts they are studying for students in lower grades who need the information to enrich their study units; or composition students may write short stories designed for younger readers and share them with classroom teachers of lower grades. Students may write directions for carrying out procedures for their classmates to follow in class or explanations of steps in scientific experiments that other students may be curious about or want to duplicate.

Deciding on an approach to the writing may include choosing a format, such as a letter, a short story, a poem, a memorandum, or an essay. It also can include choosing the manner of presenting expository information, such as comparison/contrast, chronological order, problem/solution, cause/effect, or some other organizational pattern.

Knowledge that the student already has about the topic can be activated through activities such as class discussion, brainstorming, webbing, and/or making comparison charts or feature matrixes. Students listen to the contributions of others in these class activities and remember related items to contribute. Interaction among students at this stage is extremely desirable.

Ideas may be organized through a web or map, a feature matrix, a timeline, or an outline. Students should be taught all these techniques and be allowed to choose the one that appears to fit the task best for each assignment.

Tchudi and Yates (1983) suggest the use of a project plan sheet, as shown in Example 7.4.

E X A M P L E **7.4**

Project Plan Sheet

1. What is your subject? Explain why you are interested in it.
2. Describe your audience. Why should they know about your subject and how do you hope to affect them?
3. What information is critical to your audience's understanding of the subject and material you want to present? List. What information will your audience already know prior to the presentation?
4. Describe how you want to present your ideas. What form (editorial, poster, minute-mystery, etc.) is best for your ideas and what general outline should you follow to make your ideas clear?
5. Keeping in mind your answers to questions 1–4, try writing a first draft or sketching out your ideas for visual presentation. If you get stuck or need advice, have someone read your work and ask for suggestions.

Source: *Teaching Writing in the Content Areas: Senior High School*, © 1983. National Education Association. Reprinted with permission.

Writing a Draft

The stage of writing a draft is designed to allow the writer to put his or her ideas on paper without worrying about mechanics or neatness. Ideally, the writing time should be in an uninterrupted block, so that intervening activities do not break a student's train of thought. Some sharing of ideas with classmates may take place during this period in the form of spontaneous conversation among students seated close together. This should be allowed if it is not disruptive to the other students. Piazza and Tomlinson (1985) point out that this conversation is essentially a continued rehearsal of students' writing ideas. Peer responses may help to shape the writing in some cases, and the interaction may make a sense of audience easier to attain. Certainly if the paper is to be a collaborative effort, the collaborators need to converse as the draft progresses. Although Britton and others (1975) have characterized the production stage of the writing process as a lonely one, they do perceive the value of talking about the project. They feel that the relationship of talking to writing is a central one, that good talk encourages good writing, and that talk permits writers to express tentative conclusions and opinions. They say, "It is probable that of all the things teachers are now doing to make their pupils' approach to writing more stimulating, and the writing itself a more integral part of the manifold activities of the classroom, it is the encouragement of different kinds of talk that is the commonest and most productive factor" (Britton et al., 1975, p. 29).

Teachers may need to help students overcome their reluctance to take risks related to spelling and punctuation and their reluctance to produce messy first drafts by bringing in examples of their own first drafts, which are double spaced to allow for changes, with words, phrases, and sentences struck out and others inserted between lines or in margins and with some incorrectly spelled words circled to be looked up later. Students often have the impression that the draft has to be perfect from the beginning. Thus, to avoid imperfection, they substitute less exact words for ones they cannot spell without using the dictionary and substitute shorter, less complex sentences for ones they cannot punctuate without additional thought and time.

In the midst of drafting a paper, peer and teacher conferences about the writing may take place. Quick, informal teacher conferences may occur as the teacher circulates among the students to see how work is progressing. The teacher may ask students how their writing is going, and, when problems are revealed, ask pertinent questions to help the writers think the problem areas through effectively. For example, if a student says, "I'm not sure what order to use to tell about these events," the teacher might say, "What order did the author of your history book use to tell about the events that came just before those events?" The student may answer, "Time order," and the teacher may ask, "Is that an appropriate order for you to use here, or do you have a reason to want to use another order? What would be the value of chronological order or some other order to your presentation?" These conferences are brief but help productive writing to continue. The teacher does not tell the student what to do with the writing but leads him or her to think in channels appropriate for the task.

Students may request peer conferences for the purpose of asking for help with some part of the writing that is giving them trouble. They may read their writing to one or more peers and say something to this effect: "I'm having trouble with this ending. What can I do to improve it?"

The peers should first respond to the piece by indicating their understanding of what it says; then they should offer positive comments on good points. Finally, they should give suggestions that they may have for improvement. Students often take suggestions better if they are couched as questions: "Would it help if you left out the last paragraph? How would it sound if you referred to the beginning statement here?" When a student has an entire first draft finished, he or she may wish to read it to a peer or several peers for further response. At this point in development, the student should read the work to his or her peers rather than having them read it. This procedure keeps the mechanical problems of the draft from interfering with a content analysis by the other students.

Revision

For pieces that are going to be read by others, revision is a necessary step, although it is not necessary for everything students write. Revision should not be expected, for example, in journals or class notes unless the student does it spontaneously.

The first step in the revision process is for the student to read his or her own piece carefully, considering the criteria for writing that have been established in the class. Students should realize that revision is not just editing for spelling, grammar, and punctuation, although these aspects of writing should be considered in the process. It involves reorganizing the material, clarifying ideas, and adding and deleting information as needed. Although revision is listed as the third step in the writing process here, it is important to realize that it is a recursive process "and can occur at any point in the writing process, embedded within other subprocesses. For example, revision may happen during planning either before or during the time pen meets paper. Or it may happen while writers review material that is either in their minds or on paper" (Fitzgerald, 1988, p. 124).

A list of criteria to use in judging students' written work may be cooperatively developed by the teacher and students, or the teacher may provide it. Below is a set of criteria that a group might develop:

1. Beginning — Does it arouse the reader's interest from the start? It should get the reader "hooked" right away.
2. Middle — Is the information or action presented in a logical order? Is the organizational pattern evident to the reader? It should have an organizational pattern that fits your information.
3. Ending — Does the ending tie up the piece satisfactorily? It should not leave the reader "hanging."
4. Sentence structure — Have you used complete sentences? Do your sentences make sense? Sentence fragments should be avoided, except in special cases, such as dialogue.
5. Vocabulary — Have you used words that say exactly what you want to say? Consider the precise meanings of the words that you used and make sure they fit the context.
6. Point of view — Did you maintain a single point of view in the story? Make sure that you have not shifted from third person to second person or first person, for example.
7. Focus — Does your piece stay on the main topic? Delete portions that stray from the main point.
8. Audience — Is your story appropriate for the intended audience? Read the piece with your audience in mind, and make sure that you have taken their backgrounds into consideration.
9. Mechanics — Have you used punctuation marks and capitalization correctly? Have you spelled words correctly? Proofread for punctuation,

capitalization, and spelling. (If you wrote your piece on the computer, run the grammar and spelling check programs.)

Tchudi and Yates (1983) present another possible revision guide, shown in Example 7.5.

E X A M P L E **7.5**

Revision Guide

1. As you listen to the presentation, jot down what you like best and are most interested in.
2. Write down any questions or general comments you have when the presentation ends.
3. Did you become confused or disinterested in any section? If so, identify the section and describe what happened to you.
4. Check any of the following revision methods that will help make the presentation more interesting or clearer to you:

   Add more information or pictures (show where).

   Take out confusing or unnecessary sections (point out).

   Add an interesting fact, clue, story, or idea in the beginning that helps introduce the subject (make suggestions).

   Change the order of the ideas or pictures (explain).

   Add words, signals, or sentences that explain the order of ideas (show where).

   Add words, signals, or sentences that help tie together your ideas and the information you present (point out where).

   Give some of your own opinions, ideas, or conclusions (suggest where).

   Add some interesting information or pictures at the end to reinforce your point (make suggestions).

Source: *Teaching Writing in the Content Areas: Senior High School,* © 1983. National Education Association. Reprinted with permission.

Students can make their paper and pencil revisions by using carets and writing additional material between lines, marking out or erasing unwanted material, using circles and arrows to move material around, or even cutting and pasting. Their markings need to be clear, but the paper does not necessarily need to look neat.

If the piece has been written on a word processor, the revision activity is much easier and the final copy will be cleaner. A few keystrokes will delete material, insert material, and move material around. Papers revised in this manner never need to look messy. A spelling checker can highlight suspicious words for the student to check, and other writing tools are available to check for clichés, incomplete sentences, punctuation problems, redundancies, wordiness, and other aspects of poor or mediocre writing. These tools simply alert students to potential problems in their writing; they do not make changes for the students. The students must still take responsibility for making judgments about the flagged material. These tools simply force students to take a close look at their writing. Many flagged parts may be perfectly acceptable, whereas some errors will not be flagged. Computers cannot consider meaning in their analyses, and therefore they make errors that a human editor is less likely to make (O'Donnell, 1979).

After students have read and revised their papers to the best of their abilities, they may submit their work for peer editing. They may have regular partners for peer editing, or certain students may act as peer editors for specified weeks, or writers may request different peer editors at different times. Peer editors read each other's papers with the class writing criteria in mind, write positive comments about the material, and make suggestions for changes or ask for clarification about parts of the writing. These comments and any marks related to mechanics are discussed with the student author. The author then decides which changes may be necessary and which ones are not desirable. This process should be modeled by the teacher before the students are expected to use it (Harp, 1988).

Publishing

The pieces that students carefully revise for sharing with others, as just described, are "published" in one of a number of ways. They may simply be shared orally by the student author, or they may be posted on bulletin boards, bound into a "book" to be placed in the classroom library or school library, or published in a school magazine or newspaper. Many types of writings may be "published" in various classes. Members of a shop class could develop directions for assembly of various objects. Students in a home economics class could produce meal plans to fit family members with special dietary needs, such as low cholesterol diets or low calorie diets. Literature students could turn a short story into a play for presentation in class or to a wider audience, and science students could write descriptions of science fair exhibits or class experiments.

Students see the reason for careful crafting of their writing when others are going to read it for information or entertainment. They get a great deal of satisfaction from seeing others reading their work, and they appreciate the opportunities to read the work of their peers.

Types of Writing to Learn in the Content Areas

Many types of writing are used in content area classes to enhance learning. The types discussed here are some of the more common ones from which teachers have reported positive results. Knowledge of the steps in the process approach to writing can help teachers to implement some of these writing-to-learn strategies more effectively.

Language Experience Writings

Language experience materials have already been discussed thoroughly in Chapter 6, and a description of the procedure for developing them can be found there. These materials are very meaningful types of writing for learning, because in them students record what they understand about the material under study.

Much of what the group members record will have been gained from reading the text. The students translate the writing in the text into their own words, making it more memorable for them and more accessible to those among their classmates who cannot read the text independently.

Content Journals or Learning Logs

Content journals, or learning logs, allow students to keep a written record of content area learning activities that is personal and informal. They help students to clarify their thoughts and feelings about topics under study. Students generally choose what to write in these journals, although teachers may suggest general areas of consideration and types of things they may wish to record, if appropriate. For example, the teacher may ask that the students record any questions that occur to them as they read a content chapter or listen to a class lecture and discussion, new ideas that they have gained, confusion about a topic or procedure, feelings about the subject area, predictions about the assigned reading, explanations of a recently taught concept, or some other general category — such as the answer to some broad content-related questions — at specific times. When the teacher makes a request or notes a specific thing to be recorded, there may be sharing of journal entries by volunteers (with prior warning that sharing will be invited). At other times the students may choose among the many possibilities that arise in the classroom for their daily entries.

The student who is doing the writing is the primary audience for the content journal, although the teacher may collect these journals and read them periodically. However, content journals are not graded in the ordinary sense; spelling and grammatical errors are not marked, for example, but sometimes extra credit is awarded for especially insightful entries (Santa et al., 1989).

When teachers take up journals, they may occasionally make encouraging comments to students in response to their entries. These comments should focus on the message the student was trying to convey and ignore problems with punctuation, spelling, and grammar. Red-penciling of journals is not allowed, no matter how tempting it may be. This frees students from the fear of writing something that they are not perfectly sure about and results in more comprehensive and creative journal entries.

Teacher comments should always be written in correctly spelled and punctuated standard English, and they will serve as a model to the student for future writing. If a word has been repeatedly misspelled by the student, the teacher may write a comment in the journal with that word spelled correctly, without referring to spelling. The example can be more potent than the admonition would have been.

Focused Freewriting

Some teachers have students use the journals for true freewriting — that is, writing that has no teacher restrictions on content. Students simply write in a sustained manner for a specified period of time. This freewriting is intended to make thinking conscious and visible (Collins, 1990). In content classes, however, the teacher often places some boundaries on the content of the journals, although the students still write knowing that their writing will not be graded. This type of writing may be referred to as "focused freewriting." Language teachers may obtain more direct benefit from true freewriting than other content teachers do, because part of their curriculum centers on self-expression. Freewriting can promote writing fluency and the development of the writer's voice (Vacca and Vacca, 1989). Elbow (1978, p. 67) believes, "If you are really interested in good quality writing, then you must make it your immediate goal that people write copiously, not well. Only when people begin to use writing on other occasions than when it is required — only when they have written for diverse purposes over a period of years — will they eventually come to produce good writing." Writing consistently in journals on a daily basis is valuable to development of ease in writing.

Teachers usually designate times in class for students to write in their journals. At the beginning of a class students may write summaries of what they learned on the previous day, or at the end of class they may write summaries of what they learned that day. They may write predictions about the lesson that they are about to begin, list everything that they think they already know about the topic, or do both. They may explain how they will apply the day's lesson in everyday life. They may record the progress of a laboratory experiment or observational study. Some teachers set aside the same time period each day for journal writing, and students are asked to write for the entire five or ten minutes about the class or observations related to the class, such as their difficulty in finding time at home to study for it.

Teachers can use the journals to discover gaps in understanding and confusion that the students have. They may also gain insight into students' lives that helps explain class performance. For example, if a student writes in his or her journal, "I don't know what the chapter for last night was about. My parents left me to take care of my brothers and sisters and didn't get home until two in the morning," the teacher has an idea of the reasons behind this student's failure to answer questions in class.

Reading Response Journals

Reading response journals are a type of learning log for literature classes. With these journals, the students read or listen to a chapter of a book and then write about it for three to five minutes immediately afterward. They comment about the characters, setting, plot, author's writing style and devices, and their personal reactions. The teacher writes while the students are writing and shares his or her entries frequently as a model for the students. Students also may share their material voluntarily. The sharing can become the basis for lively discussion. The teacher can collect the journals and comment on entries, clarifying points of confusion for the students and giving positive reinforcement to those who showed insight into the story (Simpson, 1986).

Jossart (1988) suggests a slightly different twist to the use of the reading response journal. She asks her students to select a character in the book and write a journal entry for that character at a particular point in the progress of the story when there is much descriptive action. The students try to write their entries so that each one takes on the point of view of only one character. Then they share the entries, and the other students try to guess which character supposedly wrote each one. This activity involves higher level thinking on the part of both the writer and the listener.

Responses to Thought Questions

Thought questions are questions that resemble the essay questions that teachers use on tests. Writing responses to essay questions is probably the most traditional writing task that teachers expect of students. Teachers often assign study questions to classes for homework as study aids. Unfortunately, they often do not prepare students to respond effectively to such questions, as was pointed out in Chapter 4. The students may not know the meanings of the terms used in the questions, and therefore may not understand what is being asked of them (Jenkinson, 1988c). Teachers should use the procedures suggested in Chapter 4 for helping students learn to answer essay questions before asking them to respond in their journals. Teachers should define terms (such as compare, contrast, discuss), model answers that fit questions with each of the important terms, and provide students with practice questions for writing and discussion in class. Since the journal activity is ungraded, this practice in answering such questions is not threatening to the students, and they can be free to experiment with the technique without fear of failure.

Langer (1986) found that, when using written question responses as a study technique, the students that she studied tended to read a question and restate it, sometimes scan their memories of the passage, look back at the passage for the answer, and write it. They tended not to rethink the question or revise their answers afterward. Langer found that when the students responded to study questions related to a selection, their topic knowledge did not increase as much as it did when they wrote essays or took notes on the topic. The study questions seemed to cause the students to focus on specific ideas chosen by the teacher and, therefore, "may best be used to invoke quick recall of isolated items of information" (p. 406). Teachers who use study questions as a part of journal writing should be aware that they will cause the students to focus on details of the content rather than on the overall picture.

Simpson (1986) teaches a procedure that she refers to as PORPE (Predict, Organize, Rehearsal, Practice, Evaluate) in response to her students' apprehension about essay examinations. This procedure, described in detail in Chapter 4, should result in better performance in answering study questions in journals or otherwise as well as better performance on essay tests by many students, because of the intense involvement with text that is required.

Creative Applications

Some teachers have students use their journals for a variety of creative applications of writing in the subject area. The students may be asked to write stories about a historical period that they are studying in social studies class, making sure that they construct characters, settings, dialogues, and plots that fit the time that has been chosen. They may also write fictional interviews with historical characters, news stories about historical events, or letters to historical figures or from one historical figure to another. Students in math classes may write their own statement problems. In a class on electronics, students can write imaginative accounts of things such as what life would be like without electron flow. Students in a home economics class can write sets of instructions for performing a specific type of task that classmates will be asked to follow. In science class, students can write scripts for weather forecasts (Hightshue et al., 1988; Jenkinson, 1988b). To come up with other ideas for assignments, teachers may wish to refer to the list of discourse forms for content writing presented by Tchudi and Yates (1983, p. 12), shown in Example 7.6.

EXAMPLE **7.6**

Discourse Forms for Content Writing

Journals and diaries
  (real or imaginary)
Biographical sketches
Anecdotes and stories:
  from experience
  as told by others
Thumbnail sketches:
  of famous people
  of places
  of content ideas
  of historical events
Guess who/what
  descriptions
Letters:
  personal reactions
  observations
  public/informational
  persuasive:
    to the editor
    to public officials
    to imaginary people
    from imaginary places
Requests
Applications
Memos
Resumés and
  summaries
Poems
Plays
Stories
Fantasy
Adventure
Science fiction
Historical stories
Dialogues and
  conversations
Children's books
Telegrams
Editorials
Commentaries
Responses and rebuttals

Newspaper "fillers"
Fact books or fact
  sheets
School newspaper
  stories
Stories or essays for
  local papers
Proposals
Case studies:
  school problems
  local issues
  national concerns
  historical problems
  scientific issues
Songs and ballads
Demonstrations
Poster displays
Reviews:
  books (including
    textbooks)
  films
  outside reading
  television programs
  documentaries
Historical "you are
  there" scenes
Science notes:
  observations
  science notebook
  reading reports
  lab reports
Math:
  story problems
  solutions to
    problems
  record books
  notes and
    observations
Responses to literature
Utopian proposals
Practical proposals

Interviews:
  actual
  imaginary
Directions:
  how-to
  school or neighbor-
    hood guide
  survival manual
Dictionaries and
  lexicons
Technical reports
Future options, notes
  on:
  careers, employment
  school and training
  military/public service
Written debates
Taking a stand:
  school issues
  family problems
  state or national
    issues
  moral questions
Books and booklets
Informational
  monographs
Radio scripts
TV scenarios and scripts
Dramatic scripts
Notes for improvised
  drama
Cartoons and cartoon
  strips
Slide show scripts
Puzzles and word
  searches
Prophecy and
  predictions
Photos and captions
Collage, montage,
  mobile, sculpture

Source: *Teaching Writing in the Content Areas: Senior High School,* © 1983. National Education Association.
Reprinted with permission.

Paraphrasing and Summarizing

Paraphrasing and summarizing material learned in content area classes and from content area textbooks provides material for content journals. A surprising number of secondary school students do not know how to paraphrase the text material in their content subjects. In fact, when asked to paraphrase, many do not realize that they are simply expected to put the material into their own words. According to Shugarman and Hurst (1986, p. 397), "research supports the view that paraphrase writing enhances reading skills and increases content comprehension and recall." A study by Patricia and James Cunningham showed that paraphrase writing resulted in improved listening, speaking, reading, and writing vocabularies (Shugarman and Hurst, 1986). Therefore, paraphrase writing in content journals seems to be a fruitful activity.

Paraphrase writing depends on the student's reading for meaning and restating content in other words. Shugarman and Hurst (1986) identify three types of paraphrases: simple paraphrases, summaries, and elaborations. Simple paraphrases are used for short passages, summaries for bringing out main points in longer passages or graphic materials, and elaboration for integrating the content of the original material with the person's prior knowledge and experiences as well as his or her creativity. With elaboration, new forms may be used to represent the meaning of the text; for example, material from written text may be described in tabular or graphic form. Dictionaries and thesauruses are helpful tools for paraphrasing.

To teach paraphrasing, teachers should define the concept, demonstrate it for the students first with short paraphrases, offer the students guided practice in providing short paraphrases, and then provide planned independent practice. After short paraphrases have been mastered, the students will be ready for summaries and, finally, elaborations. The instruction for these types of paraphrases should parallel that for short paraphrases.

Practice in paraphrasing can be enjoyable. The teacher can present students with statements such as "A fowl in the palm is of the same value as a pair in the shrub." Students can be asked to paraphrase this sentence to produce a familiar saying. Students are permitted to refer to dictionaries and thesauruses for the activity. Later the students may be asked to locate familiar expressions, paraphrase them, and present the paraphrases to the class for decoding. Eventually, the students can be asked to locate key phrases in the textbook assignment for the day and write paraphrases in clear language. Judging of the clarity and accuracy of the paraphrases can be done in small groups, with all group members presenting their own paraphrases and participating in the evaluation of those of other students. Both paraphrasers and evaluators have to examine the text material closely in order to complete this activity. Students in math classes can paraphrase statement problems; those in social studies classes can paraphrase news articles, campaign literature, and advertisements; those in shop class can paraphrase instructions for a project; and so on for any subject area.

A form of summarizing is précis writing. D'Angelo (1983) credited skill in précis writing with improving both writing and research skills, and Bromley and McKeveny (1986) suggest that the use of précis writing enhances comprehension and recall of content material. Précis are abstracts of materials that retain the point of view of the original materials — in other words, they are a special type of summary. Bromley and McKeveny offer suggestions for teaching students to write précis, including the use of paraphrasing.

Students need to understand the purposes for précis writing, including vocabulary improvement and enhanced comprehension and retention. The teacher should demonstrate the process to the students, showing them how to analyze the original material, select main ideas for inclusion in the précis, reject nonessential material, and paraphrase the ideas through use of synonyms and restructuring of sentences. Encouraging the use of the thesaurus is a good technique. Taking such a close look at the content makes learning and remembering the material much more likely than if the material were processed less actively.

Group composition of a précis is a good beginning step. This can be done by having the students dictate as the teacher or one of the students records the précis. This is an application of the language experience technique described in Chapter 6.

Bromley and McKeveny (1986) suggest that models of acceptable précis be available to students so that they can compare these models to their own products, evaluate their efforts, and perhaps revise their work. They also suggest that students save their précis for study before tests.

Summarizing can also be an effective study technique to use with reading assignments. More information on summarizing is found in Chapter 4.

Dialogue Journals

Although dialogue journals *could* be content journals, they need not be. The distinctive feature of dialogue journals is that they set up a two-way written conversation between the teacher and each student. Their primary purpose is to open lines of communication. Students write about anything they choose, including both in-class and out-of-class experiences and concerns. They may offer their opinions, state grievances, provide information, make predictions, ask questions, answer questions, apologize, make promises, offer thanks, make evaluations, or give directions, among other possibilities. The written statements, questions, or observations are not evaluated by the teachers; the teachers respond to them as personal communications (Bode, 1989; Strackbein and Tillman, 1987; Jenkinson, 1988a).

Each day, time is made available for the students to write in their journals. The teachers read all the entries (generally after school) and respond to them. The responses may include recognition of what the students are saying, clarification of things about which the students are confused, answers to students' questions, questions for students to answer related to the writing or to some common interest, and sharing of personal thoughts and feelings. Grammatical and spelling errors in journal entries are never marked. The next day the students read the teachers' responses and continue the written dialogue with another entry. Strackbein and Tillman (1987) suggest that the teacher read only a specified number of journals each day if the reading load seems too great. Teachers who follow this suggestion should take care not to omit any one student's journal more often than others. Since grading is not a part of the reading, most teachers will be able to manage reading each student's journal at least every other day.

Dolly (1990) suggests the use of dialogue journals with English as a second language (ESL) students. She points out that such journals ensure that this reading material will be somewhat adjusted to the students' individual reading abilities, because teachers can modify their writing to fit the language proficiency of the students.

RAFT Assignments

"RAFT simply stands for (R) role, (A) audience, (F) format, and (T) topic, the key ingredients for making writing assignments" (Santa et al., 1989, p. 148). RAFT assignments are explicit as to each of these factors: the student is told who the writer is, who the audience is, what form the writing will take, and the topic for the writing. Student roles may vary widely; they can be scientists, blood cells, trees, animals, or other animate or inanimate objects. The audiences can be classmates, younger children, or the general public. Formats can include letters, editorials, memoranda, and poems. A sample assignment might be as follows: You are the brother of a boy who is considering experimenting with cocaine (role). Through a letter (format) to your brother (audience), try to persuade him not to do this, backing up your arguments with facts about this drug.

Research Reports

Tone (1988, p. 76) points out values of the research paper in secondary classes: "It commonly ties reading to writing. As a writing project, it usually involves the organizing and outlining of numerous facts and details. It develops comprehension that arises from synthesis and organization of information." Research papers can promote critical thinking about topics under study. They also offer practical applications of various study skills, such as library use, reference book use, notetaking, outlining, and summarizing. Nevertheless, research papers should not be assigned without careful assessment of students' prerequisite skills, so that appropriate instruction can be offered if necessary skills are not in evidence. These skills should be taught as needed and connections made between the skills and the current task of answering the research questions that have been raised. Benson (1987) believes that students should be offered several notetaking, footnoting, and bibliographic forms from which to choose; this gives them a feeling of control over the project.

When content area teachers assign reports to be written for their classes, they sometimes allow students to choose their own topics. In other instances, a teacher may ask each student to write on a predetermined topic. Some educators feel that students should have a great deal of control over what they write. Britton and others (1975, p. 23) state: "But, however controlled the situation, the writer is *selecting* from what he knows and thinks. . ., and embodying that knowledge and thought in words which *he* produces, no matter how much he draws on the language of a book or of the teacher's notes." Therefore, from the perspective of Britton and others, having the teacher assign topics and guide students in writing procedures does not negate the ownership of the writing.

Davis and Hunter (1990) suggest having gifted students research the accuracy of historical novels as a project that would result in a research paper that solved a real problem. Anachronisms and other inaccuracies would be located by consulting reference books about the period. The students thus can have a choice of the novel to write about and a choice of focus for the paper, but they also have a well-defined task.

The process that follows can be used to help students prepare good reports. The first step listed obviously is not applicable if the teacher chooses the topic.

Step 1. Select a topic. The topic selected must be pertinent to the content area material being studied. It should be chosen because of its interest value for both the reporter and the rest of the class, if the reports are going to be shared. Ordinarily, students tend to choose topics that are much too broad for adequate coverage. The teacher needs to help students narrow their topics so that the task of preparing the report is more manageable.

Step 2. Collect information on the topic. Students should use the location skills discussed in Chapter 4 in order to collect information from a variety of sources. The organizational skill of note taking, also covered in Chapter 4, is also essential for use at this point.

Step 3. Organize the material. Outlining or webbing the information collected is the main activity in this step. Material from the different sources used must be fused together. The sequence and relationship of main ideas and details are important considerations in forming the outline or web.

Step 4. Write a first draft. Utilizing the outline or web just formulated and the notes compiled, the students write an initial draft of the report.

Step 5. Read the first draft for revision and editing. The students read the first draft and check for organization, sentence and paragraph sense, cohesiveness of the information, appropriate usage, correct spelling, and proper punctuation. They also confirm that all material is properly documented.

At this point, peer editing may be utilized. With this approach, a peer editor carefully reads the report of his or her classmate, answering questions provided by the teacher. Some sample questions are as follows: "Does the report have a title that accurately reflects its contents? Does the report have a good beginning that sparks interest in the topic? Is the sequence in which the information is presented logical? If not, what do you think is wrong with it? Is enough information included? In your opinion, what questions remain to be answered by the report? Does the report have errors in mechanics (e.g., spelling, capitalization, punctuation)? If so, mark them for the author. Does the report have a conclusion that sums up the material adequately? Do you have any questions or suggestions for the author?" After answering these questions, the peer editor returns the report and comments to the author, who revises it, carefully considering the editor's comments. The peer editor may be asked to read and react to the report again before it is submitted to the teacher. Often two students work together, each acting as peer editor for the other.

Step 6. Revise the report. The students make needed changes in the initial draft and rewrite the report in a form acceptable for submission to the teacher. Revision is easier if the report has been written using word processing software on a microcomputer.

The teacher can do much to help prepare students to perform effectively on an assigned written report. A procedure that a teacher might follow is described below.

1. Name a broad topic related to the course of study. Ask students for suggestions as to how the topic could be narrowed to make it more manageable. Consider a number of acceptable topics that might be derived from the original topic.
2. Choose one of the acceptable narrowed topics. Take the students to the library and have them locate sources of information on the topic. Ask each of them to take notes from at least one source and to record bibliographical information. Remind them to make use of skimming and scanning techniques as they search for information. (See Chapter 4 for information on skimming and scanning.)
3. Return to the classroom. As a class, synthesize the notes into a single outline. (Use the chalkboard or overhead projector.)
4. Write the report from the outline as a whole-class or small-group activity,

with the teacher working as the scribe or assigning a student to be the scribe.

5. Have the students read the draft for content, organization, and mechanics.

6. Make needed changes in organization, spelling, and expression on the basis of the proofreading.

The teacher who follows this procedure has essentially walked the students through the steps of report writing before asking them to attempt it on their own. Thereafter, the students will know what to expect when they are assigned individual reports to write. Help with skills of note taking, outlining, summarizing information, and locating information should be a prerequisite for assignment of a written report if these skills have not been mastered previously. Help should also be given with composing footnote and bibliographic entries. A guide such as *Form and Style: Theses, Reports, Term Papers* (Houghton Mifflin, 1986) can be a valuable resource. Example 7.7 shows a sample page on footnote form from this useful guide. Some dictionaries, such as the *Houghton Mifflin College Dictionary* (see sample page in Example 4.9), also offer information on footnotes and bibliographic entries.

Some computer software has been developed to help students with basic research skills. Many of these programs are not very good, and teachers should preview them carefully before buying. Some are based on a single product, such as a particular set of encyclopedias, and will have little value for a teacher who does not have access to these resources.

Davey (1987) recommends having students work in teams on research reports, following steps similar to those enumerated above. She feels that research reports are less threatening and provide more active involvement when they are completed in teams of two to five students. In addition, greater learning appears to result from team reports than from individually produced reports. Teachers must monitor team work regularly and should also encourage self-monitoring of progress by team members.

Raphael and others (1988) developed the Expository Writing Program (EPW) to help students learn how to write well-organized reports with data collected from a number of sources. The EPW is designed around "think sheets" that stimulate strategy use for planning the report, gathering data, drafting, editing, and revising. The EWP Prewriting Think Sheet focuses on planning concerns such as considering the topic, things the students already know about the topic, and the audience for the paper. The Organizing Think Sheet focuses students' attention on different sets of questions that fit different text structures, such as comparison/contrast, problem/solution, and explanation. Students use the sheet that is appropriate for their chosen organizational pattern. A lined sheet of colored paper forms the think sheet for writing the first draft. There are Edit and Peer Editor Think Sheets that provide the framework for first self-editing and then peer editing. These sheets

EXAMPLE **7.7**

Form and Style Guide Page

NOTES

Books

Basic form
    ¹ Jacob Bronowski, <u>The Ascent of Man</u> (Boston: Little, Brown, 1973), 57-67.

Two authors
    ² James G. March and Herbert A. Simon, <u>Organizations</u> (New York: Wiley, 1958), 79.

More than three authors
    ³ Marion C. Sheridan et al., <u>The Motion Picture and the Teaching of English</u> (New York: Appleton-Century-Crofts, 1965), 37.

Two authors with same last name
    ⁴ Wilma R. Ebbitt and David Ebbitt, <u>Writer's Guide and Index to English</u>, 6th ed. (Glenview: Scott, Foresman, 1978), 67.

Pseudonym, real name supplied
    ⁵ J. Abner Peddiwell, Ph.D. [Harold Benjamin], <u>The Saber-Tooth Curriculum</u> (New York: McGraw-Hill, 1939), 78-85.

Author's name missing
    ⁶ [Dorothy Scarborough], <u>The Wind</u> (New York: Harper, 1925).

or

    ⁷ <u>The Wind</u> (New York: Harper, 1925), 27.

Group or corporation as author
    ⁸ Holiday Magazine, <u>Spain</u> (New York: Random House, 1964), 52.

Editor and author, emphasis on author
    ⁹ William C. Hayes, <u>Most Ancient Egypt</u>, ed. Keith C. Seele (Chicago: Univ. of Chicago Press, 1965), 5.

Translator and author, emphasis on translator
    10 Suzette Macedo, trans., <u>Diagnosis of the Brazilian Crisis</u>, by Celso Furtado (Berkeley: Univ. of California Press, 1965), 147-53.

Two editors
    11 Arthur S. Link and Rembert W. Patrick, eds., <u>Writing Southern History: Essays in Historiography in Honor of Fletcher M. Green</u> (Baton Rouge: Louisiana State Univ. Press, 1966), 384.

Examples of Note and Bibliography Forms

Source: William Giles Campbell, Stephen Vaughn Ballou, and Carole Slade, *Form and Style: Theses, Reports, Term Papers,* 7th ed. (Boston: Houghton Mifflin Company, 1986), p. 126. Reprinted by permission of Houghton Mifflin Company.

E X A M P L E **7.8**

Sample Think Sheets

Think Sheet for Planning

Author's name _____ Date _____

Topic: _____

Who: Who am I writing for?
Why: Why am I writing this?
What: What do I already know about my topic? (Brainstorm)

1. _____
2. _____
3. _____
4. _____

How: How do I group my ideas?

Source: Taffy E. Raphael, Carol Sue Englert, and Becky W. Kirschner, "Acquisition of Expository Writing Skills," in Jana M. Mason (Ed.), READING AND WRITING CONNECTIONS. Copyright © 1989 by Allyn and Bacon. Reprinted with permission.

Think Sheet for Editing a Comparison/Contrast Paper

Author's Name _____ Editor's Name _____

Read to check information. (Authors: Read your paper aloud to your editor.)

What is the paper mainly about?

What do you like best? Put a * next to the part you liked best and tell why you like it here:

What parts are not clear? Put a ? next to the unclear parts, and tell what made the part unclear to you:

Is the paper interesting? Tell why or why not here:

Question yourself to check organization.

Did the author:

Tell what two things are compared and contrasted?   Yes   Sort of   No

Tell things they are being compared and contrasted on?	Yes	Sort of	No
Tell how they are alike?	Yes	Sort of	No
Tell how they are different?	Yes	Sort of	No
Use keywords clearly?	Yes	Sort of	No

Plan revision.

What two parts do you think should be changed or revised? (For anything marked "Sort of" or "No," should the author add to, take out, reorder?)

    1. _____

       _____

    2. _____

       _____

    What could help make the paper more interesting?

Talk.

Talk to the author of the paper. Talk about your comments on this editing think-sheet. Share ideas for revising the paper.

Source: Taffy E. Raphael, Carol Sue Englert, and Becky W. Kirschner, "Acquisition of Expository Writing Skills," in Jana M. Mason (Ed.), READING AND WRITING CONNECTIONS. Copyright © 1989 by Allyn and Bacon. Reprinted with permission.

focus on the content and organization of the paper and on planning the next step of the writing. A Revision Think Sheet encourages the students to integrate the feedback from others into a revision plan. Two types of think sheets are shown in Example 7.8. A variety of examples of various types of think sheets can be found in a recent article in *The Reading Teacher* (Raphael and Englert, 1990).

Laboratory Reports

Secondary science classes often have laboratory components for which laboratory reports must be written. A student lab guide such as the one in Example 7.9 may be used to guide students through experiments.

    The writing of a laboratory report can be modeled by doing an experiment and writing a cooperative laboratory report on the chalkboard or a transparency. The teacher can lead the students through each step in the process; then the students can use their lab guides to write reports independently. For students who need more support in becoming independent report writers, teachers may provide a framed report form, such as the one in Example 7.10. The sentence starters will cue the students to the information that they should be including. Use of framed reports should be phased out as the students become more adept at report writing (Santa et al., 1989).

E X A M P L E **7.9**

Student Lab Guide

Purpose of This Lab: Why are you doing this lab?

Problem: What problem are you investigating?

Hypothesis: What do you think the outcome of this lab will be? Think about what you already know about the topic, and make an educated guess about the outcome.

Materials: List all materials that you will need to conduct this laboratory.

Procedure: List in step by step fashion the procedure you are going to use to collect the data.

Data or Results: Draw, record, or chart all detailed observations noted from the procedure above.

Analysis or Conclusion: Reread your problem statement. Did your results resolve the problem? Explain why. If the results did not help clarify the problem, explain why.

Class Conclusion: Final conclusion after class discussion. Modify your own conclusion, if necessary.

Source: Santa/Havens/Harrison, "Teaching Secondary Science Through Reading, Writing, Studying, and Problem Solving," in CONTENT AREA READING AND LEARNING: Instructional Strategies, Lapp/Flood/Farnan eds., © 1989, p. 150. Reprinted by permission of Prenctice Hall, Inc., Englewood Cliffs, New Jersey.

Photo Essays

Sinatra and others (1990) found that the use of photo essays and various types of semantic maps was effective for building background knowledge of cultur- ally diverse students and for helping them to organize their thoughts into writing. The students worked in pairs initially to develop photo essays with meaningful conceptual frameworks and then reconstructed the photos on storyboards using semantic mapping formats. The images in the photos helped to bridge the language differences of the student population and to provide a common base for communication. The procedure was to plan topics or themes, take photos to illustrate the topics, organize the pictures on a storyboard, and then write a composition on the topic with the storyboard in view. Students brainstormed ideas for photos before the actual picture-taking was done. When the pictures had been developed, the student pairs worked together on the arrangement on the storyboards. The assignments elicited sequential, descriptive, and classification writing styles. Example 7.11 shows these three patterns for organizing essays.

E X A M P L E **7.10**

Framed Laboratory Report

Observation: After observing [state something unexplainable], I noticed

_____ .

Problem [or question]: Why does [put observation in the form of a question or problem]

_____ .

Hypothesis: I think _____ [refer to the problem or question] is _____ . An observation that led to this hypothesis is _____ . I intend to prove

_____ by _____ .

Materials:

1.
2.
3.

Procedure: [put in order your plan for proving your hypothesis]

1.
2.
3.

Data: [Accurate detailed observations of your model and how it works are recorded here. Include visuals such as tables, graphs, mathematical operations, and pictures along with written observations.]

Analysis and/or Conclusion: [Examine the problem and your hypothesis. Did your data support your hypothesis? Explain why your results supported or did not support your hypothesis.]

My problem is _____ . The results of my investigation are _____ . These results may be caused by _____ . Therefore, these results did or did not support my hypothesis because _____ .

Class Conclusions: After the class discussion, we concluded _____

_____ .

Source: Santa/Havens/Harrison, "Teaching Secondary Science Through Reading, Writing, Studying, and Problem Solving," in CONTENT AREA READING AND LEARNING: Instructional Strategies, Lapp/Flood/Farnan eds., © 1989, pp. 150–151. Reprinted by permission of Prentice Hall, Inc., Englewood Cliffs, New Jersey.

EXAMPLE **7.11**

Three Patterns of Storyboard Organization for Photo Essay and Written Composition

(A) Sequential organization

```
                    ┌──────────────────────────┐
                    │  A Day with Our Principal  │
                    └──────────────────────────┘

┌──────────┐     ┌──────────┐     ┌──────────┐     ┌──────────┐
│ Photo 1  │ ──→ │ Photo 2  │ ──→ │ Photo 3  │ ──→ │ Photo 4  │
└──────────┘     └──────────┘     └──────────┘     └──────────┘

          ┌──────────┐     ┌──────────┐
          │ Photo 5  │ ──→ │ Photo 6  │ ──→  etc.
          └──────────┘     └──────────┘
```

(B) Thematic organization

(C) Organization by classification

Source: Richard Sinatra et al., "Combining Visual Literacy, Text Understanding, and Writing for Culturally Diverse Students." *Journal of Reading* 33 (May 1990), 614. Reprinted with permission of Richard Sinatra and the International Reading Association.

Evaluation of Writing

Not all writing that students are asked to do in content area classrooms is formally evaluated. Writing done in journals, for example, is done for its learning value and is not formally evaluated for a grade. Language experience writing is generally evaluated by the students who develop it as it is produced. Generally it is not graded by the teacher but is used as a learning aid in the classroom.

If the process approach to writing is used, there is much ongoing evaluation as a written piece is developed. Students elicit feedback about their writing from their peers, they proofread their own work with revision checklists in mind, and they receive feedback from their teachers during student-teacher conferences. In addition to the evaluative efforts that have gone on as materials are written, there are times when teachers must formally evaluate a final draft of a written assignment. These grading procedures may be holistic or analytic in nature.

When holistic grading is used, the teacher evaluates the written material as a whole. The paper is read for general impression and overall effect. It may be compared with pieces that have already been graded or scored for the inclusion of features important to the particular type of writing involved (INC Sights, 1989). Scoring guides can be developed, which list the characteristics of high-quality, medium-quality, lower-quality, and lowest-quality papers for a particular assignment with a specified purpose and audience. When this approach is used, it is referred to as primary trait scoring (Graser, 1983). Kirby and Liner (1988, p. 221) point out that holistic grading "focuses on the piece of writing as a whole and on those features most important to the success of the piece. . . . The rating is quick because the rater does not take time to circle errors or make marginal notations." Kirby and Liner suggest that teachers may use a list of criteria related to the impact of the writing, the inventiveness of the approach, and the individual flavor of the writing as a guide for their holistic grading. They refer to this type of grading as impression marking.

Analytic scales not only focus readers' attention on the features that are needed for the writing to be effective but also attach point values to each feature. The reader sums the scores for each feature in determining the overall grade. The Diederich Scale is an example of an analytic scale. It leads the scorer to assign a score of 1 (poor), 2 (weak), 3 (average), 4 (good), or 5 (excellent) to quality and development of ideas *and* organization, relevance, and movement (both of which are weighted heavier than the other considerations); style, flavor, and individuality *and* wording and phrasing (both of which are given intermediate weights); and grammar and sentence structure, punctuation, spelling, and manuscript form and legibility (all of which receive the lowest weights). Content and organization represent 50 percent of the grade; aspects of style, 30 percent; and mechanics, 20 percent. Scales such as this keep raters focused on the carefully defined criteria and keep them from being unduly influenced by surface features rather than considering all the factors contributing to the effectiveness of a piece of writing (Kirby and Liner, 1988). If students are asked to keep folders of written work over the course of a semester or year, their progress can be noted by comparing the earlier pieces with the latest ones. Students may gain more satisfaction from this type of final evaluation than from many other methods because they can see the differences in the writing and often can see that early teacher comments led to improvements in later products.

SUMMARY

Writing is valuable in content area classes because it is a tool for thinking and for attaining self-knowledge and because it enhances retention of the material studied. As these benefits are gained, fluency in writing is also promoted.

Reading and writing are closely related skills. Both are written language skills, involve prediction of outcomes, are concerned with communication, involve construction of meaning, and make use of vocabulary. Still, use of random writing activities in a content course may not help students in reading. To foster reading progress, writing assignments must focus on the relationships between reading and writing. Writing before reading can help students activate their background knowledge about a topic, enhancing reading comprehension. Reading is a thinking process, and reading comprehension requires thinking at various cognitive levels, as does writing production.

A process approach to writing tends to produce superior writing products and a better understanding of the writing process than an approach in which the teacher assigns a paper and the students write it and turn it in without process guidance. The writing process can be broken down into four overlapping and recursive steps: prewriting, writing a draft, revision, and publishing. Many types of writing-to-learn activities have been used in content classes. They include language experience writings, content journals or learning logs, dialogue journals, RAFT assignments, research reports, and laboratory reports.

Not all writing done in class needs to be evaluated. Journal writing is a prime example of this. Writing that is developed through a process approach is subject to ongoing evaluation as the writing progresses. Sometimes teachers need to evaluate a final draft of a piece of writing for grading purposes. When this is the case, they may use either holistic or analytic grading procedures.

1. Why is writing considered a catalyst for learning? (a) It is a tool for thinking. (b) It leads to an ongoing process of self-knowledge. (c) It aids metalinguistic reflection. (d) All of these

2. What amount of time did Applebee find was used in content classrooms on the writing of at least a paragraph? (a) Less than 5 percent (b) 5 to 10 percent (c) 10 to 20 percent (d) 20 to 50 percent

3. What type of writing did Applebee find students primarily doing in content classes? (a) Imaginative (b) Personal (c) Mechanical and informational (d) None of these

4. What does the technique called story impressions involve? (a) Sharing reactions to a story after reading (b) Jotting down words that the story calls to mind as you read (c) Using clue words and phrases from a story to construct your own story before the story from which the words were taken is read (d) None of these

5. What types of writing may be used for content journals? (a) Focused freewriting (b) Reading response journals (c) Responses to thought questions (d) All of these

6. What is true of focused freewriting? (a) It is always graded immediately by the teacher. (b) It can promote writing fluency. (c) Punctuation, spelling, and grammatical errors are circled in red by the teacher to help students improve. (d) None of these

7. What is paraphrasing? (a) Repeating the words of the text exactly (b) Writing down your own ideas about a topic (c) Restating the material in the text in your own words (d) None of these

8. What is the distinctive feature of dialogue journals? (a) They involve having students write on an assigned topic. (b) They set up a two-way written conversation between the teacher and each student. (c) They are graded each day by the teacher. (d) They can be used only with average or gifted students.

9. What does RAFT stand for? (a) Role, audience, format, topic (b) Reading, acting, fact-finding, telling (c) Reading, activating background knowledge, facilitating writing, thinking about the product (d) None of these

10. What should be avoided in assigning written reports to students? (a) Stressing organizational skills before starting the report writing (b) Guiding the students through a report-writing experience before they are asked to write independently (c) Using a single source of information for the reports (d) None of these

11. What are the steps in the writing process? (a) Prewriting, writing a draft, revision, and publishing (b) Assigning, writing, evaluating (c) Preparation for writing, writing, turning in assignment (d) None of these

12. What are the components of effective writing lessons? (a) Free choice and absence of evaluation (b) Teacher modeling, guided practice, and feed-

back (c) Worksheet skill assignments to be completed individually (d) None of these

13. What may occur during the prewriting stage? (a) Selection and delimitation of topic (b) Determination of the audience for writing (c) Activation of the students' prior knowledge about the subject (d) None of these

14. How can knowledge that the student already has about the topic be activated? (a) Through class discussion (b) Through brainstorming (c) Through webbing (d) All of these

15. What should happen during writing of a draft? (a) Students should check all spelling and grammar as they proceed. (b) Students should write very neatly and legibly. (c) Students should share ideas with classmates if they feel the need. (d) All of these

16. What is true of teacher-student conferences on writing? (a) The teacher tells the student what to say. (b) The teacher leads the student to think about some aspects of his or her writing. (c) The teacher grades the writing during the conferences. (d) All of these

17. What is true of revision? (a) It is necessary for every piece of writing that students do. (b) It only involves editing for mechanics. (c) It is needed only for materials that are to be published for sharing with others. (d) None of these

18. What type of evaluation is typical each time the process approach to writing is used? (a) None (b) Ongoing (c) Holistic (d) Analytic

THOUGHT QUESTIONS

1. In what ways is writing valuable in content area instruction?
2. What are some types of activities in which writing can positively influence reading achievement?
3. Which types of writing to learn would be most helpful in your content area? Why?
4. Why is the prewriting stage so important to the writing program?
5. What are some advantages to publishing and sharing students' writing?
6. What method of evaluation of final drafts seems most appropriate to you? Why?

ENRICHMENT ACTIVITIES

*1. Observe one period of a content area class. List the types of writing that the students are asked to do and the length of time spent on each writing activity. Compare your findings with those of Applebee.

*These activities are designed for in-service teachers, student teachers, or practicum students.

*2. Try using one of the prereading writing activities suggested by Oberlin and Shugarman with a content reading assignment that you give. Share your feelings about its effectiveness with your classmates in written or oral form.

3. Analyze a story and prepare a story impressions clue list for it. *Try the activity with a secondary class, if possible.

*4. Try using content journals or learning logs in your classroom for a three-week period. Report your reaction to this technique to your classmates.

5. Make a list of creative applications of writing to your subject area.

6. With a partner from this class, role-play the use of dialogue journals for a specified imaginary class (for example, a tenth grade biology class). One of you write as the teacher and one as the student. Be prepared to discuss with the class your reactions to the technique.

*7. Guide a group of secondary school students through the process of writing a group report.

8. Prepare a lesson plan for using the process approach with a writing assignment. Role-play the teaching of this lesson to your classmates. *If possible, teach the lesson to a class of secondary school students.

BIBLIOGRAPHY

Applebee, Arthur N. *Contexts for Learning to Write: Studies of Secondary School Instruction*. Norwood, N.J.: Ablex, 1984.

Beatty, Jane N. "The Research Paper in a Remedial Curriculum." *Journal of Reading*, 30 (March 1987), 550–551.

Benson, Linda K. "How to Pluck an Albatross: The Research Paper without Tears." *English Journal*, 76 (November 1987), 54–56.

Bode, Barbara A. "Dialogue Journal Writing." *The Reading Teacher*, 42 (April 1989), 568–571.

Britton, James, Tony Burgess, Nancy Martin, Alex McLeod, and Harold Rosen. *The Development of Writing Abilities (11–18)*. London: Macmillan Education Ltd., 1975.

Bromley, Karen D'Angelo, and Laurie McKeveny. "Précis Writing: Suggestions for Instruction in Summarizing." *Journal of Reading*, 29 (February 1986), 392–395.

Collins, Norma Decker. "Freewriting, Personal Writing, and the At-Risk Reader." *Journal of Reading*, 33 (May 1990), 654–655.

Cunningham, Patricia M., and James W. Cunningham. "Content Area Reading-Writing Lessons." *The Reading Teacher*, 40 (February 1987), 506–512.

D'Angelo, Karen. "Précis Writing: Promoting Vocabulary Development and Comprehension." *Journal of Reading*, 26 (March 1983), 534–539.

Davey, Beth. "Team for Success: Guided Practice in Study Skills through Cooperative Research Reports." *Journal of Reading*, 30 (May 1987), 701–705.

Davis, Susan J., and Jean Hunter. "Historical Novels: A Context for Gifted Student Research." *Journal of Reading*, 33 (May 1990), 602–606.

Davis, Susan J., and Janice Winek. "Improving Expository Writing by Increasing Background Knowledge." *Journal of Reading*, 33 (December 1989), 178–181.

Dolly, Martha R. "Integrating ESL Reading and Writing through Authentic Discourse." *Journal of Reading*, 33 (February 1990), 360–365.

292

Elbow, Peter. "Why Teach Writing?" In Philip L. Brady (ed.), *The Why's of Teaching Composition*. Washington State Council of Teachers of English, 1978, pp. 57–69.

Farr, Marchi (ed.). *Interactive Writing in Dialogue Journals: Practitioner, Linguistic, Social, and Cognitive Views*. Norwood, N.J.: Ablex, 1988.

Ferris, Judith Ann, and Gerry Snyder. "Writing as an Influence on Reading." *Journal of Reading*, 29 (May 1986), 751–756.

Fitzgerald, Jill. "Helping Young Writers to Revise: A Brief Review for Teachers." *The Reading Teacher*, 42 (November 1988), 124–129.

Freeman, Marcia S., and Wendy C. Kasten. "A Secondary Model for a Young Author's Conference." *Journal of Reading*, 33 (February 1990), 356–358.

Gahn, Shelley Mattson. "A Practical Guide for Teaching Writing in the Content Areas." *Journal of Reading*, 32 (March 1989), 525–531.

Glatthorn, Allen. "Thinking, Writing, and Reading; Making Connections." In Diane Lapp, James Flood, and Nancy Farnan (eds.), *Content Area Reading and Learning: Instructional Strategies*. Englewood Cliffs, N.J.: Prentice Hall, 1989.

Graser, Elsa R. *Teaching Writing: A Process Approach*. Dubuque, Iowa: Kendall/Hunt Publishing Co., 1983.

Graves, Donald H. *Writing: Teachers and Children at Work*. Portsmouth, N.H.: Heinemann Educational Books, 1983.

Harp, Bill. "When the Principal Asks: 'Why Aren't You Using Peer Editing?' " *The Reading Teacher*, 41 (April 1988), 828–829.

Hightshue, Deborah, Dott Ryann, Sally McKenna, Joe Tower, and Brenda Brumley. "Writing in Junior and Senior High Schools." *Phi Delta Kappa*, 69 (June 1988), 725–728.

Hillocks, George, Jr. *Research on Written Composition*. Urbana, Ill.: Eric Clearinghouse on Reading and Communication Skills and National Conference on Research in English, 1986.

INC Sights: A Teacher's Guide to Writers INC. Burlington, Wis.: Write Source Educational Publishing House, 1989.

Jenkinson, Edward B. " 'I Don't Know What to Write about Today': Some Ideas for Journal Writing." *Phi Delta Kappan*, 69 (June, 1988a), 739.

———. "Learning to Write/Writing to Learn." *Phi Delta Kappan*, 69 (June 1988b), 712–717.

———. "Practice Helps with Essay Exams." *Phi Delta Kappan*, 69 (June 1988c), 726.

Jossart, Sarah A. "Character Journals Aid Comprehension." *The Reading Teacher*, 42 (November 1988), 180.

Kirby, Dan, and Tom Liner, with Ruth Vinz. *Inside Out: Developmental Strategies for Teaching Writing*. 2nd ed. Portsmouth, N.H.: Heinemann, 1988.

Konopak, Bonnie C., Michael A. Martin, and Sarah H. Martin. "Reading and Writing: Aids to Learning in the Content Areas." *Journal of Reading*, 31 (November 1987), 109–115.

Kucer, Stephen B. "Helping Writers Get the 'Big Picture.' " *Journal of Reading*, 30 (October 1986), 18–24.

Kuhrt, Bonnie L., and Pamela J. Farris. "Empowering Students through Reading, Writing, and Reasoning." *Journal of Reading*, 33 (March 1990): 436–441.

Langer, Judith A. "Learning through Writing: Study Skills in the Content Areas." *Journal of Reading*, 29 (February 1986), 400–406.

Maimon, Elaine P. "Cultivating the Prose Garden." *Phi Delta Kappan*, 69 (June 1988), 734–739.

Manion, Betty Byrne. "Writing Workshop in Junior High School: It's Worth the Time." *Journal of Reading*, 32 (November 1988), 154–157.

McGinley, William J., and Peter R. Denner. "Story Impressions: A Prereading/Writing Activity." *Journal of Reading*, 31 (December 1987), 248–253.

Murray, Donald M. *A Writer Teaches Writing*. 2nd ed. Boston: Houghton Mifflin, 1985.

Oberlin, Kelly J., and Sherrie L. Shugarman. "Purposeful Writing Activities for Students in Middle School." *Journal of Reading*, 31 (May 1988), 720–723.

O'Donnell, Holly. "ERIC/RCS Report: Children Writing: Process and Development." *Language Arts*, 56 (October 1979), 839–843.

Parsons, Les. *Response Journals*. Portsmouth, N.H.: Heinemann, 1989.

Peresich, Mark Lee, James David Meadows, and Richard Sinatra. "Content Area Cognitive Mapping for Reading and Writing Proficiency." *Journal of Reading*, 33 (March 1990), 424–432.

Piazza, Carolyn L., and Carl M. Tomlinson. "A Concert of Writers." *Language Arts*, 62 (February 1985), 150–158.

Porter, Dwight. "Précis Writing in the ESL Classroom." *Journal of Reading*, 33 (February 1990), 381.

Raphael, Taffy, Carol Englert, and Becky Kirschner. *The Impact of Text Structure Instruction and Social Context on Students' Comprehension and Production of Expository Text*. Research Series No. 177. East Lansing, Mich.: Institute for Research on Teaching, 1986.

Raphael, Taffy E., Becky W. Kirschner, and Carol Sue Englert. "Expository Writing Program: Making Connections between Reading and Writing." *The Reading Teacher*, 41 (April 1988), 790–795.

Raphael, Taffy E., and Carol Sue Englert. "Writing and Reading: Partners in Constructing Meaning." *The Reading Teacher*, 43 (February 1990), 388–400.

Reading/Language Subcommittee of IRA. "Secondary Perspectives: A Reading-Writing Connection in the Content Areas." *Journal of Reading*, 33 (February 1990), 376–377.

Santa, Carol, Lynn Havens, and Shirley Harrison. "Teaching Secondary Science through Reading, Writing, Studying, and Problem Solving." In Diane Lapp, James Flood, and Nancy Farnan (eds.), *Content Area Reading and Learning: Instructional Strategies*. Englewood Cliffs, N.J.: Prentice Hall, 1989.

Sensenbaugh, Roger. "Process Writing in the Classroom." *Journal of Reading*, 33 (February 1990), 382–383.

Sensenbaugh, Roger. "Writing across the Curriculum: Evolving Reform." *Journal of Reading*, 32 (February 1989), 462–465.

Shanahan, Timothy. "Nature of the Reading-Writing Relationship: An Exploratory Multivariate Analysis." *Journal of Educational Psychology*, 76 (1984), 466–477.

———. "The Reading-Writing Relationship: Seven Instructional Principles." *The Reading Teacher*, 41 (March 1988), 636–647.

Shugarman, Sherrie L., and Joe B. Hurst. "Purposeful Paraphrasing: Promoting a Nontrivial Pursuit for Meaning." *Journal of Reading*, 29 (February 1986), 396–399.

Simpson, Mary K. "A Teacher's Gift: Oral Reading and the Reading Response Journal." *Journal of Reading*, 30 (October 1986), 45–50.

Simpson, Michele L. "PORPE: A Writing Strategy for Studying and Learning in the Content Areas." *Journal of Reading*, 29 (February 1986), 407–414.

Sinatra, Richard, et al. "Combining Visual Literacy, Text Understanding, and Writing for Culturally Diverse Students." *Journal of Reading*, 33 (May 1990), 612–614.

Staton, J. "The Power of Responding in Dialogue Journals." In T. Fulweiler (ed.), *The Journal Book*. Portsmouth, N.H.: Boynton-Cook, 1987.

Strackbein, Deanna, and Montague Tillman. "The Joy of Journals — with Reservations." *Journal of Reading*, 31 (October 1987), 28–31.

Tchudi, Stephen N., and Joanne Yates. *Teaching Writing in the Content Areas: Senior High School*. Washington, D.C.: National Education Association, 1983.

Tone, Bruce. "Guiding Students through Research Papers." *Journal of Reading*, 32 (October 1988), 76–79.

Vacca, Richard T., and Jo Anne L. Vacca. *Content Area Reading*. 3rd ed. Glenview, Ill.: Scott, Foresman, 1989.

8

READING IN THE CONTENT AREAS: PART I

OVERVIEW

Content textbooks are designed to teach students the basic concepts of content area subjects. Successful students are active readers and independent learners who are able to read and learn concepts from school texts and other publications (Davey, 1989). Competent readers are motivated to read, and they score higher on achievement tests than their less motivated counterparts. Therefore, content reading instruction should motivate students to read extensively.

This chapter focuses on preparing teachers to help their students read and study content reading materials in the areas of social studies, science, mathematics, computer science, English (language arts), and foreign languages. Techniques are introduced to guide students into "strategic" reading. Strategies are included to develop word meanings, content understanding, and comprehension of common writing patterns in the content areas. Among the specific strategies discussed are use of study guides, including process guides and concept guides.

PURPOSE-SETTING QUESTIONS

As you read this chapter, try to answer these questions:

1. What are the reading skills that you think are necessary in fields such as social studies, science, mathematics, computer science, English, and foreign languages? Make a list of the abilities that you think are most important in the content area that you are interested in teaching. As you read the chapter, check to see if your predictions are accurate.
2. What common writing patterns appear in these different content areas?
3. Which strategies are useful before reading?

4. What are four strategies discussed in this chapter that are designed to be used during or after reading? Explain each one.

5. Does each content area have unique reading strategies? To what extent can reading strategies be adapted from one subject area to another?

KEY VOCABULARY

As you read this chapter, check your understanding of these terms:

list structure

cause-and-effect pattern

problem-solving pattern

classification pattern

experimental pattern

definition or explanation pattern

demonstration pattern

chronological order pattern

word (verbal) problems

comparison-contrast pattern

computer literacy

Introduction to Reading Content Material

Teaching any content area includes more than just sharing information with students through a lecture; it includes teaching students how to read and comprehend printed materials (Vigil and Dick, 1984). Dea (1978) estimates that over 75 percent of the learning at the secondary level is acquired through reading. Therefore, teachers must be concerned with the application of reading instruction to the content areas. The most effective and efficient content reading instruction occurs when teachers help students read and learn content concurrently with acquiring the strategic reading abilities they need to understand subject matter textbooks, trade books, and related materials. Writers carefully choose vocabulary, syntax, and organizational patterns (structures) to communicate with readers. Students need to understand these aspects of their content textbooks to learn effectively. In earlier chapters we discussed these factors, and strategies included in these chapters will aid comprehension of content material.

As subject matter experts, content teachers are the appropriate people to identify the content objectives they wish to achieve. Content area learning objectives usually specify the important ideas and concepts of the subject matter. Teachers ask themselves, "What is it about my content area that I can realistically expect my students to gain from my teaching?" (Harker, 1985, p. 27). For example, in a unit or lesson in geography, the content area learning

296

objective may be that students understand how geographic features are formed; in an English class, the objective may be understanding the ways a short story writer develops setting; or in a science course, the objective may be understanding the periodic table of elements.

After identifying content objectives, teachers must determine the reading strategies their students need to achieve these objectives. They should identify strategies to prepare students to read, those to implement during reading, and the follow-up activities that will ensure learning. In Chapter 3, Reading Comprehension, you will find prereading strategies and activities.

Content Text Structures

Secondary teachers see their disciplines as organized bodies of knowledge with defined methods of inquiry (Clarke, Raths, and Gilbert, 1989). To students, however, the facts, interpretations, principles, and theories that make up a discipline may not appear to be organized at all. Students initially tend to focus on specific facts, overlooking main ideas and the relationships among facts, theories, and concepts, often recalling content as a series of fragments that they must memorize. Students who understand the structure of knowledge in a subject can use this understanding to make a text more coherent and meaningful. However, awareness of text patterns is not an end in itself. It is one way of building schemata for different text types.

Five major patterns or organizational structures occur most frequently in content texts: chronological order, list structure, comparison-contrast, cause-effect, and problem-solution (Horowitz, 1985a). Content teachers should familiarize themselves with and teach students these text patterns to help the students build reading, writing, and thinking strategies. These structures are found in all subjects, sometimes alone and often in combination. Among these five patterns, chronological order and list structure are easiest to learn; therefore, students should examine these first (Horowitz, 1985a). Identifying these patterns in different subjects helps students achieve broader understanding and gives them a feeling of greater control over otherwise complex subject matter. After examining the easier structures, students should move on to the more difficult ones, i.e., cause-effect, comparison-contrast and problem-solution. The cause-effect pattern is difficult for many readers from the early elementary grades through college (Horowitz, 1985a). Instruction about structure should focus on the actual materials students will read in each subject area.

A number of strategies have proved successful in developing students' awareness of text patterns (Horowitz, 1985b), including

Providing examples across topics and texts
Relating text patterns to real-life exeriences
Having students identify signal words and make notes in the margins

Making visual representations of text patterns
Having students practice writing text patterns.

Content Reading Assignments

To plan content reading instruction, teachers should think through the learning task from the students' perspective, identifying the reading abilities and strategies that will enable them to achieve the objectives and incorporating those strategies into the lesson. Content reading instruction is most effective when implemented with students' current textbooks and reading materials rather than using specially prepared exercises. Reading instruction based on the students' current reading materials, real-life reading materials, and authentic reading activities is purposeful and motivating.

Authentic reading assignments lead to thinking and problem solving. Activities such as simulations, taking oral histories, and solving community problems (such as selecting toxic waste sites), lead students into active involvement with reading, learning, and application of ideas.

Each section of this chapter introduces purposeful teaching strategies that can be adapted to various types of content, although the space constraints prohibit demonstrating every strategy with each type of content. Students who learn to use these strategies can apply them in their own content textbooks.

One of the most beneficial strategies teachers implement to help students read and study is the use of study guides. Study guides direct students' attention to important ideas and to thinking about these ideas (Bean and Ericson, 1989).

Study guides are useful in every content subject. They are often developed to accompany textbook assignments. However, teachers may develop study guides to focus the students' studies, whether they are based on printed materials or audiovisual materials. Students may study materials such as trade books, magazines, and newspapers, television shows, and films to learn more about content subjects.

Social Studies Content

Social studies classes are concerned with the study of human behavior. The area of social studies encompasses many academic disciplines, including history, anthropology, geography, economics, political science, psychology, philosophy and sociology. Recently, multicultural education has become an overarching theme in curriculum development. The primary objective of multicultural education is to help all students reach their potential (Gollnick, 1980). To accomplish this, students must understand cultural pluralism (Banks, 1981). In developing an understanding of this concept, students learn

298

that our culture is composed of many cultures and that we actually live in a global village. Each of us must respect our own culture and the other cultures in our world.

Social studies students have to read many printed materials; therefore, reading is essential to understanding social studies content. Readers of social studies content need to

1. understand the ideas and viewpoints of others;
2. acquire and retain a body of relevant concepts and information;
3. think critically, and creatively, thus developing new attitudes and values and the ability to make decisions.

Readers of social studies content use reasoning abilities to understand human behavior. Although critical reading is important in all subject areas, it is especially important in social studies at this time. Current social studies research is focusing on higher-order thinking in the classroom, and social studies teachers are being encouraged to promote students' reasoning abilities (Alvermann, 1987). Social science materials offer a particular challenge for students because many people have preconceived ideas about some of the topics studied in this content area. Students' ignorance of the cultural values and beliefs of others may be a serious deterrent to comprehension. Readers tend to distort culturally unfamiliar text by making modifications consistent with their own cultural values and beliefs; they try to explain unfamiliar material in light of the familiar culture (LeSourd, 1988).

Social studies students read and reflect on diverse topics to increase their knowledge base (LeSourd, 1988). They must learn about other cultures if they are to avoid distorting culturally unfamiliar content. Readers who are studying multicultural materials must comprehend human behaviors that are outside their experiences; therefore, comprehension depends upon enriching their cultural schemata. In addition to building students' schemata in these areas, teachers should use strategies such as anticipation guides, study guides, and advance organizers to help students comprehend.

Teachers should incorporate selections from trade books, magazines, and newspapers to supplement the information offered by social studies texts in order to help students understand a topic more fully. Consulting a greater variety of sources enables students to experience more than one point of view regarding a topic. It is especially important for students to read critically when an author writes about not only what has happened but also why these events have occurred. An author's biases are likely to appear when causes of events are explained. The author's point of view is affected by the following factors:

1. Author's age
2. Author's nationality
3. Author's religion

4. Author's political views
5. Author's race
6. Author's family history
7. Author's sex
8. Audience for whom author is writing.

Social studies materials are written in an expository style, which is precise and factual. Example 8.1 illustrates this style of writing. As you read this example, note the density of concepts and the use of several technical terms that must be defined before the content can be understood. The reader must understand these terms and remember them for any future reading in economics.

EXAMPLE **8.1**

Social Studies Content

The Gross National Product

The dollar value of all the goods and services produced by an economic system in one year is called the **gross national product (GNP).** That is certainly one way of measuring how well an economic system does. When the economy suffers, the gross national product (or GNP for short) also suffers and goes down. On the other hand, if the economy is healthy, the GNP will rise.

The dollar value of all the goods and services produced by the system in one year gives you an idea of the system's size, if nothing else. In one recent year, the GNP of the United States was almost two trillion dollars. That figure represents the value of all of the goods and services produced in just one year by all of the business firms and individuals in our economic system. We not only produced more than any other country in the world, we also produced more than a hundred countries put together.

Because the GNP is an index of the health of the economy, it is used as a measure of growth. We can compare last year's gross national product with this year's. To make such comparisons not only easy but realistic, we should adjust for changes in the value of a dollar. We take one year and call that our *base year*. We say that the dollar of our base year is a **real dollar,** which means that it is a measure against which we will determine the value in purchasing power of the dollars of other years. For example, if we call 1967 our base year, the 1967 dollar becomes our real dollar. If in 1968 the real dollar can buy only 97¢ worth of goods or services, it is worth less than it was in 1967. If in 1968 the real dollar can buy $1.03 worth of goods or services, it is worth more than it was in 1967. In either event, we can measure the worth of the 1968 dollar against a constant: the real dollar of 1967. If we measure the GNP every year in terms of real dollars, our basis of comparison will remain the same.

Source: General Business: Our Business and Economic World by Betty Brown and John Clow (Boston: Houghton Mifflin Company, 1982), pp. 142–143. Reprinted by permission of Houghton Mifflin Company.

As stated earlier, use of study guides is an important strategy for helping students to comprehend content. The instructor's reasons for using a study guide and the students' needs determine the guide's composition. A study guide may cover a chapter, a larger unit, part of a chapter, or a concept that is being developed through multiple materials. Students should have the study guide prior to reading an assignment, so they can reflect about it while they read. Example 8.2 illustrates a social studies study guide.

EXAMPLE **8.2**

Social Studies Study Guide

Vocabulary

Directions: Pay attention to the words in Column A — they are important for understanding of this selection. After reading the selection, draw a line from the word in Column A to its meaning in Column B.

Column A	Column B
Gross national product	Dollar value in the base year
Base year	Value of goods and services for a given year
Real dollar	The year selected for comparison

Comprehension

Directions: Write short answers to the following questions

LITERAL

1. How is gross national product computed?
2. What are the components of gross national product?

INFERENTIAL

3. Why is the GNP considered an index of the health of an economy?

APPLIED

4. The value of goods and services is computed for the GNP. Which of the following are categorized as goods and which are categorized as services: TV repair bill, wool, house, steel, dentist's fee, lumber, draperies, dishes, lathe?
5. What practical value does the GNP have for you as an individual?

CRITICAL

Directions: Write a short essay to answer this question.

6. How could GNP be used as propaganda?

A concept guide, which is another form of study guide, is essentially concerned with developing students' understanding of an important content concept. Concept guides may be developed in a number of different ways. Following is an example of a concept guide based on the chapter that contains the selection shown in Example 8.1. This concept guide would be completed by a student after he or she has read the chapter. Concept guides are a form of reasoning guides, which are presented and explained in Chapter 3.

E X A M P L E **8.3**

Social Studies Concept Guide

Directions: Write a + before each term that is associated with gross national product, according to the information in your social studies textbook. Write a − before each word that is unrelated to the concept of gross national product. Be prepared to explain and support your answers by using your textbook.

_____ goods	_____ real dollar
_____ labor union	_____ machines and tools
_____ economic system	_____ base year
_____ specialty	_____ GNP
_____ services	_____ standard parts
_____ index	_____ durable goods
_____ growth	_____ nondurable goods
_____ manufacturing	

Vocabulary

A student must comprehend 75 percent of the ideas and 90 percent of the vocabulary of a social studies selection in order to read it on an instructional level. This level of understanding is necessary for the student to learn and to avoid frustration (Herman, 1969). Through activities like those described in Chapter 2 and the activities that follow, word meanings are reinforced and recall is enhanced.

ACTIVITIES

1. Give students practice exercises such as the following one:

   From the list of phrases below, choose a phrase that is associated with each of the words in the word list (Vigil and Dick, 1984).

   Phrases

rules of conduct	control behavior
process	making and enforcing rules

power of making rules
printed list of candidates
lawmaking branch
citizen's freedoms
people's vote
power of enforcing rules

self-government
rights of the people
indicated voters' choices
power of political unit
choosing governing nation

Word List

1. jurisdiction
2. plebiscite
3. law
4. govern
5. government

6. autonomy
7. civil rights
8. legislature
9. ballot
10. power structure

2. An activity called "Possible Sentences" encourages students to learn word meanings and to predict ideas they will encounter when reading content (Moore and Arthur, 1981). For this activity, use the following steps:

a. Identify important vocabulary in the reading selection and write the words on the chalkboard. Pronounce each word as you write it. The words below are taken from a social studies text chapter comparing democracy and communism.

democracy
socialism
capitalism
legislature

civil rights
laws
communist
welfare state

b. Ask each student to construct sentences for at least two of the words. Record these sentences on the chalkboard, underlining the important words. Continue eliciting sentences from the students as long as the sentences are creating new contexts.

Democracy means rule by the people.

The communist form of government is based on the dictatorship of the Communist party.

Laws are made by the legislature.

Civil rights are the freedoms that people have that are guaranteed by the government.

c. Have students read their textbooks to verify the accuracy of the sentences they constructed.

d. After they read the text, have the students evaluate each sentence using the text as a reference. Students may also use glossaries, dictionaries, and thesauruses. Have students modify the sentences if necessary.

e. Ask students to create additional sentences if they can think of any. The following are examples of sentences that might be provided by students:

The United States government is an example of a <u>democratic</u> government, whereas the Soviet government is an example of a <u>communist</u> government.

In a <u>socialist</u> system, the economy is controlled by the government.

A <u>welfare state</u> is one in which the government is responsible for the welfare of the people.

3. The List-Group-Label lesson, originated by Hilda Taba (1967), uses categorization to help students develop and refine concepts. This activity also encourages students to relate content to past experiences. It includes the following steps:

a. Give students a topic drawn from the materials they are studying. An appropriate topic could be "The Geography of Georgia."

b. Have students develop a list of words or expressions they associate with the topic. Record these words on the chalkboard until the list totals approximately twenty-five words.

Appalachian Mountains	Blue Ridge Mountains
The Piedmont	Atlantic Coast
Okefenokee Swamp	Stone Mountain
peanuts	shrimp
pecans	stone
lumber	peaches
tobacco	cotton
Savannah	Augusta
Callaway Gardens	Cyclorama
Altamaha River	Chattahoochee River
Savannah River	Atlantic Ocean

c. Have students group words from the large list, providing a label for each group.

Mountains	*Waterways*	*Products*
Blue Ridge Mts.	Atlantic Ocean	peanuts
Stone Mt.	Altamaha River	cotton
Appalachian Mts.	Chattahoochee River	tobacco
	Savannah River	lumber
		pecans
		peaches

Writing Patterns

As in many content areas, social studies content is structured through main ideas and details that are presented in a variety of writing patterns. The most common ones were introduced in Chapter 3 and earlier in this chapter. Following are examples of writing patterns in social studies content.

Cause-and-Effect Pattern

Each area of social studies is concerned with chains of causes and effects: one cause results in certain effects that become causes of other effects. The passage in Example 8.4 is written in the cause-and-effect writing pattern.

E X A M P L E **8.4**

Cause-and-Effect Pattern (Social Studies)

The Townshend Acts outrage the colonists. The Townshend Acts started a new wave of protest in the colonies. The writs of assistance angered merchants who thought that homes and warehouses should be safe from government officials. The colonists also objected to paying officials' salaries from tax moneys. This practice meant that colonial legislatures no longer had to approve the officials' salaries. As a result, the colonists had less influence over how the British officials carried out their duties. Finally, many colonists feared that what had happened to the New York Assembly might happen in other colonies.

The colonists were most angry about taxes on imports. Unlike the Stamp Act, the Townshend Acts did not set up internal taxes. Colonists now argued, however, that Britain did not always have the right to collect external taxes. They said that Britain could set up external taxes to regulate trade, but not just to raise revenue. The colonists said they would only accept taxes to raise revenue if the colonial legislatures gave their approval.

The colonists resist the Townshend Acts. As the wave of protest gained strength, colonists gathered in the streets and in meetinghouses to speak out against the Townshend Acts. Led by Samuel Adams, the Massachusetts legislature sent the other colonies a letter urging them to oppose the new taxes. The Virginia House of Burgesses condemned the Townshend Acts because they ignored the colony's right to vote on its own taxes. As in the case of the Stamp Act, Americans boycotted British goods. Trade between Britain and the colonies once again dropped sharply.

The Boston Massacre strengthens opposition. Anti-British feeling ran especially high in Boston. British soldiers were sent to Boston to maintain order, but their presence only made matters worse. The British wore bright scarlet uniforms, and many Bostonians taunted them with names such as "redcoats" and "lobsterbacks."

On a snowy night in March 1770, a crowd of boys began throwing snowballs at a

British sentry, who called other soldiers to his aid. Soon a threatening crowd gathered. Some of the soldiers fired into the crowd, killing several citizens. Among those who fell was Crispus Attucks, a black sailor and one of the leaders of the crowd. This incident became known as the **Boston Massacre.** The people of the city were so outraged after the shooting that the British troops had to withdraw to a fort in Boston Harbor.

Britain vs. the Colonists

British Actions	American Actions
Townshend Acts passed	British goods boycotted
British soldiers sent to keep order	Boys threw snowballs at British sentry
Soldiers fired into crowd (Boston Massacre)	Several citizens killed

Source: Howard B. Wilder, Robert P. Ludlum, and Harriett McCune Brown: *This is America's Story* (Boston: Houghton Mifflin Company, 1990), p. 144. Copyright © 1990 by Houghton Mifflin Company. Reprinted by permission of Houghton Mifflin Company.

After students have examined cause-and-effect content, the teacher may use strategies like the following to help them relate causes and effects.

ACTIVITIES

1. State some effects and ask students to identify the causes. Ask them to answer the question, "Why did this happen?" after reading the material in Example 8.4.

   The colonists' objections to taxation were caused by _____
   _____

2. State some causes and ask students to identify the effects. Have them answer the question, "What did this fact cause?"

   The passing of the Townshend Acts caused _____

Definition or Explanation Pattern

This pattern is used to define or explain important concepts. The concept is the main idea, and the supporting details constitute the elements of the definition or explanation. To comprehend this pattern of writing, the student must identify both the concept and the author's definition or explanation. This pattern is important to the reader because the knowledge included in the definition or explanation frequently serves as a basis for learning subsequent information on the topic. This pattern is illustrated in Example 8.5, which defines and explains the Articles of Confederation.

EXAMPLE **8.5**

Definition or Explanation Pattern and Outline (Social Studies)

The states plan for a national government. The members of the Second Continental Congress knew that the United States needed a permanent government. In 1777, after a year of discussion, they agreed on a plan. They proposed that the states join together in a **confederation** — a loose union of independent states. The document outlining this union was called the **Articles of Confederation.**

Before the Articles of Confederation could take effect, each state had to **ratify** — approve — them. Twelve states quickly did so. Maryland, however, refused to ratify the Articles until a land dispute was settled. At the time, about half the states claimed large areas of land west of the Appalachian Mountains. (See map on page 190.) As a small state, Maryland feared the growth of its neighbors. If these states gained more land and became more powerful, they could threaten Maryland and other small states. As a result, Maryland insisted that the western lands be turned over to the new national government.

For some time Virginia, New York, and the other states claiming western lands objected. Finally, however, they decided that the need for a central government outweighed their desire for more territory. They gave up their claims, and the Articles were adopted in 1781. By then, the War of Independence was almost over.

The Articles of Confederation set up a national government. The central government established under the Articles of Confederation took a different form from the state governments. Instead of a three-part structure, with legislative, executive, and judicial branches, the Confederation had a single governing body, Congress. Congress did not have an upper and a lower house. It was a **unicameral** — one-house — legislature made up of delegates from all the states. Each state sent between two and seven delegates to Congress. Regardless of the number of delegates, however, each state received only a single vote. As a result, small states such as Rhode Island had as much say in the government as large states such as Pennsylvania or Virginia.

Under the Articles of Confederation, more power lay with the individual states than with the central government. Each state kept control of important matters such as taxes and law enforcement. Congress's main powers were waging war and making peace, and handling foreign affairs. Congress also had authority to regulate trade with the Indians, arrange for mail service, and borrow and issue money. The government, however, could take no action unless 9 of the 13 states agreed to do so. Furthermore, any change in the Articles of Confederation, no matter how small, required approval by all 13 states.

The writers of the Articles of Confederation purposely created a weak government. Because of their experience with the British monarch and Parliament, they feared a powerful central government. Soon, however, many Americans would see the need for a stronger national government.

Source: Howard B. Wilder, Robert P. Ludlum, and Harriett McCune Brown: *This is America's Story* (Boston: Houghton Mifflin Company, 1990), pp. 189, 191. Copyright © 1990 by Houghton Mifflin Company. Reprinted by permission of Houghton Mifflin Company.

Outline

I. Articles of Confederation
   A. Proposed by Second Continental Congress
   B. Ratified after long delay
      1. Western lands a problem
      2. Claims to western lands relinquished
      3. Confederation finally accepted 1781
   C. Nature of the government formed by Confederation
      1. Single governing body, Congress
      2. Unicameral legislature
      3. Each state had 2–7 delegates
      4. Each state had one vote
      5. Could wage war
      6. Could establish foreign relations
      7. Could regulate trade with the Indians
      8. Could arrange for mail service
      9. Could borrow money
      10. Could issue money
      11. Nine states had to agree for action.

Chronological Order (Time Order) Pattern

In the chronological order pattern, events are arranged in order of occurrence. The teacher can help students develop a concept of time periods by having them consider time in relation to their own lives. Understanding time is necessary for comprehending social studies material, but reflecting on what one has read is more valuable than memorizing dates. Indefinite time references, such as "in the early days" or "in ancient times," may confuse the reader; therefore, the teacher needs to clarify these terms. The chronological order pattern is presented in Example 8.6.

E X A M P L E **8.6**

Chronological Pattern (Social Studies)

The Civil War proved to be a long, bitter struggle. Southerners fought to preserve slavery and to win independence from the Union. Northerners fought to save the Union and to end slavery. The North had the advantages of a larger population, more resources, an established government, and an army and navy. The North planned to crush the Confederacy by gaining control of the Mississippi River, blockading southern ports, and seizing the capital at Richmond, Virginia.

The South's strengths were its defensive position and its outstanding military leaders.

308

Its strategy was to hold out until the North tired of the war. The Confederates also hoped to capture Washington, D.C., and to get help from Europe.

In 1861 the first Battle of Bull Run ended with a victory for the South. The North had more success in the West and at sea. Early attempts to take Richmond, however, failed. Then, in September 1862, the North narrowly won the Battle of Antietam. This gave Lincoln a chance to issue the Emancipation Proclamation, freeing the slaves.

In the following months the picture brightened for the South. Robert E. Lee defeated Union forces in several key battles. The Battle of Gettysburg, however, proved to be a turning point. The Confederates lost badly and never regained their advantage. Ulysses S. Grant took command of all Union armies and carried out the final defeat of the South. After Sherman's march through Atlanta and the fall of Richmond, General Lee surrendered at Appomattox Court House on April 9, 1865.

The Civil War meant many casualties among soldiers and hardship for those at home. Political discontent and opposition to the draft troubled both sides. The South suffered more than the North, however, because most of the fighting took place on southern soil. While the South's economy withered, the North's grew. Abraham Lincoln was renominated for the presidency in 1864. At first the election outcome was uncertain, but Sherman's taking of Atlanta ensured Lincoln's reelection. When he began his second term in 1865, he knew that reuniting the nation would be no easy task.

Source: Howard B. Wilder, Robert P. Ludlum, and Harriett McCune Brown. *This Is America's Story* (Boston: Houghton Mifflin Company, 1990), p. 433. Copyright © 1990 by Houghton Mifflin Company. Reprinted by permission of Houghton Mifflin Company.

Understanding of chronological order may be developed by using the following techniques.

ACTIVITIES

1. Guide students to understand blocks of time. Seeking relationships among events helps students comprehend time. After reading the full text from which the material in Example 8.6 was extracted, the student should understand that the twenty years prior to the Civil War was the period when the immediate causes of the war became apparent and that a great many factors that led to the war developed during that period. The war itself lasted from 1861 until 1865.

CIVIL WAR

   1861   First Battle of Bull Run
  _____ Battle of Antietam; Emancipation Proclamation
  _____ Battle of Gettysburg
  _____ Sherman's march through Atlanta
   1865   Lee surrenders at Appomattox Court House

2. Relate a time sequence to a student's own experience with time and help the student develop a concept of the past, present, and future. The

student can relate historic occurrences to his or her own lifetime and the lifetimes of his or her parents and ancestors. For example, the Civil War probably occurred in the lifetime of the great, great grandparents of present-day students.

Past	*Ancestors*
Civil War	Great, great grandparents
World War I	Great grandparents
World War II	Grandparents
Korean War	Parents
Present	*Student*
Future	*Descendants*

Comparison and/or Contrast Pattern

When using the comparison and/or contrast pattern, an author explains social studies ideas by using likenesses and differences to develop understanding. Example 8.7 shows this writing pattern. The following techniques help readers understand the comparison-contrast pattern.

ACTIVITIES

1. The teacher and students may develop a chart to show comparisons and/ or contrasts. The following chart is based on Example 8.7 and shows the contrast between the Democratic-Republican Party and the Federalist Party.

Democratic-Republican Party	*Federalist Party*
Opposed strong federal government	For strong federal government
For strict interpretation of Constitution	For loose interpretation of the Constitution
For low taxes	For taxes

2. Using the example selection provided, the teacher may point out contrasts and ask students to locate comparisons; or the teacher may give the Democratic-Republican party's point of view and ask students to list the contrasting views of the Federalist Party.

Question and Answer Pattern

Authors sometimes use a question and answer pattern to organize social studies materials. In this pattern, the author asks a question and then answers it. Readers should be able to recall the author's questions and identify his or her answers. Example 8.8 illustrates this style of writing.

310

EXAMPLE **8.7**

Comparison and/or Contrast Pattern (Social Studies)

The Growth of Political Parties

During Washington's presidency, Americans often held conflicting ideas about the direction of government policy. By 1792 they divided into two rival **political parties** — groups organized to promote specific goals and candidates for office. Thomas Jefferson, Washington's Secretary of State, led one group. Alexander Hamilton, Secretary of the Treasury, guided the other.

Political parties develop. From the time he proposed the financial plan, Hamilton had opponents. Thomas Jefferson and others believed that Hamilton was making the federal government too powerful and too favorable toward business. Therefore Jefferson, with the assistance of James Madison, formed the **Democratic-Republican party.** This name showed their strong belief in **democracy** — government by the people — and in the republican system.

Jefferson's followers were mainly farmers and artisans. Often called Republicans, they thought taxes and government regulations should be kept to a minimum. They wanted the federal government limited to the role outlined for it in the Constitution. Republicans believed that ordinary people and the states, not Congress, should control most government matters.

Hamilton, meanwhile, supported a strong federal government. His ideas appealed mostly to business and manufacturing people from the East. Hamilton and Vice President John Adams formed the **Federalist party.** The Federalists believed that the new nation could not function without taxes and regulations. They favored a loose interpretation of the Constitution. Congress, they said, could make laws that were "necessary and proper" to carry out the principles of the Constitution. In other words, the federal government could take powers not clearly listed in the Constitution.

Source: Howard B. Wilder, Robert P. Ludlum, and Harriett McCune Brown: *This is America's Story* (Boston: Houghton Mifflin Company, 1990), p. 248. Copyright © 1990 by Houghton Mifflin Company. Reprinted by permission of Houghton Mifflin Company.

Graphic Aids

Graphic aids are particularly abundant in social studies materials. Readers must integrate graphic information with the written content. Graphic aids include maps, charts, pictures, graphs, and tables. When a graphic aid is mentioned in the text, students should examine it, its caption, and any associated material. The teacher should include specific instruction on graphic aids so that students will learn to read and interpret them and to combine this information with the ideas that are written in the text. See also Chapter 4 for more on graphic aids.

E X A M P L E **8.8**

Sample Question/Answer Writing Pattern (Social Studies)

What Made the United States an Industrial Leader?

The United States had many advantages that spurred industrial growth. It was rich in natural resources. It had hard-working and inventive people. The economic system encouraged people to organize and to invest in businesses. Good transportation and communication systems helped the country grow. In addition, people developed new methods of producing and selling goods. This, in turn, increased the demand for manufactured products.

National Resources

Throughout the early years of the country, most Americans depended on the resources of soil, water, and timber. Good soil was the source of food and cash crops. Rivers provided waterpower to turn machinery. The nation's transportation system depended on rivers and ocean harbors. Timber was the principal fuel and the main building material.

As industries grew, soil, water, and timber continued to be important resources. Rich soil, particularly in the Midwest, produced crops large enough to feed millions of city people. Waterways remained essential for transporting industrial products. Timber was used to build railroad cars, factories, ships, and apartment houses.

The United States develops rich mineral resources. As industry grew, Americans used more and more mineral resources. In the nineteenth century the most important minerals were coal and iron ore. The nation had large supplies of both. Coal provided fuel for steam engines to drive machinery. Coal was also used to produce iron and steel. Steel mills were usually located near plentiful supplies of coal and iron ore.

Source: Howard B. Wilder, Robert B. Ludlum, and Harriett McCune Brown: *This Is America's Story* (Boston: Houghton Mifflin Company, 1990), p. 483. Copyright © 1990 by Houghton Mifflin Company. Reprinted by permission of Houghton Mifflin Company.

Science and Health Content

The goal of scientific study is to help people understand the world through investigation and explanation of natural phenomena. Science education has two major objectives. The first is to develop scientific literacy, which is the ability of an intelligent layperson to read scientific literature and to understand its societal implications. Scientific literacy enables the reader (and the consumer) to recognize that although science may solve many of our universal problems, in doing so it often creates new problems. For example, the technology that gave the world cleaner, whiter laundry also contributed to the present environmental crisis because of the phosphates in detergents.

The second objective of science education is to introduce the field to young people who may be interested in pursuing scientific careers. Adolescence is a period of exploration during which students study many areas to identify special interests they may develop in the future.

The goal of health education is to help people understand themselves. The objective of health education is twofold: to help students understand both their physical bodies and their emotional growth and development.

All scientific content (including health education material) is written to convey concepts, details, generalizations, and theories. Many details are used in scientific writing, and readers must be able to relate these details to larger ideas in order to understand concepts, generalizations, and theories. Scientific content frequently includes experiments and laboratory work, which require students to apply knowledge and to follow directions precisely.

In order to comprehend scientific material, students must learn to follow scientific thinking and writing style, which is generally terse, with dense factual content. The reader must read slowly and thoroughly and pay careful attention to the concepts, details, generalizations, and theories presented in order to understand the exact meaning. Technical words and typical patterns of writing should be learned.

Many science teachers lament their students' inability to understand their textbooks; yet 90 percent of science teachers rely on textbooks to convey scientific content (Lloyd and Mitchell, 1989). Therefore, science teachers need practical suggestions to help students better understand the text. Study guides, concept guides, preview guides, directed reading activities (see Chapter 6), and SQ3R (see Chapter 4) are some of the strategies that can be used to help students understand scientific and health education content.

Vocabulary and Concept Development

Many specialized, technical terms are used in science and health materials. Scientific vocabulary changes often because new discoveries add new technical terms and cause other terms to become obsolete. Example 8.9 shows an activity that is useful for teaching students scientific vocabulary. It is an entry from a student-constructed and illustrated dictionary of scientific terms.

E X A M P L E **8.9**

Illustrated Dictionary of Scientific Terms

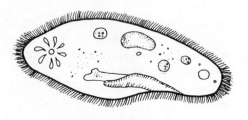

A paramecium is a one-celled animal that is found in the scum on pond water.

Paramecium

The Frayer model (Frayer and Klausmeier, 1969) is designed to develop a conceptual understanding of words and is appropriate for any subject. Example 8.10 shows an activity that is an adaptation of the Frayer model. The process of implementing this includes

1. Identify the concept to be examined.
2. Identify the factors that occur in all instances of the concept.
3. Identify the relevant factors and eliminate the irrelevant ones.
4. Give an example of the concept.
5. Give a non-example of the concept.

E X A M P L E **8.10**

Frayer Model Activity

Concept: Adaptation

ESSENTIAL ATTRIBUTES

1. Improves chance of survival
2. Improves genetic selection

NON-ESSENTIAL ATTRIBUTES

1. Seasonal changes
2. Changes that do not contribute to survival

EXAMPLES

1. Front legs of mole
2. Walrus tusks
3. Beak of black skimmer

NON-EXAMPLES

1. Albinism
2. Human beings with six fingers

Writing Patterns

The main ideas and supporting details in scientific materials are frequently organized into classification patterns, explanations of technical processes, cause-and-effect patterns, and problem-solving patterns. Another pattern used to structure scientific content is the experimental pattern.

Classification Pattern

In the classification pattern, information is ordered under common headings and subheadings. The information sorted in this way may consist of living things, objects, or general ideas. This pattern is a type of outlining that shows a classification, the distinguishing characteristics of the members of the class, and examples. The classification represents a main idea, and the distinguishing characteristics and examples are treated as details.

To understand text material written in this pattern, students should identify the distinguishing characteristics of the classification and examples of members of the classification. Outlining the material is also a useful strategy. Example 8.11 shows a passage written in this pattern and an outline based on the passage.

EXAMPLE **8.11**

Classification Pattern and Outline

Nonvascular Plants

Multicellular Algae simplest metaphytes are the multicellular plants called algae. These organisms do not have true roots, specialized leaves, or systems for transporting water and food. But they are multicellular and they photosynthesize.

Some algae, like *Spirogyra*, consist of filaments made up of cells attached in a row, and live in fresh water. Other algae are in the form of sheets of cells, like the seaweed called sea-lettuce. These algae are green in color, as you would expect.

There are other algae whose green color is hidden by other colors. These plants photosynthesize just as green plants do. However, their chlorophyll is covered up by other pigments that give them their red and brown colors. All of these plants live in the ocean. At some time during the life cycle of each there is a plant body that has an upright part as well as root-like structures.

The root-like structures serve to attach the plants to the bottom of the ocean or to rocks near the shore. The more upright portion is involved in photosynthesis and reproduction. The main plant body is made of cells joined together as branching filaments or flat blades. Some of these algae can be over 30 meters long. Others are tiny plants only a few millimeters high.

The most familiar types of brown algae are kelp and the seaweed *Fucus*. *Fucus* covers rocks in the intertidal zone; kelp lives attached to the ocean bottom in shallow water. Other seaweeds have a red color. A red alga common on both the Atlantic and Pacific coasts of North America is *Polysiphonia*. This organism is a mass of small, branching, delicate filaments.

Source: Earl D. Hanson, J. David Lockard, and Peter Jensch: *Biology: The Science of Life* (Boston: Houghton Mifflin Company, 1980), pp. 458–459. Reprinted by permission of Houghton Mifflin Company.

Outline

I. Classification — Algae
  A. Distinguishing characteristics
    1. Multicellular plants
    2. Do not have true roots
    3. Do not have specialized leaves
    4. Do not have systems for transporting food and water
    5. Photosynthesize
  B. Classified by color
    1. Green
    2. Brown
    3. Red

Definition or Explanation Pattern

The definition (or explanation) pattern occurs frequently in scientific content and health-related materials. This pattern may explain processes that are biological (the digestive process) or mechanical (the operation of an engine). It also may provide definitions for scientific terms, such as *atmosphere*. Diagrams usually accompany this kind of pattern, so the reader must integrate written content information with the diagrams (see Example 8.12).

Techniques that will help students comprehend the explanation of a process follow.

ACTIVITIES

1. Have students attempt to restate the explanation in their own words.
2. Have students reread the explanation to check their comprehension.
3. Have students study the sequence of steps in the process and attempt to explain the process by recalling the steps in sequence. For the science passage in Example 8.12, the steps would be as follows:
   a. Plasmid is taken from bacterial cell.
   b. Plasmid's molecular ring is broken open.
   c. DNA fragment is split off from the other cell.
   d. DNA fragment is added to complete the recombined plasmid.
   e. Completed plasmid is placed in new host bacterial cell.
4. Mask the labels in an accompanying diagram and have students insert appropriate labels.

E X A M P L E **8.12**

Explanation of a Process (Science)

Recombinant DNA

Scientists have recently learned how to transfer small segments of DNA molecules from the cells of one organism into the DNA of another organism. The new DNA segments are called **recombinant** (*ree KAHM buh nuhnt*) **DNA.** This transfer of bits of DNA is a remarkable achievement. Some scientists have wanted for a long time to find ways to improve the genetic make-up of organisms. Transferring DNA opens up a wide new world of research opportunities. This field of research is called **genetic engineering.** When you have seen how the transfer of DNA is accomplished, you might consider some of the possibilities and dangers of this line of research.

Transferring bits of DNA from one organism to another presented three major problems. First, scientists had to learn how to break DNA apart at specific points along the molecule. Second, they had to develop chemical methods for connecting the tiny segments of DNA with other DNA strands. And third, scientists had to find a way to insert the remodelled DNA molecules into living cells.

Scientists have been able to transfer DNA segments into certain types of bacterial cells. Bacteria contain small doughnut-shaped rings of DNA separate from the bacterial "chromosome." These rings are called **plasmids** (*PLAZ mihds*); they are found floating free within each bacterial cell. Until it became possible to transfer DNA segments, scientists paid very little attention to the presence or function of plasmids. Now, however, plasmids play a key role in DNA transfer research. Look at Figure 10.20 for a description of how DNA segments are transferred from one organism to another.

Under the right conditions, the genetic instructions contained in the foreign fragment of DNA are followed in the bacterial cell. Therefore, a bacterial cell could serve as a sort of "biochemical factory" and produce large quantities of a desired substance. For instance, the hormone insulin is missing or in low supply in people who suffer from the disease diabetes. Normally, insulin is formed by cells of the pancreas. It might be possible to move the gene coding for insulin production from a pancreas cell to a bacterium that multiplies very rapidly. This bacterium may follow the genetic instructions for producing insulin. If so, its rapid growth would then provide an inexpensive source of large quantities of insulin.

Even if the host bacterial cell does not follow the inserted genetic instructions, DNA transfer can serve another useful purpose. Many such bacterial cells are not in any way disturbed by the presence of the foreign DNA fragment. As it divides, the cell will reproduce the foreign DNA fragment. Thus, scientists would be able to use a rapidly dividing bacterium and its dividing daughter cells to produce large quantities of a particular gene for study.

FIGURE **10.20**   *A diagram of DNA transfer from two separate organisms into a new host bacterial cell.* **1.** *A plasmid is taken from a bacterial cell.* **2.** *The plasmid's molecular ring is broken open, leaving space for a fragment of DNA from the other organism.* **3.** *DNA fragment is split off from the other cell.* **4.** *DNA fragment is added to complete the recombined plasmid.* **5.** *Completed plasmid is placed within a new host bacterial cell.*

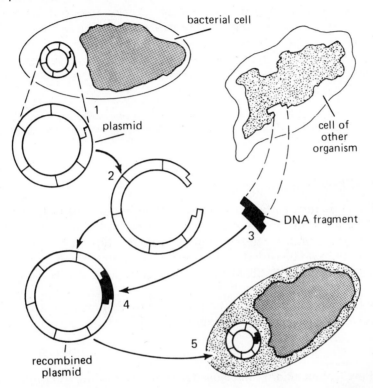

Source: Earl D. Hanson, J. David Lockard, and Peter Jensch: *Biology: The Science of Life* (Boston: Houghton Mifflin Company, 1980), pp. 294–295. Reprinted by permission of Houghton Mifflin Company.

The teacher may use the following techniques to help students read explanatory materials.

ACTIVITIES

1. Have students identify the main idea and supporting details in paragraphs that they read. For instance, a definition of the term *insomnia* is the main idea of Example 8.13.
2. Have students reread this pattern as many times as necessary to understand the information, principle, process, or definition that is being explained.

EXAMPLE **8.13**

Explanation Pattern (Health)

Insomnia *(ihn SAHM nee uh)*, or having difficulty sleeping, takes several forms. Some people have a very hard time falling asleep, or they wake up much earlier than they want to. Others may not be able to sleep more than a few hours at a time without waking up. People who have insomnia sometimes feel that they don't sleep at all, but actually they drift in and out of sleep without realizing it. They probably get more sleep than they think they do.

Source: Edward Rosenberg, Henry Gurney, and Vivian Harlin: *Investigating Your Health,* rev. ed. (Boston: Houghton Mifflin Company, 1978), p. 142. Copyright © 1978 by Houghton Mifflin Company. Reprinted by permission of Houghton Mifflin Company.

Cause-and-Effect Pattern

The cause-and-effect pattern, as it is presented in scientific or health-related materials, is illustrated by the passage in Example 8.14. The chart that follows is based on this passage. Students might create this type of chart themselves, or the activity could be varied so that the teacher supplies either the causes or effects and the students fill in the missing information in the appropriate column.

The following activities can be used to provide practice with the cause-and-effect and other writing patterns.

ACTIVITIES

1. Writing (composition) can be used to reinforce reading comprehension in any content area or of any writing pattern. In the following paragraph, the student writer connected the earth science content he read to his own experiences.

   The climate is the average pattern of weather in a place. The climate affects the habitat, which includes the water, rocks, soil, and air that all living things need. Since the plants and animals need certain things to live, they exist in places where the habitat provides the things they need to live. The kinds of water, rocks, soil, and air that are available make a difference in the kinds of plants and animals that live in that place. Woodpeckers and sapsuckers live in North Carolina because they eat the insects that live in the pine trees growing in this state.

2. Ask students to write questions about the content they read, for example,
   a. Why do some animals become extinct?
   b. If Guilford County became a desert, what animals would become extinct?

E X A M P L E **8.14**

Cause-and-Effect Pattern (Biology Text) and Chart

Concentration and the Environment

Too many stimuli from the environment can cause confusion. Have you ever tried to concentrate in a place where people are talking or moving around? You may have learned to tune out certain distracting sights and sounds. Many animals have this ability to choose which stimulus they will respond to in the environment. This is called tuning out a stimulus.

Scientists call the mind's ability to select among stimuli "gating" because the process resembles a gate opening and closing to let in or keep out information. Scientists do not know exactly where and how messages are stopped. But it appears that what is allowed through the mind's "gate" depends on what the animal is doing or intends to do.

Scientists have also found that too much stimulation from the environment can interfere with learning. Experiments with animals, including humans, have shown that if there are too many distractions, they cannot be tuned out. The animals make many errors, learn more slowly, and become restless. On the other hand, an environment with too few stimuli also slows learning and results in drowsiness. The best condition for learning seems to be an environment with a moderate amount of stimulation.

Source: Earl D. Hanson, J. David Lockard, and Peter Jensch: *Biology: The Science of Life* (Boston: Houghton Mifflin Company, 1980), p. 53. Reprinted by permission of Houghton Mifflin Company.

Chart

Cause	Effect
too many stimuli	cause confusion
distracting sounds	tune out
distracting sights	tune out
too much stimulation	interferes with learning
too many distractions	cannot tune out
cannot tune out distractions	errors, slow learning, restlessness
too few stimuli	slow learning, drowsiness
moderate stimulation	learning

Study guides can be developed to help students read the cause-and-effect pattern. Example 8.15 illustrates the cause-and-effect pattern in health-related materials and presents a study guide built on the passage.

For additional teaching suggestions to use with this style of writing, see the cause-and-effect pattern in the section on social studies.

E X A M P L E **8.15**

Cause-and-Effect Pattern (Health) and Study Guide

Being active is not just a way to improve an already healthy body — to become stronger or more attractive, for example. The fact is, if you are not regularly active, you don't just stay the same. Your health actually goes downhill.

Constantly inactive muscle fibers become smaller, and they store less energy. They exert less tension for a task, and they tire quickly. When inactive muscles are over-worked, they often feel stiff and sore for a few days afterwards. Unused joints become stiff and less flexible, and can become sore if moved too far or too fast. A lack of stress regularly exerted by muscles makes bones eventually become softer and more easily broken.

The effect of regular exercise is to make muscles and joints stronger and more flexible. Tendons and bones also become harder and stronger. Well-used muscles do not tire as quickly as flabby muscles do, even though they do more work. This is because trained muscles can take up and use glucose and oxygen from the blood at a faster rate. They also get rid of waste products faster. And trained muscles are also more efficient at turning food energy into work.

Source: Edward Rosenberg, Henry Gurney, and Vivian Harlin: *Investigating Your Health*, rev. ed. (Boston: Houghton Mifflin Company, 1978), p. 131. Copyright © 1978 by Houghton Mifflin Co. Reprinted by permission of Houghton Mifflin Company.

Cause-and-Effect Study Guide

Directions: Read the assigned selection and identify all of the causes and effects in the selection. After reading the selection, read the list of effects and the list of causes. Then place the letter of the cause in the blank before the effect with which it is associated.

CAUSES

a. smaller muscle fibers
b. overworked, inactive muscles
c. unused joints
d. regular exercise
e. trained muscles
f. lack of muscle stress

EFFECTS

_____ 1. Less energy is stored.
_____ 2. Muscles tire easily.
_____ 3. The individual feels stiff and sore.
_____ 4. Muscles and joints become stronger.
_____ 5. Tendons and bones become harder, stronger.
_____ 6. Food energy is turned efficiently into work.
_____ 7. Bones become softer.

E X A M P L E **8.16**

Problem-Solving Pattern (Science)

Unsolved Problems

In 1970, the greatest unsolved problem regarding ocean basins was their origin. By the 1980's, the development of the present basins was well established. Now the question is, "How many ocean basins have there been throughout Earth's history?" Clearly there have been more than we know today, but the puzzle requires many detailed studies of the ocean's rocks.

Have any deep-sea sediments ever formed into rocks that now occur on land? Certainly ancient rocks must have formed from such sediments, and marine geologists would like to examine them. They have not come from cores drilled in the sea floor. A geologist from the University of Hawaii believes she sampled some in the Solomon Islands in 1980. Her analysis is interesting, yet still incomplete.

Certain areas of the sea floor, far away from sources of sediment, have few deposits. Rocks are not covered with sediment, or are close to the surface of the sea floor. In 1981 oceanographers completed a study of these parts of the sea floor, and learned that they are as quiet as had been supposed.

Source: William Matthews, Chalmer Roy, Robert Stevenson, et al.: *Investigating the Earth,* 4th ed. (Boston: Houghton Mifflin Company, 1984), p. 211. Reprinted by permission of Houghton Mifflin Company.

Problem-Solving Pattern

The problem-solving style of writing is used in scientific and health-related materials to describe a real or hypothetical problem and its actual or suggested solution. For example, a writer might use this style of writing to explain how a vaccine was developed for polio. Example 8.16 contains an illustration of this style of writing that was drawn from science content.

To teach students to read and understand the problem-solving style of writing, the teacher may use the following techniques.

ACTIVITIES

1. Ask students to identify the problem presented in a passage and to state it in their own words.
2. Ask students to locate the solution or solutions suggested by the author.
3. Ask students to prepare a problem and solution statement similar to the following:
   Problem: Why don't bacteria grow and divide in the region surrounding bread mold?
   Solution: Fleming found that mold gave off a chemical that killed the bacteria. He isolated the chemical and tested it against bacteria. He tested the chemical on animals with bacterial disease and on sick human volunteers.

E X A M P L E **8.17**

Experimental Pattern (Science)

Procedure

Place a glass beaker on your desk with two objects in it. This will represent the earth, which will hold only a certain size population.

Put a row of paper cups on your desk (ten should be enough). In the first cup, place two of the objects. In the second cup, place twice as many as in the first cup, or four objects. Write on the outside of the cups the number of objects that have been placed in each cup.

In cups 3 through 10, double the number of objects that are in the previous cup (that is, cup number 3 will contain 8 and cup number 4 will contain 16). Write the amount in each cup on the outside. Determine the height of the beaker with the two objects in it. What is the approximate volume (in percent) of the empty space in the beaker? Record this at 0 time. Make a table to record your data.

In 35 seconds, add the contents of cup 1 (that is, 2 objects) to the beaker and record in the table the total population and the approximate percent of the volume of the beaker that is empty. At 35-second intervals, add the contents of cups 2 through 10. Record your results.

Make a graph of your results, with population on the vertical axis and time on the horizontal axis.

Discussion

1. The human population of the earth is thought to have had a slow start, with early periods of doubling in size as long as 1 million years. The present world population is thought to be doubling every 37 years. How would the mathematical nature of this growth rate compare to your investigation?
2. The present world population is well over 4 billion people. To answer this question, assume that it is 4.5 billion. The earth's radius is about 6400 kilometers and about 7/10 of its surface is covered with water. What is the present density of human population in terms of people per square kilometer of land surface? (Area of a sphere = $4\pi r^2$)
3. Assume that the present population growth rate will continue. What will the density per square kilometer be 37 years from now? 111 years? 1110 years?
4. Is space the only limiting factor in determining maximum human population? If not, describe others.

Source: William Matthews, Chalmer Roy, Robert Stevenson, et al.: *Investigating the Earth,* 4th ed. (Boston: Houghton Mifflin Company, 1984), p. 340. Reprinted by permission of Houghton Mifflin Company.

The experimental pattern of writing is frequently used in scientific materials because experiments are the basis of scientific knowledge and advancement. The reader must be able to read experiment directions and translate them into action. The reader must carry out the directions precisely and carefully observe the outcomes. The purpose of an experiment is comparable to a main idea, and experimental directions are comparable to details. Example 8.17 presents this pattern of writing.

Following are the steps a reader should use when reading an experiment.

1. Ask the following questions:
   a. What am I to find out?
   b. What materials are needed?
   c. What processes are used?
   d. What is the order of the steps in the experiment?
   e. What do I expect to happen?
2. Perform the experiment.
3. Observe the experiment.
4. Compare the actual outcomes with predicted outcomes. (Success or failure of an experiment is determined by the learning that takes place.)

Additional Skills

In addition to an understanding of technical terminology and the styles in which science materials are organized, the reader of science must have mathematical skills. He or she must know and be able to apply the abbreviations and equations that are found in scientific content.

Mathematics Content

The discipline of mathematics is used in many areas of work and study. "To most people, the abilities to read and to think mathematically are probably the two most valuable skills learned in school. Most quantitative information is encountered in written form, and it must be read to be understood" (Krulik, 1980, p. 248). The National Council of Teachers of Mathematics Standards (1989) points out that "all students need extensive experience listening to, reading about, writing about, speaking about, reflecting on, and demonstrating mathematical ideas." They also state that teachers should continually encourage students to clarify, paraphrase, or elaborate. Researchers have established a high correlation between problem solving in mathematics and reading comprehension (Krulik, 1980).

Mathematics is the use of numbers, symbols, and words to express qualities, quantities, and relationships. We use mathematics in our lives in many ways, such as telling time, making change, banking, and computing income taxes. Current mathematics instruction emphasizes the use of "real-world" mathematics problems and materials and of computer capabilities to develop conceptual understanding (National Council of Teachers of Mathematics, 1989).

Words and Symbols

The field of mathematics requires that students think in terms of abstract ideas and symbols. Mathematics is a highly compressed system of language in which a single symbol may represent several words; for example, the symbol $>$ represents the words *greater than*. Writing in mathematics is generally denser and contains more ideas in each line and on each page than writing in the other disciplines.

In mathematics, as in some science content, words and symbols are mixed; comprehension depends not only on words and word relationships but also on the relationships between words and symbols. The reader of mathematics must be able to read symbols, signs, abbreviations, exponents, subscripts, formulas, equations, geometric figures, graphs, and tables as well as words.

Vocabulary study is essential in teaching students to read mathematics. Students must learn to read with precision; they cannot skip words or fill in meanings from context. It is important to understand the precise meaning of every word because reading a single word incorrectly may alter the meaning of an entire passage. The reader also must integrate the words into thought units and understand relationships among words. Some words, such as *count, odd,* and *power,* have meanings in mathematics that are quite different from their meanings in everyday conversation.

Since mathematical terminology is so important, teachers should use a variety of vocabulary strategies in their instruction. For example, students can be asked to develop a dictionary of mathematical terms, adding each new term that is introduced in class. When creating these dictionaries, students should be encouraged to write meanings in their own words rather than to use standard dictionary definitions. Paraphrasing the meanings will help students understand and remember the terms.

Four types of definitions are commonly used with mathematics terminology: formal definition, listing of characteristics, simulated examples, and real-world examples (Earle, 1976). Following are examples of each type of definition.

1. *Formal definition:* A square is a parallelogram that has four right angles and four sides of equal length.
2. *Listing of characteristics:* Several things are true about any square. It has only two dimensions — length and height. It has exactly four sides, all of which are straight lines of equal length. It has four interior angles, which total exactly 360 degrees. Each angle is a 90-degree angle.

3. *Simulated example:* Squares can be drawn on a chalkboard, cut from paper or other material, or pointed out in drawings or pictures.
4. *Real-world example:* These can be natural occurrences that exemplify square formulation or manmade objects that utilize squares as industrial, architectural, or decorative features. Real-world examples of squares might include the shape of a field, a windowpane, a room, or a table top.

Students can use these approaches to defining mathematical terms when they create their mathematics dictionaries. Teachers also can use these approaches to introduce terms before students read a mathematics assignment: after the teacher has identified the new terms, students can define them in the four different ways. Discussion and comparison of definitions will help students clarify their understanding of the new terms.

Another instructional approach to mathematical terms involves defining concept characteristics. The teacher prepares a worksheet for the students and asks them to identify the characteristics that describe each mathematical term on the worksheet. This activity could be used after students finish reading a mathematics chapter. Example 8.18 is a worksheet that illustrates this strategy.

E X A M P L E **8.18**

Mathematical Terms Worksheet

Directions: Check the characteristics that describe the term.
A set

_____ is a collection of objects.

_____ has members.

_____ has common properties.

_____ includes dissimilar objects.

_____ can be an empty set.

_____ has fractional numbers.

Reading Mathematics

It is important for teachers to emphasize the fact that reading mathematics content is very different from reading a story. The reading involved in problem solving is particularly difficult, because of the variety of cognitive processes that must be employed (Thomas, 1988).

Students need linguistic and mathematics schemata in order to read mathematics; therefore, teachers need to ascertain that students have the necessary background for comprehension (Thomas, 1988). To read mathematics material effectively, the following procedures are recommended.

326

The reading rate for mathematics is slower than that for other content areas. Students should understand the appropriate reading rates for the content. They should preread a section of the text at a moderate rate to get the general idea of the concept being introduced. Then they should read it more slowly, this time taking notes and copying definitions and the information printed in bold type. As they read, students should paraphrase the content and devise questions relating to the assignments. Finally, they should reread any passages that are unclear and write questions regarding information they need in order to clarify the material. They should give special attention to understanding illustrations (Henrichs and Sisson, 1980).

A directed reading lesson gives students a guide that can help them understand mathematics texts. The following set of steps can be used for directing the reading of a mathematics chapter.

1. *Introduce the new terms, using them in sentences.* Sentences from the text may be used. Give students an activity to help them learn the new terms, such as paraphrasing the meanings for a mathematics dictionary. Students may use their texts to help work out the meanings of the words.
2. *Ask students to preview the chapter and identify the topic.*
3. *Provide students with two or three silent reading purposes.* This step may be varied. If students have some background knowledge about the topic, they can help formulate silent reading purposes.
4. *Have students read the text silently.* Students should take notes on the content and formulate questions while reading.
5. *Work on any examples provided.* Students should ask questions if they do not understand an example.
6. *Discuss the silent reading purposes* and the questions formulated by the students in step 4.

Writing Patterns

The writing patterns that occur most frequently in mathematics are the problem pattern and the demonstration pattern. In addition, graphs and charts are often used in math content reading.

Verbal Problems

Solving word problems (verbal problems) is a very sophisticated task. Many readers have significant difficulties reading and understanding word problems, which are mathematical situations that are stated in words and symbols. Even when they can read the words and sentences with facility, many students have difficulty choosing the correct process (operation) to solve the problem. Knifong and Holtran (1977) found that 95 percent of the students they studied could read all the words correctly in word problems; 98 percent knew the situation the problem was discussing; 92 percent knew what the problem was asking; yet only 36 percent knew how to work the problem.

Kresse (1984) recommends a technique similar to SQ3R for helping students solve word problems. This approach to solving verbal problems helps students identify the appropriate process or processes for solving a problem. A mathematics reading technique similar to Kresse's follows. Immediately after the description of the technique, the process is modeled as it would be applied to the mathematics problem in Example 8.19.

TECHNIQUE

1. *Survey* the problem out loud. Try to visualize the situation.
2. *Question.* What is the problem asking me to find? This step gives students a purpose for reading the problem. It helps them know why they are reading.
3. *Question.* What is the correct process? (e.g., addition, subtraction, division)
4. *Read the problem aloud.*
5. *Work the problem.*

MODELING THE READING AND SOLVING MATHEMATICS
PROBLEMS PROCESS (AS APPLIED TO EXAMPLE 8.19)

1. *Survey.* The question sentence in this problem is, "What was your average cost per mile to own and operate your car?" I see that the car was a used one that the owner bought for $4200.00 two years ago. I also see that the person drove the car 17,500 miles. The expense record for the last two years is given in the problem. This is the kind of problem that business people who travel have to figure out all of the time. They need this kind of information for their income tax records.
2. *Question.* What is this problem asking me to find? I have to determine the average cost per mile to own and run the car. This problem is an averaging task.
3. *Question.* What is the correct process? I will have to use two processes. I will add all of the expenses to figure out the total expenses. Then I will divide the total expenses into the total number of miles that the owner has driven over the last two years.
4. *Read the problem aloud.* The problem states, "You bought a used car two years ago for $4200.00. Since then, you have driven it 17,500 miles. You kept a record of all your car expenses." The car expense record follows. Then the problem continues, "What was your average cost per mile to own and operate your car?"
5. *Work the problem.* I am adding $360 + 65 + 66 + 200 + 480 + 4200 + 66 + 165 + 60 + 400 + 390 + 60. The total is $6512.00. Now I will divide $6512.00 by 17,500, which gives an answer of 37 cents per mile as the average cost per mile to own and operate the car.

Kresse recommends having students check their work by reasoning through the problem. Following is a model of this process.

1. *Question:* What processes did I use to solve the problem?
2. *Answer:* Addition and division.
3. *Evidence:* I had to determine the average cost, and you add and divide to figure out average cost.
4. *Reasoning:* I added the expenses for operating the car and the cost of the car when the owner bought it. Then I divided that total by the number of miles the owner drove the car.

One of the difficulties that students experience when reading mathematics is realizing that the information they need to solve a problem is found in the wording of the problem. A study guide can help students understand this. Example 8.19 contains a verbal problem and a reading guide based on the problem. The teacher would prepare the mathematics reading guide; students would complete it as they read a verbal problem. The guide shown here is based on a format suggested by Riley and Pachtman (1978).

EXAMPLE **8.19**

Verbal Problem (Mathematics) and Reading Guide

Problem Solving: Driving a Bargain

You bought a used car two years ago for $4200. Since then, you have driven it 17,500 miles. You kept a record of all your car expenses.

Car Expense Record

1st Year		2nd Year	
Insurance	$360	License	$ 66
Tune-up	65	Repair brakes	165
License	66	Tune-up	60
Repair clutch	200	Insurance	400
Gas	480	Gas	390
		Repair muffler	60

Problem: What was your average cost per mile to own and operate your car?

Solution Plan: Find the total of your car expenses. Figure the unit rate, in cents per mile, for your car.

Source: Bryce Shaw, Robert Kane, and Katherine Merseth: *Fundamentals of Mathematics: Skills and Applications,* 2nd ed. (Boston: Houghton Mifflin Company, 1986), p. 226. Reprinted by permission of Houghton Mifflin Company.

Reading Guide

Part I: Facts of the Problem

Directions: Read the problem. Then in Column A, check those statements that contain the important facts of the problem. You may refer to the problem to verify your responses. In Column B, check the statements that will help you solve the problem.

A   B

_____ _____ 1. The car is two years old.

_____ _____ 2. You have driven the car 17,500 miles.

_____ _____ 3. You have a record of all car expenses.

_____ _____ 4. You found it necessary to repair the muffler.

_____ _____ 5. The problem asks for average cost per mile to own and operate your car.

_____ _____ 6. You paid $4200.00 for the car.

Part II: Mathematical Ideas and Interpretation

Directions: Check the statements that contain mathematical concepts related to the problem. You may go back to Part I to review your responses.

_____ 1. The total cost for insurance was $760.00.

_____ 2. Multiply dollars times 100 to get cents.

_____ 3. "Per" often suggests that division is necessary.

_____ 4. The total cost of repair and maintenance was $550.00.

_____ 5. To find the total expenses, add initial cost, first year expenses, and second year expenses.

_____ 6. Gasoline currently costs 98¢ a gallon.

Part III: Computation

Directions: Below are possible mathematical calculations. Check those that apply to this problem. You may refer to Part I and Part II to verify your responses.

_____ 1. ($760.00 + $550.00 + $132.00 + $870.00)/2

_____ 2. $760.00 + $550.00 + $132.00 + $870.00 + $1200.00

_____ 3. $4200.00 divided by 17,500

_____ 4. $4200.00 multiplied by 17,500

_____ 5. [($4200.00 + $1171.00 + $1141.00) ÷ 17,500] × 100

Part IV: Final Computation

Directions: Compute the answer.

Another valuable approach to reading verbal problems was suggested by Earle (1976). In this technique, the teacher uses a series of steps to guide students through the written language of the problem. The following steps are based on those suggested by Earle.

1. Read the problem quickly to obtain a general understanding of it. Visualize the problem. Do not be concerned with the numbers.
2. Examine the problem again. Identify the question you are asked to answer. This question usually comes at the end of the problem, but it may occur anywhere in the problem.
3. Read the problem again to identify the information given.
4. Analyze the problem to see how the information is related. Identify any missing information and any unnecessary information.
5. Compute the answer.
6. Examine your answer. Label the parts of the solution to correspond with the question that the problem asks you to solve. Is your answer sensible?

Demonstration Pattern

The demonstration pattern is used to show students the development of processes and concepts. This writing pattern is usually accompanied by an example that illustrates the written material. It is important in mathematics materials because it is used to show students how to work problems. Following are strategies that students can use while reading the demonstration pattern.

ACTIVITIES

1. The student should work through the example to determine whether he or she understands the process. If the student does not compute the same answer as shown in the example, he or she should work slowly through the example again, rereading each step carefully to determine the point in the process at which he or she erred.
2. The reader should paraphrase the process in his or her own words.
3. The student should apply the process to other situations.

Example 8.20 shows the demonstration writing pattern.

Graphs and Charts

Graphs and charts are often used to represent mathematical concepts in math materials as well as in other content textbooks, in newspapers, and in magazines. The graph in Example 8.21 appears in a mathematics textbook. The questions that follow can be used to guide students' reading of charts and graphs.

E X A M P L E **8.20**

The Demonstration Writing Pattern

The Pythagorean Theorem

OBJECTIVES

1. Determine the geometric mean between two numbers.
2. State and apply the relationships that exist when the altitude is drawn to the hypotenuse of a right triangle.
3. State and apply the Pythagorean Theorem.

6-1 Geometric Means

Suppose r, s, and t are positive numbers with $\dfrac{r}{s} = \dfrac{s}{t}$. Then s is called the **geometric mean** between r and t.

EXAMPLE 1

Find the geometric mean between the given numbers.

a. 3 and 7   b. 6 and 15

SOLUTION

a. $\dfrac{3}{x} = \dfrac{x}{7}$ b. $\dfrac{6}{x} = \dfrac{x}{15}$

$x^2 = 21$ $x^2 = 90$

$x = \sqrt{21}$ $x = \sqrt{90} = \sqrt{9 \cdot 10} = \sqrt{9} \cdot \sqrt{10} = 3\sqrt{10}$

The symbol $\sqrt{}$ always indicates the positive square root of a number. In (b) above, the *radical* $\sqrt{90}$ could be *simplified* because the *radicand* 90 has the factor 9, a perfect square. When you write radical expressions you should write them in **simplest form**. This means writing them so that

1. No radicand has a factor, other than 1, that is a perfect square.
2. No radicand is a fraction.
3. No fraction has a denominator that contains a radical.

You should express answers involving radicals in simplest form unless you are asked to use decimal approximations.

Source: Ray C. Jurgensen, Richard Brown, and John Jurgensen: *Geometry* (Boston: Houghton Mifflin Company, 1985), p. 247. Reprinted by permission of Houghton Mifflin Company.

332

EXAMPLE **8.21**

Sample Mathematics Graph and Questions

Bar Graphs

A *bar graph* is a way to present information. Bars (rectangles) and a scale are used to compare quantities. Each quantity is represented by the length of a bar. To read a bar graph, use the scale to find the length of the bar.

A group of high school seniors were asked what they planned to do after graduation. The results are shown in the bar graph. How many plan to go to technical school?

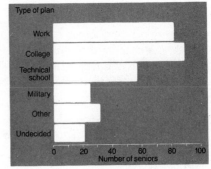

MODEL

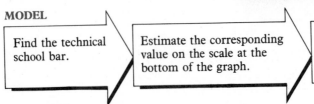

Find the technical school bar.

Estimate the corresponding value on the scale at the bottom of the graph.

About 58 seniors plan to enter technical school.

Source: Bryce Shaw, Robert Kane, and Katherine Merseth: *Fundamentals of Mathematics* (Boston: Houghton Mifflin Company, 1982), p. 238. Copyright © 1982 by Houghton Mifflin Company. Reprinted by permission of Houghton Mifflin Company.

Questions

1. What is the title of this graph?
2. What type of graph is it?
3. What is being compared in this graph?
4. Who would find the information in this graph useful?
5. State a conclusion based on this graph.

Additional information on graph reading can be found in Chapter 4.

Additional Skills

Students of mathematics must learn to read and use the special symbols, signs, and formulas that are found in mathematics textbooks. Reading and understanding these is similar to learning a foreign language. Example 8.22 is a selection from a math textbook that contains special symbols, signs, and formulas.

EXAMPLE **8.22**

Symbols in Mathematics Content

Circumference

The distance around a circle is called the **circumference** of the circle. You can use the diameter of a circle to find the circumference.

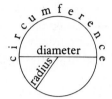

Circumference $= \pi \times$ diameter, or $C = \pi \times d$

The value of π is about 3.14. This value is the same for all circles.

MODEL

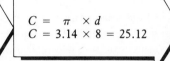

| The diameter of a circle is 8 m. Find the circumference. | $C = \pi \times d$ $C = 3.14 \times 8 = 25.12$ | The circumference is 25.12 m. |

Because the diameter of a circle is twice the radius, the circumference can be expressed as follows:

Circumference $= 2 \times \pi \times$ radius, or $C = 2 \times \pi \times r$

MODEL

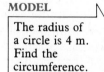 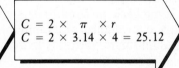

| The radius of a circle is 4 m. Find the circumference. | $C = 2 \times \pi \times r$ $C = 2 \times 3.14 \times 4 = 25.12$ | The circumference is 25.12 m. |

Source: Bryce Shaw, Robert Kane, and Katherine Merseth: *Fundamentals of Mathematics* (Boston: Houghton Mifflin Company, 1982), p. 156. Copyright © 1982 by Houghton Mifflin Company. Reprinted by permission of Houghton Mifflin Company.

Students should practice reading and translating the symbols, signs, and formulas that are used in mathematics, textbooks, rewriting formulas in words to help themselves learn the necessary symbols (Henrichs and Sisson, 1980). Activities that require the matching of words and symbols help reinforce comprehension of symbols.

Teaching a Chapter of Mathematics Content

Mathematics teachers may wish to use the following strategies. They can develop student readiness for reading a chapter by introducing key terms and concepts, writing the terms on the chalkboard or on a handout sheet, and using them in sentences. Students may be asked to associate their ideas and previous experiences (brainstorming) with the terms. This introduction can be varied with some of the strategies introduced in Chapters 2, 3, and 6.

After the concepts and vocabulary have been introduced, students may be given an advance organizer, a structured overview, a study guide, or a concept guide to use as they read through the selection. A directed reading lesson may be used instead of a study guide or concept guide.

After students have read the chapter, the teacher can monitor their comprehension by having them demonstrate their ability to apply the new concepts.

Computer Literacy Content

Computer literacy classes are becoming more prevalent at the junior and senior high school levels than ever before. They are generally concerned with familiarizing students with computers and the terminology related to them and teaching students to use computers in a variety of ways. Topics such as the history of computing, careers in computing, the social impact of computers, applications of computers, and specifics of programming may be included in such courses.

The goal of computer literacy courses is generally to make students aware of the impact of computers on our society, to acquaint them with the equipment that is available, to give them experience in using some computer applications, and to teach them some basic programming skills. A computer literacy course may be a prerequisite for regular programming courses. Computer literacy courses also offer students an opportunity to decide if they would like to prepare for computer-related careers.

The reading materials in computer literacy courses are quite varied. Students are usually asked to read from textbooks, handouts, computer displays, computer printouts, and computer magazines and journals. The content of these materials varies from expository discourse to program listings to narrative discourse.

Most of the material in computer literacy textbooks is expository in nature. It abounds with difficult vocabulary that represents abstract concepts likely to be unfamiliar to students, although with the current popularity of home computers, some students may have had prior exposure to some of the concepts. The expository discourse is generally interspersed with examples and graphic aids. The material is precise and factual, and the idea density may be extremely high.

This expository material must be read slowly and carefully. Almost every statement may present an important idea that must be grasped in order to comprehend later material.

The material read from the computer screen may be either expository or narrative in nature. The narrative material would probably be the content of applications programs that students are asked to run. This type of material is unlikely to cause as many reading problems for students as expository material may cause.

The ability to read program listings is a specialized skill that requires use of logical thinking and knowledge of technical terminology. Programs are written in computer languages that are very different from regular English and must be learned in a manner similar to the way a foreign language is learned. Every number, word, and punctuation mark in a computer program is important to the program's correct function and, therefore, is important to the comprehension of the program. Visualization of the effect that each line of the listing has on the program's operation is also important.

Vocabulary

Many specialized, technical terms are found in computer literacy materials, from the labels for the parts of the computer to the terminology used in writing programs. In this field, there are many words that stand for very complex procedures, and there are many abbreviations and acronyms (for example, RAM, ROM, BASIC, CRT, DIR).

Many words in computer literacy materials are multiple-meaning words that have a specialized meaning in this field. Examples of these words are *chip, hardware, program,* and *boot.* Example 8.23 contains sample items for a vocabulary exercise involving multiple-meaning words in computer literacy.

An exercise like that in Example 8.23 can be given to students before they read assigned material containing the vocabulary words. The teacher can

EXAMPLE **8.23**

Sample Items for a Vocabulary Exercise for Computer Literacy

Directions: Choose the correct meaning for each underlined word, depending on the context in which this sentence is found in your chapter.

1. Boot the program.
   a. kick
   b. start up
   c. footware
2. Boot the program.
   a. set of instructions for the performance of a specific task
   b. a public presentation
   c. a plan of action

instruct the students to look for the sample sentences as they read the assignment, to read the context of the sentences surrounding the sample sentences carefully, and to decide which definition the underlined words have in the specific context of the chapter. After students finish reading the selection, the teacher can conduct a class discussion of the meanings chosen, asking students to read parts of the chapter that they feel support their choices. Before students will be able to participate in a discussion of this type, the teacher will have to model the behavior of finding the supporting clues in the context and verbalizing them.

Writing Patterns

The writing patterns in computer literacy materials are much like those found in the areas of science and mathematics and include the definition or explanation of a technical process pattern; the classification pattern; the cause-and-effect pattern; and the problem-solving pattern. At times these patterns are combined. Graphic aids are also used in abundance.

Definition or Explanation Pattern

This pattern may explain processes performed by the computer or followed by programmers in software development. It may also provide definitions for specialized terms in the computer field. This pattern may be accompanied by graphic aids, such as flow charts and pictures, which must be understood in relation to the expository text that accompanies them.

The information presented in this pattern is usually densely packed with specific details that students need to acquire. For this reason, it should be read slowly and carefully, with much allowance for reflection on the meaning of each bit of information presented.

The passage in Example 8.24, taken from a computer literacy textbook, illustrates the definition pattern. Note that in Example 8.24 the definition is given in words, *and* graphic aids are also included for additional clarification. The reader must correlate the written words with the diagrams in an attempt to understand the definition.

After students have read material such as the passage in Example 8.24, have been given the meanings of all the different shapes used in the flowcharts, and have been led through the flowcharts authors have developed for a specific function, the logical method of checking their understanding would be to have the students develop flowcharts for simple, everyday tasks and explain their charts. This activity would not be appropriate for students who had read only the excerpt in Example 8.24, however, for not enough information is provided for full development of the process in this brief selection. Guidance through the process by the teacher would be imperative.

EXAMPLE **8.24**

Definition Pattern in a Computer Literacy Book

In designing a system, the systems analyst may use a special type of diagram called a **flowchart.** The flowchart is a tool that shows all the steps in a system in sequence. As you can see from the illustration, various-shaped symbols stand for input/output devices, memory or storage, and processing steps. Arrows, called **flowlines,** indicate the direction that each step in the sequence takes. A flowchart is a kind of problem-solving tool.

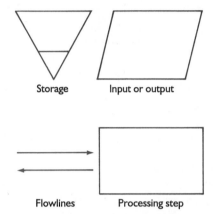

Storage   Input or output

Flowlines   Processing step

Source: June St. Clair Atkinson: *Help with Computer Literacy* (Boston: Houghton Mifflin Company, 1984), p. 58. Reprinted by permission of Houghton Mifflin Company.

Classification Pattern

In the classification pattern, information is ordered under common headings and subheadings. Generally, in this pattern, a classification is given, and the distinguishing characteristics of the members of the class are explained. Examples of class members are also usually included.

For each classification described in this way, readers must be able to identify the important distinguishing characteristics and relate them to the examples. If the reader comprehends the material, he or she should then be able to recognize examples and non-examples of class members.

Example 8.25 illustrates the classification pattern of writing.

Cause-and-Effect Pattern

In the cause-and-effect pattern, the results of particular actions by a computer programmer or operator may be revealed or the cause of particular computer output may be considered. In the passage in Example 8.26, the effect of entering certain values as variables into a computer program is explained.

338

EXAMPLE **8.25**

Classification Pattern in a Computer Literacy Book and Study Guide

Suppose, for instance, you want a printed copy as the end result. That's simple! You need a **printer.** But how do you want your printed material to look? How much will it cost? Is speed important? You can buy a printer that is relatively inexpensive but slow, or one that is expensive and fast. There are impact and nonimpact printers. It all depends on the results you want, whether in business or in your own home. The speed of printing is increasing so fast that most information about it is out of date as soon as it is printed!

An **impact printer** forces (impacts) a character against a ribbon and paper like a typewriter. Some of these so-called character printers are very much like typewriters. They can produce copy at speeds of 10 to 300 characters per second. A common type of impact printer is the ball-like unit originally introduced by IBM on the Selectric typewriter. This kind of typewriterlike printer is considered very slow as far as speed of output is concerned.

Another widely used printing element is the **daisy wheel.** As the illustration indicates, it looks like a daisy with a set of spokes, each spoke with a character at the end. A hammer mechanism strikes a character when it is in position for printing. Print quality of the daisy wheel is excellent at a rate of about 10 to 55 characters per second.

A **dot matrix printer** has wire ends that strike against the ribbon in a kind of grid, making a dot pattern. This dot pattern contrasts with the fully filled-in character made by the ball element or the daisy wheel. However, the matrix printer is faster and less expensive than the daisy wheel. It prints up to 330 characters per second.

A **chain printer** carries the characters on a loop chain. As the type moves across the paper, individual hammers strike the characters engraved on the chain links. Such a high-speed impact printer can print up to 3000 lines per minute.

Nonimpact printers do not use the method of striking with a key or a wire end. Instead, they use heat, ink jets, or laser beams. One kind of heat-process printer requires specially coated paper. The color of the paper changes as the top layer is literally burned away, leaving the desired characters. Unfortunately the resulting print is not of very high quality. The heat-process printer can print from 160 to 220 characters per second.

Ink-jet printers fire a jet of charged ink through a magnetic field onto the paper. Such a printer is expensive, but it can print up to 60,000 lines per minute.

Laser beam printers, which burn images onto specially prepared paper, are also expensive and fast.

Source: June St. Clair Atkinson: *Help with Computer Literacy* (Boston: Houghton Mifflin Company, 1984), pp. 47–48. Reprinted by permission of Houghton Mifflin Company.

Study Guide

Directions: Fill in the columns with the characteristics of the different types of printers.

Daisy wheel	Dot-matrix	Chain	Heat-process	Ink-jet	Laser

E X A M P L E **8.26**

Cause-and-Effect Pattern in Computer Literacy

Variables

ROBOT 6 COMMANDS
U — move UP
D — move DOWN
R — move RIGHT
L — move LEFT
K — KICK

nU, nD, nR, nL, where "n" is a number, repeats the step "n" times.

S — STOP
CLEAR — end exercise

n(...) where "n" is a number, repeats everything inside the parentheses "n" times

"A," "B," "C" variable names.

Using the program that takes the robot to the ball and around it, you can understand that it is simple to make the robot circle the ball once, twice, or any number of times. You simply replace the number that controls the steps within parentheses. In some computer applications, a series of steps must be repeated, but the exact number of repetitions is not known in advance. Thus, some kind of "place holder" is put into the program at the spot where the number will be needed. This is called a variable.

This robot can handle the concept of a variable. Whenever the robot comes upon the letter "A," "B" or "C" in its program, it will stop and ask you for a number to replace that variable in the program. It then proceeds with the program. If the computer came upon A(R), for example, it would stop to ask for a value of "A." If you answered "10," it would then move the robot ten spaces to the right.

Source: Stephen M. Booth et al.: *Computer Discovery* (Chicago: Science Research Associates, 1981), p. 48.

To check for mastery of the information presented in the passage in Example 8.26, the teacher might use an activity such as the one below.

Directions: Fill in the effect upon the robot if you gave the response "3" to the screen prompt when the robot encounters each of the following instructions:

Instruction	Effect
1. A(L)	_____
2. A(U)	_____
3. A(D)	_____

Problem-Solving Pattern

The problem-solving pattern may appear in computer science materials with descriptions of real or hypothetical questions and actual or suggested solutions. For example, the material may describe how reservations for tours were handled before and after computerization. A content study guide can be used with such material to help students focus on the information that they should be able to extract from the material and the applications of the information that they should try to make.

English (Language Arts) Content

The language arts are concerned with communication between the sender and the receiver of a message. Both participants must have command of the English language in order to communicate effectively; therefore, study of the language arts is involved primarily with effective use and appreciation of the English language. English has the most varied subject matter of all the content subjects. Study of English requires readers to work with grammar, composition, and many forms of literature — novels, short stories, poetry, biographies, autobiographies, newspapers, and magazines.

All too often, it is assumed that English teachers know more about teaching reading than other content teachers do. English teachers have been prepared to teach their content area, which includes reading literature; however, they generally have acquired skills in literary analysis rather than in reading instruction.

Vocabulary Development

Vocabulary development is an important aspect of English instruction because students who have a large store of word meanings at their command are better communicators. Students can expand and enrich their general vocabulary through instruction and through reading literature. In English class they can be taught technical vocabulary words such as *pronoun, hyperbole, précis,* and *haiku.* Suggestions for teaching technical words are provided in Chapter 2 of this text.

The vocabulary file is often overlooked as a method for developing vocabulary because it doesn't seem very exciting, but it can be a very effective device. Each student keeps his or her own card file containing the new words that are encountered in reading. The word cards may take the following form (or any form that appeals to the teacher).

Word _____
Sentence in which found _____
Student definition _____

For the word file to be effective, the teacher must carefully evaluate its content at regular intervals. Students may test each other in pairs, or they may construct crossword puzzles from their words for peers to complete. The teacher may evaluate an individual file by asking the student to build sentences from his or her words or to place words in categories.

Students should be encouraged to make a point of systematically adding new words to their vocabularies. A helpful technique includes the following steps:

1. Look at the word.
2. Say the word.
3. Write the word with a synonym or brief definition.
4. Use the word in conversation or writing.

In order to say the word correctly and write its meaning, students may need assistance from the teacher or a classmate, but they should first try to find the meaning of the word by using context clues. If other help is not available, they can use a dictionary or thesaurus. After adopting this system of learning new words or developing similar systems of their own, students will become more independent in acquiring new vocabulary.

Studying the etymology of words motivates some students to learn more about words and to remember them. Through this kind of word research, students will learn that meanings of certain words have changed over time. For example, the word *marshal* once meant "one who held horses," not quite as impressive as its present-day meaning. As a result of being used daily over a period of years, the words in a living language gradually change in various ways. Following is a list of the ways in which words change.

1. *Amelioration.* The meaning of the word has changed so that the word means something better than it once did. For example, a person who was called *enthusiastic* was once considered a fanatic. Currently, enthusiasm is considered a desirable quality.
2. *Pejoration.* Pejoration indicates that the word has a more derogatory meaning than it did earlier in its history. For example, a *villain* once was a feudal serf or a servant from a villa. Currently, a villain is considered to be a scoundrel.

3. *Generalization.* Some words become more generalized in meaning. When generalization operates, the meaning of words is broadened. Earlier in history, a *picture* was a painting, but now a picture may be a print, a photograph, or a drawing. In fact, a picture may not be representational at all, because in art a picture may not have a distinct form.

4. *Specialization.* The opposite of generalization is specialization. In this case, word meanings become more specific than they were in the past. At one time, *meat* was any food, not just lamb, pork, or beef. The Chinese used the word *pork* to mean any kind of meat earlier in their history.

5. *Euphemism.* This term indicates the use of an affectation to convey elegance, or the use of a more pleasant word for an unpleasant one. For example, a *janitor* is often called a "custodian" or "maintenance engineer," and a person does not *die* but rather "passes away."

6. *Hyperbole.* This is an extreme exaggeration. For example, a man who is tired might say that he could "sleep for a year." Exaggeration is being used to make the point of extreme fatigue. Many people currently use the word *fantastic* to describe almost anything unusual, although *fantastic* means strange, wonderful, unreal, and illusory.

Activities such as the following can be used to develop word meanings through etymology.

ACTIVITIES

1. Give students a list of words with instructions to determine the origin of each term and the type of changes that have occurred in its meaning. Words such as the following could be used in this activity: *city, ghetto, manuscript, lord, stench.*

2. Ask students to identify the origins of the names of the months and/or the days of the week. For example, *October* is from the Latin *Octo* (eight), because it was the eighth month of the Roman calendar. *Monday* means "day of the moon."

3. Encourage students to determine the origins and meanings of their first names and surnames. For example, Susan means "lily." Many surnames are related to occupation or geographic origin. The surname Butler means a bottlemaker; the surname *Hatfield* refers to a wooded field.

Word knowledge can be increased by exploring some of the unique characteristics of different types of words. Activities that involve acronyms, oxymorons, and homonyms, for example, will develop students' vocabularies. Following are definitions of some special types of words.

1. *Acronyms.* Words composed of the first letters or syllables of longer terms, such as SNAFU, which means "situation normal, all fouled up." This is a Navy term that originated during World War II.

2. *Oxymorons.* Two incongruous words used together, such as *cruel kindness.*

3. *Homonyms* — also known as *homophones*. Words that sound alike but are not spelled alike, such as *to, too, two; pare, pair; sum, some.*
4. *Heteronyms.* Words that have different pronunciations and meanings, although they are spelled exactly the same, such as:

    Don't *subject* me to that experience.
    What is the *subject* of your book?

5. *Coined words.* Words invented to meet specific needs. Words are often coined by using previously existing words and word parts. *Gerrymander, curfew, motel,* and *astronaut* are examples of coined words. Many product names are coined words, for example, *Pream, Tang, Jello, and Bisquick.*

The denotative and connotative meanings of words can be introduced through literature. *Denotation* is the literal definition of a word as defined by the dictionary. *Connotation* refers to the ideas and associations that are suggested by a term, including emotional reactions. For instance, the word *home* denotes the place where one lives, whereas it may connote warmth, love, and family. Readers must learn to recognize the connotations of words in order to comprehend a selection. By definition, *cunning* and *astute* are very similar, but, when the word *cunning* is used to describe a person, it usually implies a negative quality, whereas describing a person as *astute* is a compliment.

Students can look for examples of both connotative and denotative uses of words in the literary selections they read. In addition, the following activities will increase understanding of denotation and connotation.

ACTIVITIES

1. In each pair, select the word that you would prefer to use for describing yourself. Tell why you chose the word.
    a. *creative or screwball*
    b. *stolid or easygoing*
    c. *thrifty or tight*
    d. *enthusiastic or excitable*
    e. *fat or heavy-set*
    f. *conceited or proud*
2. Provide students with a list of words similar to the preceding list and ask them to write a plus (+) beside each positive word, a minus (−) beside each negative word, and a zero (0) beside each neutral word.

Figurative language is connotative use of language. The author implies ideas through figurative language, and this expressive application of language makes written language more interesting to readers. You can refer to Chapter 2 for suggestions to aid in instruction related to figurative language.

Literature

The goal of teaching literature is to develop in readers a lifelong interest in and appreciation for literature. Having students read and respond to inter-

344

esting literary selections helps teachers achieve these goals. When students read material that is related to their interests and background experience, their schemata will enable them to read with greater comprehension. Many students need guides that will help them comprehend literature, such as anticipation guides, advance organizers, and three-level study guides (Lubell and Townsend, 1989).

Novels and Short Stories

Reading novels and short stories is basic to the study of literature. A literature selection is an imaginative expression of a writer's ideas: the author shares an experience with the reader by relating incidents through a story. The longer form of the novel permits an author to develop literary elements such as characterization in greater depth than is possible within the form of the short story.

Researchers have identified eight processes that are involved in a student's response to literature (Cooper and Purves, 1973). These processes are as follows:

1. *Description.* Students can restate in their own words what they have read.
2. *Discrimination.* Students can discriminate among different writings on the basis of type, author, theme, and so forth.
3. *Relation.* Students can relate to each other several aspects of a piece of literature. For example, students could discuss the relationship between a story's setting and plot or could compare the plots of two different stories.
4. *Interpretation.* Students can interpret the author's ideas and support these interpretations.
5. *Generalization.* Students can use what they have learned in one piece of literature to understand another one.
6. *Evaluation.* Students can apply criteria to evaluate a piece of literature. For example, they might evaluate the quality of the element of characterization.
7. *Valuing.* Students can relate literature to their own lives.
8. *Creation.* Students can respond to literature by creating their own art, music, writing, drama, or dance.

When teaching novels or short stories, teachers should prepare students by activating their schemata. Then it is advisable to have students read straight through the story, although the reading may extend over a number of class sessions. This helps them to understand the entire plot, character development, setting, and theme. If the reading of a selection is broken into chapters or smaller parts, the reader does not have an opportunity to grasp the entire selection or the way the components of the selection fit together.

In addition to using the eight processes of responding to literature to guide instruction, the teacher should ask students to support answers with material from the selections they have read. Students may be asked to diagram story structure in the following manner:

Title

Setting	*Theme*	*Plot*	*Characters*
Place	Symbols	Episode #1	Main character
Time	Incidents	Episode #2	Supporting character
		Episode # 3	

A directed reading lesson such as that in Example 8.27 is another way for teachers to help students read and understand novels and short stories. Directed reading lessons are discussed in detail in Chapter 6.

Following is a sample literature lesson.

EXAMPLE **8.27**

Directed Reading Lesson: Literature

MOTIVATION AND BUILDING BACKGROUND

1. Ask the students these questions: Do you know any good ghost stories? Have you ever sat around with a group of friends telling ghost stories? How did you feel later, particularly if you had to go some place alone? You probably felt the way Ichabod Crane felt in this story after he listened to some ghost stories and rode home alone over country roads.

2. Tell the students that the story they are going to read is a ghost story. The characters in this story include a worthy pedagogue; a rantipole hero; a ripe, melting and rosy-cheeked maiden; and a contented farmer. After they read the story, they should try to name each of the characters listed.

SKILL DEVELOPMENT ACTIVITIES

3. Have the students match a number of words from the story with their definitions.

Words	*Definitions*
continual reverie	German soldier
Hessian trooper	Bible study
spectre	constant daydream
psalmody	ghost

GUIDED READING

4. *Silent* — Have the students read the story silently. Tell them to think about these purpose questions as they read: What factors created an atmosphere for the ghost to appear? What happened to Ichabod?

5. *Discussion* — After the students have read the selection, use these questions for further discussion:
   a. How would you characterize the residents of Sleepy Hollow?
   b. Is the setting important in this story? Why?
   c. Do you think Katrina was really interested in Ichabod? Why?
   d. How are Brom Bones and Ichabod Crane alike? How are they different?
   e. What was the point of view of this story?
   f. Do you agree with the old man about the purpose of this story? What do you think the purpose was?

FOLLOW-UP ACTIVITIES

6. Have students write a paragraph telling what they would have done if they were Ichabod.
7. Ask students to read another story written by Washington Irving and compare it to the "Legend of Sleepy Hollow."
8. Have students draw a picture of the way they visualize Ichabod.

Poetry

Poetry is a condensed form of writing that expresses in a succinct fashion the writer's thoughts and emotions and stimulates the reader's imagination. Frequently, a poet can inspire a reader to perceive familiar things and ideas in a new way. Poets use rhythm, rhyme, imagery, and many other devices to make a reader see or feel what they are expressing.

Teachers may use the following techniques with poetry:

1. Poems should be read aloud.
2. Poems should be read in their entirety for full appreciation of them.
3. Poems should usually be read twice in order to achieve full appreciation.
4. Prose and poetry on the same topic may be compared in order to understand the succinctness of poetry.

Drama

Drama is literature that is written to be acted. The writer intends for the characters to speak the lines and for the audience to see the action. Drama includes stage directions needed to understand the plot. The reader should pay attention to all information in parentheses and italics. The name of the speaker is printed before his or her lines, and the reader must be alert to the names of the speakers in order to determine who is speaking and how the action unfolds. In drama, the characters are responsible for telling the story.

The following teaching procedures may be used for drama.

1. Ask the students to visualize the action.
2. Have the students read the speeches aloud to aid comprehension.

3. Have the students act out the described actions in order to arrive at a better understanding of the action.

Essays and Editorials

Essays, editorials, and position papers are expository forms of writing. Exposition is used to explain information from a particular point of view. The author is usually trying to convince readers to accept his or her argument. Exposition contains a greater amount of information than fiction does. The strategies suggested in this chapter (and in Chapters 9 and 10) for guiding the reading of content materials aid the teacher in teaching exposition. Following are activities that teachers can use to help students comprehend expository materials.

1. Identify the author's purpose.
2. Identify the author's perception of his or her audience.
3. Identify the author's argument.
4. Identify the details the author uses to support his or her argument.
5. Identify the author's organization of details.
6. Identify the details that are emphasized.
7. Identify the sequence of details.
8. Identify the author's attitude toward the topic and toward the audience (Finder, 1970).

The preceding activities can be used for discussions and study guides.

Grammar and Composition

Textbooks are used in many language arts classes to teach grammar and composition. They explain the grammar and punctuation of the English language, using technical vocabulary words such as *complex sentences, interrogative,* and *adjective.* Frequently, these textbooks follow an expository pattern: a concept or idea is explained and illustrated, a definition or generalization is developed, and application exercises are provided. The many details that are packed into each page make for rather uninteresting, although clearly presented, reading. Frequently the material is almost in outline form, requiring the reader to identify supporting details and main ideas. Some of the models and examples used in language arts textbooks are written in a narrative style, so that the reader must switch from expository to narrative style. Example 8.28 shows content from a grammar and composition text that is written in a definition or explanation pattern.

Teachers can approach grammar and composition instruction by teaching students the technical vocabulary and focusing on identification of main ideas and supporting details. The outline approach that is used in some textbooks to present grammar content makes identification of main ideas and details a most important skill. To help students remember the text material, instruction

E X A M P L E **8.28**

Content from a Grammar and Composition Text

Prepositional Phrases

A preposition is usually followed by a noun or a pronoun, which is called the **object of the preposition.** The preposition, the object, and the modifiers of that object form a *prepositional phrase.*

prep.   obj.

There are deep cracks **in the moon's surface.** [The prepositional phrase consists of the preposition, *in,* the modifiers, *the* and *moon's,* and the object of the preposition, *surface.*]

In some sentences the preposition comes *after* the object. This arrangement often occurs in questions, as in the following example.

obj.   prep.

Which state are you **from?** [**Think:** From which state are you?]

A prepositional phrase may have more than one object, as in the following sentence.

prep.   obj.   obj.

The moon's surface is covered **with rocks and dust.**

Prepositional phrases usually act as modifiers. A prepositional phrase functions as an adjective if it modifies a noun or a pronoun. A prepositional phrase functions as an adverb if it modifies a verb, an adjective, or an adverb.

Used as an Adjective

prep. phrase

I still have to paint the other *side* **of the house.** [*Of the house* tells which side.]

Used as an Adverb

prep. phrase

Max *hit* the golf ball **into the pond.** [*Into the pond.* tells where Max hit the ball.]

Source: Ann Brown, Jeffrey Milson, Fran Shaw, et al.: *Grammar and Composition: Second Course* (Boston: Houghton Mifflin Company, 1986), pp. 31–32. Reprinted by permission of Houghton Mifflin Company.

should be given in paraphrasing and finding applications for content. Advance organizers, study guides, and concept guides are especially useful for teaching grammar and composition content.

Foreign Languages

The ability to read and speak foreign languages is a valuable skill in today's world because of increased travel and communication among the people of the world. Studying a foreign language has an additional value in that it helps students understand the culture of another country. Foreign language instruction should be approached through meaning-centered activities, which result in the ability to use a language functionally.

Learning to read a foreign language is very similar to learning to read one's native language. Therefore, readiness is an important factor in reading a foreign language. The teacher must build a point of contact between the reader and the content he or she is reading. Students should be exposed to oral language to develop listening comprehension of the language they are learning. Listening comprehension precedes reading comprehension. Recordings and foreign language broadcasts on radio and television provide opportunities for students to develop listening comprehension.

Students should be taught the concepts and the vocabulary used in the selections they are preparing to read. Discussion and practice of common phrases and expressions are useful in developing readiness to read. The teacher should stress the use of context as an aid to understanding vocabulary in a foreign language. In addition, the teacher should provide questions to guide the students' silent reading.

To become fluent in reading a foreign language, students need to read for global meaning rather than translating word by word through a page or passage. Students who have to stop several times on each line to check English equivalents are not actually reading because they are not able to access the ideas from the written language (Carlson, 1984). Students should have opportunities to listen to, speak, read, and write the language. These activities will help them learn both the semantics and the syntax of the language they are studying. Teachers can use the same methods in teaching students to read a foreign language that they use in teaching them to read English.

Following are some specific techniques useful for helping students develop comprehension of a foreign language.

ACTIVITIES

1. Teach students to use a foreign language dictionary.
2. Encourage students to write their own ideas in the language being studied.
3. List words in English that are derived from the language studied.
4. Ask students to describe a basketball or football game in the language they are studying.
5. Provide students with direction cards written in English. Have them state the directions in the foreign language. For example, directions for finding the children's department in a department store could be provided.
6. The above activity can be reversed, with the directions printed in a foreign language and the students stating them in English.
7. Have students write an advertisement to sell an automobile in a foreign language.

8. Provide students with grocery advertisements and ask them to write the foreign word for each item in the advertisement.
9. Provide students with objects to categorize by form, function, color, or texture in the foreign language.

SUMMARY

This chapter focuses on reading strategies that are useful for helping secondary students read content materials in the areas of social studies, science and health, mathematics, computer science, English (language arts), and foreign languages. Study guides, concept guides, directed reading lessons, and pattern guides are useful for developing comprehension in each of these content areas.

Reading materials in each of the content areas are organized differently, and they include technical vocabulary. Content in social studies is organized in patterns of cause and effect, definition and/or explanation, chronological order, comparison/contrast, question and answer, and combinations of these patterns. Science and health materials are organized by classification, definition and/or explanation, cause and effect, problem solving, and the experimental pattern. Mathematics content includes many details and is presented through written (verbal) problems, the demonstration pattern (of processes and concepts), and graphs and charts. Computer science content is organized in patterns of definition or explanation, classification, cause and effect, and problem solving. Language arts reading materials are probably the most diversified of all the content areas. These materials include narrative writing in literary selections and examples, poetry and drama, and expository writing that is used for explaining concepts of grammar and composition. Foreign language reading requires the same skills needed for reading English.

The content reading strategies presented in this chapter may be used before, during, and after reading to help students become more independent in their approaches to reading and comprehending content.

SELF-TEST

1. What level of vocabulary understanding should a student achieve in order to read social studies material at an instructional level? (a) 50% (b) 25% (c) 75% (d) 90%

2. What style of writing is used most in social studies content? (a) Fictional (b) Expository (c) Narrative (d) Stream of consciousness

3. Which pattern(s) of writing are used in social studies content? (a) Comparison/contrast (b) Chronological (c) Cause and effect (d) All of these

4. Why are graphs and charts used in textbooks? (a) To make the text more interesting (b) To brighten the book (c) To make the text more difficult (d) To present information in a concise manner

5. Which of the following is the best description of a scientifically literate person? (a) One who enjoys reading science (b) One who reads a large amount of science (c) An intelligent, understanding reader of science (d) A professional scientist

6. Why should scientific content be read slowly? (a) The vocabulary is difficult. (b) There is a high concentration of information included in scientific content. (c) The teacher prefers it. (d) Both *a* and *b*

7. Which of the following styles of writing science materials is/are used in science textbooks? (a) Experiment (b) Explanation of a technical process (e) Classification (d) All of these

8. Why is mathematics considered abstract? (a) It is difficult. (b) The symbols represent ideas. (c) It is compactly written. (d) All of these

9. Which of the following factors contributes most to the problems of reading mathematics? (a) One symbol may represent several words. (b) Mathematics is a difficult subject for many students. (c) Too many problems are introduced on a single page. (d) Too many examples are given.

10. What is the basic goal of language arts materials? (a) Understanding between the sender and the receiver of a message (b) Speaking clearly (c) Learning specialized vocabulary (d) Diagramming sentences

11. What is the purpose of computer literacy courses? (a) To familiarize students with computers (b) To familiarize students with the terminology related to computers (c) To teach students to use computers in a variety of ways (d) All of these

12. What kinds of written materials do computer science students read? (a) Novels and newspapers (b) Fiction and handouts (c) Textbooks, handouts, computer displays, and computer magazines and journals (d) None of the above

13. Why should foreign language teachers include the study of culture in their instruction? (a) To help students acquire vocabulary (b) To increase the number of words students have to memorize (c) To build background for understanding language and concepts with more examples (d) None of these

14. What language arts instructional methods are used in teaching students to read a foreign language? (a) English novels (b) Listening, speaking, reading, and writing the language (c) Listening to radio broadcasts of languages that belong to the same language family (d) Reading newspapers written in languages that belong to the same language family

THOUGHT QUESTIONS

1. How are social studies content and mathematics content alike? How are they different?
2. Why is critical reading important in social studies content?
3. Why do some students find mathematics content difficult to read?
4. How can teachers help students comprehend mathematics content?
5. What are the characteristics of science content?
6. How can the use of directed reading lessons and study guides lead to independent reading comprehension?

ENRICHMENT ACTIVITIES

1. Develop a directed reading lesson for a chapter in a social studies or science textbook.
2. Prepare a study guide for a chapter in a social studies or science textbook.
3. Prepare a study guide for a verbal problem in a mathematics textbook.
4. Develop a bibliography of trade books that could be used by students who are unable to read the textbook.
5. Prepare a cause-and-effect chart for a topic in a content area text.
6. Check professional journals such as *Social Education, Science Teacher, Mathematics Teacher,* and *English Journal* for articles dealing with reading of content material. Share your findings with the class.
7. Check the readability level of a textbook and/or supplementary material used for one of the subjects treated in this chapter.

BIBLIOGRAPHY

Alvermann, D. "Learning from Text." In D. Alvermann, D. Moore, and M. Conley (eds.), *Research Within Reach: Secondary School Reading.* Newark, Del.: International Reading Association, 1987, pp. 38–51.

Banks, J. *Education in the 80's: Multiethnic Education.* Washington, D.C.: National Education Association, 1981, pp. 42–53.

Bean, T., and B. Ericson. "Text Previews and Three Level Study Guides for Content Area Critical Reading." *Journal of Reading,* 32 (January 1989), 337–341.

Berryhill, P. "Reading in the Content Area of Social Studies." In M. Dupuis (ed.), *Reading in the Content Areas: Research for Teachers.* Newark, Del.: International Reading Association, 1984, pp. 142–152.

Carlson, J. "Reading in the Content Area of Foreign Language." In M. Dupuis (ed.), *Reading in the Content Areas: Research for Teachers.* Newark, Del.: International Reading Association, 1984, pp. 23–32.

Chase, F. "Demands on the Reader in the Next Decade." In M. King, B. Ellinger, and W. Wolf (eds.), *Critical Reading.* New York: J. B. Lippincott, 1967, pp. 1–3.

Clarke, J., J. Raths, and G. Gilbert. "Inductive Towers: Letting Students See How They Think." *Journal of Reading,* 33 (November 1989), 86–95.

Cooper, C., and A. Purves. *A Guide to Evaluation.* Lexington, Mass.: Ginn and Company, 1973.

Davey, B. "Active Responding in Content Classrooms." *Journal of Reading*, 33 (October 1989), 44–49.

Dea, W. "The Relationships Between Vocabulary Recognition and Higher Chapter Test Scores in United States History Classes." Master's Thesis, Whittier College, 1978.

Earle, R. *Teaching Reading and Mathematics*. Newark, Del.: International Reading Association, 1976.

Ennis, R. "Critical Thinking and Subject Specificity: Clarification and Needed Research." *Educational Researcher*, 18 (April 1989), 4–10.

Finder, M. "Teaching to Comprehend," *Journal of Reading*, 13 (May 1970), 611–636.

Frayer, F., and H. Klausmeier. *A Scheme for Testing the Level of Cognitive Mastery*, Working Paper No. 16. Madison: Wisconsin Research and Development Center for Cognitive Learning, 1969.

Gollnick, D. "Multicultural Education." *Viewpoints in Teaching and Learning*, 56 (Winter 1980), 1–17.

Harker, J. (ed.) *Classroom Strategies for Secondary Reading*. 2nd ed. Newark, Del.: International Reading Association, 1985.

Henrichs, M., and T. Sisson, "Mathematics and the Reading Process: A Practical Application of Theory." *Mathematics Teacher*, 73 (April 1980), 253–256.

Herman, W., Jr. "Reading and Other Language Arts in Social Studies Instruction: Persistent Problems." In R. Preston (ed.), *A New Look at Reading in the Social Studies*. Newark, Del.: International Reading Association, 1969, pp. 5–9.

Horowitz, R. "Text Patterns: Part I." *Journal of Reading*, 28 (February 1985a), 448–454.

Horowitz, R. "Text Patterns: Part II." *Journal of Reading*, 28 (March 1985b), 534–541.

Knifong, J., and B. Holtran. "A Search for Reading Difficulties Among Erred Word Problems." *Journal for Research in Mathematics Education*, 8 (May 1977), 227–230.

Kresse, E. "Using Reading as a Thinking Process to Solve Math Story Problems." *Journal of Reading*, 27 (April 1984), 598–601.

Krulik, S. "To Read or Not to Read: That Is the Question!" *Mathematics Teacher*, 73 (April 1980), 248–252.

LeSourd, S. "Using an Advance Organizer to Set the Schema for a Multicultural Lesson." *Journal of Reading*, 32 (October 1988), 12–18.

Lloyd, C., and J. Mitchell. "Coping with too Many Concepts in Science Texts." *Journal of Reading*, 32 (March 1989), 542–549.

Lubell, M., and R. Townsend. "A Strategy for Teaching Complex Prose Structures." *Journal of Reading*, 33 (November 1989), 102–106.

McClain, L. "Study Guides: Potential Assets in Content Classrooms." *Journal of Reading*, 24 (January 1981), 321–325.

Moore, D., and S. Arthur. "Possible Sentences." In E. K. Dishner, T. Bean, and J. Readence (eds.), *Reading in the Content Areas: Improving Classroom Instruction*. Dubuque, Iowa: Kendall/Hunt, 1981, pp. 119–128.

National Council of Teachers of Mathematics. *Curriculum and Evaluation Standards*. NCTM: 1989.

Riley, J., and A. Pachtman, "Reading Mathematical Word Problems: Telling Them What to Do Is Not Telling Them How to Do It." *Journal of Reading*, 21 (March 1978), 531–534.

Taba, H. *Teacher's Handbook for Elementary Social Studies*. Reading, Mass.: Addison-Wesley, 1967.

Thelen, Judith N. *Improving Reading in Science*. 2nd ed. Newark, Del.: International Reading Association, 1984, p. 18.

Thomas, D. "Reading and Reasoning Skills for Math Problem Solvers." *Journal of Reading*, 32 (December 1988), 244–249.

354   Vigil, Yvonne Tixiery, and J. Dick. "Problems and Suggestions for Improving the Reading of Textbooks: A Social Studies Focus." *The High School Journal*, 68 (December/January 1984), 116–121.

CHAPTER APPENDIX: USING NEWSPAPERS AND MAGAZINES

Strategies

Teachers in every content area can use newspapers and magazines in their classes as instructional aids. They provide interesting, relevant, up-to-date information. Newspapers and magazines are excellent media to use for reading instruction because they are readily available, they treat a wide variety of subject matter, and they are highly motivating for secondary students because they focus on the present. Students who have been turned off by formal reading materials find newspapers and magazines more interesting and personally relevant. Newspapers have the added advantage of providing a fresh set of materials each day. Magazines enable students to pursue special interests in depth. Teachers can devise newspaper and magazine activities as enrichment materials or as a substitute for the textbook for students who are unable to read it. Following are suggested activities to use with newspapers, and a directed reading lesson (Example 8.29 on page 356) based on work with newspapers.

LITERAL READING ACTIVITIES

1. Locate the main points in an article and the writer's supporting material for these points.
2. Read the classified advertisements to find a job you would like to fill. Write a letter of application responding to the qualifications listed in the advertisement.
3. Answer specific literal questions related to news stories or advertisements, such as: "Who won the baseball game?" and "Which grocery has the cheapest coffee?"
4. Locate *who, where, when, why,* and *how* in a newspaper story.
5. List in sequence the steps of a how-to-do-it article.
6. Follow directions for making an item found in a newspaper or magazine.
7. Examine a newspaper to determine the percentage of space used for advertising.

INFERENTIAL READING ACTIVITIES

1. Identify the point of view of an editorial.
2. Compare two editorials for likenesses, differences, and points of view.
3. Compare the treatment of a news event in a news story and in an editorial.
4. Find examples of an author's interpretation in a news story.

5. Ask questions such as the following:
   a. How does one reporter's writing differ from another reporter's writing?
   b. What can you learn about the author from the way he or she writes news stories?
6. State the effects you can anticipate as the result of a news event. This exercise may be developed in the form of a chart such as the following:

News Event	*Effects*

CRITICAL READING ACTIVITIES

1. Analyze articles, editorials, and advertisements for examples of fact and opinion.
2. Analyze the way connotations of words are used in newspapers to influence the reader.
3. Analyze news stories related to controversial topics for bias.
4. Evaluate the effectiveness of editorials in achieving their purposes.
5. Determine whether the writer of a news story is well informed.
6. Ask questions such as the following:
   a. Did the writer omit important information?
   b. Does the story fit with what the reader knows from past experience?
7. Analyze advertisements to find examples of various types of propaganda.
8. Analyze advertising to determine if it appeals to emotions or logic.

CREATIVE READING ACTIVITIES

1. Write an advertisement for an item or service that could be used in a newspaper or magazine.
2. Rewrite a news story to improve it.
3. Write a letter to the editor on a topic of concern.
4. Create a cartoon relating to a controversial issue or personality.
5. Write a review of a movie or a television show.
6. Dramatize a news story.

FLEXIBLE RATE ACTIVITIES

1. Suggest the rates at which you feel various sections of newspapers or magazines should be read.

2. Make a list of the purposes you have for reading newspapers and magazines.
3. Skim news stories and advertisements for main ideas.
4. Scan the entertainment section to locate the time of the late showing of a movie.

PICTURE, CHART, GRAPH, AND MAP ACTIVITIES

1. Learn to identify the different types of pictures used in newspapers, such as file photographs, on-the-spot photographs, and drawings.
2. Analyze the information provided in graphs, maps, and charts.
3. Discuss the value of pictures, graphs, maps, and charts for illustrating the news.

E X A M P L E **8.29**

Directed Reading Lesson: Fact and Opinion and Bias

OBJECTIVES

To identify fact and opinion in a news story
To identify bias in a news story
To suggest effects of a news event

MATERIAL

Articles from several newspapers relating to the Supreme Court ruling that allows lawyers to advertise routine legal services

MOTIVATION AND BUILDING BACKGROUND

Ask the students if they have heard any discussion or read anything about the Supreme Court ruling. Ask the students what they think about advertising of their services by lawyers. Have them supply reasons for their opinions.

GUIDED READING

Silent — Present these purpose questions. Then allow sufficient time for silent reading of the selections.

Do the authors of these articles agree with your opinion?
Do the writers present any advantages or disadvantages of this advertising?
Do you think the writers are biased in their presentations of the story?

Discussion: Discuss the questions posed as silent reading purposes as well as the following questions:

Did the writers of these articles all have the same attitude regarding the topic?

Were they expressing facts or opinions? How do you know?
Why do you think the writers were biased, if they were?

FOLLOW-UP ACTIVITIES

The class members may conduct a poll to determine how many people are opposed to this ruling and how many are in favor of it. The class may analyze the reasons for voting yes or no.

The students may locate further information on the topic by reading additional newspapers and magazines.

The class may develop a chart of the effects of this ruling based upon their reading, discussion, and poll.

Sources of Newspaper Teaching Materials

The following materials are available from the sources cited.

1. American Newspaper Publishers Association (ANPA) Foundation, The Newspaper Center, Box 17407, Dulles International Airport, Washington, D.C. 20041.

   NIE Development Plan
   NIE Beginner's Kit
   Why NIE?
   Newspaper Test Sample Kit
   Workshop Workbook
   Using Newspapers to Teach Reading Skills
   The Newspaper as an Effective Teaching Tool
   Films About Newspapers

2. The Canadian Daily Newspaper Publishers Association (CDNPA), 321 Bloor Street East, Suite 214, Toronto, Ontario M4WlE7.

   Canadian Newspaper in Education Bibliography
   Effective Decision Making: A Survival Skill for Today's World
   A News Beginning
   Learning from Newspapers

3. International Reading Association, 800 Barksdale Road, P.O. Box 8139, Newark, Del. 19714-8139.

   Write for annual publications catalog.

9

READING IN THE CONTENT AREAS: PART 2

OVERVIEW

This chapter focuses on vocational and performance-oriented content areas. The ability to read work- and performance-related materials with fluency prepares students for success in both occupational roles and further education. Students in these areas of study need to read a wide variety of printed materials for many different purposes. Reading competence is as important for studying these content areas as it is for studying all other subjects. Students need both general and specific reading abilities to understand the rapidly changing, challenging fields of industrial technology, business education, human environmental sciences, agriculture, physical education, driver education, art, and music. This chapter describes both of these types of reading and strategies for developing them.

The range in reading achievement among secondary students who elect to concentrate on occupationally oriented subjects tends to be broader than it is among students who choose academic areas. Some students select vocational subjects thinking they can avoid reading if they follow a vocational course of study (Lee, 1981). These students tend to begin vocational programs with lower reading achievement, which inhibits their success. However, some very capable students also choose to pursue these subjects. Thus, vocational teachers face the challenge of assisting the less able students while stimulating the competent students to achieve to their highest level.

PURPOSE-SETTING QUESTIONS

As you read this chapter, try to answer these questions:

1. Why do subjects such as industrial technology, business education, human environmental science, agriculture, physical education, driver education, music, and art require reading competence?

2. What reading skills help students understand content information in industrial technology, business education, human environmental science, and agriculture?
3. What reading skills increase comprehension of content information in physical education and driver education?
4. What reading skills are required in music and art?
5. What strategies are useful for helping students comprehend the content and applications of vocational and technical materials?

KEY VOCABULARY

As you read this chapter, check your understanding of these terms:

vocational subjects	industrial technology
expository style	human environmental science
graphics	business education

Vocational and Technical Materials

Vocational and technical students need to understand specialized vocabulary as well as recognize the language patterns found in the printed materials used for work and for instruction. Literacy in vocational and technical subjects also requires that students recognize the organization of ideas in these materials. Since authors use a large number of graphics, students must understand them and integrate the concepts represented in them with the text. Diehl and Mikulecky (1980) studied a broad cross-section of vocational and technical occupations and found that daily reading was almost universally required. Therefore, teachers must develop students' reading skills as they teach vocational and technical content materials. Sticht and others (1987) advise that combining literacy learning with technical knowledge and skill is the most practical approach.

Reading materials used in vocational and technical subjects contain concepts and terminology unfamiliar to students, and may contain unusual writing styles. Teaching students to read these materials means that teachers must introduce reading comprehension activities before, during, and after reading a passage in order to help them understand and retain text (Moore, Readence, and Rickelman, 1989). Teachers need to prepare students to read, support them during reading, and follow up after the reading. Students need reading strategies to aid their comprehension and recall of content area reading materials.

Vocational and technical education focuses on two major strands: the skills needed for vocational success and the skills needed to acquire education in these subjects. Researchers report that higher levels of literacy and literacy-related competencies are required for acheiving success in occupational training programs than are necessary for achieving success on the job (Rush, Moe, Storlie, 1986). Vocational and technical content, which is closely related to the world of work, is usually taught in a pragmatic fashion that demands practical application of textbook material. Diehl and Mikulecky (1980) reported a mean work-related reading time of 113 minutes per day in vocational occupations.

The primary objective of teaching vocational and technical subjects is to educate students to be workers who will be careful, organized, effective, and efficient and who have mastered occupational skills. Teachers also hope to foster in students positive attitudes toward work. In order to do this, instructors must not only acquaint students with particular content reading materials but also must develop in their students adequate reading skills, providing direct reading instruction so students can comprehend specialized materials. Because vocational and technical materials deal with students' direct interests and future goals, students are often motivated to read, desiring success in these work-related areas.

Reading in vocational and technical education requires extensive use of expository and descriptive prose. Students must read textbooks, reference books, and sets of complex instructions. In most required reading, students need to study carefully and learn the information presented in the text, graphics, and text/graphic formats similar to those found at the job sites. Real-life reading materials are extremely important in educating these students. Rush, Moe, and Storlie (1986) reported on the reading levels demanded by the printed materials in various occupations. These are examples: account clerks read materials that ranged in difficulty from college freshman to college graduate, printed materials for auto mechanics ranged in reading difficulty from grade 10 to college graduate, and secretaries read materials ranging in difficulty from college senior to college graduate.

Mikulecky (1982) examined the literacy demands, competencies, and strategies present in the daily reading materials of both vocational students and workers. He found that students read less often in school than most workers do on the job, that students read less competently than workers, and that students read easier material with less understanding. The reading strategies students used appeared less effective than those used by workers. Unfortunately for poor readers, there is no subject in the secondary curriculum that does not require reading ability, just as there are no jobs that do not require reading ability.

Reading is an integral part of technical and managerial jobs, and this can sometimes be frustrating or difficult for people employed in those positions. Miller (1982) found that these employees spend, on the average, fifteen to twenty hours per week doing work-related reading. Many of the participants in her study averaged fifteen pieces of reading material per day. They read the following types of materials:

technical pieces
proposals
manuals
data sheets
memos and attachments
correspondence
nontechnical pieces

People in these positions read to analyze problems, propose solutions, and carry out research. Managers and supervisors read to review, advise, assign, and develop organizational procedures and policy. However, the participants in this research reported that they were inefficient readers who were often frustrated by their work-related reading (Miller, 1982).

Aspects of Vocational Reading

Since the amount of written material used in vocational subjects appears to be smaller than that required in other subjects, students and teachers may misjudge the reading difficulty of these materials. Even brief vocational reading selections demand precise, careful reading. Vocational materials are written in an expository style that is concise and uses technical vocabulary. Readers must be able to follow directions and to apply ideas and words to actual situations.

Vocabulary

Each vocational subject includes a great deal of technical vocabulary as well as common vocabulary words that have special meanings. For example, the common word *credit* has a special meaning when used for bookkeeping, in which it refers to a bookkeeping entry that shows money paid on an account. ("You may place this entry on the *credit* side of the ledger.") Technical vocabulary words usually represent concepts essential to reading a particular subject with understanding. Fortunately for teachers of vocational subjects, the technical vocabulary terms usually represent concrete concepts, which are easier to teach than abstract ideas. For example, in human environmental science, *sauté* is a word that represents a particular way of cooking food that can be demonstrated to students; in bookkeeping, *debit* represents a specific concept that can be concretely illustrated.

Unfortunately, teachers cannot assume that students will be able to learn the precise meaning of a technical word by using context clues or a dictionary. Technical material does not always contain enough clues to help a reader define a term, and many high school dictionaries do not include the technical terms that are used in vocational materials. These factors make vocabulary instruction very important in vocational subject areas.

Teaching Technical Vocabulary

Teachers should plan direct instruction for technical vocabulary. They can point out and define new terms before having students read a textbook assignment. They can demonstrate the concrete meanings of many technical terms by showing students the objects or activities the words represent. Students can write the words in a notebook and develop a content dictionary for their own or class use.

Teachers or students can construct picture word cards that have a drawing and the word or words on one side and the definition on the other. These cards can be used individually by students or by the entire class; they may be laminated for protection and displayed around the classroom. The teacher should give the students a quiz on these words every other week to check vocabulary development. Vocabulary evaluation strategies for teachers and additional suggestions for developing word meanings are presented in Chapter 2. Example 9.1 illustrates two possible picture word cards.

Following Directions

Every technical and vocational subject requires that the student read directions and translate them into action. The reader in industrial technology must read directions for operating and repairing various pieces of equipment. The reader of human environmental science material must be able to follow the directions for writing a resumé or making a garment. The business education student must read directions for operating business machines and for setting up bookkeeping systems.

Reading directions requires that the student read slowly and precisely. The student should be prepared to reread the material in order to achieve complete understanding. When reading directions, students should be guided by the following questions.

1. What am I trying to do? (What is the task?)
2. What materials are required?
3. Do I understand all of the terms (words) used in these directions?
4. What is the sequence of steps?
5. Have I omitted anything?
6. Am I ready to perform the task?
7. Was I successful in accomplishing the task?

EXAMPLE **9.1**

Picture Word Cards

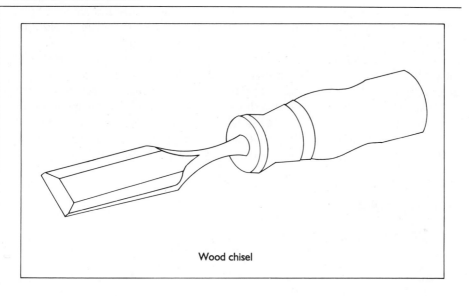

Wood chisel

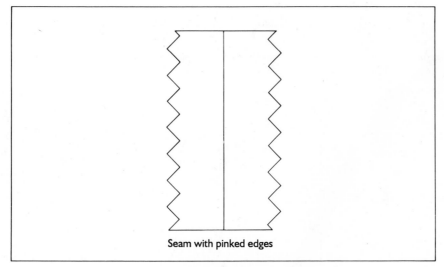

Seam with pinked edges

364

These questions can be incorporated into study guides. Suggestions for developing study guides are included later in this chapter and in Chapters 3, 6, and 8. Suggestions for following directions are also found in Chapters 4 and 8.

In using vocational materials there is immediate feedback regarding how well a student has read directions; if directions are not followed properly, the result is concrete and observable. For example, if a student has failed to follow directions for operating a machine in the industrial technology shop, it will not work properly. If a student has failed to follow directions for baking a cake accurately, the result will be apparent when the cake is seen or eaten.

Teachers — or students — can develop an illustrated dictionary of terms for each subject area. This activity is useful for all vocational and technical subjects. Following is an example of an entry in an illustrated dictionary of terms for the subject area of woodworking (Example 9.2).

E X A M P L E **9.2**

Illustrated Dictionary of Terms

Term: vise

Pronunciation: vīs

Definition: A vise is a tool with two jaws that are opened and closed by a screw. It is used to hold an object firmly while this object is worked on.

Sentence: A vise can be of a permanent type, which is bolted to a workbench or table, or it can be one of many clamp-on types.

Illustration:

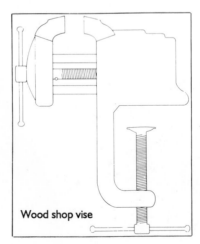

Wood shop vise

Example 9.3 is a set of directions from a human environmental science textbook. The reader could apply these questions and activities to this example.

1. What am I trying to do? (make spiced apple muffins)
2. What materials are required? (⅔ cup flour, 3 tablespoons sugar, 1½ teaspoon baking powder, ⅛ teaspoon salt, ⅛ teaspoon cinnamon, ⅓ cup milk, 1 tablespoon beaten egg, 1½ teaspoons butter or margarine, ⅓ cup raw apples for the muffins and 2 teaspoons sugar and ⅛ teaspoon cinnamon for the topping)
3. Do I understand the terms? (grease, mix, fold, preheat, dry ingredients, liquid ingredients)
4. What is the sequence of steps? a. grease muffin pan; b. mix flour, sugar, baking powder, salt, and cinnamon; c. combine milk, egg, melted butter or margarine; d. add dry ingredients to liquid ingredients; e. fold in apple; f. fill muffin pan ⅔ full; g. preheat oven; h. combine sugar and cinnamon; i. sprinkle mixture over top of unbaked muffins; j. bake; k. remove from pan and cool on a cooling rack.
5. Have I omitted anything? (no)
6. Complete the steps.
7. Was I successful in accomplishing the task? (If muffins rise, look appetizing, and have a texture that is even and small grained, the student has succeeded.)

E X A M P L E **9.3**

Directions from Human Environmental Science

Spiced Apple Muffins (makes 6)

⅔ c flour
3 tbsp sugar
1½ tsp baking powder
⅛ tsp salt
⅛ tsp cinnamon
⅓ c milk
1 tbsp beaten egg
1½ tsp butter or margarine, melted
⅓ c raw apples, finely chopped

1. Grease a 6-muffin pan.
2. Mix together flour, sugar, baking powder, salt, and cinnamon.

3. In a separate bowl, combine the milk, egg, and melted butter or margarine.
4. Add the dry ingredients to the liquid ingredients and mix. (Batter will be lumpy.)
5. Fold in apples.
6. Fill muffin pans two-thirds full.

Topping:

2 tsp sugar
⅛ tsp cinnamon

1. Preheat oven to 425°F.
2. Combine sugar and cinnamon.
3. Sprinkle mixture over top of unbaked muffins.
4. Bake 20 minutes or until toothpick inserted in middle comes out clean.
5. Remove from pan and cool on a cooling rack.

Source: Reprinted from *Teen Guide* by Valarie Chamberlain, with permission of Glencoe/McGraw-Hill, A Macmillan Company. Mission Hills, California, Copyright © 1990, p. 445.

Graphic Materials

Vocational and technical students are very often required to read a variety of graphic materials, such as blueprints, drawings, cutaways, patterns, pictures, and sketches. They must be able to visualize the items represented and understand their three-dimensional aspects. They must also be able to interpret the scales and legends that accompany many graphic materials in order to understand both the illustrations and the textual materials they are reading.

Examples 9.4 and 9.5 show two types of graphics that vocational students commonly encounter. Example 9.4 is from an architecture drafting and design text; Example 9.5 is from the human environmental sciences.

To read the floor plan in Example 9.4, the student must be able to interpret both the scale of the drawing and the special symbols such as the symbol (') for feet, the symbol (") for inches, and the symbol (×) for *by*. There are also several abbreviations for words that need to be interpreted correctly.

In reading the diagram in Example 9.5, the student must coordinate the text with the illustrations. Directions must be followed carefully and in sequence.

Teachers should give students many opportunities to convert written directions, drawings, and blueprints into models and actual objects. They can also have students match blueprints and diagrams with pictures of the finished products — an activity that will help students develop the ability to visualize written ideas. Having students prepare directions, diagrams, and blueprints for classmates to follow will help them to become more adept at understanding these written materials themselves.

EXAMPLE **9.4**

Floor Plan (Industrial Technology)

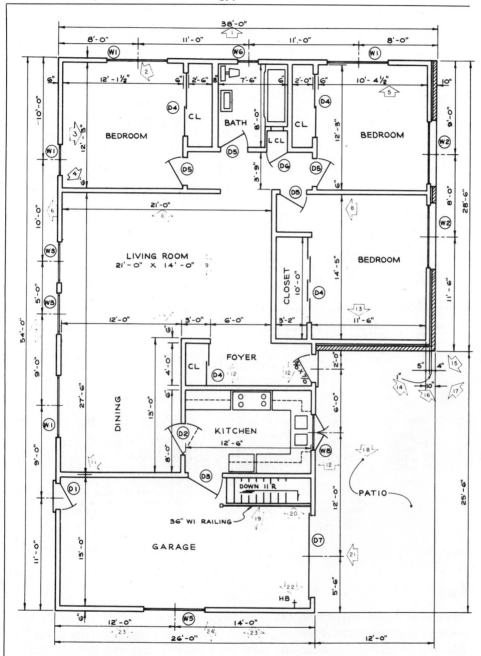

Source: Donald Hepler and Paul Wallach, *Architecture Drafting and Design,* 3rd ed. (New York: McGraw-Hill, 1977), p. 204. Reproduced by permission of Glencoe/McGraw-Hill Educational Division.

E X A M P L E **9.5**

Sewing Machine Diagram (Human Environmental Science)

Basic Parts of the Machine

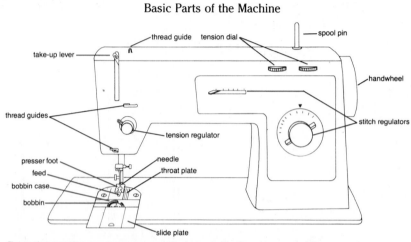

The sewing machine you see here may not look exactly like the one you use at home or school. Each brand and model of machine is a little different. However, all sewing machines have the same basic parts. These parts are shown here. Look at the box on the next page for a description of what each part does. For more information on the machine you are using, look in the machine operating manual.

How a Stitch Is Formed

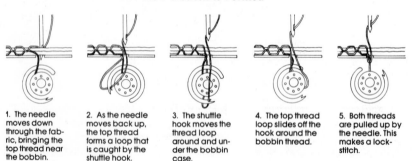

1. The needle moves down through the fabric, bringing the top thread near the bobbin.

2. As the needle moves back up, the top thread forms a loop that is caught by the shuttle hook.

3. The shuttle hook moves the thread loop around and under the bobbin case.

4. The top thread loop slides off the hook around the bobbin thread.

5. Both threads are pulled up by the needle. This makes a lock-stitch.

Source: Reprinted from *Teen Guide* by Valarie Chamberlain, with permission of Glencoe/McGraw-Hill, A Macmillan Company. Mission Hills, California, Copyright © 1990, p. 335.

Rate

Readers of vocational and technical materials must adjust their reading rates according to purpose, type of content, and familiarity with the subject. Because vocational materials are often problem-oriented and include many directions, they should be read slowly and carefully. Vocational students should learn to reread content until they fully comprehend it. Written directions are rarely understood well after only one reading and often need to be gone over many times to be followed successfully. It is important for students to realize that rereading is a normal, necessary procedure. Through problem-solving activities, the teacher can give students practice in the strategies of reading slowly and rereading.

Writing

Writing is an asset in retaining and understanding content materials (Gahn, 1989). Writing helps students clarify personal understandings of text (Shugarman and Hurst, 1986). Through writing activities, students expand their understanding of technical and vocational language and their ability to express ideas effectively. Writing activities also develop students' knowledge of technical vocabulary, sentence structure, paragraph organization, and sequencing. However, for vocational and technical teachers to teach students how to write in their content areas, they must model writing, provide guided practice, and give students feedback (Gahn, 1989). In Chapter 7, there are suggestions for content area writing activities.

Utilizing Motivation

Utilizing or building motivation is a responsibility of the teacher in vocational and technical education. Because some students are personally motivated to study these subjects, their interest can stimulate them to read. Students frequently are able to read materials with higher readability levels than usual because of the nature of the reading content (Diehl and Mikulecky, 1980). The classroom library should include trade periodicals, which provide information about new products, materials, and techniques. Periodicals also give general information about the various trades that is useful to students. Teachers can use these materials to develop their students' reading interests and understanding of the content area, thereby increasing students' ability to predict content and, consequently, to comprehend content materials. Following are some suggestions for using motivation to increase comprehension of content materials.

1. Display subject area books, magazines, and related materials that are appropriate to student interest and reading levels.
2. Suggest additional readings in magazines, newspapers, periodicals, and books.
3. Review and refer to relevant books.
4. Use learning activities such as field trips, movies, records, and radio and television programs to build background and to stimulate a desire for further information.
5. Provide time in class for reading materials related to class topics.
6. To develop interest and critical reading ability, compare and contrast the way two or more authors have treated a topic.
7. Encourage students to discuss their readings with each other.
8. Permit students to work together so that good readers can help less able ones.

The Textbook as a Reference

Teachers should make a particular effort to explain and demonstrate the use of textbooks and real-life printed materials as reference works, since vocational teachers use a wide variety of materials in a problem-solving format and students often are not acquainted with this approach. Instruction that familiarizes the students with the wealth of information provided in printed materials will help them to use these materials for acquiring knowledge and solving problems.

Reading Strategies

Reading-to-learn and reading-to-do are both kinds of reading that vocational and technical students are often required to do. Sticht (1978) discussed these two categories of reading tasks. *Reading-to-learn* is a reading task in which an individual reads with the intention of remembering and applying textual information. *Reading-to-do* is a reading task in which an individual uses the material as an aid to do something else. In the latter situation, the materials often serve as "external memories," because the individual may refer to them to check information rather than to specifically learn the content. Sticht found that most on-the-job reading is a type of reading-to-do, which may demand the following reading strategies:

1. *Read/rehearse,* which involves repeating the information or reading it again.
2. *Problem solve/question,* which involves answering questions posed by the text and/or searching for the information necessary to solve a specific problem.
3. *Relate/associate,* which is associating new information with the individual's existing store of information.
4. *Focus attention,* which involves reducing the amount of information in some way, such as by underlining, outlining, or taking notes.

Having students read to solve problems is a good way to teach the preceding reading strategies. Before having students practice the strategies on their own, the teacher should present a content-based problem and explain to the students each of the steps as it relates to the problem. The problem and the associated strategies may be introduced through overhead transparencies, posters, or bulletin board displays. Problem-solving activities such as the following might be used:

1. Industrial technology — List the tools you need to build a chair.
2. Human environmental science — Prepare menus for nutritionally balanced meals for a week for a family of three based on a budget of [$85].
3. Business — Set up an office mailing system for the [XYZ] Company.

The problem-solving writing pattern is common in vocational materials. These materials also include presentations of factual information and how-to-do-it directions. Reading instruction should focus on these types of content materials.

Directed reading lessons are also useful in helping vocational students learn to read textual materials. Following is an example of a directed reading lesson based on human environmental science content (Example 9.6).

E X A M P L E **9.6**

Directed Reading Lesson (Human Environmental Science)

MOTIVATION AND BUILDING BACKGROUND

1. Ask students the following questions: What kind of fabric is used in the clothing you are wearing today? What is your favorite kind of fabric? Here is a box of various types of fabric. Look at each piece and try to determine the contents of each piece of fabric.

SKILL DEVELOPMENT ACTIVITIES

2. Discuss and pronounce each of the following vocabulary words. Be certain students have a concept for each type of fabric by giving them labeled samples of each to examine.

wool	brocade
synthetic fabric	lamé
satin	velvet
cotton	

GUIDED READING

3. *Silent* — Provide students with *silent reading purposes* such as the following: How do you choose a suitable fabric to make a dress? How are synthetic fabrics different from natural fabrics? Have the students *read the lesson silently.*
4. *Discussion* — *Discuss* the silent reading purposes and ask discussion questions such as the following: Do you prefer natural or synthetic fabrics? Why? What are the advantages of natural fabrics? What kind of dress pattern would you choose for a brocade fabric?

FOLLOW-UP ACTIVITIES

5. Have students reread as necessary to solve the problem of selecting an appropriate fabric for their next garment.

The teacher can also prepare study guides to help students increase comprehension of vocational materials as they read. Example 9.7 shows a selection from an industrial arts textbook and includes a study guide based on the selection.

E X A M P L E **9.7**

Sample Writing in Vocational Materials and Study Guide

Painting and Enameling

Paint and enamel are protective and decorative coatings for the less expensive woods for which a transparent finish may not be desirable. Either paint or enamel can be used satisfactorily as a colorful finish on furniture and cabinets.

Paint is generally applied to exterior surfaces or to projects which are used out of doors. Enamel is suitable for interior trim and for projects used in the home. It comes in a gloss, a semigloss, or a dull (flat) finish. Enamel usually produces a harder finish than paint because varnish is an ingredient in enamel.

Both paint and enamel are available in many colors. Both can also be bought either in white or tinted with colors ground in oil. Each of the many paints and enamels has its own recommended thinner. Read the instructions on the container for the method of thinning and for the manufacturer's suggestions for applying.

Mixing and Applying Paint or Enamel

1. Prepare the surfaces for painting or enameling. They should be properly planed, scraped, and sanded.
2. Read the directions on the container before opening it. Each manufacturer of paint and enamel recommends how it should be mixed and applied. The container also specifies the drying time required.
3. If the directions call for a primer coat, apply it first.
4. Shake the can thoroughly. Remove the lid, and pour off some of the top liquid into another container.
5. Stir the base mixture with a paddle. Add the top liquid to the base mixture a little at a time, and stir them until they are thoroughly blended.
6. Add turpentine, linseed oil, or the thinner recommended on the can, if needed.
7. Select a suitable high-quality brush.
8. Dip the brush into the paint so that about three-fourths of the length of the bristles absorbs paint. Wipe the surplus paint or enamel on the edge of the can as you remove the brush.
9. Apply the paint or enamel to the surface with long, even strokes. A little practice helps to determine the proper amount to apply. It should cover the surface smoothly and evenly. Do not allow it to run.
10. Allow the coat to dry thoroughly according to the time given in the directions. Sand smooth with fine sandpaper. Wipe the surface with a clean cloth.
11. Apply a second and a third coat if needed. Do not sand the final coat, because it will dull the finish.

Source: Chris H. Groneman, *General Woodworking,* 5th ed. (New York: McGraw-Hill, 1976), pp. 247–248. Reproduced by permission of Glencoe/McGraw-Hill Educational Division.

Study Guide

Introduction

This selection discusses the value of paint and enamel as finishing materials. Directions are given for preparing a surface for paint or enamel and applying that finish.

Vocabulary

Give examples for each of the following terms: paint, enamel, transparent, gloss, semi-gloss, dull, flat, tinted, sandpaper.

Comprehension

Directions: Put the following steps for painting in the correct sequence by numbering them. Refer to the text.

LITERAL

- Apply a primer coat first, if needed.
- Dip three-fourths of the length of the bristles into the paint. Wipe the surplus on the edge of the can.
- Prepare the surface by planing, scraping, and sanding.
- Read the directions on the container. Note drying time.
- Apply the paint or enamel with long, even strokes.
- Stir the paint or enamel.
- Shake the can.
- Apply a second and a third coat if needed.
- Allow to dry thoroughly, sand smooth with sandpaper, and wipe clean.

Directions: Write a short answer to each of the following questions:

INTERPRETIVE

1. Does varnish cause a hard finish? How do you know this?
2. Which coating — paint or enamel — is probably more waterproof? Why?
3. What would happen if you did not shake the can of paint or enamel thoroughly?
4. Why does the author recommend a high-quality brush?
5. What might happen to a cabinet if you gave it only one coat of paint?

APPLIED

6. Give an example of an item that you would finish with enamel rather than paint. Why did you choose enamel for this item?
7. Give two examples of substances that could be used for thinning paint. What is the best way to choose the right thinner?
8. Can you mix paint and enamel? Why or why not?

After students read a chapter and complete a study guide similar to the one in Example 9.7, they should have an opportunity to discuss their answers and should be prepared to explain and support them by citing the text.

Applications of Reading Comprehension Skills

The sections that follow discuss how specific reading comprehension skills and strategies can be applied to particular subject areas. However, the skills and strategies that are demonstrated can be used interchangeably in the various subject areas. In addition, the activities included in Chapter 8 can be used with the content areas discussed in this chapter.

Industrial Technology (Industrial Arts)

Industrial technology content includes materials that are written about machine operation, woodworking, auto mechanics, drafting, and radio and television repair. Obviously, these areas have large technical vocabularies that must be understood by the students. Example 9.8 shows a selection from a general woodworking text.

E X A M P L E **9.8**

Industrial Technology Content

Recognizing Good Design

Recognizing the factors that constitute good design helps create a well-designed product. When you go to a store to buy furniture, you look for certain characteristics. One of the first is *pleasing appearance*. Does the piece of furniture have a graceful or pleasing shape? Is the color suitable? Will it fit well with other furniture in the room? These are some of the questions that will help in determining whether or not the customer thinks the product being considered for purchase has a pleasing appearance.

You consider *function* when you decide whether the product or object fulfills the role for which it was originally planned and designed. If the design problem calls for a bookcase to hold 50 books, and there is room for only 30, the product will not do the job for which it was intended and is therefore not useful.

High-quality craftsmanship is essential to good design. No one wants to buy a piece of poorly constructed furniture. Tight joints, smooth finish, and precise cutting and fitting of parts are a few of the important considerations in selecting a well-designed and well-constructed product.

Source: Chris H. Groneman, *General Woodworking,* 5th ed. (New York: McGraw-Hill, 1976), p. 22. Reproduced by permission of Glencoe/McGraw-Hill Educational Division.

Readers must understand the following essential words in order to understand the preceding selection:

joints	function
appearance	craftsmanship
finish	shape
surface decorations	

Many of the technical terms that are used in industrial technology classes are related to tools and equipment. Demonstrating and labeling tools and equipment clearly in the classroom can help students learn to recognize these terms when they appear in textbooks.

Demonstrating mechanical processes also can clarify printed textual explanations. For example, the teacher might illustrate the process of replacing the jets on a carburetor.

Many reading tasks in industrial technology involve the students' ability to read and implement directions. For example, students must know how to follow step-by-step directions for operating equipment, constructing furniture, or installing a carburetor. They must learn to follow the directions on "job sheets," used in industrial technology classes to assign daily work. Safety rules also are important reading content for industrial technology. Teachers should prepare study guides to help students comprehend and carry out complicated written instructions.

Example 9.9 presents a diagram taken from an automobile repair textbook. The diagram illustrates a "V"-design compressor. Teachers should encourage students to study such diagrams carefully and to associate this type of illustration with the accompanying written textual material. To fully understand this particular diagram, students need to realize that it represents a cutaway section of a compressor and that the lines with letters identify the parts of the compressor. Industrial technology materials are often coordinated with illustrative designs.

Business Education

Business education encompasses a wide variety of studies, including shorthand, typing, bookkeeping, computer courses, secretarial studies, general business, business mathematics, business law, management, economics, and business communications. Computer applications in business are extensive; therefore students who have basic computer skills can better compete for many of the jobs they want. Each of the courses in business education has considerable written content. According to Heinemann (1979, p. 239), "Courses in business have traditionally relied heavily on reading as an important part of instruction." Many people in business face an increasing volume of transactions and the accompanying paperwork due to the heavy use of computers and facsimile machines. Nevertheless, business people, like those

376

E X A M P L E **9.9**

Industrial Technology Diagram

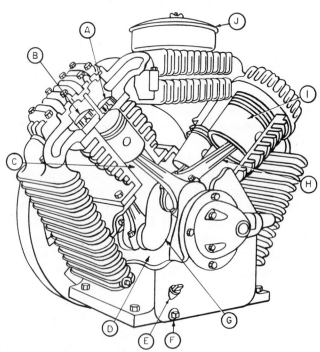

27-8. Cutaway of a two-stage "V"-design compressor: A. Intake valve assembly. B. Exhaust valve assembly. C. High-pressure connecting rod and piston assembly. D. Crankcase. E. Oil level dipstick. F. Crankcase oil drain. G. Crankshaft. H. Low-pressure connecting rod. I. Low-pressure piston. J. Air intake filter.

Source: Reprinted from Lester Duenk, W. Randolph Williams, and Clarence Brooks, *Auto Body Repair*, Glencoe/McGraw-Hill Educational Division. Copyright 1977. Reproduced by permission of Glencoe/McGraw-Hill Educational Division.

in other occupations, underestimate the reading demands of their occupations (Sticht, 1982).

Business education students and people who work in the business world read many types of content. Following is a list of written materials that they commonly read:

manuals	directions
reference materials	memos
ledgers	computer printouts
business letters	charts
invoices	graphs

directories	labels
handbooks	trade journals and professional
checklists	magazines
reports	newspapers
textbooks	

Many of the written materials used in business and industry are complex and have a high readability level (Razek et al., 1982). These materials are often filled with concepts and loaded with information (Stoodt, 1985). However, business education textbooks probably do not reflect the diversity apparent in business reading materials. Generally, these textbooks are academic in both content and format and fall into two categories: how-to-do-it manuals and informational books. Therefore students must acquire the reading skills not only to read the textbooks that are often the basis of classroom instruction but also to read the other business materials that will be important to their careers.

The reading tasks that confront business education students and people who work in business are summarized in the following list.

1. Reading directions/instructions and implementing them. Workers who have to stop others to ask for instructions or who complete tasks incorrectly slow down others and themselves (Banks, 1978).

2. Identifying main ideas and details in textbooks, magazine articles, and newspaper articles.

3. Skimming and/or scanning to locate needed information. These skills may be used to locate materials needed to solve a specific problem or to prepare a report (Banks, 1978).

4. Reading newspapers, magazines, and professional journals to learn about current trends in the business world.

5. Reading and implementing memos. Memos are organized differently than other types of written communication, often informing employees of changes in existing practices or policies in a business situation; therefore, the receiver must read these communications and remember the details.

6. Reading and responding to business letters. Business letters are organized differently, use more technical vocabulary, and use different semantics than social correspondence. Thus they require different reading skills.

7. Reading invoices to check their accuracy.

8. Reading computer printouts to locate needed information. These printouts may be used for problem solving or as a basis for planning programs to meet specific needs.

9. Reading reference materials such as interest tables, financial handbooks, and handbooks of business mathematics. Students must interpret and apply this information.

10. Reading and interpreting textbooks in order to complete class assignments that enable students to learn business skills.

11. Reading technical vocabulary. Researchers have identified both general and specific vocabulary lists for secretaries, account clerks, and others (Rush, Moe, Storlie, 1986).

Example 9.10 contains a selection from a business education textbook. Note the technical terminology, including *real estate*, *personal property tax*, *assessor*, *assessment*, *revenues*, and *tax base*. The preview guide, also shown in Example 9.10, should be completed by students before they read the selection; it helps readers anticipate the selection content, thus increasing comprehension. After students have completed the preview guide and read the chapter, they should have an opportunity to discuss and support their answers.

EXAMPLE **9.10**

Business Education Content and Preview Guide

Property Tax

Local governments get a major share of their revenues from property taxes. This includes counties, cities, towns, townships, and school districts. About one-third of all revenues at this level comes from property tax. The state and federal governments have almost no revenue from this tax.

A **real estate property tax** is one on the value of land, and anything *on* the land such as houses, barns, garages, or other buildings. A second tax is the **personal property tax,** a tax applied to movable items such as automobiles, furniture, and machinery used by businesses. Because of the ease with which personal property can be hidden, the personal property tax is being used less and less. Real estate has thus become the most important property tax base and source of revenue for local communities.

The amount of real estate taxes is determined by first estimating the value of the property, and then multiplying the tax rate by the value. The amount at which the property is valued is called an **assessment,** and the government official who does the valuation is called an **assessor.**

Source: Betty Brown and John Clow, *General Business: Our Business and Economic World*, p. 231. Copyright © 1982 by Houghton Mifflin Company. Reprinted by permission of Houghton Mifflin Company.

Preview Guide

Directions: Place a check mark under the *Yes* column if you believe the selection will support the statement. Place a check under the *No* column if you believe the text will not support the statement. After you read the selection, review your responses.

Yes   No

_____ _____   1. Property tax is levied on real estate and personal property.

_____ _____   2. Property tax is not levied on any personal property that can be bought and sold.

_____ _____   3. Personal property tax is applied to movable items.

_____ _____   4. Taxpayers may be exempted from paying tax on the full value of a property if there is a mortgage on it.

_____ _____   5. Taxpayers find it difficult to avoid paying personal property tax.

_____ _____   6. The assessed value of a property is the basis for calculating the amount of tax.

Business students must learn to combine skimming and scanning with close reading. First, they should skim for the main idea or scan for specific information they need to solve a problem, to compose a letter or memo, or to write a report. Then they should carefully and accurately read the section or sections of content containing the information they need. Close reading is important because in many situations even a small error can have serious consequences. For example, a bookkeeping error can make a company appear profitable when it is actually losing money; a secretary's error in typing and proofreading a business letter can change the entire meaning of an important communication; and a tiny error in a computer program may result in a program that will not run. Business students should understand clearly how meaning is expressed through grammar, and they should concentrate on reading to identify details that convey meaning.

Chapters 3 and 6 include suggestions for teaching students how to read for meaning. Teaching strategies such as preview guides, study guides, and directed reading lessons can help business education students refine vital comprehension skills. Each of these strategies can be applied to a specific area of business education and can focus on skills such as following directions, solving problems, and locating information. In addition, a reading strategy similar to the following one is helpful.

A Reading Strategy for Business Education Materials

Students who must read the many kinds of materials identified earlier in this section can improve their reading comprehension by using a strategy like PRC (Stoodt, 1985). Its three phases are prereading, reading, and consolidation.

Prereading. The prereading phase of the business reading process is the limbering up part. The readers survey the reading material in order to identify the type of content (e.g., memo, letter, report, text) and to set the stage for remembering it. During this phase, the readers identify topics around which they can cluster the ideas that are in the selection. They also identify the author's organization; knowing how the material is organized will help them pinpoint the main ideas when reading. During the prereading phase, the readers establish questions that will guide their reading, such as the sample questions that follow:

1. What does this selection tell me?
2. What is the main point?
3. What are the important details?
4. What questions will I be asked about this reading?

Reading. The students read carefully if close reading is necessary or scan if that is adequate. If they are reading to gather data to write an important report, close reading is in order. However, if the students are reading to locate specific pieces of information and those details are all that is needed from the content, then scanning is appropriate.

Consolidation. During this phase, readers consolidate the information acquired from reading. Processing the information helps them organize it for long-term memory and for implementing the ideas presented when that is necessary. Readers may take notes to aid remembering and should ask themselves questions similar to the following:

1. What is it that I don't understand?
2. How does this information relate to what I already know?
3. What other examples can I think of?
4. How does this information change or alter what I already know?
5. How can I implement this information?

Business education students must be able to read graphs, charts, tables, balance sheets, invoices, and tax forms. Refer to Chapter 4 for further suggestions about how to teach students to read these graphic aids.

The gloss in Example 9.11 shows a section from a computer science textbook used in secondary computer science classes. The gloss identifies the reading tasks that a student would encounter when reading this section, found at the beginning of the textbook.

Human Environmental Science (Home Economics)

Human environmental science is a multidisciplinary field that includes much of what was formerly considered home economics. However, current studies emphasize a synthesis of knowledge in the social and behavioral sciences. Today's human environmental science studies explore child and family behavior, technological innovations, health, foods and nutrition, clothing and textiles, design, management, housing, home furnishings, and personal growth and development. Secondary students pursue these studies for both

EXAMPLE **9.11**

Gloss of Computer Science Text Showing Reading Tasks
Required by the Content

1-3 Communicating with the Computer

Identify
Main Idea —→ The methods used to communicate with a computer are very important. The
computer must receive instructions in a form that it has been programmed to
accept and to which it can respond.

Detail —→ The computer itself cannot understand a human language such as English. It
Technical
language —→ in *machine language*. Machine language is based on coding in the binary
number system. (See the Computer Language Feature on page 64.) The bi-
Mathematics—→ nary number system uses only 0's and 1's to represent numbers. These
digits — 0 and 1 — can easily be related to the electronic components of the
computer, where the current (or switch) is either on (represented by 1) or off
(represented by 0). Although the computer understands machine language,
human beings sometimes have difficulty with it; an instruction telling an
Example —→ Apple computer to add one number to another looks like this: 10101101
00001010 00000011 01101101 00000111 00000011 10001101 00001000
00000011.

Description —→ Clearly, it would be easier for a human being to communicate in a familiar
language like English. Of course, the computer does not understand English
(a very complicated language, if you think about it), so a compromise was
reached. Languages less complicated than English but easier for a programmer to work with than machine language were invented. In this book, you
will learn to use the BASIC language to communicate with computers.

Acronym
Important
Idea —→ BASIC (Beginner's *All-purpose Symbolic Instruction Code*) was first developed in the early 1960's as a general purpose computer language. It was, and
is today, a language that you can learn without having a strong technical or
scientific background. BASIC is the most popular language used for microcomputers. Any computer language that a human can understand easily,

English → BASIC → Machine Language

such as BASIC, is called a *high-level language*. Many other high-level computer languages have been developed. You can learn a little about Logo,
Pascal, and others in the Computer Language features at the end of each
chapter of this book.

Source: D. Myers, V. Elswick, P. Hopfensperger, and J. Pavlovich: *Computer Programming in Basic* (Boston:
Houghton Mifflin Company, 1986), p. 8. Reprinted by permission of Houghton Mifflin Company.

vocational and avocational purposes. As more and more women work outside the home, men and women must learn how to work together to rear children and manage their homes. Therefore, this field is no longer solely the domain of women. Many secondary schools include human environmental science units for young men.

Students can read the complex materials used in human environmental sciences more effectively with teacher assistance through strategies that include guided reading lessons, study guides, and preview guides. Study guides have proved to be valuable aids to comprehension and students have, in fact, requested them. Students learn best when teachers guide them as they read a passage (Moore, Readence, and Rickelman, 1989). Included in this section are examples relating printed materials and sample teaching strategies.

Human environmental science content includes many technical terms, for example, *developmental stages, teachable moment, top sirloin, kinship networks,* and *French seam.* Example 9.12 presents a selection from a textbook in this area. Notice that the reader must understand the following terms: *warm colors, cool colors, tertiary colors, primary, secondary, analogous,* and *complementary.* The study guide that follows the selection will help students check their understanding of these terms and of the content.

E X A M P L E **9.12**

Human Environmental Science and Study Guide

Whether or not you like a garment depends very much on its color, texture, pattern, and lines. These factors are called design elements. The way that these elements work together in any one garment has much to do with how that garment looks on you. The way a garment looks on you has a great deal to do with how much you want to wear it.

A Splash of Color

Color is important to how you feel. Some colors make us happy; others tend to put us in a sad mood. Color in clothing is also important to how you look. It can make you look larger or smaller, healthy or unhealthy, or even happy or unhappy. Color can change the look of your skin. It can also change the look of other colors you wear. Try putting blue next to red. Both colors will look slightly different from the way they look alone. Now put the blue next to your face; then, the red. You may see a difference in how you look with each color.

How Colors Are Classified

Understanding how color is classified, or put into categories, makes it easier to choose what colors go together and look good on you.

Colors, themselves, are sorted into three basic groups: primary, secondary, and tertiary. Other terms having to do with light and heat are also associated with colors.

Primary Colors. The place to start in sorting out colors is with primary colors. There are three **primary colors:** red, yellow, and blue. All the other colors are made by combining these three colors. Look at the color wheel on page 297, and use it to find the colors discussed in this section.

Secondary Colors. The colors orange, green, and violet are **secondary colors.** They are made by combining equal amounts of primary colors. Red and yellow, for example, make orange. Blue and red make violet. Yellow and blue make green.

Tertiary Colors. The next group is called the **tertiary colors.** This group of six colors is made by combining secondary colors with primary colors. For example, blue, a primary color, combined with green, a secondary color, makes blue-green. Look on the color wheel to see the other tertiary colors. In the name of a tertiary color, the primary color is always used first.

Other Colors and Terms

The color wheel on page 297 has 12 colors in it. As you can see by just looking around you, there are many more colors than the 12 you see in the wheel. Where do other colors come from? These other colors come from adding black or white to the primary, secondary, and tertiary colors. A color that white has been added to is called a **tint.** A color that black has been added to is called a **shade.** Navy, for example, is a shade of blue, and pink is a tint of red. Shades and tints are also referred to as color values. A color that has a dark value is a shade, or a color to which black has been added. A color that has a light value is a tint, or a color to which white has been added.

Color is also defined in terms of intensity. **Intensity** refers to the brightness or dullness of a color. For example, rust, dark brown, and tan are dull colors, while light blue and pale peach are considered bright colors.

The last way colors are described is in terms of warmth or coolness. Colors that have red and yellow in them are referred to as warm colors. Colors that have blue in them are considered cool colors. Aqua, which contains blue, is a cool color, and gold, which contains red and yellow, is a warm color. Blue is the color of sky and water. Yellow and red are the colors of the sun. These facts help to explain why these colors are considered warm or cool.

We also think of colors as being complementary to each other. **Complementary colors** are those opposite each other on the color wheel. Red and green are complementary colors as are yellow-orange and blue-violet. A pair of complementary colors is always made up of one warm color and one cool color. This contrast creates excitement.

Source: Reprinted from *Teen Guide* by Valarie M. Chamberlain, with permission of Glencoe/McGraw-Hill, A Macmillan/McGraw-Hill Company. Mission Hills, California, Copyright © 1990, pp. 294–295.

Study Guide

Introduction

This selection discusses color, color classifications, and the relationships among colors. The classifications include primary colors, secondary colors, and tertiary colors. Some of the relationships consist of shades and tints of colors, intensity, and complementary relationships.

Vocabulary

Find an example for each of the following terms:

primary colors   shades
secondary colors   tint
tertiary colors

Comprehension

Directions: Place a + beside each statement that is supported by the reading selection and a − beside each item that is not supported by the selection.

LITERAL

_____ 1. Intensity refers to brightness.
_____ 2. Colors are sorted into two basic groups.
_____ 3. Complementary colors are contrasting colors.
_____ 4. All secondary colors are made by combining primary colors.

INTERPRETIVE

_____ 5. Wearing green and red together has a soothing effect on the wearer.
_____ 6. Special effects in decorating can be created by individuals who understand the effect that colors have on people.
_____ 7. Large areas in the home should be covered with the color red.
_____ 8. If we block off any color in the spectrum, the remaining colors form its complement.

Directions: Write short answers for the following questions.

APPLIED

9. Identify three ways in which you can use the ideas in this article for interior decorating.
10. What are your best colors? Why?
11. What color relationship is formed by your school colors?

Human environmental science students need to learn to read diagrams, patterns, drawings, graphs, and charts. They must be able to visualize the finished product of a pattern or of a floor plan and to read mathematical symbols and legends to understand the graphics. Example 9.13 shows a chart from a human environmental science textbook. Interpreting the pictures and the arrows is important to understanding this chart. Example 9.14 shows a different type of chart.

EXAMPLE **9.13**

Human Environmental Science Chart

HOW A BANK USES YOUR MONEY AS A RESOURCE

When you deposit your money in a bank, the money is put to work in a number of ways. The bank lends deposited money to individuals who need it to buy goods or to pay for services. For example, if someone wants to buy a car or needs to pay for a college education and does not have enough money, the bank will make that person a loan. The bank also lends money to companies. For example, it may lend money to help build a new factory.

Each borrower pays interest to the bank for the use of the bank's money. In this way, the bank uses your deposit as a resource to make more money for itself.

You benefit, too.

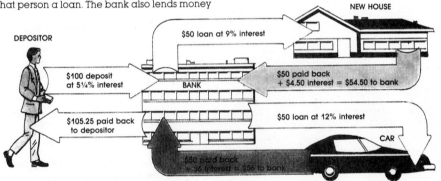

The bank receives $100.00 from the depositor. It makes loans and receives $110.50 back. It pays the depositor $105.25. Thus, the bank's profit is $5.25 on the loan it made.

Source: Teen Guide by Valarie Chamberlain, with permission of Glencoe/McGraw-Hill, A Macmillan/McGraw-Hill Company. Mission Hills, California, Copyright © 1990, p. 190.

Human environmental science students should know how to interpret labels for specific information, for example, the labels on foods, fabrics, and cleaning products that tell exactly how much of each item or ingredient is contained in the package. They must be able to determine from a label whether a certain product is suitable for their needs. When planning a special diet, the students may have to locate information about the amount of carbohydrates, fats, proteins, and other nutrients contained in a food.

The directions used in human environmental science study and in pre-

EXAMPLE **9.14**

Human Environmental Science Chart

ACCIDENTS AND EMERGENCIES GUIDE	
If a healthy family wants to stay healthy, it must be prepared to deal with accidents and emergencies.	
What Can Happen	**What to Do**
• A family member has a simple accident.	• Use first aid. A child who is alone should notify the parents. Never give medicine unless the parents or a doctor directs you to do so.
• A family member is bleeding badly, vomiting, or has a very high temperature.	• Apply direct pressure and elevate the wounded, bleeding area. Call a doctor at once. If the doctor suggests taking the victim to a hospital emergency room, call the police. They will send an emergency car. A child who is alone should call the parents while waiting for the emergency car. The child should ask a neighbor to care for the other children.
• A family member burns herself or himself.	• Submerge the burned area in cold water until the pain goes away. Cover the burn with a thick, dry, sterile bandage to keep air out. Get medical help. A child who is alone should notify the parents.
• A family member gets a dangerous substance in his or her eye.	• Wash the eye thoroughly with water for 15 minutes. Hold the eyelid open and pour the water from the inside corner of the eye out. Put a pad over the closed eyelid. Get medical help. A child who is alone should notify the parents.
• A family member swallows something you think may be poisonous.	• Do not take for granted antidote on label. Much of the information may be outdated and incorrect. Call the poison-control center or hospital emergency room nearest you for instructions. A child who is alone should notify the parents.
• A family member chokes on something.	• If the victim is breathing, do not try to remove the swallowed item by slapping the back. Ask the child to cough up the item. If necessary, use the Heimlich maneuver (see page 271).
• A fire breaks out in the house.	• Get yourself and the children out of the house immediately. Go to a neighbor's house to telephone the fire department. Do not go back into the house for any reason.

Source: Teen Guide by Valarie Chamberlain, with permission of Glencoe/McGraw-Hill, A Macmillan/McGraw-Hill Company. Mission Hills, California, Copyright © 1990, p. 110.

packaged products for the home include technical vocabulary words that the student must understand. Additionally, following directions precisely and in the proper sequence is necessary for achieving the desired outcomes. Directions require slow, precise, and careful reading. Unfortunately, many people tend to become overconfident when they see short and concise directions; this attitude seems to be a common failing and can lead to carelessness and limited understanding (Daines, 1982). Teachers can prepare students for reading the directions in their textbooks through directed reading lessons, study guides, and other instructional strategies. See Chapters 3 and 6 for more on following directions.

Agriculture

Agriculture is a complex, multidisciplinary field of study involving science and mathematics. Science is involved when agriculture students learn about the care and feeding of livestock as well as planting and cultivating crops. Prospective farmers must also have a working knowledge of basic mathematics for budgeting and accounting purposes. Business management plays a pivotal role in the study of agriculture, since farms are businesses. Because farming is mechanized, prospective farmers also must develop some mechanical skills and often need to deal with highly advanced technology and equipment. In addition, conservation of natural resources is a significant aspect of agricultural study.

Students who study agriculture read content materials in the areas of science, mathematics, social science, geology, and auto mechanics. This wide variety of reading content creates a very real challenge for students: each of these content areas involves a different technical vocabulary and its own characteristic patterns of organizing content. These patterns include cause and effect, problem solving, comparison, experiment, directions, and chronological order. In addition, authors of agricultural content often use graphs, charts, diagrams, and pictures, which students must be able to interpret. Following are some examples of agricultural content. Example 9.15 shows scientific content, and Example 9.16 shows agricultural material related to mathematics use. Example 9.17 shows a mapping activity based on the content in Example 9.15.

EXAMPLE **9.15**

Scientific Content

What Are the Causes of Diseases Among Farm Animals?

A *disease* is considered in a broad sense to be any disorder of the body. (When the word is analyzed, it really means "lack of ease," which is probably its original meaning.)

Improper Feeding as a Cause of Diseases

Some diseases are caused entirely by improper feeding methods. The disease called *rickets*, in which the bones of an animal fail to develop properly, is due to improper amounts of certain minerals and vitamins. Young animals are sometimes born with enlargements in the throat region. This ailment, which is known as *goitre*, or "big neck," is caused by insufficient amounts of iodine in the ration of the mother animals during the period previous to the birth of the young. *Colic* in horses and *bloat* in cattle and sheep are usually caused by improper methods of feeding.

Animals may be poisoned by lead, which they can get through licking paint pails or freshly painted surfaces. They may also consume feeds that have a poisonous effect on their bodies. Poisonous weeds such as loco weed and white snakeroot are examples. The latter weed, if eaten by dairy cows, may injure not only the cows themselves but also the people who drink the cows' milk. Halogeton is a weed that has spread rapidly in semi-desert areas; at times, it has caused the death of many sheep in some western states. Other plants that have a poisonous effect on livestock are alsike clover, when eaten wet; bouncing Bet, cocklebur, and corn cockle roadside plants; bracken fern, found in dry and abandoned fields; buttercup, when eaten green; larkspur; ergot; horse nettle; jimson weed; Johnson grass; nightshade; hemlock; milkweed; and wild cherry.

Ornamental plants toxic to goats include oleander, azalea, castorbean, buttercup, rhododendron, philodendron, yew, English ivy, chokeberry, laurel, daffodil, jonquil, and many members of the lily family. Even tomatoes, potatoes, rhubarb, and avocadoes contain toxic substances. Goats may also be harmed by toadstools, mushrooms, mistletoe, and milkweed.

Source: From Alfred H. Krebs, *Agriculture in Our Lives,* 5th ed. (Danville, Ill.: The Interstate Printers and Publishers, Inc., 1984), p. 405.

Physical Education

Physical education is a popular area of study today. The growing national interest in physical fitness has created a parallel surge of interest in physical education in the schools. The content of physical education studies can be used to motivate reluctant readers; students who may not be interested in reading other materials often willingly read physical education materials.

Reading serves four purposes in physical education:

1. Physical education topics can motivate students to read, and reading can motivate students to become involved in athletics.
2. Students can learn game rules and signals by reading.
3. Reading can be used to increase and refine skills.
4. Reading can increase understanding of a sport and thus can enhance the spectators' or participants' pleasure.

Physical education is frequently taught without textbooks, but students still need reading skills to read rules and directions for playing games and to read books and magazines to improve their techniques in various sports. For example, there are many books and magazine articles available to help people improve their golf swings and tennis strokes.

Reading physical education material requires a number of reading skills. There is extensive specialized vocabulary in this reading content. Each sport has a separate set of terms to be learned. (For example, *love, touchdown, foul,* and *guard.*) Notice that the word *love* from tennis and the terms *foul* and *guard,* which apply to several sports, are multiple meaning terms for which students have other uses in their everyday vocabularies.

The team and individual sports taught in physical education classes re-

EXAMPLE **9.16**

Content Related to Mathematics Use

Keeping Records for a Farm Business

In keeping farm business records, a farmer should select a good type of record book to use. Most state colleges of agriculture have developed farm record books that are quite easy to keep. Usually, directions are provided for keeping and summarizing these records. These record books may usually be purchased for a small sum from the state agricultural college or the county agricultural agent; or the high school agriculture teacher will help a farmer secure one. The most suitable record books provide for (1) figuring depreciation on machinery, buildings, and equipment; (2) making opening and closing inventories; (3) recording expenses and income; and (4) other items.

Some farmers obtain help in keeping and using records by attending adult farmer classes sponsored by high school departments of vocational agriculture. Some join with other farmers in a farm record association and cooperatively employ a field supervisor who helps each farmer-member keep records and use them in improving the farm business.

Source: From Alfred H. Krebs, *Agriculture in Our Lives,* 5th ed. (Danville, Ill.: The Interstate Printers and Publishers, Inc., 1984), p. 694.

EXAMPLE **9.17**

Mapping Activity for Cause and Effect in Agricultural Content

Improper feeding causes disease

Causes	Effects
Lack of iodine	Goitre
Improper feeding methods	Colic Bloat
Lead Weeds Ornamental plants	Toxic (poison)

quire much special equipment. In order to learn the names and functions of the various pieces of equipment, students could illustrate each piece of equipment, label it, and describe its function. A notebook could be maintained for this purpose, in which the equipment for each sport is categorized and alphabetized. Teachers may wish to develop inventories of terminology related to each sport studied. These inventories can be used both as preparation to introduce the sport and, after study, as a means to review students' understanding of this vocabulary. Students can supply synonyms or define terms in their own words and may develop an illustrated dictionary of sports terms. Following are examples of inventories of sports terms (Example 9.18).

E X A M P L E **9.18**

Sports Term Inventories

Directions: Define the following terms in your own words.

Tennis	Basketball
racket	dribble
backhand	field goal
forehand	foul
love	free throw
serve	pass
net	pivot
game point	press
deuce	rebound
match	shoot
fault	traveling
double fault	violation
volley	backboard
lob	division line
slice	basket
chop	
overhead smash	

Example 9.19 shows a referee's hand signals. The reader of these diagrams has to translate the stick-figure drawings into actual actions, and he or she must associate the signal with its name and the rule it represents. This is a complex reading task. A study guide or directed reading lesson would help the reader in this situation.

Students also can increase their understanding of physical education content by writing game rules, directions, illustrations, and suggestions for younger children. They may refine these materials and actually use them to teach games to elementary school children.

Critical reading is also important in physical education materials. Critical thinking is developed when students evaluate the strategies and/or equip-

EXAMPLE **9.19**

Diagram of Referee's Hand Signals

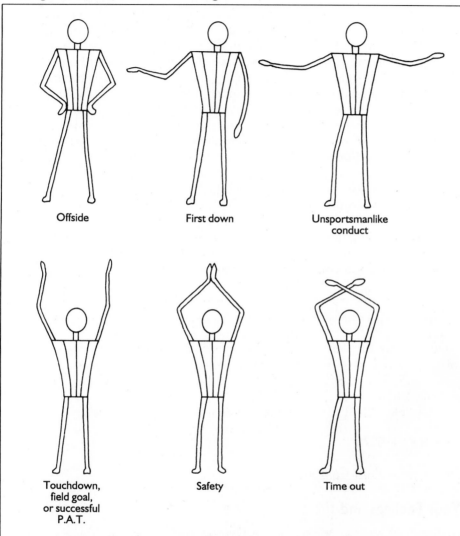

Offside

First down

Unsportsmanlike conduct

Touchdown, field goal, or successful P.A.T.

Safety

Time out

ment suggested by different authors. This is a good thinking activity, since various authorities suggest widely different approaches to a sport. Critical thinking also comes into play when students evaluate exercises and equipment for physical fitness. For example, recent television commercials recommend some equipment for exercising specific parts of the body, although physical fitness authorities consider the equipment useless.

Driver Education

Driver education classes teach secondary students to drive safely, carefully, and effectively. Driver education courses usually include a section on theory that is taught with a textbook; this is followed by practical applications of driving skills and actual driving practice. Most young people look forward with great anticipation to acquiring a driver's license. For modern American teenagers, learning how to drive is a rite of passage into adulthood. Since driving is such a significant skill for young people, reading driver education content and related materials is very important for secondary school students.

Readers of driver education content utilize abilities similar to those needed for reading in the other content areas. They have to interpret the following types of content: technical vocabulary, cause-and-effect relationships, directions, inferences, comparisons, pictures, diagrams, symbols, and mathematical material. In addition, they must read and understand the material, make inferences from it, and think critically about it. Visualizing is especially important because they have to translate words into action as they move from textbook descriptions to actual driving practice.

Understanding the technical vocabulary used in driver education materials is essential to understanding its content and translating the content into action. The technical vocabulary of such materials usually represents concrete concepts relating to driving skills and automotive equipment. The student who has had little or no experience with an automobile is at a disadvantage because he or she has had no firsthand exposure to the concepts involved in driving. Demonstrations with the equipment and processes involved help to overcome this problem. The technical vocabulary includes words such as *crosswalk, oversteering, intersection, collision, accelerator, right-of-way, regulatory signs, vehicle malfunction,* and *gauges.* (Refer to Chapter 2 for vocabulary teaching suggestions.)

Example 9.20 illustrates content from a driver education text.

E X A M P L E **9.20**

Driver Education Content

Your Feelings and the Driving Task

Changes in the way you feel can affect the way you drive. Strong emotional feelings, such as joy or anger, can "blind" you and make you less alert. If your mind isn't alert, it can't do a good job. And if you fail to see problems, you won't be able to predict, decide, or execute. The driving task requires that your mind and body work together.

Drivers who feel great anger or sadness may act in ways they would not if all were well. If they're very angry or if they're worried about being late, they may take chances they would not otherwise.

Source: Jay Davis, Donn Maryott, and Warrent Stiska, *In the Driver's Seat,* p. 22. Copyright 1978 by Houghton Mifflin Company. Reprinted by permission of Houghton Mifflin Company.

To comprehend written material, readers must be able to follow the author's organizational patterns. Activities like the following can be incorporated into driver education study guides.

1. Have students make a diagram of causes and effects. The following are based on the text in Example 9.20:

Causes	*Effects*
joy or anger	becomes "blind," less alert
lack of alertness	fails to predict, decide, execute
anger	becomes careless
worry about being late	takes chances

2. State the effects and ask students to identify the causes, as in this example:
   a. Cause: _____
      Effect: becomes careless
   b. Cause: _____
      Effect: takes chances

In addition to reading organizational patterns, readers of driver education materials frequently must identify main ideas and details in order to understand the content. (Chapters 3 and 8 suggest a number of ways to help students read for main ideas and details.)

The content of driver education materials and the actual driving process both require the student to make predictions based on inferences and comparisons. Observing traffic conditions and signs enables the driver to predict the road conditions he or she will encounter. Also, the driver can relate present conditions to past driving experiences in order to predict how to react to particular traffic situations. The reader must be able to make inferences and comparisons that are based on written information. Following is an example of a worksheet that teachers can use for helping their students develop skill in making predictions (Example 9.21).

Readers of driver education materials and drivers both must be able to identify traffic signs, which are often reproduced in textbooks, by color, size, and shape. Flash cards that show the various traffic signs are useful in helping students memorize them. Driver education textbooks also include diagrams to help students understand various driving situations and related information.

The teacher can help students understand diagrams of driving situations by using these steps:

1. Give students diagrams of a stretch of road and a written description of a driving maneuver. Students should draw the vehicle in each of the major positions needed to complete the maneuver.
2. Give students a complete diagram and ask them to write the directions for carrying out the maneuver. (See Example 9.22.)

E X A M P L E **9.21**

Inference and Comparison Worksheet (Driver Education)

1. *Inferences:* Inferences enable the driver to decide on appropriate actions. Read and answer the following question: if you are driving an automobile that is traveling at 45 miles per hour and you encounter a sign indicating a sharp curve with a sign below it saying 35 M.P.H., what inference should you make?
2. *Comparison:* It will help you as a driver to compare present conditions with previous experience. Read and answer the following comparison questions:
   a. How does driving a truck compare with driving an automobile?
   b. If you were driving through a snowstorm, what comparisons could you make that would help you decide how to drive?
   c. If you see a horse running toward the road, what should you do? What previous experiences can help you make your decision?

E X A M P L E **9.22**

Driver Education Diagram

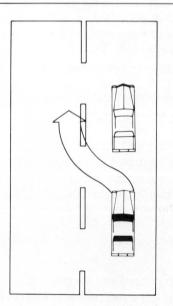 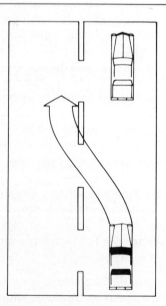

Source: Jay Davis, Donn Maryott, and Warren Stiska, *In the Driver's Seat,* p. 207. Copyright © 1978 by Houghton Mifflin Company. Reprinted by permission of Houghton Mifflin Company.

Students must also be able to read and compute mathematical material in order to understand driver education content. Example 9.23 shows the type of mathematical skills required to understand driver education materials.

The teacher may help students use a diagram like the one in Example 9.23 in the following ways:

1. Ask students to explain the main idea of the chart.
2. Ask students to explain the significance of the information given.
3. Ask students to explain how to apply this information to actual driving situations.
4. Ask students to state specific details, such as the stopping distance of snow tires on glare ice.

EXAMPLE **9.23**

Mathematics in a Driver Education Book

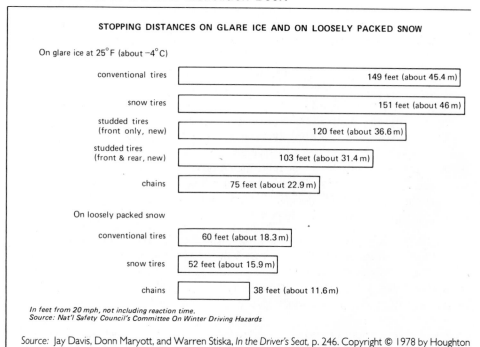

STOPPING DISTANCES ON GLARE ICE AND ON LOOSELY PACKED SNOW

On glare ice at 25°F (about −4°C)

conventional tires	149 feet (about 45.4 m)
snow tires	151 feet (about 46 m)
studded tires (front only, new)	120 feet (about 36.6 m)
studded tires (front & rear, new)	103 feet (about 31.4 m)
chains	75 feet (about 22.9 m)

On loosely packed snow

conventional tires	60 feet (about 18.3 m)
snow tires	52 feet (about 15.9 m)
chains	38 feet (about 11.6 m)

In feet from 20 mph, not including reaction time.
Source: Nat'l Safety Council's Committee On Winter Driving Hazards

Source: Jay Davis, Donn Maryott, and Warren Stiska, *In the Driver's Seat,* p. 246. Copyright © 1978 by Houghton Mifflin Company. Reprinted by permission of Houghton Mifflin Company.

Art

Art students use and study the media of artistic expression more frequently than they use and study textbooks. The study of art does not involve as much textbook reading as many other content areas, and fewer textbooks are available in this subject area than in other areas. Nevertheless, art students need to have well-developed reading skills because they read many types of written content for a variety of purposes. For example, they read to acquire information about artistic techniques, art history, and the lives of important artists. Following is a summary of the reading strategies art students commonly use:

1. Reading for information. Art students often read about exhibitions, artists, and techniques. They read to identify art styles or movements. Reading for information involves identifying main ideas and supporting details.
2. Reading to follow directions. Art students must read and follow steps in sequential order. This kind of reading would occur when they read about topics such as new media and new techniques or how to make a woodcut.
3. Reading to interpret charts and diagrams, such as a color wheel. For example, art students need to learn about complementary colors.
4. Reading critically. The art student uses this skill when evaluating reviews of art shows or the impact of a medium or a style.
5. Reading to implement information or directions. After reading about a particular medium or style, an art student may experiment with it.
6. Reading and organizing information for reports. Art students may be required to write a report on the life of an artist, a style of art, or ways of interpreting moods and feelings in art. This reading task requires that the reader identify main ideas and details.
7. Reading technical vocabulary related to art. This vocabulary includes words like *linear*, *hue*, and *perspective*.
8. Reading materials such as reference books, art history books, biographies, and magazines. The art student reads magazines such as *Arts and Activities*, *School Arts*, *Popular Photography*, and *Craft Horizons* to obtain current information and ideas.

Study guides, preview guides, and vocabulary activities are particularly helpful to art students. In addition, many of the strategies presented in Chapters 2, 3, and 6 can be used to help art students develop appropriate reading skills. Examples of art reading activities follow, including a vocabulary activity, a preview guide, and a study guide.

Activity: Art Vocabulary Game

Objective: To provide practice in associating words with colors.

Materials Needed: Set of cards with hues (as listed below), set of cards with color words.

cinnamon	indigo	burgundy	puce
ocher	magenta	cerise	ivory
sepia	vermilion	ecru	

Directions for Activity: This game is one in which a student accumulates "books" (sets of two) of matching cards (color card plus hue card). The regular rules of a card game may be used. (This activity can be played by two or more people. The person who matches the most cards correctly within a specified period of time wins.)

Example 9.24 includes material from a textbook used for teaching art. As you read this brief selection, note the many technical words and expressions used (for example, *linear perspective, diminishing contrasts, hue, value, intensity of color, texture, achieve deep penetration, two-dimensional surface, infinite concept, atmospheric perspective, pictorial composition, theme, picture plane, volume of deep space, softening edges of objects, scale,* and *middle ground*). Following the selection are two reading guides that are based on the passage.

E X A M P L E **9.24**

Art Content and Reading Guides

Problem I

In conjunction with linear perspective, artists of the past frequently used diminishing contrasts of hue, value, and intensity of color and texture to achieve deep penetration of space on a two-dimensional surface. This is known as the infinite concept of space or atmospheric perspective.

Create a pictorial composition based on the theme "Objects in Space." Conceive of the picture plane as the near side of a volume of deep space. Use the indications of space suggested in the opening paragraph, plus softening edges of objects as they are set back in depth. The human figure may be used to help suggest the scale of objects in space. Foreground, middle ground, and deep space may be indicated by the size of similar objects.

Source: Otto Ocvirk, Robert Bone, Robert Stinson, and Philip Wigg, *Art Fundamentals: Theory and Practice* (Dubuque, Iowa: William C. Brown Company, 1975), p. 114.

Preview Guide

Directions: Check *Yes* if you believe the reading selection supports the statement; check *No* if you believe the selection does not support the statement.

Yes   *No*

_____ _____   1. The infinite concept of space and atmospheric perspective are the same thing.

_____ _____   2. Artists of the past used diminishing contrasts of hue, value, and intensity of color to achieve atmospheric perspective.

_____ _____   3. Students should conceive of the picture plane as the far side of a volume of deep space.

_____ _____   4. Trees are used to suggest scale.

Study Guide

Introduction

This selection poses a problem for art students to solve. If you have questions after you have read the problem, refer to books and articles in the bibliography on linear perspective.

Vocabulary

Provide an example for each of the following words: linear perspective, diminishing contrasts, hue, value, intensity, texture, two-dimensional surface, infinite concept, atmospheric perspective, pictorial composition, theme, picture plane.

Comprehension

Directions: Write a short answer to each question.

LITERAL

1. What does this selection ask you to do?
2. What concept is explained in the first paragraph?
3. What is the theme of the pictorial composition that the student is to create?

INTERPRETIVE

4. Why does the author suggest that a human figure may be used to suggest scale?
5. Will color play an important role in this composition?
6. What similar objects might be used to indicate foreground, middle ground, and deep space?

APPLIED

7. What materials will you need to complete this problem?
8. Can you create another composition that has the same title but uses a different object to show scale? If so, what could you use?

Music

Learning music is similar to learning a language. Both tasks depend on the student's ability to perceive likenesses and differences in sounds, shapes, and symbols (Badiali, 1984). Reading words and reading music are both done left to right and top to bottom. The goal of instruction in both instances is understanding the text, and both tasks depend upon students' ability to remember the meaning of symbols (Elliott, 1982).

Many music teachers choose not to use textbooks in their instruction; however, they must remember that each piece of music can be considered a text (Morgan and Berg-O'Halloran, 1989). In studying music, students must be able to read the words, the music, and the technical language (Frager and Thompson, 1983; Mateja, 1982).

To help secondary students with the task of reading music books, teachers may use the following strategies:

1. Anticipate students' problems before they read. Standardized reading tests and teacher-made inventories can provide data regarding students' reading skills. Observing students' performance in reading music is very helpful in isolating their strengths and weaknesses.
2. Teach the necessary vocabulary before students read a selection.
3. Develop and use illustrated dictionaries of musical terms.
4. Teach students how to study and prepare assignments (see Chapter 4). Demonstrating these techniques with music content can be helpful.
5. Use strategies such as study guides, directed reading lessons, structured overviews, preview guides, and vocabulary study to help students read and understand music content.

Music instruction often requires a high level of reading ability, including knowledge of notes, lyrics, and music theory. Students must be able to understand material that is written about music in order to interpret the music. Music students must be able to read and understand the following types of content (Tanner, 1983):

expository and narrative materials about composers
critiques, reviews, and descriptions of performances
exposition — music history
reporting — current events related to music
references — research, reviews
types of media — books, magazines, newspapers, scores

Music students read and interpret a large number of musical terms, such as *sonatina, spiritoso, andante,* and *allegretto.* In addition, special symbols are used in music books and scores. These symbols aid the student in interpreting the music. Students must be able to recognize symbols for elements such as treble clef; bass clef; notes (whole, half quarter, and so on); rests (varying values corresponding to note values); sharps; flats; crescendo; and diminuendo. The teacher must frequently demonstrate the musical terms and concepts. For example, the teacher might demonstrate *pianissimo* by playing a song softly and show *forte* by playing the same song loudly; or he or she might illustrate a *crescendo* followed by a *diminuendo.*

Hicks (1980) points out that in instrumental music, the reading process involves recognizing the notes, which represent pitch; the meter symbols, which indicate time; and various other interpretive and expressive markings. At the same time, an instrumentalist must physically manipulate valves, bows, slides, and keys. Hicks suggests that teachers present the early stages of music reading as a problem-solving activity involving simple duple and triple meters. He suggests presenting all songs in the same key, emphasizing continuity and repetition and using materials that have repeated patterns and a narrow range. He also recommends including familiar elements in each new activity.

1. Provide background information about the song.
2. Present the words of the song in poem form on a ditto sheet (to avoid confusion that may result from all the accompanying signs and symbols on a music sheet).
3. Discuss any words that may not be recognized or comprehended as well as the overall meaning of the lyrics.
4. The teacher and students should divide the words into syllables cooperatively. A ditto sheet may again be prepared with words in this form.

After the musical aspects of the song are taught, the students can use the ditto sheet (with divided words) to sing from. Later, they may use the music books that contain syllabicated words along with the notes and other symbols.

When preparing to perform a composition, music students must ask themselves a number of questions regarding the composition and their performance. Michael Tanner asked a saxophone player in a high school band to identify the questions he had before playing a piece of music, and he produced a list similar to the following one:

1. What will playing this exercise show me?
2. What skills should I learn or develop?
3. From what I know about the composer, what does this piece tell me about him or her?
4. What mood is conveyed?
5. What is the key signature?
6. What is the meter (time signature)?
7. What rhythms does the composer use?
8. What intervals are used?
9. What form does the piece have?
10. How long are the phrases?
11. How did the composer want the piece played?
12. What dynamic markings are shown and why?
13. How many motives did the composer have?
14. Is this music challenging to play?
15. Can I play this successfully?
16. Do I want to play this piece?

17. Is this music too hard?
18. How can I play better?
19. Would it help me if I heard the song played by someone else?
20. Would it help me if I heard the lyrics? (Tanner, 1983)

The SQ3R study procedure can be applied to music, as shown in the following paragraphs. (See Chapter 4.) SQ3R is applied to the music selection "Chumbara," presented in Example 9.25.

EXAMPLE **9.25**

Selection from Secondary School Music Textbook and Study Guide

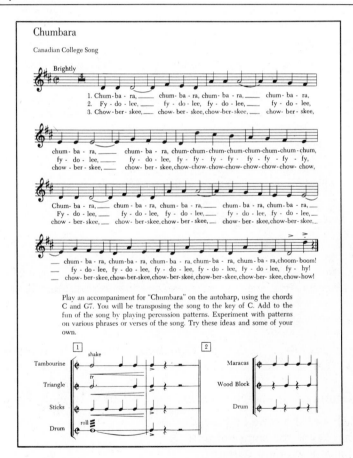

Source: Beth Landis and Lara Haggard, *Exploring Music* (New York: Holt, Rinehart and Winston, Publishers, 1968), p. 150. Reprinted by permission of the publisher.

Study Guide

Introduction

"Chumbara" is a Canadian college song that illustrates the use of nonsense words as lyrics. This music is versatile and is especially adapted for percussion instruments.

Vocabulary

Explain the meaning of each of the following terms or phrases: brightly, autoharp, chords C and C7, transposing to the key of C, percussion patterns, maracas, wood block.

Comprehension

Directions: Place a plus (+) beside statements that are supported by the selection and a minus (−) beside any statements that are not supported by the selection.

    LITERAL

_____ 1. The tambourine, triangle, and sticks can be used to play an accompaniment for this song.

_____ 2. The ♪♩♩♩♩ pattern is suggested for the triangle.

_____ 3. The ♪♩♩♩♩ pattern is suggested for the maracas.

    INTERPRETIVE

_____ 4. This song could be sung at a football rally.

_____ 5. Nonsense words are used in this song to make it difficult to understand.

Directions: Write a short answer or follow the specific directions for each item below.

    APPLIED

6. Can you think of another musical composition that is similar to this one?
7. What instruments (that are not mentioned) could be used to play this music?
8. Transpose this song into the key of C.
9. Make up your own patterns for different parts of the song.

Survey. Read the title. (*The title is "Chumbara."*) Who is the composer? (*Not identified.*) What subtitles do you see? (*Canadian College Song.*)

Question. Compose questions regarding the content to be read. For example:

    , How should the song be played?
    In what key is the song written?
    What is a percussion pattern?
    How many counts does a half-note get in this song?
    How is this song especially adapted for percussion instruments?

Read. Read the selection to answer your questions. When reading music, you may read the rhythms of the music to yourself in order to aid comprehension and retention.

Recite. Answer the questions that you composed in the question step of this study process. Answer any other questions that occur to you.

Review. Reread the content related to any questions that you could not answer. You may apply the content read by identifying examples of the same type of music. You could compare this selection to other college songs, other songs that use nonsense words, and/or other music adapted for percussion instruments.

Example 9.26 illustrates another type of content that music students read.

E X A M P L E **9.26**

Music Text

Structure of the Classical Sonata

Just as the Classical symphony is a sonata cycle for orchestra, the Classical sonata is a sonata cycle for piano, or for piano and another instrument. The number of movements in the cycle varies from three to four. The first movement is always in sonata form, although it is sometimes preceded by a slow introduction. The second movement may be in sonata, ternary, or theme and variations form. In a four-movement work, the third movement is generally a minuet and trio, while the last movement is in rondo or sonata form. Sonatas with only three movements omit the minuet.

Major Composers of Classical Sonatas

Haydn's most important works for piano are sonatas. Mozart too wrote sonatas for solo piano and sonatas for piano and violin. In the early years of the nineteenth century, Franz Schubert (1797–1828) also emerged as a major composer of solo piano sonatas. While many of their works are of fine quality, it is in the sonatas of Beethoven that the epitome of the genre is reached. His works form a bridge between Classical and Romantic styles and foreshadow many later nineteenth-century developments.

Beethoven: Piano Sonata in C Minor, Op. 13

One of Beethoven's finest and best-loved works is the *Piano Sonata in C Minor, Op. 13* (the "Pathétique"), which was published in 1799, quite early in his career. The work is in three movements.

First Movement: Grave; Allegro di molto e con brio; in Sonata Form. The first movement begins with a slow, ominous introduction. This contrasts dramatically with the main part of the movement, which is marked Allegro and cast in sonata form. The structure of the sonata form is clear, but it is further clarified by the return of the slow introductory material between the exposition and the development, and again after the recapitulation. Dramatic contrasts of theme, key, and dynamics are much greater here than in piano works written earlier in the Classical period.

Listening Guide for Beethoven's Piano Sonata in C Minor, *First Movement*

Timbre:	piano
Melody:	dotted motive prominent in introduction; first theme stresses rising motion; second theme more lyrical
Rhythm:	duple meter; tempo of introduction Grave (very slow); main tempo of movement Allegro di molto e con brio (very fast, with spirit)
Harmony:	mainly minor mode; begins in C minor, modulates most significantly to E♭ major, ends in C minor
Texture:	mainly homophonic
Form:	sonata form preceded by slow introduction

Source: Daniel T. Politoske, *Music,* 2nd ed. © 1979, pp. 204, 205. Reprinted by permission of Prentice-Hall, Englewood Cliffs, New Jersey.

SUMMARY

Efficient reading is a prerequisite for successful learning. Unfortunately, some students enroll in vocational and technical courses because they believe the reading demands in these courses are less rigorous than those in academic courses. Vocational and technical reading content is actually very demanding. Most vocational and technical content has a readability level of tenth grade or higher, which is above the reading level of many students who must read these materials.

The complexity of reading vocational and technical materials is increased by the fact that they usually include content from a variety of disciplines and subjects. For example, students in agriculture classes must read scientific and mathematics content, directions, and material on auto mechanics, as well as graphs, charts, diagrams, and pictures. Human environmental science, business education, industrial technology, and music students also are exposed to a wide variety of reading content.

Vocational and technical reading materials are written and organized to impart information, provide directions, and give solutions to problems. Teachers should plan to use vocabulary strategies, advance organizers, study guides, preview guides, directed reading lessons, mapping, and SQ3R to help students comprehend these materials. Systematic reading instruction as a part of content instruction will improve students' achievement in these courses.

SELF-TEST

1. Why do vocational students need reading instruction? (a) So they can read vocational materials in class (b) So they can read well enough to get a job (c) Both *a* and *b* (d) Neither *a* nor *b*
2. Why do poor readers often choose to study vocational subjects? (a) The subjects are more abstract in nature. (b) The students think they will be required to do less reading. (c) The students want to learn to read. (d) None of the above
3. Vocational materials usually include three writing types. Which of the following is *not* one of the three? (a) Factual information (b) How-to-do-it material (c) Stories (d) Problem solving
4. The technical vocabulary of industrial technology, business education, and human environmental science is which of the following? (a) Often concrete so it can be illustrated and demonstrated (b) Hard to pronounce (c) Difficult to teach (d) Abstract
5. How must the reader of vocational materials read directions? (a) Quickly (b) Skip them (c) Precisely and carefully (d) Memorize them
6. Why do readers of vocational subjects have an advantage when they read directions? (a) The directions are short. (b) They are easy. (c) The reader receives feedback regarding the success of his or her reading. (d) Following directions is fun.
7. What factors do *not* influence the rate used by the reader of vocational materials? (a) Purposes for reading (b) Type of content (c) Familiarity with the subject (d) None of the above
8. Why is critical reading important to industrial technology students? (a) They must evaluate material on labels. (b) They must pronounce the words. (c) Both *a* and *b* (d) Neither *a* nor *b*
9. Which of the following references might a business education student use? (a) A shorthand book (b) Interest tables (c) *Encyclopaedia Britannica* (d) All of the above
10. Which of the following is *not* a reason for critical reading in human environmental science? (a) To evaluate new equipment (b) To evaluate the contents of food products (c) To select recipes (d) To read for pleasure
11. Which content area discussed in this chapter is not complicated by the number of different disciplines involved in its written content?

(a) Mathematics (b) Industrial technology (c) Agriculture (d) Business education

12. What techniques can teachers use to help students read music more effectively? (a) Teach the sounds and rhythms students will encounter (b) Avoid the relationship between sight and sound (c) Read only the narrative portions of the music text (d) Read only the lyrics

13. Which of the following types of content are music students likely to encounter? (a) Reviews and critiques of performances (b) Musical compositions (c) Music history (d) All of these

THOUGHT QUESTIONS

1. Why do the reading materials for vocational subjects give the impression that less reading is required in these areas?

2. How does the reading in vocational subjects compare with the reading in academic subjects?

3. What kinds of reading tasks does the reader of vocational subjects encounter?

4. What strategies can teachers use to help students comprehend vocational materials?

5. How would you respond to a colleague who stated that it is not necessary for vocational students to read?

6. Discuss the eclectic nature of agriculture and human environmental science. How can teachers effectively teach the variety of content in these subjects?

ENRICHMENT ACTIVITIES

1. Select a set of directions from a subject treated in this chapter and rewrite the directions in simpler language for poor readers.

2. Develop an annotated bibliography of materials that could constitute a classroom library in one of the subjects treated in this chapter. Indicate readability levels whenever possible.

3. Make a dictionary of terms for use in one of the areas treated in this chapter. You can use drawings and pictures from magazines, catalogs, and newspapers to illustrate the dictionary.

4. Collect pamphlets, magazines, newspapers, and library books that could be used to develop understanding of vocabulary and concepts in a subject treated in this chapter.

5. Select a section in a textbook on a subject treated in this chapter and make a reading lesson plan for it.

6. Prepare a presentation, describing how you would help teach a student to read one of the following: (a) an invoice or balance sheet; (b) a con-

tract; (c) a tax form; (d) a physical education activity or game; (e) a critical review of art or music; (f) a specialized handbook; (g) a reference source.

7. Read several of the articles cited in the Bibliography on one of the subjects treated in this chapter. Report to the class on suggestions for teaching reading in this area.

8. Examine materials from industrial technology, business education, and human environmental science textbooks. Locate examples of the common reading problems.

9. Prepare a vocabulary activity to teach new terms in a textbook chapter.

10. Prepare a study guide for a selection from one of the subjects discussed in this chapter.

11. Use a readability formula and compute the readability level of a textbook for one of the content areas discussed in this chapter.

BIBLIOGRAPHY

Badiali, B. "Reading in the Content Area of Music." In M. Dupuis (ed.), *Reading in the Content Areas: Research for Teachers.* Newark, Del.: International Reading Association, 1984, pp. 42–47.

Banks, J. "Secretarial Survival Skills." *Business Education Forum,* 33 (December 1978), 45–48.

Daines, D. *Reading in the Content Areas: Strategies for Teachers.* Glenview, Ill.: Scott, Foresman and Company, 1982.

Diehl, W., and L. Mikulecky. "The Nature of Reading at Work." *Journal of Reading,* 24 (December 1980), 221–227.

Elliott, C. "The Music-Reading Dilemma." *Music Education Journal,* 59 (February 1982), pp. 33–34.

Frager, A. and L. Thompson. "Reading Instruction and Music Education: Getting in Tune." *Journal of Reading,* 27 (December 1983), 202–206.

Gahn, S. "A Practical Guide for Teaching Writing in the Content Areas." *Journal of Reading,* 32 (March 1989), 525–531.

Heinemann, S. "Can Job-Related Performance Tasks Be Used to Diagnose Secretaries' Reading and Writing Skills?" *Journal of Reading,* 23 (December 1979), 239–243.

Hicks, C. "Sound Before Sight: Strategies for Teaching Music Reading." *Music Education Journal* (April 1980), 53–67.

Lee, H. "Dealing with Reading in Industrial Arts." *Journal of Reading,* 24 (May 1981), 663–666.

Mateja, J. "Musical Cloze: Background, Purpose, and Sample." *The Reading Teacher's Journal of Business Education,* 35 (January 1982), 444–448.

Mikulecky, L. "Job Literacy: The Relationship Between School Preparation and Workplace Actuality." *Reading Research Quarterly,* 17 (1982), 400–419.

Miller, P. "Reading Demands in a High-Technology Industry." *Journal of Reading,* 26 (November 1982), 109–121.

Moore, D., J. Readence, and R. Rickelman. *Prereading Activities for Content Area Reading and Learning.* 2nd ed. Newark, Del.: International Reading Association (1989).

Morgan, H. and S. Berg-O'Halloran. "Using Music as a Text." *Journal of Reading,* 32 (February 1989), 458–459.

408

Noe, K. "Technical Reading Technique: A Briefcase Reading Strategy." *Journal of Reading*, 27 (December 1983), 234–237.

Razek, J., G. Hosch, and D. Pearl. "Readability of Accounting Textbooks." *Journal of Business Education* (October 1982), 23–26.

Rush, R., A. Moe, and R. Storlie. *Occupational Literacy Education*. Newark, Del.: International Reading Association, 1986, pp. 66–159.

Shugarman, S. and J. Hurst. "Purposeful Paraphrasing: Promoting a Nontrivial Pursuit for Meaning." *Journal of Reading*, 29 (February 1986), 407–414.

Sticht, T., W. Armstrong, D. Hickey, and J. Caylor. *Cast-Off Youth: Policy and Training Methods from the Military Experience*. New York: Praeger, 1987.

Sticht, T. *Literacy and Vocational Competence*. Columbus, Ohio: National Center for Research in Vocational Education, 1978.

Stoodt, B. *Literacy in an Information Age*. Greensboro, N.C.: Center for Creative Leadership, 1985.

Tanner, M. "Reading in Music Class." *Music Education Journal*, 60 (December 1983), 41–45.

10

ASSESSMENT

PROCEDURES

OVERVIEW

A major purpose of this chapter is to assist the content area teacher in determining whether students possess the reading and study skills necessary to deal successfully with course materials. To perform this evaluation, the content teacher must be aware of the reading and study skills appropriate to the particular subject. Salvia and Ysseldyke (1988, p. 5) describe the process of educational assessment well when they say that it is "a multifaceted process that involves far more than the administration of a test. When we assess students, we consider the way they perform a variety of tasks in a variety of settings or contexts, the meaning of their performances in terms of the total functioning of the individual, and the likely explanations for those performances. Good assessment procedures take into consideration the fact that anyone's performance on any task is influenced by the demands of the task itself, by the history and characteristics the individual brings to the task, and by the factors inherent in the setting in which the assessment is carried out." Such assessment is data collection designed to help teachers determine problem areas and make instructional decisions.

This chapter discusses five assessment procedures: (1) norm-referenced tests of reading achievement; (2) criterion-referenced tests; (3) informal measures of reading achievement; (4) other informal measures; and (5) process and holistic assessments. These are not all mutually exclusive measures; for example, process and holistic assessments may be either norm-referenced or informal.

PURPOSE-SETTING QUESTIONS

As you read this chapter, try to answer these questions:

1. What are some representative norm-referenced reading tests, and how are the test results useful to teachers?
2. What are criterion-referenced tests?
3. What are some informal measures of reading achievement, and how can the results of each be used to help teachers plan instructional programs?
4. What types of questions and record-keeping systems may be utilized for observation checklists related to reading achievement?
5. What are some self-appraisal techniques to help students evaluate their own reading strengths and weaknesses?
6. What measures of attitudes toward reading are helpful to the teacher in individualizing the instructional program?
7. What is a "reading interest inventory," and how can the results be used by the teacher to enhance an instructional program?
8. What is meant by process and holistic assessment?

KEY VOCABULARY

As you read this chapter, check your understanding of these terms:

norm-referenced reading test
informal reading inventory
group reading inventory
graded word list
criterion-referenced tests
survey reading test
validity
test norms
grade equivalent
percentile rank
stanine

normal curve equivalents
independent reading level
instructional reading level
frustration reading level
capacity (potential) reading
    level
skills inventory or test
cloze procedure
reading autobiography
holistic and process
    assessment

Norm-Referenced Tests

Content teachers may administer and interpret certain types of norm-referenced tests, especially survey achievement tests, to check student performance in a wide range of areas: reading, listening, language, mathematics, science, social studies, reference skills, and others. Test results indicate the relative achievement of the groups tested in these areas. Results also can be used to determine how a student's performance on a subtest in one subject compares with his or her performance on other subtests in a test battery. Teachers also can learn how a student's performance on a test compares with his or her earlier or later performance on the same test.

Scores from two different kinds of norm-referenced reading tests cannot be compared easily because the tests probably differ in purpose, length, and degree of difficulty. Even the results of the same test administered on successive days may vary, depending on the reliability of the test and factors related to the student.

Scores on Norm-Referenced Tests

Results of norm-referenced tests may be reported as (a) grade scores or grade equivalents, (2) percentile ranks, (3) stanines, and (4) normal curve equivalents.

Grade equivalent indicates the grade level, in years and months, for which a given score was the average score in the referencing sample. For example, if a score of 25 has the grade equivalent of 8.1, 25 was the average score of pupils in the norm group who were in the first month of the eighth grade. If a pupil (not in the norm group) who is in the first month of the eighth grade were to take the same test and score 25 correct, his or her performance would be at "grade level," or average for his or her grade placement. If that pupil were to get 30 right, or a grade equivalent of 9.1, he or she would have scored as well as the typical ninth grader in the first month of the school year. Similarly, a 6.3 grade equivalent for an eighth grader would mean that the student scored the same as the average pupil in the third month of sixth grade.

Some words of caution need to be offered about grade equivalents. Grade equivalents do not indicate the appropriate grade placement for a student. A score of 9.0 indicates only that the student who is just beginning the ninth grade had 50 items correct; it does not mean that the student who had 50 items correct can necessarily read 9.0 grade level material. In fact, the grade score a student gets on a silent reading test usually indicates that material of that level is too difficult for the student, since many of these tests give frustration level (the level at which a reader cannot perform adequately) scores, not instructional level (the level at which a reader can function adequately with assistance) scores. Certainly a grade equivalent of 9.0 does not mean that a fifth-grade test taker can read as well as a ninth grader. Another problem is that "[b]ecause the average reading level of the population flattens out during junior high school (Grades 7–9), grade equivalents have almost no meaning at these grade levels" (Lewandowski and Martens, 1990). Moreover, the grade equivalents from grade level to grade level (for example from 9.0 to 10.0) are partly hypothetical and are arrived at statistically, since tests are usually standardized at only one or two places within each grade. Because of these and other misinterpretations, some test publishers are discouraging the use of grade equivalent scores. The Board of Directors of the International Reading Association, after noting the serious misuses of grade equivalents, has recommended that grade equivalent interpretations be eliminated from tests.

Using percentiles, stanines, or normal curve equivalents is generally more acceptable than using grade equivalents to interpret test results, since grade equivalents are so frequently misinterpreted. Therefore, content area teachers need to understand these types of test results in order to apply the information gained from tests to classroom practice. Explanations of these methods of reporting results follow.

Percentile rank expresses a score in terms of its position within a set of 100 scores. The percentile rank indicates the percent of scores of the norm group that are equal to or lower than the given score. Thus a result ranked in the 35th percentile is regarded as equivalent to or surpassing the results of 35 percent of those in the norm group. A student who scores in the 83rd percentile according to the local school's norms may only score in the 53rd percentile if his or her score is based on national norms because of the differences in the sample populations on which the norms were based.

A *stanine* ranks a test score in relation to other scores on that test. (The term is derived from the words standard and nine.) A stanine is expressed as a value from one to nine on a nine-point scale. Thus, the mean score of the standard population has a stanine value of 5. Verbal descriptions often assigned to stanines are as follows:

stanine 9 — highest performance
stanines 7 and 8 — above average
stanines 4, 5, and 6 — average
stanines 2 and 3 — below average
stanine 1 — lowest performance

Stanines and percentiles may be compared as follows:

Stanines	Percentiles
9	96–99
8	90–95
7	78–89
6	60–77
5	41–59
4	23–40
3	11–22
2	5–10
1	1–4

Normal curve equivalents (NCEs) are used in some states and school systems. NCEs are represented on a scale of 1 to 99 with a mean of 50. They have many of the characteristics of percentile ranks but have the additional advantage of being based on an equal-interval scale. This scale allows a meaningful comparison to be made between different achievement test batteries and/or different tests within the same test battery. For example, if a student receives an NCE score of 62 on the mathematics test of a battery and an NCE of 53 on the reading test, it would be correct to say that the mathematics score is 9 points higher than the reading score. Tables that show the conversions of test scores to NCEs are usually supplied by test publishers.

Readers interested in further study of measurement concepts can read Salvia and Ysseldyke (1988).

Criteria for Choosing Norm-Referenced Tests

A norm-referenced test that is selected for use should meet certain criteria. Its norms should be based on a population that is similar to the population being tested, and it should have high reliability and validity.

A test is inappropriate if the sample population used to establish norms is significantly different from the class or group to be tested. A description of the norm population is usually contained in the test manual. Even a test that is based on populations of students from a wide variety of rural and urban centers, of various social and ability levels, and of different sexes and races is not always the most appropriate. Some publishers have begun to standardize tests according to a particular geographic region or a particular educational reference group. In many cases, local norms may be more appropriate to use, because the students in a particular locality may be more homogeneous in terms of particular social, ethnic, and other factors than is the national population. The ways that students may differ are discussed in detail in Chapter 5. Salvia and Ysseldyke (1988) point out that, when the performance of a student is compared with that of a normative sample population in an effort to predict the student's future behavior, an assumption is made that the student has had a chance to acquire skills and concepts comparable to those of the students in the sample population. If that assumption is incorrect, the test is unfair to the students because it cannot indicate how well they will perform if they are given the opportunities for acquiring skills and concepts that the students in the sample population have already had. On the other hand, the same test can fairly show that the student does not *currently* have a particular skill or concept.

Some people feel that students who are different in some ways from the majority of the population have an unfair disadvantage in taking many tests because the tests contain a cultural bias. Any time that the background experiences of a group of students differ from those of the sample population on which the test was standardized, the test's norms are inappropriate for that group, and relying on the results of this test may lead to incorrect educational decisions. It is important to note that the cultural bias that the test would contain against this group of students would be based on variant experiential backgrounds, *not* specifically on race or ethnic origins (Salvia and Ysseldyke, 1988).

The concepts of validity and reliability need to be understood thoroughly by teachers who are using tests. A valid norm-referenced reading test represents a balanced and adequate sampling of the instructional outcomes (e.g., knowledge and skills) that it is intended to cover. Validity is best judged by comparing the test content with the related courses of study, instructional materials, and educational goals of the class. Evidence about validity is nearly always given in the test manual of directions or in a technical information pamphlet; such information may be checked against the impartial opinions of educational professionals and should be given a careful inspection to see if the test is designed to measure what the teacher wants to measure.

Some people believe that tests that do not yield the same pattern of scores when administered to various groups of students and do not exhibit approximately equal means for all of the subgroups in the sample population are not valid. Johnston (1984) points out that this makes test validity a sociopolitical issue. He believes that placing these constraints on test construction can make the tests invalid for other reasons. Test makers would have to construct tests that were not influenced by differences in prior knowledge. Reading comprehension depends so much on prior knowledge to predict outcomes, make inferences, and administer self-correction when misconceptions result from the reading that this would be very difficult. If the tests were set up with only passages about which none of the students had any prior knowledge, they would no longer resemble normal reading tasks, in which prior knowledge is used constantly.

In addition to measuring the skills it claims to measure (validity) and having subtests that are long enough to yield reasonably accurate scores, a test should not result in a chance score, with students obtaining high scores by luck, guessing, or other factors (reliability). The reliability of a test refers to the degree to which the test gives consistent results.

One way that test authors establish reliability is to give the same test twice to a large group of pupils. If each student achieves practically the same score in both testing situations, the test is highly consistent and reliable. If many students attain higher scores in one testing situation than in the other, the test has low reliability. Another method of measuring reliability is to compare students' scores on the odd-numbered items with their scores on the even-numbered items; if they are in the same rank order, or if they have a high correlation, the test is reliable. A third method of measuring reliability is to compare scores obtained on one form of a test to those obtained by the same students on an equivalent form. When measuring the level of achievement of an individual student, only a test of high reliability should be used, since it is necessary to find that student's specific, not comparative, level of achievement. To be considered reliable, tests should have internal consistency reliability coefficients of .85 or above and test-retest reliability of .70 or above (Lewandowski and Martens, 1990). Although a test of low reliability cannot be valid, high reliability does not guarantee that a test is valid.

Readers who are interested in more detailed descriptions of particular tests can consult the following collections of reviews on reading tests.

Mitchell, James V., Jr., ed. *The Ninth Mental Measurement Yearbook.* 2 volumes. Lincoln, Neb.: Buros Institute of Mental Measurements, 1985. (A 1988 *Supplement to the Ninth Mental Measurements Yearbook* edited by Jane C. Conoley, James V. Mitchell, and Jack J. Kramer is also available.)

————. *Tests in Print, III.* Lincoln, Neb.: Buros Institute of Mental Measurements, 1983.

Keyser, Daniel J., and Richard C. Sweetland, eds. *Test Critiques, Vols. I–VI.* Kansas City, Mo.: Test Corporation of America, 1987.

————. *Test Critiques Compendium: Reviews of Major Tests from the Test Critiques Series.* Kansas City, Mo.: Test Corporation of America, 1987.

Compton, Carolyn. *85 Tests for Remedial and Special Education.* Belmont, Calif.: David S. Lake Publisher, 1989.

A service is provided by the Buros Institute of Mental Measurements that teachers should find valuable. It consists of a computerized data base that can be accessed through most major libraries. The *Ninth Mental Measurements Yearbook* is currently in the data base, and the new information that will appear in the *Tenth Mental Measurements Yearbook* is being added on a monthly basis (Salvia and Ysseldyke, 1988). In addition to these sources, articles dealing with testing that often appear in professional journals (for example, the *Journal of Reading*) may prove useful.

Norm-Referenced Tests of Reading Achievement

Norm-referenced reading tests yield objective data about reading performance. They are designed so that each response to a test item is subject to only one interpretation. Authors of norm-referenced tests sample large populations of students to determine the appropriateness of test items, and they seek to verify the validity and reliability of test results so that schools can be confident that the tests measure what they purport to measure and do so consistently.

There are various types of norm-referenced reading tests:

1. Survey tests, which measure general achievement in a given area — in this case, reading.
2. Study skills tests, which measure a student's ability to utilize techniques essential for enhancing comprehension and retention, such as study methods, locating and organizing information, and adjusting rate of reading.
3. Diagnostic tests, which help teachers identify specific strengths and weaknesses. An analysis of test results may suggest causes for the identified strengths and weaknesses.

Survey Tests and Study Skills Tests

Of the three types of norm-referenced reading tests described earlier, the content teacher will have most direct contact with survey tests and study skills tests.

A reading survey test measures general achievement in reading. The results can show how well students are performing. By examining a student's score in relation to the scores of others, the teacher obtains an impression of the student's reading achievement. Looking at a number of students' scores gives an indication of the range of reading achievement in the class.

TABLE **10.1**

Range of Reading Scores in a Tenth-Grade Class

Grade Score	Number of Students
15.0–15.9	1
14.0–14.9	1
13.0–13.9	4
12.0–12.9	4
11.0–11.9	2
10.0–10.9	6
9.0– 9.9	2
8.0– 8.9	3
7.0– 7.9	5
6.0– 6.9	1
5.0– 5.9	1
	$N = 30$

For example, the distribution in Table 10.1 approximates the range of reading achievement scores for a tenth-grade class. A cursory examination of the distribution shows that one-third of the students are performing well below grade level, one-third within a year or two of grade level, and one-third well above grade level. A teacher who has this information at the beginning of the school year knows that it is necessary to make provisions for individual differences.

A single score on a survey test represents the student's overall reading achievement and does not reveal how the student will perform on specific reading tasks. However, some reading survey tests designed for secondary school students have separate sections on vocabulary, comprehension, and reading rate. Such tests yield separate scores for each section. A wise teacher is not merely concerned with a student's total achievement score but wants to determine if the student is equally strong in all areas tested or if he or she is stronger in one area than another. Furthermore, a careful examination of student responses to individual test items might provide the teacher with information about more specific reading needs. One way to learn more from testing is to go over the test items with the student to see if he or she can explain his or her responses. It is possible that correct responses were reached in inappropriate ways or that a student guessed at a number of the answers.

Some survey and reading achievement tests include:

1. *California Achievement Tests.* Forms E and F. Monterey, Calif.: California Test Bureau, McGraw-Hill, 1985. (Includes subtests on reading vocabulary, comprehension, reference skills, and content areas of language and mathematics. Level 17 for 6.6–7.9; Level 18 for 7.6–9.9; and Level 19 for 9.6–12.9.)

2. *Stanford Test of Academic Skills.* Cleveland, Ohio: The Psychological Corporation, 1983. (Includes subtests on reading vocabulary and comprehension, and content areas of mathematics, spelling, English, social studies, and science. Level 1 for grades 8 through 12; Level 2 for grades 9 through 13.)

3. *Comprehensive Test of Basic Skills.* Monterey, Calif.: CTB/McGraw-Hill, 1981. (Includes subtests on reading vocabulary, comprehension, reference skills, and content areas of spelling, language, mathematics, science, and social studies.)

4. *Gates-MacGinitie Reading Tests.* 2nd ed. Chicago: Riverside, 1978. (Includes subtests on vocabulary and comprehension. Level E for grades 7–9; Level F for grades 10–12.)

Notice that the first three survey tests listed provide achievement measures in some of the content areas, whereas the last two tests provide information about reading achievement only. In addition to being interested in the results of the content subtests, content teachers should be concerned with the reading achievement levels of students in terms of knowing what printed materials are appropriate for study. Reference skills tests measure the student's ability to utilize essential study techniques, such as study methods, locating and organizing information, and adjusting rate of reading. Such techniques are of major concern to content area teachers, since these skills are very important aspects of learning from texts. Using results from such tests, the content area teacher may need to include material to develop these study skills within the framework of the content course; or he or she may need to refer low-achieving students to the special reading teacher, who, in turn, could use the content textbook to help develop the students' comprehension, retention, and study skills.

Diagnostic Tests

Diagnostic reading tests are used most frequently by special teachers of reading. Content teachers find it helpful to have some basic information about this type of test in order to discuss test results with a special reading teacher.

Diagnostic reading tests help to locate specific strengths and weaknesses of readers and sometimes suggest possible reasons for them. Such tests often include subtests for comprehension, vocabulary, word identification skills, and rate of reading. Group diagnostic tests (such as the *Stanford Diagnostic Reading Test*, New York: Harcourt Brace Jovanovich, 1984) may be given by reading specialists or sometimes by classroom teachers. Administration of individual diagnostic reading tests requires experience and training, and most classroom teachers do not have sufficient training. Actually, even if classroom teachers were experienced in administration of diagnostic tests, time constraints make their use in the content area classroom impractical.

Several oral reading tests are available for students at the secondary level. These tests must be given on an individual basis. Presumably the kinds of errors a student makes when reading orally serve as a clue to the kinds of errors he or she makes when reading silently. This may or may not be true, but oral reading tests are valuable diagnostic tools for some students with serious reading problems. Oral reading tests usually check for accuracy of word recognition, comprehension, and reading rate.

Criterion-Referenced Tests

Criterion-referenced tests (CRTs) have become popular in recent years. Whereas norm-referenced tests compare the test taker's performance with that of others, CRTs check the test taker against a given performance criterion as a predetermined standard. Thus a criterion-referenced test might read: "Given ten paragraphs at the ninth-grade reading level, the student can identify the main idea in eight of them." In short, a CRT indicates whether or not the test taker has mastered a particular objective or skill rather than how well his or her performance compares with that of others. A norm-referenced test, on the other hand, may indicate that the student can identify the main idea of a paragraph better than 90 percent of the test takers in his or her age group.

The results of criterion-referenced tests can be used as instructional prescriptions; that is, if a student cannot perform the task of identifying the contraction for *cannot*, the need for instruction in that area is apparent. These tests are therefore useful in day-to-day decisions about instruction.

However, there are a number of unresolved issues related to criterion-referenced tests. For example, the level of success demanded is one issue. Often the passing level is set arbitrarily at 80 or 90 percent, but there is no agreement as to the nature of mastery or how to measure it. Additionally, many criterion-referenced tests give the appearance that there are hundreds of discrete reading skills that must be mastered separately, overlooking the fact that the skills are highly interactive and must be integrated with each other if effective reading is to occur. There is some question about whether CRTs can measure complex domains such as critical/creative reading skills, reading appreciation, or attitude toward reading. CRTs may also be questioned in terms of reliability and validity. Any type of test *may* measure only knowledge of rules rather than ability to use them, and a short set of items over a particular reading objective can be less than reliable, particularly in terms of individual measurement.

It seems likely that both criterion-referenced tests and norm-referenced tests will continue to be important reading assessment tools, serving different purposes. In fact, both kinds of interpretation — individual and comparative — are offered by a number of tests, including the *Stanford Achievement Test* and the *Metropolitan Achievement Test*.

Below is a listing of some criterion-referenced tests:

1. *MULTISCORE*. Riverside Publishing Company, 8420 Bryn Mawr Avenue, Chicago, Ill., 60631.
2. *Objectives-Referenced Bank of Items and Tests* (ORBIT). CTB/McGraw-Hill Publishing Company, Del Monte Research Park, Monterey, Calif., 93940.
3. *Prescriptive Reading Inventory*. CTB/McGraw-Hill Publishing Co., Del Monte Research Park, Monterey, Calif., 93940.
4. *Reading Yardsticks*. Riverside Publishing Company, 8420 Bryn Mawr Avenue, Chicago, Ill., 60631.

This listing includes CRTs that are related to reading programs. These are utilized mainly by the special teacher of reading, but content teachers may also make frequent use of certain CRTs. They may construct these measures themselves, using banks of criterion-referenced test items that are available for all subject areas from some state educational departments or from places such as Educational Testing Services, in Princeton, New Jersey. Teachers may choose appropriate items from such collections to construct tailor-made CRTs, or they may construct their own items.

For many years, content teachers have been using their own criterion-referenced measures to assess the results of instruction. In such cases, definite instructional objectives are tested, and there is a definite standard of judgment or criterion for "passing." Example 10.1 shows an objective that is measured by six items on a test prepared by a teacher. The criterion for demonstrating mastery of this objective is set at five out of six; that is, the student must answer five out of six items correctly to show mastery.

Note that each question in Example 10.1 is related to the objective. The criterion level for "passing" must be determined by the teacher. Results give the teacher precise information concerning what each student can or cannot do; the test results can be used to improve classroom instruction. Thus, criterion-referenced tests are useful for planning further instruction.

420

EXAMPLE *10.1*

Criterion-Referenced Test

Objective: Utilizing the information found on the content pages of the almanac.

Directions: Find answers to the following:

1. Who was the fifteenth president of the United States?
2. Who holds the world record for high diving?
3. What was the Academy Award winner for the Best Picture of 1979?
4. What are the names of the Kentucky Derby winner of 1985 and the jockey who rode the horse to victory?
5. Where is the deepest lake in the United States?
6. How many American League baseball teams have won the World Series since 1965?

Informal Tests

Informal tests (tests not standardized against a specific norm or objective) are an invaluable aid to the content teacher. Although some are commercially available, many are constructed by the teachers themselves. These informal measures offer the content teacher ongoing assessment information about both the students' reading achievement and their nonreading behaviors and attitudes that may affect their reading.

Informal Tests of Reading Achievement

There are several informal measures of reading achievement that can be useful to the teacher in revealing student reading achievement. Eight of these measures are discussed in the sections that follow: (1) sight vocabulary assessment, (2) assessment of background knowledge, (3) group reading inventory, (4) skills inventories, (5) informal reading inventories, (6) cloze procedure, (7) observation checklists, and (8) self-assessment techniques.

Sight Vocabulary Assessment

In this section, we will focus on one informal diagnostic measure of sight vocabulary. The San Diego Quick Assessment (LaPray and Ross, 1969) is a graded word list that may be used to determine approximate reading level and detect errors in word analysis. The information provided by the assessment may be used to group students or to help teachers select appropriate reading materials for them. To administer this device, the teacher should follow these steps:

1. Type each list of ten words on an index card.
2. Begin with a card that is at least two years below the student's grade level.
3. Ask the student to read the words aloud; if he or she misreads any on the initial list, drop to easier lists until no errors are made.
4. Encourage the student to attempt to read the unfamiliar words aloud so that the techniques the student uses for word identification can be determined.
5. Have the student read from increasingly difficult lists until he or she misses at least three words on a list.

The level at which a student misses no more than one out of ten words is a rough indication of his or her *independent reading level* (the level of material that he or she can read successfully without teacher aid). Two errors on a list indicate an approximate *instructional level* (the reading level of the material to be used with teacher guidance). Three or more errors indicate that the level is too difficult for the student (called the *frustration level*).

Lists are available for preprimer level up to the eleventh grade. For practical purposes, only the lists for grades 4 through 11 are presented in Table 10.2. This type of vocabulary assessment will give the content area teacher only a rough estimate of the student's reading ability. Such data can be used when there is a need to match a student quickly with printed material of appropriate difficulty level for varying situations, such as independent or instructional reading. This is a particularly helpful assessment to administer to a student who is new to the class. One important caution: this test gives information about the reader's ability to recognize words out of context, not his or her ability to comprehend material in which these words appear. Also, the use of graded word lists does not produce as accurate an estimate of the reading levels as can be obtained from other measures, such as informal reading inventories.

Assessment of Background Knowledge

Since the background knowledge of the students plays a vital role in their comprehension of reading material (see Chapter 3), it is wise to assess background knowledge about a topic before asking students to read about that topic. When prior knowledge of the topics covered in the reading passages is lacking because students with diverse home backgrounds and mental capabilities have been exposed to or have acquired different sets of background information, teachers should take steps to develop missing concepts before assigning the reading. Students with varying backgrounds will often have difficulties with concepts in different content fields.

Background knowledge may be assessed in a variety of ways. Oral

TABLE 10.2

Graded Word List for Quick Assessment

Grade 4	Grade 5	Grade 6	Grade 7
decided	scanty	bridge	amber
served	business	commercial	dominion
amazed	develop	abolish	sundry
silent	considered	trucker	capillary
wrecked	discussed	apparatus	impetuous
improved	behaved	elementary	blight
certainly	splendid	comment	wrest
entered	acquainted	necessity	enumerate
realized	escaped	gallery	daunted
interrupted	grim	relativity	condescend

Grade 8	Grade 9	Grade 10	Grade 11
capacious	conscientious	zany	galore
limitation	isolation	jerkin	rotunda
pretext	molecule	nausea	capitalism
intrigue	ritual	gratuitous	prevaricate
delusion	momentous	linear	risible
immaculate	vulnerable	inept	exonerate
ascent	kinship	legality	superannuate
acrid	conservation	aspen	luxuriate
binocular	jaunty	amnesty	piebald
embarkment	inventive	barometer	crunch

Source: M. LaPray and R. Ross, "The Graded Word List: A Quick Gauge of Reading Ability." *Journal of Reading*, 12 (January 1969), 305–307. Reprinted with permission of the authors and the International Reading Association.

methods of assessment may be better for less advanced students because they may actually know more than their writing skills allow them to express.

Holmes and Roser (1987) suggest that there are five ways to assess prior knowledge: free recall, word association, structured questions, recognition, and unstructured questions. Free recall involves asking students to tell or write down all the facts they know about a topic. It is a time-efficient method, but it is more successful with older skilled readers than with younger students and less skilled older readers, who do not appear to be able to retrieve their knowledge as easily. Word association involves giving the students words that are subtopics of the main topic, one at a time, and asking them to tell everything they can think of about the terms as they relate to the main topic. This technique usually provides more information about prior knowledge than does free recall. The teacher may prepare structured questions about subtopics of the main topic to probe prior knowledge, but this approach requires expertise in question formulation and time for preparation of questions. Structured questioning offers the largest amount of information of the five types of assessments suggested by Holmes and Roser, and it provides the largest number of facts per minute of administration time. When a recognition task is used, questions about the subtopics of the main topic with a modified multiple-choice format are used. There may be more than one correct answer to each question. This method is relatively efficient and effective in assessment of prior knowledge. Unstructured discussion of the students' prior experiences with a topic is the least effective of the five approaches mentioned.

Langer (1981) developed the PreReading Plan (PReP) technique to help teachers to assess students' background knowledge about a content area topic and to activate prior knowledge they possess about the topic before they are asked to read the material. The PReP is basically a discussion activity for a group of approximately ten students, in which the teacher selects a key word, phrase, or picture about the topic to start the discussion. First, the teacher has the students brainstorm about the presented stimulus by saying something like, "What do you think of when you hear (the particular word or phrase) or see (the selected picture)?" The responses are recorded on the board. Then the students are asked what made them think of the responses that they gave, which helps them to develop an awareness of the network of ideas they possess in their experiential backgrounds and exposes them to the associations that their classmates have made. Finally, the teacher asks them if they have any new ideas about the word, phrase, or picture related to the topic of the content passage before they begin to read the text. The opportunity to elaborate on their prior knowledge often results in more refined responses than those given previously, since they can use input from others to help in shaping responses. After the discussion ends, the teacher can analyze the responses to discover the students' probable ability to recall the content material after they have read it. Students who have much prior knowledge about the topic under discussion usually respond with superordinate concepts, definitions, analogies, and comparisons with other concepts. Those with some prior knowledge about the topic generally respond with examples or attributes of the concept. Those with little prior information about the topic usually make low-level associations, offering word parts (prefixes, suffixes, and/or root words) or sound-alike words or sharing not quite relevant personal experiences. Initial responses may fall into one category and responses during the final elaboration may fall into a higher category of knowledge, showing that the process may activate knowledge as well as assess it. Langer states that responses that show much and some prior knowledge indicate that the students will be able to read the text with sufficient understanding. Responses that show little prior knowledge indicate that the students need direct instruction related to relevant concepts before they are asked to read the material.

Group Reading Inventory

The content teacher may administer a group reading inventory (GRI) before asking students to use a particular text for study. A GRI of content material may be given by having students read a passage of 1,000 to 2,000 words from their textbooks and then asking them certain types of questions. This procedure can give some indication of how well students will be able to read a particular textbook. Content books to be studied should be written on a student's instructional or independent reading level (instructional for material to be worked on in class with the teacher's assistance; independent for material to be used by the students outside of class); trade and supplementary books should be on a student's independent level, since they are generally used for outside reading assignments. Therefore, by using a Group Reading Inventory, the content teacher can decide whether or not to use material from a particular book for in-class or homework assignments and can decide which materials are inappropriate for use with particular students at any time.

Usually the selection used in an inventory is chosen from an early part of the textbook, but it should be material that has not been read previously by the students. The teacher introduces the selection and directs the students to read it for the purpose of answering certain kinds of questions. As students read, the teacher writes the time on the chalkboard at 15-second intervals; each student writes down the last time recorded when he or she finishes reading the passage. Later, a words-per-minute score is computed by dividing the time into the total number of words in the passage. For example, if the passage is 1,000 words long and the student reads it in 4 minutes, the student would divide 4 into 1,000 to get a 250-words-per-minute score. When he or she is finished reading, the student closes the book and answers a series of questions of such types as

1. vocabulary (word meaning, word recognition, context, synonyms, antonyms, affixes),
2. literal comprehension (main ideas, significant details, sequence, following directions), and
3. higher-order comprehension (inferential and evaluative).

A sample GRI from a secondary level history textbook is provided in Example 10.2.

Materials are suitable for instructional purposes if the student can comprehend 75 percent of what he or she reads (answers six out of eight questions correctly). If students can comprehend 75 percent of what they read, their comprehension will probably increase if teachers introduce specialized vocabulary words, help with comprehension, teach a study method, and provide specific purposes for reading. Of course, students have many different reading levels, depending on their interests and the background information they possess on any specific topic. Thus, there is a need to apply GRIs to

E X A M P L E **10.2**

Sample Group Reading Inventory

Name: _____ Date: _____

Motivation Statement: Read to find out why the Confederation Congress was unable to settle its foreign problems.

Selection: Dealing with Other Countries

The men who represent one country as it deals with other nations are called diplomats. Their work is called *diplomacy,* or the *foreign relations* of their country. The foreign relations of the Confederation were not very successful. Congress did not have the power to make the states or the people follow the agreements that it made with other countries. Under these conditions other nations had little respect for the United States.

The British had promised in the Treaty of Paris to leave the territory they had agreed was now part of the United States. Instead, they remained in their forts along the Great Lakes. They also used their Indian friends to keep settlers out of the Northwest Territory. There was much fighting between the frontiersmen and England's Indian allies.

Why did the English hold these forts? They hoped to keep their fur trade and the control it gave them over some Indian tribes. They even hoped to set up an Indian nation north of the Ohio River. Suppose the American government failed to last. Some British leaders thought that they could then move back into control of their former colonies. The reason they gave for keeping their grip on the Northwest was that the United States had not kept its treaty promise to help British creditors collect their debts in America.

In 1784 Congress tried to settle some of its problems with England. It sent John Adams to London. He tried to get the British to give up the forts on American soil and to increase trade with the United States. The British refused to give up the forts until American debtors had paid the money owed to British creditors since before the Revolutionary War. They refused to make any kind of trade treaty. Adams tried for three years, but could not get the British to change their minds.

Congress also tried to settle its troubles with Spain. In the Treaty of Paris, England had given Americans the use of the Mississippi River and the right to store their goods at New Orleans. This agreement was most important to the people who had moved into Kentucky and Tennessee. They had to use the Mississippi to get their goods to market. They also needed the right to deposit, or keep, their goods in New Orleans until a ship could load them for the trip across the ocean.

Spain held the lower Mississippi and New Orleans. Its rulers would not accept the agreement made by the British and Americans. They also hoped the new nation would not succeed so they could take part of it. Spanish officials urged the settlers south of the Ohio to secede, or take their territory out of the United States. They could then join the Spanish empire. Spain would give them the use of the Mississippi and New Orleans. Spain was still a strong nation. It proved this by getting Indians to attack the pioneers who settled near Spanish territory, and by holding onto Natchez, in American territory.

426

But Spain was willing to discuss such problems. In 1785 Don Diego de Gardoqui became the first Spanish minister to America. He and John Jay, the American Secretary of Foreign Affairs, soon began to bargain. By this time Spain had closed the lower Mississippi to American trade. Jay was told by Congress that he must get Spain to allow such trade. Don Diego was willing, but only if Spain would control the Mississippi, most of what is now Alabama and Mississippi, and parts of Tennessee, Kentucky, and Georgia. Spain claimed this land because it had held parts of it while fighting the British as allies of the United States during the Revolutionary War. Don Diego also asked that Spain should hold all lands south of the thirty-fifth parallel.

John Jay refused to accept such claims. He insisted that the United States would accept only the terms of the Treaty of Paris, which made the thirty-first parallel the boundary between Florida and the United States. Businessmen in the North and East wanted to build up their trade with Spain. In August, 1786, Congress changed its position. It told Jay that he could give up American rights on the Mississippi River for 25 years, if Spain would in turn agree to allow more American trade in Spanish ports. This would have helped the businessmen of New England, but would have hurt the farmers and settlers in the South and West. There was a bitter debate in Congress, and the men who represented seven of the states voted for this plan. This was two states less than the nine that had to agree before Congress could make a treaty. The talks between Spain and the United States then ended. The problems between the two countries were not settled until the Pinckney Treaty of 1795.

Relations with France were also poor. Thomas Jefferson became our minister to France. He wrote that the French showed him little respect. The leaders of the French government were angry because the United States could not repay its wartime debts. However, Jefferson did get them to agree to allow more trade by American ships. The Confederation had no army, and could not do much about Indian attacks. It could not open up the Mississippi, build up trade with Europe, or make needed agreements with foreign governments. More people began to wonder why they had to have such a weak national government.

Source: Boyd Shafer, et al., *A High School History of Modern America,* 3rd ed., pp. 104–105. Copyright 1977. By permission of LAIDLAW BROTHERS, A Division of Doubleday and Company, Inc.

Inventory Questions

Directions: Write a short answer to each question.

VOCABULARY

1. What is meant by the term *diplomacy?*
2. Define *secede.* Define *allies.*
3. What is a synonym for the word *treaty?*
4. Write the definition of the word *relations* as used in the passage.
5. What did the author mean by "keeping their grip on the Northwest"?

LITERAL COMPREHENSION

1. What job did John Jay have in the Confederation government? (Detail)
2. Why did the English remain in forts along the Great Lakes? (Detail)
3. Why was the Treaty of Paris important to the people of Tennessee and Kentucky? (Detail)
4. List, in order, the sequence of steps in the discussion of problems with Spain. (Sequence)

INTERPRETIVE AND CRITICAL COMPREHENSION

1. Do you agree with the directive of Congress to Jay in 1786? Why or why not? (Evaluation)
2. What do you think the people began to want from their national government? What makes you think this? (Inference)
3. Why did the U.S. have so much difficulty in dealing with other nations as described in this selection? (Conclusion)

the text in each specific content area. When the student comprehends 90 to 100 percent of what he or she reads (answers 9 questions out of 10 correctly), the material can be classified as being on his or her *independent* reading level. When the student comprehends 50 percent or less of what he or she reads (answers 5 questions out of 10 correctly), the material is on his or her *frustration* level. Students scoring 70 percent or below on a set of materials should be given an inventory on easier material; those who score 90 percent or above should be given an inventory on more difficult material.

Skill Inventories

Content teachers may want to know if students have developed the reading skills that are necessary to understand textbooks and other printed materials in their particular content areas. When the teachers are preparing to teach particular chapters or units that involve reading content area materials, they should be aware of the nature of the material that is going to be read and, it is hoped, understood. To help them decide the level and amount of instruction needed to accommodate the many differences among students, the teachers can prepare and administer to class members skill inventories that are based on textbook chapters or units, modeling them after the skill inventories presented in this section. On the basis of the results, the teachers will become more aware of what activities are needed to prepare students to read and understand the assigned materials. Activities suggested by such inventories are particularly good to use with students who are not profiting from their reading assignments and who may need special help and additional practice in the required skills.

Skill inventories may serve as a part of the total assessment program; that is, part of a test by a science teacher may require students to read a table or graph that appears in the text; questions about interpretation of a map that appears in the text might be used as part of a social science teacher's chapter or unit test; symbol knowledge and diagram-reading ability might be included in a mathematics teacher's test; questions on vocabulary words may be used to check understanding of the special terms in a content chapter or unit; assignments in outlining or note-taking or adjusting reading rate to purpose and degree of difficulty may be included in tests by all content teachers. The ultimate purpose of skill inventories is that students master and comprehend the content found in their textbooks and in other printed materials used in the classroom. The following skills are common to all content areas.

1. Understanding and using parts of textbooks (table of contents, index, list of illustrations, appendices, bibliography, glossary)
2. Interpreting maps, tables, charts, graphs, diagrams, cartoons
3. Knowing specialized vocabulary
4. Using reference materials (encyclopedias, dictionaries, supplemental reference books)
5. Recognizing special symbols, formulas, and abbreviations

Other necessary general skills are using study methods, outlining, taking notes, and reading at a flexible rate. Of course, general comprehension skills are involved in all content areas, as suggested in the GRI. The following items may be used to prepare skill assessments:

1. Parts of textbooks — Have students make use of different elements in their textbooks, such as preface, index, vocabulary lists, and appendices.
2. Maps, tables, charts, graphs, diagrams, cartoons — Use examples from the students' textbooks and ask students to answer questions you have prepared.
3. Specialized vocabulary — Use words from the glossaries of textbooks or supplemental materials.
4. Reference materials — Use the reference materials that are available for your content area and develop questions to see if students know the various reference sources and how to use them.
5. Symbols, abbreviations, and formulas — See if students can recognize the most frequently used symbols and abbreviations in the content material.

The following examples (Examples 10.3 through 10.9) provide some sample reading skills tests. The examples deal with several different content areas.

EXAMPLE *10.3*

Using Parts of a Textbook — Skill Inventory

Directions: Below are two columns of words or phrases. Match the expression from the righthand column with the one that means the same, or almost the same, thing in the lefthand column.

_____	Index	*1.* Name of book
_____	Table of contents	*2.* Part of book giving additional information, such as notes and tables
_____	Bibliography	
_____	Appendix	*3.* Introduction
_____	Glossary	*4.* List of books for further reading
_____	Preface	*5.* Alphabetical list of topics with the page on which each is found
_____	Title	
_____	Copyright date	*6.* Year when book was published

7. List in front of book with chapter headings or topics in sequence and page on which each begins

8. List of words with their meanings

Directions: Use your textbook to answer the following questions:

1. What is the title of your book?
2. When was it published?
3. Who wrote the book?
4. What are the titles of the first three chapters?
5. How are the chapters arranged or grouped?
6. On what page does Chapter 4 begin?
7. Find the meaning of the term _____ .
8. On what page is there a chart showing _____ ?
9. What does the map on page _____ tell you?
10. On what page does the book explain the construction of a _____ ?
11. What index entries are given for _____ ?

E X A M P L E **10.4**

Reading Tables, Maps, and Graphs — Skill Inventory

Tables

Directions: Look at the table below and answer the following questions.

Element	Symbol	Number of Protons	Number of Neutrons	Number of Electrons in Neutral Atoms
hydrogen	H	1	0	1
helium	He	2	2	2
lithium	Li	3	4	3
beryllium	Be	4	5	4
boron	B	5	6	5
carbon	C	6	6	6
nitrogen	N	7	7	7
oxygen	O	8	8	8
fluorine	F	9	10	9
neon	Ne	10	10	10
sodium	Na	11	12	11
magnesium	Mg	12	12	12
aluminum	Al	13	14	13

Source: Faith Fitch Hill and Jeffrey C. May, *Spaceship Earth: Physical Science* (Boston: Houghton Mifflin Company, 1981), p. 382. Copyright © 1981 by Houghton Mifflin Company. Reprinted by permission of Houghton Mifflin Company.

Questions

1. What is the symbol for helium?
2. What is the number of neutrons for carbon?
3. Ten is the number of protons for which element?
4. What is the number of electrons in neutral atoms for aluminum?
5. Which element has no neutrons?

Maps

Directions: Study the map below. Tell whether the statements about the map are true or false.

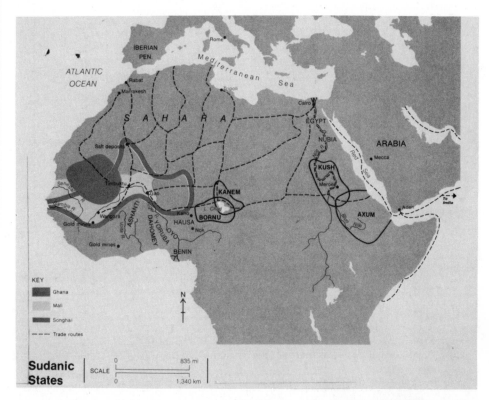

Source: Marvin Perry, *Unfinished Journey: A World History* (Boston: Houghton Mifflin Company, 1980), p. 221. Copyright © 1980 by Houghton Mifflin Company. Reprinted by permission of Houghton Mifflin Company.

True or False

_____ 1. The Sahara is located south of the Iberian Peninsula.

_____ 2. The Senegal River intercepts the Gambia River.

_____ 3. One could sail from Mirot to Cairo on the Nile River.

_____ 4. It would be closer to take a land journey than to travel by sea from Rome to Tripoli.

_____ 5. Rabat is located on the coast of the Atlantic Ocean.

_____ 6. It would take longer to walk from the gold mines to Wangara than from the gold mines to Nok.

Graphs

Directions: Look at the graph and answer the questions about it.

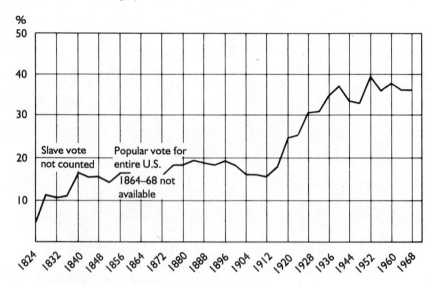

Source: Historical Statistics and Statistical Abstract.

Questions

1. Was there a steady growth of voters from 1824 to 1860?
2. Around what year was there a sudden increase in popular votes cast in presidential elections?
3. Does the graph show the percentage of voting-age citizens participating in presidential elections?
4. For what years are complete data not provided?
5. About what percentage of Americans voted in the 1972 presidential election?

E X A M P L E *10.5*

Using Reference Sources — Skill Inventory

Directions: Answer the following questions (based on English classroom reference sources).

1. What library aid will tell you the library number of a book?
2. What is a biography?
3. What is the difference between fiction and nonfiction?

4. Explain what each circled numeral of this entry from *Readers' Guide to Periodical Literature* refers to.

       ①   AIRPLANES
          ②   Electra on public trial.   L. Davis   II Flying
                                          ⑦   ⑧   ⑨

      68: 46—7$^+$ F′ 61
       ③   ④   ⑤   ⑥

5. Describe the content of *Dictionary of American Biography.*
6. Describe the content of *Granger's Index to Poetry.*
7. Where could you find an alphabetical listing of words with synonyms and antonyms instead of definitions?
8. What information may be found in the *Reader's Encyclopedia?*
9. Where might you find short stories listed by title, author, subject?
10. What information may be found in the *Book Review Digest?*
11. What information may be found in *Cumulative Book Index?*
12. Where might you go to find the answer to the question, "Is Steinbeck's *The Grapes of Wrath* considered to be one of his better works?"

Directions: Find the following words in a dictionary and list the guide words and numbers of the pages on which they fall.

Word	Guide Words	Page Number
anachronism		
aphorism		
assonance		
denouement		
epigram		
foreshadowing		
irony		
soliloquy		

Directions: Use a set of encyclopedias, such as *The World Book.* Answer the following questions.

1. What is the purpose of an encyclopedia?
2. What are the meaning and purpose of the guide letter or letters on the cover of each volume?
3. What are the meaning and purpose of *guide words?*
4. What is meant by *cross reference?*
5. What is the purpose of the bibliographies at the ends of articles?
6. Where is the index located in the encyclopedia?

Vocabulary — Skill Inventory

Directions: Explain the following terms concisely. (The source of these vocabulary items is Chapter 27, Parts 1 and 2, "An Industrial Society" and "New Scientific Ideas," in *History of the World,* by Marvin Perry and others, Boston: Houghton Mifflin, 1990.)

vaccination
pasteurization
radiation
evolution
genetics
sociology
psychology

Directions: Study the list of words above. Use your knowledge of meanings of any of the word parts to help you understand the meanings of the whole words. Answer the following questions:

1. What are the root words of the following words: *vaccination, pasteurization, radiation, evolution,* and *genetics?*
   If you know the meanings of the root words, use these meanings to help you determine the meanings of the new words.
   How is the word *pasteurization* different from the others? Does knowing the root word for this word help you? Why, or why not?
   Does being familiar with common suffixes help you figure out the meanings of these words?
2. What are the combining forms that make up the words *sociology* and *psychology?* If you know the meanings of these combining forms, use them to help you determine the meanings of the new words. Notice how knowing the meaning of one combining form can help you with two different words.

Directions: Define the italicized words.

1. When a person has been given a *vaccination,* an injection of a solution of weakened germs, he or she may be protected from contracting the disease.
2. The process of *pasteurization* of milk was invented by Louis Pasteur when he realized that bacteria could be killed by heat.
3. Uranium gives off *radiation* that is similar to X-rays.
4. The *evolution* of living things over time could result in one species slowly evolving into another, according to Darwin.
5. Genes carry the traits that are passed from parents to their children. Mendel did work that established the foundation of the science of *genetics.*
6. When searching for a set of laws under which human society operates, Comte invented the term *sociology* to describe his scientific study.
7. Those who wish to learn more about the mind and behavior may wish to major in *psychology.*

The inventory in Example 10.7 checks symbol knowledge and diagram-reading ability. Skills in these areas are required for reading of most content area textbooks. The inventory shown here is somewhat different from the other inventories — it is an actual page from a textbook, not a teacher-made instrument. However, its use — as a diagnostic tool — is similar to that of the other inventories.

E X A M P L E **10.7**

Special Symbols for Flow Charting

1. The *oval* is used to signal the *start* or *end* of the instructions.
2. The *diamond* is used to tell you that a question is being asked. You should be able to answer the question with a *yes* or *no*. The diamond indicates a decision point.
3. The *rectangle* is used to tell you that some process must be carried out. The rectangle indicates a do-something point.
4. The *parallelogram* tells you to record or copy or remember something. If you were writing flow charts for giving instructions to a computer, you would be very careful to use enough of these. The computer is a quick accurate machine, but it is also absolutely without imagination. It needs to be told everything it must do, down to the smallest detail.
5. The *arrow* indicates the sequence of the steps in a flow chart. The arrow tells you which box to go to next.

Here is a flow chart for simplifying numerical expressions which contain parentheses. The flow chart on page 42 is referred to as "Procedure A."

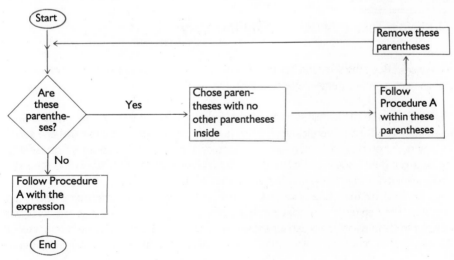

Exercises

Copy the flow chart on page 43 and number the parts as shown in the figure.

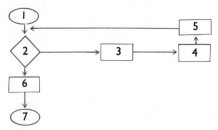

1. For each expression given, write the number of each step in the order which would be used to simplify the expression.
Sample: $10 - [2 - (1 + 1)]$ would use $1 \rightarrow 2 \rightarrow 3 \rightarrow 4 \rightarrow 5 \rightarrow$
$2 \rightarrow 3 \rightarrow 4 \rightarrow 5 \rightarrow 6 \rightarrow 7$

a. $3 - (5 - 4)$
c. $2 \times [10 - (2 + 2)]$
e. 3×5
g. $10 - (13 - (16 - (10 - 3)))$
h. $8 \div \{[1 + (4 - 3) - 2] \times 3 + 1\} - 2$

b. $2 \times 3 - 5 \div 4$
d. $(2 + 5) \times (4 - 2)$
f. $(2 \times (5 - 3) + 1) \times 7$

2. Using the flow chart of Exercise 1, what is the greatest number of steps there can be in simplifying an expression?

Source: William H. Nibbelink and Jay Graening, *Algebra 1,* Teacher's Annotated Edition (Columbus, Ohio: Charles E. Merrill, 1975), pages 43 and 44.

EXAMPLE **10.8**

Outlining/Taking Notes — Skill Inventory

Directions: Read the selection below. Outline what you have read as you would a reading assignment in your course. (Use one main idea and four subtopics.)

Signs of promise. The philosophes of the Enlightenment believed that humans were essentially good. They were confident that humans could improve themselves and society if they relied on reason. Two major developments in modern European history seemed to bear out their hopes. These were the French Revolution (1789–1799) and the Industrial Revolution, which began in England about 1760.

Inspired by the philosophes, reformers in France sought to advance liberty and equality. They ended the special privileges of the clergy and aristocracy, did away with absolutism, and established parliamentary government in France. During the nineteenth century the ideas of the Enlightenment and the French Revolution spread throughout

Europe and to other parts of the world. Reformers sought to imitate the achievements of the revolution. Many lands drew up constitutions, established parliaments, and granted equality under the law. In the tradition of the Enlightenment, they established public education.

At the same time advances in science and technology were transforming the material conditions of life. New inventions dramatically improved the standard of living, opened up new opportunities, and gave people more leisure. Discoveries in medicine prolonged life.

In the nineteenth century most thinkers believed that they were living in an age of progress. They saw their age as a fulfillment of the dreams of the philosophes. And they expected that this progress would continue indefinitely.

Source: Marvin Perry: *Unfinished Journey* (Boston: Houghton Mifflin Company, 1980), p. 346. Copyright © 1980 by Houghton Mifflin Company. Reprinted by permission of Houghton Mifflin Company.

E X A M P L E **10.9**

Adjustment of Rate to Purpose and Difficulty — Skill Inventory

Directions: Read this selection carefully. Try to comprehend the author's point of view and remember the main ideas, details, and what might be implied by the author. (A selection with appropriate questions would follow.)

Read as rapidly as you can to understand the main points. The questions for the selection will deal with the main events it covers. (A selection and appropriate questions would follow.)

Scan the following selection to answer the questions. (Appropriate questions would precede the selection.)

A skills chart can be developed for recording the instructional needs of students. Skills charts include a list of skills down the right side of a page and a list of students' names across the top of the page. The teacher places a check mark beside a skill under the name of a student who successfully achieves the skill. A glance at the chart provides a guide as to which students need special help in developing a required skill. If most students need help with a particular skill, the teacher may plan a total class instructional session around that skill. If only certain students lack a skill, the teacher may set up a small skill group to help students who need it. Skill groups are temporary groups in that they are dissolved when the members have mastered the skill. A skills file (collection of materials, equipment, and supplies) may provide the needed practice activities for some students.

A sample record-keeping chart is provided in Example 10.10.

EXAMPLE 10.10

Sample Skills Record

Student Names

Skills

1. Parts of textbook
2. Interpretation of maps, tables, charts, diagrams etc.
3. Specialized vocabulary
4. Reference sources
5. Special symbols/abbreviations
6. Study methods
7. Outlining/taking notes
8. Flexibility of rate

Key. Pupil Performance Code

I — needs introduction and teaching
R — needs review and reinforcement
S — satisfactory (regular instruction adequate)
M — has mastered (no more practice needed)

Informal Reading Inventory

There are published, commercial inventories to gauge a student's reading levels. They are compilations of graded reading selections with questions prepared to test the reader's comprehension. These types of inventories are often administered by the special or remedial reading teacher to students identified as problem readers, but they can also be used by regular classroom teachers for special situations. According to Bader and Wiesendanger (1989, p. 403), "If we examine the definitions of *informal* (not prescribed or fixed) and *inventory* (appraisal) we realize that the intention behind these devices is to provide a window on the reading process. The reader's confidence, willingness to risk error, ability to make semantically and syntactically sound substitutions, fluency, perception of organization, and a host of other understandings and abilities can be observed." They further point out that it may be inappropriate to expect reliability coefficients for alternative forms of informal reading inventories because of "the effect of content on attention, understanding, and recall." Professional judgment is needed to make decisions when greater prior knowledge about or interest in the content of a particular passage results in unusually high performance on that passage or when limited prior knowledge or interest in the content of a passage results in unusually low performance on that passage.

Four widely used inventories are

1. Roe, Betty D. *Burns/Roe Informal Reading Inventory.* Boston: Houghton Mifflin Company, 1989. (For grades preprimer–12.)
2. Johns, Jerry L. *Secondary & College Reading Inventory.* Dubuque, Iowa: Kendall/Hunt, 1988. (For grades 7–college.)
3. Woods, Mary Lynn, and Alden Moe. *Analytic Reading Inventory.* Columbus, Ohio: Merrill, 1989. (For grades primer–9.)
4. Silvaroli, Nicholas. *Classroom Reading Inventory.* Dubuque, Iowa: William C. Brown, 1989. (For grades preprimer–8.)

The chief purpose of these inventories is to identify the independent, instructional, frustration, and capacity reading levels of the student. Such inventories are valuable in that they not only provide an overall estimate of the student's reading ability, but they also make possible identification of the specific strengths and weaknesses of the reader. They are helpful in determining what books a student can read independently and how difficult assigned reading can be if it is to be used as instructional material. Although a reading specialist might give a student an entire series of inventory selections and locate all four of these levels, the content teacher may give a similar inventory based on textbooks used in a particular class to find out if students can benefit from using those books.

Although it is time-consuming, it is possible for the teacher to construct and administer an informal reading inventory. The steps below are suggested for this procedure.

1. Select a set of books (or other materials) used at various grade levels (such as seventh, eighth, ninth, tenth, eleventh, and twelfth), preferably a series used in the class.
2. From each book, select one passage to be used for oral reading and one passage to be used for silent reading (each of 200 words or more).
3. Make a copy of each of the passages from each book. (Later, as the student reads from the book, the teacher marks the errors on the copy.)
4. Make up approximately ten questions for each passage. The questions should be of various types, including:
   a. Main idea — Ask for the central theme of the selection.
   b. Detail — Ask for bits of information conveyed by the material.
   c. Vocabulary — Ask for meanings of words used in the passage.
   d. Sequence — Ask for a listing of events in the order of their occurrence.
   e. Inference — Ask for information that is implied but not directly stated in the material.

      f. Cause and effect — Ask for related factors that establish a cause-effect relationship.

5. Direct the student to read the first passage orally. Mark and count his or her errors. Follow these directions for marking errors:

      a. Place *p* above each unknown word that must be supplied by the teacher.

      b. Underline each word or word part that is mispronounced, indicating pronunciation given by the student above the word.

      c. Circle each omitted word or word part.

      d. For student insertion of words not in the text, use a caret to mark the location of the inserted words, and write the words above the caret.

      e. Use reversal mark (∿) to indicate reversals of word order or word parts.

      f. Use wavy underline to indicate repetition.

    Spontaneous corrections may be marked as well, although they should not be scored as errors. Mispronounced proper names and differences attributable to dialect should also not be counted as errors. This, of course, requires the teacher to be familiar with the dialects spoken by the students in order to score the inventory properly. Some teachers have found it effective to tape a student's oral reading, replaying the tapes to note the errors in performance.

    Then ask questions prepared for the oral reading. Count the number of questions answered correctly.

    Direct the student to read the second passage silently. Ask questions prepared for silent reading. Again, count the number of questions answered correctly.

6. Count the number of errors in oral reading. Subtract the number of errors from the number of words in the selection. Then divide by number of words in the selection and multiply by 100 for the percent correct:

$$\frac{\text{Number of words correct}}{\text{Number of words in selection}} \times 100 = \% \text{ correct}$$

    Total the number of correct answers to questions for both the oral and silent reading passages. Then divide by number of questions and multiply by 100 for the percent correct:

$$\frac{\text{Number of questions right}}{\text{Number of questions asked}} \times 100 = \% \text{ correct}$$

7. Read higher levels of material aloud to the student until you reach the highest reading level for which he or she can correctly answer 75 percent of the comprehension questions. (The highest level achieved indicates the student's probable *capacity*, or potential, reading level.)

The following chart will help the teacher in estimating the reading levels of the reader:

Level	Word recognition		Comprehension
Independent	99%	and	90%
Instructional	95%	and	75%
Frustration	<90%	or	<50%
Capacity			75%

Various writers in the field suggest slightly differing percentages relative to independent, instructional, frustration, and capacity levels. Originally, the criteria to establish the levels were developed by Betts (1946). Ekwall (1974) has presented evidence that the Betts criteria should be maintained, particularly if repetitions are counted as "errors." Since the authors of this text do recommend counting repetitions as errors, we have utilized the criteria as presented above. The set of criteria for the reading levels is basically the one proposed by Johnson, Kress, and Pikulski (1987). An example of an informal reading inventory selection is found in Example 10.11.

Cloze Test Procedure

An alternative method of assessment that can provide information similar to that provided by the informal reading inventory is the cloze test procedure. This test is easy to construct, administer, and score, and it takes much less time to administer than the informal reading inventory. For these reasons, content area teachers are likely to find the cloze procedure more attractive for classroom use than the informal reading inventory.

For a cloze test, the student is asked to read selections of increasing levels of difficulty and to supply words that have been deleted from the passage. A sample cloze passage is given in Example 10.12.

Following are the steps used for constructing, administering, and scoring the cloze test:

1. Select a set of materials typical of those used in your classroom; from each level of these materials, select a passage of about 250 words. The chosen passages should be ones the students have not read previously.
2. Delete every fifth word until you have about fifty deletions. Replace the deleted words with blanks of uniform length. Do not delete any words in the first sentence.
3. Ask the student to fill in each blank with the exact word that has been deleted. Allow time to complete the test.
4. Count the number of correct responses. Do not count spelling mistakes as wrong answers; do not count synonyms as correct answers.
5. Convert the number of correct responses into a percentage.

EXAMPLE 10.11

Informal Reading Inventory Selection

◆◆11 PASSAGE ▮ FORM A ▮ TEACHER 11◆

MOTIVATIONAL STATEMENT: Read this story to find out some things Johnny Appleseed did.

There is some disagreement concerning the way in which Johnny went about planting apple trees in the wild frontier country. Some say that he scattered the seed as he went along the edges of marshes or natural clearings in the thick, almost tropical forests, others that he distributed the seeds among the settlers themselves to plant, and still others claim that in the damp land surrounding the marshes he established nurseries where he kept the seedlings until they were big enough to transplant. My Great-Aunt Mattie said that her father, who lived in rather a grand way for a frontier settler, had boxes of apples brought each year from Maryland until his own trees began to bear, and then he always saved the seeds, drying them on the shelf above the kitchen fireplace, to be put later into a box and kept for Johnny Appleseed when he came on one of his overnight visits.

Johnny scattered fennel seed all through our Ohio country, for when the trees were first cleared and the land plowed up, the mosquitoes increased and malaria spread from family to family. Johnny regarded a tea brewed of fennel leaves as a specific against what the settlers called "fever and ague," and he seeded the plant along trails and fence rows over all Ohio.

Source: Louis Bromfield, "Johnny Appleseed and Aunt Mattie," in *Pleasant Valley* (New York: Harper and Row, 1945).

COMPREHENSION QUESTIONS

___ main idea
1. What is the main idea of this story? (Johnny Appleseed planted apple trees and fennel seed.)

SCORING AID

WORD RECOGNITION

%—MISCUES
99—3
95—12
90—22
85—33

COMPREHENSION

%—ERRORS
100—0
90—1
80—2
70—3
60—4
50—5
40—6
30—7
20—8
10—9
0—10

217 WORDS (for Word Recognition)
217 WORDS (for Rate)

WPM
13020

___ detail
2. In what kind of country did Johnny plant trees? (wild frontier country; marshes; thick forests)

___ vocabulary
3. What does the word "distributed" mean? (handed out to different people)

___ vocabulary
4. What are the nurseries mentioned in the story? (places where trees, shrubs, and vines are grown until they are large enough to transplant)

___ inference
5. Was Great-Aunt Mattie's father rich or poor? (rich) What in the story caused you to answer that way? (He lived in a grand way for a frontier settler and had boxes of apples brought from Maryland until his own trees began to bear.)

___ detail
6. What did Great-Aunt Mattie's father save for Johnny? (seeds from his apples)

___ sequence
7. Name, in order, the two things Great-Aunt Mattie's father did with the seeds. (He dried them on the shelf above the kitchen fireplace and then put them in a box.)

___ cause and effect/inference
8. What caused the spread of malaria through Ohio? (The increase in mosquitoes when the trees were first cleared and the land plowed up.)

___ inference
9. What did the settlers call malaria? (fever and ague)

___ inference
10. What did Johnny believe would help malaria sufferers? (a tea brewed of fennel leaves)

Source: Betty D. Roe, Burns/Roe Informal Reading Inventory: Preprimer to Twelfth Grade (Boston, Houghton Mifflin Company, 1989), p. 90. Reprinted by permission of Houghton Mifflin Company. Excerpt shown: "Johnny Appleseed and Aunt Mattie" from PLEASANT VALLEY by Louis Bromfield. Copyright 1945 by Louis Bromfield, renewed 1972 by Hope Bromfield Stevens and Harper & Row, Publishers, Inc. Reprinted by permission of HarperCollins Publishers, Inc.

EXAMPLE 10.12

Sample Cloze Passage

Rocks exposed to the atmosphere slowly change. Air, water, and materials _____ living things can react _____ minerals in rock to _____ or even
     (1)   (2)   (3)
remove them.

_____ is the process by _____ rocks change to soil. _____ may result
  (4)   (5)   (6)
from both _____ and physical action on _____.
            (7)   (8)
In a common form _____ chemical weathering, minerals containing
                     (9)
_____ are broken down. Iron _____ to moisture and air _____ a red-brown
 (10)   (11)   (12)
coating or _____. The iron combines with _____ and becomes a new
            (13)   (14)
_____, iron oxide (rust). Similar _____ occur in rocks exposed _____ air
 (15)   (16)   (17)
and water. Some _____ are more easily changed _____ than others. In the
                 (18)   (19)
_____ of air and moisture, _____, for instance, changes to _____
 (20)   (21)   (22)
minerals. Quartz, however, is _____ to chemical changes.
                               (23)

Physical _____ acting on rocks cause _____ weathering. In mechanical
          (24)   (25)
weathering, _____ are broken down by _____ forces as windblown
             (26)   (27)
sand, _____ water, and temperature changes _____ cause rocks to
       (28)   (29)
shrink _____ expand.
        (30)

Plants also weather _____. Simple plants called lichens _____ grow on
                     (31)   (32)
unweathered rocks. _____ the lichens weather the _____, other types of
                    (33)   (34)
plants _____ themselves. Plants remove chemicals _____ developing soil.
        (35)   (36)
Living and _____ plants may also add _____ such as acids to _____. Besides
            (37)   (38)   (39)
their chemical effects, _____ roots may act upon _____ physically. Some
                         (40)   (41)
plant roots _____ work their way into _____ and crevices and split _____
             (42)   (43)   (44)
apart. Plants also have _____ great effect on soil _____ it is formed.
                         (45)   (46)
Soil _____ might otherwise be carried _____ by wind or water _____ be
      (47)   (48)   (49)
held in place _____ a dense mat of plant roots.
               (50)

Answers:

1. from, 2. with, 3. alter, 4. Weathering, 5. which, 6. It, 7. chemical, 8. rocks, 9. of, 10. iron, 11. exposed, 12. develops, 13. rust, 14. oxygen, 15. substance, 16. changes, 17. to, 18. minerals, 19. chemically, 20. presence, 21. feldspar, 22. clay, 23. resistant, 24. forces, 25. mechanical, 26. rocks, 27. such, 28. moving, 29. that, 30. and, 31. rocks, 32. can, 33. As, 34. rocks, 35. establish, 36. from, 37. decaying, 38. chemicals, 39. rocks, 40. plant, 41. rocks, 42. can, 43. cracks, 44. rocks, 45. a, 46. after, 47. which, 48. away, 49. can, 50. by.

Source: Norman Abraham et al., *Interaction of Earth and Time,* 2nd ed. (Chicago: Rand McNally Co., 1976), pp. 262–265.

The following criteria may be used in determining levels:

Accuracy	*Reading level*
57% or greater	Independent reading level
44–57%	Instructional reading level
Below 44%	Frustration level

A student who achieves a percentage of accuracy at or above the instructional level is asked to complete the next higher level cloze test until that student reaches his or her highest instructional level. The teacher can probably assign instructional reading of tested material to any student who achieves a score of between 44 and 57 percent on that material. A score of 57 percent or better on any passage means the teacher can use the material from which the passage was taken for independent reading. A score of less than 44 percent accuracy on a passage would indicate that the material from which the passage was taken is probably not suitable for that particular student.

Students should be given an explanation of the purpose of the procedure and a few practice passages to complete before a cloze test is used for assessment. Students need to be encouraged to use the information contained in the material surrounding each blank in order to make a decision about the correct word to place in the blank, or they may simply guess without considering all of the available clues. Some students exhibit anxiety with this form of test, and practice may help alleviate this anxiety.

Readers who wish to know more about the cloze procedure should refer to the references cited in Thought Question 7 at the end of this chapter and/or an explanatory article by Bormuth (1968) in *Elementary English,* which answers frequently asked questions about the cloze procedure. These references explain the research that supports the following statements:

1. Scores on cloze readability tests correlate with scores on conventionally designed comprehension tests.
2. Cloze difficulties of passages correlate with the difficulties of the passages as determined by conventional tests.

3. The traditional fifth-word deletion pattern appears to be the best pattern.
4. For test purposes, there is no advantage in giving credit for synonyms when the purpose is to differentiate among students' reading performances.
5. The established level criteria are comparable to scores judged as instructional, independent, or frustration level on conventional comprehension tests.

An alternative cloze test has been proposed by Burron and Claybaugh (1974). They suggest that when constructing a cloze test for content materials, a passage of 520 words should be selected and every tenth word deleted; this modification is intended to compensate for the denseness of concepts and technical language in content materials.

Another modification of the cloze test has been proposed by Baldauf and others (1980) for lower secondary school ESL students. This is a "matching" cloze: students select from the five words randomly ordered in the margin and copy the correct ones into the five blank spaces for one set of sentences of the passage, continuing this procedure for other sections of the passage.

Teachers who wish to discover the ability of their students to use semantic and syntactic context clues effectively may wish to administer the cloze test and accept as answers synonyms and reasonable responses that make sense in the passage. To obtain very specific information about students' use of particular types of context clues, a teacher may wish to delete specific categories of words in specific contexts, rather than every nth word (Johnston, 1983). For example, only nouns or only adjectives might be deleted. Of course, such modifications would make determination of reading levels according to the criteria indicated in this section inappropriate, but they would allow the teachers to see how the students process language as they read.

According to Johnston (1983, pp. 62–63), a cloze test does not present "a normal reading task because often one must hold an empty slot in memory until one can locate information to fill it and construct a meaning for the segment. This places quite a demand on short-term memory, and there are search skills involved." Therefore, because of the short-term memory demands, some students may not score as well on a cloze test as they would on another type of test.

Observation Checklist

Systematic daily observation of students' reading performances can provide teachers with clues for planning effective instruction. Such observation of reading behaviors can and should take place continuously in content classrooms. These observations will be more directed if systematic records are kept. Every reading activity the students engage in, whether instructional or recreational, provides a possible source of diagnostic information that can be recorded for analysis. Over a period of days or weeks, patterns of student

446   development will become apparent, and consistent needs can be noted. Growth of the student and other changes will be more evident when effective record keeping is used.

The teacher should keep questions such as the following in mind during observation of each student:

1. Does the student approach the assignment with enthusiasm?
2. Does he or she apply an appropriate study method?
3. Can he or she find answers to questions of a literal type (i.e., main idea, details, sequence)?
4. Does he or she understand ideas beneath the surface level (answering inferential and critical level questions)?
5. Can he or she ascertain the meanings of new or unfamiliar words? What word recognition skills does the student use?
6. Can he or she use locational skills in the book?
7. Can he or she use reference skills for various reference sources?
8. Is he or she reading at different rates for different materials and purposes?

In addition, when a student gives an oral report or reads orally, the teacher has the opportunity to observe the following:

Oral report	*Oral reading*
pronunciation	methods of word attack
general vocabulary	word recognition problems
specialized vocabulary	rate of reading
sentence structure	phrasing
organization of ideas	peer reactions
interests	

During use of computer programs, the teacher can observe students in order to make evaluative decisions about their progress. When drill-and-practice or tutorial programs are used, they may look for such things as whether the student chooses to use the software voluntarily, responds well to the rewards offered for successful responses, understands that particular commands cause particular responses, recognizes repeated language patterns presented in the programs, becomes more successful with practice, remembers new information that is presented, uses study strategies when working with the lessons, needs repetition of the information before it is understood, is enthusiastic about using the program, or becomes frustrated when using the program. When problem solving/adventure programs (simulations, gaming programs, interactive fiction, and creative art programs, for example) are used, the teacher may observe to see such things as whether the student uses previously learned problem-solving strategies, organizes information for later recall, predicts solutions to the problem based on information provided in the program, relates personal experiences to the situation, and follows directions and hints provided (Shannon, 1989).

Observation may suggest a need for an individual interview with the student. In this conference, a teacher can learn whether a student has successfully completed a given assignment and can assess the student's attitudes toward reading, school, and self, as well as his or her relations with other students. The student also may divulge the uses he or she has for reading.

Self-Assessment

Self-assessment techniques can be used to help students evaluate their own reading strengths and weaknesses. Such techniques include

1. *Discussion.* Self-assessment may focus on a single topic, such as word recognition, meaning of vocabulary, comprehension, study skills, or problems in reading a particular textbook. With guiding questions from the teacher, the students can discuss, orally or in writing, their strengths and weaknesses in regard to the particular topic.
2. *Structured interview or conference.* After the student has written a reading autobiography (see the section on "Attitude" in this chapter), such questions as the following may be asked:
   a. How do you figure out the pronunciation or meaning of an unknown word?
   b. What steps are you taking to develop your vocabulary?
   c. What do you do to get the main ideas from your reading?
   d. Do you use the same rate of reading in most of your assignments?
   e. What method of study do you use most?
   f. How do you organize your material to remember it?
   g. What special reference books have you used lately in the writing of a report?
   h. How do you handle graphic aids that appear in the reading material?
   i. How do you study for a test?
   j. What could you do to become an even better reader?
3. *Self-rating checklist.* A sample checklist is provided in Example 10.13. It deals with several broad areas. Similar checklists could be prepared that focus on particular skills, such as reading to follow directions.

For teachers who are interested in a self-report instrument to determine awareness of strategic reading processes, Schmitt (1990) has developed such an instrument for elementary school students that appears to be easily adapted for use with older students. The instrument was developed for middle and upper elementary grade students and appears in the March 1990 issue of *The Reading Teacher.*

EXAMPLE **10.13**

Self-Rating Checklist

Name _____   Date _____

Subject _____

Please rate yourself on these items:

	Good	Average	Need help
1. Pronouncing and knowing the meaning of most of the words in your content book	____	____	____
2. Using parts of textbooks	____	____	____
3. Using the dictionary	____	____	____
4. Using strategies to help increase vocabulary	____	____	____
5. Answering questions that call for critical thinking	____	____	____
6. Being flexible in reading rate	____	____	____
7. Knowing a good study method	____	____	____
8. Outlining, summarizing, and taking notes	____	____	____
9. Locating materials in books and reference sources	____	____	____
10. Writing a report	____	____	____
11. Following printed directions	____	____	____
12. Interpreting graphic aids	____	____	____
13. Remembering material	____	____	____
14. Test taking	____	____	____

Other Informal Measures

In addition to testing and measuring reading achievement, informal assessment tools can be used by the content teacher to measure such nonreading behaviors as attitudes and interests. Each of these behaviors can directly or indirectly affect a student's reading achievement.

Attitude

A student's affective response to reading selections has a critical influence on whether or not he or she will become a willing reader. Therefore, some kind of measure of the student's attitudes toward reading experiences is an important aspect of the total assessment program. Reading takes many forms and means many different things to different students; a student might enjoy reading the sports page but be bored or even dislike reading a library book to complete an English assignment.

Whether or not a student likes reading depends on what he or she is reading and for what purpose. Therefore, perhaps the most valid measure of a student's attitude toward reading would be his or her responses to individual selections. A scale such as the one presented in Example 10.14 could be given to students after they have read particular selections.

EXAMPLE **10.14**

Response Scale

Directions: Rate the selection you have just read by circling the appropriate letter for each item.

A = strongly agree
B = agree
C = disagree
D = strongly disagree

1. I enjoyed reading this selection.

    A   B   C   D

2. This selection was boring to me.

    A   B   C   D

3. This selection held my attention.

    A   B   C   D

4. I disliked reading this selection.

    A   B   C   D

Students are not expected to respond positively to all their reading experiences, but if the majority of their responses indicate negative attitudes toward reading, something is amiss. A profile of individual scores may be kept as an ongoing assessment of each student's attitude toward reading. Content teachers should be concerned about the attitudes of students toward reading material; students who have negative attitudes may not comprehend well and will probably need additional motivation for reading. An assessment of this type carried out near the beginning of the school term should be valuable to content teachers.

To undertake a more comprehensive study of the student's reading, some authorities suggest the use of the reading autobiography — a developmental history of a student's reading experiences. Some accounts give details concerning the student's early reading experiences, when and how he or she was taught, the range and variety of his or her reading, home background, and use of available resources. Other autobiographies reveal the writer's attitude, special reading interests, and perhaps reading difficulties. Sometimes they include the writer's ideas about ways to overcome the difficulties that he or she has recognized.

Other attitude assessment instruments include one prepared by Kennedy and Halinski (1975), which is a seventy-item instrument in which students respond to statements according to a four-point scale — Strongly Agree, Agree, Disagree, and Strongly Disagree. A copy of the instrument may be found in the April 1975 issue of the *Journal of Reading*. Another instrument, which was developed by Estes (1971), can be found in the November 1971 issue of the *Journal of Reading*. Dulin and Chester (1974) provide a validated study of the Estes Attitude Scales.

Interests

In reading, as in other areas, interest is often the key that unlocks effort. Consequently, study of students' reading and other interests is an important part of the teaching process. Teachers should plan ways to motivate students and show how a subject is related to their personal lives.

Subject-matter teachers need to know the *specific* interests of each student in order to capitalize on them in recommending reading materials. One of the ways to learn a student's reading interests is through observation in daily classes. The teacher notes the books the student chooses to read, the degree of concentration and enjoyment with which he or she reads them, his or her eagerness to talk about them, and the desire expressed to read more books of similar nature or books by the same author.

More detailed information about reading interests may be obtained from an interest inventory. An inventory should include both general and reading interests. A sample inventory is presented in Example 10.15.

EXAMPLE **10.15**

General and Reading Interests Inventory

Name: _____   Grade: _____   Age: _____

GENERAL INTERESTS

1. What do you like to do in your free time?
2. What are your favorite TV shows?
3. What are your favorite hobbies?

4. What games or sports do you like best?

5. What clubs or other groups do you belong to?
6. Do you have any pets? If yes, what kinds?
7. What is your favorite type of movie?
8. What is your favorite school subject?
9. What is your most disliked school subject?
10. What kind of work do you think you want to do when you finish secondary school?

READING INTERESTS

1. How often do you go to the public library?
2. What are your favorite books that you own?
3. What things do you like to read about most?
4. Which comic books do you read?
5. Which magazines do you read?
6. What are some books you have enjoyed?
7. What parts of the newspaper do you read most frequently?
8. Do you like to read?

Process and Holistic Assessments

In general, current standardized reading tests do not seem to reflect what we now know about the reading process and reading comprehension. Farr and Carey (1986) have pointed out the fact that tests used by schools for monitoring of student progress have not reflected advances in educational research. Current tests treat reading as if it were simply skill mastery of a variety of skills (a product) rather than a constructive, strategic process in which readers make use of their prior knowledge and techniques for unlocking meaning in the text in order to understand its message (a process). Valencia and Pearson (1987) enumerate the dangers of looking at reading from the new perspective but continuing to assess students' achievements and needs from the old one. They also mention that teachers who want their students to score well on the traditional testing instruments may allow the tests to influence the curriculum, resulting in inappropriate instruction in light of the current understanding of the reading process. Wittrock (1987, p. 736) explains to teachers that process oriented comprehension measures "will not tell what your students have learned about a text passage. Nor will they tell you where your students' reading achievement lies in relation to that of other students. But process oriented tests will tell you about the strategies your students use to make sense out of the text they read in your class. They will provide a way for you to understand the instruction in comprehension your students need."

The following chart from Valencia and Pearson (1987) helps to put the problem of the mismatch between current theory about reading and current assessment techniques into perspective.

FIGURE 10.1

Contrasting Views of the Reading Process and Assessment Practices

A Set of Contrasts Between New Views of Reading and Current Practices in Assessing Reading

New Views of the Reading Process Tell Us That . . .	Yet When We Assess Reading Comprehension, We . . .
Prior knowledge is an important determinant of reading comprehension.	Mask any relationship between prior knowledge and reading comprehension by using lots of short passages on lots of topics.
A complete story or text has structural and topical integrity.	Use short texts that seldom approximate the structural and topical integrity of an authentic text.
Inference is an essential part of the process of comprehending units as small as sentences.	Rely on literal comprehension test items.
The diversity in prior knowledge across individuals as well as the varied causal relations in human experiences invite many possible inferences to fit a text or question.	Use multiple choice items with only one correct answer, even when many of the responses might, under certain conditions, be plausible.
The ability to vary reading strategies to fit the text and the situation is one hallmark of an expert reader.	Seldom assess how and when students vary the strategies they use during normal reading, studying, or when the going gets tough.
The ability to synthesize information from various parts of the text and different texts is hallmark of an expert reader.	Rarely go beyond finding the main idea of a paragraph or passage.
The ability to ask good questions of text, as well as to answer them, is hallmark of an expert reader.	Seldom ask students to create or select questions about a selection they may have just read.
All aspects of a reader's experience, including habits that arise from school and home, influence reading comprehension.	Rarely view information on reading habits and attitudes as being as important information about performance.
Reading involves the orchestration of many skills that complement one another in a variety of ways.	Use tests that fragment reading into isolated skills and report performance on each.
Skilled readers are fluent; their word identification is sufficiently automatic to allow most cognitive resources to be used for comprehension.	Rarely consider fluency as an index of skilled reading.
Learning from text involves the restructuring, application, and flexible use of knowledge in new situations.	Often ask readers to respond to the text's declarative knowledge rather than to apply it to near and far transfer tasks.

Source: Sheila Valencia and P. David Pearson. "Reading Assessment: Time for a Change." *The Reading Teacher,* 40 (April 1987), 731. Reprinted with permission of the International Reading Association.

Currently some attempts are being made to develop standardized reading tests that reflect an up-to-date view of the reading process, but obstacles stand in the way of this development. Prior knowledge of test users is difficult to assess in a concise paper-and-pencil format, whole selections sometimes take unrealistically long periods of time to read, appropriate answers to questions involving different backgrounds of experience are hard to determine, reading strategy assessment is a more abstract concept than assessment of mastery of facts, reading fluency is difficult to assess, and construction of items that tap higher-level thinking is more difficult than construction of test items at the literal level of thinking. Wixson and others (1987, p. 751) have been involved in developing statewide reading tests in Michigan that "evaluate reading in a more holistic manner" without the attempt to set up "a one to one correspondence between each stated objective and individual test items." Both these researchers and Valencia and Pearson (1987) in Illinois have worked out ways to assess background knowledge. The two techniques being used in Illinois for background assessment are having students predict if particular ideas are likely to be found in a selection on a certain topic and rating the relatedness of vocabulary terms to a central concept of a selection.

Wixson and others (1987) have chosen representative classroom materials and used complete selections from them. The reporting of results from these tests will probably "describe a reader's performance under specific conditions (for example, with a certain level of topic familiarity, a certain type of text, a certain level of interest in the text)" (p. 752). The types of test items that Valencia and Pearson (1987) are working on include items to test summary writing skills and metacognitive judgments and items with more than one acceptable response. For example, to evaluate summary writing students pick the best summary of the selection that they have read from three or four written by other students. They may be given a list of summary features and be asked to check off their reasons for choosing one as the best. To check metacognitive judgments, students may have to rate the helpfulness of several retellings of a selection that they have read to a variety of audiences, such as a teacher, a classmate, or a younger child.

As test items are developed to assess comprehension, producers of such tests must be aware of some research findings related to testing of students in grades 5 through 12. Some pertinent information from studies reported by Davey (1989) follows:

1. Poor readers are much slower than good readers in test completion times, adding a rate factor to a comprehension assessment that is to the disadvantage of some students.
2. Multiple-choice question scores are generally higher than free response scores, and free response questions are more difficult for poor readers than they are for good readers, although multiple-choice items are not.
3. Testing that allows students to look back at the passage when answering questions appears to enhance free recall responses but not multiple-

choice responses, but good readers benefit more than poor readers from lookback opportunities. Good readers appear to integrate specific text information with their background knowledge and to reason about the material when they are allowed to look back. Poor readers benefit from looking back when answers are directly stated in the text but fail to use inferential strategies.

Informal assessments may be needed in order for a teacher to assess outcomes of currently endorsed instructional procedures at present. Johnston (1987) points out that, after all, most decision making in the classroom takes place on a moment-to-moment basis, involving observation of classroom activities. Teachers, then, need to know how to look for patterns of behavior and to keep records related to the patterns observed. Teachers should try to observe students reading in instructional, recreational, interactive, individual, and formal test-taking settings in order to develop a complete picture of reading behaviors (Glazer and Searfoss, 1989). The validity of observations for assessment can be high because they exist in the context of real reading events and are a natural part of regular classroom lessons. Reliability can be high because the assessment is ongoing over an extended time period, and patterns of responses in real reading situations have time to form (Readence and Martin, 1989).

Informal classroom evaluation, according to Johnston (1987), is process oriented and involves both evaluation by the teacher and self-evaluation by the students. This self-evaluation can lead to the use of metacognitive strategies when students are reading. They ask themselves if they understand the material, and, if not, what they can do to understand it better.

Teachers may wish to ask students to react in writing to narrative passages to discover if they are attending to surface level plot structures, underlying universal themes, or character development (Readence and Martin, 1989; Purves, 1968). This could be considered a form of written retelling of the story, which has the advantage over oral retelling of not requiring one-to-one attention of the teacher during the retelling process.

Assessing comprehension of material read by having students retell a selection can be an effective, although time-consuming, technique. Readers construct a text in their minds as they read a particular selection. The texts constructed by better readers are more complete and accurate than those constructed by less skilled ones. The retelling technique shows what the students consider important in the text and how they organize that information rather than showing if the students remember what the adults doing the testing consider important. A selection to be retold should be read silently and then retold to the teacher without interruption. When the retelling is completed, the teacher may request elaboration on some points, for the students may know more about the material than they can produce in a free recall situation. Teachers should listen for such things as mention of major characters, characteristics of the characters, the story's problem and solution, and an accurate sequence of events in retellings of narrative texts. They should listen for main ideas and important supporting details in expository texts (Richek, List, and Lerner, 1989). The retellings are a type of window to the reading comprehension process that goes on within a student and can be highly valuable in selected settings. Morrow (1989) cautions that retelling is difficult for students and suggests that teachers offer students guidance and practice with retelling before it is used for formal evaluation of their skills. She also stresses that students should be told before they read a story that they will be expected to retell it, and they should be given a purpose for the reading that is congruent with the information the teacher is looking for in the evaluation.

Retellings can be evaluated by counting the number of idea units included (probably weighted for importance) and checking for appropriate sequence. The number of recalled units at each level of importance can be divided by the total number of units at that level to produce percentages that show how much the student's comprehension is slanted toward more or less important units. Retellings can also be checked to determine such things as inclusion of literal and implied information, attempts to connect background knowledge to text information or to apply information to the real world, affective involvement with the text, appropriate language use, and control of the mechanics of spoken or written language (Morrow, 1989; Clark, 1982).

Johnston (1984) believes a natural extension of the oral reading test could be an approach in which the students verbalize their thought processes while reading. The students would think aloud as they read, predicting and testing hypotheses about the material while the teacher listened and analyzed the approaches taken to the reading.

Wade (1990) describes the use of a think-aloud procedure for comprehension assessment. With this procedure, students read short segments of passages in which they cannot be certain what the topic is until they have read the last segment. After reading each segment, they think aloud about the passage's meaning, generating hypotheses about the meaning from the clues in the segment just read. At the completion of the passage, the reader retells the complete passage. Example 10.16 shows a procedure for administering and scoring a comprehension think-aloud exercise.

Use of the think-aloud procedure can reveal students who are good comprehenders, those who over-rely upon bottom-up (text based) or top-down (knowledge based) processing, and those who fail to integrate information found in the different segments of the passage. Knowing these approaches to reading can help the teacher plan appropriate instruction, such as focusing on developing or activating prior knowledge to help students understand the text; helping them to understand the function of background knowledge in comprehension; helping them link information from various sentences to form a unified, coherent idea; helping them develop flexibility in interpretations; and helping them learn to use metacognitive skills.

Baumann (1988) points out that the cloze procedure is a type of process

456

EXAMPLE *10.16*
=====

Think-Aloud Administration and Scoring

Procedure for Administering and Scoring a Comprehension Think Aloud

PREPARING THE TEXT

Choose a short passage (expository or narrative) written to meet the following criteria:

1. The text should be from 80 to 200 words in length, depending on the reader's age and reading ability.
2. The text should be new to the reader, but on a topic that is familiar to him or her. (Determine whether the reader has relevant background knowledge by means of an interview or questionnaire administered at a session prior to this assessment.)
3. The text should be at the reader's instructional level, which can be determined by use of an informal reading inventory. Passages at this level are most likely to be somewhat challenging while not overwhelming readers with word identification problems.
4. The topic sentence should appear last, and the passage should be untitled. Altering the text in this way will elicit information about the reader's strategies for making sense of the passage and inferring the topic.
5. The text should be divided into segments of one to four sentences each.

ADMINISTERING THE THINK ALOUD PROCEDURE

1. Tell the reader that he or she will be reading a story in short segments of one or more sentences.
2. Tell the reader that after reading each section, he or she will be asked to tell what the story is about.
3. Have the student read a segment aloud. After each segment is read, ask the reader to tell what is happening, followed by nondirective probe questions as necessary. The questions should encourage the reader to generate hypotheses (what do you think this is about?) and to describe what he or she based the hypotheses on (what clues in the story helped you?).
4. Continue the procedure until the entire passage is read. Then ask the reader to retell the entire passage in his or her own words. (The reader may reread the story first.)
5. The examiner might also ask the reader to find the most important sentence(s) in the passage.
6. The session should be tape-recorded and transcribed. The examiner should also record observations of the child's behaviors.

Ask the following questions when analyzing the transcript:

1. Does the reader generate hypotheses?
2. Does he/she support hypotheses with information from the passage?
3. What information from the text does the reader use?
4. Does he/she relate material in the text to background knowledge or previous experience?
5. Does the reader integrate new information with the schema he/she has already activated?
6. What does the reader do if there is information that conflicts with the schema he/she has generated?
7. At what point does the reader recognize what the story is about?
8. How does the reader deal with unfamiliar words?
9. What kinds of integration strategies does the reader use (e.g., visualization)?
10. How confident is the reader of his/her hypotheses?
11. What other observations can be made about the reader's behavior, strategies, etc.?

Source: Suzanne E. Wade, "Using Think Alouds to Assess Comprehension." *The Reading Teacher,* 43 (March 1990), 445. Reprinted with permission of Suzanne E. Wade and the International Reading Association.

assessment because readers have to respond *while* they are working on figuring out the text. The readers use the semantic and syntactic clues in the supplied text to construct a meaningful whole text. The cloze procedure is described fully earlier in this chapter.

Brozo (1990) makes a case for interactive assessment for at-risk readers that resembles a directed reading lesson. First, there is a diagnostic interview to collect background information about the student's ideas about reading purposes and his or her reading strategies and ability, interests, and attitudes. Then passage placement in an informal reading inventory is determined by letting the student work through the word lists, providing assistance with difficult words and strategies for unlocking them. Activation and expansion of prior knowledge of the topic of the passage, preteaching of vocabulary, and purpose setting for the reading are used to prepare the student to read. The student reads silently first and then orally. As the student reads orally, the teacher observes use of strategies, asks questions about strategies, and models effective strategies as needed. After the reading takes place, the student retells the material. The teacher may probe for additional information through questions, allowing the student to look back through the passage to find answers. Comprehension is then extended through activities that connect the student's prior knowledge with the new content. A number of techniques found in this text — for example, semantic mapping and anticipation guides — may be used in both the preparation for reading step and this final step. This procedure is obviously time-consuming, but it has the

458

potential for uncovering a student's actual ability to perform in classwork, rather than his or her ability to perform independently.

Dynamic assessment is also suggested for at-risk readers by Kletzien and Bednar (1990). They suggest initial assessment and strategy analysis to establish the student's reading level and to determine his or her strategy knowledge and use. They also suggest an informal reading inventory for this purpose. The teacher observes the student's strategy application and questions the student about reading strategies used. Then the teacher plans a mediated learning minilesson to determine the reader's capacity for modifying his or her approach to reading. The teacher discusses the student's initial performance with him or her, stressing both strengths and limitations. Then a strategy is chosen to be taught, using independent level materials. The student is taught how, when, and why the strategy can be used. The teacher models the strategy directly through a think-aloud procedure and then offers the student guided practice and independent practice. The teacher observes the student's attempts to learn the strategy. A postassessment and strategy analysis follows, using another form of the informal reading inventory that was used initially. Comparing the student's performance on the two assessment measures helps the teacher to determine his or her ability to integrate the targeted strategies into the reading process. This approach also takes quite a bit of time, although it yields useful information.

Portfolios of students' work can be an important factor in process assessment. The portfolios should include materials showing each student's accomplishments as a reader and a writer (Wolf, 1989). These materials could be writing samples judged to be the student's best efforts chosen for inclusion in the portfolio at regular intervals, audiotapes of a student's best oral reading (done with prior preparation) collected at regular intervals, written responses to literature that has been read and discussed in class (which can be analyzed for inclusion of information on theme, characters, setting, problem, events, solution, application, and personal response), and reading logs that show the number and variety of books read in various time periods (Au and others, 1989).

SUMMARY

Teachers at the secondary school level often need to interpret norm-referenced reading test results to learn about individual students' reading abilities and about the range of reading abilities within the classroom. Both survey and diagnostic tests can be useful.

Criterion-referenced tests, which check the test-taker's performance against a performance criterion as a predetermined standard, can also be helpful in assessment. Results of criterion-referenced tests can be used as instructional prescriptions, making them useful in decisions about instruction.

Perhaps more useful to content teachers are informal tests, such as sight vocabulary assessments; the group reading inventory (GRI), which gives an indication of how well students read a particular textbook; the informal reading inventory, which provides an overall estimate of a student's reading ability as well as a picture of some of his or her strengths and weaknesses; and the cloze procedure, which provides the teacher with two types of information — an overall view of the student's reading ability and the appropriateness of text material for the student.

The type of assessment measure used most frequently by secondary school content teachers is the skill inventory, which provides information about whether students have developed the specific reading skills necessary to understand content material in the teacher's particular area.

Since careful judgment enters into decisions about the level of each student's performance, the classroom teacher must carefully observe students as they perform daily tasks with printed materials. Beyond that, teachers can help students utilize self-appraisal techniques as a way of evaluating their strengths and weaknesses in handling printed materials.

Student attitudes toward the reading experiences in the content classroom are an important aspect of the overall assessment program. Besides observation and discussion, there are teacher-made devices, self-evaluation devices, and other instruments available to show attitude. Similarly, since interest is often the key that unlocks effort, content teachers who know the general and reading interests of students can plan ways to motivate the students and can capitalize on these interests when selecting and using materials.

Achievement tests given by schools do not generally reflect current views of the reading process as a constructive strategic process in which readers make use of their prior knowledge and techniques for unlocking meaning in the text. Work is being done to develop standardized process and holistic assessment procedures, however. In the meantime, teachers may need to use informal assessments to make classroom decisions about reading progress. Observations, retellings, written responses to writing, and portfolios for students are all informal procedures that, along with more common informal testing procedures, can facilitate process assessment.

SELF-TEST

1. What type of norm-referenced test measures general achievement in reading? (a) Survey (b) Diagnostic (c) Oral (d) Study skills

2. What feature about a norm-referenced test is assessed when the results on one form of a test are compared with results of an equivalent form of the test? (a) Validity (b) Reliability (c) Population (d) None of these

3. What is the term for expressing test scores in terms of position within a set of 100 scores? (a) Grade equivalent (b) Percentile rank (c) Stanine (d) Median score

4. What should internal consistency reliability coefficients for tests be? (a) Above .50 (b) .65 or above (c) .85 or above (d) .80

5. What level is usually indicated by the score achieved on a norm-referenced silent reading test? (a) Independent (b) Instructional (c) Frustration (d) Each of the above

6. If a student misses no more than one out of ten words on a list of graded words, what level does this represent? (a) Independent (b) Instructional (c) Frustration (d) Capacity

7. What classification may be given to material on a group reading inventory that was read with a comprehension score of 50 percent or less? (a) Independent (b) Instructional (c) Frustration (d) Capacity

8. For which areas common to all content classes can sample skill inventories be prepared? (a) Parts of a textbook (b) Reference sources (c) Specialized vocabulary (d) All of the above

9. What is (are) the chief purpose(s) of an informal reading inventory? (a) Identifying reading levels (b) Analyzing oral reading errors (c) Providing an exact assessment of reading ability (d) Both *a* and *b*

10. In using cloze test procedures as recommended in this text, which words are deleted? (a) Every fifth (b) Every eighth (c) Every twelfth (d) Every fifteenth

11. What would be perhaps the most valid measure of a student's attitude toward reading? (a) Reaction to specific selections (b) A reading autobiography (c) "Incomplete sentences" (d) None of these

12. What technique may be utilized in self-appraisal by students? (a) Discussion (b) Conference (c) Checklist (d) All of these

13. Which type of score is the NCE most similar to? (a) Grade equivalents (b) Stanines (c) Percentiles (d) None of these

14. Which is the least desirable way of expressing test results? (a) Percentile ranks (b) Stanines (c) Grade equivalents (d) Scale scores

15. What type of score uses the specific content skills or objectives measured by the test as a reference point? (a) Norm-referenced score (b) Criterion-referenced score (c) Anticipated achievement score (d) Normal curve equivalents

16. When holistic assessment is used, what characteristic(s) are present in the testing? (a) Reading is treated as skill mastery of a variety of skills. (b) Reporting of results describes a reader's performance under specified conditions. (c) Single sentence items are used in preference to lengthier text. (d) All of the above

17. Which of the following could be used for holistic or process assessment?
(a) Retellings (b) Portfolios of students' work (c) Cloze procedure (d) All of the above

THOUGHT QUESTIONS

1. What do you consider to be the major strengths and weaknesses of each of the major assessment procedures discussed in this chapter?
2. Which way of reporting results of norm-referenced tests do you think is the most helpful? Why?
3. What are some of the major strengths and weaknesses of CRTs?
4. In what ways may a group reading inventory be useful to a content area teacher?
5. Which reading skill inventory do you think would be most helpful to you as a content area teacher? Why?
6. Why might secondary teachers prefer the cloze test procedure to the informal reading inventory?
7. Consider these questions about the cloze procedure: "Why must the replacement be the exact word?"; "How were the percentages/levels established?" Research these questions and report your findings. Two helpful resources are Michael C. McKenna and Richard D. Robinson, *An Introduction to the Cloze Procedure: An Annotated Bibliography*, rev. ed., Newark, Del.: International Reading Association, 1980, and Eugene A. Jongsma, *Cloze Instruction Research: A Second Look*, Newark, Del.: International Reading Association, 1980.
8. Do you think a self-assessment checklist would help you learn more about a student's reading of a content area textbook? If so, prepare a self-rating checklist that would be most appropriate in your classroom. If not, explain why not.
9. How would you revise the general and reading interests inventory to be most appropriate to your specific content area?
10. Are process and holistic assessments likely to be more helpful to teachers than current standardized tests in planning for reading instruction? Why, or why not?

ENRICHMENT ACTIVITIES

*1. If feasible, administer a norm-referenced reading rate test to a student and interpret the results.
*2. Administer the San Diego Quick Assessment to a student. Share your findings about reading levels with peers.

*These activities are designed for in-service teachers, student teachers, and practicum students.

*3. Prepare a group reading inventory, using content area reading materials. Administer your inventory to a student, record your results, and share the findings with the class.

4. Using a textbook of your choice, develop at least two sample questions on each of the book parts listed. (If a particular book part is not included in your text, select examples from supplemental materials.)
   a. Preface, Introduction, or Foreword
   b. Table of Contents
   c. Index
   d. Appendix
   e. Glossary
   f. Unit or Chapter Introduction and/or Summary

*5. Prepare a reading skills inventory for a content area textbook. Administer it to a student, record your results, and share the findings with the class.

*6. Secure a published informal reading inventory and administer it to a student. Report the results to the class.

*7. Prepare an informal reading inventory selection using content area reading materials. Administer it to a student, record the results, and share your findings with the class.

*8. Prepare a cloze procedure test for a passage of content area reading material. Administer it to a student. Report the results to the class.

*9. Read the article "Using Think Alouds to Assess Comprehension" by Suzanne E. Wade in the March 1990 issue of *The Reading Teacher*. Try using this procedure to assess a student's comprehension skills. Tell the class your conclusions about the comprehension instruction needed by this student.

*10. Prepare a self-appraisal checklist of some aspect of reading (see sample on study skills, Example 10.14). Administer to a student and report your findings to the class.

*11. Administer an interest inventory to a student. What information may be utilized in the instructional program?

*12. Prepare an interest check on one topic of study in your content area. If feasible, administer it to a student.

13. Prepare a criterion-referenced test, using content area reading materials.

*14. If possible, administer a criterion-referenced test to a group of secondary students.

BIBLIOGRAPHY

Au, Kathryn H., Judith A. Scheu, Alice J. Kawakami, and Patricia A. Herman. "Assessment and Accountability in a Whole Literacy Curriculum." *The Reading Teacher*, 43 (April 1990), 574–578.

Bader, Lois A., and Katherine D. Wiesendanger. "Realizing the Potential of Informal Reading Inventories." *Journal of Reading,* 32 (February 1989), 402–408.

Baldauf, Richard B., Jr., et al. "Can Matching Cloze Be Used with Secondary ESL Pupils?" *Journal of Reading,* 23 (February 1980), 435–440.

Baumann, James F. *Reading Assessment: An Instructional Decision-Making Perspective.* Columbus, Ohio: Merrill Publishing Company, 1988.

Betts, Emmett A. *Foundations of Reading Instruction.* New York: American Book Company, 1946.

Bormuth, John. "The Cloze Readability Procedure." *Elementary English,* 45 (April 1968), 429–436.

Brown, Carol S., and Susan L. Lytle. "Merging Assessment and Instruction: Protocols in the Classroom." In Susan Mandel Glazer, Lyndon W. Searfoss, and Lance M. Gentile (eds.), *Reexamining Reading Diagnosis: New Trends and Procedures.* Newark, Del.: International Reading Association, 1989, pp. 94–102.

Brozo, William G. "Learning How At-Risk Readers Learn Best: A Case for Interactive Assessment." *Journal of Reading,* 33 (April 1990), 522–527.

Burron, Arnold, and Amos L. Claybaugh. *Using Reading to Teach Subject Matter: Fundamentals for Content Teachers.* Columbus, Ohio: Merrill Publishing Company, 1974.

Clark, Charles H. "Assessing Free Recall." *The Reading Teacher,* 35 (January 1982), 434–439.

Davey, Beth. "Assessing Comprehension: Selected Interactions of Task and Reader." *The Reading Teacher,* 42 (May 1989), 694–697.

Dulin, Kenneth L., and Robert D. Chester. "A Validated Study of the Estes Scale Attitude Scales." *Journal of Reading,* 18 (October 1974), 56–59.

Ekwall, Eldon E. "Should Repetitions Be Counted As Errors?" *The Reading Teacher,* 27 (January 1974), 365–367.

Estes, Thomas H. "A Scale to Measure Attitude Toward Reading." *Journal of Reading,* 15 (November 1971), 135–138.

Farr, Roger, and Robert F. Carey. *Reading: What Can Be Measured?* Newark, Del.: International Reading Association, 1986.

Glazer, Susan Mandel, and Lyndon W. Searfoss. "Reexamining Reading Diagnosis." In Susan Mandel Glazer, Lyndon W. Searfoss, and Lance M. Gentile (eds.), *Reexamining Reading Diagnosis: New Trends and Procedures.* Newark, Del.: International Reading Association, 1989, pp. 1–11.

Henk, William A. "Reading Assessments of the Future: Toward Precision Diagnosis." *The Reading Teacher,* 40 (May 1987), 860–870.

Holmes, Betty C., and Nancy L. Roser. "Five Ways to Assess Readers' Prior Knowledge." *The Reading Teacher,* 40 (March 1987), 646–649.

Johnson, M. S., R. A. Kress, and J. J. Pikulski. *Informal Reading Inventories.* 2nd ed. Newark, Del.: International Reading Association, 1987.

Johnston, Peter H. "Assessment in Reading." In P. D. Pearson et al. (eds.), *Handbook of Reading Research.* New York: Longman, 1984.

Johnston, Peter H. *Reading Comprehension Assessment: A Cognitive Basis.* Newark, Del.: International Reading Association, 1983.

Johnston, Peter. "Teachers as Evaluation Experts." *The Reading Teacher,* 40 (April 1987), 744–748.

Kennedy, D., and Ronald S. Halinski. "Measuring Attitudes: An Extra Dimension." *Journal of Reading,* 18 (April 1975), 518–522.

Kletzien, Sharon B., and Maryanne R. Bednar. "Dynamic Assessment for At-Risk Readers." *Journal of Reading,* 33 (April 1990), 528–533.

Langer, Judith A. "From Theory to Practice: A Prereading Plan." *Journal of Reading,* 25 (November 1981), 152–156.

463

464

LaPray, M., and R. Ross. "The Graded Word List: A Quick Gauge of Reading Ability." *Journal of Reading*, 12 (January 1969), 305–307.

Lewandowski, Lawrence J., and Brian K. Martens. "Test Review: Selecting and Evaluating Standardized Reading Tests." *Journal of Reading*, 33 (February 1990), 384–388.

Morrow, Lesley Mandel. "Retelling Stories as a Diagnostic Tool." In Susan Mandel Glazer, Lyndon W. Searfoss, and Lance H. Gentile (eds.), *Reexamining Reading Diagnosis: New Trends and Procedures*. Newark, Del.: International Reading Association, 1989, pp. 128–149.

Pikulski, John J. "Informal Reading Inventories." *The Reading Teacher*, 43 (March 1990), 514–516.

Purves, A. C. *Elements of Writing About a Literary Work*. Champaign, Ill.: National Council of Teachers of English, 1968.

Readence, John E., and Michael A. Martin. "Comprehension Assessment: Alternatives to Standardized Tests." In Susan Mandel Glazer, Lyndon W. Searfoss, and Lance M. Gentile (eds.), *Reexamining Reading Diagnosis: New Trends and Procedures*. Newark, Del.: International Reading Association, 1989, pp. 67–80.

Richek, Margaret Ann, Lynne K. List, and Janet W. Lerner. *Reading Problems: Assessment and Teaching Strategies*. Englewood Cliffs, N.J.: Prentice Hall, 1989.

Salvia, John, and James E. Ysseldyke. *Assessment in Special and Remedial Education*. 4th ed. Boston: Houghton Mifflin, 1988.

Schmitt, Maribeth Cassidy. "A Questionnaire to Measure Children's Awareness of Strategic Reading Processes." *The Reading Teacher*, 43 (March 1990), 454–458.

Shannon, Albert J. "Effects of Methods of Standardized Reading Achievement Test Administration on Attitude Toward Reading." *Journal of Reading*, 23 (May 1980), 684–686.

Shannon, Albert J. "Using the Microcomputer Environment for Reading Diagnosis." In Susan Mandel Glazer, Lyndon W. Searfoss, and Lance M. Gentile (eds.), *Reexamining Reading Diagnosis: New Trends and Procedures*. Newark, Del.: International Reading Association, 1989, pp. 150–168.

Tullock-Rhody, Regina, and J. Estill Alexander. "A Scale for Assessing Attitudes Toward Reading in Secondary Schools." *Journal of Reading*, 23 (April 1980), 609–614.

Vacca, Richard T., and Jo Anne L. Vacca. *Content Area Reading*. 3rd ed. Boston: Little, Brown and Company, 1989.

Valencia, Sheila, and P. David Pearson. "Reading Assessment: Time for a Change." *The Reading Teacher*, 40 (April 1987), 726–732.

Valmont, William J. "Creating Questions for Informal Reading Inventories." *The Reading Teacher*, 25 (March 1972), 509–512.

Wade, Suzanne E. "Using Think Alouds to Assess Comprehension." *The Reading Teacher*, 43 (March 1990), 442–451.

Wittrock, Merlin C. "Process Oriented Measures of Comprehension." *The Reading Teacher*, 40 (April 1987), 734–737.

Wixson, Karen K., Charles. W. Peters, Elaine M. Weber, and Edward D. Roeber. "New Directions in Statewide Reading Assessment." *The Reading Teacher*, 40 (April 1987), 749–754.

Wolf, D. P. "Portfolio Assessment: Sampling Student Work." *Educational Leadership*, 46, No. 7 (1989), 35–39.

11

SECONDARY SCHOOL READING PROGRAMS

OVERVIEW

This chapter considers the personnel who are responsible for reading instruction and different types of secondary school reading programs. These reading programs include total-school reading programs, special English sections and units, remedial reading classes, reading laboratories, and reading improvement classes. The total school organization for reading is much more comprehensive than the other programs, which are often combined so that two or more are initiated at the same time.

Any school reading program, regardless of its complexity, requires special planning. Responsibility for execution of the various aspects of the program must be assigned. Cooperation of staff members is essential, as is in-service training for them. Program goals and instructional techniques must be determined cooperatively by the involved personnel, and materials for the program must be chosen carefully.

PURPOSE-SETTING QUESTIONS

As you read this chapter, try to answer these questions:

1. What responsibilities for reading instruction in the secondary school belong to the content area teacher, the administrator, the reading consultant, the special reading teacher, and the librarian or media specialist?
2. What are necessary activities related to the development of a total-school reading program?
3. What are some techniques that should be used in working with remedial readers?
4. What are some skill areas considered in reading improvement classes?
5. What are some types of equipment that may be found in reading laboratories?
6. What are some questions that a teacher should ask about materials being evaluated for use in a secondary school reading program?

466

As you read this chapter, check your understanding of these terms:

corrective instruction

developmental instruction

diagnostic test

in-service training

special reading teacher

reading achievement test

reading laboratory

remedial instruction

reading consultant

Personnel Responsible for Reading Instruction

The secondary school reading program is the responsibility of a number of individuals. Those responsible for various portions of the program include content area teachers, administrators, reading consultants, special reading teachers, and librarians or media specialists.

Content Area Teachers

The responsibility of the content area teacher is to help students read their textbooks and supplementary materials more effectively in order to learn the content more effectively. Content teachers need to know what reading skills are necessary for successful reading of the materials in their particular disciplines, and they need to be capable of assisting students in applying these skills as they complete their content area assignments. In most cases, such as in teaching technical vocabulary, reading instruction and content instruction are identical. Content teachers may often find that brief instruction in a particular reading strategy will pay large dividends in the students' understanding of an assignment.

Content area teachers are not expected to be *primarily* engaged in teaching reading strategies, however. Students who have significantly impaired reading abilities are helped by a special reading teacher outside the content class. The content teachers do have to make adjustments for these students and their reading levels when making content assignments. It is necessary to provide alternate materials and teaching methods for these students if their content learning is to be successful.

Following are the requirements for content area teachers if they are to meet their responsibilities to their students and the reading program:

1. Knowledge of the reading skills that are needed by secondary students in order to read content materials in their disciplines
2. Knowledge of assessment measures that can help them identify students who cannot read the standard assignments, students who can read the assignments only with much assistance, or those who can read the assignments with ease

3. Ability to identify specific learning problems that should be referred to a specialist in order to provide appropriate help for students who require it
4. Knowledge of ways to help students learn specific skills needed for their content areas
5. Knowledge of study aids and procedures that can help students be more successful in content area reading
6. Knowledge of effective ways to differentiate assignments for students reading at different levels of proficiency
7. Willingness to cooperate with other school personnel, such as the special reading teacher, in helping students reach their full potential in reading to learn content

Special Reading Teacher

The special reading teacher works directly with students. He or she may be either a diagnostic-remedial specialist or a developmental reading-study skills specialist. This person should have a graduate degree in reading or the equivalent, have several years of teaching experience, and be certified as a reading specialist.

Although the specific responsibilities of the reading specialist may vary from locale to locale, the following are fairly typical:

1. Knows reading strategies, formal and informal instruments for assessing reading (can administer and interpret them), and a variety of methods and materials for reading instruction.
2. Plans and teaches reading classes for average readers, accelerated readers, and disabled readers.
3. Works with paraprofessionals and parents who may assist with the reading program.
4. Works with content area teachers whose students are in reading classes; assists content area teachers in selecting instructional materials to meet the needs of students; when called upon, helps content teachers develop and utilize reading instruction within content classrooms; provides suggestions on establishing learning centers within content classrooms, especially involving use of tape-recorded instruction for the severely disabled reader.
5. Assists the reading consultant as a demonstration teacher and resource person.

Reading Consultant

The reading consultant works with administrators and other school personnel to develop and coordinate the schoolwide reading program. This person is freed from classroom teaching or instruction of special reading classes. He or she should have a high degree of professional skill and knowledge, have had formal study in reading and related areas and several years successful teaching experience, and have met certification qualifications as a special teacher of reading.

Again, although the specific responsibilities of the reading consultant may vary somewhat from locale to locale, the following are typical:

1. Studies the population to be served — both students and teachers
2. Assists principal/supervisor/administrator in planning a comprehensive reading program that includes (a) development of basic skills, (b) correction/remediation, (c) content area reading and study skills, (d) development of interests and tastes in leisure reading
3. Orients beginning teachers to philosophy, procedures, and materials for school reading program and keeps all school staff informed about new developments in reading
4. Evaluates the program through supervisory activities and research, making recommendations for changes as needed
5. Provides in-service instruction, conducting workshops, seminars, conferences, and minilessons on topics such as readability formulas, informal reading inventories, and construction of teaching or study guides
6. Evaluates and recommends reading materials
7. Works as resource person with special cases when difficulty or complexity requires a high degree of professional competence
8. Keeps the school community informed about the purposes and progress of the reading program

Principal or Administrator

A most significant prerequisite for a good secondary reading program is administrative direction. The administrator alone possesses the prestige and authority to carry through a sound reading program. He or she must encourage the staff and ensure that the reading philosophy is implemented in logical and innovative ways. He or she needs to provide the impetus for defining the reading program's philosophy and must facilitate that philosophy by extending it to the entire school. Example 11.1 presents an administrator's self-evaluation checklist that outlines the responsibility of the administrator in the reading program.

Several points may be made that elaborate on the checklist in Example 11.1. The administrator should consider the following as important ultimate goals of a comprehensive reading program:

1. The students like to read and have acquired an abiding interest in reading a wide variety of worthwhile material.
2. The students make efficient use of skills to identify words and increase meaning vocabulary (understanding of words) through reading.
3. The students make efficient use of skills needed to read informative (content) reading materials.

EXAMPLE *11.1*

Administrator's Self-Evaluation Checklist

(Please respond yes or no to these items)

GENERAL GOAL FOCUSING

1. The teachers and I have in mind the basic goals of the reading program.
2. The teachers and I keep in mind the interdependency of the instructional reading phases.
3. To remain knowledgeable about reading and students,
   a. I read books on the role of the administrator and reading.
   b. I take formal courses in reading and attend reading workshops and conferences.
   c. I visit often with outstanding reading teachers.
   d. I study the reading materials used in the school.
   e. I maintain a professional reading library.
4. The teachers and I have arrived at basic principles of reading instruction.
5. I help stimulate reading improvement opportunities by
   a. evaluating the present program with teachers.
   b. observing classrooms for reading instruction practices and noting items such as the following:
      How are the students prepared for reading?
      How is the reading material interpreted?
      How are skills/abilities extended?
      How are interests extended?
   c. providing for intervisitation demonstrations, videotaping.
   d. focusing on reading topics of interest in faculty meetings and workshops.

RESOURCE COMMITMENT

6. I make a real effort to reduce teacher-pupil ratio.
7. I try to meet and exceed requirements for library resources.
8. I try to involve parents, paraprofessionals, and students in the reading program.
9. I make decisions about reading materials for school use only after tryouts on a limited scale and by following selection guidelines.
10. I recognize that organization is a technique or a system — not a "method of instruction" — and that organization can only facilitate — or hinder — effective instruction.

PROGRAM MONITORING

11. The teachers and I maintain appropriate record forms for indicating reading progress of each student.
12. The teachers and I understand and use reading survey tests, diagnostic reading tests, informal reading inventories, and other assessment techniques.

13. The teachers and I have provided corrective/remedial services for appropriate students.
14. I am prepared to answer the questions about reading most frequently asked by parents and others.
15. The time allocated for reading instruction is sufficient for the task.
16. I attempt to designate space for a central resource center.
17. The teachers and I periodically review results of our efforts to improve reading instruction.
18. I use the data from these review sessions to make needed changes.

HIRING PERSONNEL

19. I hire classroom teachers who are informed about reading problems in their special areas.
20. I hire reading personnel who have adequate expertise in reading.

INTERPERSONAL RELATIONSHIPS

21. The teachers perceive me as a facilitator rather than as a dictator.
22. The teachers feel free to come to me when problems related to the reading program develop.
23. I communicate well with parents concerning their children's reading difficulties and the steps being taken to help them.
24. Students are not afraid to approach me with problems related to their reading program or other areas.

4. The students can understand literally; can interpret, evaluate, and react to printed ideas; and can organize and remember what they read.
5. The students can adjust reading rates to the purpose and nature of the reading material.

There are nine major functions of the administrator in the reading program:

1. *Knowing about reading and students.* Ways to increase knowledge are suggested in Example 11.1 (see points 3b through 3e). The administrator should arrive at some basic principles or understandings about reading, such as (a) reading is a complex act with many factors that must be considered; (b) reading depends on the interpretation of the meaning of printed symbols — it is not just "decoding"; (c) there is no one correct way to teach reading — the teacher is the focal point; (d) learning to read is a continuing process; (e) reading and other language arts are closely interrelated; and (f) reading is an integral part of all content area instruction.

2. *Stimulating improvement opportunities.* This can be accomplished through the four procedures suggested in Example 11.1 (points 5a through 5d). Reading topics of interest to many teachers — such as methods of group-

ing students, classroom analysis of reading needs, methods of improving comprehension and recall, methods of teaching word recognition strategies, teaching study and research skills, methods of individualizing instruction in the various content areas, and ways of planning a balanced reading program — provide critical issues for consideration at faculty meetings, workshops, and conferences.

3. *Enhancing teaching/learning environment.* Three major contributions that can be made by the administrator in this area involve items 6 through 8 in Example 11.1.

4. *Selecting effective materials.* Publishers and their representatives are in business to make money; they produce material that they believe will sell well. Valid standards and procedures for selection of superior materials are needed to avoid ill-considered purchases. Many schools have in their storerooms materials and learning aids that never should have been bought but that were purchased hastily when money suddenly became available from an unexpected source. The best way to avoid such mistakes is to pre-evaluate materials. Decisions to purchase should not be made by a single individual, and in most schools they are not. Tentative decisions should be reached by a group that includes representatives who know (a) what the local resources are, (b) what alternatives are available, and (c) what opinions and preferences the potential users have. Potential users should be a part of the group. Final decisions on major purchases should come only after tryouts on a limited scale whenever this can be arranged.

Assistance in choosing appropriate materials may also be obtained from sources such as university faculty. Some universities have entire courses devoted to materials selection. (More on selection of materials is included later in this chapter.)

5. *Creating appropriate organizational plans.* In organizing for reading instruction, the administrator should be aware of important guidelines: (a) there are vast differences among the instructional needs of students of similar age/grade placement; (b) organizational patterns should be flexible and altered as better ways are discovered; (c) more emphasis should be placed on methods of providing for individual differences by teachers than on methods of grouping; and (d) organization is a technique or system — not a "method of instruction"; therefore organization can only facilitate or hinder effective instruction.

6. *Helping to collect and interpret test data.* Appropriate reading progress forms need to be maintained by the school in the student's cumulative folder. The administrator realizes that reading survey tests should show in a general way how well students are performing (they indicate the range of reading achievement in the class), whereas diagnostic reading tests help teachers to locate specific reading strengths and weaknesses and possibly to determine

472

causes. The administrator should be sensitive to the fact that the best tests are those for which the sample population used to standardize the test resembles the class to be tested; he or she should also be aware that a test score on a standardized reading test frequently reflects the student's frustration level (the material is too advanced) rather than instructional level (best level for effective teaching) or independent reading level (student can read on his or her own). The administrator values informal reading inventories, informal skills checks, and interest inventories. (See Chapter 10 for a detailed description of such assessment tools.)

7. *Providing corrective/remedial services.* The administrator (a) is sensitive to the basic principles of corrective reading instruction; (b) helps identify students reading below capacity level; (c) focuses on possible instructional weaknesses throughout the curriculum, such as failure to adjust content material to the students' reading levels and ineffective motivation for developing reading interests; (d) provides appropriate materials; and (e) wisely utilizes the reading specialist and the reading consultant for this specialized service.

8. *Communicating about the reading program.* The administrator should be aware of the following questions frequently posed by parents and be prepared to answer them reasonably: How is reading taught in the school? Is my youngster reading at grade level? What can I do to help my child like reading? What about the use of computers? What can we parents do to help our child who is a poor reader? Does my child have dyslexia? Should I hire a tutor for my disabled reader? What special programs do you have for poor readers? How fast should my teenager be able to read?

9. *Hiring capable personnel.* All teachers are expected to understand about reading difficulties that may occur in their content area assignments and to adjust assignments to fit the students' reading capabilities. The administrator should give special consideration to candidates who have had courses in reading methods.

Teachers who are hired specifically as reading personnel should meet the guidelines established by the International Reading Association (Professional Standards and Ethics Committee, 1986). These guidelines address roles and responsibilities, academic preparation, and competencies for classroom teachers, reading specialists, and allied professionals. Areas in which levels of competency are designated for each of ten roles are linguistic and cognitive bases for reading, comprehension, word identification and vocabulary, appreciation and enjoyment, diagnostic teaching, and continuing program maintenance planning and improvement.

Teachers should exhibit personal characteristics that enhance their effectiveness in interactions with students: empathy, patience, and positive attitudes are important.

Sanacore (1988) believes that the school principal can and should support schoolwide independent reading, since it can have a positive effect on students' reading habits and achievement. He laments the fact that some principals see independent reading as frivolous and delegate it to time after skills instruction, ignoring the fact that it provides prior knowledge of content that will be studied, helps students build reading interests, allows students to apply skills in realistic text, and helps students develop a love of reading. Sanacore believes that in each subject area five weeks of independent reading could be offered to students, allowing them to be exposed to independent reading in at least one class throughout most of the school year without sacrificing content instruction in any one class. This approach would, of course, require large numbers of books appropriate to the different instructional areas from which students could choose their independent reading. Sanacore's position is congruent with that of Hillerich (1983, p. 100), who has stated that "independent reading should be half of the total program in reading instruction."

Wilhite (1984) questioned principals in DuPage County, Illinois, about their views of the principal's ideal leadership role. All the respondents felt that evaluation of the reading staff was part of their role. Ninety-six percent felt that ensuring funding and hiring specialized reading personnel were their responsibilities. Eighty-seven percent judged both evaluation of the reading program and establishment of guidelines for hiring specialized reading personnel to be part of their jobs. Participation in planning in-service programs and planning and implementing the reading program were seen as the principal's responsibility by 83 percent and 78 percent of the respondents, respectively. Seventy-four percent felt that promotion of staff involvement in reading for the content areas and provision of guidelines for staff communication with the community were their responsibility. Very few felt that participation in the daily operation of the reading program (26 percent) and selection of equipment and instructional materials for reading (35 percent) were part of the principal's responsibility. This study shows that, although principals do view reading-related activities as a part of their responsibility, they may not want to be directly involved in these activities on a day-to-day basis. It would be interesting to discover if the instructional programs in which the principals participated more had superior results when compared to results of the other programs.

Ward and Bradford (1983) found that achievement of junior high school students is positively influenced when they are taught under the supervision of an administrator (often an assistant principal) who is eligible for certification in reading or who has earned additional college credits in reading. If the teachers of these students perceive the supervisor to have reading expertise, the effect on students' reading achievement is also positive.

Librarian or Media Center Specialist

The librarian or media center specialist provides assistance to the special reading teacher and the content area teacher alike by locating books and other printed materials on different subjects and reading levels, making available audiovisual aids that can be used for motivation and background building, and providing students with instruction in location skills related to the library. The librarian may set up special displays of printed materials on specific subjects at different reading levels at the request of the teachers and may provide students with direct assistance in finding and using appropriate materials. Recreational reading may be fostered by the librarian's book talks or attractive book displays on high-interest topics.

Teamwork

The content area teacher is a part of a team of personnel who are all concerned with the development of reading skills of secondary school students. The content area teacher is concerned with the level of reading proficiency largely because it can enhance or adversely affect the learning of content. Content area teachers may ask for the reading consultant's assistance when determining which approaches will best meet the special reading needs of students in their content classes. They may send students who are reading far below the level of the instructional materials assigned for the grade to the special reading teacher for diagnosis and remedial instruction; they should work closely with the special reading teacher in planning reading assignments for students who are currently enrolled in special reading classes for remedial assistance; they should consult with the special reading teacher about instructional materials that will meet the reading needs of their students; and they may ask the special reading teacher to demonstrate lessons in some aspects of reading. Content area teachers should expect to work hand-in-hand with the librarian and/or media center specialist when assembling materials for teaching units and when teaching library skills. Content magazines, reference materials, and recreational reading materials should be a part of the library's yearly budget allocation, and content teachers should be the ones who recommend appropriate materials.

Content teachers in the Polk County, Florida, district found that assistance from reading specialists/consultants was beneficial to their programs. Particularly useful were their services in conducting class presentations on various topics, preparing study guides for content texts, diagnostic testing, determining readability levels of materials, and conducting in-service sessions on reading components (Woods and Topping, 1986).

The principal sets the tone of the school's reading program. The content area teacher should be able to approach the principal for funding for instructional materials that are needed to meet the diverse reading needs of the students in content classes and for help with organizational arrangements, such as special grouping practices that he or she may wish to use to enhance the content area reading program.

When the principal or administrator, reading consultant, special reading teacher, and librarian or media specialist work together and with the content area teachers to produce a good reading program for a school, success for the program is likely. Each staff member needs to understand his or her own job and the jobs of colleagues. This understanding helps to enhance cooperation.

Total-School Programs

A total-school reading program is one in which all school personnel cooperate and all students are offered reading instruction according to their needs. Reading instruction is offered in special reading classes and clinical settings and is a priority in content area classes as well. The skills are taught as their use is required; therefore, the instruction is meaningful to the students because they see a direct application for it. Developmental instruction is offered to students who are progressing satisfactorily in building reading skill, and corrective and remedial instruction is offered to students who are experiencing difficulties. In such a program, all aspects of reading are included:

1. Developmental reading is taught.
2. Content area reading is taught.
3. Recreational reading is encouraged.
4. Remedial reading is offered.

Implementing a total-school reading program is a difficult, demanding assignment, but the energy invested in it is well spent. Teachers in one survey indicated that such programs are promoted by recognition of need, effective in-service training, cooperative planning time, support of the administration, and leadership to coordinate development of the program (Gee and Forester, 1988), all factors that can indeed make a difference in the success of a program. The process of implementation can be diagrammed as shown in Figure 11.1.

Figure 11.1 shows a sequence of activities through which a school's staff can move in developing a total-school reading program. The sequence shows movement from defining a reading philosophy to evaluating the program. Throughout the entire sequence, constant in-service training of one type or another is offered to the staff involved in the program development. Suggestions provided during in-service activities will be most helpful if they can be implemented immediately. Therefore, the training sessions should be offered when a need for the particular information is current. Results of each step in the sequence provide input, which may affect subsequent in-service sessions for the director(s) of the in-service training.

Staff In-Service Training

A first glance at this plan of implementation may result in the reaction that in-service training is being overemphasized. Careful consideration, however,

476

FIGURE II.I

Implementation of a School Reading Program

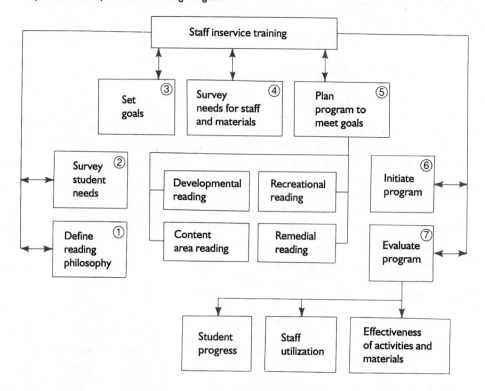

reveals that this is not the case. Many secondary teachers (in some schools, most teachers) have little background knowledge concerning the nature of reading; the reading strategy needs of students, available formal tests of reading progress, informal measures of reading achievement, reading interests and tastes of adolescents, and other topics related to helping secondary students progress in reading. In addition to this lack of knowledge, some of the teachers are opposed to the idea of teaching reading strategies. They often fail to realize that helping their students read the subject matter with more understanding will help these students learn subject matter concepts more effectively.

The first in-service training sessions should be designed to help the school's staff members recognize not only the need for reading instruction in the school but also the benefits to them as subject matter specialists if this need is adequately met. These sessions may involve "selling" the idea of a total-school program. Both teachers and administrators may need convincing, since many administrators have had no more background in the area of reading instruction than the subject matter specialists on the faculty have had. If the attempts to convince the staff are not effective, the chances of success for the program are greatly diminished. In-service sessions should involve the entire school staff — administrators, faculty members from all departments, media specialist(s), and guidance personnel.

Subsequent in-service sessions may deal with such topics as

1. Setting realistic program objectives
2. Determining reading skill needs of students
3. Locating and using appropriate materials for meeting student needs
4. Learning techniques for teaching specific strategies
5. Teaching directed reading lessons in content areas
6. Differentiating instruction in content area classes
7. Fitting reading assignments in the content areas to the reading achievement of the students
8. Using the library to full advantage
9. Learning techniques for evaluating the program's effectiveness

The in-service training may take a variety of forms, including the following:

1. Workshops in the school, conducted by the school's reading consultant or reading teacher
2. Workshops in the school, conducted by an outside expert on the topic under consideration
3. Reading conferences and conventions
4. Demonstration lessons
5. Faculty planning sessions (teachers working together to plan implementation of the program in their special areas using the resources available in the school)
6. Teachers observing the teaching of innovative peers
7. Consultants teaming with individual teachers or small groups of teachers to solve teacher-identified instructional problems
8. University courses

In-service sessions that involve hands-on activities seem to be more successful with teachers than straight lecture sessions. Stier (1978) describes one way to give secondary content area teachers some hands-on in-service sessions that can transfer into their classroom teaching. Any in-service session should include practical suggestions of immediate usefulness in addition to necessary theoretical background. Demonstrations of techniques, handouts, and displays of useful materials are more effective than mere "pep talks."

There should be teacher input into the planning of the in-service activities. Teachers should help to determine the topics to be considered, the format for the sessions, and the scheduling.

Reading Committee

Although all staff members need to believe in the concept of a schoolwide program and need to be willing to cooperate in implementing it, much planning can be done by a small staff group initially and then plans can be submitted to the entire staff for input, endorsement, and implementation. This planning group is sometimes referred to as the reading committee. It should be composed of people with the ability and enthusiasm to offer effective guidance of the program. A good composition for such a committee might be the principal, the reading consultant, all special reading teachers, a representative from each department, the media specialist, a guidance counselor, and perhaps a school board member or representative from a parent group (such as the Parent-Teacher Association). The principal or another knowledgeable person such as the reading consultant may chair the committee. In some schools, reading improvement teams have been formed to work on developing or improving the schoolwide reading program. The members of the team negotiate about and collaborate on reading program improvements in a school. They enter into extended dialogues aimed at reaching agreements about future working conditions for the teachers and learning arrangements for the students, for example, grouping and testing policies (Erickson, 1990). Although these teams do not always focus on total-school reading programs, this is one possible direction that they could take. Such teams encourage interactive decision-making rather than "mandates from above," which are often resented by teachers who are expected to implement them.

Anders (1981) offers five justifications for having a reading committee that has representatives from each content area within a school. The same advantages can be advanced for a similar composition of a reading improvement team.

1. The committee allows working relationships between the reading specialist and other faculty members to be developed in a natural and efficient way.
2. The committee facilitates the reception of feedback on old practices and new ideas related to the reading program.
3. Committee members from specific departments may be more able to communicate ideas to their department members because the department members are more willing to listen to them than to a reading specialist.
4. Reading specialists can share their expertise in reading while relying on the content teachers who are on the committee to share knowledge about the processes involved in learning content area concepts.
5. All faculty members — content area teachers and the reading specialist — share the responsibility for the total-school reading program.

Defining Reading Philosophy

The reading committee may elicit ideas from the other members of the staff concerning the nature of reading, the reading abilities that are necessary for comprehending printed material in the respective subject areas, the importance of recreational reading, and other similar areas. These ideas should be integrated with carefully researched published materials. The committee may then produce a statement of the school's reading philosophy and share the results with the entire staff. Representative statements from such a document might include:

1. Reading is the process of getting meaning from printed symbols.
2. Secondary school students need reading instruction, although the type of instruction needed may differ from student to student.
3. Students need help in learning to read printed materials before they can read these materials to learn concepts.
4. Special reading skills are needed in order to read certain content area materials with understanding.

Surveying Student Needs

The idea of starting a total-school reading program may come about because of low student scores on standardized reading achievement tests or because various faculty members have detected reading deficiencies in their students. If test results have motivated the effort, these results may be used as a beginning for surveying student needs. Reading achievement tests generally reveal the students' accomplishments in broad areas of reading (comprehension, vocabulary, rate). If an achievement test in reading has not previously been administered, the reading committee will probably wish to choose an appropriate test and make arrangements for its administration. After broad areas of difficulty among the student body have been identified, the committee may wish to choose either standardized or informal diagnostic measures for administration in order to pinpoint specific difficulties. Measures of reading interests and attitudes toward reading also may be used at this time to help the staff clarify the needs of the students. Suggestions for conducting a needs assessment have been offered by Siedow (1985), including ideas for assessment documents.

Setting Goals

When embarking on a new endeavor such as an all-school reading program, it is helpful to have some goals in mind. The reading committee may formulate a list of goals for the program and submit them to the rest of the faculty for input and approval. All faculty members need to have a part in deciding on goals because these goals will have a great deal of influence over each teacher's classroom activities. Some goals that might be stated include the following:

1. All students will be offered an opportunity to develop and refine their basic reading skills through special reading classes.
2. All students will be helped to develop reading skills specific to particular content areas during the content area classes.
3. Each student will be offered reading assignments that are appropriate to his or her reading achievement level.
4. All students will be encouraged to read for recreation in a variety of interest areas.
5. All students will be given opportunities to utilize the resources of the school's media center.
6. All students who are classified as remedial readers will be given special instruction by a qualified specialist.

Surveying Needs for Staff and Materials

The reading committee can take the list of goals for the school's program and analyze the needs of the school relative to meeting these goals. For example, the committee may discover that another qualified reading teacher will be needed if each student classified as a remedial reader is to receive special help. It may not be possible to meet such a need at midyear, and the total implementation of the remedial portion of the program may have to be postponed; however, the program goal will at least clarify the need for specialized staff in the coming year.

If each student in the school is going to be offered an opportunity to develop and refine basic reading skills, the committee may find that rooms must be set aside for reading laboratories. These laboratories should be staffed by reading teachers and equipped with reading materials and equipment suitable for use by students who are reading on a wide variety of levels and need help with a variety of different skills. Once again, the committee may find that complete implementation is not immediately possible, but a beginning can be made, and future plans can include the needed changes.

Taking into account the amount of money available for implementing the program, the committee members may study catalogs of materials and equipment, may preview or examine available items, and may choose the items needed most to implement the program. The committee may continue to preview promising materials even after the program goes into full operation, or the reading consultant and reading teachers may assume that responsibility at some time in the process. Naturally, all staff members should be encouraged to suggest appropriate materials, especially those related closely to particular disciplines.

When the committee has obtained information about the skill needs of the students and the goals of the program, specific plans for a program can be made. Plans may center around the four major aspects of reading instruction — developmental reading, content area reading, recreational reading, and remedial reading.

Developmental Reading. Basic reading strategies and skills are often taught in developmental reading classes that are staffed by a reading teacher; they are also taught in remedial classes and, as needed for understanding the content, in content classes. Developmental reading classes frequently feature group instruction. However, some programs are individualized: teachers often assign materials on different levels to different students or make use of individual student contracts. The individualized programs often utilize a laboratory setting. Areas that usually receive attention in developmental reading classes include study skills, vocabulary building, general comprehension, critical reading, appreciation, and rate. The developmental reading classes also may go beyond basic skills instruction and offer help with special reading problems in the content areas, in cooperation with the content area teachers, who also will stress such assistance. In order to teach these skills, instructors often use demonstrations, lectures, class discussion, workbooks or computer drill-and-practice programs, and mechanical equipment.

Demonstrations of the application of reading strategies are perhaps the most effective approach to use in developmental classes. Teacher modeling of the strategies for the students through think-aloud presentations allows students to see what they are expected to do. Such demonstrations should be followed by guided practice and independent practice of the strategies presented.

Presentation in lecture form of material on how to improve reading proficiency is likely to elicit questions from the students, and the ensuing discussion can be valuable to the class as a whole. In addition, some students are auditory learners — they learn things better through hearing them. Lecture-demonstration combinations are especially effective for helping students acquire techniques for increasing rate of reading.

Most developmental reading programs make use of workbooks or worktexts either as the basic texts for the programs or as supplementary materials. Many programs use a number of different workbooks, and instructors assign appropriate sections to individual students. Some programs are now using computer drill-and-practice programs instead of workbooks.

Following are some important considerations concerning the selection of workbooks for a class:

1. Does the book include information about development of reading strategies and skills as well as exercises designed for practice of such strategies

and skills? (If you intend to lecture on development of strategies and skills yourself, you may want only exercises. If the student is expected to learn some techniques through reading, the book should probably contain a balance of exercises and instructional material.)

2. Does the book cover all of the areas of reading that you wish to cover in your class? (If you wish to use a basic text, you should choose one that covers all of the areas in which you are interested. If you are using the book as a supplement to other materials, check to be sure that the areas covered are ones for which you need additional material.)

3. Are purposes indicated for each textbook assignment? (If not, you will need to provide purposes for the assignments in order for the students to gain maximum benefit from the material.)

4. Are answers to the exercises included in the workbook? (If you wish the students to use the book independently, answers should be included.)

5. Are the reading selections ones that students consider interesting and relevant? (Lack of relevance of selections can result in decreased student enthusiasm for course activities.)

6. Does the book contain charts and/or graphs that are designed to help the student keep a record of his or her progress? (Such visible signs of progress serve as motivation for future effort. If the book does not include such aids, you may want to devise some for your students.)

7. Are the directions for the activities clear? (Vague directions may result in students' following incorrect procedures. As a result, no learning may occur, or the students may learn incorrect responses.)

8. Is the workbook durable? (Students become understandably irritated by books that fall apart in the middle of a course.)

Although mechanical devices can contribute to a reading program, they are not essential to the development of a good program. They seem to function primarily as motivational devices for the students. Many types of equipment are utilized in reading programs. Some of them include (1) controlled reading devices, (2) tachistoscopes, (3) reading accelerators or pacers, (4) tape recorders (often with listening stations), and (5) computers (with appropriate software). (See Chapter 4 for additional discussion of rate improvement devices.)

Controlled readers, tachistoscopes, and reading accelerators or pacers are ordinarily utilized to help students build reading speed. The printed material accompanying the controlled reading filmstrips is also designed to aid in vocabulary development and comprehension. Computer programs have been developed to work on rate improvement and may eventually replace the other types of hardware completely. At present, not all schools have a sufficient number of computers available for wide use of these programs.

Since the various devices for increasing rate are adjustable to speeds appropriate for different individuals, these devices can contribute to individualization of a program. Group use of projected controlled reading materials, however, may cause teachers to neglect individual differences. The rate chosen may frustrate some students if it is too fast and may bore others if it is too slow for them. Controlled reading devices in general can help individuals realize that it is possible for them to read faster. However, the skills so acquired must be transferred from reading with machine aid to reading without artificial assistance before the student will have truly acquired a useful reading technique.

In a study of the kinds of reading courses taught in junior and senior high school, nearly half of the sixty-one respondents from across the United States indicated that developmental reading was offered in their schools, and more than a third indicated that accelerated reading courses (for students reading above grade level) were also offered (Greenlaw and Moore, 1982).

Content Area Reading. All of the basic areas of reading discussed earlier — vocabulary, general comprehension, critical reading, study skills, appreciation, and rate — are important in content area reading because they are necessary to the understanding of content material. A good content teacher will address all these areas at times when students need them to understand the particular content that is being presented. Thus, the strategies and skills are taught as a means to the end of better content understanding. The developmental reading teacher, on the other hand, has as his or her main goal the teaching of the reading strategies and skills themselves.

As explained and highlighted in Chapters 8 and 9, each content teacher is especially concerned with the specific applications and reading strategies and skills that are particular to his or her content area. For instance, the social studies teacher will be very attentive to the cause-and-effect and chronological order patterns of organization, whereas the science teacher must be especially concerned with the classification pattern, the cause-and-effect pattern, and the following of directions. Although the special reading teacher will also work on these patterns, it is the content teacher who can observe the students' ability or inability to understand a particular pattern within the actual content materials and can provide instruction as needed to facilitate the learning of the content. Since many content area teachers have had no previous training in helping students with reading strategies, these teachers may need in-service training to help them prepare for these tasks.

Recreational Reading. Recreational reading is reading purely for pleasure. Many secondary school students today do not read recreationally. Outside distractions, such as movies, television, and readily available cars, are partially responsible for the fact that many young people do not read for pleasure. Also, students may not have adult role models who read for pleasure and may never have been exposed to enjoyable reading materials that stimulate personal interests. All teachers and other school staff members — principals, librarians, and guidance counselors — can help to encourage recreational reading. They can provide reading materials and information about reading materials and can act as positive role models by reading recreationally themselves in the presence of students.

Newman (1982) suggested the development of a readers' club to encourage students to read in their free time. The club can meet during lunch to discuss interesting books. Members can rate the books read and develop a list of recommended books. The club can be billed as being for students who love to read, but, if activities are interesting enough (for example, book parties and guest authors), others will be tempted to join as well.

Recreational reading courses are sometimes offered by schools, but they are offered less frequently than remedial and developmental courses (Greenlaw and Moore, 1982).

Remedial Reading. Remedial instruction is generally designed for those students who read two or more years below the level at which they could be expected to read with understanding. Such instruction is given by a reading specialist in a special reading class or a reading laboratory. In most cases the student-teacher ratio for a remedial program is lower than that for a developmental program, and each student is given more individual attention by the teacher.

Diagnosis of needs for remedial readers is generally quite extensive, with both formal and informal diagnostic measures being utilized. Attitude, interest, and personality inventories are frequently used to supplement the reading test information, and counseling personnel are often involved in the testing and advisement of the students. See Chapter 10 for a discussion of formal and informal tests that may be used.

Teachers strive to use high interest, low vocabulary materials with remedial readers. Care must be taken to avoid choosing materials that are obviously written for much younger readers. When high interest, low vocabulary materials are not available, teachers often resort to rewriting materials to lower levels of difficulty or to using the language experience approach described in Chapter 6.

Because of repeated failures in the past, remedial students often enter reading programs with extremely poor self-concepts. Counseling, along with help in improving reading strategies, may be needed for these students.

Remedial programs are generally individualized as much as staffing will allow. To offer more individual and small-group help than a single teacher can manage, schools often use paraprofessionals in addition to the regular instructor. The diagnosis and prescription for each remedial student are done by the reading teacher. Then the teacher shows each paraprofessional how to conduct help sessions with a specific student or a small group of students. Paraprofessionals are shown how to help students use the printed materials and equipment prescribed in the students' individual programs; how to offer encouragement and reassurance; how to help the subjects correct poor reading habits; how to monitor attendance; and how to keep the reading teacher apprised of either positive or negative changes in the subjects' reading performances. While paraprofessionals work with individuals and small groups, the reading teacher is free to offer intensive individual and small-group help to students who have problems that the paraprofessionals are not qualified to handle. The instructor also must continuously monitor the activities of the paraprofessionals.

Other attempts at individualization have some students working on tutorial or drill-and-practice computer programs that have been chosen to meet their particular needs while the teacher works directly with other students. Programs that have a management component that records scores and/or errors for each student, which can be examined by the teacher later, are particularly useful in this type of situation.

Remedial reading instruction needs to be as practical as possible. The students need to be able to see how it is going to help them cope with real-life needs. Therefore, reading instructors would do well to confer with each student about his or her personal concerns and to try to tailor the remedial program to reflect the perceived needs of the individual.

Remedial students often need initial instruction in, or reteaching of, basic word recognition and comprehension strategies and skills. Therefore, decoding skills, vocabulary building, and comprehension are generally stressed in remedial programs, whereas little attention is given to rate. The basic skills are necessary prerequisites to programs for increasing rate, but in a remedial program some attention may be given to developing flexibility of rate. Flynn (1977) suggests that attention to skimming skills can be highly beneficial for students who have been indoctrinated with the idea that every word must be read, even if the students are remedial students who need much help with the basic skills. She describes a program in which the students' enthusiasm for the skimming exercises seemed to lead to widespread improvement.

Sanacore (1987) believes that a reading program for a remedial student should be intensive and that in the most effective programs remedial activities are offered throughout the school day. The reinforcement of the material taught, by emphasis during the entire day and even on subsequent days, can help the student to master the material more completely.

Remedial courses were found to be more numerous than any other type of course in each grade from grade six to grade twelve (Greenlaw and Moore, 1982). More discussion of remedial reading may be found in the section on Special Reading Classes later in this chapter.

Case Study: Total-School Reading Plan. The way one school developed a total-school reading plan to meet specific goals is shown in the sample case described below.

INTRODUCTION

The school's faculty has recognized the fact that all the students in the school can improve their basic reading skills in some way. They wish to offer possibilities for improvement to students who are reading above grade level, as well as students who are reading on grade level and students who are reading below grade level. They realize that many students have the capacity to read much better than they do, even though they are reading at grade level or above, and that some students reading below grade level are making satisfactory progress when their capacity levels are taken into consideration.

AREA ONE: DEVELOPMENTAL READING

To meet the basic skills needs of the students, the faculty decides to include in each ninth grade student's schedule one semester of reading instruction. Since there are approximately 200 ninth graders in the school, about 100 students are assigned to reading classes each semester. A special reading teacher is designated to teach five classes of approximately 20 students each semester. Because the students within each class vary greatly in reading achievement and needs, the class is conducted as a laboratory with individual and small-group instruction rather than whole-class instruction. The teacher studies test results for each student and plans an individual course of study for each one, based on the student's current achievement level and needs. If several members of a class have similar needs, the teacher plans small-group sessions. Otherwise, the students work independently with materials on appropriate reading levels and meet regularly with the teacher for teacher-pupil conferences concerning the assignments. During the conferences, the teacher sometimes gives specific strategy or skill instruction, but conferences are also used to help students choose reading materials from a pool of appropriate ones, to check on word recognition and comprehension skills, and to help students plan ways to share their reading experiences with their classmates.

On Friday of each week, five or more of the students share with the rest of the class something they have read. The sharing may take a number of forms: oral reading of episodes from a book, illustrations of scenes from a book, panel discussions presented by several students who have read the same book, skits presented by students who have read the same book, and many others.

The reading laboratory is arranged in the following way: the room includes seven carrels in which students can carry on individual work with a minimum of distraction, a listening station where up to eight students can listen to an audio presentation over headsets at the same time, two large tables at which small groups of students can work on common projects, a group instruction area in which up to nine students can receive small group instruction from the teacher, and a glassed-in teacher's work area where the teacher can conduct individual conferences privately without having to leave the classroom totally unsupervised.

Plans are made to develop a second reading laboratory for students in the tenth, eleventh, and twelfth grades who are developmental readers but feel a desire to work to improve their basic reading skills and are willing to attend the laboratory during their regularly assigned study periods or free periods.

FIGURE **11.2**

Sample Reading Laboratory

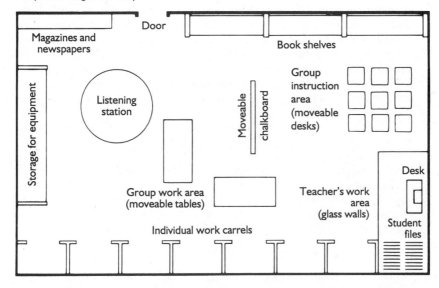

Setting up this second laboratory has to be postponed until the second year of the program because another qualified reading teacher will be needed to provide specialized help for the students.

AREA TWO: CONTENT AREA READING

The reading committee members identify reading strategies and skills that they feel are vital for content understanding in many content areas. Then they arrange for in-service training sessions to help the content teachers learn to teach these strategies and skills in their subject areas when needed. A particular strategy or skill is emphasized each month of the year. At the beginning of each month, in-service training for the selected strategy or skill is offered to the teachers for whom the training is appropriate. This approach is taken in order to gradually introduce the content teachers to the application of appropriate instruction of different types, since in-service training about, and application of, instruction in all reading strategies and skills at once could be too overwhelming to content teachers to be effective. Once teachers learn a technique, they are expected to continue to use it in all subsequent months as it is needed. Teachers who already have knowledge of the strategy or skill being taught in a particular in-service session are not required to attend, although they are encouraged to do so to refresh their knowledge and perhaps acquire some new ideas for presentation. Sometimes these teachers are enlisted to help with the in-service presentations.

The ideas identified for focus are vocabulary building; recognizing and understanding prefixes and suffixes; using study methods; recognizing main ideas; following directions; locating information in textbooks and in the library; developing flexibility of rate; detecting sequence; using context clues, drawing conclusions and making inferences; reading maps, tables, charts, and graphs; detecting propaganda; recognizing facts and opinions; and detecting the author's motives or biases. During the first year, the faculty has chosen the following nine areas for emphasis: study methods, prefixes and suffixes, main ideas, sequence, context clues, following directions, flexibility of rate, locating information in textbooks, and reading maps.

The content area teachers also learn how to teach directed reading lessons in their respective content classes. They learn to utilize study guides to direct the silent reading portions of the directed reading lessons.

The job of the media specialist is defined as helping the teachers locate appropriate materials for use in their subject areas. These materials include books, magazines, and pamphlets written on a variety of reading levels. The teacher attempts to match the materials to the students' abilities.

The reading consultant is available to offer help to content area teachers in planning for the teaching of reading strategies and skills related to each content area. The consultant is available to teach specific demonstration lessons in the content area classes when the content area teachers request such help.

AREA THREE: RECREATIONAL READING

All content area teachers are encouraged to make students aware of materials available for leisure-time reading in their respective disciplines. The English teachers have decided to make one day a week available during their classes for recreational reading and the sharing of books and other materials read for pleasure. In addition, all students are encouraged to make use of the media center during their free periods.

A reading club has been formed during the homeroom-club period. The reading consultant and special reading teacher sponsor the club. Members read books on areas of mutual interest and discuss them with fellow club members.

AREA FOUR: REMEDIAL READING

The faculty has decided that all students reading two years or more below capacity level should be offered individual or small-group (ten or fewer students) assistance by a qualified reading specialist. For ninth graders, this instruction is in addition to the special reading class provided in basic skills and is offered during the semester when the basic reading class is not scheduled. For tenth through twelfth graders, instruction is offered two days a week during the study period. No student is forced to enroll in the remedial course, but conferences are held with students who need help, and they are invited to take part.

Initiating the Program

Initiating a total-school program is a difficult undertaking. For this reason, some schools initiate such a program gradually. One possible method of gradual initiation might take place over a two-year period, as shown in Table

TABLE **11.1**

Plan for Initiating Program

	Developmental Reading	Content Reading	Recreational Reading	Remedial Reading
1st year	9th-grade, developmental classes	Content teachers teach study methods; use DRA; emphasize vocabulary	Media center Reading clubs	9th-grade remedial classes (voluntary)
2nd year	9th-grade classes plus voluntary 10th–12th-grade classes	Content teachers learn and emphasize, when applicable, a reading skill each month	Media center English class time Reading clubs	9th–12th-grade remedial classes (voluntary)

11.1. Another approach might be to initiate the program one or more grade levels at a time over a period of years.

Evaluating the Program

A total-school reading program must constantly be evaluated in a variety of ways. Evaluation can be considered in three areas — student progress, staff utilization, and effectiveness of activities and materials.

1. Student progress can be evaluated through standardized and informal achievement tests, as well as through teacher observation. Teacher observation may serve to help evaluate progress in areas rarely covered by tests. For example, students' attitudes toward, and interests in, reading can often be detected through observation, whereas tests may give no information about these areas. If progress has been unsatisfactory, reasons for the situation must be investigated.

2. The staff members need to look at the functions that are being performed by different people to determine whether there is unwarranted overlap of responsibility, inadequate coverage of some area or areas by qualified personnel, or insufficient staff to handle the needs of the students in some areas (perhaps remedial reading). If any inadequacies are detected, the staff members need to make plans to alleviate the problems in the future.

3. Teachers can keep records of the activities and materials that seem to be most effective in meeting the objectives of the program. Use of ineffective activities and materials should be discontinued, and the advice of the reading consultant should be sought about other possible approaches to the students' problems.

A program should be evaluated regularly throughout the school year, not only at the end of the year, although the end of the year is generally one good checkpoint for evaluation. Periodic evaluation sessions can help keep teachers aware of the need for continuous assessment of progress toward program goals.

Needs Assessment

A school's evaluation of its established reading programs can take the form of a "needs assessment." Basically, a needs assessment is an attempt to measure the gap between "what is" and "what should be." Such an evaluation overlaps program planning, implementation, and periodic checkups by internal or external personnel. It is presented below as an isolated phase only for ease of exposition. The following items suggest the components of a needs assessment.

1. *Student Performance.* What is the present reading level of students? What specific types of reading problems are the students having? What are the reading potentials of students? What may be the reasons for underachievement, if this exists? What reading attitudes and interests exist?

2. *Personnel.* Who are the personnel involved in the reading program, including classroom teachers and reading teachers? What are their training, experience, and abilities? What other personnel are available (e.g., psychologists, speech and hearing therapists, guidance counselors)?

3. *Present Reading Program.* What are the locations of the reading classroom, reading laboratory, and so forth? What basic pattern or type of reading program exists? What materials and equipment (e.g., books, periodicals, computers) are being used? How much time is provided for reading instruction and when is it provided? What use is made of reading specialists? What in-service program in reading is provided for specialists and classroom teachers? What is the present reading evaluation program? What recordkeeping patterns are maintained?

4. *School Plant.* What are the size, location, and resources of the school library? What reading resources and materials are available in the classrooms or elsewhere in the building?

5. *Fiscal Resources.* What money is available to the reading program from the local school budget? From other sources?

6. *Professional Resources.* What use is made of specialized clinics, reading centers, nearby college and university departments, private reading specialists, and others? What consultant help is available from sources such as these?

Special English Sections and Units   *491*

In some schools, special sections of English are designated as classes for students who have reading difficulties. In these classes English teachers instruct the students in reading rather than in grammar and composition.

Meints (1977) describes a task system that has been used to individualize instruction in reading in sections of Corrective Reading/English in one high school. With this system, students are responsible for completing seven types of activities each week: reading skills, silent reading, writing, listening, word games and puzzles, cloze passages, and group activities. For a passing grade, ten tasks, each taking about twenty minutes, must be completed each week. Two tasks that involve reading skills, two that involve silent reading, and two group activities must be completed, as well as one task of each of the other four types. The reading skills tasks are keyed to individual needs as assessed by diagnostic tests. This approach certainly has positive features, because it takes into account the need for individualization of instruction in a class of students with diverse strengths and weaknesses.

However, one problem with these programs has been that the students object to being placed in the special class. Another common problem may be even more serious. Some English teachers have no training in teaching reading strategies because their teacher preparation programs did not include these techniques. These teachers may lack the ability to identify the reading deficiencies of the students and to help students attain proficiency in reading. They also often resent being asked to perform a function for which they lack sufficient training. With reluctant students and reluctant teachers, these classes are likely to be ineffective.

Many English teachers assigned to such special sections take the responsibility very seriously, however. They take reading courses at a nearby university, study professional literature, and attend conferences. These teachers can do a great deal of good for their students if they can find effective ways to motivate them.

Some schools include reading units as a part of all English classes, instead of designating certain classes as special English classes. For example, using a special reward system, English teachers in a Minnesota junior high school taught students to use the SQ3R method when reading English, social studies, and science materials. This instruction, although it was carried out in the English classes, was part of a total-school reading program. Content teachers in the school also utilized the method in their classes (Gruber, 1973).

Although reading-study skills such as outlining, summarizing, and note taking fit into the English curriculum fairly well and some interpretive and critical reading skills are given attention as literature is taught, the inclusion of special reading units only in English classes should not be considered a comprehensive attack on the reading needs of the student population. English classes should not be expected to solve the entire school's reading problems, especially if the English teachers have not had special training in identifying reading needs or in teaching reading. Even if teachers know how to approach teaching the comprehension strategies needed in literature study, it is unlikely that they will be equipped to handle a student with severe word recognition difficulties.

Special Reading Classes

In some schools, students who are identified through testing procedures as remedial readers are assigned to special reading classes, whereas students who classify as corrective or developmental readers receive no outside help. In other schools, developmental and corrective readers are offered direct reading instruction in "reading improvement classes" or in reading laboratories.

Remedial Reading Classes

Different schools define remedial readers in different ways. A common definition of a remedial reader is a student who reads at a level two years behind where he or she should be reading.

Many teachers translate this definition into "a student who is reading two years below grade level." These teachers overlook the fact that not all students have the ability to read up to grade level and that some students who read two years below grade level are doing as well as can be expected, according to their capacities. (Approximate capacity or expectancy levels for reading can be obtained from such assessment measures as informal reading inventories, described in Chapter 10.) Remedial readers should always be defined in terms of capacity level rather than in terms of grade placement level. If a large gap exists between capacity level and reading achievement level, there is a good chance for rapid student progress with adequate instruction. If the gap is small, little progress may result, even with excellent teaching, because the student is already performing at close to his or her potential.

Ideally, remedial reading classes should be small, and the work should be conducted in small groups and on a one-to-one basis. Each remedial reader requires a great deal of individual attention. As Kress (1989, p. 370) points out, "Individualized instruction based on individualized diagnosis has long been acknowledged as the best in remediation, but . . . it is not the predominant delivery for remediated readers at present."

Diagnostic tests must be given to each reader to determine specific areas of strength and weakness. Many of these tests are designed to be administered individually. After a student's weaknesses have been detected, a program that overcomes these weaknesses and that capitalizes on the student's strengths must be developed. Several students with the same needs may be helped together, but students should not be forced into group activities that are not appropriate for their personal needs. Individualization of assignments requires careful planning. Each student's weekly assignments may be planned on a special sheet so that both teacher and student can see at a glance what needs to be done and what has been accomplished. Such a system provides both structure for the student and a record of progress.

Students must be helped to recognize their specific reading needs and must understand how each activity used in the remedial work can help to overcome their difficulties. A teacher who develops good rapport with a student at the outset of the remedial instruction will find it easier to communicate with the student about specific needs and how to overcome problems than will a teacher who thinks only of lesson presentation and ignores the influence of the student's attitude. When students recognize the goals they are working for, they are generally much more receptive to techniques designed to help achieve these goals.

Remedial readers need to see indications of progress. Graphing their comprehension scores from week to week may help them to see that they are improving as they apply themselves to their reading activities. Keeping a record of books read and satisfactorily reported on to the teacher provides another visible sign of progress.

Remedial readers often lack interest in conventional "reading resource room" activities because they have been exposed to these activities so often throughout their school years. "Secondary level remedial reading programs, then, must provide more than competent teachers, boxes and shelves of materials, and instruction based on the diagnosed needs of each student if they are to succeed. They must also capture the interest of the students and involve students actively in the learning process" (Lehr, 1981, p. 350).

Computer-assisted instruction has entered the remedial reading scene for a number of reasons: the computer is a patient dispenser of information, not showing irritation at slow responses or the need for repetition; the computer offers "interactive" instruction — the student responds to prompts and receives feedback from the computer; feedback offered about correctness of responses can be immediate; and some programs can branch to explanations and additional practice for students who are having problems. Computers are not enough in a remedial program, however, because they cannot observe student behavior in ways that teachers can, and they cannot administer responses that are as individualized to a particular student's needs (Kress, 1989).

Voluntary remedial reading classes seem to produce more impressive results than required classes. Subjects may resent being placed unwillingly in a remedial reading course; they may become sullen and noncommunicative and resist all of the reading teacher's attempts to help.

In many cases, a remedial reader has never been successful in reading

494

activities. Since success is a powerful motivator, the remedial reading teacher should plan some activity that is designed to allow the student to experience success with each session. Progressing through the instruction in a series of small steps makes success more likely. One suggestion for offering students a chance for success involves basing some grades on effort instead of product. Kitchens (1987) has developed a plan in which students spend a particular amount of time every week on individualized reading and language activities and receive grades on the effort expended, as evidenced by student reports of time expenditures and activities completed and effort reflected in the material that is given to the teacher.

Students should probably be given course credit for a remedial reading class, which is, in fact, as much a skill development class as an English composition class or a speech class. Students get credit for English composition and speech — why not for remedial reading? The credit may serve as an added incentive to some students to do well. At the least, students will not resent being required to work at a task they would not have chosen without credit.

Since improvement is the aim of remedial reading classes, these classes are a means to an end, not an end in themselves. Ideally, students will overcome their reading deficiencies through participation in these classes and will move on into more developmental reading activities and full participation in the regular reading assignments for content classes. Placement in a remedial reading class should not constitute a "life sentence" to such classes.

Reading Improvement Classes

"Reading improvement classes" is a term that is often applied to developmental reading classes offered in the secondary school, although remedial programs, as described earlier, are sometimes also included under this title. In this section, only developmental classes are considered.

Realizing that every reader has areas of reading in which he or she could improve if given the opportunity and assistance, many schools have initiated reading improvement classes for developmental readers. Developmental readers at the secondary level generally have good backgrounds in word recognition skills and general comprehension skills of a literal nature. In many cases, however, they have much room for improvement in interpretive, critical, and creative reading skills as well as in reading/study skills.

Evaluative instruments should be used to determine the skill profiles of the various members of a developmental reading class. Since these profiles will differ, grouping within the class and offering some individualized help will be necessary. Approaching any reading class with a "shotgun approach" — requiring the same activities of all students — wastes valuable instructional time and bores students who do not need help in the chosen area.

Reading improvement classes often focus extensively on developing rate with comprehension. Mechanical devices such as tachistoscopes, pacers, and controlled readers are often used, in addition to timed readings. Flexibility of rate is another topic commonly included in such programs. Students who have a firm foundation in basic word recognition and comprehension skills and strategies are ready for some emphasis on rate, but the basic skills should be emphasized first.

Recreational reading is also frequently emphasized in these classes. Time in class is often utilized for recreational reading activities, and teachers may use many motivational techniques to encourage reading for pleasure, both in class and outside of class.

Reading improvement classes can be slightly larger than remedial classes, since the students generally require less one-to-one attention. In most programs, however, no more than twenty students are placed in a class of this type because of the diversity of needs that the teacher is trying to meet.

Some reading improvement classes are required; others are voluntary. Voluntary classes generally accomplish larger mean gains in reading achievement.

Some reading classes offer credit toward graduation; others do not. As in the case of remedial classes, it seems logical to offer some credit for the reading class if credit is given for English composition and speech, two other communication classes.

Farrell (1982) described a junior high reading class that was based on sustained silent reading (SSR), a procedure in which students read self-selected material silently, while the teacher also reads. Some techniques other than SSR were also used in the class, including vocabulary development activities and discussion and writing of reports on material read. Students were graded on vocabulary tests, class reading, number of books read and reported on, and special forms of book reports. Most students in the program (90 percent) gained between one and two years in their reading levels on a standardized reading test during the year. The remaining students gained either less than one year or more than two. Farrell further noted that by May all students were reading above grade level.

Beers (1986) designed and implemented an advanced developmental reading class for ninth-grade college preparatory students who needed help in study skills, test-taking skills, and critical reading. Part of the class time was devoted to improving rate of reading. Not only were different rates discussed, but flexibility of rate was emphasized. There was excellent growth in reading skills and rate by students in the program, resulting in a decision to continue the one-semester course for ninth graders.

Reading Laboratories

Many secondary schools have established reading laboratories for improving reading skills. Although reading classes as described in the previous two

496

sections can be held in a reading laboratory, reading laboratories are not usually bound to class organization, and the pupils work more independently than in a typical class situation. Reading laboratories are generally equipped with a wide variety of materials and equipment designed to be used individually by students. The laboratory instructor administers diagnostic instruments and plans a special program for each student that the student can follow independently to overcome his or her weaknesses. Many of the materials are self-scoring. Rate machines are usually available, and sometimes other machines are utilized. Programmed materials are valuable also. The laboratory instructor is available to help students when needed.

It is important for the laboratory instructor to monitor the students' activities and progress constantly. If this is not done, a student can become locked into an unsuitable program that is not challenging enough or that he or she finds frustrating.

Reading laboratory sessions may be required or voluntary, and attendance in the laboratory may be either scheduled or offered at the convenience of the students. Each school must make decisions about these points according to the needs of the student population and the available staff.

Webber (1984) describes how one senior high school in Ohio has implemented flexible planning and scheduling in the use of the reading laboratory. Sometimes individual students who are having difficulty reading are assigned to attend the reading lab on a daily basis. At other times, the reading laboratory instructor and content area teachers work together to identify weaknesses among the students in a skill area, and the reading lab teacher schedules a lab session one or two days a week during the content class time to work with students on these weaknesses. One half of the students attend the lab while the rest attend the content class, and the two groups change places on alternate days. In still other cases, the content class and the reading laboratory are scheduled during consecutive periods, with the students in the content class attending reading lab following their content class. The content teacher and the laboratory instructor work together to plan work on strategies and skills that the students lack. Still another option is for the entire content class to attend reading lab instead of the content class one day each week. One additional option is available: The content teacher may ask the lab instructor to develop a particular skill in a limited time frame, perhaps several consecutive days.

Combination Programs

Some schools that do not have total-school reading programs utilize a combination of two or more of the other programs. A typical combination involves remedial reading classes and reading improvement classes. A reading laboratory may house either remedial reading courses or reading improvement courses or both, or in a different situation the laboratory might be available for *independent* work by students. In this case, regular reading classes of one or both types are held elsewhere in the school or special "English" sections or units are utilized. In *all* cases and combinations, even when they are not part of a centralized total school reading program or when they are partially covered within another setting such as "English" classes, content area reading instruction — within each content room — should be a priority.

Choosing Materials for a Secondary School Reading Program

A wide variety of reading materials is available for use in secondary school reading programs. Some materials are printed; others are audiovisual. Some are intended to teach strategies and skills; others are designed primarily to offer practice in strategies and skills already taught. Selection of the best materials for a particular situation is of primary importance. The burden of selection should not rest on one individual; instead, materials should be chosen through the cooperative efforts of a variety of people, including school administrators, reading consultants, special reading teachers, and content area teachers.

Following are some of the questions that should be asked about materials being considered:

1. Is the philosophy behind the material sound?
2. Is the material designed to teach the strategies and skills the students in this school need?
3. Is the material appropriate to the maturity levels of the students with whom it is to be used? (This criterion is particularly important when choosing materials for secondary school students. Childish material should be avoided.)
4. Is the material appropriate to the backgrounds of experience of the students for whom it is intended?
5. Is the material interesting to the students who will be using it?
6. Are provisions made to encourage application of strategies and skills taught by the material to reading situations outside the reading class, including reading in the content areas?
7. Is the material free from role stereotypes (of different nationalities, ethnic groups, sexes)?
8. Is the material up-to-date?
9. Is proper emphasis given to all components of the reading process?
10. Does the material provide for continuous diagnosis of reading difficulties?
11. Does the material include an adequate teacher's manual?

12. What kinds of written material are covered? Poetry? Prose? Nonfiction? Fiction?
13. Does the material have a good format (e.g., easy-to-read print, adequate margins, good quality paper)?
14. If the material is audiovisual, can it be operated independently by the students?
15. Is the material easy to use with students?
16. Is audiovisual material technically acceptable (good sound, color, and so forth)?
17. Does multilevel material make provisions for placing students appropriately within a sequence?
18. Are all directions clearly given in written or oral form?
19. Does the material have pretest and post-test activities available?
20. Is the material adaptable to groups of students with different needs?
21. Does the material suggest follow-up activities to help reinforce the strategies and skills presented?
22. Has the material been field tested? With what results?
23. Have controlled research studies shown this material to be effective in teaching strategies and skills?
24. Is the cost of the material reasonable?

Cheek (1983) suggests a number of documents that can be helpful in choosing good supplementary materials for secondary classrooms, including sources concerned with selection of print materials for content classrooms of various types, for reading classrooms, for student interest, and for avoidance of sex and minority bias. The materials he cites are all ERIC documents that are readily available to teachers.

Krause (1984) has provided suggestions for choosing useful and appropriate computer software. Some of his suggestions are similar to those Cheek makes for application to any material purchased. In addition, Krause recommends not buying software without trying it first and inquiring about the following concerns: existence of a warranty on the software, possibility of using portions of the material without using the entire program, availability of a built-in management or record-keeping system, possibility of making a printout from the program's management system, possibility of controlling rate of presentation, and policy on obtaining upgrades of the program.

Evaluating Textbooks for Use in Content Classrooms

When evaluating a textbook for use in any content classroom, educators must decide what role that textbook is expected to play in that classroom. Will it be a reference manual for the teacher or students, the basis for instruction, or the entire curriculum for the course? Without knowing the role of the textbook, a decision about its use may not be appropriate (Muther, 1985). If the text is to serve primarily as a reference manual for the teacher in the content area, it may be written at a higher readability level, have fewer motivational materials included, and have a greater concept density than if it is to serve as a reference manual for the students. A reference manual for the students or a text that is the basis for instruction should be written at a readability level that is accessible to a majority of the students (100 percent is unlikely) and should be designed to interest the students in the material. The content density of a text that is to be the basis of instruction should be lower than that of one that is a reference manual. A text that forms the entire curriculum for a course should be comprehensive in coverage of topics important to the subject, whereas a reference manual may have less comprehensive coverage and still be useful.

For each textbook adoption decision, of course, a key consideration is how well the book fits the course for which it will be used. Are important topics included and covered thoroughly rather than simply being mentioned? Bernstein (1985, p. 464) has pointed out that "textbooks in nearly every category tackle too many subjects and cover them so superficially that the students have difficulty understanding what is being said." Important and trivial material may be given equal attention.

Content should be checked for accuracy and currency. Treatment of controversial issues should be handled fairly. The representation of various segments of society should be handled fairly in textbooks. Women, minorities, the elderly, and the handicapped have sometimes been treated as stereotypes, and such treatment should not be considered acceptable.

If the coverage of material is good, there is still the concern that students need to be able to understand the material. Bernstein (1985), Armbruster and others (1985), and Armbruster (1984) have denounced the use of short, choppy sentences in which many connectives have been deleted, the use of vague words instead of more exact ones, and the stilted language patterns found in many textbooks. "Writing to formula" has caused some of these problems. Inappropriate editing to reduce the length of texts after many topics have been added may also be a problem.

Farr and Tulley (1985) mention the importance of logical organization, as well as clarity, in textbooks. Osborn and others (1985) suggest the need for advance organizers and other devices to highlight the structure of the text. They point out that researchers have found that students learn best from organized and readable text, sometimes referred to as "considerate" text. Text that is not considerate "requires the reader to organize its content and establish relationships between parts of the content" (p. 12). Deficiencies that have been cited in some textbooks are inadequate tables of contents, not enough chapter headings, and chapter subheadings that are cute, rather than informative (Bernstein, 1985).

The background experiences of the audience for the textbook should be considered when choices are made (Osborn et al., 1985). The material should provide sufficient information for the development of concepts but should not be repetitious in presenting material that is likely to be generally known by the target audience. In addition, Armbruster and Anderson (1981, p. 46) point out that "[a]nalogies, metaphors, and other types of figurative language should be used only if their referents are well known by the reader." Adults often overlook the fact that their students' backgrounds of experiences may not have included the referents necessary for such material to be understood.

Pedagogical aids, such as chapter overviews, chapter and unit objectives, chapter summaries, discussion questions, and practice activities should be well designed and written, focusing on important material. Discussion questions should include higher-order questions as well as literal-level ones. Practice activities should be directly tied to chapter content and should be extensive enough to enhance learning.

Textbook format should be considered in an evaluation. The format should be attractive and should enhance the readability through adequate white space, appropriate text size and style, good quality paper, and clarity of organization through headings and subheadings.

Teachers' editions of textbooks should give teachers ideas about how to build prerequisite knowledge for studying a topic, how to activate the students' prior knowledge before the instruction begins, and how to present certain material in a way that will encourage students to integrate the prior knowledge with the new material in the chapter (Osborn et al., 1985). The teachers' editions should provide ideas for teaching that encourage students to read the textbooks for meaning and to search for supplementary information in other sources. They should provide teachers with questions on various levels of thinking that are appropriate for purpose-setting, discussion, and testing purposes. They should have suggestions for adjusting textbook use for different types of learners (good and poor readers, students with varying learning styles, and students with varying handicaps). Ways to arouse interest in the material to be studied should also be included in the teachers' editions, and teachers should be provided with lists of supplementary reading material that both they and their students can use during the study of the topic.

Effective Programs

Baumann (1984) reviewed the research on reading programs that are effective. The research shows that the presence of a strong instructional leader is very important. Teachers who are effective accept primary responsibility for student achievement and expect their students to learn. Effective teachers have clearly formulated instructional objectives and can communicate these objectives to their students. They provide frequent opportunities for their students to experience success, keep instruction at a brisk pace, have minimal transition time between activities, set unambiguous rules, prevent misbehavior, and monitor their students' progress. These teachers are well prepared for teaching and engage in direct instruction.

Effective programs allot enough time to reading instruction to allow students time to learn, and the time on task is high in these programs. The classrooms have warm, nonthreatening atmospheres. Achievement is greater when the students work in homogeneous groups.

SUMMARY

Among the personnel responsible for the development of reading ability at the secondary school level are the content area teacher, the school administrator, the special reading teacher, the reading consultant, and the librarian or media center specialist. It is essential for all content teachers to have an understanding of reading, since such understanding helps to facilitate the teaching of their particular subjects.

Reading programs in secondary schools may fall under several different classifications: total-school reading programs, special "English" sections and units, remedial reading classes, reading improvement classes, and reading laboratories. The total-school reading program is the most comprehensive type, since it involves all school personnel in a cooperative effort. Much inservice training is necessary for the program's implementation, and it is important to have a carefully chosen reading committee. All aspects of reading are considered in a total-school reading program: developmental reading, content area reading, recreational reading, and remedial reading. Other types of programs do not involve all school personnel and are much less comprehensive. Frequently, two or more of these less extensive programs are implemented simultaneously in a school.

Choice of materials for a secondary reading program is important and should be the result of the cooperative efforts of all personnel involved with the school's reading program.

SELF-TEST

1. What is true of a total-school reading program? (a) Developmental reading is taught. (b) Content area reading is taught. (c) Remedial reading is offered. (d) All of the above
2. If a total-school reading program is to be established, when should inservice training sessions be held? (a) Only at the beginning of the planning period (b) Only at the end of the planning period (c) Only after

implementation of the program (d) Throughout the process of planning and implementation

3. Who should be involved in in-service sessions? (a) Administrators (b) Faculty members from all departments (c) Media specialists (d) All of the above

4. Which statement is true of a school reading committee? (a) It should be composed of only the school's reading teachers. (b) It should be composed of people who can offer effective guidance to the school's reading program. (c) It should never include an administrator. (d) It should never include faculty members from departments other than English.

5. Which statement is true of reading achievement tests? (a) They are of little use when planning a total-school reading program. (b) They generally pinpoint specific skill difficulties. (c) They generally reveal the student's accomplishments in broad areas of reading skills. (d) None of the above

6. Which statement is true of recreational reading? (a) It is unimportant for inclusion in a school's reading program plans. (b) It can be encouraged through reading clubs. (c) It is not a concern of content area teachers. (d) None of the above

7. What should evaluation of a total-school reading program include? (a) A measure of student progress (b) Consideration of staff utilization (c) Consideration of the effectiveness of activities and materials (d) All of the above

8. Why are English teachers often chosen to teach reading in special "English" classes? (a) They are well prepared to do so by their teacher-preparation programs. (b) Other faculty members perceive English and reading as being closely related. (c) Both *a* and *b* (d) Neither *a* nor *b*

9. Which statement is true of reading instruction offered as special units in "English" classes? (a) It constitutes a comprehensive attack on the reading needs of the student population. (b) It is useless to most students. (c) It is useful for developing some types of reading strategies. (d) None of the above

10. How are remedial readers defined? (a) Students who are reading at levels two or more years behind where they should be reading (b) Books for students reading below grade level (c) Students who dislike reading (d) None of the above

11. What do remedial readers need? (a) Much individual attention (b) To see some evidence of progress (c) Both *a* and *b* (d) Neither *a* nor *b*

12. Which statement is true of developmental readers at the secondary level? (a) They generally have a good background in word recognition strategies and skills. (b) They often need help with critical reading strategies and skills. (c) They often need help with reading/study skills. (d) All of the above

13. Which statement is true of reading laboratories? (a) They are generally set up to allow much independent work by the students. (b) They need to have a lab instructor present at all times. (c) Both *a* and *b* (d) Neither *a* nor *b*
14. Who should choose materials for a secondary school reading program? (a) The administrator (b) The special reading teacher (c) The content teacher (d) All three of the personnel mentioned above, plus the reading consultant
15. What does research indicate about effective reading programs? (a) The teachers expect their students to learn. (b) The instruction is kept at a brisk pace. (c) There is a strong instructional leader. (d) All of the above
16. Which personnel are primarily responsible for finding subject matter materials appropriate to varying levels of reading ability? (a) Administrators (b) Reading consultants (c) Special reading teachers (d) Content area teachers

THOUGHT QUESTIONS

1. List and elaborate on the steps you would follow if you were given the assignment of planning the initiation of a total-school reading program. Which steps would you be able to handle alone? For which steps would you need assistance? Which people could supply the expertise you would need in helping you set up the program?
2. After a total-school reading program has been initiated, what evaluation procedures should be utilized to determine its effectiveness? When should evaluation of the program take place? Who should be responsible for the evaluation?
3. Can sufficient reading instruction for all students in a secondary school be provided through special "English" classes? Why, or why not?
4. How do remedial reading classes differ from developmental reading classes? Why do these differences exist?
5. Should remedial classes be elective or required? Why?
6. Should students receive credit toward graduation from remedial reading classes? Why, or why not?
7. What are some advantages of reading laboratories for improving reading skills?
8. What is the best procedure for choosing materials for use in a secondary school reading program?
9. Do you agree with the list of seven requirements for content area teachers presented at the beginning of this chapter? Why, or why not? Be specific.
10. How does the principal of a secondary school influence the reading program?
11. What factors are most important in evaluating content area textbooks?

ENRICHMENT ACTIVITIES

 1. List the duties that a member of a school reading committee might be expected to perform. Compare your list with the lists your classmates have developed. Discuss differences of opinion.

*2. Report to the class on the provisions for reading instruction in your school.

*3. Check with your principal and fellow teachers about reading problems of students in your school. After identifying the two most common problems perceived by the educators in your school, write a plan for solving each problem. Share your findings and your plan.

*4. Draw a plan for a reading laboratory that would be adaptable to the needs of your school.

 5. Make a list of reading strategies and skills that might be taught in a developmental reading class. Check the ones that could be taught by a content area teacher. Discuss your list with your classmates.

 6. With a group of your classmates, design a total-school reading program. Include physical plant needs, materials and equipment needs, staff needs, organizational plans, and staff responsibilities.

 7. Examine some reading material that could be used in a secondary school reading program. Ask yourself the questions presented in the section of this chapter entitled "Choosing Materials for a Secondary School Reading Program." Share your evaluation with your teacher and classmates.

*8. List the personnel in your school who are concerned with reading instruction. Briefly describe the responsibilities of each.

*9. Go over the administrator's checklist with a secondary school principal. Share his or her reactions to it with the group.

 10. Interview a reading consultant and a special reading teacher. What are their functions and roles? Share your findings with the class.

 11. With a partner, examine a secondary level textbook for your content area. Evaluate it, and report to the class on your findings.

BIBLIOGRAPHY

Anders, Patricia. "Dream of a Secondary Reading Program? People Are the Key." *Journal of Reading*, 24 (January 1981), 316–320.

Armbruster, Bonnie B. "How Is a Turtle Like a Frog?" *American Educator* (Summer 1984), 14–17.

———, and Thomas H. Anderson. *Content Area Textbooks*. Reading Education Report No. 23. Champaign, Illinois: University of Illinois at Urbana-Champaign, July 1981.

———, Jean H. Osborn, and Alice L. Davison. "Readability Formulas May Be Dangerous to Your Textbooks." *Educational Leadership*, 42 (April 1985), 18–20.

*These activities are designed for in-service teachers, student teachers, or practicum students.

Baumann, James F. "Implications for Reading Instruction from the Research on Teacher and School Effectiveness." *Journal of Reading*, 28 (November 1984), 109–115.

Beers, Penny G. "Accelerated Reading for High School Students." *Journal of Reading*, 29 (January 1986), 311–315.

Berger, Allen, and H. Alan Robinson (eds.). *Secondary School Reading: What Research Reveals for Classroom Practice*. Urbana, Ill.: National Conference on Research in English, 1982.

Bernstein, Harriet T. "The New Politics of Textbook Adoption." *Phi Delta Kappan*, 66 (March 1985), 463–466.

Bruce, Bertram, Andee Rubin, and Kathleen Starr. *Why Readability Formulas Fail*. Reading Education Report No. 28. Champaign, Ill.: University of Illinois at Urbana-Champaign, August 1981.

Cheek, Dallas H. "Secondary Reading Materials: Selection Criteria for the Classroom Teacher." *Journal of Reading*, 26 (May 1983), 734–736.

Davison, Alice. *Readability — Appraising Text Difficulty*. Reading Education Report No. 24. Champaign, Ill.: University of Illinois at Urbana-Champaign, July 1981.

Erickson, Lawrence G. "How Improvement Teams Facilitate Schoolwide Reading Reform." *Journal of Reading*, 33 (May 1990), 580–585.

Farr, Roger, and Michael A. Tulley. "Do Adoption Committees Perpetuate Mediocre Textbooks?" *Phi Delta Kappan*, 66 (March 1985), 467–471.

Farrell, Ellen. "SSR as the Core of a Junior High Reading Program." *Journal of Reading*, 26 (October 1982), 48–51.

Flynn, Peggy. "Speed Is the Carrot." *Journal of Reading*, 20 (May 1977), 683–687.

Gee, Thomas C., and Nora Forester. "Moving Reading Instruction Beyond the Reading Classroom." *Journal of Reading*, 31 (March 1988), 505–511.

Greenlaw, M. Jean, and David W. Moore. "What Kinds of Reading Courses Are Taught in Junior and Senior High School?" *Journal of Reading*, 25 (March 1982), 534–536.

Gruber, Paulette M. "Junior High Boasts Super Stars." *Journal of Reading*, 16 (May 1973), 600–603.

Hillerich, Robert L. *The Principal's Guide to Improving Reading Instruction*. Boston, Massachusetts: Allyn and Bacon, 1983.

Kitchens, Roger. "Getting More Effort Out of Remedial Readers in High School." *Journal of Reading*, 30 (May 1987), 726–728.

Krause, Kenneth C. "Choosing Computer Software that Works." *Journal of Reading*, 28 (October 1984), 24–27.

Kress, Roy A. "Trends in Remedial Instruction." *Journal of Reading*, 32 (January 1989), 370–372.

Lehr, Fran. "New Approaches to Remedial Reading Programs at the Secondary Level." *Journal of Reading*, 24 (January 1981), 350.

Meints, Donald W. "The Task System in an Individualized Reading Class." *Journal of Reading*, 20 (January 1977), 301–304.

Mehlinger, Howard D. "American Textbook Reform: What Can We Learn from the Soviet Experience." *Phi Delta Kappan*, 71 (September 1989), 29–35.

Muther, Connie. "What Every Textbook Evaluator Should Know." *Educational Leadership*, 42 (April 1985), 4–8.

Newman, Fran. "Let's Join the Readers' Club!" *Journal of Reading*, 25 (April 1982), 693.

Nicely, Robert F., Jr. "Higher-Order Thinking Skills in Mathematics Textbooks." *Educational Leadership*, 42 (April 1985), 26–30.

Osborn, Jean H., Beau Fly Jones, and Marcy Stein. "The Case for Improving Textbooks." *Educational Leadership*, 42 (April 1985), 9–16.

506

Professional Standards and Ethics Committee. *Guidelines for the Specialized Preparation of Reading Professionals.* Newark, Del.: International Reading Association. April 1986.

Rickelman, Robert J., and William A. Henk. "Reading Technology: Telecommunications in the Reading Classroom." *The Reading Teacher*, 43 (February 1990), 418–419.

Rowe, Mary Budd. "Science Education: A Framework for Decision-Makers." *Daedalus: Scientific Literacy* (Spring 1984), 123–142.

Sanacore, Joseph. "Needed: A Better Link Between the Learning Center and the Classroom." ERIC document, 1987, 15 pp. [ED 286 151]

———. "Schoolwide Independent Reading: The Principal Can Help." *Journal of Reading*, 31 (January 1988), 346–353.

Sewall, Gilbert T. "American History Textbooks: Where Do We Go from Here?" *Phi Delta Kappan*, 69 (April 1988), 552–558.

Shanker, James L. *Guidelines for Successful Reading Staff Development.* Newark, Del.: International Reading Association, 1982.

Shannon, Albert J. "Monitoring Reading Instruction in the Content Areas." *Journal of Reading*, 28 (November 1984), 128–134.

Siedow, Mary D. "Assessing Needs." In Mary D. Siedow, David M. Memory, and Page S. Bristow (eds.), *Inservice Education for Content Area Teachers.* Newark, Del.: International Reading Association, 1985, pp. 8–26.

Spiegel, Dixie Lee. *Reading for Pleasure: Guidelines.* Newark, Del.: International Reading Association, 1982.

Stier, Peggy F. "Inservice Program Helps Teachers Learn by Doing." *Journal of Reading*, 22 (November 1978), 131–133.

Ward, Stephen D., and Eugene J. Bradford, "Supervisors' Expertise in Reading Affects Achievement in Junior High." *Journal of Reading*, 26 (January 1983), 362.

Webber, Elizabeth A. "Organizing and Scheduling the Secondary Reading Program." *Journal of Reading*, 27 (April 1984), 594–596.

Wilhite, Robert K. "Principals' Views of Their Role in the High School Reading Program." *Journal of Reading*, 27 (January 1984), 356–358.

Woods, Alice R., and Mary H. Topping. "The Reading Resource Specialist: A Model." *Journal of Reading*, 29 (May 1986), 733–738.

SELF-TEST ANSWERS

Chapter 1

1. a	3. a	5. d	7. d
2. c	4. b	6. c	8. a

Chapter 2

1. b	5. d	9. c	13. d
2. a	6. b	10. a	14. c
3. b	7. a	11. a	
4. a	8. a	12. b	

Chapter 3

1. b	8. a	14. c	20. c
2. a	9. b	15. a	21. a
3. a	10. c	16. d	22. c
4. b	11. b	17. b	23. b
5. c	12. a	18. c	24. a
6. b	13. b	19. d	25. d
7. c			

Chapter 4

1. a	5. c	9. b	13. c
2. d	6. a	10. b	14. d
3. b	7. c	11. d	
4. d	8. b	12. c	

Chapter 5

1. b	4. c	7. b	10. b
2. d	5. c	8. c	
3. c	6. b	9. d	

Chapter 6

1. b	4. b	7. a	10. a
2. a	5. d	8. b	11. d
3. d	6. c	9. d	12. b

Chapter 7

1. d	6. b	11. a	16. b
2. a	7. c	12. b	17. c
3. c	8. b	13. d	18. b
4. c	9. a	14. d	
5. d	10. c	15. c	

Chapter 8

1. d	5. c	9. a	13. c
2. b	6. d	10. a	14. b
3. d	7. d	11. d	
4. d	8. b	12. c	

Chapter 9

1. c	5. c	8. a	11. a
2. b	6. c	9. d	12. a
3. c	7. d	10. d	13. d
4. a			

Chapter 10

1. a	6. a	10. a	14. c
2. b	7. c	11. a	15. b
3. b	8. d	12. d	16. b
4. c	9. d	13. c	17. d
5. c			

Chapter 11

1. d	5. c	9. c	13. c
2. d	6. b	10. a	14. d
3. d	7. d	11. c	15. d
4. b	8. b	12. d	16. d

INDEX

STUDENT

RESPONSE

FORM

Many of the changes made in this edition of *Secondary School Reading Instruction: The Content Areas* were based on feedback and evaluations of the earlier editions. Please help us respond to the interests and needs of future readers by completing the questionnaire below and returning it to: College Marketing, Houghton Mifflin Company, One Beacon Street, Boston, MA 02108.

1. Please tell us your overall impressions of the text.

	Excellent	Good	Adequate	Poor
a. Was it written in a clear and understandable style?	———	———	———	———
b. Were difficult concepts well explained?	———	———	———	———
c. How would you rate the frequent use of illustrative examples?	———	———	———	———
d. How comprehensive was the coverage of major issues and topics?	———	———	———	———
e. How does this book compare to other texts you have used?	———	———	———	———
f. How would you rate the activities?	———	———	———	———
g. How would you rate the study aids at the beginning and end of each chapter?	———	———	———	———

2. Please comment on or cite examples that illustrate any of your above ratings.

———————————————————————————————

———————————————————————————————

———————————————————————————————

3. Were there any topics that should have been included or covered more fully?

_____

_____

_____

4. Which chapters or features did you particularly like? _____

_____

_____

5. Which chapters or features did you dislike? _____

_____

_____

6. Which chapters taught you the most? _____

_____

_____

7. What changes would you like to see in the next edition of this book? _____

_____

_____

8. Is this a book you would like to keep for your classroom teaching experience?

_____ Why or why not? _____

_____

_____

9. Please tell us something about your background. Are you studying to be a secondary school classroom teacher or a reading specialist? Are you in-service or preservice? Are you an undergraduate or graduate student? _____

_____

_____